LIVES

OF THE

LORD CHANCELLORS OF ENGLAND

GREAT SEAL OF GEORGE I.

LIVES

OF

THE LORD CHANCELLORS

AND

KEEPERS OF THE GREAT SEAL

OF

ENGLAND,

FROM THE EARLIEST TIMES TILL THE REIGN OF QUEEN VICTORIA.

BY

LORD CAMPBELL.

SEVENTH EDITION.

ILLUSTRATED.

VOL. VI.

WILDSIDE PRESS

CONTENTS

OF

THE SIXTH VOLUME.

CHAP.	PAGE
CXXV.—Continuation of the Life of Lord King till the death of George I.,	1
CXXVI.—Conclusion of the Life of Lord Chancellor King	15
CXXVII.—Life of Lord Chancellor Talbot from his birth till he received the Great Seal,	37
CXXVIII.—Conclusion of the Life of Lord Talbot,	48
CXXIX.—Life of Lord Chancellor Hardwicke from his birth till he was appointed Attorney General,	73
CXXX.—Continuation of the Life of Lord Hardwicke till he was appointed Lord Chancellor,	91
CXXXI.—Continuation of the Life of Lord Hardwicke till the death of Queen Caroline,	108
CXXXII.—Continuation of the Life of Lord Hardwicke till the resignation of Sir Robert Walpole,	134
CXXXIII.—Continuation of the Life of Lord Hardwicke till the breaking out of the Rebellion of 1745,	148
CXXXIV.—Continuation of the Life of Lord Hardwicke till the death of Frederick, Prince of Wales,	157
CXXXV.—Continuation of the Life of Lord Hardwicke till he resigned the Great Seal,	184
CXXXVI.—Continuation of the Life of Lord Hardwicke till the death of George II.,	198
CXXXVII.—Conclusion of the Life of Lord Hardwicke,	209
CXXXVIII.—Life of Lord Chancellor Northington from his birth till he received the Great Seal,	237
CXXXIX.—Continuation of the Life of Lord Northington till the death of George II.,	249
CXL.—Continuation of the Life of Lord Northington till he resigned the Great Seal,	259
CXLI.—Conclusion of the Life of Lord Northington,	274
CXLII.—Life of Lord Chancellor Camden from his birth till the death of George II.,	287

CONTENTS.

CHAP.	PAGE
CXLIII.—Continuation of the Life of Lord Camden till he received the Great Seal,	302
CXLIV.—Continuation of the Life of Lord Camden till he became an ex-Chancellor,	318
CXLV.—Continuation of the Life of Lord Camden till he was first appointed President of the Council,	348
CXLVI.—Continuation of the Life of Lord Camden till the King's illness in 1785,	369
CXLVII.—Continuation of the Life of Lord Camden till the breaking out of the French Revolution,	388
CXLVIII.—Conclusion of the Life of Lord Camden,	397
CXLIX.—Life of Lord Chancellor Charles Yorke from his birth till he was returned as a Member of the House of Commons,	407
CL.—Continuation of the Life of Lord Chancellor Charles Yorke till he was appointed Solicitor General,	423
CLI.—Conclusion of the Life of Lord Chancellor Charles Yorke,	437
CLII.—Life of Lord Chancellor Bathurst from his birth till he was made a Puisne Judge,.	481
CLIII.—Continuation of the Life of Lord Bathurst till he resigned the Great Seal and was made President of the Council,	492
CLIV.—Conclusion of the Life of Lord Bathurst,	513

LIVES

OF THE

LORD CHANCELLORS OF ENGLAND.

CHAPTER CXXV.

CONTINUATION OF THE LIFE OF LORD KING TILL THE DEATH OF GEORGE I.

ON what strange chances and vicissitudes does official promotion depend! When Sir Peter King had been ten years Chief Justice of the Common Pleas, he and his friends thought of his terminating his honorable, but comparatively obscure, career in this office, leaving a name only to be found in musty blackletter law Reports, or in chronological tables of the twelve Judges. But a madness seized the nation, during the South Sea Bubble, unknown before or since, till the coming up of railways: the Masters in Chancery caught the infection, and, losing large sums of suitors' money intrusted to them, became defaulters, and attracted public notice to the manner in which they were appointed, and to the abuses in their department of the Court. Suddenly a storm of indignation arose against the Lord Chancellor, who had only been a little more rapacious than most of his predecessors; he who, a few weeks before, had been in the plenitude of power and popularity, was driven to resign; there being no one who could conveniently be at that moment appointed to succeed him, the Great Seal was put into commission; the Chief Justice of the Common Pleas having more leisure than the Chiefs of the other Courts in Westminster Hall, Sir Peter King was appointed Speaker of the House of Lords: there he conducted himself with such dignity and propriety during an impeachment, that he was made Lord Chancellor and a Peer; so he became a character in English history, and is regarded as the founder of a distinguished family in the nobility of England.

Sir Joseph Jekyll, and his brother Commissioners, being appointed on the 7th of January, 1725,—in obedience to the royal admonition,¹ applied themselves diligently to business, but found the concerns of the suitors in a state of deplorable confusion from the deficiencies of the Masters, and were greatly perplexed and divided in opinion with respect to the remedies which ought to be applied. Sitting daily during Hilary and Easter Terms, and in the intervening vacation, their time was almost wholly occupied with motions respecting the abstraction, the replacing, and the securing of trust money.

Meanwhile the trial of the Earl of Macclesfield proceeded. When parliament assembled, after the Christmas recess, Sir Peter King took his place on the woolsack as Speaker of the House of Lords, leaving his puisnes to do the ordinary business of the Court of Common Pleas, and questions of difficulty being reserved for his advice. On the 13th of February a message from the Commons was announced; and Sir Peter King having put on his hat, Sir George Oxenden, attended by many members, "in the name of all the Commons of England, impeached Thomas, Earl of Macclesfield, of high crimes and misdemeanors, declaring that the House of Commons would, in due time, exhibit particular articles against him, and make good the same."

Sir Peter, not being a peer, of course had no deliberative voice; but during the trial, as the organ of the House of Peers, he regulated the procedure without any special vote, intimating to the managers and to the counsel for the defendant when they were to speak, and to adduce their evidence. After the verdict of *Guilty*, he ordered the Black Rod to produce his prisoner at the bar; and the Speaker of the House of Commons having demanded judgment, he, in good taste, abstaining from making any comment, dryly, but solemnly and impressively, pronounced the sentence which the House had agreed upon.²

The Lords Commissioners were still going on very indifferently, and complaints becoming loud against their inefficiency, Walpole felt that, to secure the popularity

¹ Ante, vol. v. p. 386.
² 16 St. Tr. 801, 938, 1080, 1258, 1265, 1330; Ante, vol. v. p. 403.

which he had justly acquired by sacrificing the late Chancellor to the public indignation, another enjoying the public confidence should be appointed. Sir Philip Yorke, the Attorney General, who had made such a brilliant start, was not much turned of thirty; and a head of the law, and keeper of the King's conscience, so youthful, would have been the subject of gibes instead of reverence. Sir Clement Wearg, the Solicitor, had distinguished himself much in supporting the bill for the banishment of Atterbury, and as manager of the House of Commons in conducting the impeachment of Macclesfield; but though considerably senior in age, and in standing at the bar, he was considered of inferior ability, and there were strong objections to puting him over the head of the Attorney General.[1] The Sergeants and King's Counsel offered no better choice. Sir Joseph Jekyll, the Master of the Rolls, had rather lost reputation by acting as a Commissioner of the Great Seal. A selection was to be made therefore of a Common-Law Judge, and none could have a higher character than Chief Justice King, whose conduct during the impeachment both parties had concurred in praising.

Accordingly he was fixed upon, and it was agreed that he should at once be declared Lord Chancellor without being Lord Keeper; and that he should simultaneously be raised to the Peerage (likewise an unusual rapidity of honor), and that he should receive a salary of £6,000 a year payable out of the Post-office, and £1,200 a year payable out of the Hanaper-office, in consideration of the sale of the offices in the Court of Chancery being adjudged to be illegal.

I have now the advantage of a diary which Lord Chancellor King, on his new appointment, began to keep in short-hand, without any view to authorship. From this I shall occasionally make extracts, and at other times I shall refer to it as the authority for my narrative. Thus he commences:—

"1725.—*Tuesday, June* 1. Monday, the 31st May, being the last day of the sitting of Parliament, I was introduced into the House of Lords as Lord King, Baron of Ockham, in the county of Surrey. My introducers were Lord Delaware and Lord Onslow. Baron's robes lent me by Lord Hertford. And this day at noon I went to St.

[1] Life of Sir Clement Wearg, by Duke, 1843.

James s, and being called into the King's closet, he delivered the Seals to me as Lord Chancellor; and soon after, I went to the council-chamber, carrying the Seals before him. The first thing that was done was to swear me Lord Chancellor, after which I took my place as such. The King then declared that he was going beyond sea, and had appointed a regency, whose names were then declared.[1]

"*2nd.*—In the morning I received the visits of several Lords and others of my friends, and at noon went to wait on the Prince and Princess, and kissed their hands. This day I surrendered my place of Chief Justice of the Common Pleas.

"*3rd.*—About ten o'clock I waited on the King to have two bills signed, the one for Eyre to be Chief Justice of the Common Pleas, the other for Gilbert to be Chief Baron, and as soon as I left him, he went on his voyage to Hanover. And inasmuch as several of the nobility were to wait on him to Greenwich, so that they could not attend me, according to custom, to Westminster Hall, I did from thence take an occasion to go privately to Westminster Hall, which I did this day, being a day of motions. I here took again the oath of a Chancellor, which the Clerk of the Crown read, and the Master of the Rolls held the book."

The new Chancellor probably abstained from all parade in his installation, out of delicacy to the melancholy condition of his predecessor, who was now a prisoner in the Tower of London. Had he chosen to have the usual procession to Westminster Hall, I doubt not that, notwithstanding the King's absence, it would have been one of the most splendid seen for many years, as his promotion was universally approved of, and there was a general expectation that he would turn out to be one of the greatest Chancellors that had ever sat upon the woolsack. He himself did not labor under any serious misgivings, having

[1] "1st June, 1725. His Majesty having received the Great Seal of Great Britain from the Lords Commissioners this day, and having been pleased to deliver it the same day to the right Honble. Peter, Lord King, with the title of Lord Chancellor of Great Britain, his Lordship on Thursday, the 3rd of the same month, came privately from his house in Norfolk street to the Chancery Court in Westr Hall, and did then in the Court of Chancery take the oaths appointed to be taken by the 1st of William & Mary, and the oath of Lord Chancellor, the Master of the Rolls holding the book, and the Clerk of the Crown read the said oaths."—*Roll, 1714-1727.*

long been such a complete master of his work on the common-law bench.

However, there was soon considerable disappointment experienced by the public, as well as anxiety by himself. He succeeded a Judge who not only had a fine legal understanding, but to whom the doctrine and practice of the Court had become "familiar as his garter." Lord King had not only never practiced in the Court of Chancery, but, there seeming no possibility of his leaving the Common Pleas during his life, he had been contented with well understanding "pleading in actions real and personal;" and he had neither read Chancery Reports nor paid the slightest attention to Chancery proceedings. He now saw daily pleading before him, Yorke, Talbot, Wearg, and other counsel regularly trained in the court,—and he found himself in the painful and humiliating situation of knowing much less of the subject than the advocates on whose arguments he was to decide. He was even in a more perilous predicament than a man at once taken from the bar and placed in a judicial situation for which he is not quite prepared; for, by presiding ten years over the phlegmatic sergeants, he expected always to be treated with extreme deference, and he was apt to show impatience and peevishness if an ill-considered opinion thrown out by him was roughly handled. He was much frightened by the approach of "a Seal ," and he had little sleep the night before the dreaded day when he was to be assailed by all manner of motions, of which he had no previous notice. He could pretty well manage the regular hearing of a cause—when the bill and answer were opened very tediously, as was then the custom,—the evidence was all read at full length,—counsel were heard on both sides,—and time could be taken to consider the decree. He could even dispose of pleas and demurrers with tolerable composure, as a little patience and discreet reserve to conceal ignorance might lead to a shrewd and tolerably safe guess at the right conclusion. But when there came motions for injunctions and for sequestrations, and for the appointment of receivers, and for the payment of money into court and out of court, and for divers other things about which the little he had read in his youth had long faded from his memory, and which he was obliged to decide off-hand,—he sadly repented that for "the thorns of Chancery" he had ever exchanged "the cushion of the Common Pleas."

Although his perception was not so quick as it had been, and all his faculties were beginning to be a little rigid,—as soon as he discovered his deficiencies he nobly struggled to supply them. Disregarding amusement and recreation, and regardless of health and even of life itself, he boldly began and he steadily pursued a course of reading to qualify himself for the discharge of his duties as an Equity Judge. There were then hardly any published Chancery Reports; there were no systematic treatises on Equity pleading or practice; and there was but little for the Equity student in print beyond the heads "Subpœna" and "Chancery," in the general ABRIDGMENTS. But Lord King, besides confidentially conversing with some practitioners in his court, borrowed MS. treatises respecting Chancery, and MS. reports of the decisions of former Chancellors which were in private circulation. By a diligent perusal of these he made himself a very pretty Equity lawyer, and he had a tolerable notion of the newest fashions which his predecessor had introduced. Still he never could remove the impression which he had made at the commencement of his Chancellorship. It is said that there were more appeals from the Court in his time than during any equal period, either before or since, and that there were more of his decrees reversed than there have ever been of any other Chancellor. But the fate of appeals depends greatly on the general reputation of the Judge appealed from, and the temper of the Judge or Judges appealed to. Lord King was not, like Lord Hardwicke, the only law Lord, so as to make an appeal from the Court of Chancery to the House of Lords "ab eodem ad eundem," and Lords Lechmere and Trevor were not sorry to have an opportunity of civilly pointing out his mistakes.

Reading Lord King's Equity judgments, as they appea in Peere Williams,[1] I believe they will be generally es

[1] The cases heard before Lord Chancellor King from 17-6 to 1730 are also published by a reporter of inferior merit, named Moseley, whose volume has generally been *vilipended*. However, in Mr. Hargraves's copy of it in the British Museum is to be found the following notice:—" Lord Mansfield, in 5 Burr, 2629, says, 'this book should not be quoted,' and in *Myddleton* v. *Lord Kenyon*, Lord Chancellor Loughborough observed to Mr. Fonblanque, upon his citing a case from it, 'that he had not heard it cited.' But I took the

teemed sound, and they are to be praised for the same clearness and precision which distinguished him as a Common-Law Judge.

No very important case came before him in the Court of Chancery, and he can not be said to have added very materially to our Equitable code, but a few of his decisions may be found generally interesting.—He settled the rule that a will of lands in England, though made abroad, must be signed by three witnesses, according to the English Statute of Frauds, as a will of lands is to be governed by the *lex loci rei sitæ*, and a will of personalty by *lex domicilii*.[1] Where by a marriage settlement the wife is entitled to pin-money, he decided that if the husband and wife lived together, and he maintains her, she is not entitled to claim the arrears of her pin-money.[2]

A man having seduced a modest girl, and had a child by her, entered into an executory agreement to pay £2000 to be laid out in purchasing an annuity for the mother and child. When a bill was filed for a specific performance of this agreement after the child's death, objection was made that, this being a matter of *terpitude*, Equity ought not to interfere,—*Lord Chancellor King:* "If a man does mislead an innocent woman, it is both reason and justice that he should make her reparation: but this case is stronger in respect of the innocent child whom the father has occasioned to be brought into the world in this shameful manner, and for whom in justice he ought to provide; and though the child be now dead, yet the case is to be taken as it was when the agreement to provide for them was signed, and then the child was living."[3]

Lord Chancellor King established the very salutary rule, that although, by the law of England, all personal property bequeathed to a wife belongs to her husband, Equity will not aid in compelling payment of the legacy without seeing a settlement of the property made for the wife's benefit.[4] What seemed a more doubtful rule laid down by him has been since adhered to, that *lis pendens* shall be tantamount to actual notice; so that a purchaser for valuable

liberty of saying that 'I had often heard it cited, and that I had found very good matter in it.'"

[1] *Coppin* v. *Coppin*, 2 P. W. 293.   [2] *Thomas* v. *Burnet*, 2 P. W. 341.
[3] *Marchioness of Annandale* v. *Harris*, 2 P. W. 434. This decree was affirmed on appeal by the House of Lords, 1 Brown's P. C. 250.
[4] *Brown* v. *Elton*, 3 P. W. 202.

consideration may lose the property for which he has paid, having bought it from a person who had a legal right to sell,—if a suit of which he was ignorant had been commenced to establish an equitable interest in it.[1]

A curious case came before him, showing that towards the middle of the last century the custom of marrying infants of tender years, which had formerly been very common, still prevailed in England. One of several guardians to an heiress took her from a boarding school when she was only nine years old, and married her to his own son, who had no estate. The Lord Chancellor, on motion, ordered this guardian to bring into court the infant whom he had married to his son, and that he, the son, and the infant should attend. All attending, the counsel for the application pleaded, "that this guardian having, in so perfidious a manner, broken his trust, and married his ward to his own son, who was worth nothing, the Court of Chancery, the guardian of all infants, with the superintendency and cognizance of all trusts, ought to commit him, and not suffer the girl, now but nine years old, to continue to cohabit with her husband, who ought not to be indulged with opportunities of inveigling her, and preventing her from disagreeing to the marriage when she should come to the age of twelve years, which it would be for her interest to do." *Lord Chancellor:* "The infant girl never having been under the care of the Court, nor committed by the Court to the care of this guardian, I do not think he can be considered guilty of a contempt of Court; but then it is a very ill thing in him to marry this child to his own son, and he is punishable by an information. I will, therefore, have him bound over with sureties to appear to answer an information to be filed against him by the Attorney General. As for the child, let her be handed over by this knavish guardian to the other guardian named in her father's will, who, it is to be hoped, will take proper care of her, and do what is for her advantage in advising her to confirm or to renounce the marriage."[2]

I will only mention one other case, which occurred soon after, and illustrates the manners of the age. Sir John Chaplyn, a young baronet, nineteen years of age, of great estate in Lincolnshire, was drawn in by a "bumbailiff" in

[1] *Sorrell* v. *Carpenter*, 2. P. W. 482. [2] *Goodhall* v. *Harris*, 2 P. W. 561.

Clare Market to marry his daughter, a girl of sixteen, and to make a will bequeathing all his personal estate to her. In two months he died, leaving three sisters, who were his heirs at law, if there were no issue by this marriage. The widow pretending to be pregnant, the sister petitioned for a writ "*de ventre inspiciendo*," and that "residing at her late husband's house in Lincolnshire, this might be as her castle, wherein she should be inclosed,[1] and continue until the time of her delivery, and that some woman might be always resident with her both before and at the birth." Her counsel argued "that she was guilty of no crime in marrying Sir John, who was of sufficient age to choose a wife for himself, and who might think beauty and virtue a sufficient portion, especially when his fortune had put him above the want of money; that, as it had not appeared any fraud or collusion was intended, it was very unreasonable to suspect she would be guilty of imposing a false child on the family; that it would be a hardship on a lady of such tender years to send a jury of matrons to inspect her; that, she being now with child, the inspection might be of dangerous consequence, and occasion a miscarriage, a thing possibly wished for by the other side; that the 'castle' in Lincolnshire was an old house in the fens, much out of repair; and that, she having no relations or friends in that country, it would be cruel to imprison her there." Lord Chancellor : " I take this writ '*de ventre inspiciendo*' to be of common right—for the security of the next heir, to guard against fraudulent or supposititious births. But as it may be a hardship to oblige the lady to live in Lincolnshire, far from her relations and friends, and since the marriage appears to have been in March last, consequently, no probability of her being brought to bed before Christmas, and as her father consents she shall be in town before Michaelmas, and reside in St. James's parish in Middlesex, let the writ '*de ventre inspiciendo*' issue at Michaelmas, directed to the Sheriff of Middlesex. In the meantime, the present heirs may send two women at reasonable times to see whether she is with child, they giving reasonable notice beforehand, so that this may be

[1] At common law a jury of matrons must be impanneled, and if they find the widow with child, she is to be shut up in a castle, where the sheriff of the county keeps her in safety till she is delivered.

attended with as little inconvenience as possible to Lady Chaplyn. There is no occasion to execute the writ with all the strictness of the common-law, provided people of skill from time to time have access to her, and may be present at the birth."[1]

I shall afterwards have occasion to consider the beneficial changes which Lord King introduced in the Master's offices, in the administration of the funds of the suitors, and other departments,—which place him high in the rank of law reformers. But we must now survey him in the exercise of his political functions.

Immediately after his appointment the King had gone to Hanover, leaving him and other great officers of state "Lords Justices." They had their first meeting as soon as news was received of the King's arrival in Holland; there was afterwards a formal assembly of the whole body once a fortnight, and a committee (of which Walpole was chief) met from time to time as occasion required. The first question they had to deliberate upon was the propriety of granting a pardon to Lord George Murray, who had been attainted when only eighteen years of age, and had petitioned for mercy. The Chancellor would only say that there was nothing in law to obstruct a pardon, but refused to give any further opinion,—on the ground that he was not sufficiently acquainted with the facts. The Duke of Argyle was strongly for rigor, "because this man's treason was attended with perfidy in deserting the King's troops and running away to the rebels; and if he were pardoned, others would immediately make the same application." Walpole, however, took the merciful side, and, carrying a majority with him, a letter was ordered to advise the King to pardon him.[2]

Much consultation took place with respect to the granting of commissions of the peace for Scotland, then in a very distracted state on account of the Malt Tax. The Earl of Islay was "called in, and gave an account of having made up lists for all the counties.—which had taken three months in preparing, and which he vouched were made up with great exactness and attention to the gentlemen to be appointed." "On this," says the Diary, "I told

---

[1] *Ex parte Aiscough*, 2 P. W. 391 This writ continues to be granted not only to the heir, but to a devisee, either for life in tail or in fee. 1 Coxe, 297; 4 Brown, C. C. 90.   [2] June 5.

the Regency that though in England the Great Seal would be a little more consulted in matters of this nature, yet, considering the urgency of affairs, if their Excellencies would order me to pass those commissions of the peace as now settled, I would do it. Thereupon they ordered me to pass them."[1]

Then comes an exceedingly curious entry.—"*June* 24. Sir Robert Walpole went with me to Ockham, and lodged there the night. He entered into a free discourse with me about foreign affairs." [After a copious account of the disputes with Spain, &c., no longer interesting, he adds:—] "Another negotiation had lately been on foot in relation to the the two young Princes, Frederick[2] and William.[3] The Prince[4] and his wife[5] were for excluding Prince Frederick from the throne of England, but that, after the King and Prince, he should be Elector of Hanover, and Prince William King of Great Britain; but that the King said it was unjust to do it without Prince Frederick's consent, who was now of age to judge for himself; and so this matter now stood. But that Sir Robert Walpole had told the King that if he did not in his lifetime bring over Prince Frederick, he would never set his foot on English ground, so that he did not know whether the King, when he returned from Hanover, would not bring that Prince with him." This is a curious proof of the early dislike of George II. and Queen Caroline to their eldest son, Frederick, Prince of Wales. Lord King must have looked forward with some dismay to the dissensions in the royal family, which had proved so perilous to his predecessors. But he contrived to retain the favor of the reigning Sovereign, without giving fresh offense to the heir apparent; and although Prince Frederick for some unaccountable reason was not brought over from Germany during the present reign, George I., while alive, thwarted the plan for disinheriting his grandson, and on the accession of George II. the national cry was so strong against continuing to rear as an alien him who was to fill the throne of England, that in two years it was found necessary to send for him. He had his revenge by perpetually

---

[1] July 1st.   [2] Afterwards Fritz, Prince of Wales.
[3] Afterwards Duke of Cumberland, the hero of Culloden.
[4] The then Prince of Wales, afterwards George II.
[5] Afterwards Queen Caroline.

disturbing the government of his father, till the joyful exclamation was uttered—" Fritz is dead!"

During the King's absence in Germany, the Chancellor was at the head of the Regency.[1] The Lords Justices, besides carrying on routine business at home, were occupied with intricate foreign negotiations, (now happily uninteresting), with a view to the aggrandizement of his Majesty's hereditary dominions by the addition of some little patches of territory; but some of the Chancellor's entries in the Diary are worth copying, as showing how business was transacted between his Majesty and his representatives:—

"*July* 26.—Received by Lord Townshend from the King a warrant to pass a commission under the Great Seal to Lord Townshend to treat and contract with such princes and states as the King should direct, which I accordingly passed under the Great Seal." " 29.—The Duke of Newcastle was with me to explain the meaning of the commission to Lord Townshend, which was that the Emperor and King of Spain living now in strict amity, there was a necessity to enter into a league with other powers to preserve the peace of Europe; that France and the King of Sardinia were ready, and it was hoped that the Protestant Princes of the Empire and Holland would likewise come into it." "*Sept.* 7.—Tuesday night, a messenger came to me (at Ockham) from Mr. Delafaye with ten instruments from Hanover, with the King's warrant countersigned by Lord Townshend to fix the Great Seal to them. I returned back word by the messenger that I was coming to town, and would there do what was necessary." " 8.—Wednesday at night I came to town. The Duke of Somerset came to me, and I asked him, when he was in the Regency and the King abroad, as had happened in King William's time, and the King made a treaty abroad, whether this was communicated to the Regency or Council here? or whether, upon the King's warrant

---

[1] I do not believe that he ever enjoyed much political power, but in foreign countries he was regarded as a very important personage. I have now in my hands a letter to him from a Frenchman of the name of Neville, giving him some important information, thus addressed:—

"HIS EXCELLENCE MILOR PITER KING
HIG CANCELLOR CF GREAT BRITTAGNE &
ONE OF MILORS OF REGENCE
LONDON."

from beyond the sea, the Great Seal was affixed to them here? He said it was always the custom, on the King's warrant, for the Chancellor to affix the Great Seal. The next day Mr. Delafaye told me this was always the custom, and that it would be absurd to lay them before the Regency, because the King had agreed and signed them already. I therefore put the Seal to them."

Looking to Wolsey's impeachment and other sources of constitutional information, respecting the exercise of the royal authority, the result seems to be, that the Great Seal can only be used within the realm, but that it may lawfully be applied on the warrant of the Sovereign signed beyond the seas; and that the Regent, Guardian of the Realm, or Lords Justices, are bound to obey any directions they may receive from the Sovereign, either before his departure or during his absence abroad, but that in all matters respecting which they are left without instructions their act is equally valid and potent as if done by the Sovereign in person. It is probable that in after times there will be no deputation of the royal authority, unless to open or prorogue parliament, or to give the royal assent to bills.

I will conclude this head with an entry after the King's return, which proves that the Chancellor, who used to be of yore the sole foreign secretary, still imagined that, as he was to affix the Great Seal to treaties, he was to exercise a superintendence over foreign affairs:

"*Thursday, March* 10, 1726.—At the desire of Lord Townshend I was this evening at the Duke of Devonshire's, with the Dukes of Argyle and Newcastle, and Sir Robert Walpole." [He then gives a long account of a written declaration signed by the Landgrave of Hesse, promising 8,000 foot and 4,000 horse for the defense of Hanover.] "Lord Townshend saying, that 'this was not properly a treaty, but only a declaration by the Landgrave on what terms he would furnish the King with so many soldiers, and that there was nothing more to do than for the King to show his approbation by a ratification under the Great Seal,' I thought that 'the form of this instrument made no alteration in the substance, and that this was really nothing else than a treaty, and that there was no instance wherever the Great Seal made a treaty by itself, or ratified a treaty, which was not first agreed to by some minister or commissioner.' And thereupon it was agreed that inquiry should be made in the Secretary's office whether there had been anything of this nature before; and on inquiry the next day it being found that there was none such, it was agreed that Diemar and Lord Townshend should both mutually sign the agreement by way of treaty, and that after such signing the ratification should pass according to the usual forms. And I have hinted to Lord Townshend *that when I was to be concerned in the conclusion of an affair it was but reasonable I should know the beginning and progress*, he did send me the copy of this matter drawn up in the form of a treaty between him and Diemar."

Lord King took his place as Chancellor in the House of Lords on the 20th of January, 1826, and then read the royal speech, the King not even repeating the effort he made when he first came to the throne, to say, in English, that "I have ordered my Lord Chancellor to declare the causes of calling this parliament." The custom was now introduced of the two Houses echoing the words of the speech, and on this occasion the address was carried unanimously. Opposition was almost annihilated, and Sir Robert—graced with the order of the Bath, which he revived to increase his patronage, and with the order of the Garter, the importance of which he enhanced by deigning to accept it—was now in the zenith of his power, although not of his glory, for as yet he had not encountered in mortal strife Pulteney, Carteret, or Pitt. There was not a division in the House of Lords during the session, the entire repose of which was only occasionally interrupted by that luckless wight, Lord Lechmere, who, struggling in vain for office and fame, occasionally made motions from habitual restlessness, but met with so little support that the Lord Chancellor had no trouble beyond putting the question, and declaring that the "Non-contents" had it.

The following session was equally tranquil, and at the close of it the Lord Chancellor read George I.'s last speech to parliament, thanking them for the zeal and harmony with which they had dispatched the public business. His Majesty, having appointed Lords Justices, immediately set off for the Continent, and never again touched British ground, dying, on the 10th of June, on his way to

Osnaburgh, and being interred, with his ancestors, in Hanover.

During his reign of thirteen years, the public attention was so completely devoted to the struggle for the throne between the old and new dynasties, that no regard was paid to legal reform. Lord Somers's "Statute of Jeofails" continued the most recent attempt to correct the abuses of Westminster Hall.

The penal code had been rendered more severe by the Riot Act, and by several fiscal regulations encroaching on the liberty of action which had formerly prevailed in England. Even the impeachment of Lord Macclesfield had produced little beyond salutary exposure, no measures being yet taken effectually to prevent the recurrence of similar evils. But Lord Chancellor King was not forgetful of his duty to struggle for the improvement of our institutions; and, amidst the difficulties which surrounded him, he afterwards accomplished in this department as much as could reasonably be expected from him, and more than was attempted by his successors during the rest of the eighteenth century.

CHAPTER CXXVI.

CONCLUSION OF THE LIFE OF LORD CHANCELLOR KING.

THE Lord Chancellor's own Diary will best introduce his proceedings in the new reign:—

"*Wednesday, June* 14, 1727.—About five in the evening I had a letter from Sir R. Walpole, informing me that the King was dead, and desiring me to meet him immediately at the Duke of Devonshire's.[1] I went there immediately, and found that Sir R. Walpole, on receipt of the news from Lord Townshend, had instantly gone to Richmond and acquainted the Prince with it, and that thereupon the Prince had resolved to be in town as fast

[1] The original of this letter, in the handwriting of Sir R. Walpole, lies before me:— (Copy.)
"My Lord, "Wedn. 5 o'clock.
"The melancholy news is just come of the King's death. Pray hasten way to my Lord President's, where I wait your coming.
"Yours, &c. "R. WALPOLE."

as he could that evening. In the meantime we prepared, by the Attorney and Solicitor General, the draft for proclaiming the King, and settled the other things necessary to be done. The King, in the mean time, came to town, and sent us word that he was ready whenever we were ready to wait on him. Accordingly, we who were at the Duke of Devonshire's, except the Duke himself, who had the gout, went to Leicester House, and there being joined by several others of the nobility, we sent in to the King to desire an audience: and although the Archbishop was present, yet I made a short speech to the King, according to agreement, setting out the great sorrow we were under by the unexpected death of the late King, and that nothing could relieve or mitigate it but the certain prospect of happiness under his future administration: and that being now become our liege Lord, we desired leave to withdraw into the council-chamber to draw up a form of proclamation for proclaiming him, and to sign it as usual; which being granted, we retired into the council-chamber, and there the form, which we had before agreed upon, was produced, engrossed, and thereon all the Lords of the Council then present, first signed it. Then the doors were opened, and the Peers in the outer room were desired to walk in and sign it, which they did; then it was delivered to the gentlemen in the outer room to sign, as many as they pleased. And after it had been some time out, the Lords of the Council sent for the parchment, which being returned, secret intimation was given to the King that the Council were ready to receive him. Whereon he immediately came in, and, seating himself in the royal chair, he there read the declaration, that was printed at the desire of the Lords of the Council: it had been prepared at the Duke of Devonshire's, by Sir R. Walpole and the Speaker. After that, orders were given for the proclaiming of the King the next morning at ten o'clock, and several other orders of course were made, which are to be seen in the council-book, particularly one for proroguing the Parliament, being now, by reason of the King's demise, immediately to meet. *Thursday, 15th.*— A little after ten, I came to Leicester House, and the heralds and all being ready, about eleven, the Archbishop of Canterbury, myself, and other Lords, went into the yard before Leicester House, and there the heralds proclaimed the King, we being there on foot uncovered. As soon as that was done, we went into our respective coaches, and in the street before Leicester House, the King was again proclaimed. From thence we went and proclaimed him at Charing-Cross, Temple Bar, the corner of Wood Street, and the Royal Exchange. After that, I came home, and about four o'clock got to the House of Lords, where the Parliament met, and all the Lords present taking the oaths, I then informed the House that I had a commission from the King to prorogue the Parliament to the twenty-seventh instant, which was the day it stood prorogued to in the late King's time. And thereon the Lords Commissioners seated themselves as usual in such cases, and on message by the Usher of the Black Rod, the Speaker and Commons coming to the bar, the commission was read, and I declared the Parliament prorogued to the twenty-seventh instant. From hence I went to Leicester House, a Council being appointed this evening, and there several other orders were made, which had been omitted the evening before, and particularly the same proclamation which had been issued out upon the death of Queen Anne on the foundation of the act *Sexto Annæ* for continuing persons in their offices, and requiring them to take the oaths according to the said act. *Friday, 16th.*—A Council in the evening, wherein I delivered up the Seals to the King, who redelivered them to me as Chancellor, and thereon I was sworn Chancellor in Council. *Saturday, 17th.*—I was sworn Chancellor in the Chancery Court in Westminster Hall, and this day I swore all the Judges *de novo*, and the King's Council, and some of the Welsh Judges pursuant to the act of parliament *Sexto Annæ*. *Sunday, 18th.*— Received the sacrament at Ockham to qualify myself. *Tuesday, 20th.*—Took the oaths in the King's Bench; went to Kensington and presented the Judges, both English and Welsh, Masters in Chancery, and the King's Council, who all kissed the King's and Queen's hands. *Saturday, 24th.*—At a Cabinet Council at Lord Townshend's office the King's speech settled. There then arose a question whether the King was to take the test on his first coming to parliament next Tuesday, and the Lords desired me to look into that matter, and I promised them to do it by Monday morning, and lay what I could find before them for their determination. *Monday, 26th.*—At Lord Townshend's in the morning, where were present Harcourt, Trevor, Walpole, Newcastle, the Speaker, Townshend, Godolphin, and myself, and I stated the matter to them." [After discussing the matter at great length, he adds.] "On these reasons the Lords all present agreed that there was no need for the King now to take the test; but he might do it at his coronation if that intervene before a new parliament should be chosen."

Lord King might consider himself in luck to retain the Great Seal under him whose pretensions to educate his children and to consent to their marriage he had treated so unceremoniously; but George II. would not avenge the injuries of the Prince of Wales, and he now became reconciled to doctrines which would add to his power over his own son, whom he so much detested. He therefore received the Chancellor very graciously, saying, "Your Lordship has always shown yourself, and no doubt will continue to show yourself, a zealous servant of the Crown, and a warm friend to the Protestant succession." His Majesty, however, made an attempt to usurp patronage, which, we learn from the Chancellor's Journal, was manfully and successfully resisted:—

"The King, when he came to the throne, had formed a system both of men and things, and to make alterations in several offices, as to their power, and particularly as to mine. About July 8th he told me that he expected to nominate to all benefices and prebendaries that the Chancellor usually nominated to. I told him, with great submission, that this was a right belonging to the office, annexed to it by act of parliament and immemorial usage, and I hoped he would not put things out of their ancient course. He told me my Lord Cowper told him, that in the latter part of his Chancellorship, in the Queen's time, he laid before the Queen a list of all persons whom he recommended to benefices, that she might be satisfied they were good Churchmen.[1] I did not give up this point,

[1] Extract from Lord Cowper's Diary.—"*November 13th, 1705.* I had the Queen's leave to bestow my livings of £40 and under without consulting her." "*June 25th, 1706.* At Cabinet. Before it begun I had discourse with the Archbishop about disposing of the livings in my gift, and my having promised the Queen to present, as she directed, in all the valuable ones; he said he feared it would be under a worse management than under the late Keeper's servants, by the importunity of the women and other hangers-on at court, and promised to endeavor to get that matter into a proper method."

b it directly desired him to consider it; and afterwards, at another time, he told me that I should go on as usual. *Sunday, July* 16*th.*—I then saw him again: he seemed now very pleasant, and I gave him a list of all the Judges, both in England and Wales, King's Sergeants, and Counsel, and other subordinate officers in the law, in his invariable nomination, and told him, that as to those which were not Judges in England, they were many of them parliament men, and some now stood again. So he ordered me to make out *fiats* for such of them as were like to be parliament men."

The system which his Majesty then proposed for the appointment of magistrates is very amusing:—" He also told me, now that he had heard that I had acted prudently in his father's time as to the commission of the peace, that his pleasure was, that I should put into the commission of the peace all gentlemen of rank and quality in the several counties, *unless they were in direct opposition to his Government;* but still keep a *majority* of those who were known to be most firmly in his interest, and he would have me declare the former part as his sentiment."

Lord King's Journal gives an interesting statement of the manner in which it was then conceived that Walpole had established his ascendency, which had been for some time endangered by the King's old partiality for Sir Spencer Compton, now Speaker of the House of Commons:—

"On the King's coming to the throne, he ordered Sir R. Walpole and Sir S. Compton to confer together about his affairs, and let him know what they thought fit to be done for his service from time to time. Sir R. Walpole seemed so sensible that he should be laid aside, that he was very irresolute what to do, whether to retire into the House of Lords and give up all business, or whether to continue. But the King and the Speaker persuading him to continue, he went on and undertook what the King expected from him, as to the Civil List and the Queen's jointure, which he forwarded in parliament. During which time by his constant application to the King by himself in the mornings, when the Speaker, by reason of the sitting of the House of Commons, was absent, he so worked upon the King, that he not only established himself in favor with him, but prevented the cashiering of many others, who otherwise would have been put out. The Speaker for some time came constantly to the King every afternoon, and had secret conferences with him; but in about three weeks' time he saw his credit diminish, and so left off the constancy of his attendance. The Tories and others, who expected great changes and alterations, finding these things not to answer their expectations, began to retire about the end of the short session of parliament that was held for settling the Civil List."

It has since appeared, however, that the Lord Chancellor was not altogether in the secret as to the manner in which the Premiership was then settled. Walpole, receiving Lord Townshend's dispatch announcing the death of the late King, hastened to the palace at Richmond, where he was admitted to the bedroom of the Prince, who had retired for his *siesta*. Kneeling down, and kissing his hand, the anxious minister inquired " whom his Majesty would be pleased to appoint to draw up the necessary declaration to the Privy Council?" being sanguine in the hope that the choice would fall upon himself. " COMPTON," answered the King shortly; and Walpole withdrew in the deepest disappointment. This " best of Speakers," however, was so little acquainted with real business, that he confessed his incapacity to perform the task imposed upon him, and begged Walpole to draw up the declaration for him. Sir Robert willingly complied, and wrote the declaration, which Compton carried to the King. For a few days a change of administration was confidently expected; but the weakness of the favorite was so apparent, that Walpole said confidently to his friend, Sir William Younge, "I shall certainly go out; but let me advise you not to go into violent opposition, as we must soon come in again." He continued uninterruptedly in his office by the discernment of Queen Caroline, who fully appreciated his talents,—and by a well-timed offer to obtain from parliament a jointure for her Majesty of £100,000 a year—whereas £60,000 was the highest sum which had been proposed by Compton.[1]

Walpole afterwards owned to the Chancellor his obligations to the Queen, and that with all her influence he had great difficulties to encounter:—

[1] Coxe's "Walpole." ii. 519.

"*Nov. 24th.*—At this time Sir Robert took occasion to tell me of the great credit he had with the King, and that it was principally by the means of the Queen, who was the most able woman to govern in the world; however, he wished now he had left off when the King came to the throne, for he looked upon himself to be in the worst situation of any man in England : that he was now struck at by a great number of people. All those who had hopes on the King's coming to the throne, seeing themselves disappointed, looked upon him as the cause. All the discontented Whigs, and Carteret, Roxburgh, Berkley, Bolingbroke, the Speaker Compton, and Pulteney, were entered into a formal confederacy against him: and if he could once retire, he never would meddle by way of opposition, but would comply with the Government in everything."

The Lord Chancellor stood well with Walpole, who consulted him confidentially on all legal and constitutional questions which arose. I observe by the Journal, that Sir Robert as seldom as possible called meetings of the whole Cabinet—and he never had what we should call "Cabinet dinners,"—but his favorite mode of preparing business was to invite two or three more particularly connected with the department to which the subject belonged, or whose opinion he particularly regarded, to dine with him,—and after the most unrestrained conversation with them, he settled what was fit to be done. Thus he would invite the two Tory law lords, Lord Harcourt and Lord Trevor, to meet the Chancellor, that he might consider with them respecting the reforms of the Court of Chancery.[1]

I do not think that the Chancellor ever was consulted by Sir Robert out of his own immediate department, or that he had any influence in the general measures of the Government. Indeed, the same thing might be said of Sir Robert's other colleagues during the whole course of his administration. If Lord King, like Lord Townshend had made a struggle to share power with the Premier, he very speedily would have been obliged, like Lord Townshend, to retire.

[1] "*August 11th.*—At Sir Robert Walpole's; dined there with Lord Harcourt and Lord Trevor. The end of our dining was to consider what was fit to be done with Lord Macclesfield's £30,000."

When parliament first met for the dispatch of business in the new reign, the Chancellor was relieved from the task of reading the royal speech, George II. having learned to speak English, although with a strong foreign accent;[1] and the Lord Chancellor had no other duty to perform than to present the speech to his Majesty in the fashion now adopted instead of receiving the speech from his Majesty according to the fashion of the reign of George I. The Opposition was still so feeble, that in the House of Lords the Chancellor's place was a sinecure. His name does not once appear in the printed debates; but this does not prove much, as they are so defective and scanty

The orders against publishing the proceedings of parliament were enforced by both Houses with greater rigor than ever. Upon a complaint against one Raikes, a printer at Gloucester, that he had printed speeches purporting to have been delivered in the House of Commons, there was an unanimous resolution "that it is an indignity to, and a breach of the privileges of, this House for any person to presume to give, in written or printed newspapers, any account or minutes of the debates or other proceedings of this House, or of any committee thereof; and that upon discovery of the authors, printers, or publishers, this House will proceed against the offenders with the utmost severity." The House of Lords enforced their order with equal rigor, and—by their superior power of fining and imprisoning for a fixed term, notwithstanding a prorogation—more effectually; insomuch that the magazines hardly ventured to give even a touch of their orations under feigned names, as delivered in Athens, Rome, or Liliput.[2] Upon consulting other

[1] He said he never could pronounce P or G. Hence two of his noted sayings, "I hate all *B*oets and *B*ainters,"—and "I do love old Brentford; it reminds me so much of *Y*armany."

[2] There is nothing in our constitutional history which surprises me so much as the long continuance of this restriction; for, besides that the publication of parliamentary debates is favorable to liberty, it is highly flattering to the vanity of the members, and now pleases them so much, that when the reporters' gallery is shut, all speaking is suspended. I suspect that, originally, when printing was introduced, and parliamentary proceedings excited curiosity, the Government was afraid that popular haranguing would be encouraged by the publicity of the debates, and that every successive Administration, even after the Revolution, thought they had an interest in making parliamentary proceedings as secret as possible, forgetting that from the circulation of their own speeches they might acquire popularity and strength. —At last the officer of the House of Commons who was to enforce the stand-

sources of information, however, I think there is reason to believe that Lord Chancellor King spoke very rarely, except in bringing forward the bills for reforming the Masters' offices, and for the improvement of the administration of the law, which I shall notice hereafter. Judging from his Diary, which is almost entirely filled with the deliberations of the Cabinet on pending negotiations, he seems to have taken a lively interest in foreign affairs, but, when they came to be publicly discussed, he very prudently remained silent; nor did he speak upon the "Pension Bill," the "Mutiny Bill," or on the "Civil List Bill," almost the only other subjects which seem to have caused much excitement in the House of Lords, while he remained Chancellor. This was a most remarkably tranquil period in the history of parliament. Walpole's Excise scheme excited a storm in the Commons, but it never reached the Upper House.

Although there must have been still going forward at Court a number of intrigues in which the Chancellor was concerned, his Diary unfortunately takes no notice of these, and, abounding with discussions on continental politics, contains very few personal anecdotes of himself or his contemporaries;—but I will give one other extract from it, which may cause regret that he did not write oftener in the same strain, availing himself of the private communications of the Premier:—

"*Monday, 2nd September,* 1729, went to town.—The next day saw the Queen at Court: from thence went to Sir R. Walpole's in his chariot, and dined with him and his lady only. He told me, that since the last time I saw him, they had received the draught of articles for a definitive peace concerted between our Plenipotentiaries and the Cardinal and the *garde des sceaux;* that they were so plain and good, that they did not think it worth the while to send for me to come to town to see and agree to them, or to give any further instruction; that they were as good as we could desire, he was afraid too good—but, however, the Cardinal said that he was sure Spain would come into it; that, for expedition, as soon as they were agreed on in France, they were immediately sent to Spain, and were there by this time. In talking with him about the King's

ing order was committed to prison; and now, in one session, there are more reports than during the first sixty years of the last century.

orders, that orders for the fleet and the negotiations with Spain should be all from hence without first sending to Hanover, he told me that Lord Townshend was very much displeased at it; that he, in concert with the Queen, gained it by a stratagem; that the Queen wrote a letter to the King intimating that some people thought the orders for the fleet were too long coming from Hanover, but that she would not for the world desire the King to send a power to her or to any one here to give immediate orders; that would be to execute a power which belonged only to him, and should be only executed by him. Whereon he wrote her a letter, that he would trust his throne and kingdom entirely with her, and thereupon ordered, that not only the fleet, but also the Plenipotentiaries at Paris, should receive their immediate orders from hence, and not stay for his.—On this occasion he let me into several secrets relating to the King and Queen—that the King constantly wrote to her by every opportunity long letters of two or three sheets, being generally of all his actions—what he did every day, even to minute things, and particularly of his amours, what women he admired . . .; and that the Queen, to continue him in a disposition to do what she desired, returned as long letters, and approved even of his amours, not scrupling to say, that she was but one woman, and an old woman, and that he might love more and younger women. . . .[1] By which means, and a perfect subserviency to his will, she effected whatsoever she desired, without which it was impossible to keep him within any bounds."

This certainly is a very singular correspondence between husband and wife, and we should not be justified in remarking upon it had they not been the King and Queen of these realms: but it is matter of history, and discloses to us the real influences by which the nation was governed. There must have been an extreme intimacy between her Majesty and Walpole, that she should show him these letters; and we can not help suspecting that, as a method of perpetuating her favor with his Majesty, and consequently his own ministerial stability he framed the answers—which could scarcely have been spontaneously suggested by her own mind. Indeed, it is possible that

[1] Diary, p. 111. I have been obliged to omit some other expressions imputed to her Majesty as too coarse to be copied.

the whole was the invention of Walpole, who over his wine might wish to mystify the Chancellor. Queen Caroline is generally, and I believe truly, represented to us as not only chaste and pure in her own conduct, but as a zealous patron of religion and morality.'

The Diary, which had been kept very irregularly, entirely breaks off in October, 1729. I will try to supply its place by here introducing several letters addressed to Lord King while Chancellor, which will throw light upon his conduct and upon the manners and customs of his age.

On the sudden death of Sir Clement Wearg, there was a keen contest about the filling up of his office. Sir John Willes, afterwards Attorney General and a distinguished Judge, did not consider it beneath his dignity thus to address the distributor of legal patronage:—

"The occasion of this is humbly to beg your Lordship's favor that I may succeed the late Solicitor General. I have been King's Counsel above seven years, and none of my seniors, as I am informed, desire it. During my whole life, in whatever station I have been, I have never omitted any one opportunity of showing my zeal for the present establishment; and your Lordship, I believe, can bear me witness that I was not wanting in my poor endeavors to promote his Majesty's interest at a time when it was not only very unfashionable, but very dangerous to do so. My behavior in this respect will, I hope, be thought sufficient to balance my other imperfections, of which I am fully sensible."

Lord King, however, espoused the interest of Mr. Talbot, who was now appointed Solicitor General, and afterwards succeeded him as Chancellor.

It is curious to observe how judges who wished to resign on account of age and infirmity, were obliged to beg for a pension or retired allowance. Sir Littleton Powys, in a letter to Lord Chancellor King, after describing a severe illness from which he had recently recovered, thus proceeds to state his claims:—

"I was in arms myself with three servants, at the time of the Revolution, under the then Lord Herbert, who chose me to read the Prince of Orange's Declaration, at

---

¹ I am sorry to say that the "Memoirs of Lord Hervey," recently published, have removed all doubt as to the genuineness of the disgusting correspondence between George II. and Queen Caroline.—*Note to 3rd Edit.*

the head of many hundreds of the best of the county then met at Shrewsbury, which I did with a very loud voice, and I am sure with very great heartiness. I was, the first circuit after that, made Second Justice of Chester, and afterwards, by the great favor of my Lord Chancellor Somers, I was advanced into the Exchequer. I was afterwards, by the approbation of my Lord Chief Justice Holt, removed into the King's Bench, where I have been twenty-three years—so that I have now sat a Judge in Westminster Hall thirty years, and in three reigns, and I have had the protection of the clause 'Quamdiu se bene gesserit,' without any misbehavior ever imputed to me. I am sure I have been most hearty and zealous for his Majesty's person and government, and the present establishment." [Having described his terrible attacks of the gout, he says:] "I might, by the help of the bath, and other means, try to restore my health, and endeavor to die a Judge, but my success in such restoring meets with a most untoward objection, that I am now fourscore years old wanting but one, and I am therefore thinking it better to resign my place if I may be admitted by the great favor and generosity of his Majesty, after so long and faithful service, to go off with honor, by having a pension, in like manner as my brother Powel had, who was a Judge in Westminster Hall eight years fewer than I have been, and my brother Blencowe now hath, who was my junior one year."

He continues at great length to urge his petition—hinting that it might be very convenient for some worthy friend of the Lord Chancellor, that there should be a vacancy on the bench.

The Prime Minister does not seem to have encroached by any means improperly on the Lord Chancellor's legal patronage. Thus he good-naturedly solicits him for the most inconsiderable appointment which could be held by a barrister:—

"My Lord,

"Mr. Green, the bearer, has desired me to recommend him to your Lordship to be continued a Commissioner of Bankrupts. He is now a Fellow of King's College in Cambridge, was clerk to Sir Edward Northey for ten years,—is well known to Lord Chief Justice Raymond and others from whom you may have his character. Our education

at the same place and college entitles him to my good wishes, and is the occasion and excuse for my giving you this trouble.
"I am very truly, my Lord,
"Your Lordship's most faithful humble Servant,
"R. WALPOLE."

In the disposals of livings, however, I suspect that for election purposes Sir Robert interfered pretty freely—without very scrupulously considering the merits of candidates. Here is a specimen:—

"My Lord,
"I am afraid you will think me a hackney solicitor about Church preferments, but my friends will make me the canal to your Lordship's favor, which must plead my excuse. I have just received an account that the vicarage of Lostwithiel, in Cornwall, is vacant. My son being now chosen for that borough, makes my troubling your Lordship more excusable, and begging that you will not be engaged for this vacancy till I receive my instructions in whose behalf I shall be obliged to receive your Lordship's favor,
"I am very truly,
"Your Lordship's most faithful humble Servant,
"R. WALPOLE."

I will give another application to Lord King for a living—from the head of my clan in favor of a poor countryman:—

"My Lord,
"This letter will be delivered to your Lordship by the young man I had the honor to recommend to you. He has been hitherto instructing the good people of England *for nothing* in the primitive style, but now giving in to the modern taste of prophesying for money, and having at present nothing, will be glad to have any preferment, from the prelacy of Canterbury to the least living in your gift. If your Lordship will be so good as to enable him to tread in the paths of his brethren, you will do a great favor to
"Your most faithful and most obedient
humble Servant,
"ARGYLL AND GREENWICH."

The next letter shows that in those days the Lord Chancellor, both in England and Ireland, was enabled to conciliate the good will of persons of the highest eminence in church and state by a lavish distribution of stationery at the public expense. Thus writes the Most Reverend Father in God, JOHN, LORD ARCHBISHOP OF DUBLIN, &c., &c., &c., to Lord King:—

"My Lord,

"Ever since I have had the honor of being acquainted with Lord Chancellors, I have lived in England and Ireland upon Chancery paper, pens, and wax. I am not willing to lose an old advantageous custom. If your Lordship hath any to spare me by my servant, you will oblige your very humble Servant,

"JOHN DUBLIN."[1]

I shall add one letter more, showing that the King thought the surest way to attach the citizens of London to his dynasty was by giving them a good dinner. The Treaty of Vienna being made public, whereby Austria and Spain had engaged to place the Pretender on the throne of Great Britain, a loyal address was voted by the Lord Mayor, Aldermen, and Common Council, to his Majesty,—and the Secretary of State sent the following mandate to the Lord Chancellor:—

"My Lord,

"The King having ordered a dinner to be provided at St. James's for the citizens who shall accompany the address which is to be presented to-morrow, and it being proper that his Majesty's servants should dine with them, which they can not conveniently do in case the House of Lords should sit, I must beg your Lordship will be so good as to get the House adjourned till Wednesday next. I am, with the greatest truth and respect,

"My Lord,

"Your Lordship's most obedient humble Servant,

"TOWNSHEND."

I have now only to consider Lord King as a juridical reformer. He found the Court of Chancery in the most deplorable state of confusion. The old usage for the Lord Chancellor, on taking possession of his office, like the Roman Prætor, to revise the procedure by issuing a

---

[1] Very different from the economy of modern times!—when the Attorney General, deprived of his salary, on which he still pays the land-tax, is obliged gratuitously to draw public acts of parliament with his own pens and ink on his own paper, being deprived of his stationery, and of the pecuniary compensation for some time substituted for it.

new set of Orders (or an Edict), had been long laid aside, and abuses for the profit of the practitioners, the officers, and the Chancellor had been greatly multiplied and aggravated. The most crying grievance was the loss which many suitors had sustained by the insolvency of the Masters in Chancery, who, to indemnify themselves for the large sums paid for their places, had been speculating in the South Sea Bubble with the trust-money in their hands. Lord King, upon his appointment, framed various regulations to enforce those lately issued by the Lords Commissioners of the Great Seal, for the purpose of compelling the Masters to do justice to the injured suitors.[1] At his desire the Lords of the Regency directed that Mr. Paxton, the Solicitor to the Treasury, should prepare an account of the deficiency of the Masters to be laid before the Council, and the Attorney and Solicitor General were required to take care that the suitors might receive satisfaction for their several demands. There were four offices found deficient to the amount of £82,301 19*s.* 11½*d.*, the whole of which would have been lost—to the utter ruin of many families, the loss falling particularly on widows and orphans—if a legislative remedy were not found. In the first place, Lord Macclesfield's fine of £30,000, was most righteously applied to this purpose, and the remainder was made up by an expedient too often resorted to in Chancery reform—by mulcting future innocent suitors:[2] a tax was imposed for thirty-two years on writs and other proceedings; and on the credit of this the requisite sum was borrowed, so that the suitors who had been robbed were all fully indemnified. To check the like abuses in time to come, Lord King, with the concurrence of the Master of the Rolls, remodeled Lord Macclesfield's order, forbidding Masters in Chancery any longer to make any use of suitors' money for their own advantage, and commanding them forthwith to pay all sums received by them into the Bank of England.[3]

This for the future secured the principal of the money, but would not have done justice to the suitors, whose fortunes might be locked up many years in the course of administration or pending a complicated litigation. A

---

[1] Sanders's Orders, i. 506–537.
[2] Thus in 1843, on the abolition of the Six Clerk's office, the indemnities were directed to be paid by heavy fees.   [3] Sand. Orders, i. 514.

plan was therefore devised, whereby interest should be allowed to them in the mean time, the money being vested in public securities in the name of a new officer, acting under the control of the Lord Chancellor, to be called the ACCOUNTANT-GENERAL. This was carried into effect by two acts of parliament, the one entitled "An Act for better securing the Moneys and Effects of the Suitors of the Court of Chancery,"[1] and the other, "An Act for the Relief of the High Court of Chancery."[2] "Happy had it been," says Oldmixon, "if the acts had further relieved the suitors in that Court, by regulating the litigious, tedious, and expensive suits, and the enormous extortions of hungry solicitors, and the vexatious and chargeable attendances upon Masters, which render even a Court of Equity in too many instances equally ruinous and terrible."[3] But the difficulties in the way of further improvement were probably then insurmountable. A contemporary writer says, "If an order is but made to cut off a burdensome expense, to shorten the old lengths for the benefit of suitors, a defalcation never so small runs to the very quick in Chancery Lane. Malice goes to work, clamors, outcries, and oppositions arise, and in the end may grow worse than one man perhaps could tell how to deal with."[4] We must recollect that not only the Lord Chancellor himself, but that all the officers in the Court down to the doorkeepers, were chiefly paid by fees; that the Chancellor of the Exchequer and the public would not have tolerated a proposal to pay them by fixed salaries out of the public revenue; and that the fund arising from unclaimed sums of money now found so very convenient for Chancery improvements, was then in embryo. When we censure those who have gone before us for inefficiency in law reform, we should recollect that we ourselves have never solved the problem of recompensing professional labor, without the test of the length of law proceedings, and that till this is done all attempts to check prolixity will be vain.[5] Under the auspices of Lord King, returns were

[1] 12 Geo. I. c. 32.   [2] Ibid. c. 33.   [3] Vol. iii. 784.
[4] History of Chancery, &c. 1726. 12mo.
[5] A striking illustration of the brevity which lawyers could attain, there being no interest to be verbose is the judgment of death upon a felon, which, as there was no fee according to the number of words contained in it, was thus recorded—"SUS. PER COL."

obtained of all fees and emoluments of officers in courts of justice; and these were referred to a commission, that their legality and reasonableness might be thoroughly scrutinized in order to their being regulated and reformed. But the report of the commissioners was not presented till after his death.[1] It should be mentioned to Lord King's credit that he made several attempts to improve the practice of the Court respecting applications to rectify the minutes of decrees; respecting appeals from the Master of the Rolls, and respecting petitions for rehearings;[2] but he had little success in this department, and the complaints of the delays and expense of Chancery proceedings were as loud as at any former period.

There was one great improvement in law proceedings which, while he held the Great Seal, he at last accomplished. From very ancient times the written pleadings, both in criminal and civil suits, were, or rather professed to be, in the Latin tongue; and while the jargon employed would have been very perplexing to a Roman of the Augustan age, it was wholly unintelligible to the persons whose life, property, and fame were at stake. This absurdity had been corrected in the time of the Commonwealth, but, along with many others so corrected, had been reintroduced at the Restoration, and had prevailed during five succeeding reigns.[3] The attention of the public was now attracted to it by a petition from the magistracy of the North Riding of the county of York, representing the evils of the old law language being retained in legal process and proceedings, and praying for the substitution of the native tongue. The bill, by the Chancellor's direction, was introduced in the House of Commons, and it passed there without much difficulty. In the Lords it was fully explained and ably supported by the Lord Chancellor; but it experienced considerable opposition, several noble lords being greatly alarmed at such an innovation, and contending that, "if it were

[1] In 1730, an act was passed to terminate certain disputes respecting the orders and decrees of the Masters of the Rolls—confirming them subject to an appeal to the Lord Chancellor.—3 Geo. 2, c. 30; Com. Journ. xxi. 563. It was not thought necessary to introduce any bill to forbid the sale of masterships in Chancery, this being considered adjudged in Lord Macclesfield's case to be illegal, though constantly practiced.

[2] Sand. Orders, i. 506, 511, 521.

[3] See an instance of it, ante, vol. v. p. 444, where the question arose whether the word "impressit" could properly be used to mean *he printed*.

sanctioned, our records would be neglected, and the true knowledge of the law would be lost; that much uncertainty and confusion would be produced by attempting to translate the well-established Latin forms into English; that great delays would arise in the administration of justice; that a wide door would be opened to fraud; that prosecutions for crimes would be rendered more difficult and expensive; that the recovery of small debts would become almost impossible, and that the supposed reform would multiply law-suits instead of bringing ease to the people." Lord Raymond, the Chief Justice of the King's Bench, speaking, I presume, the sentiments of all his brother Judges, strongly opposed the measure—availing himself of the weapons of ridicule as well as of reason, and saying, " that, if the bill passed, the law might likewise be translated into Welsh, since many in Wales understood not English." The Duke of Argyll, after a general defense of the bill, said he was glad that nothing could be brought forward against it by the Chief Justice of the King's Bench, as wise and learned a lord as ever sat in that House—beyond a joke. Amidst heavy forebodings of future mischief the bill passed, and mankind are now astonished that so obvious a reform should have been so long deferred.[1]

Lord Chancellor King's career, most honorable, if not very brilliant, was now drawing to a close. His fall was not by a revolution in the state, by the death of a Sovereign, or by a ministerial crisis. With health and fitness for his office, he might have continued to hold it for many years. But, after a long and arduous struggle, he

[1] Geo. 2, c. 26; and see 6 Geo. 2, c. 14, allowing technical expressions, such as *nisi prius, quare impedit,* &c. still to be used. Blackstone laments the loss of the old law Latin (Com. iii. 322); and I have heard the late Lord Ellenborough from the bench regret the change, on the ground that it has had the tendency to make attorneys illiterate. Sergeant Heywood, the vindicator of Fox, seriously acted upon Lord Raymond's jest. As I have been told by the counsel who were present, while he was sitting as Chief Justice of the Caermarthen Circuit on a trial for murder, it appeared that neither the prisoner nor the jury understood one word of English, and it was proposed that the evidence and the charge should be translated into Welsh; but his Lordship said that " this would be repealing the act of parliament, which requires that all proceedings in courts of justice shall be in the English tongue, and that the case of a trial in Wales, the prisoner and the jury not understanding English, was a case not provided for, although it had been pointed out by that great Judge, Lord Raymond." The jury very properly brought in a verdict of *not guilty,* the evidence, to those who understood it, being decisive to prove that the prisoner had murdered his wife.

thought it would be decent and becoming that he should voluntarily resign. He had materially injured his constitution by the intense application to which he began to submit for the purpose of qualifying himself as an Equity Judge, soon after he received the Great Seal, and his supervening illnesses were aggravated by the anxiety and mortification to which he was exposed from perceiving that he did not enjoy the confidence of the Bar, as he had done when he was a Common-Law Judge. As early as November, 1727, he enters in his Journal his refusal to a pressing request from the Duke of Newcastle to come to town, from Ockham, to attend a cabinet: "To this I returned answer, that my constant and continued application to the business of the Court of Chancery had brought upon me rheumatical and sciatical pains; and if I had any regard to myself or family, I must, for remedy, stay three or four days in the country." He had a very able and experienced Master of the Rolls, but Sir Joseph (piqued, probably, that a common lawyer should have been put over his head), instead of cordially assisting him, kept aloof as much as he could, and sometimes actually thwarted him in the framing of orders respecting the practice of the court.[1] He made extraordinary exertions to clear off arrears, often sitting in court to a late hour; but even for these exertions he was censured. The author of a pamphlet, then published, "Upon the Abuses of the Court of Chancery," bitterly exclaimed, "It was not lawful for the PRÆTOR URBANUS to hear causes after sunset; but ours we see post on till *midnight*, to master and put down the business of his Court."[2] This complaint of late sittings appears very sulky and capricious, but I am afraid it might be excused by what was to be spied in the Court of Chancery in the latter days of Lord Chancellor King. The celebrated Jeremy Bentham, in a letter to Cooksey, the author of the "Lives of Lord Somers and Lord Hardwicke," has given, from the relation of his father, an eminent solicitor, a very lively picture of the manner in which equity business was then disposed of:—

"Lord King became so far advanced in years when he held the seals as Chancellor, that he often dozed over his

---

[1] Diary, p. 19. "His secretary delivered me a letter from him, whereby he declares that he will prevent as much as he can the usher submitting to any such bills." [2] History of Chancery, &c. 1726, 12mo.

causes when upon the bench; a circumstance which I myself well remember was the case; but it was no prejudice to the suitors; for Sir Philip Yorke and Mr. Talbot were both men of such good principles and strict integrity, and had always so good an understanding with one another, that, although they were frequently, and almost always, concerned for opposite parties in the same cause, yet the merits of the cause were no sooner fully stated to the Court, but they were sensible on which side the right lay; and, accordingly, the one or the other of these two great men took occasion to state the matter briefly to his Lordship, and instruct the Register in what manner to minute the heads of the decree."[1]

At last, when Lord King had been Chancellor eight years—from the exertions he made beyond his strength, he was struck by a paralytic affection, which happily left him conscious of the propriety of his retirement. He yielded to the necessity with decency and firmness, and intimated, first to the Minister, and then to his Majesty, his determination to resign. Not being in a state of health to go to St. James's to surrender the Great Seal with his own hand,—at his request George II., on the 19th of November, 1733, sent the Secretary of State to his house to receive it, and to bear warm acknowledgments of his long and faithful services.

Having delivered up the bauble with little regret, the ex-Chancellor felt that he was now completely disabled for public life, and that the time that might be spared to him was to be devoted to contemplation. He immediately hastened to his favorite retreat at Ockham, and, having a mind early tinctured with literature and devotion, he was not sorry to exchange the distractions of business for the resumption of his theological studies and the settlement of that great account which he was about to render of his thoughts and of his actions in this mortal state. He seemed to rally from repose and the pure air

---

[1] Cooksey's "Somers," p. 60. When business is divided in a court between two great leaders without competitors, justice may thus be substantially administered, although not always to the satisfaction of the losing party, who expects his counsel to make the best fight he can in return for his fees. The late Chief Justice Gibbs told me that when he led the Western Circuit against Sergeant Lens, they kept a weak Judge right. "Thus," said he, "I once, knowing I had no case, opened a nonsuit before my brother Graham. He was for deciding in my favor; but I insisted on being nonsuited, and saved my client the expense of having a verdict in his favor set aside."

of the country, but on the 22nd of July in the following summer, about noon, he had a fresh and much more severe attack of his disorder, and, at eight o'clock in the evening of the same day, he expired, in the sixty-sixth year of his age.

His body was interred in the parish church at Ockham, where there was erected a most splendid and tasteful monument to his memory by Roubiliac—with these words engraved on an urn :—

"DEPOSITUM
PETRI DOMINI KING,
BARONIS DE OCKHAM."

And the following inscription on a tablet underneath:

"He was born in the City of Exeter, of worthy and substantial parents,
but with a genius superior to his birth.
By his industry, prudence, learning, and virtue,
he raised himself to the highest character and reputation,
and to the highest posts and dignities.
He applied himself to his studies in the Middle Temple,
And to an exact and complete knowledge in all parts and history of the Law,
added the most extensive learning, Theological and Civil.
He was chosen a member of the House of Commons in the year 1699;
Recorder of the City of London in the year 1708;
Made Chief Justice of the Common Pleas in 1714, on the accession of King George I.;
Created LORD KING, BARON OF OCKHAM,
and raised to the post and dignity of Lord High Chancellor of Great Britain,
1725;
under the laborious fatigues of which weighty place,
sinking into a paralytic disease, he resigned it Novr. 19, 1733,
And died July 22, 1734, aged 65.
A Friend to true Religion and Liberty."

This panegyric is modest and well deserved. The voice of posterity re-echoes "A friend to true religion and liberty!" He was not celebrated for his eloquence: he has not enriched our literature with any very attractive compositions; and he did not, in his highest elevation, equal the expectation that had been formed of him; but he was a most learned, enlightened, and upright magistrate, ever devoted to the conscientious discharge of the duties of his station. He rose from obscurity to high distinction by native energy and self-reliance,—without courting the favor of any patron or of the multitude, and without ever incurring the suspicion of a dishonorable or mean action. If he did not dazzle by brilliant qualities, he gained universal good-will by such as were estimable and amiable.

He himself unostentatiously ascribed all his success in life to his love of labor, and he took for his motto, " Labor ipse voluptas,"—upon which I find in the Biographia Britannica the following paraphrase by one of his admirers :—

> " 'Tis not the splendor of the place,
> The gilded coach, the purse, the mace,
> Nor all the pompous strains of state,
> With crowds that at your levee wait,
> To make you happy, make you great ;
> But whilst mankind you strive to bless
> With all the talents you possess,
> Whilst the chief joy that you receive
> Arises from the joy you give,
> Duty and taste in you unite
> To make the heavy burden light ;
> For pleasure rightly understood,
> Is only labor to be good." [1]

I have not been able to discover much of him in private society, but he seems, notwithstanding his addiction to divinity and law, to have had no inconsiderable share of humor, and he must have been a most determined punster if we may judge from the following epitaph, which he is said, when Chancellor, to have written upon an old carpenter of the name of Spong, and which is still to be read on a square granite grave-stone covering this "plane" man's remains in Ockham churchyard :—

> " Who many a sturdy oak had laid along,
> Fell'd by DEATH's surer hatchet, here lies SPONG.
> *Post* oft he made, but ne'er a *place* could get,
> And liv'd by *railing* tho' he was no wit,
> Old *saws* he had, although no antiquarian,
> And *styles* corrected, yet was no grammarian.
> Long liv'd he Ockham's premier architect ;
> And lasting as his fame a tomb t' erect
> In vain we seek an artist such as he,
> Whose pales and gates were for eternity.
> So here he rests from all life's toils and follies,
> O spare awhile, kind heaven, his fellow-laborer Hollis." [2]

---

[1] When Lord King was about to be raised to the peerage, a gentleman of the name of Whatley sent him a long dissertation on " MOTTOES," warning him against a punning or "canting" one, as " A Rege pro Rege," and submitting three for his choice : " Est Modus in Rebus," " Discite Justitiam," and " Vincit Ratio." This is preserved among the " Somers' Tracts," edited by Sir Walter Scott.

[2] Hollis was bricklayer to the family, as Spong had been carpenter.—*Gent. Mag.* vol. lxx. p. 113. The present of Earl of Lovelace denies that his ancestor was the author of these lines on Spong's tombstone : it is stated that he died Nov. 17, 1736, which is two years and four months after Lord Chancellor King ; so that if the Chancellor wrote the *jeu d'esprit* it must have been to amuse the old carpenter in his lifetime.

Lord King, as I have before stated, was married early in life, and he continued to live with the object of his affections to the day of his death in perfect harmony and happiness. By her he left four sons, three of whom successively inherited his honorable title and ample estate. Though all well-behaved, none of them appear to have in any way gained much renown. The eldest, for dabbling in poetry, is grouped in the DUNCIAD with other dull sons of distinguished sires :—

> " Great C**, H**, P**, R**, K**,
> Why all your toils? your sons have learned to sing;
> How quick ambition hastes to ridicule!
> The sire is made a peer, the son a fool."

But in another generation the talent of the founder of the family again broke out with fresh luster. The late Lord King, so eminent for wit, eloquence, and every great and amiable quality, was the grandson of the youngest of the four brothers. The Chancellor is now represented in the direct male line by the Earl of Lovelace, whom I rejoice to see deservedly raised in the peerage, but whom, from my regard for the memory of old Sir Peter, I should have been still better pleased to have hailed as "EARL KING."[1]

CHAPTER CXXVII.

LIFE OF LORD CHANCELLOR TALBOT FROM HIS BIRTH TILL HE RECEIVED THE GREAT SEAL.

WE have now bid a final adieu to the stirring times of William III. and of Anne, in which the six last preceding Chancellors played a distinguished part. Those who are to follow did not enter public life till the House of Hanover was securely on the throne; and, without being engaged in revolutionary intrigues, they rose to high office merely by professional eminence. The Georgian period of English history, to which we are to be confined, was comparatively tranquil; but it presents us with great men at the head of the law, who would have been capable of guiding the destinies of the nation under

[1] Grandeur of the law, p. 114.

any circumstances, however arduous. The first of these was praised in a more vehement and less qualified manner than almost any one who ever held the office of Lord Chancellor. Historians and poets were equally eager to celebrate his good qualities. But this arose in part from the sympathy excited by his fate, for he was only shown as a Judge to excite the admiration of mankind when he was snatched away to an early tomb.

CHARLES TALBOT sprang from a very ancient and illustrious family, which has produced a great number of distinguished warriors and statesmen,—having for his ancestor the companion of Henry V., who, after the death of that monarch, so heroically sustained the interest and glory of the English name in France. He was of a younger branch of the Talbots—settled first at Grafton and then at Salwarp, in Worcestershire.[1] His father, a younger brother, went into the Church, and, displaying learning and liberality of sentiment, was successively Dean of Worcester, and Bishop of Oxford, of Salisbury, and of Durham. The Earl of Shrewsbury, the early friend of Lord Somers,—head of the house at the close of the seventeenth and beginning of the eighteenth century,—who took a leading part in two revolutions,—in bringing in King William, and bringing in King George,—no doubt assisted the merits of his kinsman in procuring these promotions. Bishop Talbot was, as might be supposed, a zealous Whig. From him was inherited the eloquence in debate which distinguished his son. He seems to have had considerable weight in the House of Lords. Burnet particularly celebrates his speech in favor of the Union with Scotland, and his speech against Dr. Sacheverell. On this last occasion, he boldly denied that the Church condemned resistance in cases of extreme tyranny, and he relied upon the instance of the Jews, who, under the brave family of the Maccabees, revolted against Antiochus, and formed themselves into a free and independent government. "Our homilies," he said, "only condemn willful rebellion against our kings *while they are governing by law.*"[1] These sentiments he instilled into the minds

---

[1] This branch was descended from Sir Gilbert Talbot, third son of John, second Earl of Shrewsbury.

Vol. iv. 176, 286. He seems even to have been ready to draw his sword in a good cause, like Bishops of old. In the account of a royal review in Hyde

of his descendants, who, steadily defending the just prerogatives of the Crown established for the good of the people, were zealous friends of civil and religious liberty.

The Bishop, by his wife Catherine, daughter of Alderman King, of London, had eight sons. Of these, the eldest, the subject of this memoir, was born in the year 1684, while his father was only a country parson. I have not discovered anything respecting his school education, and there seems reason to think that he continued under private tuition till he was sent to the University. The diligent habits and taste for polite literature, which afterwards distinguished him, he must have contracted at an early age. In Michaelmas Term, 1701, he was entered a gentleman commoner at Oriel College, Oxford, where his father likewise had been educated. Learning had then fallen to a low ebb in this once famous University, Jacobite politics being the chief business of the place, and hard drinking its chief recreation :—

> " Now Isis' elders reel, their pupils sport,
> And Alma Mater lies dissolv'd in port."

Luckily for young Talbot, he was generally regarded with a sort of horror, as the son of a Whig bishop who had opposed the " Bill against Occasional Conformity," and he was excluded from the coteries where measures were debated to put down Dissenters, along with Low Church divines—if possible, more odious,—and to atone for the national sin of the Revolution (in which the Church had for a short time been implicated), by re-establishing the doctrine of divine right, and by recalling the true heir to the throne. Our banished student consoled himself with the Orations of Cicero and Demosthenes, and he surreptitiously got possession of a copy of the works of John Locke, which, carefully concealing it from his tutor, he pored over late at night, in his bed chamber, where he thought he was in no danger of a visit from the proctors. Now, likewise, he most usefully devoted much of his time to the study of the Roman Civil Law,—which was probably the secret of his afterwards turning out so skilful a jurist, and such an admirable

Park, to be found in the "Flying Post" of June 14th, 1722, it is said that "Bishop Talbot was finely mounted in a long habit of purple, with jack boots, and his hat cocked, and black wig ty'd behind him like a militant officer."

Judge. Being impatient to breathe in a freer atmosphere, he claimed, under the statutes of the University, an honorary degree as the son of a bishop, before the ordinary time for his graduating had arrived ; and it was found that, notwithstanding the loose opinions which he was supposed to have inherited from his father, this could not be refused to him, for he had been remarkably regular in his attendance at chapel and at lectures, and no breach of academical discipline could be imputed to him. He proceeded B.A. in Trinity Term, 1704. Forthwith, he left the University with the highest reputation for his accomplishments ; and his manners were so agreeable, that in the following year, although known to be a Whig, and, what might be equally alarming, known to be more than "*mediocriter doctus*," he was elected a fellow of All Souls.[1]

He spent two or three years very agreeably, having his college for his head quarters,—not yet determined on a profession, and with a strong inclination for the easy life he might expect to enjoy in the Church. But he grew more and more sick of the monotony of Oxford, and falling into the company of Lord Chancellor Cowper, that discerning man soon discovered his extraordinary talents and fitness for public life, and advised him to study the law. Accordingly, on the "28th of June, 1707, Charles Talbott, Esq., son and heir apparent of William, Lord Bishop of Oxford, was admitted of the Honorable Society of the Inner Temple,"[2] and he took up his residence in chambers.

I have not been able to obtain any authentic account of him while he remained *in statu pupillari* there. He must have been exposed to the disadvantage of a com-

[1] It is said that by the statutes of this college, those to be elected Fellows are required to be " bene nati, bene vestiti, et mediocriter docti ;" but in modern times, the Fellows have often been distinguished for their learning as well as their social qualities.—*1st edit.*

I have since been informed that the current story of the Fellows of All Souls being required to be only " moderately good scholars, so that they are well-born and smartly dressed," is a calumny upon them and the Founder, and that the following is the true reading of the statute referred to :—

" Statuentes præterea quod nulli alii scholares in prædicto collegio eligantur nisi qu rudimentis grammaticæ sufficientur, et in plano cantu competenter, prius fuerint eruditi, et qui primam tonsuram clericalem habentes ad sacerdotium sint habiles et dispositi, liberæ conditionis, de legitimo matrimononati, bonis conditionibus et moribus peronnati, et in studio proficere coupentes, et re ipsâ proficientes."—(1849.)   [2] Admission Book, 1693-1707.

fortable home at the west end of the town while his father was attending parliament, and to the danger of easy access to fashionable society—more formidable to a law student than penury and friendlessness. But, on the other hand, he had a powerful stimulus to exertion and perseverance in recollecting that his father had such a numerous family, and that a finished education was all the patrimony he had to expect.[1]

From extraordinary proficiency in his studies, or from family interest, the period of his studentship was abridged. According to the rules then subsisting in the Inns of Court, he could not be called to the bar till he was of seven years' standing, and had kept sixteen terms; but on the 11th of February, 1711, he had a "call of grace." [2]

[1] Instead of inheriting large possessions from his father, he is said afterwards to have contributed generously to pay his father's debts; who, in princely magnificence spent more than his princely revenue at Durham.

[2] "* Interius Templum   } Parliamentu
     Ricus Webb, Armiger. | tentm undecimo
     Thesaurarius ibm.   } die Februarij
                           Anno Dom. 1710.

"At this Parliament Mr Charles Talbott is called to the Bar, and to be utter Barrister of this Society."

The following entries likewise appear in the books of the Inner Temple, respecting Lord Chancellor Talbot:—

" Interius Templum   } Parliament. tentum
   Nathan^l Manlove, Ar. } Sexto die Maij
   Thesaurar. ibm.   } Anno Dom. 1726.

"At this Parliament Charles Talbott, Esqr., his Majesties Soll General, is called to the Bench."

" Interius Templum   } Parliamentu tentum
   Nathl Manlove Arm. | decimo nono die
   Thesaurarius ibm.   } Novembris Anno
                           Dom. 1726.

"At this Parliamant, it is ordered that Charles Talbot, Esqr, his Majesty's Sollicitor-General, one of the Masters of the Bench of this Society, be and is hereby unanimously elected Treasurer for the year ensuing."

" Intius Temp'um   } Parliamentum tentum
   Carolus Talbot, Ar. | undecimo die
   Soll Genal Dni R^s. } Februarij Anno Dom
   Thesaurarius ibm.   } 1726.

"At this Parliament, Charles Talbot, Esqr, his Majesties Sollicitor-General, Trearer of this Society, is chosen Reader for the next Lent Vacation (in the

* "Bench Table, 5 Feb. 1710–11.—Ordered that notice be given to the Masters of the Bench that a call to the Barr will be proposed at the Table on Friday next. And it is also ordered that Mr. Charles Talbot, eldest son of the Bishop of Oxford, be put into the paper in order for such call."

During the reign of Queen Anne he seems to have abstained from politics, and to have devoted himself entirely to his profession. His success was rapid and steady. He went the Oxford Circuit, where he got into good practice, but he chiefly flourished in the Court of Chancery. He was one of the first who, early in their professional career, confined themselves to the sittings of the Lord Chancellor, which, since the abolition of the Star Chamber, were held, during the seasons of business, every morning, and in the afternoons of Wednesdays and Fridays,—and to the sittings of the Master of the Rolls, held in the afternoons of Mondays, Tuesdays, and Thursdays. But he had laid a solid foundation of common law, and continued to go the circuit till he was appointed Solicitor General to the King. An equity draughtsman's office was not thought a sufficient school for Chancellors till a century afterwards.

On the accession of George I., Talbot's father succeeded the famous Gilbert Burnet as Bishop of Salisbury; and, at the general election which soon followed, he was himself returned to the House of Commons as member for Tregony. His name is hardly ever mentioned in the printed debates, but it is quite certain that he spoke frequently and well; and such a position had he established for himself, that although a lawyer, he was selected to second the nomination of Spencer Compton as Speaker. The seconder seems to have made the best speech on that occasion. Although the mover was the celebrated Philip Earl of Chesterfield, then Lord Stanhope, he seems to have said little more than, "considering the present circumstances of the times, and the many important affairs that seemed urgent to come before the House, and the House ought, in this first step, to give his Majesty and the whole nation convincing proofs of their firm adherence to our present happy establishment, by choosing for their Speaker a person of unshaken fidelity to his Majesty, and of undoubted zeal for the Protestant succession." But, according to the slight sketch we have of Talbot's oration, after congratulating the House on the numerous attendance, which he hailed as an earnest of public spirit in the new parliaroome of Richard West, Esqr, late Lord <u>Chancellor</u> of Ireland, and one of the Masters of the Bench of this Society, deced.).

ment, he said "he hoped every gentleman came there resolved to support the liberty of the subject, the just rights of the Crown, and our present happy establishment in church and state: that it would be impossible to give a more striking proof of these laudable feelings than by placing in the chair the honorable person named, who had been ever distinguished for his love of freedom and his unalterable adherence to a government framed for the good of the people. If there be any enemies to our peace, who have entertained imaginary hopes that the people of this kingdom are inclined to exchange Protestant for Popish rule, let us show by the known character of the person we place at our head, what is to be expected from this House of Commons." He then goes on to give the form, which has been followed ever since on such occasions;—to enumerate all the qualifications of a perfect Speaker, and to assert that they are all concentrated in the individual whom it is proposed to call to the chair.[1]

In 1717 a feather was put into Talbot's cap by appointing him Solicitor General to the Prince of Wales; but he had been eleven years in parliament before he had any valuable professional advancement. Lord Chancellor Macclesfield entertained a prejudice against him, or, at any rate, sacrificed him to the indulgence of his excessive partiality for a favorite—certainly a very deserving one—Philip Yorke, who was made Solicitor General while almost a boy. Talbot, having resented this promotion, incurred the decided displeasure of the Lord Chancellor, and was passed over on the next move in the law, which took place on the elevation of Sir Robert Raymond to be Lord Chief Justice of the King's Bench.

At last, after the fall of Lord Macclesfield, Lord King, the new Chancellor, expressed himself sensible of the injustice hitherto done to Mr. Talbot, who had continued to enjoy high distinction both in his profession and in parliament; and on the sudden death of Sir Clement Wearg, although a strong effort was made in favor of Sir John Wiles, Mr. Talbot was appointed to succeed him as Solicitor General to the King. He escaped knighthood, and continued Charles Talbot, Esquire, till made Lord Chancellor and a Peer. He had some time before been returned member of parliament for the city of Durham,

[1] 8 Parl. Hist. 22.

where his father was now Prince Bishop. On his promotion he vacated his seat under the recent act of parliament, but he was re-elected without opposition.[1]

Notwithstanding former jealousies, a perfect friendship was now established between him and his colleague, and seldom has the crown of England had such law officers,—Sir Phillip Yorke being Attorney General, while Talbot was Solicitor. They continued to serve together cordially, zealously, and honorably, for above six years. Sir Robert Walpole was sensible of their great value, and on the death of George I., as soon as he found that his own power was to continue, took care that their patents should be renewed.

The members of the Government, for a long while, had easy work in the House of Commons, for, as yet, there

[1] Talbot, remaining a member of the Inner Temple, had for the convenience of occupying chambers in Lincoln's Inn been admitted of that Society, and was now made a bencher and treasurer. The following entries respecting him appear in our books:—

"London ff. Carolus Talbot de Interiori Templo London Armiger admissus est in Societatem hujus Hospicij tricesimo primo die Januarij anno regni Dni nri Georgij Dei Gra Magne Britanie Franc et Hibnie Regis quinto. Annoq. Dni 1718. Et solvit ad usum Hospicij p'd. £iij iijs. iijd."

"At a Council held the 10th day of December, 1722.

"Upon the nomination in writing of Sr John Williams and Sr Edward Gould, Knt, touching a certain chamber situate in Series Court, Lincolnes Inne, &c. to Charles Talbot of Licolnes Iinne, aforesaid, Esqre. It is ordered that the said Mr Talbot be admitted to ye said Chamber, he first paying the fine of ten pounds to ye Treasurer of This Society, and the usual ffees to the Officers of ye House, and all arrears due on ye said chamber."

"At a Council held the 27th day of April, 1726.

"Ordered, that Charles Talbott, Esqre, his Majesty's Sollr Generall, be invited to the Bench of this Society; and that Mr Willes and Mr Hungerford, do waite upon him and acquaint him therewith."

"At a Council held the 11th day of May, 1726.

"Upon the report of Mr Willes and Mr Hungerford, two of the Masters of the Bench of this Society, who were by Order of Council of ye 27th April last desired to attend Mr Sollicitor Generall with an Invitation to the Bench, 'That they had attended the said Mr Sollr Generall, who accepted of the said Invitation.'—Ordered, that ye said Mr Sollicitor Generall be called to the Bench of this Society and that he be published at the next Exercise in the Hall, first paying all his arrears of duties to this Society."

"At a Council held the 27th day of July, 1726.

"Ordered, that Charles Talbot, Esqre, his Majesties Sollicitor Generall, be Treasurer of this Society for the remaining part of this yeare, in the place of John Browne, Esqre, who hath lately resigned his place of Treasurer."

"At a Council there held the 28th day of Novr, 1726.

"Ordered, that Mr Sollicitor Generall be Master of the Library for the year ensuing."

was no organized opposition, and a session would go off with a tame discussion on Spanish intrigues, or a complaint about publishing proceedings in parliament.

Sir Robert, at last, brought forward his famous Excise scheme;[1] and although the measure is now allowed to have been highly favorable to free trade, and well calculated to improve the revenue and to lessen the weight of taxation, such was the clamor against it, that it had nearly caused a change of administration. During this crisis, the Minister was nobly supported by the Solicitor, General, who was not a mere equity practitioner, but an enlightened statesman, capable of understanding and discussing any question on which the safety or prosperity of the country might depend. In answer to the Minister's most masterly statement of his plan, Sir John Barnard, Pulteney, and Sir William Wyndham having attacked and misrepresented it, Talbot gallantly rose, and having first shown that instead of being a "General Excise," it was merely an alteration of the mode of levying the tax on tobacco and wine, to facilitate commerce in these commodities, by requiring the tax to be paid when they were to be used, instead of when they were imported; he proved that, by the operation of the bill, infinite frauds would be prevented, the fair dealer would be protected, prices would be reduced, consumption would be doubled, and the revenue would be proportionably improved, so that the land-tax might be entirely remitted. He further argued, that by the extension of the same system, all the ports in Great Britain might be made free ports, and our trade and our wealth might be infinitely increased. The legal profession shone much in this debate, for the measure was likewise ably defended by the Attorney General, and by Sir Joseph Jekyll, the Master of the Rolls. It was carried through the first stage by 266 to 205; but this majority dwindled away on subsequent divisions, and the opposition was so tremendous out of doors, that it was abandoned—to the great joy and loss of the nation.[2] The session was as soon as possible closed by a prorogation, and Talbot never again appeared in the House of Commons. Before parliament re-

---

[1] In this instance he violated and proved the wisdom of his maxim "quieta non moveas."
[2] 8 Parl. Hist. 1268-1328; 8 Parl. Hist. 1-48; Coxe's Walp. i. 404.

assembled, there were very important changes, by which he was removed to another scene of action.

In the Life of Lord King, I have related how, in his declining days, Talbot and Yorke, who led against each other in the Court of Chancery, amicably settled between them the decrees and orders to be pronounced by the Chancellor, but that in November, 1733, this mode of disposing of the business came to an end. It so happened that a little time before Lord King's resignation, Lord Raymond, the Chief Justice of the King's Bench, suddenly died, and no successor to him being yet appointed, the highest Equity Judgeship and the highest Common-Law Judgeship were vacant at the same time. "Although Sir Philip Yorke, then Attorney General, was considered as such to be entitled to the Seals in preference to Mr. Talbot, yet the latter having confined himself very early to the practice of the Court of Chancery, and not having been much conversant with the practice of the Common-Law, he thought himself not sufficiently qualified to preside in the Court of King's Bench; on which account, Sir Philip Yorke being equally competent to preside either in that Court, or the Court of Chancery, it was agreed between them that Sir Philip should waive his pretensions in favor of Mr. Talbot; and the King and the Ministry so well approved of it, that it was settled among them that Sir Philip Yorke should have the place of Chief Justice of the King's Bench, and should have £2,000 a year added to his salary as Chief Justice,—which, however, Sir Philip, to his honor, refused to accept without its being made permanent to the office of Chief Justice of that Court, by being secured to his successors; and upon these terms the Seals were delivered to Mr. Talbot. In consequence of which, Sir Philip was created Lord Hardwicke, and Mr. Talbot Lord Talbot."[1]

I have thought it right to state this transaction in the very words of Bentham, the philosopher of Queen's Square, who had good means of information, and whose sincerity may be depended upon. But I can not help suspecting that there were other reasons for conferring the higher office upon Talbot besides his supposed want of qualification for the lower. Although for the last

---

[1] Jeremy Bentham's Letter to Cooksey.—*Cooksey 61.*

eight years he had confined his practice to the Courts of Equity, he had been familiarly acquainted with the Common Law, by private study, and by going circuits, and he must have been as well prepared to be a Chief Justice as Lord Eldon was, who presided with full as much applause in the Court of Common Pleas as in the Court of Chancery. Nor can the true solution be, that Yorke, having the first choice, preferred, as others have done, the certainty of tenure to splendor of present enjoyment, for he afterwards willingly resigned for the Great Seal the office which he now accepted. Some have supposed that the arrangement was the result of political intrigue, and that the descendent of the Earls of Shrewsbury by family connection triumphed over the son of the country attorney. But this is a merely gratuitous conjecture, and is at variance with Talbot's open and upright character and the cordial intimacy that now subsisted between these rivals for honorable distinction. The probability is, that Walpole, much as he no doubt valued Sir Philip Yorke, thought that Talbot would be a still more desirable associate in the Cabinet, and would be still more useful to him presiding on the woolsack than in a court of law. In such arrangements political convenience has ever had more weight than nice considerations of judicial fitness. From a very long official career Lord Hardwicke has left a far greater reputation as a judge and as a statesman than Lord Talbot, who was so suddenly cut off when beginning to gather his fame; but, while they were running the race of glory together, the latter seems to have excited the most applause, and if his life had been prolonged, a statue would have been erected to him in the new palace at Westminster, by the side of Lord Somers and Lord Mansfield. The circumstance of their relative rank as law officers of the Crown, when the vacancies occured, would be of small importance; for although it has always been considered that the Attorney General may claim as of right any Common-Law Judgeship which is vacant, the disposal of the Great Seal in earlier times was the personal act of the Sovereign, and more recently was left to the Prime Minister, who was not guided by any fixed rotation, but considered what would most conduce to the credit and strength of his government. Upon this occasion, the Attorney General could not consider himself aggrieved with the Chiefship of the King's Bench, a Peerage, and a large addition to his salary; and the two continued cordially to co-operate in the public service without any envious or jealous sentiment arising to disturb their friendship.

The Great Seal having been received from Lord King, it was delivered to Mr. Talbot as Lord Chancellor, by his Majesty George II., at a council held on the 29th of November, 1733. The same day he was sworn a Privy Councillor, and on the 5th of the following month he was raised to the Peerage by the title of Lord Talbot, Baron Talbot of Hensol, in the county of Glamorgan.

CHAPTER CXXVIII.

CONCLUSION OF THE LIFE OF LORD TALBOT.

AN illustration was now given of the excellence of the English practice of selecting for the Bench men of the highest eminence at the Bar, who have distinguished themselves as law officers of the Crown,—instead of following the French system of keeping the order of advocates and judges distinct. If men are appointed Attorney and Solicitor General from family interest, or from considerations of party convenience, without looking forward to their fitness for their judicial destiny, their promotion is a heavy misfortune to the public; but it is only from the long experience in the administration of justice obtained as an advocate that the public could have the advantage of such consummate Judges as Hardwicke and Talbot. Their appointment gave universal satisfaction; and as the latter was the more popular, great delight was expressed that he was placed at the head of his profession, and that the wrong formerly done to him was completely redressed.

A few days after receiving the Great Seal, the new Chancellor sat for the dispatch of business in Lincoln's Inn Hall, but he was not formally installed in his office till the 23 of January following, the first day of Hilary Term,—when, after a most splendid procession to Westminster Hall, he was placed in the marble chair in the Court of Chancery with all the ancient solemnities.[1]

A grand "Revel" was given in honor of the new Chancellor by the Inner Temple,—being the last royal festivity at an Inn of Court till the visit of Queen Victoria to Lincoln's Inn, more than a century after,—when the Prince Albert, her Consort, vouchsafed to become a member of that Society, and was called to the degree of an utter barrister.

It would require the pen of a Dugdale to do justice to such scenes, but the following not ungraphic account of the "Talbot pageant" has been transmitted to us:—

"On the 2nd of February, 1733-4, the Lord Chancellor came into the Inner Temple Hall about two of the clock, preceded by the Master of the Revels, Mr. Wollaston, and followed by the Master of the Temple, Dr. Sherlock, Bishop of Bangor, and by the Judges and Sergeants who had been members of that House. There was a very elegant dinner provided for them and the Lord Chancellor's officers; but the barristers and students of the house had no other dinner provided for them than what is usual on GRAND DAYS; but each mess had a flask of claret besides the common allowance of port and sack. Fourteen students waited at the bench table, among whom was Mr. Talbot, the Chancellor's eldest son, and by their means any sort of provision was easily obtained from the upper table by those at the rest. A large gallery was built over the screen, and was filled with ladies, who came for the most part a considerable time before the dinner began; and the music was played in the little gallery at the upper end of the Hall, and played all dinner time. As soon as dinner ended the play began, which was—'*Love for Love*,' with the farce of '*The Devil to Pay.*' The actors

[1] "Anno 7timo Georgii 2^{di} Regis. 29 Nov. 1733. Memorandum, that on Thursday, the 29th of November, 1733, at the request of Peter, Lord King, Lord High Chancellor of Great Britain, his Majesty sent to his Lordship for the Great Seal; and about three in the afternoon of the same day, his Majesty was graciously pleased to deliver the same to Charles Talbot, Esq., with the title of Lord Chancellor, and his Lordship was sworn in council at the same time; and though he sat at Lincoln's Inn Hall the 4th day of December following, yet his Lordship was not sworn by the Clerk of the Crown till the 23rd of January, being at Westminster Hall the first day of the then next Hilary Term, when his Lordship took the oaths appointed to be taken by the 1st of William and Mary, and the oath of Lord Chancellor, the Master of the Rolls holding the book, and the Clerk of the Crown giving the oaths." —*Roll, 1727-1760.*

who performed in them all came from the Haymarket in chairs, ready dressed, and (as it was said) refused any gratuity for their trouble, looking upon the honor of distinguishing themselves on this occasion as sufficient. After the play, the Lord Chancellor, Master of the Temple, Judges and Benchers entered into their parliament chamber, and in about half an hour after came into the Hall again, and a large ring was formed around the fire-place (but no fire or embers were on it). Then the Master of the Revels, who went first, took the Lord Chancellor by the right hand, and he by his left took Mr. Justice Page, who, joined to the other Judges, Sergeants and Benchers present, danced or rather walked 'round about the coal fire,' according to old ceremony, three times, during which they were aided in the figure of the dance by Mr. George Cook, the prothonotary, then sixty: and all the time of the dance the ancient song, accompanied with music, was sung by one Toby Aston, dressed in a bar gown, whose father had been formerly Master of the Plea Office in the King's Bench. When this was over, the ladies came down from the gallery, went into the parliament chamber, and stayed about a quarter of an hour, while the Hall was being put in order. Then they went into the Hall, and danced a few minuets. Country dances began at ten, and at twelve a very fine collation was provided for the whole company, from which they returned to dancing, which they continued as long as they pleased, and the whole day's entertainment was generally thought to be very genteelly and liberally conducted. The Prince of Wales honored the performance with his company part of the time; he came into the music *incog.* about the middle of the play, and went away as soon as the farce of 'walking round the coal fire' was over."[1]

[1] "Wynnes Eunomus. Notes." A newspaper of the day says, "The ancient ceremony of the Judges 'dancing round the coal-fire' was performed with great decency."

As these festivities in the Inns of Court are not only closely connected with the history of the Law, but possess permanent interest as illustrating the manners of the age, I will here insert, from the records of our Society, the official record of Queen Victoria's visit on the occasion of the opening of the New Hall at Lincoln's Inn, in the year 1845. After describing an audience with which the Treasurer and two other Benchers were honored to invite her Majesty and her Royal Consort, her Majesty's gracious intimation that they would be present at a "déjeuner" on the 30th of October, and the preparations made to receive them—it thus proceds:—

"The Queen's Counsel wore their silk gowns, and the long full-bottomed

As an Equity Judge, Lord Talbot exceeded all the high expectations which had been formed of him, In my wig. Lord Cottenham, Lord Campbell, and the Speaker wore their black velvet court dresses; the three Vice-Chancellors their full dress, Judges' wigs, and Lord Bexley his blue and gold official dress, as a former minister of the Crown.

"At the top of the Hall a table was placed upon the dais for the Queen, his Royal Highness, Prince Albert, and the other guests who accompanied the Queen, the benchers and the preacher of the Inn; and then, transversely, four tables reaching to the bottom of the Hall were devoted to the Bar and such of the students as attended.

" The band of the Coldstream Guards attended, and played during the time her Majesty was in the Hall.

" All the benchers being assembled, and the hour of arrival drawing nigh, the procession for receiving her Majesty, headed by the Treasurer, made its way down the Hall, and placed itself at the south-east entrance of the Hall, and shortly afterwards the Queen, with Prince Albert, attended by four of the ladies in waiting, and certain high officers of her household, arrived. The party came in five private carriages, attended by a body of the Life Guards; and soon in the Hall the National Anthem was heard. Her Majesty immediately entered, passing up the middle of the Hall, leaning on Prince Albert's arm, and preceded by the Treasurer walking backwards, and amidst loud and hearty cheering, her Majesty walked to the library, followed by her ladies, the Cabinet Ministers, Officers of State, and the Benchers, who came two and two, according to the date of their election to the bench.

" The Queen wore a blue drawn silk bonnet with a blue feather, a dress of Limerick lace, and a scarlet shawl with a broad gold edging.

" In the Library, the Queen, seated on a chair of state, held a levee, and received an address from the benchers, the barristers represented by the four seniors, and the students or fellows, two of whom were also present. The address was read by the Treasurer to the Queen, on his knee, and was as follows:—

"'Most Gracious Sovereign,

"' We, your faithful subjects, the Treasurer and Masters of the Bench, the Barristers and Fellows of the Society of Lincoln's Inn, entreat your Majesty's permission humbly to testify the joy and gratitude inspired by your august presence. The edifice in which, under such happy auspices we are for the first time assembled, is adorned with memorials of many servants of the Crown, eminent in their talents, their learning, and their integrity. To the services as recorded in history of these our distinguished predecessors, we appeal in all humility for our justification in aspiring to receive your Majesty beneath this roof.

"' Two centuries have nearly passed away since the Inns of Court were so honored by the presence of the reigning prince. We can not, therefore, but feel deeply grateful for a mark so conspicuous of your Majesty's condescension, and of your gracious regard for the profession of the law.

"' It is our earnest desire to deserve this proof of your Majesty's favor, by a zealous execution of the trust reposed in us, to guard and maintain the dignity of the Bar of England.

"' In our endeavors to this end, we shall but follow in the course which it has been your Majesty's royal pleasure to pursue. Signally has your Majesty fostered the independence of the Bar and the purity of the Bench, by distributing the honors which you have graciously bestowed on the profession among the members of all parties in the State.

"' Permit me also, most gracious Sovereign, to offer your Majesty our

long journey from the reign of Ethelred to that of George IV., I find this Chancellor alone without an accuser; sincere congratulations on the great amendments of the law which have been effected since your Majesty's accession to the throne throughout many portions of your vast empire.

"'The pure glory of these labors will be dear to your Majesty's royal heart ; for it arises from the welfare of your subjects.

"'That your Majesty may long reign over a loyal, prosperous, and contented people, is our devout and fervent prayer to Almighty God.'"

"The following reply, which her Majesty received from Sir James Graham, was then read:—

"'I receive, with cordial satisfaction, this dutiful address. My beloved Consort and I have accepted with pleasure your invitation, for I recognize the services rendered to the Crown at various periods of our history by distinguished members of this Society; and I gladly testify my respect for the profession of the law, by which I am aided in administering justice, and in maintaining the prerogative of the Crown and the rights of my people.

"'I congratulate you on the completion of this noble edifice ; it is worthy of the memory of your predecessors, and the station which you occupy in connection with the Bar of England.

"'I sincerely hope that learning may long flourish, and that virtue and talent may rise to eminence, within these walls.'"

"A chair was placed for the Prince on the left of her Majesty ; he did not occupy it, but remained standing.

"The above address, and its answer, having been read, the Treasurer was knighted ; and his Royal Highness, Prince Albert, was invited to become a member of the Inn, to which he at once agreed, and the admission book being handed to her Majesty and Prince Albert, they were graciously pleased to sign their names therein, as also did the following persons:—The Lord Chancellor, the Duke of Wellington, the Marquis of Exeter, the Earl of Aberdeen, Lord Liverpool, the Earl De La Warr, the Earl of Jersey, the Earl of Hardwicke, the Earl of Lincoln, Lord George Lennox, Sir James Graham, the Honorable Colonel Grey, the Honorable Captain Alexander N. Hood, Colonel Bouverie, and Captain Francis Seymour.

"The ceremony being over in the Library, her Majesty accompanied by the above party, then proceeded to the Hall. Grace being said by the chaplain, the assembly received the permission of the Queen to be seated ; her Majesty, occupying a chair of state with a canopy, partook of the refreshment provided, appearing pleased and well contented.

"On the right of the Queen sat Prince Albert ; next to his Royal Highness the Lord Chancellor, then came the Duke of Wellington, and then the Earl of Aberdeen, and then Lord Cottenham.

"On the left of her Majesty sat the Treasurer, Sir Francis Simpkinson, and then one of the ladies in waiting; next the Earl of Hardwicke and Lord Campbell. At the end of the banquet, which lasted about half an hour, grace was again said; and then the Treasurer having received permission from her Majesty to propose a toast, proposed 'the health of her Majesty the Queen, who had that day honored them with her Royal presence.' This was responded to with plaudits. After some minutes, the cheering having subsided, the Treasurer stated that his Royal Highness had that day become a member of the Inn, and begged, with the permission of her Majesty, to propose the health of their new member, 'His Royal Highness Prince Albert.' This also was received with loud cheering, and was rendered even more interesting by the manner in which the Queen joined in it. Holding a glass of port wine in her hand, she stood up all the time, and drank it off to the bot-

without an enemy; without a detractor; without any one, from malice or mistake, to cavil at any part of his character, conduct, or demeanor. While in no respect deficient in judicial gravity and dignity, the flowing courtesy of his manners seems to have won all hearts. Well acquainted with the most abstruse branches of the law of real property, he had himself heard delivered in court all the important judgments of Lord Harcourt, Lord Cowper, Lord Macclesfield, Lord King, and Sir Joseph Jekyll, and he knew familiarly the most minute details of practice, which are only to be learned thoroughly by experience, and to which there was then hardly any printed guide. In addition to these qualifications, he was energetic and indefatigable in business, punctual in his hours of sitting —till he had subdued his arrears, eager to avoid, instead of to make, a holiday, and to postpone, instead of hastening, the adjournment of the Court. He was under the influence of no leader at the bar, and he on no occasion showed peculiar favor to any counsel, unless to those who required encouragement from their modesty and timidity. He never even incurred a suspicion of corruption in the disposal of office or of undue influence in his decrees.[1]

tom. His Royal Highness, in a peculiarly distinct voice, returned thanks, and said he had received her Majesty's commands to propose ' Prosperity to the Honorable Society of Lincoln's Inn,' which was drunk. Soon after the Queen, accompanied by the ministers and benchers, withdrew, amidst loud cheering. Her Majesty and her party retired into the council-room; from whence, after her carriage had been summoned, she came again into the Hall, and, accompanied by the Treasurer and benchers, she proceeded amidst loud cheering into her carriage, and departed.

"It is further to be noticed that Prince Albert, on withdrawing after the feast, put on a student's gown over his Field Marshal's uniform, and so wore it on returning from the Hall."

Afterwards his Royal Highness Prince Albert was in due form called to the Bar, and was elected a Bencher.

On the grand day of the following Trinity Term, his Royal Highness dined in the Hall as a Bencher—when he most gracefully entered the dining hall, after Henry Tancred, Esq., M.P. for Banbury, the Treasurer. Such intercourse tends to strengthen the throne, and to perpetuate the liberties of the people!

[1] It is related of him, that he much valued a maxim taken for the motto to a law book, published by Judge Jenkins. "The common law has been from the beginning of the world, for it is common reason;" and that "he quoted and avowed this maxim from the bench whenever anything repugnant to it was offered from the bar." But I think he was too sensible a man to set up for law his own notion of what was reasonable or unreasonable, expedient or inexpedient. It was well said by Mr. Justice Burrough, "Public policy is an unruly horse, which, if a Judge unwarily mounts, ten to one he is run away with."

Some of his decisions are to be found in Peere Williams, but his chief reporter is Forrester, a barrister who practiced before him, and has left us an octavo volume, entitled, "Cases Tempore Talbot." This gentleman, with an adequate share of professional knowledge and accuracy, possessed little skill in composition, so that he gives us a very faint notion of the lucid reasoning and felicity of illustration universally ascribed to the Judge whose fame he ought to have perpetuated.

I can do little more than show how Lord Chancellor Talbot disposed of a few of the principal questions which came before him. He first decided that the Court will assist a testamentary guardian to prevent an improper marriage of an infant heir. The son of the late Lord Raymond, Chief Justice of the King's Bench, while a boy of seventeen, was about to marry a Miss Chetwynd. Thereupon his guardians, under his father's will, filed a bill in the Court of Chancery, and presented a petition, stating that it would be a great disadvantage to the minor to marry at this time, and that it had been necessary to keep him in close custody to prevent his marrying, and praying that the Lord Chancellor would give such directions as he should think fit for the benefit of the minor. *Lord Chancellor:* "I am glad that this application has been made. The Court will prevent the marriage if it has the power to do so. It is admitted that the young lady is of a good family, and it is not shown what fortune the young peer has, so that I can not tell whether this be a Smithfield bargain or not; but his age is improper for marriage; that is the consideration which weighs most with me, and upon which I think myself bound to interfere. In order to strengthen the hands of the guardians, I order them to retain the Lord Raymond in their care and custody, and that they do not permit him to marry without the consent of the Court. But it has been said that it would be very cruel and unnatural in a father not to suffer his daughter to marry to her advantage, and she would have reason to blame him for it ever after. Now, to prevent that charge upon Mr. Chetwynd, I order him not to suffer his daughter to marry the Lord Raymond without the consent of the Court—which prevents any imputation or charge upon Mr. Chetwynd from the lady, or anybody else; since, if there be any fault in it, it will fall upon the Court, and I shall be very willing to bear it." [1]

In *Cray* v. *Rooke*, he had to determine whether a bond which a testator had given to his mistress should be set aside; and if not, in what order and from what fund it should be satisfied. After great deliberation, he held that, as it had not been obtained by fraud, it should not be set aside in favor of the legitimate children or heir; that it should not be paid out of the personal estate until after simple contract debts; but that it should be paid out of the real estate if the personal estate should fall short.[2]

The question arose in *Heard* v. *Stanford*, "whether, if a man marries a woman of large personal property which comes to him by the marriage,—after her death he is liable for the debts due from her before marriage?" It was strongly urged that, as he would be liable for them during her life, her fortune in his hand should be considered equitable assets for the benefit of her creditors. *Lord Chancellor:* "The question is, whether the husband, as such, be chargeable for a debt of his wife after her death, in a court of Equity? As, on the one hand, the husband is liable to all his wife's debts during the coverture, though he did not get one shilling portion with her; so, on the other hand, it is as certain that if the debt be not recovered during the coverture, the husband is no longer chargeable as such, let the fortune he received with his wife be ever so great. The case, perhaps, may be hard, but the law has made it so,—that it may be equal on both sides, as well where the husband is sued during the coverture for a debt of his wife's with whom he had no fortune, as when by her death he is discharged from all her debts, notwithstanding any fortune he may have received in marriage with her. So is the law; and the alteration, if desirable, is the proper work of the legislature only."[3]

In Barbuit's case it was debated "whether a foreign minister resident in England, by engaging in commerce, forfeits his privilege not to be arrested, and whether a foreign consul is privileged as a minister." Barbuit, com-

---

[1] Lord Raymond's case.—Cas. Temp. Talbot, 58.
[2] Cas. Temp. Talbot, 155.
[3] *Heard* v. *Stanford*, Cas. Temp. Talbot, 173.

missioned by the King of Prussia " to do what his Prussian Majesty should think fit to order with regard to his subjects trading in Great Britain," exercised the trade of a tallow-chandler in London, and, being imprisoned under an order made in a Chancery suit, he claimed, as an ambassador, to be discharged. *Lord Chancellor:* "Though this is a very unfavorable case, yet if the defendant is truly a public minister, I think he may insist on his privilege after allowing the suit to go on ten years against him without objection; for the privilege of a public minister is to have his person sacred and free from arrests, not on his own account, but on the account of those he represents: and this arises from the necessity of the thing, that nations may have intercourse with one another in the same manner as private persons, by agents, when they can not meet themselves. And if the foundation of this privilege is for the sake of the prince by whom an ambassador is sent, and for the sake of the business he is to do, it is impossible that he can renounce the privilege introduced not for his own benefit. He may deserve to be thrown into prison, but we must protect the state which he represents. The exception in the statute of Anne of persons trading, relates only to the servants of ambassadors, for the parliament never imagined that the ambassadors themselves would trade. The question is, whether the defendant be a public minister? If he had been accredited to negotiate a commercial treaty, he would have been so. It is of no weight with me, that he was not to concern himself about other matters of state. The commission need not be general to entitle him to protection. But this person is not to transact affairs between the two Crowns: the Commission is to assist his Prussian Majesty's subjects here in their commerce. Although he is called an agent of commerce, I do not think that the name alters the case. At most he is only a CONSUL, and it is the opinion of Barbeyrac, Wiquefort, and other writers on public law, that a Consul is not entitled by the *Jus Gentium* to the privileges of an ambassador. I therefore can not discharge him." [1]

In *Duke of Somerset* v. *Cookson*, from a desire to do complete justice, he a little stretched his authority by

[1] Cases Temp. Talbot, 181. But to please the Prussian Government, the Secretary of State satisfied his creditors, and he was discharged.

holding that a bill in Equity lies to compel the preservation and the delivery to the right owner of a valuable piece of art. The plaintiff, as lord of the manor of Carbridge, in Northumberland, having a grant of "*treasure trove*," was entitled to an antique silver altar dug up there, which had a Greek inscription upon it, and was dedicated to Hercules. The altar had been purchased by the defendant with notice of the claim to it, and he threatened to deface it or melt it down. On a demurrer to a bill filed by the Duke for an injunction, and to have the altar delivered up to him, it was objected that the remedy was at law by action of trover or of detinue ; that Equity had not yet gone further than to allow a suit for the recovery of title deeds, which *savor of the realty ;* and that if the present plaintiff were to succeed, all actions of trover and detinue would be turned into bills in Chancery. But Lord Talbot held, "that this suit was maintainable on the ground that the thing sued for was matter of curiosity and antiquity ; that it would be very hard if a person who wrongfully gets possession of such a relic might destroy or retain it, paying the intrinsic value of it ; and that the law being defective in this respect, such defect is properly supplied in Equity."[1]

One other case of general interest I find to have been decided by him—*Hunter* v. *Murray*—in which the question arose, " whether, since the Union with Scotland, under a writ of *ne exeat regno*, a party might be prevented from going into that part of the United Kingdom." *Lord Chancellor :* " This, in its origin, was a mandatory writ to prevent the King's subjects from going into foreign parts to practice treason with the King's enemies : but since, it has been made ancillary to the jurisdiction of this Court, that persons residing within the realm of England may be compelled to do justice to their fellow-subjects. How can I alter the terms or the operation of the writ by reason of the legislative Union with Scotland, which in no respect enlarges or affects the jurisdiction of any Court in England? It is dangerous to alter established forms. I will make no order, but leave parties to proceed in the old beaten path."[2]

These specimens of Lord Talbot's decisions may not exalt him in our view above the level of modern Vice-

[1] Peere Williams, 390.   [2] *Hunter* v. *Murray*, Cas. Temp. Talb. 196.

Chancellors, but by his contemporaries he was regarded as almost a superior being. His great dispatch, and the admirable manner in which he comported himself, caused a prodigious influx of business into his Court, and "Chancery" having for the first time in England become a popular word, it was said that "a new era had begun in the administration of Equity." I ought likewise to mention to his credit, that he powerfully assisted the inquiries which were going on respecting the taking of excessive fees from the suitors, and that he had important measures in preparation for correcting judicial abuses. Thus was Lord Talbot successfully laboring as a magistrate, and if his life had been spared, I make no doubt that the praise of perfecting our equitable system would have been bestowed upon him still more loudly than it has been upon his successor.[1]

As a politician we read hardly anything of Lord Talbot from the time of his appointment as Chancellor. This arises from the profound tranquillity of the times—the masterly policy of Walpole having warded off foreign war, suppressed Jacobitism, and, for a season, paralyzed faction. After the tremendous storm excited by the Excise scheme had subsided, the nation was pleased by the marriage of the King's eldest daughter, the Princess Anne, to the Prince of Orange; the apprehension of plots was allayed by Bolingbroke's retirement into France, and for three years nothing more memorable occurred than hopeless motions for the repeal of the Test Act and of the Septennial Act, the passing of the Gin Act, Porteous's

[1] In mentioning the universal satisfaction which Lord Talbot gave as a Judge, perhaps I ought to have excepted old Sarah, Duchess of Marlborough; but, as we say in Scotland, "her tongue is no scandal," and her abuse may be considered a necessary addition to the commendation of others—to make out a perfect character. Pope was wrong in saying that her ruling passion was gratified, for it ever remained craving and insatiable:

"From loveless youth to unrespected age,
No passion gratified except her rage."

Lord Talbot, soon after his appointment, pronounced a decree against her; and she scurrilously abused him to all her correspondents. Thus, in a letter to Lord Marchmont, dated June 11th, 1734, writing about election petitions to the House of Commons, she says, "There will be one against my Lord Chancellor, who has done most unbecoming and unjustifiable things to make a return for his son against Mr. Mansell for Glamorganshire. This is a step very bad to begin his reign with; but it is certain he is a man of no judgment, whatever knowledge he may have in the law; nor does he know anything of the world, or the qualities of a gentleman."

1734.] LORD TALBOT. 59

riots in Edinburgh, and the blowing up of a little gunpowder in Westminster Hall to frighten the Judges. Lord Mahon says, "It was to stem in some degree the formidable attacks expected in the Upper House on his dismissal of Chesterfield, Clinton, Burlington, Montrose, Marchmont, and Stair, for their opposition to the Excise scheme, that Walpole determined to send there two of his most eminent commoners, the Attorney and Solicitor General."[1] But for a long time in that assembly hardly any show of opposition appeared. The circumstance of the Prime Minister continuing a commoner—then quite unexampled—diminished the consequence of the Lords, and they were rapidly falling from the palmy state which they had occupied in the beginning of the ceutury, and which without more energy, I see little prospect of their ever resuming. Lord Talbot's name is seldom mentioned in their deliberations.

He took his seat as a Peer on the 17th of January, 1734, being the first day of the seventh session of the seventh parliament of Great Britain. The account of this ceremony as recorded in the Journals[2] may be amusing:—

"The Lord President acquainted the House that his Majesty had been pleased to create Charles Talbot, Esq., Lord Chancellor of Great Britain, a Peer of this realm. Whereupon his Lordship, taking in his hand the purse with the Great Seal, retired to the lower end of the House; and having there put on his robes, was introduced between the Lord Harrington and the Lord Delawarr (also in their robes),—the Gentleman Usher of the Black Rod, Garter King of Arms, the Lord Great Chamberlain, and the Deputy Earl Marshal of England preceding. His Lordship laid down his patent on the chair of state kneeling; and from thence took and delivered it to the Clerk, who read the same at the table. [The entry, having described the reading of the patent, and the writ, and the taking of the oaths, thus proceeds :] which done, he took his place on the lower end of the Barons' bench, from whence he went to the upper end of the Earls' bench, and sat there as Lord Chancellor, and then returned to the woolsack."[3]

Lord Talbot is mentioned this year as having spoken

[1] Vol. ii. 257. [2] 9 Parl. Hist. 1822.
[3] Lord Hardwicke took his seat as a Peer the same day.

once, and once only. In consequence of the commencement of hostilities on the continent of Europe, between the Spaniards and the House of Austria, a message was brought down from the King recommending that power should be given to augment the forces, and a motion to this effect was made by the Duke of Newcastle. This being opposed by Lord Carteret, Lord Chesterfield, and Lord Bathurst, the Lord Chancellor left the woolsack and spoke as follows:—

"The present situation of affairs in Europe is so well known to every noble Lord that it does not require to be detailed by me to justify the course proposed by the Government. Considering the heavy war actually begun, and the different powers already actually engaged in it, there can be no doubt that it may produce imminent dangers to this nation, for which, in prudence, and for the preservation of our own neutrality, we ought to be prepared. By his Majesty's message he asks no powers beyond those already constitutionally vested in him, and the message may be considered only as an application from his Majesty for the advice of his parliament with relation to what may be thought most proper to be done at such a critical juncture. The most dutiful and becoming return we can make, is, in my opinion, the address proposed by the noble Duke. If, without any appeal to parliament, ministers had augmented our forces by sea and land, can there be a doubt that parliament would have approved of what was necessary for our defense, and would have provided for the necessary expense thereby occasioned? If the increased force should be unnecessary, and the expense of it thrown away, there is nothing in the address to justify such mismanagement, and the next parliament will be at full liberty to animadvert on his Majesty's advisers as if no such message had been brought down, and no such address had been quoted. As between parliament and the government, the power of censure and of punishment remains untouched. I will grant, my Lords, that by the address proposed the ministers may have a little more credit among the people than otherwise they might have had. I will allow that by the address the honor of parliament will be engaged to provide for the expense to be incurred, whether inevitable or unnecessary. But this is the very reason why I support the course proposed for our adoption. Surely, in our dangerous situation from the disturbed state of Europe, we are not to be left defenseless for fear a bad use should be made of the means granted for our defense. Without confidence, neither the affairs of individuals nor of nations can be conducted. There may be a breach of trust; yet trustees must be appointed. Ministers may be guilty of delinquencies, but you must vest in them power to provide for the public safety, and that power must be increased in proportion to the perils which surround you. His Majesty tells us there is nothing he has more at heart than to see the flame of war extinguished before we are involved in it; and to strengthen his hands for this purpose, nothing can be so effectual as to show to the world the perfect harmony which is subsisting between his Majesty and his parliament. This address will prove to Europe that his Majesty has all the resources of this mighty nation completely at his command, and will enable him to arbitrate irresistibly for the general good. This parliament must very speedily be dissolved, as nearly seven years have expired since it was summoned. Let its last act be to declare that as we are free at home, we are determined to be respected abroad. 'Britons never will be slaves.' This sentiment will be repeated by all the constituent body at the coming elections, and will be the rallying cry of the new House of Commons. When his Majesty is thus seen to be warmly supported by a parliament which is to last seven years, we may rest assured that he will be able to restore tranquillity to the Continent on equitable terms, and that at all events he will effectually provide for British interests, and make the British name respected all over the world."

The address was carried by a majority of 101 to 58.[1]

In the following session, the business which seems chiefly to have occupied the Upper House arose out of a complaint respecting intimidation and undue influence in the election of the sixteen peers for Scotland. The Lord Chancellor had to speak frequently on the subject, and to write letters by order of the House to the complainants, who were Scotch Peers; but their petition was at last dismissed, the nomination remaining with the Government, —and the subject was without permanent interest.[2] The

[1] 9 Parl. Hist. 520–559.   [2] Ibid. 720–796.

proper remedy was pointed out in Lord Sunderland's Peerage Bill,—by giving a certain number of hereditary seats in the House of Lords to the Scotch Peerage.—The only other subject on which the Chancellor is stated to have spoken this session was the quartering of soldiers at elections, and no intelligible account of his speech is preserved. He maintained that there was no law for taking troops from places where parliamentary elections are going forward; that an express law against their being allowed to be present would destroy a useful discretion in cases of necessity; that the difficulties surrounding the subject would forever prevent legislation upon it; and that the wise course would be to leave all to the Ministers of the Crown upon their parliamentary responsibility.[1]

During the session of 1736, the Lord Chancellor is not mentioned as having spoken once, and the only subjects of debate recorded in the Lords were respecting the collection of Quakers' tithes, and the prevention of smuggling.[2]

On the first day of the session of 1737, the Speaker and the Commons having come to the bar, the Lord Chancellor spoke as follows:—

"My Lords and Gentlemen,

"In pursuance of the authority given us by his Majesty's Commission under the Great Seal, amongst other things, to declare the causes of holding this parliament, we are, by his Majesty's command, to state to you that his Majesty has been graciously pleased to direct us to acquaint you that he hath seen, with the greatest satisfaction, the unwearied application of this parliament in framing good laws, for advancing the prosperity and securing the welfare of his loving subjects; and that it hath been one of his Majesty's principal cares to enforce them by a due execution, with the strictest regard to the rights and properties of the people, no invasion whereof can with any color be suggested by the most malicious enemies of the present establishment. Whilst this hath been our condition, his Majesty can not but observe that it must be matter of the utmost surprise and concern to every true lover of his country, to see the many contrivances and attempts carried on in various shapes, and in

[1] 9 Parl. Hist. 885–887 [2] Ibid. 969–1270.

different parts of the nation, tumultuously to resist and obstruct the execution of the laws, and to violate the peace of this kingdom. These disturbers of the public repose, conscious that the interests of his Majesty and his people are the same, and of the good harmony which happily subsists between him and his parliament, have leveled their sedition against both, and in their late outrages have either directly opposed, or at least endeavored to render ineffectual, some acts of the whole legislature. His Majesty, in his great wisdom, thinks it affords a melancholy prospect to consider to what height these audacious practices may rise, if not timely suppressed, and that it deserves no small attention that they may go on to affect private persons in the quiet enjoyment of their property, as well as the general peace and good order of the whole. His Majesty apprehends it to be unnecessary to enlarge upon a subject of this nature, and therefore hath commanded us barely to mention it to you, who, by the constant tenor of your conduct, have shown that you consider the support of his government as inseparable from the preservation of the public tranquillity and your own safety."

This speech referred to riots in London in consequence of the act to check the drinking of gin,—to an insurrection in the West against turnpike gates,—to a dispersion of libels in Westminster Hall while the Judges were sitting there by means of an explosion of gunpowder,—and above all, to the murder of Captain Porteous by a general rising of the citizens of Edinburgh.

It is a curious fact, that the first measure brought in by the Ministers as a cure for these evils was opposed by Lord Chancellor Talbot, as well as by Lord Chief Justice Hardwicke and several other Peers. This was a bill to prevent smuggling, which contained a clause " subjecting any three persons traveling with arms to the penalty of transportation, on proof by two witnesses that their intention was to assist in the clandestine landing or carrying away prohibited or uncustomed goods." The opposers said, " We have in our laws no such thing as a crime by implication, nor can a malicious intention ever be proved by witnesses. Facts only are admitted to be proved, and from these facts the judge and the jury are to determine with what intention they were committed ; but no judge or jury can ever by our laws suppose, much less determine, that an action in itself innocent or indifferent was attended with a criminal and malicious intention. Another security for our liberties is that no subject can be imprisoned unless some felonious and high crime be sworn against him. This with respect to private men, is the very foundation-stone of all our liberties ; and if we remove it, if we but knock off a corner, we may probably overturn the whole fabric. A third guard for our liberties is that right which every subject has, not only to provide himself with arms proper for his defense, but to accustom himself to the use of those arms, and to travel with them wherever he has a mind. But this clause is repugnant to all the maxims of free government. No presumption of a crime can be drawn from the mere wearing of arms, an act not only innocent, but highly commendable,—and to admit witnesses to swear ' that men are armed in order to assist in smuggling,' would be admitting witnesses to prove *an intention,* which is inconsistent with the whole tenor of our laws." They objected to another provision, subjecting a party against whom a charge was preferred that he intended to assist in smuggling, to imprisonment without bail, though the offense in itself were in its nature bailable ;—to another, which made informations for assaults upon revenue officers triable in any county in England ;—and still more to the protection thrown round the same favored class, " that the justices should be bound to admit them to bail on charges of killing or wounding any one in the execution of their duty."[1] The bill was carried, though by a small majority, and, still remaining in force, is mentioned by Mr. Hallam as an illustration how, in framing our fiscal code, "'a sad necessity has overruled the maxims of ancient law," so that " it is to be counted as a set-off against the advantages of the Revolution, and has, in fact, diminished the freedom and justice which we claim for our polity."

Lord Talbot took up the prosecution of the Porteous rioters with much vigor, and expressed his hearty concurrence in the resolution of the Government to bring them to condign punishment. An order was made that the Lord Provost of Edinburgh, the four Bailies, the Commander of the City Guard, and the Commander of the

[1] Const. Hist. iii. 384; Parl. Hist. ix. 1229.

King's troops in the castle of Edinburgh, should attend at the bar of the House. But a great calamity was now impending over the nation.

Before the day for the attendance of the parties arrived, Lord Talbot was no more. When apparently in the enjoyment of perfect health, when in the full possession of the confidence and esteem of his Sovereign, and of all classes in society,—while equally respected by his countrymen of all political parties, and all religious persuasions,—while he was supposed to have before him a long career of usefulness and glory,—he was suddenly seized with a spasm in the heart, which from the first was pronounced to be fatal. Being made sensible that his dissolution approached, he prepared for it with fortitude and serenity. He had a brief space allowed him to settle his worldly affairs, and, having received the last consolations of religion, he set a pattern of dying, as he had always lived,—like a Christian. Early in the morning of Wednesday, the 14th of February, 1737, he expired at his house in Lincoln's Inn Fields, in the fifty-third year of his age.

The news was received with consternation, not only in Westminister Hall and the House of Lords, where he had been that day expected to preside, but a gloom was cast over the whole metropolis, as if every family had been visited with the loss of a beloved relative.

A general desire was felt that he should have a public funeral, and that his remains should be deposited in Westminster Abbey; but, according to a wish which, when dying, he had intimated, he was buried, attended only by his children and nearest connections, in the chancel of the parish church of Barrington, in Gloucestershire, where some of his ancestors reposed.[1]

Instead of now attempting to draw a character of Lord Talbot, I shall best please my readers by introducing some of the contemporary eulogiums pronounced upon

---

[1] On his coffin were engraved his arms, the purse, mace, and regalia, on a brass plate, with this inscription:—
"The Right Honourable
CHARLES, LORD TALBOT,
BARON OF HENSOL,
Lord High Chancellor of England,
And one of His Majesty's most Honourable Privy Council,
Died Feb. 14, 1736-7,
In the 53rd year of his age."

him; for every notice of him was an unqualified eulogium. Those who value him as I do can never tire of the repetition of his praise.

The obituary of the succeeding number of the "Gentleman's Magazine" contained the following statement:—
"Feb. 14. Charles Talbot, Lord Talbot, &c., in whom all the qualities that can constitute a good man, or can adorn a wise one, were eminently united. No man ever arrived to his high dignity with such universal approbation, nor conducted himself in it with such universal applause; no man was ever more the delight of his country, or had a larger share of the hearts and affections of the people, and yet he never made use of any other method to please than a constant course of wisdom and virtue. He had the peculiar felicity to join together those contrary qualities so rare to be met with in the same person, the mildest disposition with the greatest firmness of mind; and at the same time that he had a heart susceptible of the strongest impressions of tenderness and compassion, he maintained inviolably the strictest justice and most inflexible integrity. He had a mind so enlightened, that no falsehood could ever elude his sight, but, with inimitable sagacity, he would pursue her through all the intricate labyrinths which she took to escape him. His judgment was so clear, that he could at one view discover the most entangled points; and yet he had patience and temper to hear everything that could be said on the most plain and obvious. He always chose to make truth appear in native simplicity, though he could have adorned it with all the graces of rhetoric. He was, in all characters and relations of life, one of the ablest, greatest, uprightest men that any age or nation has produced, and was not only an honor to his country, but an ornament to human nature."

In another periodical work, in great circulation at the time, though long forgotten,[1] he was thus characterized by one who seems to have known him well in domestic life:—"His religion was his governing principle; it was well grounded and active; his piety was rational and manly. He was a sincere son of the Church of England, and ready to maintain her in her just rights and legal possessions. He was an enemy to persecution, and had

[1] See Biogr. Brit. title "Talbot."

a diffusive general and Christian charity, which made him a friend to all mankind. He had a great regard for such of the most worthy of the clergy as were distinguished by their learning, sincerity, moderation, and charity. He was a careful and indulgent father, and as no man ever deserved more of his children, no man could be more affectionately beloved by them; there was something so peculiar in this respect, that none seemed to know how to be in such friendship with his sons as my Lord Chancellor. The harmony which subsisted in his house was a very great pleasure to all who beheld it."

Another notice of him, written by a friend, said,—" He was the delight and honor of his country, both in his judicial and ministerial capacity. Eloquence never afforded greater charms from any orator than when the public attention listened to his sentiments delivered with the most graceful modesty. In apprehension he so far exceeded the common rank of men, that he instantaneously, or by a kind of intuition, saw the strength or imperfection of any argument; and so penetrating was his sagacity, that the most intricate and perplexing mazes of the law could never so involve and darken the truth as to conceal it from his discernment. So excellent was his temper, so candid his disposition in debate, that he never offended those whose arguments he opposed. When intrusted with the Great Seal, his universal affability, his easiness of access, and his great dispatch of business, engaged to him the affection and almost veneration of all who approached him. By clearly delivering, with his decrees, the reasons on which they were founded, he made his court a very instructive school of equity; and his decisions were generally attended with such conviction to the parties against whose interest they were made, that their acquiescence in them prevented any further expense. When he could obtain a short interval from business, the pompous formalities of his station were thrown aside; his table was a scene where wisdom and science shone, enlivened and adorned with elegance of wit. There was joined the utmost freedom of dispute with the highest good breeding, and the vivacity of mirth with primitive simplicity of manners. When he had leisure for exercise he delighted in field sports, and even in those trifles showed that he was formed to excel in whatever he engaged. If he had relaxed more from the fatigues of office, the nation might not yet have deplored a loss it could so ill sustain. But though he was removed at a season of life when others but begin to shine, he might justly have said 'se satis et ad vitam et ad gloriam vixisse,' and his death united in one general concern a nation which scarce ever unanimously agreed in any other particular; and, notwithstanding the warmth of our political divisions, each party endeavored to outvie the other in due reverence to his memory."[1]

These characters of Lord Talbot were supposed to come from men of the same political party with himself; but the "CRAFTSMAN," then under the influence of Bolingbroke and Pulteney, and in such bitter opposition to Sir R. Walpole's government as to be several times prosecuted *ex officio*, thus spoke of him who, when a law officer of the Crown, had assisted in these prosecutions:—" He rose by merit to the head of his profession, and not only supported himself in it with dignity, but adorned it, and acquired every day new praise and esteem. His prudence, moderation, and patience in the execution of his office, even amidst the highest provocations, make one shining part of his character, and are hardly to be paralleled by any instances of those who have sat before him upon that bench. Yet, notwithstanding this amiable disposition of mind, he discovered such courage and resolution upon all occasions, as could not be shaken by the tricks of the wealthy, the applications of the powerful, or the tears of the distressed. In a word, he possessed all the great talents of his most renowned predecessors, without any of their frailties, and hath left a noble example to all his successors; so that he was not only a blessing to the age in which he lived, but may possibly derive the same happiness to his posterity, by exciting those who follow him in that high office to an emulation of his virtues. The great increase of business in the Court of Chancery since the Seal was put into his hands, is an evident proof of that confidence which the suitors reposed in him, and will do immortal honor to his memory, though it proved fatal to his life; for the constant fatigue of his employment was one of the principal causes of his death, and therefore he may be truly said to have fallen *a martyr to the*

[1] See Biog. Br. Chalmers, "Lord Talbot."

public good! He died full of glory, but, to the great misfortune of his country, not full of years; and the general sorrow which his death has occasioned will do his noble family more honor than the highest titles or the most sumptuous monuments."[1]

Smollett, who seldom rises above a dry and uninteresting narrative of political facts, characterizes Lord Talbot as possessing " the spirit of a Roman senator, the elegance of an Atticus, and the integrity of a Cato."[2]

All subsequent historians who treat of that period, swell the note of praise. Says Tindal,—" He was an illustrious exception to the venality charged upon the profession of the law: his life was moral, his heart was good, and his head was clear; nor did ever man fill that high station with greater abilities and approbation of the public. But just as the nation was in a manner beginning to reap the benefits of his virtues, he was snatched away by death."[3]

I will only further quote our most recent historian, who, after referring to Lord Hardwicke, says—" Lord Talbot is less conspicuous in history only because he was more brief in life; he died at the age of fifty-two, and, even amidst the strife of parties, was universally lamented as a man of the highest legal talents, of unimpeachable character, and of most winning gentleness of manners."[4]

The Muses likewise were invoked to do honor to the memory of Lord Talbot. Soon after his death, there was printed and privately circulated the following Elegy, which shows at least a deep feeling of the virtues of the deceased:—

> " Magnos sæpe viros cecinit cum Musa, repente
> Obstrepuit miseræ turba maligna lyræ.
> Scilicet arguitur carmen, quia displicet heros,
> Et mala quæ jactat fama, Poeta luit,
> At vos securi Talbotum dicite Vates !
> In quo nil livor quod male rodat habet.
> Jura humana a se qui nulla aliena putavit [1]
> Delicium humanæ gentis habendus erat.
> Partium in hoc non est studio locus, omnibus idem
> Ut vixit charus, flebilis interiit."

---

[1] Craftsman, A.D. 1737.   [2] Vol. iii. p. 54.
[3] Tind. Cont. xx. 340. Tindal in stating Lord Talbot's appointment as Chancellor, had said—" He was looked upon as one of the clearest-headed as well as the best-hearted lawyers that ever practiced."
[4] Lord Mahon, vol. ii. 257.
[5] Alluding to his motto " Humana nihil lienum."

The most eminent English poets joined in the same strain. Pope, in the early editions of his Epistle to Lord Bathurst, " on the Use of Riches," thus sung :—

> " The sense to value riches with the art
> T' enjoy them, and the virtue to impart,
> Not meanly nor ambitiously pursued,
> Nor sunk by sloth, nor rais'd by servitude.
> To balance fortune by a just expense,
> Join with economy magnificence,
> With splendor charity, with plenty health,
> O teach us TALBOT ! thou 'rt unspoil'd by wealth,
> That secret rare, between th' extremes to move
> Of mad good nature and of mean self-love.
> Who is it copies TALBOT'S better part,
> To ease th' oppress'd, and raise the sinking heart ?
> Where'er he shines, O, Fortune, gild the scene,
> And angels guard him in the golden mean.
> At Barrington shall English bounty stand,
> And Hensol's honor never leave the land,
> His glories in his progeny shall shine,
> And propagate the virtue still divine." [1]

A most touching poetical tribute to the memory of Lord Talbot comes incidentally from the author of THE SEASONS, in lamenting the early death of a pupil who was thought destined to inherit the title and virtues of an illustrious sire. The Chancellor, always eager to patronize literary merit, had formed an acquaintance with Thomson soon after the publication of *Winter*, had appointed him to the office of " Secretary of Briefs," and sent him to make the tour of Europe with his eldest son. This promising youth died of a fever soon after his return from his travels, and his sorrowing tutor and friend thus opens the poem on Liberty, which was to have been dedicated to him :—

> " O my lamented Talbot! while with thee
> The Muse gay rov'd the glad Hesperian round
> And drew th' inspiring breath of ancient arts ;
> Ah, little thought she her returning verse

---

[1] For some reason which no commentator has explained, in the later editions of this epistle the name of TALBOT is entirely excluded, and it i turned into a dialogue between the poet and Lord Bathurst. Warton, in hi. " Life of Pope," in reference to Lord Bathurst, says,—" I never saw this very amiable old nobleman, whose wit, vivacity, and integrity are well known, but he repeatedly expressed his disgust and his surprise at finding in later editions this Epistle awkwardly converted into a Dialogue, in which he has little to say. And I remember he once remarked that this line,

' P. But you are tir'd ; I'll tell a tale.
B. Agreed,'

was insupportably insipid and flat."—p. xxxiii.

> Should sing our darling subject to thy shade.
> And does the mystic veil, from mortal beam,
> Involve those eyes where every virtue smil'd
> And all thy father's candid spirit shone?
> The light of reason, pure, without a cloud;
> Full of the generous heart, the mild regard;
> Honor disdaining blemish, cordial faith,
> And limpid truth, that looks the very soul."

Thomson afterwards published a long poem to the memory of Lord Talbot, which is rather diffuse, but from which some passages may fitly be extracted:—

> " Let the low-minded of these narrow days,
> No more presume to deem the lofty tale
> Of ancient times in pity to their own,
> Romance. In Talbot we united saw
> The piercing eye, the quick enlighten'd soul,
> The graceful ease, the flowing tongue of Greece,
> Join'd to the virtues and the force of Rome."
> . . . . " All his parts,
> His virtues all, collected, sought the good
> Of human kind. For *that* he, fervent, felt
> The throb of patriots when they model states:
> Anxious for *that*, nor needful sleep could hold
> His still-awaken'd soul : nor friends had charms
> To steal with pleasing guile one useful hour;
> Toil knew no languor, no attraction joy." . . . .
> " How the heart listen'd while he, pleading spoke!
> While on th' enlighten'd mind, with winning art,
> His gentle reason to persuasion stole,
> That the charm'd hearer thought it was his own." . . . .
> " Plac'd on the seat of justice, there he reign'd,
> In a superior sphere of cloudless day,
> A pure intelligence. No tumult there,
> No dark emotions, no intemperate heat,
> No passion e'er disturb'd the clear serene
> That round him spread. . . . .
> Till at the last, evolv'd, it full appear'd,
> And ev'n the loser own'd the just decree.
> But when in Senates, he, to freedom firm,
> Enlighten'd freedom, plann'd salubrious laws,
> His various learning, his wide knowledge, then
> Spontaneous seem'd from simple sense to flow." . . . .
> " I, too, remember well that cheerful bowl,
> Which round his table flow'd. The serious there
> Mix'd with the sportive, with the learn'd, the plain;
> Mirth soften'd wisdom, candor tempered mirth;
> And wit its honey lent without the sting."

Lord Talbot delighted in the society of eminent men in every department of literature; and Bishop Butler, of whom he was the friend as well as the patron, dedicated to him his celebrated "Analogy between Natural and Revealed Religion."

I have only further to state, that Lord Talbot, soon after he was called to the bar, married Cecil, daughter of Charles Matthews, Esquire, of Castle-y-Menich, in Glamorganshire, and great-granddaughter of the famous Judge Jenkins, who defied the tyranny of the Long Parliament, and from whom descended to the Chancellor's family the estate of HENSOL. With her he lived in a state of great connubial happiness, and she brought him a numerous offspring. The eldest son, of whom such hopes were entertained, the pupil of Thomson, died, as we have seen, before his talents and accomplishments could be of service to his country. William, the next brother, succeeded to his father's title, estates, and virtues. Of him it is related, that in the debate, in 1741, on the dismission of Sir Robert Walpole, being rudely called to order by Lord Cholmondley, " he declared himself an independent Peer, a character which he would not forfeit for the smiles of a court, the profit of an employment, or the reward of a pension; he said, when he was engaged on the side of truth, he would trample on the insolence that would command him to suppress his sentiments."[1] He was afterwards created Earl Talbot and Baron Dynevor, with a remainder of this barony to his daughter, an only child. She married the heir of the ancient family of the Rices, in the county of Caermarthen; and their son, Lord Dynevor, is the heir-general of the Chancellor.[2] The earldom becoming extinct, the barony of Talbot descended on John Chetwynd Talbot, the Earl's nephew, who was himself, in 1784, created Earl Talbot and Viscount Ingestre. His son, the second Earl Talbot, who at a critical period filled the office of Lord Lieutenant of Ireland with much ability, is the Chancellor's representative in the male line.

[1] Smollett, ii. 397.
[2] This venerable nobleman is in possession of all the Chancellor's papers, but, after some misunderstanding, for which he is not to blame, I have been politely informed by him that none of them are of any public interest.

CHAPTER CXXIX.

LIFE OF LORD CHANCELLOR HARDWICKE FROM HIS BIRTH TILL HE WAS APPOINTED ATTORNEY-GENERAL.

WE now come to the man universally and deservedly considered the most consummate judge who ever sat in the Court of Chancery—being distinguished not only for his rapid and satisfactory decision of the causes which came before him, but for the profound and enlightened principles which he laid down, and for perfecting English Equity into a symmetrical science. He is at the same time to be honored as a considerable statesman, co-operating powerfully for some years with the shrewdest minister this country produced during the eighteenth century, and after the fall of that chief being the principal support of his feeble successors in times perilous to the national independence, and to the reigning dynasty.

Yet the task of his biographer is by no means easy. Though he never said or did a foolish thing, he is not to be regarded with unmixed admiration. There were shades on his reputation which ought to be delineated. Personally, he does not much excite our interest or our sympathy. His career is not checkered by any youthful indiscretions or generous errors. He ever had a keen and steady eye to his own advantage, as well as to the public good. Amidst the aristocratic connections which he formed, he forgot the companions of his youth; and his regard for the middle classes of society, from which he sprung, cooled down to indifference. He became jealous of all who could be his rivals for power, and, contracting a certain degree of selfishness and hardness of character, he excited much envy and ill will amidst the flatteries which surrounded him. To do justice to the qualities and actions of so extraordinary a person would require powers of discrimination and delineation which I greatly fear I do not possess. However, after bespeaking the indulgence of my readers, I proceed,—resolved not to be sparing of praise, nor to shrink from censure, when I think the one or the other is deserved.

It is curious to observe, that the three greatest Chancellors after the Revolution were sons of attorneys, and that two of them had not the advantage of a university education. The illustrious Earl of Hardwicke was the son of a small attorney at Dover, of respectable character, but in very narrow circumstances. The family, though much reduced in the seventeenth century, is said anciently to have held considerable possessions in Wiltshire, of which county Thomas Yorke was thrice High Sheriff in the reign of Henry VIII. Philip, the father, was married to Elizabeth, daughter and coheir of Richard Gibbon, of Rolvenden, in Kent.[1] They had three children who grew up—two daughters and a son. They were glad to marry one daughter to a dissenting minister, and the other to a tradesman in a country town.

Philip, the son, the subject of this memoir, was born at Dover on the first day of December, 1690. He never was at any school except a private one, kept at Bethnal Green by a Dissenter, of the name of Samuel Morland, who is said to have been an excellent teacher. Here he won the

[1] Gibbon, the historian, being of this family has given us a very pompous account of it—showing how, being settled in "the great forests of Anderida," now the *Weald of Kent*, they, in 1326, possessed lands which still belong to them; that one of them was "Marmorarius," or Architect to Edward III.; that they had for arms "a lion rampant gardant, between three schallop-shells, argent on a field azure;" and that they were allied to Jack Cade's Lord Say and Seale, "who had most traitorously corrupted the youth of the realm in erecting a grammar-school, who had caused printing to be used, and contrary to the King, his crown, and dignity, had built a paper-mill—talking of a noun and a verb, and such abominable words as no Christian can endure to hear."—*Misc. Works.* i. 4.

Lord Hardwicke when Chancellor, erected a monument to his father and mother, with the arms of Yorke and of Gibbon impaled upon it, and with the following simple inscription, which he composed:

" Here lieth the body of PHILIP YORKE, Gent.,
who married Elizabeth, the only child
of Richard Gibbon, Gent.
They had issue
three sons and six daughters,
of whom one son and two daughters are surviving.
The other six are buried near this place.
He died June 18th, 1721, in the 70th year of his age.
Here lieth also the body of the said ELIZABETH,
Wife of the above mentioned Philip Yorke,
who died October 17th, 1727, in the 69th year of her age.
QUOS AMOR IN VITA CONJUNXIT
NON IPSA MORS DIVISIT."

The Gibbon arms are quartered in the Chancellor's shield in the Temple Hall, and in Charles Yorke's in Lincoln's Inn Hall.

good opinion of this worthy pedagogue, by displaying the quickness of parts and steady application which afterwards distinguished him through life.

When he had reached the age of fourteen, being noted as a "'cute lad," the father desired that he should be bred to his own profession of an attorney; but the mother, who was a rigid Presbyterian, very much opposed this plan. She expressed a strong wish "that Philip should be put apprentice to some *honester trade;*" and sometimes she declared her ambition to be that, breeding him a parson in her own religious persuasion, "she might see his head wag in the pulpit." However, her consent to Philip's legal destination was at last obtained on an offer being received from Mr. Salkeld, a very eminent London attorney, who had been many years Mr. Yorke's town agent, to take the boy as articled clerk without a fee.

Philip Yorke, when transferred to the metropolis, exhibited a rare instance of great natural abilities, joined with an early resolution to rise in the world, supported by acquired good habits and aided by singular good luck. A desk being assigned to him in Mr. Salkeld's office, in Brooke Street, Holborn, he applied to business with the most extraordinary assiduity, and, at the same time, he employed every leisure moment in endeavoring to supply the defects of his limited education. All lawyers' clerks were then obliged in a certain degree to understand Latin, in which many law proceedings were carried on; but he, not contented with being able to construe the "Chirograph of a fine,"[2] or to draw a "*Nar*,"[3] took delight in perusing Virgil and Cicero, and made himself well acquainted with the other more popular Roman classics, though he never mastered the minutiæ of Latin prosody, and, from the apprehension of a false quantity, ventured with trembling on a Latin quotation. Greek he hardly affected to be acquainted with.

"By these means he gained the entire good-will and esteem of his master; who, observing in him abilities and

---

[1] The "Biographia Britannica" confounds this Mr. Salkeld with Sergeant Salkeld, author of the well-known "Reports," and erroneously supposes that Philip Yorke was sent to the Sergeant as a pupil when destined for the bar.

[2] The record of a fictitious suit, resorted to for the purpose of docking estates tail and quieting the title to lands.

[3] Familiar contraction of "*Narratio*," the "Declaration" or statement of the plaintiff's grievance or cause of action.

application that prognosticated his future eminence, entered him as a student in the Temple,¹ and suffered him to dine in the Hall during the terms. But his mistress, a notable woman, thinking she might take such liberties with a *gratis clerk*, used frequently to send him from his business on family errands, and to fetch in little necessaries from Covent Garden and other markets. This, when he became a favorite with his master, and intrusted with his business and cash, he thought an indignity, and got rid of it by a stratagem, which prevented complaints or expostulation. In his accounts with his master there frequently occurred, '*coach-hire for roots of celery and turnips from Covent Garden, and a barrel of oysters from the fishmonger's, &c.*,' which Mr. Salkeld observing, and urging on his wife the impropriety and ill housewifery of such a practice, put an end to it."²

There were at the same time in Mr. Salkeld's office several young gentlemen of good family and connections, who had been sent there to be initiated in the practical part of the law—Mr. Parker, afterwards Chief Baron of the Exchequer, Mr. Jocelyn, afterwards Lord Chancellor of Ireland, and Mr. Strange, afterwards Sir John Strange, Master of the Rolls. With these Philip Yorke, though an articled clerk, associated on terms of perfect equality, and they had the merit of discovering and encouraging his good qualities.

He now received from time to time Latin letters from his former preceptor, to encourage him in his career, and to give him the news of Bethnal Green. In one of these, Morland, after dwelling with complacency on the talents of his pupil, confidently predicts the youth's future celebrity, and pronounces that to have been the most auspicious day of his life when the cultivation of so happy a genius was first committed to his charge:—" Non mirandum est si futuram tui nominis celebritatem meus præ-

" Novembris 29°, 1708°,
die et anno p'dict.

Mr Philippus Yorke filius et heres apparens Philippi Yorke de villa et porte de Dover in Com. Kant. gen. admissus est in Societatem Medij Templi spealiter et obligatur una cum . . } 04 .00 .00."
Et dat ℔ fine . . . .
—*Books of Middle Temple.*

¹ Letter to Cooksey, from "an old man of the law who knew him well."—*Cooksey,* p. 71.

sagiat animus. Quas tantopere olim vices meas dolui, eas hodie gratulor mihi plurimum, cui tale tandem contigerit ingenium excolendum. Nullum unquam diem gratiorem mihi illuxisse in perpetuum reputabo, quam quo te pater tuus mihi tradidit in disciplinam."

But the young man still had to struggle with many difficulties, and he probably would have been obliged from penury to go upon the roll of attorneys, rising only to be clerk to the magistrates at petty sessions, or perhaps to the dignity of town clerk of Dover, had it not been for his accidental introduction to Lord Chief Justice Parker, which was the foundation of all his prosperity and greatness. This distinguished Judge had a high opinion of Mr. Salkeld, who was respected by all ranks of the profession, and asked him one day, if he could tell him of a decent and intelligent person who might serve as a sort of law tutor for his sons,—to assist and direct them in their professional studies. The attorney eagerly recommended his clerk, Philip Yorke, who was immediately retained in that capacity, and giving the highest satisfaction by his assiduity and his obliging manners, gained the warm friendship of the sons, and the weighty, persevering, and unscrupulous patronage of the father. He now bade adieu to the smoky office in Brooke Street, Holborn,[1] and he had a commodious chamber assigned him in the Chief Justice's house in Lincoln's Inn Fields. Released from the drudgery not only of going to Covent Garden market, but of attending captions and serving process, he devoted himself with fresh vigor to the abstruse parts of the law and to his more liberal studies. Further, he took great pains to acquire the art of correct composition in English —generally so much neglected by English lawyers that many of the most eminent of them will be found, in their written "opinions," violating the rules of grammar, and without the least remorse constructing their sentences in a slovenly manner, for which a schoolboy would be whipped.[2] The "Tatler" had done much to

---

[1] " Three years he sat his smoky room in
Pens, paper, ink, and pounce consumin'. "

[2] This undoubted fact shows strikingly the difference between speaking and writing; for some of those who did not at all know the division of a discourse into sentences, or the grammatical construction of a sentence, have been listened to with great and just admiration, when addressing a jury,—without their inaccuracies and inelegancies being discovered. Erskine could compose

inspire a literary taste into all ranks. This periodical had ceased, but being now succeeded by the "Spectator," Philip Yorke "gave his days and nights to the papers of Addison."

Although he never approached the excellence of his model, he was so far pleased with his own proficiency that he aspired to the honor of writing a "Spectator." Accordingly, with great pains, he composed the well known Letter, signed "PHILIP HOMEBRED," and dropped it into the Lion's mouth. To his inexpressible delight, on Monday, April 12, 1712, it came out as No. 364, with the motto added by Steele :—

——"Navibus atque
Quadrigis petimus bene vivere."

As a lawyer desirious of upholding our craft by all fair means, I should have been proud to have warmly praised his performance, but I am sorry to acknowledge that I can not honestly object to the terms in which it was "vilipended" by Dr. Johnson.[1] I will, however, select one or two of the best passages, in the hope that the reader may form a more favorable judgment of it. Having described a foolish mother, who is persuaded that "to chain her son down to the ordinary methods of education with others of his age, would be to cramp his faculties, and do an irreparable injury to his wonderful capacity," Mr. Philip Homebred, trying to imitate the manner of Addison, thus proceeds: "I happened to visit at the house last week, and missing the young gentleman at the tea-table, where he seldom fails to officiate, could not, upon so extraordinary a circumstance, avoid inquiring after him. My Lady told me he was gone with his woman, in order to make some preparations for their equipage ; for that she intended very speedily to carry him to travel. The oddness of the expression shocked me a little ; however, I soon recovered myself enough to let her know that all I was willing to understand by it was, that she designed this summer to show her son his estate in a distant county in which he had never yet been.

with accuracy and elegance, but this could be said of very few of his contemporaries.

[1] "He would not allow that the paper (No. 364) on carrying a boy to travel, signed *Philip Homebred*, which was reported to be written by the Ld. Ch. Hardwicke, had merit. He said, 'it was quite vulgar, and had nothing in it luminous.'"—Boswell's *Life of Johnson*, vol. vi. p. 152.

But she soon took care to rob me of that agreeable mistake, and let me into the whole affair." . . . "When I came to reflect at night, as my custom is, upon the circumstances of the day, I could not but believe that this humor of carrying a boy to travel in his mother's lap, and that upon pretense of learning men and things, is a case of an extraordinary nature, and carries on it a particular stamp of folly. I did not remember to have met with its parallel within the compass of my observation, though I could call to mind some not extremely unlike it. From hence my thoughts took occasion to ramble into the general notion of traveling, as it is now made a part of education. Nothing is more frequent than to take a lad from grammar and taw, and under the tuition of some poor scholar, who is willing to be banished for thirty pounds a year and a little victuals, send him crying and sniveling into foreign countries. Thus he spends his time as children do at puppet-shows, and with much the same advantage, in staring and gaping at an amazing variety of strange things; strange, indeed, to one who is not prepared to comprehend the reasons and meaning of them; while he should be laying the solid foundations of knowledge in his mind, and furnishing it with just rules to direct his future progress in life, under some skillful master of the art of instruction." Here we have good sense and grammatical language, but does the writer give us " thoughts that breathe, and words that burn?"—has he succeeded in attaining " an English style, familiar but not coarse, and elegant but not ostentatious?" Had he taken to literature as a trade, he would have had poor encouragement from Lintot and Cave, and he would hardly have risen to the distinction of being one of the heroes of the Dunciad. I fear me it will be said that a great lawyer is made *ex quovis ligno*, and that he who would starve in Grub Street from his dullness,—if he takes to Westminster Hall, may become " the most illustrious of Chancellors."

This paper, though not of the highest excellence, is said to have gained for the writer the notice of Lord Somers; and there is now at Wimpole a pocket Virgil, on the fly-leaf of which are the following words, in the handwriting of Lord Somers, " Sum Johannis Dryden, 1685,"—supposed to have been given to him by the great poet, and on this occasion presented to Mr. Yorke as an incentive to literary exertion. It was rumored that our law student wrote another, which was published in a subsequent volume, but it probably had less applause, for he did not distinctly own it, and his family could never identify it. He wisely adhered to juridical studies, and labored more and more assiduously to qualify himself for his profession.

He now regularly attended the courts in term time, taking notes of the arguments and judgments,—which in the evening he revised and digested. He likewise devoted himself to oratory, and acquired that close and self-possessed manner of speaking before the public by which he was afterwards distinguished. I do not find anything expressly said about his politics in early life, but from his father's connection with the Dissenters, he was probably bred in the Low Church party. He, no doubt, was a zealous Whig when patronized by Lord Parker; and I do not find any charge of inconsistency ever brought against him.

The house of Brunswick was actually on the throne prior to his appearance in public life. He was called to the bar in Easter Term, 1715, being then in his twenty-third year.[1]

His progress was more rapid than that of any other *débutant* in the annals of our profession. He was immediately pushed by old Salkeld, who himself had many briefs to dispose of, and who had great influence among his brother attorneys. Several young men with whom he had formed an intimacy while in his clerkship, now being "upon the roll," were perhaps of still greater use to him.

He began his practice in the Court of King's Bench, where he enjoyed the marked favor of Lord Chief Justice

---

[1] "Parliament, tent. 6° die Maij, 1715.—Mr Simpson T. proposed by M. Jauncy, Mr York P. proposed by Mr Mulso, Mr fforster J. proposed by Mr Harcourt, Mr Newton J. proposed by Mr Offley, Mr Idle J. proposed by Mr Avery, Mr Brabant H. proposed by Sr William Whitelock, and Mr Sherwood J. proposed by Mr Attorny Genall, for the Degree of the Utter Barr."

On the 20th of the same month Mr. Philip Yorke was admitted to a set of chambers.

The following is the only other entry relating to him in the Books of the Middle Temple:

"Ad Parliament tent. 10ᵐᵒ ffebij. 1720ᵐᵒ.—It is ordered—That Sr Philip Yorke, Knt, his Majties Sollr Generall, be called up to the Bench of this Society in order to his Reading."

Parker. It soon happened that he had to argue a special case upon an important and intricate point of law. The judgment of the Court was with his client, and he received high compliments from the Chief Justice for the research, learning, and ability which he had displayed.[1] From that day forth he was much employed in the "special argument line," although it was some years before he acquired the reputation of a "leader."

By Mr. Salkeld's advice, he chose the Western Circuit, where, although he had no natural connection,—by means which must have excited some jealousy and distrust, but which could not be proved to be incorrect, he was suddenly in good junior business at every assize town.[2] About two years after his start, Mr. Justice Powys, who had been eminent in his profession, but was now bending under the weight of years, went to the Western Circuit, and, surprised to see so young a man in every cause, was anxious to know how he had got on so rapidly. It has been said since, that early success on the Circuit must arise from "sessions, a book, or a miracle." The practice of barristers practicing at Quarter Sessions had not then begun, and, miracles having ceased, Powys thought that young Yorke must have written some law book, which had brought him into notice. The bar dining with the Judges at the last place on the Circuit, and the party being small on account of so many having taken their departure for London, before the toast of "Prosperity to the Western Circuit," and "*Quinden. Pasch.*" were given,[3] there was a pause in the conversation, and Mr. Justice Powys, addressing the flourishing junior, who was sitting nearly opposite to him, said, "Mr. Yorke, I can not well account for your having so much business, considering

[1] We are not told how he received these compliments. He was probably pleased and grateful; but I once heard a young barrister, who entertained a very high, and perhaps somewhat excessive opinion of his own merits, say, under similar circumstances, "I think the Judges use a very great liberty in presuming to praise me for my argument."

[2] He afterwards had the satisfaction of rewarding Mr. Salkeld for all his kindness by appointing him Clerk of the Errors in the Court of King's Bench.

[3] It would appear that the present custom then prevailed of the Judges, when the barristers dine with them, giving as a toast when the party is to break up, "Prosperity to the O. Circuit," except that, at the last place on the Spring Circuit, they afterwards give, "*Quinden. Pasch.*" being the first return of Easter Term; and on the Summer Circuit, "*Cras. Animarum*," being the first return of Michaelmas Term; which is as much as to say, "To our next merry meeting in Westminster Hall."

how short a time you have been at the bar: I humbly conceive you must have published something; for look you, do you see, there is scarcely a cause before the Court, but you are employed in it, on one side or other. I should, therefore, be glad to know, Mr. Yorke, do you see whether this is the case?"—*Yorke.* "Please ye, my Lord, I have some thoughts of publishing a book, but, as yet, I have made no progress in it." The Judge, smiling to think that his conjecture was not quite without foundation, became importunate to know the subject of the book, and Yorke, not being able to evade his inquiries, at at last said, "I have had thoughts, my Lord, of doing Coke upon Littleton into verse; but I have gone a very little way into it."—*Powys.* "This is something new, and must be very entertaining; and I beg you will oblige us with a recital of a few of the verses." Mr. Yorke long resisted, but finding that the Judge would not drop the subject, bethought himself that he could not get rid of it better than by compounding a specimen of such a translation, something in the Judge's own words, and introducing the phrases with which his Lordship was in the habit of interlarding his discourse upon all occasions, let the subject be grave or gay. Therefore, accompanying what he intended to say with some excuses for not sooner complying with the Judge's request, he recited the following verses, as the opening of his translation:—

> " He that holdeth lands in fee
> Need neither to quake nor to quiver,
> I humbly conceive; for look, do you see,
> They are his and his heirs' forever." [1]

A knavish speech sleeps in a foolish ear. Although all others present perceived the jest, the learned Judge was not struck by the peculiarity of the diction, and was so much convinced that this was a serious attempt to impress upon the youthful mind the great truths of tenures, that, meeting Mr. Yorke a few months afterwards in

---

[1] The first section of Littleton in prose says—" Tenant in fee simple is he which hath lands or tenements to hold to him and his heirs forever." Of which we have another metrical transiation:—

> " Tenant in fee simple is he,
> And needs neither to shake or shiver,
> Who has his lands free from demands,
> To him and his heirs forever."

Westminster Hall, he inquired "how he was getting on with the translation of Littleton?"

The wicked wag, out of revenge, turned into rhyme the Judge's last charge to the grand jury,—of which I give a specimen:—

> "Next libelers, gentlemen present,
> Which all mistakes for to prevent
> I thus define: it is, to wit,
> Not what is spoke but what is writ,
> Or printed upon paper sheets,
> And cry'd by wenches 'bout the streets.
> Most generally it is a lye
> To blacken King or ministry." [1]

But our poet continued to deal in profitable prose in the courts of justice, and was now so prosperous that he thought he might not improperly contract a matrimonial alliance. In the object of his choice he showed his usual prudence and good sense. This was a gay widow with a good jointure, the niece of Lord Somers, and the niece by marriage of Sir Joseph Jekyll, the Master of the Rolls, at whose house in Chancery Lane he became acquainted with her.[2] Yorke was a remarkably handsome young man, and his addresses were well received by the lady, but she referred him to her father, Mr. Cocks, a Worcestershire squire. Fortified by a letter of introduction from

---

[1] Duke Wharton says, in the once popular lines,—
> "When honest Price shall trim and truckle under,
> *And* POWIS *sum a cause without a blunder;*
> Then shall I cease my charmer to adore,
> And think of love and politics no more."

Yet the simplicity of the Judge in believing in the metrical translations of Littleton is not so great as unlearned readers may suppose. My professional brethren have all read and tried to recollect "The Reports of Sir Edward Coke, Knt. in verse." This volume was first printed in 1742, and a new edition of it was published so lately as 1825. It professes, in two lines,—with the name, to give the point decided in every case which Coke has reported: *e. g.*

> "*Archer*, if he for life infeoff in fee,
> It bars remainders in contingency."
> "*Shelley*, whose ancestors a freehold take,
> The words (his heirs) a limitation make."
> "*Monopolies* granted by King are void.
> They spoil the trade in which the youth's employed."

When I was in a special pleader's office, a brother pupil thus began to versify "Tidd's Practice:"—
> "Actions are all, and this I'll stick to,
> *Vel ex contractu vel delicto.*"

[2] Her maiden name was Cocks, she being a daughter of Charles Cocks, and a sister of Lord Somers.

Sir Joseph, who encouraged the match, he repaired full of confidence to the residence of his intended father-in-law. The old gentleman received him politely, but learning the object of his visit asked him for his *rent roll*, and Mr. Lygon, his daughter's first husband, having had a very ample one, was surprised to hear that all Mr. Yorke's estate consisted of "a perch of ground in Westminster Hall." However, in answer to a letter to the Master of the Rolls, asking "how he could think of introducing into the family a young man incapable of making a settlement," his Honor so strongly represented the brilliant prospects of the rising lawyer, that the required consent was given, and the union took place,—which turned out most auspicious, for the married couple lived together till old age in uninterrupted affection and harmony, sharing the most wonderful worldly greatness, and seeing a numerous family of sons and daughters grown up—all well-behaved and prosperous, and as fully fixed among the high aristocracy as if they had descended from companions of the Conqueror.[1] Mr. and Mrs. Philip Yorke began their married life in a very small house near Lincoln's Inn, the ground floor of which served him for an office, and saved him the expense of chambers in the Temple, then considered by him a very great object.

In the year 1718, upon the resignation of Lord Cowper, Chief Justice Parker, shortly after created Earl of Macclesfield, received the Great Seal, and Mr. Yorke transferred himself to the Court of Chancery, still continuing to go the Western Circuit.[2] Equity business soon flowed in upon him—partly from his own merit, and partly from the favor of his patron, testified in a manner which gave mortal offense to the seniors at the bar. Sergeant Pengelly, in particular, was so disgusted at frequently hearing the Chancellor observe—"*what Mr. Yorke said has not been answered*," that he one day threw up his brief, saying in a loud voice, "I will no more attend a Court where I find Mr. Yorke is not to be answered." Some have gone so far as to ascribe Lord Macclesfield's subsequent ruin to

---

[1] The Lord Chancellor wrote him a letter to congratulate him, "y^t an affair of ye greatest importance in life was so happily over."

[2] For more than half a century afterwards the Chancellor's sittings were so arranged as to allow the counsel practicing in his Court to go circuit, and Equity men had the advantage of keeping up their common-law learning.

this favoritism, asserting that "Sergeant Pengelly's resentment, joined with that of others in the same situation, brought upon the Chancellor that investigation of his private management, and the abuses committed or connived at by him in his appointment of the officers of his Court, which terminated in his impeachment and conviction."[1]

However, there can be no doubt that the discontent of the old Chancery pleaders arose very much from the superior talent of the young common lawyer, whose invasion was so formidable to their empire. Most of them had been contented to pick up a knowledge of Chancery practice from experience, referring *pro re natâ* to what was to be found on the subject in the Reports and Abridgments; but he entered upon a systematic course of study, qualifying him to be a great advocate or a great judge in the Court of Chancery—tracing the equitable jurisdiction of the Court to its sources, and thoroughly understanding all the changes it had undergone.

In the case of *Rex* v. *Hare and Mann*,[2] in which Sir Robert Walpole's family was interested, he had an opportunity, of which he fully availed himself, of showing that he was deeply skilled in the history and practice of this tribunal, and he raised his reputation as high among the Solicitors here as it had been among the Attorneys in the King's Bench. In his celebrated letter to Lord Kames, on the distinction between Law and Equity, written many years after, he speaks with much complacency of his argument on this occasion, and insinuates that it contributed greatly to his elevation. "It was," says he, "when I was a very young advocate, before I was Solicitor General, but it is correctly reported; for I remember Sir John Strange borrowed my papers to transcribe, so that the faults in it are all my own. In arguing that cause, which turned upon a critical exception to the return of a writ of *scire facias* in Chancery, I found, or at least fancied it to be necessary to show, that all the various powers of that court were derived from, or had relation to, the Great Seal, and I endeavored to prove that the equitable jurisdiction exercised by the Chancellor took its rise from his being the proper officer to whom all applications were made for writs to ground actions at common law, and

---

[1] Cooksey, 72. Sergeant Pengelly was certainly the most bitter manager of the impeachment. [2] 1 Strange, 146, Feb. 1719, 5 Geo. 2.

from many cases being brought before him, in which that law would not afford a remedy, and thereby being induced through necessity or compassion to extend a discretionary one."

Lord Macclesfield now determined on the first vacancy to make a resolute effort to have his *protégé* appointed a law officer of the Crown, notwithstanding the shock such a promotion might give to aged Sergeants who had been in vain expecting advancement ever since the coming in of King William; and with this view he prevailed upon the Duke of Newcastle, who had immense borough interest, to return him to the House of Commons for Lewes.[2]

Parliament met on the 11th of November after Yorke was elected, and, with the exception of the Christmas recess, continued sitting till he went on the Spring Circuit in the beginning of March; but I can not find that he opened his mouth in this interval, and it is probable that he prudently remained silent; for the only measure of public interest then debated in the House of Commons was Sunderland's Peerage Bill, on which the Whigs were divided, and it might have appeared presumptuous for a young lawyer to give any opinion.[3]

[1] This very learned argument arose out of a seemingly very trifling objection to a writ of *scire facias*, which required the defendant " to appear in Cancellariâ nostrâ in Octobris, &c. ubicunque tunc fuerit." Objection, that it ought to have been " ubicunque eadem Cancellaria tunc foret in Angliâ," on the ground that since the Union with Scotland there was only one Great Seal for Great Britain ; that the Chancery might be held in Scotland; that for matters arising in England, suitors could not lawfully be summoned to Scotland ; and therefore that this return, which might call the defendant into Scotland, was bad.— *Yorke*, for the defendant, gave a learned history of the jurisdiction of the Court of Chancery, contending that it arose entirely from the Great Seal ; and as the Great Seal was the Great Seal of Great Britain, the Chancery had become the Chancery of Great Britain. But Lord Macclesfield said, that " although the Act of Union had made the Great Seal the Great Seal of Great Britain, it had not made the Chancery so. The powers of the Chancery as a Court are over private property ; and the articles of Union preserving to each country its municipal jurisdictions, the English Court of Chancery could not be held in Scotland, although the Great Seal might be carried to Scotland, and for some purposes used there."—1 Str. 158.

[2] So little squeamish were they then about peers interfering in elections, that the electors of Lewes presented an address to the Duke, " thanking him for having recommended to them so respectable a representative, and testifying their desire, on all future occasions, to show their sense of the favors his Grace had been pleased to lay upon them."

[3] A list of the majority and of the minority was published, but his name does not appear in either.—7 Parl Hist. 624.

Before he had made his maiden speech in parliament,—the folly as well as the favor of others working for his advantage,—an opportunity most unexpectedly arose for promoting him in his profession. The Attorney and Solicitor General, though not free from personal dislikes and jealousies, have almost always preserved ostensibly a mutual good understanding, and have cordially co-operated in the public service. But Mr. Lechmere and Sir William Thompson, the then Attorney and Solicitor General, hated each other so intensely that they had several very indecent quarrels in private causes at the bar and in the transaction of official business. Their enmity was whetted by a sordid competition,—" which of them should be most resorted to in granting charters of incorporation to Joint Stock Companies?" Now was raging the fever of speculation throughout the nation, of which the " South Sea Bubble" was a symptom, and companies were formed which, both for object and means, equaled in extravagance anything witnessed in our own times. They brought a great harvest to the law officers of the Crown, but of this Lechmere, being more popular, and supposed to have more influence, carried off by far the largest share. Thompson at last, openly, in the House of Commons, preferred a charge against him of corruptly taking excessive fees and recommending improper grants. The charge was indignantly denied by Lechmere, who said that " he had the honor to be a Privy Councillor, Chancellor of the Duchy of Lancaster, Attorney General, a Member of that House, and, more than all, *a gentleman;* that such an accusation could not therefore but fall upon him more heavily; that he defied all the world—the worst and bitterest of his enemies—to prove him guilty of corrupt or unwarrantable practices, and that he demanded an immediate inquiry." Thompson undertook to make good the accusation, and a committee sat to hear the evidence. It appeared that the Attorney General's clerk had been rather eager to make joint stock companies pay handsomely," but there did not rest even a passing shadow of suspicion on his master; whereupon it was unanimously resolved, " that the informations of Sir William Thompson were malicious, scandalous, and false, and that the Right Honorable Nicholas Lechmere had discharged his trust in the matters referred to him with honor and integrity." Thompson was immediately dismissed from his office of Solicitor General.[1] Lechmere tried to procure the appointment for an attached friend of his own, that he might no more be exposed to such squabbles; but the Lord Chancellor claimed the appointment as his patronage,—and he was at this time all powerful, both with the King and the minister.

Philip Yorke had joined the Western Circuit during this controversey, little thinking that he had any personal interest in it, but while he was attending the assizes at Dorchester he received the two following letters. The first was from the Lord Chancellor, and was directed to "Philip Yorke, Esq., Counselor at Law, M.P., at the Assizes of Dorchester."

"Sir,

"The King having declared it to be his pleasure that you be his Solicitor General in the room of Sir Wm. Thompson, who is already removed from the office, I with great pleasure obey his Majesty's commands, to require you to hasten to town immediately upon receipt hereof, in order to take that office upon you. I heartily congratulate you upon this first instance of his Majesty's favor, and am with great sincerity,

"Sir,
"Your faithful and obedient Servant,
"PARKER, C."

The second was from Mr. Secretary Craggs:

"Dear Sir,

"You will be informed from other hands of what has happened between the Attorney and Solicitor General. In the squabble the latter has lost his employment, and the first, I believe, will not succeed in his recommendation of Mr. Denton to be his successor, for I believe the King has resolved to appoint you, which I am glad of, for his service, and for my particular satisfaction: Who am entirely,

"Your most faithful Servant,
"J. CRAGGS.

"Cockpit, March 17, 1719 [1720]."

Mr. Yorke, on reading these letters, after receiving the hearty congratulations of his brother circuiteers, who re-

---

[1] However, he was afterwards made Recorder of London and a Baron of the Exchequer.

joiced sincerely in the elevation of such a formidable competitor, returned his briefs, and set off post for London. On the 22d of March he was sworn in Solicitor General before Lord Macclesfield, and a few days after, on being presented by him to the King, he received the honor of knighthood.

With the exception of the members of the Western Circuit, the profession considered Sir Philip's appointment a very arbitrary act. He was only twenty-nine years of age, and had been little more than four years at the bar. He had displayed great talents, but Wearg and Talbot, who were considerably his seniors, and had always deserved well of the Whig party, were men of distinguished reputation, and qualified to do credit to any office in the law, however exalted. Others of inferior merit were disappointed, and the blame being all laid on the Lord Chancellor, the resentment which he had before excited by his partiality for the tutor of his sons was greatly exasperated.

It is said that even the attorneys and solicitors looked askance at the new law officer, though disposed to be proud of the elevation of a gentleman so closely connected with them. Very much run after as a junior, he as yet had not got into any leading business, and they were alarmed by seeing him, with so little experience, suddenly put over the heads of the gentlemen with silk gowns, whom they had been accustomed to employ. When Easter Term came round, and he took his place within the bar in the Court of Chancery, he was left out of most of the new causes which came on to be heard, and some of his discontented rivals were sanguine enough to hope that his premature elevation had ruined him for ever. But by the exertions of his personal friends among the solicitors, by being supposed to have "the ear of the Court," by his own great talents, by his indefatigable industry, by the gentleness of his manners, and by the insinuating complacency of his address, he rapidly overcame these prejudices, and was retained in every suit.[1]

His acceptance of office having, under the recent statute, vacated his seat in the House of Commons, he was re-elected for Lewes without opposition. He after-

[1] One account of his *début* as Solicitor General says, "The storm which was raised by his premature promotion fell wholly on his patron."—*Cooksey*, 73.

wards sat for Seaford, being always returned without trouble or expense,—which was considered by some of his contemporaries as an instance of his luck, and by others as a proof of his management, in having so effectually insinuated himself into the good graces, first of Lord Macclesfield, and then of the Duke of Newcastle. But for some years to come his name is never mentioned in printed parliamentary debates, and we are left in great doubt as to the part he acted in the House of Commons.

It happened in little more than a year, that, Lechmere retiring from the bar with a peerage, there was a vacancy in the office of Attorney General, and some supposed that the Chancellor would recklessly thrust his juvenile favorite into it, although only thirty years of age; but prudence prevailed, and it was filled up with the experienced Sir Robert Raymond, afterwards Lord Chief Justice of the King's Bench.[1]

Sir Philip Yorke continuing Solicitor General, first gained great public applause on the trial of Christopher Layer for high treason in conspiring to bring in the Pretender. The prisoner, after being ably defended by counsel, himself spoke so clearly and ingeniously in his own defense as to make a considerable impression on the Jury, and to endanger the conviction—then considered of the last consequence, not only to the safety of the ministry, but of the family on the throne.

The Solicitor General rose to reply when it was late at night, and delivered a speech between two and three hours long, which, during the whole of that time, riveted the attention of all who heard it, and was most rapturously praised as a fine specimen of juridical eloquence. Certainly it is what is technically termed a " hanging speech "—very quiet and dispassionate; seemingly candid, and even kind to the accused; but in the most subtle manner bringing forward all the salient points of the evidence against him—and by insinuation and allusion, taking advantage of the prepossessions of the jury. He thus concluded:—

" It has been said, indeed, that he is but an inconsiderable man—of no rank or fortune fit to sustain such an un-

[1] There is extant a curious joint opinion given by them, " that the King might lawfully grant a pardon to a malefactor under sentence of death, on condition that he would suffer himself to be inoculated for the small-pox."

dertaking. That observation may be true : but since it is plain that he did engage in it, this, with other things, clearly proves that he was set on work and supported by persons of more influence. And, gentlemen, this is the most affecting consideration of all. But I would not even in this cause, so important to the King and to the State, say anything to excite your passions: I choose rather to appeal to your judgments ; and to these I submit the strength and consequence of the evidence you have heard. My Lord, I ask pardon for having taken up so much of your time. I have only further to beg, for the sake of the King, for the sake of the prisoner at the bar, and for the sake of myself, that if, through mistake or inadvertency, I have omitted or misrepresented anything, or laid a greater weight on any part of the evidence than it will properly bear, your Lordship will be pleased to take notice of it, so that the whole case may come before the Jury in its just and true light."

The conviction was certainly according to law; and if Layer's head had been immediately placed on Temple Bar, his execution, though lamentable, might have been thought a necessary severity: but all concerned in the prosecution and the punishment incurred and deserved obloquy—by the delay interposed with a view to elicit from the prisoner the accusation of others, and by his execution long after the verdict, when he had disappointed the hope of further disclosures.[1]

CHAPTER CXXX.

CONTINUATION OF THE LIFE OF LORD HARDWICKE TILL HE WAS APPOINTED LORD CHANCELLOR.

ON the 31st of January, 1723, Sir Robert Raymond being promoted to be Chief Justice of the King's Bench, Sir Philip Yorke, with general applause, succeeded him as Attorney General. This situation he held above thirteen years, exhibiting a model of perfection to future law officers of the Crown. He was punctual and conscientious in the discharge of his public duty,

[1] 16 St. Tr. 319.

never neglecting it that he might undertake private causes, although fees were supposed to be particularly sweet to him, and, having felt the ills of penury, he was, from the commencement to the close of his professional career, eager to accumulate wealth. Considering this propensity, he had likewise great merit in resisting the temptation to which others have yielded of accepting briefs in private causes, when he could not be present at the hearing of them, or could not do fair justice to the client who hoped to have the benefit of his assistance. I may likewise mention that, although he was afterwards supposed to have become stiff and formal in his manners, while he remained at the bar he was affable and unassuming, courteous to his brethren of longer standing, making himself popular with the juniors, and trying to soften the envy excited by his elevation. In parliament he never displayed any impatience to gain distinction, but he was regular in his attendance, and he was always ready to render fair assistance to the government, and to give his opinion on any legal or constitutional question for the guidance of the House. Without being a "prerogative lawyer," he stood up for the just powers of the Crown; and, without being a "patriot," he was a steady defender of the rights and privileges of the people.

As public prosecutor in Revenue cases in the Exchequer, he is universally lauded. "Though advocate for the Crown, he spoke," says one contemporary, "with the veracity of a witness, and the impartiality of a judge." When defending Walpole's Excise scheme against the misrepresentations of its opponents, he not ungracefully appealed to his own practice in prosecuting those who attempted to defraud the revenue and to injure the fair dealer; pronouncing a eulogy upon himself to which, we are told, "the whole House assented with universal applause."

He was not so fortunate in his prosecutions for libel. In his time sprang up the controversy respecting the rights of juries, which was not settled till the close of the eighteenth century. He contended for the doctrine, that the jury were only to decide upon the sufficiency of the evidence of publication, and upon innuendoes; *i. e.*, whether particular words or abbreviations in the alleged libel had the meaning imputed to them by the indictment or information, as, whether "the K——g" meant "our Sovereign Lord the King;" but that the lawfulness or criminality of the writing prosecuted was pure matter of law for the opinion of the Court. The judges coincided with him in their directions, but juries were sometimes rebellious. The obnoxious journal of that day was the "Craftsman," conducted by Bolingbroke, Pulteney and the principal leaders of the opposition to Sir Robert Walpole. Sir Philip Yorke succeeded in obtaining a conviction in the case of the famous Hague letter, written by Bolingbroke;[1] but he was foiled in his prosecution of a subsequent violent attack upon the Government, supposed to be from the pen of Chesterfield, for though the Chief Justice laid down the same law, and there could be no doubt about publication or innuendoes, the jury, very much approving of the sentiments of the supposed libel, and thinking them not only innocent but laudable, found a general verdict of *not guilty*. It was then that Pulteney composed his famous ballad, with the oft-quoted stanza:

> " For Sir Philip well knows,
> That his innuendoes
> Will serve him no longer
> In verse or in prose;
> For twelve honest men have decided the cause,
> Who are judges alike of the facts and the laws."[2]

But, considering how the law of libel had been laid by Lord Holt and other Judges deemed constitutional, I believe that Sir Philip is to be deemed forbearing in instituting prosecutions against the press, and mild in conducting them.[3]

[1] 17 St. Tr. 625: and see a very amusing account of this trial by Lord Mansfield, 21 St. Tr. 1037. "There was a great concourse of people: it was a matter of great expectation, and many persons of high rank were present to countenance the defendant."

[2] The last two lines were misrepresented in the Dean of St. Asaph's case by Lord Mansfield; who, to suit his purpose, or from lapse of memory, said Pulteney had admitted that "libel or no libel?" was a question only for the Court, by saying in his ballad—
"For twelve honest men have decided the cause,
 Who are judges of fact, though not judges of laws."
—21 St. Tr. 1037.

[3] Lord Chesterfield thus speaks of him as a law officer of the Crown: "Though he was Solicitor and Attorney General, he was by no means what is called *a prerogative lawyer*. He loved the constitution, and maintained the just prerogative of the Crown; but without stretching it to the oppression of the people. He was naturally humane, moderate, and decent; but when, by his employmen's, he was obliged to prosecute state criminals, he discharged

While Attorney General, he was not entirely absorbed in the routine of official and professional business. He contrived to have leisure, not only to attend to the literature of the day, but, when occasion required, to investigate thoroughly, by a reference to rare books and ancient records, questions respecting our judicial history. In consequence of some clashing of jurisdiction between Lord King as Chancellor, and Sir Joseph Jekyll as Master of the Rolls, he wrote and published "A Discourse of the Judicial Authority belonging to the Office of Master of the Rolls," which is full of recondite learning, and on which the declaratory act was passed, placing the jurisdiction of "His Honor" on its present footing.[1]

His first appearance as Attorney General in the House of Commons was in conducting the bill of pains and penalties against Bishop Atterbury, by which that learned and factious prelate was banished for life, and it was made high treason to correspond with him. There was no difficulty in producing a moral persuasion of the existence of a plot to bring in the Pretender on which it was founded, but no ingenuity could justify the departure from the rules of evidence established for the safety of the subject, or an attempt to punish, by a ministerial majority, where there must have been an acquittal before the regular tribunals of the country. The Attorney General had to carry through similar bills against Plunket and Kelly, implicated in the conspiracy. In support of the last, he is said to have been particularly energetic, but no fragment of his speech is preserved.[2]

---

that duty in a very different manner from most of his predecessors, who were too justly called *the blood-hounds of the Crown.*

[1] 3 Geo. 2, c. 30; 3 Bl. Com. 450.

[2] See 3 Parl. Hist. 54-293; 16 St. Tr. 323-693. Swift tried to revenge his friend Atterbury, by ridiculing this plot in "Gulliver's Travels,' published soon after:—"Another professor showed me a large paper of instructions for discovering plots and conspiracies against the government. He advised great statesmen to examine into the diet of all suspected persons, 'their time of eating, upon which side they lay, with what hand,' &c." and then he describes a certain method "by an examination of the *ejecta*, of ascertaining whether the design of the traitor be to murder the King, or only to raise an insurrection, or to burn the metropolis."—*Voyage to Laputa*, ch. vi. Kelly having been confined thirteen years in the Tower, was allowed to make his escape. Atterbury, it is well known, died in exile; and when his body came over for interment, the coffin was opened at the Custom House, "lest it should be made the medium of a treasonable correspondence, contrary to the act of parliament."

In the year 1725, Sir Philip was placed in a very disagreeable predicament by the impeachment of his patron —originating, as some thought, in the Chancellor's violent predilection for Sir Philip himself. He has been accused of heartlessness and ingratitude on this occasion, and of standing a silent and unconcerned spectator of the distress of the man to whom he owed all his advancement in life.[1] But I think the charge is unjust, or greatly exaggerated. If by resigning his office, he could have become the strenuous defender of his patron, with the remotest chance of saving him, it would have been his duty to have made the attempt. But the current ran so strong against the denounced "trrafficker in judicial offices, and robber of widows and orphans," that to stem it was impossible,-- and useless self-immolation could not be demanded from any one. The Commons were almost unanimous for the impeachment, although some thought there ought to have been a previous inquiry by a committee. When there appeared an opening for embarrassing the proceeding by a motion to recommit the articles of impeachment, Sir Philip Yorke strenuously, though ineffectually, supported it against Sergeant Pengelly, and Sir Clement Wearg, the Solicitor General.

On the appointment of managers to conduct the prosecution at the bar of the House of Lords, the Attorney General ought to have been of the number, but he begged to be excused on account of the private friendship subsisting between him and the late Lord Chancellor; and we are told that he had great "difficulty in obtaining his request."[2] It is not easy to specify any other step he could have taken to show his sympathy. Yet I confess I should have been gratified to hear that he had tried to turn the tide of public opinion, by a pamphlet "On the Sale of the office of Master in Chancery, proving that it has been at all times transferred for a valuable consideration," or that he had made one gallant speech in his place in the House of Commons, for the man who had such claims to public applause, and who had drawn down ill-will upon himself by befriending the friendless. Surely Sir Robert Walpole, who was not without generosity of sentiment as well as good nature (although he was anxious to rescue his government from the imputation of screening

[1] Cooksey, 73.   [2] 8 St. Tr. 414–480

high delinquency), would not have discarded his Attorney General for one solitary indiscretion. At all events, it would have much consoled me to know that Sir Philip visited Lord Macclesfield in the Tower, was in the habit of cheering his retreat at Derby, and showed a grateful solicitude to vindicate his memory. But I am afraid that he left the condemned Chancellor to his fate, like others whom " his former bounty fed,"—eager only for his own aggrandizement.

I must now pursue the prosperous career of the wary Sir Philip. Having, upon the introduction of Lord Macclesfield, made the acquaintance and gained the good graces of the Duke of Newcastle, on the fall of his first patron he devoted himself to that " place-loving nobleman," who, hardly gifted with common understanding, and not possessing the knowledge of geography and history now acquired at a parish school,—from the rotten borough system then in prime vigor, was in high office as a minister longer than Burleigh, and had much more power and patronage than that paragon of statesmen. Among other advantages which Yorke derived from this connection, he was always returned to parliament free of expense, although Willes, and other competitors at the bar, were involved in contests which made a serious inroad upon their professional gains, and kept them poor, while *he* was advancing to be a " millionaire." Lord Hardwicke's detractors allow that he never forgot these obligations. " The best thing that can be remembered of the Chancellor," says Horace Walpole, " is his fidelity to his patron; for, let the Duke of Newcastle betray whom he would, the Chancellor always stuck to him in his perfidy, and was only not false to the falsest of mankind."

On the vacancy occasioned by Lord Macclesfield's conviction, although Yorke had pretensions to the Great Seal, he was much better pleased to remain Attorney-General—with the bar as a certain resource—than to accept a precarious office, the loss of which was likely soon to leave him without employment or profit,—considering that George I. was old and infirm, and that an entire change of ministry was anticipated at the accession of the Prince. When that event did take place, he was delighted to find himself, by the skillful management of Walpole, more secure than ever—in the enviable situation of Attorney General to a powerful government, with the certainty of succeeding to the highest offices in the law.'

In the session of 1730, he was called into action by the combination between the Tories and discontented Whigs, which began to annoy, without being formidable to, the minister. With the view of crippling the Austrians, with whom there were some differences pending, and who wished to negotiate a considerable loan in London, the Attorney General brought in an Act to forbid the lending of money to any foreign power without the King's license, and to compel all persons to answer a bill in Equity to discover if they were concerned in such transactions. This measure being strongly opposed by Pulteney, and by Sir Wm. Windham, Sir Philip Yorke ably urged all that could be said in its defense. He tried to support it on the principles of the common law; according to which the King has the perogative to prevent his subjects from entering into the service of a foreign Prince by the writ of *ne exeat regno*, or by proclamation to recall them,—urging that "their money, the sinews of war, might be more useful and dangerous than their persons. The Dutch might have the advantage of being the lenders of the money if we were not, but the measure was not to be judged by mere commercial considerations of profit and loss, but was framed with a view to a question of peace and war, and to the balance of power in Europe : it was only a temporary restraint, and might be compared to an embargo, which interfered with trade more directly,

[1] His position at this time may be estimated by the following letter of introduction, addressed to him from Tickell, the friend of Addison:

"Tho⁸ Tickell, Esq. to S' Philip Yorke, Attorney General.
"Sir,   "Dublin Castle, Nov. 4, 1725.

"Mr Broughton, whom my Lord Lieutenant has sent over with the Irish Money Bill and some private ones, has so often heard me boast of being known to you, that he has desired me to introduce him to you, by a Letter. He indeed thinks too highly of my interest in you, in imagining that my recommendation may incline you to give him the utmost dispatch in his business. But I will take upon me to say, that his conversation is so agreeable, that for your own sake you will endeavor to put a speedy end to the serious part of it, and fall into that, for which you have so nice a taste. I should not presume to take this liberty, if I did not honor you more for your humanity, than others can for your great talents; and if, upon that account, I was not with the truest respect,
"Your most humble and most obedient servant,
"THO. TICKELL.

" To the Honble. S' Philip Yorke, his Majesty's Attorney General."
Bibl. Birch. Add. MS. 4325, p. 125.

yet when necessary for the public safety was not complained of. As to the clause compelling a discovery it was indispensable, as without it, from the facility of secretly entering into such transactions, the act would be wholly nugatory." [1] It passed by a large majority; and Coxe says, "a sufficient justification of the measure was, that the want of money compelled the Court of Vienna to submit to terms of accommodation;" [2] but the Dutch practice of selling ammunition to their enemies is probably more in accordance with true statesmanship as well as the principles of political economy.

The next time that Sir Philip Yorke's name is mentioned as taking a part in the debates, is in the session of 1732, when, upon a great muster of opposition under the auspices of Bolingbroke, the minister was so hard run for speakers as to be obliged to put up the Attorney General to defend the augmentation of the army. Thus called upon, he was not quite so *bellicose* as he is said to have been on a subsequent occasion when Walpole is represented to have hailed him as a military officer; but he contended that, with a view to peace, the proposed force was necessary. "It is certainly," said he, "the interest of this nation to render itself as considerable as possible amongst our neighbors, for the greater opinion they have of our strength and power the less apt they will be to undertake any expeditions or invasions against us, and the more easy it will be for us to obtain from them any advantages or immunities which we may think necessary for improving the trade and increasing the riches of the kingdom. The factions and divisions which are springing up at home, encourage our enemies abroad, and render a commanding attitude on the part of the government more indispensable. His Majesty only asks that which is required for the public safety, and any apparent disagreement between him and his parliament will be the signal for internal commotion and foreign war." [3] After the most furious debate which had been known since the reign of Queen Anne, the Minister had a majority of 241 to 171.

In the following year was brought forward the "Excise Scheme,' when Sir Philip Yorke is said to have delivered one of the best speeches in favor of that measure; but in

[1] 8 Parl. Hist. 187.   [2] Coxe's Walpole, vol. ii. p. 358.   [3] 8 Parl. Hist. 893.

print it is extremely vapid. The most valuable part of it probably was where he showed, from his professional knowledge and experience as Attorney General, that the laws of *Excise* under which it was proposed to put the collection of the duties on wine and tobacco, were not more severe than the laws of the *Customs* from which they were to be transferred. He denied that the measure encroached on the constitution, "unless frauds in the collection of the revenue by long usage had become a part of the constitution," and he maintained that "the only liberty which would be subverted was the liberty of smuggling."

A violent opponent of the measure had, during the debate, asserted that its object was to revive the worst practices of Empson and Dudley. So grossly ignorant of English history was the Prime Minister, that he had been obliged to ask Sir Philip Yorke, sitting by him on the Treasury bench, "*who Empson and Dudley were;*" and he was afraid to trust himself (lest he should commit some ludicrous blunder) to repel the charge. Sir Philip now took occasion to reprobate the conduct of the wicked tools of Henry VII., and drew a comparison between his own past conduct and that of his predecessor, Mr. Attorney General Dudley, which drew forth cheers from all parts of the House.—We ought not to doubt that the speech deserved the high praise bestowed upon it, the report of it which we have being prepared by some one who probably (according to the usage of the time) had heard not a word of it, and who, at all events, was evidently ignorant of the principle and details of the bill.[1] Sir Philip had ample time to prepare, and he had strong motives to put forth all his strength; for now was the first occasion of his experiencing the danger of being turned out of office by a hostile majority.

He never again spoke in the House of Commons. Here he had now sat fifteen years, being heard respectfully on the rare occasions when he took part in the debate, but never having acquired much reputation as an orator. In addition to the prejudice then prevailing against him by reason of his profession, he was too didactic and logical for the understandings of the country gentlemen, and he did not sufficiently deal in personal,

[1] 8 Parl. Hist. 1287.

ities, and in clap-trap declamations, to suit himself to the somewhat mobbish taste of that assembly.

His elevation to the woolsack had been for some time anticipated from the age and growing infirmities of Lord King, whose immediate successor he was generally regarded. The secret history of the arrangements actually made on the resignation of Lord King, and the death of Lord Raymond, is not authentically known, and it would be vain to speculate further upon them.[1]

The profession and the public were highly satisfied with the new Chancellor and the new Chief Justice. Talbot was considered of a more open and generous nature than his colleague; and all who knew him were pleased that he had recovered the precedence of which he had been unjustly deprived by Lord Macclesfield's partiality for another; while the learning, ability, and strict integrity which the world admitted in Sir Philip Yorke, though he was less remarkable for his amiable qualities, gave assurance that the duties of the important office of Lord Chief Justice of the King's Bench would be discharged in the most exemplary manner. He might not, himself, be perfectly contented with the allotment to him of the lower dignity, but this was no slight which he would have been justified in resenting; and, acquiescing with a good grace, he professed his determination to support the Government, and to back the new Lord Chancellor in the House of Lords to the utmost of his power. At the same time that he was made Chief Justice of England he was elevated to the peerage, by the title of Baron Hardwicke, of Hardwicke, in the county of Gloucester; and he was likewise sworn a member of the Privy Council. It has been said that he was now admitted into the cabinet; but this is certainly a mistake, although on particular subjects, he was confidentially consulted by Walpole.[2]

He took his seat in the Court of King's Bench in Michaelmas Term, 1733, and continued to preside in that Court above three years. No case of very great importance, either civil or criminal, came before him as a common-law Judge, but we know, as well by the general testimony of contemporaries as by the printed Reports of

---

[1] Ante, Ch. CXXVI.   [2] See Biog. Brit. "Hardwicke."

his decisions,¹ that he uniformly displayed, in addition to the strictest impartiality, much acuteness of intellect and great depth of legal erudition. Following such men as Holt, Parker, and Raymond, he found the principles of the old common law well defined, and they were still tolerably sufficient for the exigencies of society. He assisted a little in adapting them to the new commercial transactions and changed manners which were gradually springing up: but to his successor, Lord Mansfield, was reserved the glory of relieving the poverty of our feudal jurisprudence from the spoils of foreign codes. Although Lord Chief Justice Hardwicke showed high capacity while he presided in a common-law court, and did ample justice to the suitors, he did not make his name very distinguished by any considerable improvements in the system which he there administered. He subsequently exhibited greater powers when he had to expatiate in a new field.

The business of the Court of King's Bench now chiefly rested on his shoulders. Lee, his senior puisne, who afterwards succeeded him, was of some service from his knowledge of pleading; but Probyn, who came next, was a mere cipher; and Page, the junior, required to be kept in strict subjection, for he was ignorant, foolish, and presumptuous. In cases of importance, with a view to check the babbling of the puisnes,—after the arguments were finished, the Chief Justice insisted always that time should be taken to consider, and he afterwards delivered the decision in a written judgment, which he himself prepared. Thus he closed their mouths, unless they ventured to differ in opinion, which rarely happened.—So much for Lord Hardwicke as a common-law Judge.²

During his Chief Justiceship his political importance was greatly enhanced. Many had expected that he would

---

¹ See "Reports Temp. Hardwicke," by Lee.
² Horace Walpole says, that while Chief Justice, "he had gained the reputation of humanity by some solemn speeches made on the circuit at the condemnation of wretches for low crimes;" but I know not to what the sarcasm refers, and I suspect that it is introduced to give point to the charge of inhumanity on the trial of the rebel Lords.—Lord Thurlow is represented as having thought Lord Hardwicke a better common-law, than equity, Judge: "I have heard the late Lord Thurlow say, that he thought the Earl of Hardwicke was more able as Chief Justice of the King's Bench, than he was as Lord Chancellor; but I could never discover on what ground."—Nich. Recoll. ii. 119. This must have been with a view of lowering Lord Hardwicke in the latter capacity, rather than exalting him in the former.

succeed better as a debater in the Upper than he had done in the Lower House of Parliament, and this expectation was not disappointed. He now seemed to feel more at home, and, with increased confidence, his speaking rapidly improved. Not so graceful as Chesterfield, he was more argumentative and forcible; and after he had had a little experience in his new sphere, it may be truly said that, between the attainder of Bolingbroke and the appearance there of Lord Mansfield and Lord Chatham, the House of Peers presented no one who could attack or defend with more skill or success.

His first encounter was with Lord Chesterfield, who, smarting from his dismissal on account of his opposition to the Excise Scheme, made a furious attack on the Government, when an address of thanks was moved in answer to a message from the King, proposing an augmentation of the forces, in order to be prepared for a threatened war. Indulging in the commonplaces about the danger to liberty from military violence, the " Wit among Lords " maintained that as a standing army in time of peace was contrary to law, it could only be legalized by an act of parliament, so that the proposed address would be nugatory. Lord Hardwicke immediately followed, and thus began :—

"As the noble Earl who has just sat down has based his objections to the motion so much on legal and constitutional grounds, perhaps, my Lords, I may be excused n now offering myself to your Lordships' notice, although I must confess that the marshaling of troops, and the sufficiency of military establishments are not subjects with which I have ever been familiar. While the King by his prerogative may enlist soldiers when he pleases, I agree that a standing army can not be maintained in time of peace without the authority of parliament, because of his own authority he could not punish them by martial law, nor could he raise funds for their support. But we have passed the 'Mutiny Bill,' and we shall pass the 'Appropriation Bill,' by which the army may be disciplined and paid,—and, with great submission to the noble Earl, no further legislation will be necessary to gain the object recommended by the message from his Majesty. Under such checks, the maintenance of a sufficient force to preserve internal tranquillity, and to command the respect of foreign nations, while it is indispensable for the protection of our persons and our property, can raise no danger to liberty. Being summoned here to advise his Majesty *de arduis regni*, he now consults you whether the existing force is sufficient? If you are of opinion that it ought to be augmented, you will say so by the address which has been moved. According to the usage of parliament, the Crown and the two Houses communicate by message and address; from the usage of parliament we know the law and the constitution,—and there is no pretense for the ingenious suggestion of the noble Earl, that on such an occasion you are to proceed by an act of parliament."

He then went into the general merits of the question, and from the state of Europe and our foreign relations, showed the prudence as well as the legality of the proposed measure.[1]

In the session of 1735, Lord Hardwicke is not mentioned as taking part in any debate except upon the bill respecting the withdrawing of troops from parliamentary elections,—when he tried to calm the fears that were entertained of the military overawing the electors, and to show how little necessity there was to provide new punishments for such offenses.[2]

The following year he rendered essential service to the public by supporting a bill to amend the mortmain acts,—which, instead of being repealed (as some now wish), will, I hope, be extended to bequests of personal property,—for it is essentially necessary in all cases to guard death-beds from improper solicitations, by which superstition may be encouraged, and those for whom dying persons ought to provide may be left destitute.[3] He next opposed and threw out a well-meant but impracticable bill for regulating the payment of tithes by Quakers, which seems to have excited very great interest at the time, but which, from the general commutation of tithes, is now unimportant.[4]

The last speech he made while Chief Justice, was in a debate which took place a few days before the death of Lord Talbot, on the murder of Captain Porteous, at Edinburgh, and the riots which had lately occurred in different parts of England. He now took occasion to refer

[1] 9 Parl. Hist. 538.   [2] Ibid. 886–910.
[3] Ibid. 1119.   [4] Ibid. 1218.

to the explosion of gunpowder, and the dispersion of libels, which had happened the preceding term in Westminster Hall. Between one and two in the afternoon, while all the courts were sitting,[1] a loud report was heard, and the Hall was filled with smoke. This was found to be an ingenious device for dispersing a mass of libels on the government. Some of these being carried into the Court of King's Bench, and shown to the Chief Justice, he immediately made a comment upon their wickedness, ordered them to be laid before the Grand Jury, who were then sitting, and prevailed upon the Queen, acting as Regent, to offer a large reward for the discovery of the offender. The author of this "Gunpowder Plot" turned out to be a crack-brained, nonjuring parson, who had acted without any associates,—so that the affair was laughed at,—and it had been treated with some ridicule by the opposition peers. The indignant Chief thus expressed himself :—" The attempt which noble Lords opposite make the subject of their jests, was certainly one of the most audacious affronts ever offered to an established government, and was leveled directly at the illustrious family now upon the throne. I do not, mean, my Lords, the powder or rockets then blown up, for I do not believe that the guilty contriver meant to destroy the Hall, or to injure any one in it ; but I mean the scandalous and seditious libels spread about the Hall by the explosion, and afterwards dispersed over the whole of this vast metropolis. These libels not only reflected most indecently on the proceedings of the two Houses of Parliament, but denied his Majesty's right to the Crown, and asserted the Pretender to be our true and only lawful sovereign. If vigorous steps had not been taken to detect and punish the offender, the world would have believed that the established government was so feeble that it might be insulted with impunity, and this insult would soon have been followed up by an organized insurrection, and by foreign invasion." Having commented upon the death of Captain Porteous, which he denounced as " an atrocious murder, the authors of which must be brought to condign punishment," he described

[1] Hours had now greatly altered; and the Courts, instead of meeting at seven and breaking up at eleven, met at nine and sat till two. For many years after, however, there were *post-prandian* sittings.

the formidable nature of the riots in different parts of England, and justified the suppression of them by the military. He strongly combated the notion that there was anything illegal in employing soldiers to preserve the public peace. "I am surprised, my Lords," said he, "to hear it said that if the King's troops should now and then, upon extraordinary occasions, be called to the assistance of the civil magistrate, we should on that account be supposed to live under a military government. I hope it will be allowed that our soldiers are our fellow-citizens. They do not cease to be so by putting on a red coat, and carrying a musket. Now, it is well known that magistrates have a power to call any subject of the King to their assistance, to preserve the peace, and to execute the process of the law. The subject who neglects such a call is liable to be indicted, and, being convicted, to be fined and imprisoned for his offense. Why, then, may not the civil magistrate call soldiers to his assistance, as well as other men? While the King's troops act under the directions of the magistrate, we are as much under civil government as if there were not a soldier in the island of Great Britain. The calling in of these armed citizens often saves the effusion of innocent blood, and preserves the dominion of the law."[1]

On this day Lord Talbot, who took an active share in the debate, was in excellent health, and seemed likely for many years to fill the office of Chancellor, establishing a reputation as the greatest Equity Judge of the century in which he flourished.[2] If these expectations had been realized, Lord Hardwicke would have attracted little comparative notice, and, having gained no conspicuous place in history, would only have been recollected by lawyers, like Lord Raymond, as an eminent common-law judge. But he was destined to be nearly thirty years a cabinet minister,—to form cabinets himself,—and, a century after his death, to have a statue erected to his memory by the English nation as the greatest contributor to our Equity code.

On the day Lord Talbot died, the Great Seal was delivered by his executors into the hands of George II. at

[1] 9 Parl. Hist. 1294.
[2] It appears from the Lords' Journals, that down to the 9th of Feb., 1737, Lord Talbot was present in the House, and presided as Chancellor.

St. James's Palace. There never was any doubt as to his successor, for Lord Hardwicke was now regarded as decidedly the most useful man to be introduced into the cabinet and to preside on the woolsack as Chancellor,—and he himself, placing just confidence in the stability of the administration, did not hesitate to agree to a move which promised to gratify his love of fame, his love of power, and his love of money. But there being some difficulty with respect to salary and pension, and other accompanying arrangements requiring consideration, the Great Seal remained for a whole week in the personal custody of the King.[1]

Meanwhile, as parliament was sitting, and there was no Lord Chancellor or Lord Keeper, it was necessary to provide a Speaker for the House of Lords, and the Great Seal, while in the King's possession, was (somewhat irregularly) put to a commission authorizing Lord Hardwicke to act in that capacity.[2] He accordingly did act for several days as Speaker without being Chancellor.[3] During this interval, it is related that Walpole resisting some of Hardwicke's demands, said to him by way of threat,—"I must offer the Seals to Fazakerly." "Fazakerly!" exclaimed Hardwicke, "impossible! he is certainly a Tory!—perhaps a Jacobite!" "It's all very true," coolly replied Sir Robert, taking out his watch, "but if by one o'clock you do not accept my offer, Fazakerly by two becomes Lord Keeper, and one of the stanchest Whigs in all England." The bargain was immediately

[1] This is the last instance of such an occurrence. Since then no Chancellor has died in office; and the usual course has been, that the Great Seal has been surrendered up by the outgoing Chancellor at a Council, and, at the same Council, has been delivered to his successor.

[2] This, on principle, seems as objectionable as the act of Charles II. in sealing Lord Danby's pardon with his own hand. See ante, vol. iv. p. 217.

[3] "Feb. 10.—The Lord Chancellor being absent, the Lords were informed by the Duke of Newcastle that his Majesty had been pleased to grant a commission under the Great Seal to Philip, Lord Hardwicke, Lord Chief Justice of the Court of King's Bench, to supply the room and place of Lord Chancellor in this House."

"Feb. 11.—The Lord Hardwicke sat Speaker by virtue of his Majesty's commission." On the 11th the House was adjourned to the 16th.

"Feb. 16.—The Lord President signified to the House that the Lord Chancellor being dead, his Majesty has been pleased to grant another commission under the Great Seal to Lord Hardwicke to supply the room and place of the Lord Chancellor or Lord Keeper of the Great Seal in this House during his Majesty's pleasure." This is the irregularly sealed commission. On the 21st Feb. Lord Hardwicke sat as Lord Chancellor.

closed, and Lord Hardwicke was contented with the promise that the next Tellership should be bestowed upon his son.

Sir John Willes, the Attorney General, being provided for by being made Chief Justice of the Common Pleas, and it being settled that Lee should be Chief Justice of the King's Bench, and that Sir Dudley Ryder and Sir John Strange should be the new Attorney and Solicitor General,—on the 21st of February the Great Seal was delivered to Lord HARDWICKE, with the title of Lord Chancellor. However, he continued Chief Justice of the King's Bench till the commencement of Easter Term, and on the first day of that Term, after a grand procession to Westminster Hall, attended by Sir Robert Walpole and many of the nobility, having been sworn in and transacted business in the Court of Chancery, he went into the Court of King's Bench, and there delivered a judgment in a case which had been previously argued,—so that he had the glory of presiding on the same day in the highest civil and the highest criminal Court in the Kingdom.[1]

[1] "Memorandum—that on Monday, the 14th day of February, 1736-7, Charles, Lord Talbot, Lord High Chancellor of Great Britain, departed this life; and on the evening of the same day, the Great Seal was delivered by the Duke of Newcastle to his Majesty, who kept it in his custody till Monday, the 21st of the same month of February, during which time there was nothing sealed but a commission appointing Philip, Lord Hardwicke, Speaker of the House of Lords during pleasure; and, on the said 21st of February, his Majesty was graciously pleased to deliver the Great Seal to the aforesaid Philip, Lord Hardwicke, with the title of Lord Chancellor, who was sworn at the same time in Council, and took his place accordingly; and his Lordship sat in Lincoln's Inn Hall during the Seals after Hilary Term, but he was not sworn in Westminster Hall till the 27th day of April, 1737, being the first day of the then next Easter Term, when his Lordship took the oaths of allegiance and supremacy, and the oath of office, the Master of the Rolls holding the book, and the deputy clerk of the Crown giving the oaths. After which, the Attorney General moved that the oath might be recorded, but his Lordship did not take the oath of abjuration till another day, in the King's Bench."—*Roll, 1727-1760.*

CHAPTER CXXXI.

CONTINUATION OF THE LIFE OF LORD HARDWICKE TILL THE DEATH OF QUEEN CAROLINE.

I AM sorry to be obliged to begin my account of Lord Hardwicke, as Chancellor, by reprobating that conduct which his indiscriminate admirers have justified, and which some moderate men have attempted to palliate.

I have related how Lord Chancellor Talbot, from his admiration of the genius of Thomson the poet, and from personal kindness for him, had rescued him from the penury and dependence, then the fate of men of letters, by appointing him "Secretary to the Briefs." This was an office in the Court of Chancery which, in strictness, was held only under the Chancellor making the appoinment, but the holder of which was generally continued in it by the succeeding Chancellor. Of all the cases ever known, Thomson's is the one where it might have been expected that the usage of confirmation would have been most eagerly adhered to.[1] The author of The Seasons was not only a man of genius and most amiable in his private character, but he was warmly attached to the Whig party, and had essentially promoted its interests by his writings. He had received the office, on which he was entirely dependent, from the colleague and personal friend of the present Chancellor, as a reward for his public services, as well as for his attachment to young Talbot, with whom he had traveled, and to whose memory he had offered a touching tribute of applause.

I give the most mitigated account I can find of the affair—in the words of Dr. Johnson,—who disliked Thomson, as a Scotchman, as a Whig, and as the author of "LIBERTY," and was willing to cast blame in this affair upon him, rather than upon the Chancellor. After stating

[1] There are several such offices held under the Attorney General. When I was first appointed to that office in 1834, I had the usual applications to be continued in them, which of course were granted. When I was reappointed in 1835, I intimated that such applications were unnecessary; and my successors, Sir Frederick Pollock, Sir William Follet, and Sir Frederick Thesiger, have behaved in the same spirit.

the poet's appointment to his office by Lord Talbot, he thus proceeds:—"Thomson now lived in ease and plenty, and seems for a while to have suspended his poetry; but he was soon called back to labor by the death of the Chancellor, for his place then became vacant; and though Lord Hardwicke delayed for some time to give it away, Thomson's bashfulness or pride, or some other motive, perhaps not more laudable, withheld him from soliciting; and the new Chancellor would not give him what he would not ask. He now relapsed to his former indigence: but the Prince of Wales was at that time struggling for popularity, and, by the influence of Mr. Lyttleton, professed himself the patron of wit; to him Thomson was introduced, and being gaily interrogated about the state of his affairs, said, 'that they were in a more poetical posture than formerly,' and had a pension allowed him of one hundred pounds a year."[1]

We can not without indignation think or a man in Lord Hardwicke's situation seeking to subject Thomson to the humiliation of asking a favor, when it might naturally have been expected that his continuance in the office of secretary would have been spontaneously and earnestly pressed upon him. Even Mr. Salkeld's "gratis clerk" had shown some degree of pride, and disliked carrying home cabbages from Covent Garden, and oysters from the fishmonger's! An attempt has been made to praise Lord Hardwicke as a patron of literary merit, because he afterwards obtained a pension from the public purse for Mallet as a reward for his pamphlet against Admiral Byng; but, says a contemporary, "let it be recollected that the same man, on his succeeding Talbot as Lord Chancellor, deprived Thomson, a poet and patriot of the first class, of the place of Secretary of Briefs, which had been given him by his predecessor, and was the poor poet's only subsistence and support."[2] Although Lord Hardwicke always took care not only to have the law on his side, and was generally solicitous to have something plausible to say in his own defense, should his conduct be questioned, —it must be confessed that he was not only rather selfish, but that, from heartlessness, he even lost opportunities of doing acts which would have been considered generous, and which would have given him popularity—without

[1] Dr. Johnson's Life of Thomson.   [2] Cooksey, 36.

depriving him of money, or of any family aggrandizement.

We are now to see him in his glory as an Equity Judge. Although he by no means distinguished himself in framing laws to be enacted by Parliament—viewed as a magistrate sitting on his tribunal to administer justice, I believe that his fame has not been exceeded by that of any man in ancient or modern times; and the long series of enlightened rules laid down by him having, from their wisdom, been recognized as binding on all who have succeeded him, he may be considered a great legislator. His decisions have been, and ever will continue to be, appealed to as fixing the limits, and establishing the principles, of that vast juridical system called EQUITY, which now, not only in this country and in our colonies, but over the whole extent of the United States of America, regulates property and personal rights more than the ancient COMMON LAW.

The student, animated by a generous ambition, will be eager to know whence this great excellence arose?—Like everything else that is valuable—it was the result of earnest and persevering labor. A complete knowledge of the common law was the foundation on which he built. This he had gained not only by reading but by circuit experience, by continuing frequently to plead causes in the King's Bench and Exchequer while he was Attorney General, and by presiding above three years in a common-law court. Having been initiated in Chancery practice during his clerkship with Mr. Salkeld, he had read attentively everything to be found in the books connected with equity, and he had actually been a regular practitioner in Chancery during the whole of the Chancellorships of Lord Macclesfield and Lord King. He now revived his recollection of that learning by again going over the whole of it as if it had been new to him; and he obtained MS. notes of such of Lord Talbot's decisions as were of any importance,—so that in all branches of professional information he was equal, and in many superior, to the most eminent counsel who were to plead before him. But that to which I mainly ascribe the brilliancy of the career on which he was entering, was the familiar knowledge he acquired of the Roman civil law. The taste for this study he is said to have contracted from the necessity of preparing himself first to argue as an advocate, and then to decide, as a judge, appeals to the House of Lords from the Court of Session in Scotland. In that country he found the Roman civil law regulating the enjoyment and succession of personal property, and even frequently alluded to by way of illustration in questions respecting entails. Like most English lawyers, in preparing for the bar, he had hardly paid the slightest attention to it. While Attorney General, he was retained in many Scotch appeals, and for the occasion, he was obliged to dip into the Pandects and into the commentaries upon them; but although he had the discernment to discover the merit of these admirable compilations, it was not indispensably necessary for the discharge of his duty that he should examine them systematically, and his time was filled up with more urgent occupations. Now that he was to sit in the House of Lords as sole Judge to decide all appeals from Scotland, he saw the necessity of making himself a profound Scotch lawyer, and he found that this was impossible without being a good civilian. Therefore, having gone through Mackenzie, Bankton, and Stair,[1] he regularly proceeded to the Corpus Juris Civilis with Vinnius, Voet, and other commentators, and his mind was thoroughly imbued with the truly *equitable* maxims of this noble jurisprudence. I delight in recording how his unrivaled eminence as an Equity Judge was achieved,—lest the aspiring but careless student should think it could be reached by natural genius and occasional exertion:—

> ——" Pater ipse colendi
> Haud facilem esse viam voluit....
> ....curis acuens mortalia corda."

Lord Hardwicke, having bestowed unremitting pains in qualifying himself for the discharge of his high duties, —when occupying the judgment-seat, exhibited a pattern of all judicial excellence. Spotless purity—not only an abstinence from bribery and corruption,[2] but freedom from

[1] He took special delight in "*Dirleton's Doubts*," saying " his *doubts* are more valuable than other people's *certainties*."

[2] One attempt was made to bribe Lord Hardwicke. Thomas Martin, mayor of Yarmouth, being threatened with a bill in Chancery, wrote a letter to the Lord Chancellor, bespeaking his favor, and inclosing a bank-note for £20, of which his acceptance was requested " for his trouble in reading the papers." An order being made upon his worship, to show cause why he

undue influence, and a hearty desire to do justice—may at that time, and ever afterwards, be considered as belonging to all English Judges. But I must specially mention of this Chancellor, that he was not only a patient, but an eager listener, conscious that he could best learn the facts of the case from those who had been studying it, and that, notwithstanding his own great stores of professional learning, he might be instructed by a junior counsel, who for days and nights had been ransacking all that could be found scattered in the books on a particular topic, actuated by a desire to serve his client, and to enhance his own reputation. While the hearing was going on, the cause had the Chancellor's undivided and devoted attention. Not only was he undistracted by the frivolous engagements of common life, but during a political crisis, when there were to be important changes in the cabinet, when his own continuance in office was in peril, he was, as usual, calm and collected; and he seemed to think of nothing but whether the injunction should be continued or dissolved, and whether the bill should be dismissed with, or without costs? Some said that he was at times acting a part, and that he was considering how he should conduct a political intrigue, or how he should answer an opponent in debate,—when he pretended to be listening to a thrice-told tale; but so much is certain, that no argument ever escaped him, and that, in taking notes, it was observed that " his pen always moved at the right time."[1] He used to declare, that " he did not take his place upon the bench to write letters to his correspondents, or to read the newspaper."[2] His voluminous note books are

should not be committed to the Fleet for his contempt, he swore " that the said letter was wrote, and the said bank-note inclosed therein by him through ignorance, and not from any ill intent whatsoever" Upon his paying all expenses, and consenting that the £20 should be distributed among the poor prisoners in the Fleet, the order was discharged.—27th April, 1748. *Sanders's Orders*, ii. 628.—Lord Sidmouth prosecuted in the King's Bench, for an offer to bribe him, a simpleton who, when the criminal information came down, joyfully showed it to his family and his friends, believing that it was a patent for the office he wished to purchase.

[1] *i. e.* I presume, when anything was said worthy of being noted.

[2] I must say, that this last practice has occasionally been carried to an indecorous and inconvenient length. A glance at a newspaper may be permitted to a Judge during a tedious reply, as a hint to the counsel against prolixity; and such was the habit of Lord Mansfield, who was ever completely master of all the facts, and all the law of every case that came before him. But I have seen a Judge indulge his curiosity by turning over the un-

still extant, containing, at great length, the material proceedings of the Court during each day,—the statement of the case, the evidence, and the arguments of counsel,—with the answers to be given to them inclosed within brackets. When he took time to consider, he generally wrote his judgments either in his note books or on separate papers, to which his note books refer. Unlike some Judges, deservedly of high reputation, whose impression on hearing a case stated was never known to vary, he appears not unfrequently, upon further argument and maturer consideration, finally to have arrived at an opinion quite different from that which he had at first entertained, and even expressed: and he certainly well merited the character he gave of himself in this respect, when he said, "These are the reasons which incline me to alter my opinion, and I am not ashamed of doing it, for I always thought it a much greater reproach to a Judge to continue in his error than to retract it."[1] He never interrupted, to show his quickness, by guessing at facts, or anticipating authorities which he expected to be cited. Not ignorant that the Chancellor can always convulse the bar with "counterfeited glee," he abstained from ill-timed jocularity, and he did not level sarcasms at those who, he knew, could not retort upon him. He had a complete control over his temper, and, from the uniform urbanity and decorum of his own demeanor, he repressed the petulance and angry passions of those who practiced before him, insomuch that it was remarked, that not only was he never himself led into any unbecoming altercation, but that he taught the rival leaders to behave to each other with candor and courtesy. It is likewise stated, to his credit, that, although in society he was supposed rather to be supercilious, presuming too much upon his acquired dignity, he was in Court uniformly affable to the solicitors, remembering that they were the class to which he expected himself to have belonged, and to whose kindness he had been greatly indebted for his advancement.

The arguments being finished, if the case seemed clear,

---

wieldy pages of the "Times," while a counsel has been opening, in a condensed manner, a very important and complicated case—requiring the closest attention of a Judge, however quick, learned, and discriminating.

[1] 2 Atk. 438.

and did not involve any new question, he immediately disposed of it; but wherever his decision was likely to be quoted as regulating the "doctrine of the Court," he took time for consideration, and having perused his notes and referred to the authorities cited, he came with a prepared and often a written judgment. On such occasions he was likened to "the personification of wisdom distributing justice and delivering instruction."

These performances certainly do come up to every idea we can form of judicial excellence. They are entirely free from any parade of learning, or the affectation of pointed or antithetical sentences. Two objects seem entirely to absorb the attention of the Judge: 1. Properly to adjust the disputed rights of the parties. 2. To establish a rule by which similiar questions may be solved in future. He was anxious to bring every case within the scope of some general principle which he enunciated and defined, guarding it with its proper conditions and exceptions. He did not decide every case upon its "*specialties*" or peculiar circumstances,—leaving the profession entirely at a loss with respect to the general principle which had been discussed,—nor did he wrest the peculiar circumstances of the case to make it conform to his canon. Having lucidly stated the allegations on each side, and accurately enumerated the facts which were established, he propounded the question or questions which they raised, and on which his decree must depend. Then recollecting the observation of Lord Bacon, that "his equity was to be taken from his books, and not from his brains," and that "the Chancery was ordained to supply the law, not to subvert the law," he reviewed all the authorities upon the subject, and, if none of them were expressly in point, he tried to educe from them by analogy a rule which harmonized with them in principle, and which might equitably govern all cases similarly circumstanced. He never resorted, however, to forced interpretations or fanciful analogies, and he was always anxious to support his opinion by legal precedents—in the selection and application of which he was particularly happy. Nor was he betrayed into the seductive and dangerous practice of laying down rules in loose and sweeping terms, which might carry their authority far beyond the point necessarily to be decided, and mischievously include cases which were not then in contemplation. He, therefore, expressed himself in the most guarded terms, and mentioned distinctly the qualifications with which he meant his opinion to be received. There was no enthusiasm in his nature, but he really had a passion (such as I have seen exhibited by the cool-headed Tenterden) to do justice, and to advance the science over which he presided;—most unlike the reckless judge who is only anxious to escape open censure—indifferent as to the rights of parties, the improvement of jurisprudence, and his own permanent fame.

Lord Hardwicke's judgments are deservedly praised for luminous method in the arrangement of the topics, and elegant perspicuity of language in the discussion of them. But I will venture to point out what I consider their peculiar excellence—the fair and manly manner in which the arguments are stated which are to be overruled. I have known Judges who, in important cases, have entirely omitted to notice the most powerful objections to their view of the case—not, probably, from any disingenuous motive, but from not understanding them. Lord Hardwicke always fully sees and appreciates the arguments against the side which he adopts—restates them with additional force and clearness, and refutes them so satisfactorily as almost to bring conviction to the minds of those who had invented them, and had for a time been the dupes of their own subtlety.

He was particularly praised for the manner in which he dealt with cases coming before him on exceptions to the Masters' Report, and on appeal from the Master of the Rolls. He showed no propensity whatever to reverse what had been decided, but he freely and boldly considered every question submitted to him as the superior Judge. Not shrinking from trouble or responsibility, he formed his own opinion upon it, and resolutely corrected what appeared to him to be amiss. There were four Masters of the Rolls successively under him, and he will be found to treat them all with great respect, but with great freedom.

By these means Lord Hardwicke, in a few years, raised a reputation which no one presiding in the Court of Chancery has ever enjoyed, and which was not exceeded by that of the great Lord Mansfield as a common-law Judge. The wisdom of his decrees was the theme of universal eulogy. "Etiam quos contra statuit, æquos et placidos dimisit." Such confidence was there in his administration of justice, that the business of the Court was greatly increased, and it is said that more bills were filed under him than at any subsequent time, although the property administered by the Court of Chancery has since been increased sevenfold. There were still rare complaints of delays in Chancery, from the intricate nature of the inquiries, the death of parties, and other inevitable obstructions to the final winding up of a suit; but by great exertions arrears were kept down, "and this is fondly looked back upon as the golden age of Equity." [1]

I hardly think it worth while to mention the statement which is so much harped upon by the common herd of Lord Hardwicke's petty biographers, that only three of his decrees were appealed against, and that in each of these cases the decree was affirmed. The truth is, that during the whole of his time, through management which I shall afterwards have to consider, he was the sole law Lord, and substantially the Chancery was a court of the last resort.

But I should do injustice to his memory if I were not to praise what hitherto has attracted little notice—the admirable manner in which he disposed of the judicial business in the House of Lords. His demeanor on the woolsack appears to have been a model for all Chancellors. While he was affable and courteous, he studied to preserve order. He himself attended to the debates,[2] and his example and influence generated a habit of attention and decorum among others. Though, in strictness, without more authority than any other Peer, all sides recognized him as *moderator*, and, by his quiet and discreet exertions, unseemly altercations and excessive familiarity were effectually discouraged. In his time a meeting of the Peers had somewhat the air of a deliberative assembly,—instead of being a lounging place to hear the news of the day before dressing for dinner.

Although there were only three appeals from Philip to

[1] Lord Hardwicke,—abstaining from drinking his bottle after dinner—a sacrifice too great for his successor,—regularly, in addition to his morning sitting, sat twice a week in the afternoon or evening.
[2] There are extant copious notes, taken by him of debates which, with those of Archbishop Secker, have filled up *lacunæ* in the Parliamentary History.

Philip, in all of which the decrees were affirmed without difficulty, there were a good many writs of error from the common-law courts, which, with the assistance of the Judges, he disposed of in a very masterly manner; and there were a great many appeals from Scotland, which, without assistance, he decided to the universal satisfaction of that country, where he was much honored, till he abolished heritable jurisdictions, and compelled the inhabitants to wear breeches.

I am now desirous of laying before the reader specimens of Lord Hardwicke's performances as a civil Judge; and there are ample materials for doing so : for, besides his own note-books and his judgments in his own handwriting, there are several MS. collections of his decisions, by very able hands, during the whole time he sat in Chancery,[1] and the principal cases before him have been digested and published by Atkyns, Vesey, Sr., and other reporters. Although these " Vates sacri " prevent his name from perishing,—from their condensation, they do not render justice to his copious illustrations, his lucid arrangement, and his elegance of diction. Yet they give us the pith and substance of his discourses in pronouncing his decrees, and they afford an exquisite treat to the scientific reader. From these stores I am rather embarrassed with my riches, and, instead of writing a volume to give a sketch of Lord Hardwicke's new doctrines, with the restrictions and expansions of what had been before laid down,—being confined to the selection of a few detached points decided by him, I am much afraid of being thought to re-

[1] Of one of these, by the great kindness of my friend, Mr. Charles Purton Cooper, I am now in possession. It consists of four quarto volumes, beautifully written by Mr. Jodderell, an eminent Chancery barrister. He often does more justice to Lord Hardwicke than Atkyns or Vesey, Sr.; and I am told that, upon a reference to the register's book, he is found to be more accurate.

[2] It seems strange to us, who see reports of all judgments in print almost as soon as they are delivered, that none of Lord Hardwicke's were printed till after he had resigned the Great Seal. The newspapers and magazines of that day thought as little of the Court of Chancery as of the Court of Pekin. The first volume of Atkyns did not come out till 1757; nor the second till 1767. The first edition of Vesey, Sr., was published in 1771.

At that time MS. notes were much quoted; and counsel depended on recollection,—which had this advantage, that it always made the case recollected, and the case at bar *on all fours*. There are decisions of Lord Hardwicke to be found in Strange, Ambler, Barnardiston, Ridgeway, and West, published subsequently.

semble the Σχολαστικος in Hierocles, who, to prove the fine proportions of a building, produced a brick which he had taken from it. The Equity lawyer who feels the little justice I do to the object of his adoration, will best appreciate the difficulty of my task.

Lord Hardwicke established the rule that persons, though not Christians, if they believe in a divinity, may be sworn according to the ceremonies of their religion, and that the evidence given by them so sworn is admissible in courts of justice, as if, being Christians, they had been sworn upon the Evangelists. This subject first came before him in *Ramkissenseat* v. *Barker*, where, in a suit for an account against the representatives of an East India Governor, the plea being overruled that the plaintiff was an alien infidel, a cross bill was filed, and an objection being made that he could only be sworn in the usual form, a motion was made that the words in the commission, "on the holy Evangelists," should be omitted, and that the commissioners should be directed to administer an oath to him in the manner most binding on his conscience :—

Lord Chancellor: "I have often wondered, as the dominions of Great Britain are so extensive, that there has never been any rule or method in cases of this sort. All persons who believe a God are capable of an oath; and what is universally understood by an oath is, that the person who takes it imprecates the vengeance of God upon him if the oath he takes is false. It was upon this principle that the Judges were inclined to admit the Jews, who believed a God according to our notion of a God, to swear upon the Old Testament ; and Lord Hale very justly observes, 'it is a wise rule in the kingdom of Spain, that a heathen and idolater should be sworn upon what he thinks is the most sacred part of his religion.' In order to remove the difficulties in this case, I shall direct that the words 'on the holy Evangelists' be left out. The next consideration is, what words must be inserted in their room? On the part of the plaintiff in the cross bill, it is desired that I should appoint a solemn form for the oath : I think this very improper, because I may possibly direct a form that is contrary to the notions of religion entertained by the Gentoo people. I will, therefore direct that the commissioners may administer such oath in the most solemn manner as in their discretion shall seem meet; and if the person, upon the usual oath being explained to him, shall consent to take it, and the commissioners approve of administering it (for he may perhaps be a Christian convert), the difficulty is removed; or, if they should think proper to administer another oath, that then they shall certify to the Court what was done by them,—and afterwards will come the proper time to controvert the validity of such an oath, and to take the opinions of the Judges upon it, if the Court should have any doubt."[1]

The point was afterwards finally settled in the great case of *Omychund* v. *Barker*, where a similar commission to examine witnesses having issued, the Commissioners certified "that they had sworn the witnesses examined under it in the presence of a Bramin or priest of the Gentoo religion, and that each witness touched the hand of the Bramin,—this being the most solemn form in which oaths are administered to witnesses professing the Gentoo religion." Objection was made that the depositions so taken could not be read in evidence; and, on account of the magnitude of the question, the Lord Chancellor called in the assistance of the three chiefs of the common-law courts. After very long, learned, and ingenious arguments, which may be perused with pleasure, they concurred in the opinion that the depositions were admissible:—

Lord Chancellor : As this is a case not only of great expense, but of great consequence, it will be expected that I should not decide without giving my reasons for the decision I am to pronounce. It is certified to us that these witnesses believe in the being of a God, and in his providence; and we know that they appealed to his favor or vengeance in the manner in which they considered the most solemn. The first author I shall mention is Bishop Sanderson, ' De Jurisjuramenti Obligatione.' 'Juramentum,' says he, 'est affirmatio religiosa.' All that is necessary to an oath is an appeal to the Supreme Being, as thinking him the rewarder of truth and avenger of falsehood. This is not contradicted by any writer that I know of but Lord Coke, who has taken upon him to insert the word ' Christian,' and he alone has

[1] 1 Atk. 19.

grafted this word into an oath. As to other writers, they are all concurring (vid. Puff. lib. 4, c. 2, s. 4). Dr. Tillotson, in his sermon upon the lawfulness of oaths, taking a text which applies to all nations and to all men, 'an oath for confirmation is to them an end of all strife' (Heb. vi. 16), says, 'the necessity of religion to the support of human society, in nothing appears more evidently than in this, that the obligation of an oath, which is so necessary for the maintenance of peace and justice among men, depends wholly upon the sense and belief of a Diety.' The next thing I shall notice is the form of the oath. It is laid down by all writers that the outward act is not essential to the oath. Sanderson is of that opinion, and so is Tillotson in the same sermon. 'As for the ceremonies in use among us in the taking of oaths, they are not found in Scripture, for this was always matter of liberty; and several nations have used several rites and ceremonies in their oaths.' *Secondly*, whether, upon special circumstances, such evidence may be admitted according to the law of England? The Judges and sages of the law have laid it down that there is but one general rule of evidence, '*The best the nature of the case will admit.*' The first ground Judges have gone upon, in departing from strict rules, is an absolute necessity; then a presumed necessity. Writings subscribed by witnesses are to be proved by those witnesses, but, if they are all dead, the proof of one of their hands is sufficient. Where the original is lost, a copy may be admitted; if there be no copy, then the proof by witnesses who have read the deed, although the law abhors the memory of man for evidence of that which is written. Persons of the Gentoo religion must be admitted in courts of justice in their own country to prove facts and transactions within their own knowledge. One of the parties changing his domicil, and suing here, can he deprive his opponent of evidence which would have been admissible had he sued in the country where the cause of action arose? Suppose a heathen should bring an action at common law, and the defendant should file a bill for a discovery, will any body say that the plaintiff at law may not be admitted to put in an answer according to his own form of an oath? otherwise the injunction for not putting in the answer would be perpetual, and would be a manifest de-n'al of justice. This is the view of the subject taken by Lord Stair, Puffendorf, and other jurists. It has been the wisdom of all nations to administer such oaths as are agreeable to the religious notions of the person taking them. This course does not in the slightest degree affect the conscience of the persons administering the oath, and is no adoption by them of the religion conformed to by one of its votaries. Concurring in opinion with my Lords the Judges that these depositions are admissible, I do order that the objection to them be overruled, and that they now be read as evidence." [1]

Lord Hardwicke settled some important questions respecting literary property. The infamous Edmund Curle had printed a volume of private letters to and from Pope, who immediately applied for an injunction. There had been hitherto no instance of a Court of Equity interfering under such circumstances, and the defendant's counsel argued that Mr. Pope had parted with all property in his own letters which he had sent to his correspondents; that he never had acquired any property in those which he had received; that there could be no property in the letters the defendant had printed, as they were not written for publication, and the statute of Anne for protecting copyright did not extend to them:—

Lord Chancellor. "As to the first objection, that where a man writes a letter, it is in the nature of a gift to the receiver, I am of opinion that the receiver only acquires a qualified interest in it. The paper on which it is written may belong to him, but the composition does not become vested in him as property, and he can not publish it against the consent of the writer. Then, as to the objection that the statute does not apply to these letters, because 'they are on familiar subjects, containing little more than inquiries after the health of friends, and not deserving the name of a learned work,' I am of opinion that we can not inquire into their nature or merits, and that the bookseller who has published them can not avail himself of their frivolity if they were frivolous. But it is certain that no works have done more service to mankind than those which have appeared in this shape upon familiar subjects, and which, perhaps were never intended to be published. This it is which renders them so valuable;

[1] 1 Atk. 21–50; Phillipps on Evidence, 9.

for I must confess, for my own part, that letters which are very elaborately written, and originally intended for the press, are generally the most insignificant, and very little worth any person's reading. However, as for the letters in this volume written *to* Mr. Pope, I think that *he* can not be heard to complain. They may possibly be published with the authority of the writers of them, and from copies taken before they were sent to him.

The injunction was granted as to the one set of letters, and refused as to the other.[1]

This decision seems very reasonable, but I must own, that I much question another rule he laid down with respect to literary property, although it has not yet been upset. The question arose whether, within the period for which copyright is secured to the author, an *Abridgment* of the work may be published without his consent?—

Lord Chancellor. "When books are only colorably shortened, the statute is evaded, and the law will give redress. But this must not be carried so far as to restrain persons from making a real and fair abridgment. An abridgment may, with great propriety, be called a new book. Not only are the paper and printing the abridger's, but in his task he may show invention, learning, and judgment. In many cases, abridgments are extremely useful, though sometimes they are prejudicial, by curtailing and mistaking the sense of the author."[2]

Before the passing of the Marriage Act, Lord Hardwicke had much trouble with his female wards, for their marriage without his consent was valid, and he could only punish those concerned in contriving it. Mr. Charles, a clergyman, who married Miss Sophia More, a ward of Chancery, without leave, to John Peck, and others who were present when she was married, appeared to answer the contempt of the Court.—*Lord Chancellor.* "These are mischiefs which want the correction and reformation of the legislature. John Ubank must, in the first place, stand committed, who assisted in conducting Miss More

---

[1] 2 Atk. 342.
[2] *Gyles* v. *Wilcock*, 2 Atk. 142; and see Lofft, 775; 1 Bro. C. C. 451. I confess I do not understand why an abridgment, tending to injure the reputation and to lessen the profits of the author, should not be considered an invasion of his property.

out of her guardian's house, and gave her away at the wedding. The giving away a woman as her father, though not essential, is a custom or ceremony which clergymen always require." Having dealt with others upon the consideration whether they were concerned in the marriage, knowing the infant to be a ward of Court, he comes to Mr. Charles. 'Next comes the priest. It is surprising that the canons of the Church, with respect to marriage, are so little regarded by the clergy; but for a violation of them I have no right to pronounce sentence, and Mr. Charles does not seem to me to have been at all concerned in the contrivance or design of doing this wrongful act: therefore he is not guilty of a contempt of the Court; but I would recommend him to be more cautious for the future." [1]

On another occasion he severely punished persons concerned in clandestinely marrying a girl of fifteen with a large fortune to the son of a nobleman's steward, who was under twenty, although they were ignorant of her being a ward of Court:—

Lord Chancellor. "Lord Ossulston, by his affidavit, admits, that at the request of Pearson he procured Barry, the parson, to celebrate this marriage, and he denies knowledge of any orders of the Court. It is positively sworn by the petitioner that the match was made by the contrivance of Pearson with Lord Ossulston; that Lord Ossulston went to London and fetched the parson from the Fleet for a fee of one hundred guineas, and that Lord Ossulston being present at the marriage gave away the lady as a father, in a room at Up Park. Barry, the parson, having been committed by a former order, let Pearson, Mary Tench, the maid servant, and Lord Ossulston be now committed to the Fleet for their contempt." [2]

One of the nicest points which ever came before Lord Hardwicke, was how a widow is affected by her husband in his lifetime having pledged her paraphernalia. Lord Londonderry had given Lady Londonderry a diamond necklace, and afterwards pledged it as a collateral security for £1,000, with a power to sell it for £1,500. After his death the question arose whether the necklace ought not to be redeemed out of his personal estate for her benefit:

[1] 2 Atk. 157.
[2] *Edes* v. *Brenton*, West, 348. The Marriage Act was not passed till 1753.

Lord Chancellor. "The necklace is not to be considered as given for the separate use of the wife. I have admitted that a husband may make such a gift, but where he expressly gives jewels to a wife to be worn as ornaments of her person, they are to be considered only as *paraphernalia;* and it would be of bad consequence to consider them otherwise, for if they were a gift to her separate use, she might dispose of them absolutely in his lifetime, which would be contrary to his intention. But in this case it will be the same to Lady Londonderry, if she can prove that she wore the necklace as an ornament of her person on birthdays and other public occasions,—which it has been proved she did. The question arises 'whether there was an alienation of it by the husband in his lifetime, although he can not deprive her of them by his will?' Here there was a pledge with a power of sale, and at the husband's death the necklace remained unredeemed and unsold. I am of opinion that this was not an alienation, and that his personal estate being sufficient to redeem the pledge, and pay all his debts, she shall be entitled to have it redeemed and delivered to her."[1]

This decision in favor of the female sex was supposed to be overbalanced by the alleged harshness of another, whereby a lady was compelled, in answer to a bill of discovery, to disclose a fact which subjected her to a forfeiture. A husband left the whole of his personal estate to his wife, "but if she married again, his brother to have a moiety of it." The brother filed a bill against her for an account of the moiety, and for a discovery whether she was married again. She demurred to the discovery, relying on the case of *Chancy* v. *Tahourdin,* 1 Atk. 392:—

Lord Chancellor. "That was a forfeiture of the whole portion, the testator being a father bound by nature to provide for a child. This is to be considered a conditional limitation to the wife if she remained single, and she must show whether the condition has been performed. She must answer, whatever may be the consequence."[2]

He held, with much reluctance, that a bond given for payment of an annuity to a young woman, who, living in the family of a *married man,* had been seduced by him, was void:—

[1] 3 Atk. 393. [2] Ibid. 260.

Lord Chancellor. " This case is new. The Court has sustained such a bond as *præmium pudicitiæ*, where a young woman previously of good character has been provided for by her seducer,—their cohabitation ceasing. But I know no instance occurring where the obligor was a married man. This circumstance differs the case from those in which the Court has gone great lengths to make provision for such unfortunate persons. When a young woman appearing to be modest submits to improper solicitation, she is much to blame: but if the man be single, she knows the crime is not so aggravating as adultery; she may be inclined to suppose that he will be induced to marry her; there may be such a promise which can not be legally proved; where both parties are single, there is room for presuming such a promise: the subsequent marriage takes off from the enormity of the offense, and in most countries of Europe even legitimates the issue. At all events, under these circumstances, people are aware that they are doing that which is not of such bad consequence in families. Whereas when a man takes and keeps a mistress under the nose of his wife, who thereupon leaves him, that is such a crime as stares every one in the face. The unhappy plaintiff knew too well the situation of her seducer, and if the real consideration for the bond had been stated on the face of it, it would have been void at law. In *Lady Annandale* v. *Harris*, Eq. Cases Abridged, 87, the commerce was wholly after the death of the first wife, and before the second marriage. This Court ought not to sanction what would be of bad example in the case of married persons, and encourage people to enter into agreements of this kind. Had she not known that he was married, as if the wife had been at a distance, or any imposition had been practiced upon her, she might be entitled to relief. But she entered into the family, the husband and wife living together, and she caused a separation between them. The Court must endeavor to preserve virtue in families. Let the bill be dismissed,—but without costs." [1]

In the great case of the *Earl of Derby* v. *Duke of Athol*, he decided that the laws of England do not extend to the Isle of Man:—

Lord Chancellor. " This case concerns a very noble and

---

[1] *Priest* v. *Parrot*, 2 Ves. Sr. 160.

ancient family, and perhaps the most honorable inheritance any subject of this kingdom can enjoy. Many things are admitted on both sides: that Man is not part of the realm of England; parcel only of the King's crown of England; a distinct dominion now under the King's grants, and so for a long time past granted; held as a feudatory dominion by *Liege Homage* of the Kings of England. I am of opinion that the laws of England as such do not extend to it; neither our common law, nor statute law, unless it be expressly named or clearly included in some general legislative enactment. Though the Isle of Man be granted under the Great Seal of England, English law does not necessarily prevail in it. The Great Seal of England operates in all territories subject to the crown of England, whatever their laws may be. The King can grant, under the Great Seal of England, lands in Ireland, in the plantations, and in Guernsey and Jersey, because they are all parts of his crown."

He then enters at great length into the history of the Isle of Man, showing in a masterly manner how it was to be governed as a separate dominion, subject to the prerogative of the King, and the supreme power of parliament.[1]

There are no regular reports of the decisions in the House of Lords on appeals from the Court of Sessions till the time of Lord Chancellor Eldon. I am enabled, however, to give a statement of the most important case which came before Lord Hardwicke from Scotland, that of "Gordon of Park," respecting the effect of attainder for treason on the descent of entailed estates. Sir James Gordon had entailed the Barony of Park, with prohibitory, irritant, and resolutive clauses, on his eldest son William and his heirs male;—whom failing, on his second son James and his heirs male, &c. After the death of the entailer, his eldest son, Sir William Gordon, engaged in the rebellion of 1745, and escaped to France, but was attainted. The question then arose as to who was entitled to his estate,—the Crown, or his younger brother, Captain James Gordon, who had remained loyal to King George? An act of the Scotch Parliament, passed in 1690,[2] had provided that attainder for treason should not affect entailed estates; but the United Parliament had in-

[1] 2 Ves. Sr. 337–357. [2] C. 33.

troduced the English law of treason into Scotland, and enacted that " all persons convicted or attainted of high treason in Scotland should be subject and liable to the same corruption of blood, pains, penalties, and forfeitures as persons convicted or attainted of high treason in England."[1] The Scotch Judges unanimously held that Sir William Gordon having forfeited the estate, it should immediately, as if he had died without issue male, descend to his brother James. The Lord Advocate having appealed against this decision, Lord Hardwicke called in the assistance of the English Judges, to whom he submitted certain questions, molding the terms of the Scottish tenures as nearly as he could to those of England. He then, in accordance with their opinion, advised a reversal, saying:—

" I am sorry to be obliged to differ from the unanimous decree of the Supreme Court in Scotland, so much entitled to our respect. But the learned senators of the College of Justice are not very familiar with our law of treason, which has been introduced into their country, and they may unconsciously be inclined to adhere to the law which they had to administer before the Union. I do not see how the attainder of the heir of tailzie in possession can be considered as equivalent to his death without issue. He is not a mere tenant for life; he is the ' fiar:' the fee is in him, and our doctrine of remainders and reversions does not strictly apply;—so that, on a rigid construction of the 7 Anne, c. 21, on his attainder, there is room for contending that there ought to be an absolute forfeiture to the Crown of the entailed lands, to the entire extinction of the rights of all substitutes in the entail. But the milder interpretation of the Act will be to hold that the heir of tailzie has in him, and forfeits by his attainder, the same interest as tenant in tail in England—so that upon his attainder the Crown takes the lands during his lifetime, and while there exists issue who would take by descent through him,—leaving other substitutes in the entail unaffected. I would, therefore, advise your Lordships, reversing the interlocutor appealed against, to declare that the Barony of Park is forfeited to the Crown during the life of Sir William Gordon, and during the existence of issue male who through him would be inheritable thereto—but that upon his death

[1] 7 Anne, c. 21.

and the extinction of such issue, the remainder in favor of the respondent, Captain James Gordon, will take effect."[1]

But I am sadly afraid that, however interesting such matters are to the jurisconsult, they are very tiresome to the bulk of my readers, male and female; and I hasten to survey Lord Hardwicke in another sphere.

It is mortifying to consider that although he deserves such high commendation for his upright and enlightened administration of justice, he can not be praised for any attempt to amend our institutions by legislation. During the twenty years of his sway, the act requiring legal proceedings to be carried on in the English language, passed by Lord Chancellor King, still remained the most recent improvement, and the principle was acted upon which was soon after brought forward by Blackstone, in his "Commentaries," that our whole juridical system had reached absolute perfection. The only change introduced was a great addition to the severity of the penal code. Many felonies were now rendered capital, which before were only liable to be punished by transportation, and many frauds which at common-law were simple misdemeanors, such as forgery of deeds and negotiable instruments, being made capital felonies, in practice were always punished with death—although this bloody code did not reach its full measure of atrocity till towards the close of the reign of George III., when it was defended and eulogized by Lord Eldon.

In pursuance of an address of the House of Commons to the Crown, in the year 1732, a commission had been appointed to inquire into all fees in all the superior Courts both of Law and of Equity; and, after a period about as long as was employed in the siege of Troy, the

---

[1] Morr. Dec. 1728; Kame's Elucidations, 371; Sandford on Entails, 177. Lord Kames highly disapproved of this decision, saying, "A remainder with respect to forfeiture is introduced into our law hitherto unknown in Scotland;" and Lord Hardwicke had a sharp correspondence with him upon the subject. But I know not that a better rule could have been laid down.—A curious question subsequently arose as to the application of it. Sir William Gordon, after his attainder, married, and had two sons born abroad. On his death, Captain James again claimed the estate, on the ground that as these children were aliens, and could not inherit, the substitution in his favor had come into effect. The Court of Sessions decided against him; but he succeeded on an appeal to the House of Lords; and, in the lifetime of his nephews, became "Laird of Park."

Commissioners presented a Report, in which they point out various abuses, and suggest various amendments,—with very great tenderness to existing interests. I will present, as a specimen, what they say of the practice of writing only a few scattered words on a folio sheet of paper, the fee being so much a folio—an abuse which had been denounced by Hudibras:

> " To make 'twixt words and lines large gaps
> Wide as meridians in maps,
> To squander paper and spare ink,
> Or cheat men of their words, some think."

"A great part of the expense of the suitors," says the timorous Report, " arises from the copies of the proceedings, the bills, answers, interrogatories, depositions, orders, and decrees, being often very long, and the copies of them necessary to be taken by the complainant or defendant, and sometimes by both, having but six words to a line, and fifteen lines in a sheet, the expense of taking out such copies amounts to a very great sum of money. How this great expense to the suitor may be lessened, whether by reducing the length of such proceedings, by leaving out the immaterial and unnecessary parts of them, or by inserting more words in a line or more lines in a sheet, for which there is more than sufficient room in every sheet, or by reducing the fee usually taken for such copies, or by what other ways or means, the Commissioners humbly submit to the consideration of those who may be better able to judge, and have authority to provide suitable expedients and remedies, and to establish proper regulations whereby justice may be administered to your Majesty's subjects with as much dispatch and as little expense as conveniently may be." [1]

But the prevailing abuses withstood all the long labors of the Commissioners:—" Non anni domuere decem ;"—no act of parliament was passed, no orders were made, to correct them. The length of the proceedings might have been reduced; more words might have been inserted in a line and more lines in a sheet, and the fees for the copies might have been lowered. But the proceedings continued equally prolix: neither were there more words in a line or

---

[1] This Report, bearing date 8th November, 1740, is signed by Lord Hardwicke himself, who had been appointed a commissioner when at the bar.

more lines in a sheet; the copy money per folio continued equally exorbitant, and no ways or means were discovered to save the suitor from being plundered. The Judge and all the officers of the Court were paid by fees, and Lord Hardwicke could not have made a vigorous effort to regulate them without some sacrifice of his own pecuniary gains, and without danger of incurring ill-will from others. Hence the sarcasm upon him by his political opponent, Henry Fox: "Touch but a cobweb of Westminster Hall, and the *old spider of the law* is out upon you with all his younger vermin at his heels."[1]

That I may clear the way for following him in his political career, which must be more interesting to the general reader, I have now only to consider how he executed that most important function of a Chancellor—the appointment of Judges and law officers of the Crown,—and here he is entitled to unmixed praise. Lee, Willes, and Parker, with able puisnes, presided satisfactorily under his auspices in the Common-Law Courts, and the bar could not have furnished better men for the offices of Attorney and Solicitor General than Ryder, Strange, and Murray. It is objected to him that "he prevented the creation of law lords whereby his power in the House of Peers he apprehended might be diminished;" "the peerage of Lee, Ryder, Willes, and even of Parker, Chief Baron," says Cooksey, "though acknowledged due to their long services of the state, were delayed or denied; thus he remained the sole law lord during the whole term of his Chancellorship."[2] There is here, however, considerable exaggeration. Ryder's patent was too long delayed, and he unfortunately died before the Great Seal was put to it. The others, though respectable men, had never gained great distinction in parliament or in their profession, and law peerages ought not to be (as they have sometimes been) wantonly and inconveniently multiplied.

When we view Lord Hardwicke as a magistrate, it might be supposed that he could have had no political functions to disturb him; but now that we are to view him immersed in politics, we might suppose that he had nothing to think of but how he might please the King, and not offend the heir apparent—how he might intrigue

[1] Speech on the Marriage Bill.   [2] Cooksey, 76.

to keep up ministerial majorities—how he might assist in modeling measures to make the session come smoothly to a conclusion—how on a rupture in the cabinet he might reunite some of its scattered fragments—and how he might make all things work together for his own aggrandizement. It will be found that to advance the interests of his party and of his family he displayed great shrewdness and dexterity. His character as a statesman, about which he was very solicitous, is more doubtful. "Men are apt to mistake," says Lord Chesterfield, "or at least to seem to mistake, their own talents—in hopes, perhaps, of misleading others to allow them that which they are conscious they do not possess. Thus Lord Hardwicke valued himself more on being a great minister of state, which he certainly was not, than upon being a great magistrate, which he certainly was. All his notions were clear, but none of them were great. Good order and domestic details were his proper department: the great and shining parts of government, though not above his parts to conceive, were above his timidity to undertake."

From the disputes in the Royal Family, he had a difficult and disagreeable task assigned to him at the very moment when he received the Great Seal. George II., who had been disliked by his own father, actually hated his own son. Prince Frederick being at last permitted to come to England long after the accession of his family to the throne, now headed a powerful party in opposition to the government, and was banished from court, without being allowed a sufficient income decently to maintain himself and his wife and children. A motion was to be made in the House of Commons by his friends, for an address to the crown to assign him £100,000 a year out of the Civil List. According to the court scheme, this was to be counteracted by a proposal to parliament to vote him £50,000 a year, and at the same time he was to be reprimanded for his factious proceedings. A controversy arose with respect to the bearer of the reprimand, and the matter happened to be debated at the very cabinet at which Walpole had announced that Lord Hardwicke was to be the successor of Lord Talbot. Some one proposed that the new Chancellor should be the messenger. This was unanimously agreed to, and he was summoned to attend a council next day at twelve o'clock to receive the Great Seal. Accordingly, while he was waiting in the ante-chamber at St. James's, with the Dukes of Newcastle and Argyle, the Earl of Wilmington, and other Privy Councillors,—Sir Robert Walpole came out of the King's chamber, in a great hurry, holding a paper in his hand, and read to them the draught of a message, in his own handwriting, and acquainted them that "it was the King's pleasure that the Lord Chancellor, accompanied by the Lord President, Lord Steward, and Lord Chamberlain, should immediately carry it to the Prince." Lord Hardwicke, expecting nothing but smiles and congratulations on this auspicious day, was greatly shocked at such a commencement of his cancellarean career, and wished that he had allowed Fazakerly to be made a Whig. What added to his embarrassment was, that the King was then laboring under a low fever, from which some foretold that he would not recover. To the expressions in the reprimand "the undutiful measures which his Majesty is informed your Royal Highness intends to pursue," he positively objected; but it was replied by the minister, that the King insisted on the word "undutiful," and that he had with great difficulty been dissuaded from using harsher terms. A concession was made, however, by changing "intends" into "*hath been advised* to pursue." Still Lord Hardwicke took Walpole aside and expostulated with him on the hardship of making such a painful errand his introduction to the heir apparent. The minister answered that he had hinted this to the King *as far as he durst venture in so nice a case*, but the King prevented all further discussion by exclaiming, "My Chancellor shall go." To soften matters, it was agreed that the whole cabinet should attend in a body when the message was to be delivered, but Sir Robert contrived to slip away—on pretense that his presence was indispensably required in the House of Commons. Lord Hardwicke was then admitted into the King's closet, and received the Great Seal, with many gracious expressions of royal favor, but without a word respecting the reprimand. Having taken the usual oaths, he retired to make himself, as he apprehended, forever odious to the Prince, who might in a few weeks be upon the throne. He had a wonderful escape, however, from the "forlorn hope" on which he had been put: Frederick considered it politic on this occasion to be very civil to the Chancellor, and to use dutiful language towards the King; and he was swept off to an early grave, while the Great Seal remained in the firm grasp of its present possessor.[1]

A debate on the subject arose in the House of Lords the very day that Lord Hardwicke took his place on the woolsack as Chancellor; but he left the defense of the government to the Duke of Newcastle, and took no part in the proceedings beyond communicating the King's message to the Prince, and the Prince's answer.[2]

The first occasion of the new Chancellor's coming forward in debate was to defend the bill to punish the citizens of Edinburgh for the murder of Captain Porteous,— by repealing the city charter, by razing the city gates, and by abolishing the city guard. This measure being furiously attacked by the Duke of Argyle, who, in answer to the threat of the Queen as Regent to turn Scotland into "a hunting-ground," had said "he must go down to prepare his hounds," Lord Hardwicke justified all his enactments, observing in answer to the argument derived from the ancient loyalty of the citizens of Edinburgh, that "the merit of ancestors in a former age can never atone for the degeneracy of their posterity." This was considered by Macallamore a reflection on himself and his clan, and called forth from him a statement of their services in placing and retaining the present royal family on the throne. The Lord Chancellor declared "that the noble Duke had mistook his meaning; that he entertained the highest opinion of the noble Duke's candor and loyalty, as well as of his talents and gallantry, and that it never was his intention to insinuate anything to the disadvantage of any Campbell whatsoever." The division was in favor of the government, but the bill was so flagrantly unjust, and was so strenuously opposed by all the Scotch members in both Houses of Parliament, and by the whole Scotch nation, that the minister prudently abandoned it, and it was turned into a bill to impose a fine of £2,000 on the city of Edinburgh for the benefit of Captain Porteous's widow. "All these fierce debates ended only in making the fortune of an old cookmaid, for such had Mrs. Porteous been before the

---

[1] Com. Walp. iii. 537.   [2] 9 Parl. Hist. 1448

Captain made her a lady." [1]—A melancholy event was impending, from which important consequences were apprehended.

CHAPTER CXXXII.

CONTINUATION OF THE LIFE OF LORD HARDWICKE TILL THE RESIGNATION OF SIR ROBERT WALPOLE.

IN the end of this year Lord Hardwicke was much alarmed by the death of Queen Caroline, on whose great influence with the King, notwithstanding his infidelities to her, the ministry was supposed chiefly to depend; but her dying recommendation of Walpole sunk deep into the King's mind, and, his Majesty's health being completely re-established, the opposition party melted away. Horace Walpole says, that, "on the Queen's death, Lord Chancellor Hardwicke went deep into the scheme of governing through the Princess Emily; this scheme was to be built on the ruin of Sir Robert Walpole, who had no other trouble to make it miscarry than in making the King say, *Pho!*" [2] But this is a mere imaginary plot. From the hour of Caroline's decease the King lavished greater kindness than ever on Walpole, and it was not till long afterwards that Newcastle or Hardwicke thought of his removal.

The assailants of the government in the House of Lords, although not numerous, were active and unscrupulous. When the "Mutiny Bill" was brought forward in the session of 1738, Lord Carteret moved that the number of forces to be kept on foot for the British empire should be reduced from 18,000 to 12,000 men; and he was warmly supported by Lord Chesterfield and Lord Bathurst, who, like him, declaimed against the danger to liberty from a standing army, laughed at the idea of there being longer anything to be apprehended from the Jacobites, and contended that the best mode of allaying the

---

[1] See "Tales of my Grandfather," and "Heart of Midlothian." I can not justify the manner in which the Captain came to his end, but no true Scotsman can sincerely regret it.

[2] Memoirs of Ten last Years of George II.

prevailing discontents would be by disbanding every regiment in the service. The Duke of Newcastle made such a sorry figure in attempting to answer their sophistries, that before the debate closed the Lord Chancellor thought it proper to leave the woolsack, and he made a speech which, even from the imperfect report of it, appears to have been marked by uncommon excellence. Having pointed out the serious apprehension to be entertained from foreign invasion, and still more from internal disturbances, he thus proceeded:—

" But, say some Lords, '*all the discontents we now complain of arise from your keeping up such an army: Disband but your army, or a great part of it, and the people will be satisfied.*' This, in my opinion, my Lords, would be like a man throwing away his arms in order to be reconciled with his enemy,—which I am sure no man of courage or prudence would do. The recent riots which caused such alarm in the metropolis, and all over the country, have been produced by useful acts of the legislature for the erection of turnpike-gates, and to put down the beastly excesses of gin-drinking. The real danger to liberty arises from the machinations of desperate and ambitious men, who wish at all hazards to get into their own hands the supreme power of the state, under pretense of being attached to the exiled royal family, and who are ready to turn to their own account the delusions which may prevail among the people. If the noble Lords who ridicule our apprehensions feel none, my apprehensions are only the greater. My Lords, I warn you, that before long an attempt will be made to subvert our present happy establishment. Notwithstanding the uninterrupted peace and increasing prosperity which the nation has enjoyed since the accession of the present royal family, for reasons which I can not explain, discontents with the government are now general and deep, and without prudence and energy on our part these discontents will soon lead to open rebellion. The violence, the oppression, the subversion of law, liberty, and religion, which made the nation for a brief space almost unanimously concur in the Revolution, are forgotten; many are now so ungrateful as to censure that glorious event; many are so silly as to think, that by recalling the exiled family they may get rid of all fancied grievances, and continue to enjoy all the securities for the church and the constitution which the Revolution has achieved. While the late King James was alive, the doctrine of 'divine right' could not be acted upon without opening our arms to receive him who, by his blind bigotry, had brought us to the brink of destruction; whereas now the scene is changed, and delusive hopes may be entertained from a young Prince who personally has inflicted no wrong, although all reflecting men are aware that his family in their exile have learned nothing and forgot nothing, and that Popery and slavery would be recalled along with them. The small army which is asked is indispensably necessary for the safety of the well disposed. They will cherish it,—while it is hated by the seditious, because it prevents them from spreading war, bloodshed, and desolation over the face of their country." [1]

As soon as the Chancellor had resumed the woolsack, the House divided, when the motion was negatived by ninety-nine to thirty-five.

After this defeat the opposition made a much more skillful, though a very profligate, move. Because the Spaniards objected to our carrying on a contraband trade with their American colonies, most frightful stories were propagated of their cruelty to our countrymen, of which " the fable of Captain Jenkins's ears" was a fair specimen; and, under color of taking revenge, there was an eager desire in the nation to fit out expeditions for the purpose of capturing their galleons, and seizing possession of their gold mines. Here was an opportunity to bring obloquy upon the pacific Walpole, who was represented to be " a furious mastiff to his own countrymen, but a fawning spaniel to the Spaniards." His opponents determined to give him only the alternative of a Spanish war or resignation, and it was generally believed that, fond as he was of power, he was fonder of peace, and that his political extinction was at hand. With this view certain resolutions were moved in the House of Lords, affirming the outrageous conduct of Spain, denying the right of search which she claimed, and praying that English commerce might be protected against her aggressions. The task of combating these was cast upon the Chancellor, but he did it feebly and ineffectually, hardly venturing to go further

10 Parl. Hist. 555, 561.

than to point out that the resolutions were so framed as to condemn the belligerent right to search neutral vessels which might be carrying contraband of war—a right essential to the maintenance of our own naval ascendency. Finding that he was making no impression on the House, he withdrew his opposition, and the resolutions passed unanimously.[1]

In the following session the same policy was pursued by the opposition leaders, whose great object was to attack a preliminary convention with Spain, by which Walpole had hoped that all differences might be adjusted, and peace might be preserved. They were now encouraged by the faithless Duke of Newcastle, who thought this a favorable opportunity for becoming prime minister; and it has been represented even that another member of of the cabinet, from whom a very different line of conduct might have been expected, joined in the war cry. "The Chancellor, Lord Hardwicke," says Coxe, "a man of moderation, good sense, and candor, was of the same opinion with the Duke of Newcastle, and spoke with such vehemence in the House of Lords against the depredations, and in favor of compulsory measures, that Walpole, who stood behind the throne, exclaimed to those who were near him, '*Bravo! Colonel Yorke: Bravo!*'"[2] In justice to his memory, however, I am bound to declare that the printed reports of the proceedings of the Lords do not show the slightest foundation for this charge, and, if they are to be relied upon, they effectually repel it. He could not resist the motion for hearing witnesses at the bar, so that an opportunity was given for Captain Jenkins's celebrated declaration, that, when under the hands of the torturing Spaniards, "he committed his soul to God, and his cause to his country;" but in the debates on the convention, Lord Hardwicke appears to have defended it at great length, and boldly and manfully to have attempted to dispel the public delusion. He showed, that while we have a right to the free navigation of the American seas for the purpose of carrying on an unrestrained intercourse with our own colonies, according to the laws we are pleased to lay down for the regulation of their commerce, the Spaniards had a right to lay down laws to regulate the commerce of their colonies, and to prevent the carry-

[1] Parl. Hist. 731, 754.   [2] Coxe's Walpole, iv. 118; Lord Mahon ii. 407.

ing on of a contraband trade in violation of those laws.

"The mode in which these respective rights shall be enjoyed and enforced," said he, "is the fair subject of negotiation and treaty, and can not be satisfactorily adjusted by an appeal to arms. For this reason, plenipotentiaries were appointed on both sides, who, if they are permitted to proceed, may be expected to bring about a settlement for the mutual honor and advantage of the two nations. We have just reason to complain of the manner in which, in some instances, the Spaniards have exercised the right which we can not dispute they possess; but let us try whether we may not obtain indemnity and security without rushing headlong into a war, the result of which can not certainly be forseen, although the vulgar be captivated by the golden prospects which it is supposed to hold out. Having shown that no reasonable objection can be made to the treaty now before us, I must beg your Lordships to consider the present circumstances of Europe, the peculiar situation of this nation, and the relation we stand in to Spain. It must be allowed that no nation ought to enter into a war against a neighboring nation for any object which may be attained by peaceable means. Of all nations, we ought to be the last unnecessarily and wantonly to engage in hostilities. A great part of our people subsist by trade; our landed gentlemen owe a great part of their yearly revenue to the commerce and manufactures we carry on. Not only should we, by the wished-for war, lose our intercourse with the dominions of Spain, allowed to be so profitable, but a shock would be given to our trade with the rest of the world. Considering our heavy debt and many taxes, we are in no very good condition for engaging in a dangerous, and expensive, and perhaps protracted war. The rest of Europe will not quietly look on and see us make conquests in Spanish America, if the fortune of war should at the outset be in our favor. The Spaniards would soon be assisted by France, and perhaps by other powers we little dream of at present. Then think, my Lords, of the numerous party in this country, who, I am sorry to say, are so little solicitous about the national glory, that they are ready to join an invading army, and to receive a despotic master from our natural enemies. Some of them are actuated by the hopes of making or mending their fortunes, some by malice and an unjust hatred of those employed in the administration. There are many at present disaffected to the government from principle, but their number is decreasing every day. The rising generation see the absurdity and ridiculousness of the prejudices in which their parents were bred, and in a few years we may expect to witness a general concurrence in the principles on which the change of dynasty was found necessary, and a general attachment to good order, and to the cause of civil and religious liberty. Prudence will, by-and-by, dictate submission even to the unprincipled, when they no longer see well-meaning men whom they can hope to make the tools of their wicked designs."[1]

I must, therefore, absolve Lord Hardwicke from the charge of contributing to that madness which, a few months after, took possession of the nation, when Walpole, rather than quit office, agreed to a declaration of war against Spain,—when the heir apparent to the throne headed the mob in the streets of London, drinking "*Success to the War!*"—when, the treasures of Potosi being grasped in anticipation, and the golden dreams of the South Sea again deluding the public mind, there were greater rejoicings than followed the victories of Blenheim or of Waterloo,—and when the conscience-stricken minister exclaimed, "They are now *ringing their bells;* before long they will be *wringing their hands.*" With that minister rests, I think, the greatest share of the disgrace of commencing this war—the most unprovoked and unjustifiable in our annals. Walpole's opponents were deeply to blame, and still more were his colleagues, who wished, by making him unpopular, to supplant him; but with him the responsibility rested, and, rather than part with power, even for a time, he consented to involve the country in hostilities which he knew to be unjust, and which he expected to be disastrous. Had he honestly resisted, the nation would speedily have been restored to reason, and he would have been restored to power. By tardily yielding to the public delusion, he did not recover the popularity he had lost by resistance, and he was, ere long, forced into permanent retreat. Fit punishment, likewise, fell upon the nation; for, during the contest,

[1] 10 Parl. Hist. 1048, 1147.

although the heavy calamities which several times seemed impending were averted, the military enterprises which were undertaken produced disappointment and disgrace; we were indebted to chance, and the blunders of our enemies, that our shores were not trod by invading armies; a Stuart prince, being recognized by all Scotland, was within a few days' march of the English metropolis, where there were many friends to receive him; and we were finally obliged to agree to a treaty of peace, by which Spain did not make a single concession on the points which had been the pretense for hostilities.[1]

When Lord Hardwicke had exerted himself to the utmost to avoid a rupture with Spain, and had delivered a speech which ought to have called forth the exclamation, "Well done, Grotius!"—although he can not be much censured for remaining in office, as his resignation would only have made way for some more pliant lawyer,—I must confess that I think he would have done better by remaining quiet in parliament and watching a favorable opportunity for the restoration of peace. But Sir Robert having for the present out-maneuvered his opponents by going over to the war party, the now blustering Chancellor strenuously defended a subsidy to Denmark, that she might assist us in the quarrel, and he exclaimed,—"Whatever others may say who advocate forbearance, I am for instantly entering upon action."[2] He had for some time been regarded as the organ of the government in the House of Lords, no weight being attached to what fell from the Duke of Newcastle, who was ostensibly at the head of it. His Grace himself seems to have been aware of his own insignificance there, and thus writes to the Chancellor:—"It is no disagreeable circumstance in the high station in which your Lordship is, that every man in the House of Lords now knows that yours is the sense of the King's administration, and that their interest goes

---

[1] This is a case in which, as the lawyers say, we have "confitentes reos"—all the accused parties pleading *guilty*. Walpole at the time, with his usual openness, admitted that he was doing wrong. "Some years after," says Burke, "it was my fortune to converse with many of the principal actors against that minister, and with those who principally excited that clamor. None of them, no, not one, did in the least defend the measure, or attempt to justify their conduct. They condemned it as freely as they would have done in commenting upon any proceeding in history in which they were totally unconcerned."—*Regicide Peace.*

[2] 10 Parl. Hist. 1373, 1383, 1412, 1420.

with their inclinations when they follow your Lordship." [1]

During the Spanish war a discussion arose on a subject of more permanent interest—the Liberty of the Press,—when Lord Hardwicke delivered a speech with which he had taken great pains, and which is peculiarly interesting as coming from one who had been ten years Attorney General, and was so long afterwards at the head of the law. With a view, as it was thought, of intimidating Pope, who had cruelly lampooned Lord Hervey [2] and other peers, and kept the whole House in a state of apprehension, a complaint was made against [3] a very inferior poet, Paul Whitehead, who had recently published a satire called "MANNER," reflecting upon several peers, and whose commitment to Newgate would not have excited much public sympathy. The author absconded; but Dodsley, his publisher, appearing at the bar, a motion was made that he should be taken into the custody of the Usher of the Black Rod, which was opposed by Lord Carteret and Lord Abingdon, on the ground that such a proceeding was contrary to the liberty of the Press.

The Lord Chancellor. "My Lords, the liberty of the press ought to be sacred with every Englishman, and, I dare answer for it, will ever be so with your Lordships. But I am afraid that there is nothing less understood than the nature of that liberty. I have often, my Lords, desired an opportunity of delivering to your Lordships my sentiments upon this subject, and I may be excused if I embrace the present. It is said that the liberty of the press is about to be invaded. I know, my Lords, that the liberty of the press is generally taken for a liberty to publish every indecency against the most respectable persons either in public or in private life; and so strongly does this notion prevail, that I have never known an instance of a libeler being prosecuted without a loud cry of *oppression*, he being considered an impersonation of the liberty of the press. But has there been introduced into the law of England since the invention of printing, a right of pub-

---

[1] The Duke of Newcastle to Lord Hardwicke, 1739.
[2] "Let SPORUS tremble! What? that think of silk,
   SPORUS, that mere white curd of ass's milk," &c.
[3] It is said that Pope really was frightened by the "brave orts at the pridge," and he certainly was more cautious afterwards in meddling with high names, although his malignity to Grub Street continued to increase.

lishing to the world any defamatory matter to the prejudice of superior, inferior, or equal? Before the art of printing was known in Europe, learning was confined to a very few. At that time the copyers of books were a separate body of men, and were under particular regulations in different countries. When printing was introduced these regulations necessarily fell to the ground, and every one for a while could communicate his thoughts to the world on any subject, till printing under new regulations became an affair of state. Thence, my Lords, arose the expression of THE LIBERTY OF THE PRESS. But, my Lords, in England, the mode of publication made no change in the law of defamatory libel. The press acquired no liberty which was not known in the most remote times. If anybody, my Lords, is of opinion that authors acquired any new privileges when printing was discovered, he ought to prove either that the old laws on that subject were repealed, or that new ones were made in favor of typographical slander. Character must be protected as much as property, and an invasion of either demands an award of compensation, and punishment for the sake of public example. It is true, my Lords, that in bad reigns very great severities have been inflicted on authors and printers for publishing what was harmless or useful; but this only proves that the law was abused by power. The law of treason, allowed in this country to be wise and merciful, was abused much more; but for that reason a man may not imagine the King's death, or levy war against him with impunity. I am very sensible, my Lords, of how much use the press was at the time of the Revolution, but the authors who then espoused the side of liberty advanced nothing that was not agreeable to the constitution; they were warranted by law for what they wrote, and they had the sense of the nation on their side. I must add that the authors who are so justly praised for supporting the Revolution communicated their sentiments with the greatest deference to the persons and characters of their adversaries, without any mixture of malice or calumny. Let not modern libelers, when called to account in a legal manner, compare the present government to that of Charles II. or of James II., till they prove that they write with as much caution and as much decency as those who then lawfully availed themselves of the liberty of the press to defend the constitution of their country. The libel we are now considering is of the more virulent quality, as the noble Lords libeled could not have given any just cause of offense to the author, probably not knowing him by sight, and never having heard of his name till it was impudently affixed to this infamous publication. I therefore think it deserves all the severity of your Lordships' censure."

Lord Talbot (son of the Chancellor) pithily answered: "My Lords, if this be so, in Heaven's name let those aggrieved by this libel have recourse to the inferior courts of justice, and do not let such a charge lie against us as that we are judges, jury, prosecutors, and parties in the same suit."

On a division the motion was carried by 72 to 32, and I am only surprised that the minority was so large, or that any noble Lord had the courage to divide the House on such a question. Paul Whitehead's dull poems had nothing to do with the proceedings of their Lordships as a branch of the legislature, while he made free with the manners of individual Peers. But at this period no one ever thought of questioning any decision of the Lords upon privilege, and the standing order passed unanimously, of which I was obliged to move the repeal before I could venture to offer to the world my "Lives of the Chancellors,"—"that no one presume to publish the Lives of any Lords spiritual or temporal, deceased, without the permission of their heirs and executors."[1] The reckless perversion of privilege to the punishment of private injuries, which marked the eighteenth century, is very much to be condemned; but perhaps the other extreme into which we are inclined to run may be more injurious—a refusal to enforce privilege in cases where it is essentially necessary to enable the two Houses of Parliament to exercise the legislative and inquisitorial functions vested in them for the public good.

Parliament being called together in November to vote supplies for the Spanish war, the Chancellor had a very troublesome session. Walpole's enemies now complained of the manner in which the war had been commenced, and the manner in which it had been conducted; and they were particularly fierce against a passage in the

[1] Standing Orders, No. 113.

King's speech respecting "the heats and animosities prevailing throughout the kingdom," which was construed into a reflection on "his Majesty's opposition," who declared themselves to be the only true friends of loyalty and order. Newcastle, Hervey, Cholmondeley, and Devonshire were no match in debate for Carteret, Chesterfield, Bedford, Sandwich, and Argyle; and the Chancellor was frequently obliged to leave the woolsack, and to talk on subjects with which he was by no means familiar. In the debate on the address, the defense of the government rested chiefly upon his shoulders, and he contended with some success that his Majesty, as the father of his people, had a right to exhort all classes to cultivate mutual love and harmony—insinuating at the same time pretty broadly, that the noble Lords, whom no measures would content which they did not themselves originate and guide as ministers, were ready, for their own selfish ends, to endanger the internal tranquillity of the country and the national honor.[1]

But they had their revenge of him soon after, when the government having by inadvertence sent a message to the House of Commons respecting supplies for carrying on the war, without any similar message being sent to the House of Lords, and the omission being there taken up as a breach of privilege, the Chancellor, in a very elaborate speech, contended that "the message was in the nature of an estimate which was exclusively to be submitted to the Lower House:" but he was unmercifully dealt with by Chesterfield and Carteret, who ridiculed with much pleasantry this piece of special-pleading sophistry. The ministers did not venture on an attempt directly to negative the vote of censure moved upon them—but carried the previous question.[2]

The Chancellor was again "turned out for a day's sport" when he had to defend the manner in which Admiral Vernon's expedition had been equipped for the attack on Porto Bello, and the whole conduct of the war. The Duke of Argyle characterized his speech as " a toying with words," and the learned Lord does seem to have treated the subject as if he had been in the Court of Chancery, overruling objections to the Master's report. The minority rose to 40 against 62

[1] 11 Parl. Hist. 11, 60, 79.   [2] Ibid. 449–480.

At last came the delightful task of declaring in the King's name that parliament was prorogued. Still, the Chancellor had not the calm which he expected: for the King being gone to Germany, there were violent altercations among the Lords of the regency, and it was with the greatest difficulty that he could prevent Walpole and Newcastle from coming to an open rupture.

In the ensuing session of Parliament, he was called upon repeatedly to speak respecting the conduct of the war, the amount of the forces to be kept on foot, the reinforcements supplied to Admiral Vernon, and the instructions sent to Admiral Haddock;[1] but I do not think that his speeches, from the briefs delivered to him on these subjects, are of any interest, and I at once proceed to a great crisis in his history—the dismissal of Sir Robert.

Horace Walpole imputes treachery to him on this occasion, and considers that the ruin of the minister was brought about by his two colleagues, the Chancellor and the Duke of Newcastle. After describing their supposed attempt to turn him out on the death of the Queen, he says: "Their next plot was deeper laid, and had more effect; by a conspiracy with the chiefs of the opposition they overturned Sir Robert Walpole, and in a little time the few of their associates that they had admitted to share the spoil."[2]—Although it is quite certain that against such powerful opponents and such a load of public obloquy the Premier, having completed his twenty years of absolute sway, could not have stood much longer, I think there is some foundation for the charge against Newcastle, who, willing to submit to any indignity rather than not possess office at all, was ever ready to sacrifice every thing (good faith included) for the chance of increasing his power. "His name," said Sir Robert, "is *Perfidy*." "It would have been strange indeed," writes Macaulay, "if his Grace had been idle when treason was hatching."[3]

"Ch' i' ho de' traditor' sempre sospetto,
E Gan fu traditor prima che nato."

However, as far as Hardwicke is concerned, the statement is not only unsupported by any proof, but is con-

[1] 11 Parl. Hist. 615, 629, 700, 756, 760, 773, 813, 901, 918, 1000, 1016, 1027.   [2] "Ten last Years of George II.," p. 139.   [3] Essays, ii. 131.

trary to all probability. He had nothing to gain by a disruption of the ministry, and, although he had the good luck to survive it, he must have foreseen the danger that, if Pulteney and Carteret were to triumph, they would insist on naming a new Chancellor. On the only occasion when the subject was brought forward in the House of Lords, in February, 1741, when Lord Carteret made his celebrated motion for an address to the King, praying him "to dismiss Sir Robert Walpole from his presence and councils for ever," Lord Hardwicke defended his chief with much ability, and, seemingly, with zeal and sincerity. We have his speech, as reported by Dr. Johnson for the "Gentleman's Magazine," and though a few epithets may have been added, to give additional point to an antithesis or to round a period, I make no doubt that the report is substantially correct. Notwithstanding what has been said about "Johnson's Debates" being the invention of his own brain, it now appears, by comparing them with contemporary notes, particularly Archbishop Secker's, that they contain accurately the sentiments, and often the very words, of the different speakers, so that they must have been prepared from genuine information, or (what is more probable still) from the notes or recollection of the compiler, who may have been actually present when they were delivered. On this memorable occasion Lord Hardwicke spoke in answer to the Duke of Argyle, who had gone over the whole of the foreign and domestic policy of the government, pointing out how the autocrat had engrossed all the power of the state into his own hands, and, acting tyrannically at home and feebly abroad, had sacrificed the constitution and the national honor to his own personal aggrandizement. We care little now about the treaty of Hanover, the treaty of Vienna, or the conduct of the Spanish war; and I will not even quote the Chancellor's ingenious comparison between a campaign and "an equity suit, in which the client takes great delight till the solicitor brings in his bill." He seems to have been most happy on the vague charge, much dwelt upon, of Sir Robert having made himself "sole minister." This he likened to the old common-law high treason, called "accroachment," or assumption of the royal authority, for which, till treasons were defined by the statute of Edward

III., every great man obnoxious to the ruling faction was prosecuted and beheaded. The weakest part of his case was Sir Robert's practice (which would not now be endured) of cashiering military officers who were in parliament—from generals down to cornets—if they voted against the government:—[1]

"I shall grant, my Lords, that it is a right maxim for the King not to notice a gentleman's behavior in parliament with respect to the distribution of those favors which the Crown has to bestow. But even this maxim may admit of some exceptions. We know there is in this kingdom a party of professed Jacobites; we know there is, likewise, a party of professed Republicans. I do not say there are any of either of these parties now in parliament; but if they should get into parliament, if they should there pursue Jacobite or republican schemes, I believe it will not be said that the King ought to wink at such conduct, or that it would be any invasion of our constitution should he turn such officers out of his service. I am far from applying this to any case that has lately happened; nor do I think that his present Majesty ever dismissed any one from his service on account of his behavior in parliament, for he may have many other reasons for dismissing any officer, civil or military; and if an officer, who otherwise deserves to be dismissed, happens to have a seat in parliament, is he therefore dispunishable? But whatever reasons his Majesty may, at any time, have to make use of his prerogative to dismiss an officer from his service, I am convinced he will not allow any minister to advise him to make use of this prerogative for preventing a member's declaring his sentiments freely about any measure of government, *provided he does it with that decency which is due to the Crown, and without any factious or seditious manner of expressing himself upon the subject under debate.*"

So the opponents of Sir Robert Walpole must be Jacobites or Republicans;—and the Chancellor sanctions the doctrine of the Judges in the time of Charles I., that "Parliament men are not to be questioned before the Council for what they say in Parliament, *provided it is said in a parliamentary way.*" Sir Robert had a majority

[1] *e. g.* The Duke of Bolton and Lord Cobham deprived of their regiments and Cornet Pitt dismissed from the Blues.

of 108 to 59,[1] and all the hope of upsetting him was from proceedings in the Lower House after the dissolution of Parliament, which was now impending.

These discussions had a powerful effect to weaken the minister out of doors; the elections went against him — particularly in Scotland, where it used to be supposed, by their "second sight," they could see the shadow of a coming change; and when the House of Commons met, the appointment of "Chairman of Ways and Means" being carried against him, it was plainly seen that his official end was rapidly approaching. The old statesman made a gallant struggle; but the divisions on election petitions, then thought fair opportunities for a trial of party strength, continuing to go with the opposition,[2] he saw that he must soon be in a minority on all questions, and his colleagues, and his own family, telling him that he could stand out no longer, he announced his determination to resign.

CHAPTER CXXXIII.

CONTINUATION OF THE LIFE OF LORD HARDWICKE TILL THE BREAKING OUT OF THE REBELLION OF 1745.

LORD HARDWICKE was for some time in a state of much anxiety. He dreaded that the termination of his official career had arrived, and he regretted that he had ever left the secure position of Chief Justice of the King's Bench. Whatever Newcastle's expectations might be, he certainly had not made terms with the opposition leaders, and the probability was,

[1] 12 Parl. Hist. 1047-1233.
[2] The last of these was the Chippenham case, in which there was a majority against him of 16,—241 to 225. Nothing shows so strikingly how these were considered party questions, as the anecdote of Walpole's demeanor while the tellers were ascertaining the numbers. "Anticipating his fate, but bearing it with his usual fortitude and good humor, he beckoned to the opposition member for Chippenham, whom he had attempted to eject, to sit by him, spoke to him with great complacency, animadverted on the ingratitude of several individuals who *were voting against the government*, although he had conferred great favors upon them, and declared that he would never again sit in that House."—*Coxe's Walpole*.

that he and those most intimately connected with him must share Walpole's fate. Strange to say, the victors had formed no plan to improve the victory for which they had so eagerly fought, and which they had for some time anticipated. Meanwhile, the nation was in a state of unexampled ferment. All classes had been taught to look forward to the fall of Walpole as the cure for the evils of which they complained, and as the certain means of gaining their own favorite measure for reforming and governing the State. The counties and great cities sent instructions to their representatives all equally peremptory, but of very different import,—some insisting that the Septennial Act should be repealed, and that parliaments should be triennial or annual,—some that all placemen, as well as pensioners, should be excluded from sitting in the House of Commons,—some that all offices should be in the gift of the House of Commons,—more, that Walpole's head should now answer for his misconduct,—but most of all, that the decay of trade and other national calamities might be immediately remedied by an act to forbid the exportation of wool! The King and his private admirers, of whom the retiring minister, now Earl of Orford, was one, saw that the only chance of preserving the semblance of government or order in the country was to call in Pulteney, though personally so odious at Court that he had not been there for many years,[1] and to allow him, according to his own fancy, to form a new administration, of which it was of course supposed that he would himself be the head. The Duke of Newcastle and Lord Hardwicke were appointed to be the bearers to him of the keys of the royal cabinet. They opened the conference by saying, that "the King, convinced that Sir Robert Walpole was no longer supported by a majority of the House of Commons, had commanded them to offer the places held by that minister to Mr. Pulteney, with the power of forming his own administration —on the sole condition that Sir Robert Walpole should not be prosecuted." Pulteney refused this condition, saying, that, "even if he himself had been inclined to agree to it, it might not be in his power to fulfill his engagement, *the heads of parties being like the heads of*

[1] His name had been struck out of the list of the Privy Council, and he had been denied the commission of the peace.

snakes, carried on by their tails." The confusion increasing, the Chancellor and the Duke, at a subsequent meeting, declared that they were commissioned by the King to repeat the former offers, without urging the condition of not prosecuting the fallen minister, and his Majesty only requested that if any prosecution was commenced against Sir Robert, Mr. Pulteney, if he did not choose to oppose it, would at least do nothing to inflame it. Pulteney answered, that " he was not a man of blood, and that, in all his expressions of pursuing the minister to destruction, he had meant only the destruction of his *power*, but not of his *person;* though he was free to own that he thought some parliamentary censure at least ought to be inflicted for so many years of mal-administration." Then, to the infinite relief and delight of the messengers, he declared that " although he demanded an alteration of men and measures, and that the strong forts of government should be delivered into the hands of his party, viz., a majority in the cabinet, the nomination of the boards of Treasury and Admiralty, with the restoration of the office of Secretary of State for Scotland,—he did not require an entire sweep of all who held place under the Crown, and that he would beg the two noble Lords, who had so courteously borne to him the gracious pleasure of the King, to retain their respective situations of Chancellor and Secretary of State." To their utter amazement, he added: " As the disposition of places is in my hands, I will accept none myself: I have so repeatedly declared my resolution on that point, that I will not now contradict myself." He then named the Earl of Wilmington First Lord of the Treasury; Sandys, Chancellor of the Exchequer; Carteret, Secretary of State; and the Marquis of Tweeddale, the new Secretary for Scotland— while for himself he required an earldom, and a seat in the cabinet. On this footing the new administration was patched up. The Chancellor had the sagacity to see that it could not last long, but exulted in reflecting that he had not only escaped a great peril, but that among such colleagues his personal influence must be greatly increased, and that future changes might be under his own control. Pulteney, become " Earl of Bath," soon discovered the error he had committed, and, meeting in the House of Lords his former great rival, become " Earl of

Orford," exclaimed to him, "We are now the two most insignificant fellows in all England!" He made an effort to regain his position, but he found that his reputation and his power had perished irrecoverably.

The first occasion of the Chancellor coming forward in public, as the organ of the new administration, was in opposing the bill to indemnify witnesses who should give evidence upon the inquiry into the conduct of Sir Robert Walpole. The proceedings against him in the House of Commons had been immediately checked by the objection of those who were examined, that "they were not bound to criminate themselves;" and a bill was introduced in very general and sweeping terms, enacting "that all persons who, being examined before either House of Parliament, or any committee of either House, respecting the charges against Robert, Earl of Orford, should make any discoveries respecting his misapplication of public money, or his improper disposition of offices, or other misconduct of the said Earl, while a minister of the Crown, should be freed and discharged from all forfeitures, penalties, punishments, disabilities, and incapacities, to which they might be liable for or by reason or means of any matter or thing which, being examined as aforesaid, they should faithfully and truly discover, disclose, and make known." The bill rapidly passed the House of Commons, and, although not only the members of the late administration, but those now in office who had so often cried out for "*Walpole's head*," disliked it, no show of opposition could there be offered to it: but when it came before the Upper House, Lord Hardwicke resolutely attacked it in the finest speech which distinguished his parliamentary career. Having shown how it violated all the rules of evidence established for the protection of innocence, and the danger of offering rewards for convictions, lately testified by a club of miscreants going about from assizes to assizes to invent crimes and to accuse the innocent for the sake of "*blood-money*,"—he pointed out the unprecedented atrocity of the measure in offering a reward for evidence to implicate a particular individual, without the proof or even assertion of any *corpus delicti*. In conclusion, he indignantly exclaimed:—

"The promoters of this bill, like the tyrant Nebuchadnezzar, require first to know 'what was their dream; and, secondly, what is the interpretation thereof.'[1] But, says a noble Lord,[2] '*if we have not here a* corpus delicti, *we have what is sufficient for the purpose, a* CORPUS SUSPICIONIS;' a new expression and a new invention—*the body of a shadow*—and on this foundation he calls upon you to build his new superstructure of injustice! In my opinion, my Lords, it is a bill calculated to make defense impossible, to deprive innocence of its guard, and to let loose oppression and injustice upon the world. It is a bill to dazzle the wicked with a prospect of security, and by impunity for one crime to incite them to the perpetration of another. It is a bill to confound the distinction of right and wrong, to violate the essence of our constitution, to leave us without any rule for our actions, or any protection for our property, our lives, or our good fame So iniquitous is the law, my Lords, that I would sooner suffer by it than vote for it."[3]

The bill was thrown out by a majority of 109 to 57. This decision, though made the subject of a violent protest in the Lords, and some inflammatory resolutions of the Commons, was approved of by the public, who who began to think that the reports of the secret committees appointed to inquire into the misconduct of Sir Robert Walpole, disappointed all their expectations by dis-

---

[1] Daniel, ch. 11. [2] The Earl of Chesterfield.
[3] This pithy conclusion, which we know to be genuine, from the MS. notes of Archbishop Secker taken at the moment, is thus expanded and spoiled by Dr. Johnson:—"So clearly do I now see the danger and injustice of a law like this, that although I do not imagine myself endued with any peculiar degree of heroism, I believe that, if I were condemned to a choice so disagreeable, I should more willingly suffer by such a bill passed in my own case, than consent to pass it in that of another." A comparison of the two reports, however, will clearly prove that Johnson had either been present at the debate, or had been furnished with very full and accurate notes of the speeches.—12 Parl. Hist. 637-38. 643-711. When Cave was examined at the bar of the House of Lords as to the Reports which appeared in the "Gentleman's Magazine," he certainly *lied* by representing that he had prepared them himself from his own notes,—with the exception of some speeches sent to him by members. He said "he got into the House and heard them, and made use of a black lead pencil, and only took notes of some remarkable passages, and from his memory he put them together himself." Being asked "Whether he printed no speeches but such as were so put together by himself from his own notes," he answered, "Sometimes he has had speeches sent him by very eminent persons; that he has had speeches sent him by the members themselves." Being asked "If he ever had any person whom he kept in pay to make speeches for him?" he said "he never had."—14 Parl. Hist. 60. This seems to have been an attempt to get at JOHNSON, whom he considered himself bound at all hazards to screen.

closing nothing, *because there was little to be discovered*, and who were now ready to point all their indignation against those who, having pledged themselves to bring him to the block, were treading in his footsteps.

Lord Hardwicke's importance (as he had expected) rose considerably in the new government. The Earl of Wilmington, the nominal chief, was a mere cipher. Lord Carteret had great influence, particularly in foreign affairs, but domestic measures were left chiefly to the Chancellor, and he was called upon to defend in debate the treaties that were entered into, and the arrangements which were made for the prosecution of the war and for the defense of the kingdom. The grand object of attack with the Jacobites, Tories, and disappointed Whigs, was the measure of taking 10,000 Hanoverian troops into British pay,—which was so unpopular that many who pretended to be well-wishers to the Protestant succession joined in the cry of "no Hanoverian King!"

In the spring of 1743 this subject was brought forward in the House of Lords, in a very offensive manner, by Earl Stanhope (the son of the Minister), who moved an address to the King, praying " that his Majesty, out of compassion to his English subjects, would exonerate them from those mercenaries who had been taken into pay without the consent of parliament." A furious debate was closed with a very able pleading by the Chancellor, which was much applauded at the time, although it has now nearly lost all its interest. One passage of it might have really called forth the exclamation,—" Well done, Colonel Yorke!" In answer to the observation that, under the present administration, the nation was reduced to poverty and had lost all its spirit, he replied,—" If our wealth is diminished, it is time to ruin the commerce of that nation which has driven us from the markets of the Continent,—by sweeping the seas of their ships and by blockading their ports. Our courage is depressed—not by any change in the nature of the inhabitants of this island, but by a long course of inglorious compliance with the demands, and of mean submission to the insults, of other nations. Let us put forth all the strength we can command, and we are secure. The complaint is, that we have the aid of a friendly state. My Lords, we had auxiliaries in our pay at Blenheim and at Ramillies, and by the same means equal victories may still be won." He then, as a lawyer, combated the objection that this arrangement with Hanover should have been the subject of a treaty,—contending that such a mode of proceeding was impracticable:—" It is well known that no power in this kingdom can enter into a treaty with a foreign state except the King, and it is equally certain that with regard to Hanover the same right is limited to the Elector. This proposed treaty, my Lords, is therefore a treaty of the same person with himself—a treaty of which the two counterparts are to receive their ratification from being signed by the same person, and exchanged by being conveyed from his left hand to his right, and reciprocally from his right hand to his left." He insisted that if Hanover had been governed by another Sovereign wholly unconnected with the present royal family of England, the arrangement would have been highly advantageous to English interests, and would have met with general applause. This speech made Lord Hardwicke ever after a special favorite with George II., who had a high opinion of his own skill in the art of war, and was now burning to eclipse the glories of Marlborough,—a wish which he soon after thought he had actually accomplished at Dettingen, —although the French claimed the victory, and his undutiful nephew, Frederick of Prussia, represented him as "standing all the day with his drawn sword in his hand, in the attitude of a fencing-master who is about to make a lunge in *carte.*"

The Chancellor, amidst the plaudits bestowed upon his great Hanoverian speech, was this summer in some anxiety about ministerial arrangements. The Earl of Wilmington was dying, and Pulteney, Earl of Bath, finding too late that he could not have influence without office and patronage, made a vigorous effort to succeed him. Such a proposal was highly alarming to Lord Hardwicke, for their cordiality had been fleeting, and their ancient enmity had lately burst out afresh. He therefore stirred up Henry Pelham, brother of his patron, the Duke of Newcastle, to claim the office, although this quiet, judicious man, with characteristic timidity, shrunk from the dangerous eminence. He further prevailed upon the fallen minister, who, in his retreat at Houghton, still had much influence over the royal mind, to back the application. On Wilmington's death, the King, who was abroad, sent a dispatch announcing his decision in favor of Pelham. Lord Hardwicke was of course asked to continue Chancellor. The Duke of Newcastle then wrote to him, giving a hint, in a very amusing manner, about his over-caution: "My brother has all the prudence, knowledge, experience, and good intention that I can wish or hope in man; but it will or may be difficult for us to stem alone that which, with your great weight, authority, and character, would not be twice mentioned. Besides, my brother and I may differ in opinion, in which case I am sure yours would determine both. There has been for many years a unity of thought and action between you and me; and if I have ever regretted anything, it has been (forgive for saying it) too much caution in the execution, which I have sometimes observed has rather produced than avoided the mischief apprehended."

For many years afterwards Lord Hardwicke held the Great Seal as securely as his fee-simple estate at Wimpole. All divisions in the Cabinet were obviated by the dismissal of Carteret, become Earl Granville, the most accomplished, but the most fantastical, politician of that age. The opposition was soon after weakened by the death of Lord Hervey and the Duke of Argyle, and by Lord Chesterfield's acceptance of the vice-royalty of Ireland. Horace Walpole considers that from this time the Chancellor was Prime Minister, saying, "When Yorke had left none but his friends in the Ministry, he was easily the most eminent for abilities."[1]

Yet great difficulty was sometimes experienced in managing the King, who long remained sulky for the loss of Carteret, and was not at all reconciled to the English notion of "parliamentary government." Lord Hardwicke, in his Diary, has left us a very amusing account of a royal audience which he had demanded (January 5th, 1744-5):—

Chancellor.—"Sir I have forborne for some time to intrude upon your Majesty, because I know that of late your time has been extremely taken up; but as the Parliament is to meet again in a few days, I was desirious of an opportunity of waiting on your Majesty, to know if you had any commands for me. [Pause for above a min-

[1] "Ten last Years of George II." p. 139.

ute; the King stands silent.] Sir, from some appearances which I have observed of late, I have been under very uneasy apprehensions that I may have incurred your Majesty's displeasure; and though I am not conscious to myself of having deserved it, yet nothing ever did, or ever can, give me so great concern and so sensible a mortification in my whole life. [Another pause of above a minute; the King still quite silent.] I beg your Majesty will have the goodness and condescension to hear from me a few words upon the motives of my own conduct, the nature of your present situation, and the manner in which I think it may be improved for your service." [A long discourse follows, which was listened to without interruption, till a remark was made about measures taken for the defense of Hanover.] *King.*—" I can call home my troops for the defense of my own dominions." *Chancellor.*—" I mention it as part of the general system of carrying on the war, and as an instance of the readiness of your ministers to get over their old prejudices. But, sir, there still remains something very material behind." *King.*—" I have done all you asked of me. I have put all power into your hands, and I suppose you will make the most of it." *Chancellor.*—" This disposition of places is not enough if your Majesty takes pains to show to the world that you disapprove of your own work." *King.*—" My work! I was forced; I was threatened." *Chancellor.*—" I am sorry to hear your Majesty use these expressions. I know of no force; I know of no threats. No means were used but what have been used in all times—the humble advice of your servants, supported by such reasons as convinced them that the measure was necessary for your service." *King.*—" The changes might have been made by bringing in proper persons, and not those who had most notoriously distinguished themselves by a constant opposition to my government." *Chancellor.*—" If changes were to be made in order to gain strength, such persons must be brought in as could bring that strength along with them. On that account it was necessary to take in the leaders; and, if your Majesty looks round the House of Commons, you will find no man of business, or even of weight, capable of heading or conducting an opposition. [Pause. King silent.] Sir, permit me to say, the advantage of such a situation is a real advantage gained to the Crown. Your ministers, sir, are only your instruments of government." *King* [*smiles*].—" Ministers are the King in this country." *Chancellor.*—" Sir, I ask your Majesty's pardon for troubling you so long, but I thought it my duty to lay my poor thoughts before you."

According to this representation, it must be admitted that the Sovereign does not appear to so much advantage as the Keeper of his Conscience.

CHAPTER CXXXIV.

CONTINUATION OF THE LIFE OF LORD HARDWICKE TILL THE DEATH OF FREDERICK, PRINCE OF WALES.

WE now approach the rebellion of 1745, with respect to which we shall find Lord Hardwicke acting an important part in the measures to suppress it,—in the trial of the rebel Lords,—and in the new laws framed to introduce order and subordination into the country in which it originated. On the 15th of February, 1744, he brought down a message from the King, stating that " his Majesty had received undoubted intelligence that the eldest son of the Pretender, having arrived in France, was making active preparations to invade the kingdom, in concert with disaffected persons here." Both Houses joined in an address of thanks and assurance of support. This had been drawn by the Lord Chancellor, and concluded in the following eloquent and touching terms:—

"Loyalty, duty, and affection to your Majesty; concern for ourselves and our posterity; every interest and every motive that can warm or engage the hearts of Britons and Protestants, call upon us on this important occasion to exert our utmost endeavors, that, by the blessing of God, your enemies may be put to confusion; and we do all sincerely and earnestly assure your Majesty, that we will with zeal and unanimity take the most effectual measures to enable your Majesty to frustrate so desperate and insolent an attempt, and to secure and preserve your royal person and government, and the religion, laws, and liberties of these kingdoms."

However, a general supineness prevailed, and in about ten days afterwards a rebuke was administered to the Chancellor and his colleagues by the Earl of Orford, who had never before opened his mouth in the House of Lords. By command of his Majesty, they had laid some papers before the House containing information on oath of the arrival of Prince Charles Edward at Dunkirk, and of the equipment of a fleet, and the assembling of an army there, for the invasion of England. No motion being made, except "that the papers should lie on the table," the ex-Premier said:—

"I little expected that anything would happen to make it necessary for me to offer my sentiments in this assembly, but I feel that I can not continue silent without a crime. Little did I expect that the common forms of decency would have been violated by this august assembly. It is with the greatest surprise and emotion that I see such a neglect of duty. When his Majesty has communicated to you intelligence of the highest importance, is he to receive no answer from the House? As such treatment, my Lords, has never been deserved by his Majesty, so it has never before been practiced. And sure, my Lords, if his hereditary council should select for such an instance of disrespect a time of distraction and confusion, a time when the greatest power in Europe is setting up a Pretender to his throne, and when only the winds have hindered an attempt to invade his dominions,—it may give our enemies occasion to imagine and report that we have lost all veneration for the person of our Sovereign. It can not be thought consistent with the wisdom of your Lordships to be employed in determining rights of private property, when so weighty a case as the title to the Crown ought to engross all your attention.[1] [Here he looked hard at the Chancellor.] At this instant the enemy may have set foot upon our coasts,—may be ravaging the country with fire and sword, and may be openly threatening us with extirpation or servitude. If this attempt succeed, we shall be ruled over by a viceroy

[1] On a reference to the Journals it appears that one of the only three decrees of Lord Hardwicke ever appealed against was this day heard and affirmed.—*Countess of Warwick* v. *Earl of Cholmondeley*.

of the French King, and your Lordships, who sit in this House with a dignity envied by every class of nobility in the world, will be no better than the slaves of a slave to an ambitious and arbitrary tyrant. Permit me to rouse you from this lethargy. Let the noble and learned Lord on the woolsack submit to the sacrifice of postponing for a little while the calling in of counsel to argue about costs, while we show so much regard for the great, the universal, the national interest, as to concert a proper form of address to his Majesty, that he may not appear laboring for our safety, while we neglect what is due to our Sovereign and to ourselves."[1]

An apology being offered, on the ground that, after what had lately passed, no further declaration of their Lordships' sentiments upon the present state of affairs was deemed necessary, the Chancellor moved an address "to give his Majesty the strongest assurances that this House will, at the hazard of their lives and fortunes, stand by and support his Majesty against France, and any other power whatsoever, that shall presume to assist or countenance the Pretender, or any of his descendants or adherents, or to invade or commit any hostilities against his Majesty's kingdoms,"—which was unanimously agreed to. The government, so little prepared for defense as not to have in all England an army of more than 7,000 men, and only a few invalids in Scotland, escaped present danger by the dreadful storm which dispersed the French squadron, and wrecked many of their transports. "AFFLAVIT DEUS ET DISSIPANTUR." But it was ascertained that while there was in the country a powerful, zealous, and active

---

[1] At this is probably the last time I shall have to mention Walpole, whom I have had occasion to introduce from time to time ever since the impeachment of Lord Somers, I may be allowed to observe, that, after much unjust abuse heaped upon him, there seems now to be a great disposition to bestow upon him unqualified praise. He was probably the most dexterous party leader we have ever had,—equally skilled to win royal favor, to govern the House of Commons, and to influence, or be influenced by public opinion. He likewise well understood the *material* interests of the country, and, as far as was consistent with his own retention of power, he was desirous of pursuing them. But, that he might run no personal risk, he would make no attempt to improve our institutions; he was regardless of distant dangers; he plunged into a war which he admitted to be unjust and impolitic—and by his utter neglect of literature and literary men, in spite of the example set him by his immediate predecessors, Whig and Tory, he gave to official life in England that aristocratic feeling, and vulgar business-like tone, which it has ever since retained.

party for the Pretender, great indifference was manifested by almost all other classes. "I apprehend," said old Horace Walpole, "that the people may perhaps look on and cry, *Fight dog! fight bear!* if they do no worse."

Lord Hardwicke, much alarmed by the aspect of affairs, had recourse to an expedient which I can not think a very wise one;—he resolved to render more stringent the laws against high treason—instead of trying, by reforms, to make the government more popular. Accordingly he caused a bill to be introduced in the House of Commons to attaint the sons of the Pretender, if they should land, or attempt to land, in Great Britain or Ireland; and when the bill came up to the Lords, he added clauses to make it high treason to correspond with the sons of the Pretender, and to postpone till their death the mitigation of the English law of treason, agreed to on the union with Scotland, by which, after the death of the Pretender, corruption of blood in all cases of treason was to be done away with, so that innocent children might not be punished for the crime of their parents.

These clauses were most strenuously opposed, particularly by John, Duke of Bedford, who made a very fine speech against them, in which he alluded, with much pathos, to the fate of his grandfather, Lord Russell; and observed, that if it had not been for the circumstance of his great-grandfather still surviving at that time, all the property of his family would have been confiscated, and his name would have been extinct. Lord Hardwicke, in answer, delivered an elaborate harangue, which, however, was a mere repetition of a very ingenious pamphlet lately written by his son, the Honorable Charles Yorke, entitled "Considerations on the Law of Treason."[1] His most difficult point was to reconcile the postponement of the stipulated mitigation to the compact entered into with Scotland, whereby the English law of treason was admitted into that country, on an express condition which was to

---

[1] I have myself known several instances of a pamphlet being converted into a speech. One of the most remarkable of these was in a debate on the Catholic question, when, there appearing a great coincidence of sentiment and language between a speech delivered by Sir John Copley, and a pamphlet recently published by Dr. Philpotts, the present Bishop of Exeter, the old song was very happily quoted:—

"Good Sirs, this brown jug that now foams with mild ale,
In which we now drink to sweet Nan of the vale,
Was once TOBY PHILPOTTS."

be now violated, and he was obliged to resort to such quibbles as, that "it was not then foreseen that the Pretender would have sons;" that "as he was in a green old age, and likely to live as long as them, the postponement was inconsiderable;" and that "if *they* had sons, a further postponement would be unnecessary, as, in a few years, the title of the reigning family would be universally recognized."[1] The Chancellor had large majorities, but I doubt whether he added to the security of the existing government by any of his enactments. The general feeling upon the subject was expressed by the oft-repeated exclamation,

"See Hardwicke's quibbles voted into law."[2]

Cameron, of Lochiel, cared little for acts of parliament when he said, "I will share the fate of my Prince, whatever it be, and so shall every man over whom nature or fortune has given me any power!" The dread of attainder had no influence on the movements of Charles Edward, and if he had been captured, he must have been treated as a prisoner of war, for the voice of the whole world would have been raised against the meditated deed of executing him as a traitor. And the very fact of James III. being then a healthy man, little turned of fifty, showed that by the proposed violation of the compact respecting the law of treason, odium was wantonly brought upon the reigning dynasty.

During the session of parliament which began on the 24th of November, 1744, and was closed on the 2nd of May, 1745, there was the lull before the tempest: no business of any importance seems to have been transacted, and there has not been handed down to us the fragment of any debate in the House of Lords, from the opening of it till the prorogation.[3] The King, as usual,

[1] 13 Parl. Hist. 704-854.
[2] "What help from Jekyll's opiates canst thou draw?
   Or Hardwicke's quibbles voted into law?"
   —*Pope's Fragment, 1740.*

[3] It is a curious fact, that toward the middle of the last century, the public interest in parliametary proceedings, instead of increasing, seems almost entirely to have died away, for the prohibition against publishing debates would have had little effect if there had been any demand for them. Of the laborious and useful compilation, entitled, "The Parliamentary History," there is only one volume between 1743 and 1747; one between 1747 and 1753; and one between 1753 and 1765. After Dr. Johnson ceased to report for the "Gentleman's Magazine," it contained few debates worth reading; and the "London Magazine," which rivaled it, falls off in the same proportion.

then went abroad, and Lord Hardwicke, as a Lord Justice, was left at the head of the regency.

In a most difficult situation was he placed. First came the news of the battle of Fontenoy, which not being connected with his administration of the government, and bringing no disgrace on the national character, though unfortunate, did not probably give him much concern: but in the course of a few weeks he was thrown into deep consternation by hearing of the landing of Prince Charles Edward in the Highlands of Scotland, of his erecting the royal standard in Glenfinnan, with the motto TANDEM TRIUMPHANS,—of the gathering of the Highland clans around him,—of his march to Edinburgh,—of his enthusiastic reception in that metropolis,—of his festivals in Holyrood House,—of his victory over Cope at Prestonpans,—of the flight of the English troops to Berwick,—and of the preparations of the rebel army to cross the border. No blame was to be imputed to the Lords of the Regency. A requisition was sent to the Dutch for the six thousand auxiliaries they were bound by treaty to furnish in case of invasion; several regiments were recalled from Flanders; the militia of the northern counties was called out; Marshal Wade was directed to collect at Newcastle all the troops of every sort that could be mustered; and all suspected persons were taken up and confined in prison by virtue of a suspension of the *Habeas Corpus* Act. But there was an entire apathy in the public mind, and the " fight-dog—fight bear " prophecy seemed about to be fulfilled. Thus writes a colleague of Lord Hardwicke, well affected to the government, and not of a desponding turn of mind: " England, Wade says, and I believe, is for the first comer; and if you can tell whether the six thousand Dutch and ten battalions of English, or five thousand French or Spaniards, will be here first, you know our fate."[1] " The French are not come, God be thanked! But had five thousand landed in any part of this island a week ago, I verily believe the entire conquest of it would not have cost them a battle."[2]

The King returned in a hurry from Hanover, on the 31st of August, but although thereby Lord Hardwicke's personal responsibility was relieved, his anxiety was rather increased; for his Majesty could not be made

[1] Henry Fox to Sir C. H. Williams.   [2] Same to same.

aware of his danger, and it was considered contrary to court etiquette to say that the Stuarts had any adherents. "Lord Granville and his faction," says Horace Walpole, "persist in persuading the King that it is an affair of no consequence; and for the Duke of Newcastle, he is glad when the rebels make any progress, in order to confute Lord Granville's assertions. His Majesty uses his ministers as ill as possible, and discourages everybody that would risk their lives and fortunes with him."[1] Lord Hardwicke, at the request of the cabinet, and in the name of the whole of them, presented another strong remonstrance to his Majesty on his want of confidence in his servants, but it was heard, like the preceding, with silence and disgust. Their object now was, by language of kindness, and by measures of conciliation, to rouse some spirit in defense of the present establishment, and to try to impress upon the public mind a sense of the benefits obtained, and the evils avoided, by calling in the family which the nation, in their folly, appeared desirous of seeing ejected.

Parliament met on the 18th of October, when the King was persuaded to deliver a well-conceived speech, written by the Chancellor, containing the following stirring appeal:—

"I have throughout the whole course of my reign made the laws of the land the rule of my government, and the preservation of the constitution in church and state, and the rights of my people, the main end and aim of all my actions: it is, therefore, the more astonishing that any of my Protestant subjects who have known and enjoyed the benefits resulting from thence, and have heard of the imminent dangers these kingdoms were wonderfully delivered from by the happy Revolution, should, by any arts and management, be deluded into measures that must at once destroy their religion and liberties, introduce Popery and arbitrary power, and subject them to a foreign yoke. I am confident you will act like men who consider that everything dear and valuable to them is attacked, and I question not, but, by the blessing of God, we shall in a short time see this rebellion end, not only in restoring the tranquillity of my government, but in procuring greater strength to that excellent constitution

[1] To Sir H. Mann, 20th September, 1745.

which it was designed to subvert. The maxims of this
constitution shall ever be the rules of my conduct. The
interest of me and my people is always the same, and inseparable. In this common interest let us unite, and all
those who shall heartily and vigorously exert themselves
in this just and national cause, may always depend upon
my protection and favor."[1]

His Majesty's gracious speech was generally circulated
throughout the nation, while lower, and perhaps more
effectual, arts were used to rouse the people to the belief
that they had an interest in the quarrel. Thus the
butchers were specially apostrophised—on the ground
that Paptists abstain from eating meat in Lent,—and
handbills were hawked through the streets, representing
that the tartaned Highlanders not only violated virgins,
but ate young children for supper. A little reflection
only was wanting to convince all reasoning men that they
ought to stand by the present establishment. Setting
aside the doctrine of indefeasible hereditary right, which
had now few adherents in England, there was, unquestion-
ably, a better prospect of constitutional and wise government under the House of Hanover than under the recalled Stuarts. The two Georges, though not destitute
of some respectable qualities, certainly were not very
interesting or amiable characters; their utter contempt
for literature and the arts placed them disagreeably in
contrast with the two Charleses,[2] and some ground existed for the charge that substantial British interests had
been sacrificed to the object of procuring petty additions

---

[1] 13 Parl. Hist. 1311. In the Earl of Marchmont's Diary, under date October 7, 1745, it is said that "the Chancellor, starting as from a lethargy, remarked that he had thought lightly of the Highlands, but now saw they made a third of the island in the map." It is very possible that he might have made this geographical observation; but there is no pretense for saying that he had been blind to the danger which now threatened the government. On the contrary, he had long observed and lamented the growing activity of the Jacobites, and the growing indifference of the rest of the nation; and, from the landing of Prince Charles, was an *alarmist* as well Newcastle, of whom the characteristic story was invented, that "for a whole day he shut himself up, considering how he might best make terms with the Pretender."

[2] I have often been at a loss to understand how all the good songs, all the good tunes (with the exception of "The Campbells are coming") and the poetry, and all the wit, were on the side of the Jacobites. Is it to be ac-counted for by the apprehension, that the heads of the House of Brunswick would not endure to have their cause supported by the effusions of genius and taste?

to the Electorate. But, upon the whole, the change of dynasty had answered well. During the half century which had elapsed since the expulsion of James II,—notwithstanding the blind rage of contending factions, there had been, with slight interruptions, profound tranquillity in the country; the nation had made rapid and steady progress in wealth and power, and Britons had enjoyed civil and religious liberty to a degree hitherto unknown in the world. What could be expected from a RESTORATION pronounced by Mr. Fox to be "the worst of revolutions," and which, in this instance, must have been fatal to our free constitution, from the arbitrary principles on which it was to be defended? The objection was most forcible, that the family claiming the throne were of a different religion from the great majority of the people, and, looking to their personal qualities, it could not be overlooked that the Old Pretender, calling himself James III., was a narrow-minded bigot, while Prince Charles, notwithstanding his romantic adventures, and the attempts to exalt him into a hero, being, in reality, a very ill-educated and very silly young man, had shown a mixture of rashness and obstinacy which, combined with his hereditary notions of prerogative, rendered him wholly unfit to rule over a free people.

The King himself became apprehensive, when news arrived of the Rebels having crossed the border—having captured Carlisle—having been kindly welcomed at Manchester—and having advanced to Derby, within little more than 100 miles of the capital. Lord Hardwicke and the Duke of Newcastle were for the time in favor with him, and he heartily co-operated with them in marching the Guards to Finchley,[1] and taking the most vigorous measures for the public safety. But when the danger seemed to have passed away by Prince Charles's retreat,[2] his disaster at Clifton, and the recapture of Car-

[1] See Hogarth.
[2] The most recent and the most able historian of those times says that "had Charles marched onward from Derby, he would have gained the British throne" (3 Lord Mahon, 415); but, without a rising in his favor in England, his little army must have been extinguished at Finchley: the English Jacobites, who had been lavish of promises, faltered when it came to the push; and, after all, their numbers were not sufficient to have effected anything without the general assistance of the squires and the clergy, who again began to have the same fear for the Protestant religion by which they were actuated in 1688. The general apathy arose a good deal from too great a contempt

lisle by the Duke of Cumberland, his Majesty's dislike of the Duke of Newcastle again broke out in the saying, that it *was hard he should have for his minister a man hardly fit to be a Chamberlain in a petty German court;* and he formed a new ministry under Lord Granville, which lasted exactly forty-eight hours. It was said, when the crisis was over, that Lord Hardwicke was ready to have resigned with his colleagues; but he warily abstained from doing so, recollecting that it is easy for a minister to go out, and often very difficult to get back again.

A little temporary dismay, with mutual recriminations, arose from the news of the fight at Falkirk, but exultation and complacency were diffused by the victory of Culloden. Now Lord Hardwicke had the satisfaction of reading an address of congratulation unanimously voted by the Lords, in which he had dexterously introduced the following sentence, most soothing to the royal ear:—" It is with the greatest pleasure and admiration we behold in how eminent a manner this signal victory has been owing to the valor and conduct of his Royal Highness the Duke; if anything could add to our joy on such an event, it is to see a prince of your Majesty's blood, *formed by your example, and imitating your virtues,* the glorious instrument of it; and happy should we be in any opportunity of testifying the high sense we have of such illustrious merit." [1]

Next followed the painful but necessary task of trying the rebel Lords. The victory of Culloden was followed by wanton severities on the vulgar, which justly gave its hero an appellation immortalized by Byron; but, for the good order of society, the leaders of an attempt to subvert an established government must make it at the peril of their own lives, and they are bound to consider not only the justice of their cause, but the probabilities of success or failure. Against the Earls of Kilmarnock and Cromarty, and Lord Balmerino, bills of indictment wer found by a grand jury for the part they had taken in the siege of Carlisle; and these being removed by certiorari before the House of Lords, the trials were ordered to

of the danger. · If Charles had advanced to take London, his attempt would have more resembled Louis Bonaparte's attack on Boulogne than Napoleon's triumphant entrance into Paris from Elba.

[1] 13 Parl. Hist. 1405.

take place in Westminster Hall. Lord Hardwicke was appointed Lord High Steward.

On this occasion he is bitterly censured by Horace Walpole, who says, "Though a most comely personage, with a fine voice, his behavior was mean, curiously searching for occasion to bow to the prime minister, that is no peer; and not even ready at the ceremonial. To the prisoners he was peevish; and instead of keeping up to the humane dignity of the law of England, whose character it is to point out favor to the criminal, he crossed them, and almost scolded at any offer they made towards defense."[1]

. . . . . "He lost the character for humanity he had before tried to establish, when he sat as Lord High Steward at the trials of the Scotch Lords, the meanness of his birth breaking out in insolent acrimony."[2] This censure is greatly overcharged, but I can not defend the propriety and good taste of all his Grace's observations to the noble prisoners; and he forgot that—although their attempt, not having prospered, was called *treason*, and the law required that they should be sentenced to death—they were not guilty of any moral offense, and that if they had succeeded in placing Charles Edward on the throne of his grandfather they would have been celebrated for their loyalty in all future ages. When they had been marched to the bar, the gentleman jailer standing by their side, holding the ax, the edge still turned from them, he addressed a preliminary speech to them, which thus began:—

"William, Earl of Kilmarnock, George, Earl of Cromarty, Arthur, Lord Balmerino, your Lordships are brought before the most august judicature in this kingdom, in order to receive your several trials upon different charges of high treason. As the crimes whereof you stand accused are of the most heinous nature, so the accusations against you are grounded on no slight founda-

[1] *Letter to Sir H. Mann.*—He afterwards goes on to tell the following amusing anecdote of Lord Mansfield, which is a gross misrepresentation, as Mr. Solicitor's conduct to all the prisoner's during the trial was most courteous. "While the Lords were withdrawn, the Solicitor General Murray (brother of the Pretender's minister) officiously and insolently went up to Lord Balmerino, and asked him how he could give the Lords so much trouble. Balmerino asked the bystanders who this person was? and being told, he said, 'Oh, Mr. Murray, I am extremely glad to see you; I have been with several of your relations; the good lady, your mother, was of great use to us at Perth.'" [2] Memoirs of Ten last Years of George II.

tions. But though your charge is thus weighty and solemn, it is but a charge, and open to all such defenses as the circumstances of your several cases and the rules of law and justice will admit. The law is the solid basis and support of the King's throne: it is the great bulwark of the property, the liberty, and life of every subject, and it is the security of the privileges and honors of the Peerage. By this measure, which is uniform and equal to every member of the community, your actions which are now called in question are this day to be examined and judged. If your Lordships are innocent, this will be one ground of a reasonable confidence in your present unhappy circumstances. But to this consideration your own thoughts can not fail to add another; I mean that the rules of this law are to be expounded and disclosed to you by this illustrious assembly, the whole body of the Peers of Great Britain, in whose noble and discerning minds nothing can have weight but evidence and justice. Guilt alone can endanger you, and innocence alone can acquit you."

He then sarcastically told them of their felicity in being tried under the law made to regulate the trial of high treason since the Revolution. "However injuriously that Revolution has been traduced," said he,—"whatever attempts have been made to subvert this happy establishment founded upon it, your Lordships will now have the benefit of that law in its full extent."—Lords Kilmarnock and Cromarty pleaded *guilty*, but Lord Balmerino pleaded *not guilty*—only, however, to show the stoutness of his heart, and that he might glory in what he had done, for he had been taken with arms in his hands, and he attempted no legal defense beyond objecting that he was improperly described in the indictment as being "late of Carlisle," and that on the particular day laid in the indictment on which he was charged with assaulting that city he was more than twenty miles off; but the Lord High Steward told him that his description was an immaterial form, and that, according to English procedure, the overt act of treason might be alleged on one day, and proved on another.¹ Of course he was unanimously found

---

¹ The last Duke of Queensberry (old Q.) whom I knew on my first coming to London, used to complain of the shameful manner in which he had once been used, by losing a great cause simply for not doing what those who required it knew to be impossible. "When the trial was nearly over," said he,

guilty,—a verdict which he heard undismayed, being resolved on the scaffold, in response to the prayer "God bless King George," to say "God bless King James!"[1] The Lord High Steward now proceeded to pronounce sentence on all the three:—

"By this conviction it is now finally determined that your Lordships are guilty of that crime which not only the laws of Great Britain, but of all other countries, for the wisest reasons, adjudge to be the highest. As it gives the deepest concern to every one of my Lords, your peers, to find persons of your birth and quality stained with so foul an offense, so it must give them some satisfaction that all of you, in effect, have confessed it. Charity makes one hope that this is an indication of some disposition to that repentance which your guilt so loudly calls for. To attempt to aggravate crimes of so deep a dye, and in themselves so incapable of aggravation, against persons in your unhappy circumstances, would be a vain as well as a most disagreeable task. And yet the duty of that place in which I have the honor to sit requires that I should offer some things to your consideration, to explain more fully the necessity of that justice which is this day to be administered, and to awaken in your minds a due sense of your own condition." [Having then, at most unjustifiable length, given a partial view of the campaign, and of the motives and objects of the opposite sides, he thus concludes:] "If from any unforeseen accidents, not uncommon in military operations, delusive hopes were for some time kept alive, it seems to have been judicially designed by Providence to render the more signal that vengeance which was reserved for them at the battle of Culloden. How much was owing, on that memorable day, to the bravery and discipline of his Majesty's troops, to the animating example, the intrepid valor, and the wise conduct of a Prince descended from him who is so deeply graven on the heart of every member of this great assembly, that I could only repeat what their own grateful minds have already suggested to themselves, and

---

"proclamation was made that I, who was the plaintiff, should come forth; and because I did not come forth, I was nonsuited and cast, although Judge, jury, and counsel, all were well aware that I was not then attending the Kingston Assizes, but was shooting grouse in the highlands of Scotland."

[1] From him Walter Scott has taken the exit of Fergus MacIvor.

represented to the throne! Then was experienced how much that courage which virtue, true loyalty, and the love of our country inspire, is superior to the rashness and false fire of rebellion, accompanied by the terrors of guilt. I will add no more. It has been his Majesty's justice to bring your Lordships to a legal trial; and it has been his wisdom to show that, as a small part of his national forces was sufficient to subdue the rebel army in the field, so the ordinary course of his laws is strong enough to bring even their chiefs to justice. What remains for me is a very painful, though a necessary part. It is to pronounce that sentence which the law has appointed for crimes of this magnitude; a sentence full of horror! such as the wisdom of our ancestors has ordained as one guard about the sacred person of the King, and as a fence about this excellent constitution, to be a terror to evil-doers, and a security to them that do well. The judgment of the law is, and this High Court doth award,———"

And so he went through the drawing, hanging, cutting down alive, burning their bowels before their faces, and the other particulars which he had eulogized as necessary for the protection of the King and constitution.[1] Cromarty was pardoned out of compassion to his wife. The other two were beheaded, the rest of their sentence being remitted.

Without imputing blame in this instance to the government, their tragical end excited much commiseration:—

> "Pitied by gentle minds, Kilmarnock died,
> The brave, Balmerino, were on thy side."

The next victim, notwithstanding the courage he displayed, fell unlamented:—

> "But Lovat's fate indifferently we view,
> True to no King, to no religion true;
> No Tory pities, thinking what he was,
> No Whig compassions, for he left the cause.
> The brave regret not, for he was not brave,
> The honest mourn not, knowing him a knave."

As he had committed no overt act of treason in England, —to bring his case before the House of Lords, it was necessary to proceed against him by impeachment. Articles being presented at the bar, the Chancellor was again ap-

[1] 18 St. Tr. 442–530.

pointed Lord High Steward, and the trial took place in Westminster Hall.

Lord Hardwicke on this occasion can not be accused of any departure from the rules of law or justice; but he was too solicitous to praise the existing government, and he betrayed, under assumed moderation of tone, great internal exultation at finding such a victim in his power. All parties knowing that there was the certainty of a conviction on the clearest evidence, in his preliminary address to the prisoner when placed at the bar, he said:—

"The weight of this accusation, the solemn manner of exhibiting and prosecuting it, and the awfulness of this supreme judicature, the most illustrious in the world, are circumstances that may naturally strike your mind with anxious and alarming apprehensions. Reasonable and well-grounded must those apprehensions be if they proceed from that greatest of all terrors, a consciousness of guilt. But if your Lordship is innocent, if you have really preserved yourself untainted with the heinous crimes laid to your charge these very awful circumstances, when duly considered, ought to have a contrary effect, and to afford you support and consolation."

After the verdict of guilty came a speech of culpable length and virulence; for the punishment provided by the law in cases of high treason did not include torturing and mangling while still alive by the Judge as well as by the hangman. Having described how Lord Lovat had forced out his clan to fight for the Pretender, he thus introduced a dissertation on clanship, much fitter for a debate in the House when sitting as a legislative assembly:—

"Permit me to stop here a little and lament the condition of part of this united kingdom; happily united in interests, both civil and religious; happily united under the same gracious monarch and the same public policy. Yet the common people, in some of the remote northern counties, are kept in a state of bondage to certain of their fellow-subjects, who, contrary to all law and every true principle of government, have erected themselves into petty tyrants over them, and arrogate to themselves the right of compelling them into rebellion against their lawful sovereign, under the peril of fire and sword. Astonishing it is that such a remain of barbarism should have subsisted so long in any quarter of this civilized, well-governed island. But let it be accounted one good fruit of this inquiry, that it has been so clearly made manifest. Such a knowledge of the disease points out the remedy. This usurped power was audaciously made use of over your clan. It is true your Lordship's activity in exercising it rose and fell in proportion to the appearance of the good or bad success of the Pretender's cause; but after the advantage gained by the rebels at Preston Pans, which you vainly called a *victory not to be paralleled in history*, you thought it right to throw off the mask, and openly to espouse a party which you then hoped might be espoused with impunity."

After a history of the rebellion, and many other topics, political, economical, military, and religious, at last came the sentence, which, though frightful, it must have been a relief to hear. Lovat died bravely, exclaiming, "*Dulce et decorum est pro patriâ mori!*" but his treachery and cruelty were so notorious, that a savage shout of exultation was raised when he laid his head on the block.

About this time another execution took place, which was universally condemned, and which I think reflects great disgrace upon Lord Hardwicke. As the legal adviser of the Crown, he was chiefly answerable for it, although he did not ostensibly take any part in the proceeding. Charles Radcliffe, when quite a boy, had been engaged in the rebellion of 1715, and, being attainted, had escaped from Newgate. His elder brother, the Earl of Derwentwater, had then been beheaded, all the possessions of the family had been confiscated, their blood had been corrupted, he had lost all the rights of citizenship in his native land, and he had chosen another country in which, for thirty years, he had lived quietly and respectably. During the insurrection in Scotland, having been captured on board a French vessel bound for that country, it was resolved that he should be arraigned on his original sentence, which had slumbered so long. The only trial now conceded to him was confined to his identity, and, although there was no doubt of the fact, I do not think that it was satisfactorily established by legal evidence.[1] For such a course there was no precedent, except in the case of Sir Walter Raleigh, which had brought shame upon the reign of James I. The con-

[1] 18 St. Tr. 430-442.

stancy of this unfortunate gentleman to his cause, and the calmness of his demeanor, powerfully excited the public sympathy in his favor:

> "Radcliffe, unhappy in his crimes of youth,
> Steady in what he still mistook for truth;
> Beheld his death, so decently unmoved,
> The *soft* lamented, and the *brave* approved."

The general opinion was, and is, that, with more opportunity for clemency, there was at this time greater severity than on the suppression of the rebellion of 1715;[1] and although the blame of it is laid upon the Duke of Cumberland, who personally ordered the military executions which rendered his name so odious in Scotland, Lord Hardwicke ought to be held responsible for what was done judicially in England.[2]

However, I am glad to be able again to praise him, in stating his admirable measure for abolishing heritable jurisdictions in Scotland, by which that country was more benefited than by any legislative measure ever passed. The feudal system had been there pushed to more oppressive lengths than in any part of Europe. The relation of lord and vassal, which elsewhere is consistent with personal and civil freedom, among the Caledonians approached that of master and slave. Almost every manor or barony was a little independent state, subject to the most arbitrary laws—or rather to no law except the will of the little tyrant called the *laird* or *chief*. He had power of life and death under a grant of "*fossa et furca*," or "pit and gallows;" and, for lack of evidence

---

[1] Hall's Const. Hist. iii. 312.

[2] The subsequent execution of Dr. Alexander Cameron, in 1753, I regard as a wanton atrocity. He was a man of literature and science, who, having studied surgery, had accompanied his brother, the famous Lochiel, into the field in 1745, that he might take care of him when wounded; and had escaped with Prince Charles after the battle of Culloden. His name was included in the act of attainder, and he was appointed surgeon to a regiment in the French service. Some years after, in a time of profound tranquillity, when all real danger of Jacobitism had passed away, he visited his native country to arrange his private affairs; and, being betrayed, he was sent to London, arraigned on the act of attainder, and, without trial, executed as a traitor at Tyburn; displaying the highest qualities of a philosopher and a Christian. Although Lord Hardwicke's name is not mentioned in this affair, he must have been consulted about it; and he must have been present in council when the death warrant was signed.—See 19 St. Tr. 733–746. A beautiful marble monument has lately been erected in the chapel of the Savoy, with the consent of the Chancellor and Council of the Duchy of Lancaster, to the memory of the unfortunate Alexander Cameron.

to convict a prisoner of theft, it was enough to urge that "the young laird had not yet seen a man hanged." In the larger jurisdictions the forms of justice were more regularly observed; but it sometimes happened that the judge was a Highland cheiftian, that the prosecutor and the jury were all of the same name and blood, and that the accused was of a rival clan at mortal enmity with them—from mutual depredations and acts of vengeance reciprocally inflicted for many generations.[1] The interference of the King's regular courts was prohibited, and the only control that could be exercised over these judicial enormities was by the Scottish Privy Council, the most cruel, remorseless, and arbitrary tribunal ever established in any country,—compared to which the English Star Chamber was mild, compassionate, and regardful of law and justice. One striking consequence of the system was, that the mass of the population were almost unconscious of the general government of the country, and looked only to the will of the superior to whose rule they were subjected, and under his banner they were equally ready to fight for King James or King George. This consideration led to the abolition of heritable jurisdictions in Scotland, without much regard being paid to the private oppression which they generated. The evils of the system had been long lamented, but, from the whole aristocracy being interested in perpetuating them in a country where there was no middle class and the people had no voice, a remedy for

---

[1] I am sorry to say that in one of the most noted instances of this sort the Judge was the Duke of Argyll, the jury were all Campbells, and a poor Stewart was tried for the murder of a Campbell. The clannish spirit which prevailed may be guessed from the boast of an old Campbell, when taunted with this affair, and told that Stewart was innocent:—"It was—to be shure! That's the very thing! Ony body can get a man hanget that's guilty; but it's only Callumore can hang a man wha's no guilty ava."

Note to 4th Edition, 1857.—I have since received from an eminent Scottish Judge the following account of this trial, which may be implicitly relied upon:—"The trial alluded to did not occur till 1725, five years after the abolition of the heritable jurisdictions; and the Duke presided at it, not as Baron of his own Court, but (contrary to all precedent) as Lord Justice General in a *Circuit* Court of Justiciary. The name of the accused was *Stewart* (a clan then in open hostility to the Campbells), not *Macdonald*; and the Lord Advocate (Grant of Prestongrange) attended the trial, a thing also without precedent at a circuit. The jury were not *all* Campbells, but 11 out of 15 were, and of the other four none was a *Stewart*. The trial was that of James Stewart in Aucham for the murder of Colin Campbell of Glenure. It was a very bad case—one of the grossest instances on record of a judicial murder."

them was considered hopeless. James I., in his BASILICON DORON, addressed to Prince Henry, had observed:—
"Sed nihil est, quod legum usum magis impediat, quàm juris regalis hæreditariæ apud quosdam nobiles potestas; vera totius regni calamitas. Nihil mihi in presentia consilii hic succurrit, nisi ut severissimam à singulis exigas officii rotionem et quantùm leges persimerint, cessantium castiges ignaviam. Et si quis potestatem hanc suo vitio amiserit, nemini post illum hæreditario jure eam concesseris. Verùm ad laudabilem Angliæ consuetudinem omnia hæc paulatim aptare studebis."[1] At the time of the Union in the reign of Queen Anne, there was an express stipulation without which that measure could not have been carried,—" That all heritable offices, superiorities, heritable jurisdictions, and offices for life should be reserved to the owners thereof as rights of property, in the same manner as they were then enjoyed by the laws of Scotland."[2]

But Lord Hardwicke, like a true statesman, seeing that it was for the manifest advantage of Scotland, and of the whole empire, that they should be abolished, seized the favorable opportunity of the suppression of the rebellion to effect this great reform. Immediately after the trial of Lords Kilmarnock, Cromarty, and Balmerino, he opened the subject in the House of Peers, and procured an order to be made on the Lords of Session to prepare the draft of "a bill for remedying the inconveniences arising from heritable jurisdictions in Scotland, and for making more effectual provision for the regular administration of justice throughout that part of the United Kingdom by the King's courts and judges there," and that they should inquire into and make a report upon the nature and extent of those jurisdictions. The Scotch Judges, at that time all landed proprietors, who for little emolument contentedly filled the judicial office in consideration of the power and influence it conferred, resolved to thwart the English Chancellor in this salutary measure. They presented a report in which, on frivolous excuses, such as that some records were damaged, and others were locked up with the Scottish regalia, they pretended that they could not prepare the draft of the required bill, nor give an accurate account of the nature and extent of the

[1] Opera Jacobi Regis, p. 150. [2] Art. 19.

heritable jurisdictions; and they remonstrated against the abolition of these jurisdictions as a measure contrary to the articles of Union, and wholly impracticable.¹

Lord Hardwicke, nothing daunted, caused a bill to effect his object to be prepared under his own superintendence in London, and this he introduced at the commencement of the following session, in a most lucid and argumentative speech, of which we have an authentic report edited by himself. In this he animadverts with decency, but with the most cutting severity, on the conduct of the Scotch Judges, saying, among other things equally bitter, "The interference of the legislature is now proved to be indispensable, for after the discovery made by the Lords of Session to all the world, that there is no record by which the nature and extent of these heritable jurisdictions can be ascertained, they may be claimed and stretched by all who think fit, and the poor people who are oppressed are told by those to whom they might fly for refuge that there is no redress for oppression in its worst form." His chief difficulty was to combat the argument arising from the treaty of Union. After some rather sophistical criticisms upon the language of the different articles, he assumes a manly tone, and boldly contends that the parliament of the United Kingdom had in it all the powers which belonged to the parliament of Scotland, and could now legislate on the subject as that parliament might have done,—insisting, that if the measure was clearly required by existing circumstances, and must be for the general good of Scotland, it ought to be adopted were it forbidden by the articles of Union in terms the most express and peremptory. He showed that an attempt to fetter the supreme legislative power in any state is a contradiction in terms. "In all countries," he said, "the legislative power must, to a general intent be absolute; and therefore, upon treaties of this nature, strict and rigid constructions ought not to be made and may prove dangerous. If they should too easily be given way to, incorporating Unions would become impractic-

¹ It was soon after this that a Lord of Session spoke so contemptuously of Cromwell's Judges, who he could not deny had administered justice impartially and satisfactorily, but whom he deprived of all merit because they were free from local and party connections, saying, "No thanks to them, KITHLESS LOONS!"

able or mischievous."[1] Out of policy, I presume, but not very sincerely, he declared that he was not moved to bring forward this measure by the rebellion, or by the supposed disaffection of Scotland, or by a belief that the present possessors of these heritable jurisdictions were not fit to be intrusted with such powers, there being before his eyes Scottish chiefs of distinguished loyalty, as well as high birth, worthy to be trusted with any powers which it is proper for the Crown to confer upon a subject.

"My Lords," said he, "my true reasons are drawn from known and allowed maxims of policy. I think that the parceling out in this manner the power of jurisdiction originally lodged in the Crown, was an erroneous and a dangerous model of government. I look upon the administration of justice as the principal and essential part of all government. The people know and judge of it by little else. The effects of this are felt every day by the meanest in the business and affairs of common life. Statesmen look abroad into foreign countries, and consider our remote interests and connections with other nations. But of what utility are those views, however great and just, unless they be referred back to our domestic peace and good order? The chief object of the social compact is to secure to us the regular course of law and justice. When the King, therefore, grants away jurisdiction, he parts with so much of his government; it is giving away so many jewels of his crown. It is certainly

[1] This, however, is perhaps, by a fallacy, begging the question. There may be a legislature with limited powers, like the American Congress,—and it is possible that after an incorporating union the power of the united legislature may be made to be limited by the conditions of the treaty of union declaring that any law to infringe these conditions is void, and by erecting a tribunal like the Supreme Court of the United States to decide whether any law is contrary to these conditions—or, in a rougher manner, by providing that an infraction of these conditions shall work a dissolution of the union. However, I entertain no doubt that by the just construction of the treaty of Union with Scotland, and of the treaty of Union with Ireland, the united legislature was to be vested with supreme and absolute power over the whole empire. The fact that a proposed law repeals or alters any article of the Union is a very strong, but not a conclusive objection to it. On this doctrine I acted when I supported the entire abolition of the Court of Admiralty, and the substantial abolition of the Court of Exchequer in Scotland, both declared by the articles of Union to be forever established in that country; and by this doctrine I should be guided if any law were proposed for modifying the Protestant Episcopal Church in Ireland.—See the opinion of Mr. Burke, *Works*, vol. x. 6.

putting so much of the protection of his people into other hands; and this tends directly to dissolve the bond of allegiance and affection between King and people; while the subjects do not see the King either in the benefits they enjoy, or the punishments they undergo. Hence arises a dangerous and unconstitutional dependence. The people will follow those who have the power to help or to hurt them; and this dependence will operate most strongly in the uncivilized part of any country remote from the seat of government. The ill effects of it in Scotland were felt long since, and will continue to be felt till the appropriate remedy is applied."

He then stated the details of the measure, by which the whole of the heritable jurisdictions in Scotland were at once to be swept away, root and branch, and the King's judges were to make circuits twice a year for the trial of all offenders.

Lord Hardwicke concluded by laying his bill upon the table, and moving that it be read a first time; but, as compensation was to be given, he stated on a subsequent day that it must commence in the House of Commons. There it was brought in by the Attorney General, Sir Dudley Ryder, and passed with little opposition. When it came up to the Lords it was strongly opposed by the Duke of Beaufort, and other Jacobitically inclined peers; but the Chancellor left the defense of it to the Duke of Argyle, without again entering into its merits. The opponents of the bill did not venture to divide the House upon it, and satisfied themselves with a violent protest.[1] It certainly does high honor to its author. From the time that it came into full operation, and not from the Union, commences the prosperity of Scotland, which, having been the idlest, poorest, and most turbulent country in Europe, has become one of the most industrious, the most improving, and the most orderly.

But such is the imperfection of human wisdom, such a mixture of praise and censure is meted out to the most clear-seeing legislators, that I am obliged immediately to record another Scottish measure of Lord Hardwicke, which greatly endangered and considerably retarded the good effects of that which I have so cordially applauded. Provision being made for the due administration of jus-

[1] 14 Parl. Hist. 1-57.

tice, conciliation was now the obvious policy to reclaim the Highlands; but because a deep resentment was manifested against the barbarities of the Duke of Cumberland, and there were enthusiastic rejoicings at the escape of the young Chevalier after all the perils to which he had been exposed, and because there had been a not unnatural combination to oppose the abolition of the heritable jurisdictions between the Lords to be restrained, and the vassals to be protected by it, who all cried out with equal violence that it was an encroachment on the ancient rights and privileges of Scotsmen,—Lord Hardwicke, instead of affording a little time for those feelings to subside, in the ensuing session introduced a "Coercion Bill," which added insult to injury, for it not only contained clauses for universally disarming the Highlanders, but forbade them to use the *tartan*, which they said and believed had distinguished their ancestors since the time of Ossian, and long before. Instead of plaids and philibegs, and trews, they were, henceforth, to be clothed in coats and in waistcoats, and, (worst of all) in BREECHES! ! ! This unpopular bill was strongly opposed in both Houses, but was carried by large majorities, for there was then a strong prejudice against the Highlanders. People had not forgotten the alarm and consternation into which a small band of them had thrown all England; most unfounded stories were propagated respecting atrocities imputed to them in their march to Derby, and it was highly popular in the South by acts of parliament to heap upon them all sorts of indignity. Unfortunately the debates upon the bill are lost, except respecting one insignificant clause about preventing priests from officiating in Scotland who were ordained by nonjuring bishops. This the English bishops assailed as an attack on the spiritual jurisdiction of Christ's church, and they rejected it in the committee,[1] but, on the report, Lord Hardwicke made a strong speech in its favor. In reference to Charles's landing at Moidart, he said,—

"Rebellion may take its rise in one of the remotest,—one of the smallest and least populous corners of this island:—

'Mobilitáte viget, viresque acquirit eundo;
Parva metu primo; mox sese attollit in auras,
.... et magnas territat urbes.'

---

[1] 32, including 20 Bishops, against 29 lay Lords.

I am astonished, my Lords, to hear any regulation called *cruelty* that may tend towards preventing such a rebellion for the future. What is the form of ordination among those who call themselves nonjuring bishops, or what confessions, promises, or vows, they exact from the persons they ordain, I do not certainly know; but I believe that no man will be ordained by one of them who is not a Jacobite in his heart; and an exclusion of all such from the exercise of their function in any part of his Majesty's dominions is, I think, absolutely necessary for the public safety. As to the encroachment made by this clause upon the rights or privileges of the Christian church, I do not pretend to be so good a judge as the Right Reverend Prelates; but, as far as I am master of the subject, I cannot conceive what the rights and privileges of the Christian church have to do in this question. We do not by this clause pretend to annul the holy orders granted by a nonjuring bishop, nor do we pretend that the civil magistrate has any power to determine whether a priest has been regularly ordained, or a bishop duly consecrated; but, surely, the supreme legislature in every state has power to determine who shall be allowed to exercise the office of priest or bishop within its territory."

The clause was restored.[1] To the enactments for the universal seizure of arms, the most captivating objection was, that they made no distinction between Jacobites and Georgites. The loyal clans murmured " that, after having defended the King upon the throne, they were forbidden for the future to defend themselves, and that the sword was forfeited which had been legally employed." I believe such measures are powerless to put down disaffection, and rather excite irritation than cripple the means of annoying the established government. The Highlanders were first reconciled to the House of Hanover by the great Lord Chatham, who pursued towards them a policy very different from that of Lord Hardwicke's "Coercion Bill," for he put arms into their hands and called upon them, with confidence, to fight against the enemies of their country.[2] It is amusing to find Dr. Johnson ascrib-

---

[1] 37 to 32.
[2] " I remember how I employed the very rebels in the service and defense of their country. They were reclaimed by this means; they fought our battles; they cheerfully bled in defense of those liberties which they had at-

ing the tranquillity he observed in the Highlands, in the year 1773, to an act which, having prolonged agitation for a while, had soon become a dead letter,—the very memory of it having been blotted out by a more generous and wiser policy. "The last law," says he, "by which the Highlanders are deprived of their arms, has operated with efficacy beyond expectation." His remarks are more amusing, and therefore more valuable, on the clauses respecting the tartan garb. "In the Islands the plaid is rarely worn. The law by which the Highlanders have been obliged to change the form of their dress has, in all the places that we have visited, been universally obeyed. I have seen only one gentleman completely clothed in the ancient habit, and by him it was worn only occasionally and wantonly. The common people do not think themselves under any legal necessity of having coats; for they say that the law against plaids was made by Lord Chancellor Hardwicke, and was in force only for his life; but the same poverty that made it then difficult for them to change their clothing hinders them now from changing it again." Instead of breaking the spirit of the clans, this tyrannical law only helped to keep up clannish distinctions and customs. In Lord Hardwicke's lifetime it was evaded by Highlandmen carrying a pair of breeches, suspended by a stick, over their shoulders; for the Highlanders wearing a short petticoat like the Romans,— thought, like the Romans, with contempt of all to whom the line of Ovid might be applied,—

———"laxis arcent mala frigora *braccis.*" [1]

Jacobitism was not completely extinguished in the Highlands till Lord Hardwicke's obnoxious act was repealed on the motion of the late Duke of Montrose, who showed

tempted to overthrow but a few years before."—*Lord Chatham's Speech in the House of Lords*, 2nd Dec. 1777.

[1] Trist. v. 7. Pronouncing the *c* before *i* as the Italians do, and the Romans probably did, it is wonderful with how little change of sound this word has descended to us from our Scythian ancestors.—See Luc. i. 430.

The etymon is equally apparent, whether we take the Scotch or English name for this garment,—"breeks" being an abbreviation of "breeches," as "steeks" of "stiches."

"Wha made your *breeks?*
He that sewed the *steeks.*
Wha sewed the *steeks?*
He that made the *breeks.*"

himself a wiser man than the Chancellor, and who, for his patriotism, was thus celebrated in the Rolliad:

> " Thee, Graham ! thee the frozen chieftains bless,
> Who feel thy bounties through their fav'rite dress,
> By thee they view their rescued country clad
> In the bleak honors of their long-lost plaid
> Thy patriot zeal has bar'd their parts behind
> To the keen whistlings of the wintry wind.
> While lairds the dirk, while lasses bagpipes prize,
> And oat-meal cake the want of bread supplies;
> The scurvy skin white scaly scabs enrich,
> While contact gives, and brimstone cures, the itch ;
> Each breeze that blows upon these brawny parts
> Shall wake thy lov'd remembrance in their hearts;
> And while they freshen from the northern blast,
> So long thy honor, name, and praise shall last."

Lord Hardwicke, after these exertions, talked so much of his fatigue, and desire of ease, as actually to create a belief among those who did not know him well, that he was going to give up his office for one less laborious: "We talk much," writes Horace Walpole to his correspondent at Florence, "of the Chancellor resigning the Seals from weariness of the fatigue,—and being made President of the Council—with other consequent changes: but as this has already been a discourse of six months, I don't give it you for certain."[1] Had the Chancellor been suddenly required to resign, he would have felt like the old man when Death actually appeared to him to relieve him of his burden.

For several succeeding years his political career becomes obscure, partly from the quietness of the times, and partly from the growing deficiency of our parliamentary records. The treaty of Aix-la-Chapelle excited no discussion in the Lords, and, notwithstanding the machinations of the Prince of Wales and his party, the Chancellor, sitting on the woolsack, seems to have enjoyed nearly a sinecure. Mr. Pelham, with his unostentatious virtues, enjoyed the confidence both of the Sovereign and of the people, and, while he lived, faction was stilled almost into silence. The Chancellor in these halcyon days only came forward on occasions of ceremony, such as the choice of a Speaker, and, to keep his name before the public, he then tried to say something smart, which he would not have thought of had he been taking part in a debate on which

[1] Letter to Sir H. Mann, 2nd Dec. 1748.

the fate of the ministry depended.¹ Compliments to Speaker Onslow, and such commonplaces, however prettily turned, have lost all their interest.²

The Mutiny Bill, which now passes as quietly as any road bill, still continued an annual occasion for patriots to declaim against a standing army. In 1749, the Lord Chancellor found it necessary to reply to them in a speech curious for the view it gives of the state of public feeling which prevailed while Prince Charles was advancing to Derby, and of the danger to which the government was then exposed:

"When the late Rebellion broke out, I believe most men were convinced that, if the rebels had succeeded, popery as well as slavery would have been the certain consequence; and yet what a faint resistance did the people make in any part of the kingdom!—so faint, that had we not been so lucky as to procure a number of regular troops from abroad time enough to oppose their approach, they might have got possession of our capital without any opposition, except from the few soldiers we had in London, and the fate of the kingdom would have depended upon a battle fought within a few miles of this city. While the people therefore remain in their present unarmed and undisciplined condition, let the consequence be what it will, we must keep up a standing force, and no one ever heard of an army being long kept up in any country in the world without military laws and courts martial for holding the officers and soldiers to their duty. But these officers and soldiers are still our fellow-citizens, actuated by the same feelings with ourselves, and, while they preserve internal quiet and defend us from foreign aggression, they would join us to preserve the constitution instead of combining against us to overturn it." ³

After a few patriotic sallies on the subversion of liberty by military violence, the bill was carried, and dullness again overspread the House—till a great excitement was produced by a melancholy event which changed the succession to the throne.

¹ 14 Parl. Hist. 93; 15 Parl. Hist. 328.
² About this time Lord Hardwicke was elected High Steward of the University of Cambridge, an honor which he held for his life, and which was long enjoyed by his posterity. ³ 14 Parl. Hist. 451.

CHAPTER CXXXV.

CONTINUATION OF THE LIFE OF LORD HARDWICKE TILL HE RESIGNED THE GREAT SEAL.

THE sudden death of Frederick, Prince of Wales, in the flower of his age, which was little regretted at Court, placed Lord Hardwicke in a situation of considerable embarrassment, but he extricated himself from it with his usual prudence. The present heir-apparent, afterwards George III., being no more than twelve years old, and George II. being sixty-seven, it was indispensably necessary that provision should be made for the exercise of the royal authority on a demise of the Crown. The King wished much that the Regent to be named should be his favorite son, the Duke of Cumberland, who was himself strongly of opinion that the distinction was due to his station as first Prince of the blood, and to his services as the victor of Culloden; but this Prince, notwithstanding some high qualities which belonged to him, was now so unpopular, that when his brother's death was announced, the general cry was,—"*Oh! that it were the Butcher!*" and his appointment as Regent would only have been satisfactory to the Jacobites. Lord Hardwicke suggested to Pelham and the Duke of Newcastle that preference should be given to the Dowager Princess of Wales, who had been obnoxious to the Court during her husband's life, but on his death had behaved with such great propriety that no personal objection could be started to her. The King reluctantly acquiesced, on the condition that she should be controlled by a Council of Regency, of which the Duke should be President. The difficulty now was to announce the plan to his Royal Highness; and this task was assigned to the Chancellor, who accordingly waited upon him, and in the most respectful manner showed him the heads of the proposed Regency Bill, enlarging on the weight which he would have in the council. Deeply disappointed at not grasping the whole royal power as Regent, he said sternly,—" Return my thanks to the King for the plan of the Regency. As to the part allotted to me, I shall submit because he commands it!" The bill passed both Houses with little difficulty, and Lord Hardwicke still preserved his ascendency.

This year he deserves the credit, which I am sorry to say does not always belong to Chancellors, of supporting a useful measure proposed by a political opponent. Lord Chesterfield, dismissed from his offices, embraced every opportunity of annoying the government. and then brought forward, with the assistance of Lord Macclesfield, son of the Chancellor, his famous bill for the reformation of the Calendar, according to the Gregorian computation of time, by making the year commence, for all purposes, on the 1st of January, instead of the 25th of March, by suppressing, in September, 1752, the eleven days the old style had fallen behind, so that the day following the 2nd of that month should be called the 14th, and by inserting certain intercalary days in time to come.[1] During some Chancellorships, I am afraid the noble and learned president of the assembly, disliking trouble and responsibility,—perhaps grudging a little credit to a rival, —perhaps meaning to bring in the same bill himself at a future time,—would have left the woolsack, and with faint compliments to the good intentions of the mover, would have pointed out the danger of innovation,—the disturbance of contracts which the change would occasion,—the height of prosperity and happiness which the nation had reached under the old computation of time,— and the degradation of copying the example of the French, our natural enemies, and the Pope, the foe of our holy reformed faith. Had Lord Hardwicke followed this course, he might easily have defeated the opposition leaders, and we might still have been adhering, like the Muscovites, to the old Calendar, exploded by all civilized nations. But he candidly supported the bill, and, with his countenance, it passed so easily that people were astonished the reformation had been so long delayed.[2]

[1] 24 Geo. 2, c. 23.
[2] 14 Parl. Hist. 979; Lord Chesterfield's Letters to his Son; Dr. Matty's Life of Lord Chesterfield. Had Lord Hardwicke been inclined to crush the measure, he had an ample pretext in the manner in which it was first received by the Duke of Newcastle, the ostensible head of the government in the House of Lords. Says Chesterfield: "His Grace was alarmed at so bold an undertaking, and entreated me not to stir matters that had been long quiet; adding, that he did not love new fangled things."

In 1752, the only public measure in which Lord Hardwicke took an ostensible part was a bill for annexing the forfeited estates in Scotland to the Crown, and encouraging Englishmen and lowland Scotsmen to settle upon them. This measure, in the result, operated favorably, by preserving the estates for the families of the individuals who had been attainted; but I can not commend it, for it was meant as a measure of severity against them. Lord Hardwicke defended it on the ground that, if the estates were sold they would be purchased at a low price for the former owners, and that there were fictitious charges upon them which would run away with the whole of the purchase-money—censuring, but in a manner not very mortifying to them, the whole Scottish nation, whom he seems to have considered "aliens in blood, language, and religion." "The noble Duke," said he, "is so sanguine as to hope that all these fraudulent claims may be detected; but, from experience, I am inclined to entertain no such hopes. The people of that country are so faithful to one another, in every case in which they think their honor concerned, that no reward can tempt them, no terror frighten them, to betray their trust: they will take any oath you can frame rather than discover what they think their honor obliges them to conceal, and this fidelity reaches even to the very lowest of the people. Their contempt of rewards is proved by the escape of the young Pretender, and their disregard of threats by the impunity of the murder of Captain Porteous."[1]

The year 1753 is memorable in the life of Lord Hardwicke by his JEW BILL and his MARRIAGE BILL, for both of which I think he deserves credit. From the fatuous fears and furious cries which the former occasioned, it has generally been represented as "a bill by its own vigor at once to confer all the rights of natural-born British subjects on all foreign Jews who might set foot on English ground;" whereas it merely allowed bills to be brought in for naturalizing Jews without their having taken the sacrament of the Lord's supper according to the rites of the Church of England, or, in other words, to allow that a Jew might be naturalized by act of parliament. After some sharp debates, the bill passed both Houses, and received the royal assent; but, from there being then no

[1] 14 St. Tr. 1237, 1248.

reports of parliamentary proceedings printed, its nature was so grossly misrepresented, that great odium was cast upon the Chancellor as its author; and the Bishop of Norwich, who voted for it, soon after, holding a confirmation, was called upon by the mob "to administer the rite of circumcision," and a paper was affixed to the church doors, stating that "next day being Saturday, his Lordship would confirm the Jews, and on the day following the Christians." Such was the ferment in the nation that ministers became alarmed—particularly as a general election was approaching,—and in a very dastardly manner they agreed to abandon this measure, which, if persisted in, might have introduced, upon reflection, a more liberal feeling into the public mind, and accelerated by a century the religious freedom which we now enjoy.[1]

Lord Hardwicke's Marriage Act, with considerable modifications and improvements, remains in force, and regulates in England the most important of all contracts, —upon which civil society itself depends. Hitherto the old canon law had prevailed, according to which a valid marriage was constituted either by the mere consent of the parties, or by the presence of a priest in orders, at any time or place, without the sanction of parents or guardians, although one or both of the parties might be under age,—and without any registration or public act affording the means of knowing whether such a marriage had been contracted. This does seem to me a very defective state of the law, although it exists in the northern part of the island, and is there defended by sensible men. It is of importance for the protection of minors that they should not be permitted to enter into this contract by their own mere fantasy, when they are wholly incapacitated to enter into others of the most trifling nature; and it is important to society in general, that a form—simple and notorious—should be specified, which shall be essential, and which shall be sufficient, for constituting the con-

---

[1] 14 Parl. Hist. 1365–1442; 15 Parl. Hist. 91–163. By way of apology, Lord Hardwicke said—" However much the people may be misled, yet in a free country I do not think an unpopular measure ought to be obstinately persisted in. We should treat the people as a skilful and humane physician would treat his patient; if they nauseate the salutary draught we have prescribed, we should think of some other remedy, or we should delay administering the prescription till time or change of circumstances has removed the nausea."

tract, and the evidence of which shall be open to all mankind. Although we reject the Roman Catholic doctrine that marriage is a sacrament, it is highly desirable that a religious service should accompany the celebration of it, to create a deep sense of the solemnity of the obligation thereby contracted; but as some may object to such a service, and all should be permitted to marry, it ought not to be considered indispensable.

Various striking instances of the inconveniences and hardships resulting from the then existing law had recently occurred. Young heirs and heiresses, scarcely grown out of infancy, had been inveigled into mercenary and disgraceful matches; and persons living together as husband and wife for many years, and become the parents of a numerous offspring, were pronounced to be in a state of concubinage, their children being bastardized, because the father had formerly entangled himself in some promise which amounted to a pre-contract, and rendered his subsequent marriage a nullity. In the public prisons—particularly in the Fleet—there were degraded and profligate parsons ready, for a small fee, to marry all persons at all hours there, or to go when sent for to perform the ceremony in taverns or in brothels. The public attention had been particularly drawn to the subject by a case of very flagrant oppression which had appeared on the hearing of an appeal before the House of Lords, and the Judges were ordered to prepare a bill to remedy the evils complained of. Their bill did not please the Chancellor, who himself undertook the task with great earnestness. His own performance did not deserve applause. He declared null all marriages which were not celebrated by a priest in orders, either under banns or license, declaring in the case of minors the license void without the consent of parents or guardians—the banns to be for three successive Sundays in the parish church—and the granting of ordinary and special licenses to be subject to certain regulations—the ceremony to be performed by a priest according to the liturgy of the Church of England. The first great blot upon the measure was, that it required Roman Catholics, Dissenters, and others who might have serious scruples of conscience against being married according to the prescribed service (the least felicitous in the English liturgy) to submit to it,—or debarred them from matrimony altogether. Another serious defect was, that no provision was made by it respecting the marriage out of England of persons domiciled in England, so as to prevent the easy evasion of it by a trip to Gretna Green. The measure was likewise highly objectionable in making no provision for the marriage of illegitimate children—who had no parents recognized by law, and could only have guardians by an application to the Court of Chancery,—and in declaring marriages which were irregular by reason of unintentional mistakes in banns or licenses absolutely void, although the parties might live long together as man and wife, having a numerous issue considered legitimate until the discovery of the irregularity.

Lord Hardwicke laid the bill on the table, and explained its provisions at the commencement of the session. On the second reading, the Duke of Bedford made a speech against it; but it passed easily through the Lords. In the Commons, however, it experienced the most furious opposition, particularly from Henry Fox, who was supposed to feel very deeply on the subject, because he himself had run off with Lady Caroline Lennox, eldest daughter of the Duke of Richmond, and married her without the consent of her family.

I can not compliment him, or the other opposers of the bill, on the topics they employed. Instead of pointing out its real defects, which in practice were found oppressive and mischievous, they absurdly denied the right of Parliament to legislate upon the subject; they dwelt upon the aristocratic tendency of the bill; they denounced it as leading to vice and immorality; they prophesied that it would thin our population, and endanger our existence as a nation. Fox, who kept the bill in committee many nights, became so heated by his own opposition to it against Murray, the Solicitor General, and other lawyers who defended it, that he inveighed bitterly against all lawyers and their jargon. He even indulged in a personal attack upon its author, whom he designated "the great MUFTI," whom he accused of pride and arrogance, and whose motives in bringing it forward he described as selfish and sordid.[1] On a subsequent evening he made an

[1] I suppose it was from this vituperation that the vulgar said out of doors that the Chancellor was afraid his own children would form some low connection in marriage—whereas they were all already married in the first families.

apology for these expressions, and declared his high respect for the learning and integrity of the noble and learned Lord he was supposed to have alluded to.

The bill at last passed the Commons by a majority of 125 to 56, and was sent back to the Lords. When the amendments were to be considered, the MUFTI resolved to have his revenge; and as the parliament was to be prorogued the following day, he knew that he was safe from a rejoinder. In a most unusual manner, he read his observations from a paper which he held in his hand, as if he were afraid to trust himself to express his excited feelings; and he commented, with much warmth and asperity, on the conduct of Fox, whom he designated as "a dark, gloomy, and insidious genius, an engine of personality and faction;"—thus concluding his philippic: "I despise the invective, and I despise the retraction; I despise the scurrility, and I despise the adulation."[1] Fox, who had that evening attended some ladies to Vauxhall, being soon told by a good natured friend how he had been abused in the House of Lords, gathered some young members of parliament round him, and told them, with great eagerness, that he wished the session had lasted a little longer, as, in that case, "he would have paid off the Lord Chancellor with interest."[2]

About this time Lord Hardwicke was elected High Steward of the University of Cambridge. In his address to the Vice-Chancellor and Senate on this occasion, he said, "Though I had not the happiness to receive my education among you, yet my high sense of and value for this university have manifestly appeared by committing so many of my sons to your care."[3]

[1] According to Cooksey, in the warmth of his invective he called his antagonist "that bad, black man."—*Cooks. 103.*

[2] 15 St. Tr. 84-86. It is curious how this hatred of Lord Hardwicke's Marriage Bill descended to Henry Fox's posterity. His son, the celebrated Charles James, several times abused it in the House of Commons; and I myself have frequently heard his grandson, the late Lord Holland, in private, express high disapprobation of it—still adhering to the old doctrine, that marriage should be contracted when, and where, and how the parties please—and therefore still censuring the last Marriage Bill, which I had the honor to assist in framing, and which I consider quite perfect. I excuse a churchman who says that the Church alone ought to lay down regulations for marriages, and judge of their validity; but I can not understand how a statesman who allows it to be a civil contract can deny that the manner of entering into it may be regulated by law as much as the manner of entering into a contract to purchase goods or to let land. [3] 15th June, 1753.

The session of 1754 passed over without a single debate in the House of Lords: but, in the midst of the profoundest quiet, a storm of short duration was suddenly raised by the death of the prime minister, Mr. Pelham. Till his brother could decently appear, Lord Hardwicke was called into Council by the King, and, according to his own account, he was for some days prime minister. A letter which he then wrote to Archbishop Herring shows that the arrangement was left entirely to him, "so that he did not recommend any person who had flown in the King's face" (meaning Mr. Fox); and discloses his intrigues with the leaders of different parties.[1] Soon after, he wrote an interesting account of this crisis to Mr. Pitt. After apologizing for not sooner replying to a communication he had received from that statesman, he proceeds:—

"Besides this, I have lived in such continual hurry ever since the day of our great misfortune, Mr. Pelham's death,—

——Ille dies, quem semper acerbum,
Semper honoratum (sic Dii voluistis) habebo,

that I have no time for correspondence.

"The general confusion called upon somebody to step forth; and the Duke of Newcastle's overwhelming affliction and necessary confinement threw it upon me. I was a kind of minister *ab aratro*, I mean the Chancery plow, and am not displeased to be returned to it, laborious as it is to hold. I never saw the King under such deep concern since the Queen's death. His Majesty seemed to be unresolved; professed to have no favorite for the important employment vacant, and declared that he would be advised by his cabinet council, with the *Duke of Devonshire added to them.*"[2]

[1] March 14, 1754.
[2] The writer proceeds at great length to try to persuade Mr. Pitt that he had been laboring to bring him into office; and having stated the opposing difficulties, he thus concludes:—"I agree that this falls short of the mark, but it gives encouragement. It is more than a *color for acquiescence* in the eyes of the world; it is a demonstration of fact. No ground arises from hence to think of *retirement rather than of courts and business*. We have all of us our hours wherein we wish for those *otia tuta;* and I have mine frequently; but I have that opinion of your wisdom, of your concern for the public, of your regard and affection for your friends, that I will not suffer myself to doubt that you will continue to take an active part. There never was a fairer field in the House of Commons for such abilities, and I flatter myself that the

In a few days the Duke of Newcastle was placed at the head of the Treasury, and Lord Hardwicke was again secure in his office of Chancellor, and, if possible with more influence.

Now he was created Earl of Hardwicke and Viscount Royston.[1] It is said that he might sooner have enjoyed this elevation, as far as the King was concerned, had not a superior power interposed. One of his biographers, in giving an account of his two daughters and of his wife, thus explains the delay:—

"Both these young ladies my informer has often seen at Powis House (his town residence) opening the door of their mother's apartment (where he had the honor of attending her during the settling her domestic accounts, on Monday mornings), and, with the most graceful deference, asking what company was expected, and in what manner they should dress for the day? Having received her Ladyship's directions, they courtesied and withdrew. On this she observed, that the Lord Chancellor was in a hurry to be made an Earl, which the King would make him any day he chose it, but I delay it as much as I can. These girls you see submitting, with so much humility and observance, to consult me even in the little article of dress, would perhaps, by the acquisition of titles, be transformed into fine ladies, and abate in their respects to me. Their fortune, too, on marriage must be doubled. Ten thousand pounds, which would be deemed a sufficient fortune for a Miss Yorke, must be made twenty to a Lady Elizabeth and Lady Margaret."[2]

These young ladies had been recently married, the one to the celebrated navigator, Lord Anson, and the other to Sir Gilbert Heathcote.

In the year 1755 the political horizon began to blacken. Domestic politics were much perplexed by the machinations of Leicester House, and by the Duke of Newcastle's

---

execution of them will complete what is now left imperfect."—*Lord Hardwicke to Mr. Pitt, 2nd April, 1754.*

[1] A rumor being spread that he had selected the title of Earl of Clarendon, then dormant, Lady Charlotte Hyde, descended from the great Lord Chancellor Clarendon, remonstrated with him, and received from him an answer, in which he said—" Permit me to assure you that there is not one syllable of truth in the story of the title which they have forged for me, and that your Ladyship might have been excused for taking so much pains to dissuade me from a thing which never entered into my thoughts."   [2] Cooksey, 38.

doubts whether he should ally himself with Pitt or with Fox; while hostilities being ready to break out on the Continent, the King, for the protection of Hanover, had entered into subsidiary treaties with Russia and Hesse Cassel, which were exceedingly unpopular. On the meeting of parliament these treaties were furiously assailed in the House of Lords, and the defense of them rested chiefly on the Chancellor; for the new Prime Minister, although he had considerable volubility of gabble, was quite incapable of reasoning, and was only listened to that he might be laughed at. There is no tolerable report of Lord Hardwicke's speech on this occasion, but we have what must be considered more curious and more valuable—the notes which he made for it, in his own handwriting, showing the immense pains which he still took to prepare himself, notwithstanding all his experience and all the authority which he possessed.[1]

The last speech which Lord Hardwicke ever delivered in the House of Peers, as Chancellor, was at the close of the session of 1756, when the disagreeable task was assigned to him of throwing out the Militia Bill. Hostilities with France had now commenced: the Duke of Richelieu had sailed on his expedition against Minorca; serious apprehensions were entertained of invasion; some German mercenaries were in English pay; there was still a strong prejudice in the country against any considerable increase of the regular army; and the rage was for a national militia, in which all should be liable to serve for a limited period, which should be officered by country gentlemen, and which should not be sent out of the kingdom. A bill for establishing such a force, being introduced into the Commons and supported by Pitt, was so popular that the Government did not venture to oppose it there; but it was highly disagreeable to George II., as he thought it would interfere with his plan for hiring some additional Hanoverian regiments,—and the Duke of Newcastle was in too tottering a state to venture to thwart the King's wishes. The bill was therefore doomed to meet its fate in the Upper House. When it had been ably supported by Earl Stanhope and the Duke of Bedford, the Lord Chancellor left the woolsack, and delivered a very ingenious pleading against it, of which we have a

[1] See 15 Parl. Hist. 643.

full report corrected and circulated by himself. He first tried to show that the bill was unconstitutional, and dangerous to the just prerogatives of the Crown; comparing it with the Militia Bill proposed, and at last carried without the royal assent, in the Long Parliament. "The scale of power," said he, "in this government has long been growing heavier on the democratical side. I think that this would throw a great deal of weight into it. What I contend for is, to preserve the limited monarchy entire, and nothing can do that but to preserve the counterpoise." He next attached very undue weight to the omission of a clause to take away a writ of *certiorari*, to remove into the King's Bench proceedings against persons employed in the militia, whereby "the Judges of that Court would be made inspectors-general of this army." But he afterwards boldly and forcibly contended that it was much better that a state should be defended by a certain portion of the population, who should permanently take to arms as a profession, than that all the citizens in rotation should embrace a military life. "For my own part," said he, "I never was more convinced of any proposition than of this,—that a nation of merchants, manufacturers, artisans, and husbandmen, defended by an army, is vastly preferable to a nation of soldiers. It is a self-evident proposition, that being educated and trained to arms must give a distaste for all civil occupations. Among the common people it introduces a love of idleness, of sports, and at last of plunder. Consider, my Lords, the case of the northern parts of Scotland, and what you have been doing there for several years past. The practice and habit of arms made that people idle, averse to the labors of agriculture as well as the confinement of a factory,—followers of sports,—next of thieving,—and last, of rebellion, as a *more extensive source of plunder*. I say a *more extensive source of plunder*, because I have always been of opinion that the love of thieving and rapine has been one main ingredient in the Highland insurrections as well as Jacobitism and clanship. In order to cure this mischief, and to lead or compel them to be industrous, you have been obliged to disarm them by law. After having pursued these maxims, of which you are beginning to feel the benefit, will your Lordships now, by a new law, endeavor to introduce the same disposition and habit into the common people of England, hitherto remarkable for their love of industry and their love of order."[1] He likewise very strenuously opposed a clause in the bill, which, though petitioned against by the Dissenters, had passed without disapprobation from the Established clergy, enacting, after the example of Switzerland and other Protestant states on the Continent, that the militia should be exercised on Sundays after divine service. "If this institution," said he, "be established among us by a law, I will venture to foretell that, notwithstanding the injunction to go to church, there will be a constant fair and scene of jollity in the several parishes where those exercises are kept, and the face of religion will soon be abolished in this country."

The bill was rejected by a majority of 59 to 23, but its rejection materially contributed to the overthrow of the administration,—now at hand.

Parliament being prorogued in a few days, Newcastle tried to strengthen himself by fresh negotiations with borough proprietors and with popular leaders, but news arrived of the retreat of Admiral Byng without an effort to relieve Port St. Philip's, and of the entire loss of Minorca. The nation was in a greater ferment than at the time of the Excise Bill. Not without reason, the loss and disgrace so deplored were ascribed to the inefficiency of the present head of the government; and although he was strong in numbers in the House of Commons, and could do what he chose in the House of Lords, no one would join him.[2]

The immediate cause of the change of ministry was the sudden death of Sir Dudley Ryder, Lord Chief Justice of

[1] 15 Parl. Hist. 706-769.
[2] When the defects of the Reform Bill are considered, the working of the old system should not be forgotten,—a striking instance of which is, that it imposed upon the King and the nation for several years, as prime minister, the Duke of Newcastle, a man disliked and despised by both. I suppose this was the weakest administration that ever was intrusted with power in a free country. Lord Hardwicke was the only man of any capacity for business in the cabinet; and, after all, he was more of a lawyer than a statesman. Lord Waldegrave gives us a lively picture of one of their deliberations, when the subject was what orders should be sent out to Admiral Hawke:—"The Chancellor had more courage than the Duke of Newcastle; but, agreeable to the common practice of the law, was against bringing the cause to an immediate decision."—*Lord Waldegrave's Mem.* p. 46.

the Court of King's Bench. Pitt was at this time in hot opposition, and, with such a theme as the disgrace of our flag, was ready on the meeting of parliament actually to crush the trembling Premier. The only person in the House of Commons who "had courage even to look him in the face,"[1] was Murray, the Attorney General, who, indeed, had fought many a stout battle with him, and who, if so inclined, might still have entered the lists against him as the champion of the Government, but who now peremptorily insisted on his right to the vacant chiefship. He was not only, after Pitt, the best speaker in the House of Commons, but he was decidedly the greatest lawyer at the English bar; he had served many years as a law officer of the Crown, with the highest distinction, and, having gallantly and faithfully exerted himself in the conflict while there was a chance of victory, now that a general defeat was inevitable, he considered that he might honorably act upon the principle "*sauve qui peut.*" Newcastle, eager to retain him in the House of Commons, as a forlorn hope, plied him with various proposals,—a Tellership of the Exchequer, or the Duchy of Lancaster for life, or a pension of £2,000 a year for life, in addition to the profits of his office as Attorney General. Nay, the bidding rose to £6,000 a year of pension: but Murray was inexorable; nor would he, even on any terms, agree to remain in the House of Commons, only one session longer, or one month, or one day to support the address. He declared, in plain terms, that if they did not choose to make him Lord Chief Justice he was determined to resign the office of Attorney General, and that they must fight their own battles in the House of Commons, as he never again would enter that assembly. This spirited conduct had its proper effect; he was made Chief Justice, and a Peer, by the title of Baron Mansfield. On the day when he took his seat in the Court of King's Bench, the Duke of Newcastle, not daring to face parliament, resigned.

Lord Hardwicke, who had prompted him in all his negotiations,[2] finding that they had all failed, expressed a

[1] Lord Waldegrave's Mem. p. 82.
[2] "My Lord Chancellor, with whom I do everything, and without whom I do nothing, has had a most material hand in all these arrangements. He sees and knows the truth of what I write; and he judges as I do, that no other method but this could have been followed with any prospect of success."—*Duke of Newcastle to Mr. Pitt*, 2nd April, 1754. Lord Waldegrave

resolution to share his fate, and publicly intimated that he only retained the Great Seal for a few days to enable him to dispose of some causes which he had heard argued in the Court of Chancery. He was strongly urgued to continue Chancellor, with a view to strengthen the feeble administration now forming under that very honorable— not very able—man, the fourth Duke of Devonshire; but he peremptorily refused. It is generally said that, from age, and apprehended decline of faculties, he was anxious to retire. There is not the smallest foundation for this statement. His health and strength remained unimpaired, and his mind was as active, his perception as quick, and his judgment as sound, as when he served under Walpole;[1] and although his fortune was now enormous, his passion for increasing it, by all lawful means, had grown in the same proportion. Others say (and they may be right) that he did not consider it honorable to continue in office after his great patron and friend had been obliged to resign; but the new ministry was still a Whig one, and no material change of policy was announced, either domestic or foreign, although the men now coming in had clamored for the "Militia Bill," and against the employment of Hanoverian troops. He more probably resigned because he knew that the ministry was very weak, and must be short lived—perhaps anticipating that Newcastle, from his genius as a place-hunter, though contemptible in every thing else, might soon extricate himself from his present difficulties, and that they might return to office together, with a fair prospect of being able

gives a curious account of Lord Hardwicke's demeanor; when, as one expedient for strengthening the government, it was proposed to bring in Lord Bute, then supposed to be not only the leader of Leicester House, but the lover of the Princess of Wales:—"The Chancellor, with his usual gravity, declared that for his own part he had no particular objection to the Earl of Bute's promotion; neither would he give credit to some very extraordinary reports; but that many sober and respectable persons would think it indecent, for which reason he could never advise his Majesty to give his consent."—*Lord Waldegrave*, 67.

[1] One is surprised to find such nonsense written by so clever a man as Jeremy Bentham: "At length perceiving, or imagining he perceived, his faculties growing rather impaired, he thought proper to resign the Seals, and accordingly waited upon the King, and delivered them into his Majesty's own hands," as if his resignation had been wholly unconnected with any political crisis. "Dreading the loud cry of the people for impeachments and inquiries," writes another, "into the authors of those counsels which had brought the nation into such a calamitous and desperate situation, he wisely

to carry on the government.¹ Whatever his reasoning or his motives might be,—at a Council held at St. James's on the 19th of November, 1756, he actually did resign the Great Seal into the hands of the King, who received it from him with many expressions of respect and regret. After noticing the event in his Diary, he adds,—

"Jam mihi parta quies, omnisque in limine portus."

But I suspect that his own mind dwelt more upon the preceding line,—

"Frangimur heu fatis, inquit, ferimurque procella."

CHAPTER CXXXVI.

CONTINUATION OF THE LIFE OF LORD HARDWICKE TILL THE DEATH OF GEORGE II.

LORD HARDWICKE, after his resignation, continued to possess in a high degree the respect of all classes and of all parties. Lord Waldegrave, rather disposed to depreciate him, says that "he resigned the Great Seal much to the regret of all dispassionate men, and indeed of the whole nation. He had been Chancellor near twenty years, and was inferior to few who had gone before him, having executed that high office with integrity, diligence, and uncommon abilites. The statesman might, perhaps, in some particular be the re-

shrunk from the storm he thought he saw bursting on his head, and in 1756 resigned the Seals."—*Cooksey, 81.* Historians and biographers make sad mistakes when they begin to assign motives—which, however, they often do as peremptorily as if they had lived in familiar confidence with those whose actions they narrate.

¹ The following letter shows that the Duke most earnestly urged his resignation, and was under great apprehensions that he might remain in office:—

"Newcastle House, Nov. 2, 1756.

"My dearest, dearest Lord,—You know—you see—how cruelly I an treated, and indeed persecuted, by all those who now surround the King The only comfort I have is in the continuance of your Lordship's most cordial friendship and good opinion. The great and honorable part which you are resolved to take will be my honor, glory, and security, and upon which I can and do singly rely. I despise testimonies from others, who, for their own sakes as well as mine, I should desire not to give any of that kind at this time. But, my dearest Lord, it would hurt me extremely if yours should be long delayed. I submit the particular time entirely to you—grateful for it whenever it shall happen."

verse of the judge; yet even in that capacity he had been the chief support of the Duke of Newcastle's administration."[1]

He had no retired allowance, but, besides his own immense fortune, not only his sons, but all his kith, kin, and dependents, were saturated with places, pensions, and reversions. If he had been required to sacrifice the patronage which enabled him to confer such appanages upon them, he would have looked with contempt upon the retired allowance of a modern Chancellor.

It is a curious fact, that—although George II. had taken leave of him very tenderly, and had pressed him to come frequently to Court—when he presented himself a few days after at the levee, in a plain suit of black velvet with a bag and sword, he was allowed to make his bow in the crowd without the slightest mark of royal recognition. But as he was retreating, surprised and mortified, he was called back by the lord in waiting: the King apologized for not having known him when he first appeared without his full bottom, his robes, and the purse with the Great Seal in his hand, and renewed to him the assurance that his great services to the Crown were well known and remembered.[2]

His conduct as an ex-Chancellor deserves commendation. He now resided more than he had formerly been permitted to do at Wimpole, but, instead of torpidly wasting his days there, he tried to find pleasure in literature; he took a lively interest in public affairs, and he carried on a frequent correspondence with his political friends. Always when parliament was sitting, and at other times when his presence in London could be serviceable to his party or the public, he was to be found at his town house in Grosvenor Square. He attended as sedu-

[1] Lord Wald. Mem. 1756, p. 84.
[2] Cooksey's Memoirs. Another account says, Lord Hardwicke was much diverted with the King's looking at him the first time he went to the levee after giving up the Seal, and knowing him no more in a common coat, and without the Chancellor's wig, than if he had never seen him. The lord in waiting, observing this, told his Majesty Lord Hardwicke was there; but this was a name the King did not know the sound of, and it only brought out the usual cold question, "How long has your Lordship been in town?"—*Miss Catherine Talbot's Correspondence.*

Had he worn such a uniform as that invented by George IV. for ex-Chancellors (very much like a Field Marshal's), he could not have been mistaken for a common man.

lously as ever to the judicial business of the House of Lords, where the judgments were moved and dictated by himself, his successor not being a Peer, and being sometimes obliged to put the question for reversing his own decrees without being at liberty to say a word in their defense. Lord Hardwicke also diligently attended at the Council Board when juridical cases came before that tribunal. Although the common opinion is that he considered himself as having bid a final adieu to office, I can not but suspect that he contemplated the chance of his being again Chancellor, and that with this view he was anxious to keep himself before the public, and from time to time to burnish up his legal armor.

The first occasion of his taking any open part in politics after his resignation, was respecting the condemnation of Admiral Byng. A bill had passed the House of Commons to release the members of the court-martial, who had sentenced him to death, from their oath of secrecy, so that they might disclose the consultations which took place among themselves when deliberating upon his sentence.[1] In the House of Lords its fate depended entirely upon Lord Hardwicke, and he opposed it. For its rejection he was very severely blamed, and a cry was raised that "he wished Admiral Byng to be shot to screen the late administration,"—the multitude being misled by the unfeeling words blurted out by the Duke of Newcastle, when a deputation waited upon him from the City, complaining that Minorca had been abandoned: "It is the fault of the Admiral; he shall be tried immediately, he shall be hanged directly." The sentence of death upon Byng was erroneous,—the Court, acquitting him of treachery and cowardice, having only found that "he had not done his utmost to relieve St. Philip's Castle, or to defeat the French fleet, *from mistake of judgment;*" and the Government was highly to be censured for carrying it into effect,—particularly after the unanimous recommendation to mercy from the members of the court-martial. Nevertheless, I think that the bill rested on no principle, and that Lord Hardwicke would

---

[1] No one contended that Parliament, like the Pope, might dispense with oaths. The statute for the discipline of the navy required the members of naval courts-martial to take an oath "not to disclose or discover the vote or opinion of any particular member *unless thereunto required by act of parliament.*"

have been liable to severe censure if he had assisted in establishing a dangerous precedent by sanctioning it. In the course he took, he was warmly supported by Lord Mansfield, who now began to show the rare example of a lawyer having great success in both Houses of Parliament, and who was destined to contest the palm of eloquence with the Earl of Chatham, as he had done with Mr. W. Pitt. They treated the subject with judicial accuracy and precision, showing that criminal justice could not be administered satisfactorily by any tribunal in the world if there were to be a public disclosure of the reasonings and observations of those who are to pronounce the verdict or judgment while they are consulting together. They therefore framed two questions to be put to the members of the court-martial, all of whom were examined at the bar while the bill was pending. 1. "Do you know any matter that passed previous to the sentence upon Admiral Byng, which may show that sentence to have been unjust?" 2. "Do you know any matter that passed previous to the said sentence which may show that sentence to have been given through any undue practice or motive?" All (including Captain Keppel, at whose request the bill had been introduced) answered both questions in the negative. Lord Hardwicke then animadverted in a tone of the highest scorn upon the haste and heedlessness with which the bill had passed in the House of Commons, and on his motion it was rejected without a division.[1]

As every one had foreseen, the administration formed in the autumn of 1756 soon crumbled to pieces; and, after the dismissal of Pitt and Lord Temple, for nearly three months the country was without a government, although a foreign war was raging, and dangerous discontent began to be engendered among the people. But, in the midst of disgrace and despondency, the nation was on the point of seeing the most glorious period of its annals; for now, instead of a single victory in a European campaign, the flag of England was to ride triumphant on

[1] 15 Parl. Hist. 803–822; Hor. Walp. Mem. Geo. II., vol. ii. 687. The House of Lords, in this instance, instead of forbidding the publication of their proceedings, themselves very wisely made an order " that all the proceedings on the bill, with the evidence of the witnesses, should be printed and published under the authority of the House."—*Lords' Journ. 1757.*

every sea, and territories to which the island of Great Britain was a mere speck on the globe were to be added to her dominion. This state of things was brought about by a coalition between the greatest and the meanest of statesmen, Pitt and the Duke of Newcastle, which was arranged chiefly under the auspices of Lord Hardwicke.[1] The first personal interview was brought about by the following letter from him to Mr. Pitt :—

"Wednesday, May 25, 1757.

"Sir,

"I have seen the Duke of Newcastle this morning, who is extremely willing, and desirous to have a conference with you, and thinks it may be most useful to have a meeting first with yourself, before that which he will also be proud of having with my Lord Bute. He therefore proposes that his Grace and you should meet this evening at Lord Royston's, in St. James's Square, where I may attend you. The family is out of town. and that place will be better than any of our houses, and you (if you approve it) may come so far in your chair without hazard. I should think between eight and nine o'clock would be a proper time, unless you have any objection to it—and then any other hour you shall name.—I beg you will send me notice to Powis House as soon as you can."

In a subsequent stage of the negotiation we find that, while Leicester House was still a party to it, Lord Hardwicke thus addressed Mr. Pitt:—

"Powis House, 16th June, 1757.

"Sir,

"I am to desire, in the Duke of Newcastle's name as well as my own, that we may have the honor of meeting you and my Lord Bute at your house, this evening, a little before nine. I have in like manner sent notice to Lord Bute. I found the Duke of Newcastle pleased, in the highest degree, with your visit and conversation this forenoon."

The great difficulty in the way of a satisfactory settlement was the disposal of the Great Seal. The Duke of Newcastle was naturally eager to see Lord Hardwicke again Chancellor, that he might have his powerful support in that office ; and Lord Hardwicke himself, professing to

[1] Lord Mansfield had previously tried his hand at mediating between the parties, but in vain.

be tired of public life, would not have been unwilling to resume his labors, with the prospect now opening of a powerful government. They felt their way by at first proposing that he should have a seat in the cabinet, but conditions were annexed even to this concession, which showed the main object to be utterly impracticable. The fact was, that "the Great Commoner" and the ex-Premier, in the midst of much politeness and courtesy, thoroughly knew each other. The former determined to have all the power in his own hands, that he might pursue unchecked his vast plans for the nation's pre-eminence and glory:—while he was willing to throw to others all jobbing patronage, he could not bear the thought of seeing in high office a man of character and weight, who, from ancient associations, would be disposed to stand by the sordid and meddling Duke. Lord Hardwicke behaved exceedingly well upon this occasion. He did not allow his disappointment to be known to the world, and although he plainly saw that he could gain nothing for himself,—out of regard to his old patron, and (let us believe) out of regard to his country, then in imminent peril, he exerted himself to smooth away all difficulties. On the 22nd of June thus he writes to Mr. Pitt:—

"Since I had the honor of seeing you last, I have talked, by way of sounding, in the best manner I could, to all the three persons who can now come under consideration in the disposition of the Great Seal. I think I see clearly the way of thinking and inclination of them all, which differs very little from the conjectures which we had formed concerning them. It is now so late, that, if I should have any chance of finding you at home, I should only put you in danger of being out of time for the levee. . . . I am very desirous that we should meet this evening, for precious moments are lost, and not innocently wasted, but to the detriment of that great and useful system which we are laboring to establish. I am most sincere and zealous in my endeavors to bring about what you so much wish for, a present arrangement of the Great Seal; but I see vast difficulties attending it."

Willes, the Chief Justice of the Common Pleas, and now First Commissioner of the Great Seal,—a good lawyer, and no politician,—was expected for some time to be the successful candidate, but he haggled for a peerage, to which the King would not consent. A charge of treachery towards Willes in this affair has been brought against Lord Hardwicke, but it is not supported by any evidence, nor, as he had given up all thoughts of the Great Seal himself, by any probability.[1] At last Pitt fixed upon a man who could not be formidable to him, who was ready to accept the office on very moderate terms, and who might be expected to perform decently well its judicial duties,—Sir Robert Henley, the Attorney General,—and urged that his appointment was a stipulation that had been made by Leicester House to reward a man who had long and faithfully adhered to that party.

The following letter from Lord Hardwicke to Mr. Pitt throws great light on these intrigues:—

"Powis House, June 25, 1757, Saturday night.

"Dear Sir,

"However improper for a private man, yet *majora effugiens opprobria culpæ*, I did, in compliance with your commands, and those of our other friends who met on Thursday night, attend the King to-day, in order to know if he had any orders for me relating to the disposition of the Great Seal. I found his Majesty very grave and thoughtful on the news which came last night,[2] but calm. He soon entered into the matter; and it is unnecessary, as well as hardly possible, to give you the detail of my audience in writing. His Majesty expressed his desire to settle his administration on the plan fixed, but thought there was no necessity of making a hasty disposition of so important an office as the Great Seal an immediate part of it. However, the result was, that he absolutely refused to give a peerage with it,[3] which, I think, puts my Lord Chief Justice Willes out of the case; for his Lordship not only told me before, but has since repeated, that peerage is with him a condition *sine qua non*. I see the King inclines more to Mr. Attorney General; and when I stated to his Majesty what I collected or conjectured to be his views, he hearkened, and at last bade me talk to Sir Robert Henley, reduce his terms as low as I could, and bring them to him in writing, on Monday.

---

[1] See Cooksey, 82; and Life of Lord Northington, *post*.
[2] Defeat of the King of Prussia at Kolin.
[3] I suspect that Lord Hardwicke did not much combat this resolution, still wishing to have no more law lords in the House.

"Since I saw my Lord Chief Justice Willes, I have seen Sir Robert Henley, who talks very reasonably and honorably. His proposals are: First, a reversionary grant of the office of one of the tellers of the Exchequer to his son for life; second, a pension of £1,500 per annum on the Irish establishment to himself for life, to commence and become payable upon his being removed from the office of Lord Keeper, and not before, but to be determinable and absolutely void upon the office of teller coming into possession to his son. My present opinion is, that the King may be induced to agree to this on Monday: for when I hinted in my discourse at a pension upon Ireland, though his Majesty treated it pretty severely at first, yet when I stated the several contingencies in which it might in this case never become any real charge upon the revenue, he said of himself, that made the case different.

"I found to-night by my Lord Chief Justice Willes, that he is to go to Kensington on Monday, to get some warrants signed, and thinks that either the King may speak to him, or that he may say something to his Majesty on this subject; but I am persuaded that will have no effect, unless he gives up the peerage, which I am of opinion he never will.

"If the affair of the Great Seal should be settled on Monday, in the person of Sir Robert Henley, as I conjecture it will, I see nothing that can distrust your beginning to kiss hands on Tuesday. For God's sake, Sir, accelerate that, and don't let any minutiæ stand in the way of so great and necessary a work. I long to see this scheme executed for the King's honor and repose, the harmony of his royal family, and the stability of his government. I have labored in it zealously and disinterestedly, though without any pretense to such a degree of merit as your politeness and partiality ascribes to me. I see, with you, that attempts are flying about to tarnish it; but if it is forthwith executed on this foot, those will all be dissipated in the region of vanity, and, instead of a *mutilated, enfeebled, half-formed* system, I am persuaded it will come out a complete, strong, and well cemented one, to which your wisdom, temper, and perfect union with the Duke of Newcastle will give durableness. In all events, I shall ever retain the most lively impressions of

your great candor and obliging behavior towards me, and continue to be with the utmost respect,
"Dear Sir,
"Your most obedient and
"Most humble Servant,
"HARDWICKE."

From the same quarter conciliatory advice was likewise given to the Duke of Newcastle,—and Mr. Pitt's famous administration was formed, which carried so high the renown of the English name, but in which I can not boast that the lawyers played any very distinguished part. Lord Hardwicke had nominally a seat in the cabinet, but he seems to have been very little consulted by the autocratic Prime Minister.

Though now without the chance of office except through some very remote contingency, he still attended regularly in the House of Lords.[1] All opposition ceasing, insomuch that, for a whole session together, there was not a single division and hardly a debate, the hearing of appeals and writs of error was his chief labor.

Occasionally he was called upon to deliver his opinion upon measures concerning the administration of justice. In the session of 1758 there were various discussions, in which he took the principal share, upon a bill to amend the Habeas Corpus Act, by authorizing a single judge in all cases to issue a writ of *habeas corpus* in vacation, and by allowing the truth of the return to be controverted by affidavit. Conceding the defective state of the law, he opposed the bill as ill-framed, and, on his motion, certain questions were referred to the Judges, with instructions to prepare another bill to be submitted to the House at the commencement of the following session of parliament.[2] I am sorry to say that, when the next session arrived, nothing was thought of except the taking of Quebec, and the subject was not again resumed till the very close of the reign of George III., when Sergeant Onslow's Act passed, most materially advancing the remedy by Habeas Corpus for the protection of personal liberty,—the great glory of English jurisprudence.[3]

---

[1] As soon as Lord Hardwicke resigned the Great Seal, a commission appointed Lord Sandys Speaker of the House of Lords; and he acted in this capacity from 2nd December, 1756, till 4th July, 1757, when Sir Robert Henley took his place on the woolsack as Lord Keeper.—*Lords' Journals.*
[1] 15 St. Tr. 897–923.   [2] Stat. 56 Geo. 3, c. 100.

In praising Lord Hardwicke as an ex-Chancellor a deduction should be made in respect of his having done so little to improve the laws and institutions of the country, when he had abundant leisure to prepare measures for this purpose, and, one would have supposed, sufficient influence to carry them through. From his long experience at the bar and as a Judge in courts of law and equity, many points must have presented themselves to him, wanting "the amending hand." His own emoluments no longer in any degree depended upon the continuation of abuses, and he might surely have discovered some which might have been corrected without materially affecting the offices and reversions held by his family. Yet he suffered six years of health and mental vigor, allotted to him after his resignation, to pass away unmarked by a single attempt to extend his fame as a legislator. It is possible that he could get no one to second him effectually, and that if he carried very useful bills through the House of which he was a member, they would have been neglected or thrown out "elsewhere."[1] For several sessions, parliament only met to vote thanks and supplies; and the whole of the proceedings of the two Houses as reported, from the King's opening to his proroguing speech, would not fill more than a few columns of a modern newspaper.

I can find no further trace of Lord Hardwicke for the rest of this reign. During the warlike triumphs which now dazzled the nation, he seems almost completely to have sunk from public notice, and it was hardly known that he had a seat in the cabinet.[2] Indeed, unless when

---

[1] I can say, of my own knowledge, that this state of things has since actually existed. At different periods of our history, it has been very difficult to draw the notice of the representatives of the people to measures for the amendment of the law.

[2] He still continued to compose the royal speeches delivered at the commencement and close of every session of Parliament; but, judging from the two following letters on the taking of Quebec, there seems to have been very little familiarity between him and the "Great Commoner:"—

"Wimple, O:to^r 18, 1759.

"Dear Sir,—With the greatest pleasure I lay hold on this first opportunity to thank you for the honor of your very obliging note, which I received by yesterday's post.

"As a dutiful subject to my king, and a lover of my country, and a sincere friend to this administration, I do, upon the happy event of the conquest of Quebec, most cordially congratulate you in a particular manner. This important, and at the instant it came, unexpected success has crowned the

it happened that those who had favors to ask of the government were obliged to look to the Duke of Newcastle as the head of the Treasury, Mr. Pitt was regarded at home and abroad as the sole minister of the Crown. George II., though advanced in years, retained his health and his strength, and the existing state of affairs seemed likely to have a long continuance; but his sudden death brought about a party revolution, and soon placed all power in the hands of the Tories—who had been nearly banished from Court since the accession of the House of Brunswick.

campaign on the part of England in the most glorious manner. God grant that it may lead to what we all wish,—an honorable and lasting peace. The King has now great materials in his hands for this good work; and I make no doubt but his Majesty and his Ministers will make the wisest and most advantageous use of them.

"I have nothing to add but my best wishes for your health, and the sincerest assurances of that perfect respect and esteem with which I am,
"Dear Sir,
"Your most obedient and most humble Servant,
"HARDWICKE."

"My Lord,—I am too sensible to the honor of your Lordship's very obliging attention in answer to the short bulletin from my office, to defer expressing my best thanks for such a favor. The defeat of the French army, and the reduction of Quebec, are indeed matters for the warmest congratulations between all faithful servants of the King and lovers of their country. In the many and remote prosperities which have been given to His Majesty's arms, the hand of Providence is visible, and I devoutly wish that the hand of human wisdom and of sound policy may be conspicuous in the great work of negotiation, whenever this complicated and extensive war is to be wound up in an honorable and advantageous peace. Perhaps it is not too much to say, that sustaining this war, arduous as it has been and still is, may not be more difficult than properly and happily closing it. The materials in his Majesty's hands are certainly very many and great, and it is to be hoped that in working them up in the great edifice of a solid and general pacification of Europe, there may be no confusion of languages, but that the workmen may understand one another. Accepting my sincere wishes for your Lordship's health, and the assurances of the perfect respect and esteem with which I have the honor to remain

"Your Lordship's most obedient and most humble servant,
"W. PITT.

"May I here beg to present my best compliments to Lord Royston, if with your Lordship?
"Hayes, Octob' y* 20th, 1759."

CHAPTER CXXXVII.

CONCLUSION OF THE LIFE OF LORD HARDWICKE.

AS soon as Lord Hardwicke heard of the decease of George II., he hurried to Carlton House, where the new Sovereign was to hold his first council. Here he was resworn a privy councillor, and was treated with great consideration. When parliament was assembled, to him was still committed the task which he had performed ever since the Great Seal was first delivered to him, of preparing the speech from the throne. On the present occasion it was looked for with much anxiety. He drew it in a vague, commonplace style, making the young King lament the death of his grandfather, and express high regard for the civil and religious rights of his loving subjects. Now, for the first time, appeared alarming evidence of the influence of Lord Bute. He returned the draught of the speech with the following sentence, in the King's own handwriting, to be inserted in it:—" Born and educated in this country, I glory in the name of Briton ; and the particular happiness of my life will ever consist in promoting the welfare of a people whose loyalty and warm affection to me I consider as the greatest and most permanent security of my throne." The Duke of Newcastle, writing to inform Lord Hardwicke of the interpolation, said, " I make no observation, but this method of proceeding can't last. We must now (I suppose) submit. You will think '*Briton*' remarkable : it denotes the author to all the world." Lord Hardwicke was more seriously offended, and considered the favorite's words to be meant as an insult to the memory of the old King. But he was prevailed upon to acquiesce, and even to furnish this courtly response, which, he says, " I thought of upon my pillow :"—" We are penetrated with the condescending and endearing manner in which your Majesty has expressed your satisfaction in having received your birth and education among us. What a luster does it cast upon the name of '*Briton*' when you, Sir, are pleased to esteem it among your glories!" The ex-Chancellor was actually supposed to be intriguing for court favor, and his son, Colonel Yorke, wrote to a friend,—" Lord Hardwicke has been much caressed by the King, and continues to give his helping hand without place or pension."

When the King's union with the Princess Charlotte of Mecklenburg Strelitz approached, Lord Hardwicke wrote to his son, "I thought to have excused myself from the crowd on the Wedding night, but I fear I must be an old beau at that ceremony." He not only attended the ceremony, but presented himself at the crowded levee which was held at St. James's next day. Horace Walpole records the dialogue between George III., and his venerable minister on this occasion, which evinces how universally popular a topic of conversation, from the highest to the lowest, is the weather. *King:* "It is a very fine day, my Lord." *Lord Hardwicke:* "Yes, Sir, *and it was a very fine night.*"

A royal message being delivered, recommending that the Judges should not be removable on a demise of the Crown, Lord Hardwicke moved the address of thanks, and he delivered a very courtly speech, most extravagantly over-praising that measure, and creating the delusion which still prevails that till then the Judges held during pleasure. In truth, by the Act of Settlement,[1] their commissions were "*quamdiu se bene gesserint;*" and although, by a misconstruction of that act contrary to the maxim that "the King never dies," the appointment was held only during the natural life of the reigning sovereign, only one Judge was removed on the death of George I., not one on the death of George II., and no minister at any time coming would have ventured to remove a competent Judge on the commencement of a new reign. At any rate, this boon from his Majesty was entirely at the expense of his successor. Nevertheless, Lord Hardwicke represented the measure as of infinite importance to the

[1] 12 & 13 Will. 3, c. 2. The opinion of that great and upright magistrate, Sir Michael Foster, was clear, that after the Judges were required by the legislature to be appointed ' during good behavior," and it was provided that they should only be removable on the joint address of the two Houses of Parliament, they could not be removed on a demise of the Crown. "I think the last precedent was a precipitate proceeding against the plain scope and intent of the Act of Settlement, and derogatory to the honor, dignity, and constitutional independence of the Judges, and of the Crown itself. I found myself only on the Act of Settlement, and the reason of things."—Sir Michael Foster to Lord Chief Justice Wilmot.—*Life of Wilmot, 31.*

impartial administration of justice, and to the rights and liberties of the people. " For doing this," said he, " his Majesty has laid his reasons before you. They are such as might have become, as they are truly worthy, the most renowned legislators of antiquity." After praising our judicial system, subject to the capital defect that *quamdiu se bene gesserit* means " during the natural life of the King," he proceeds :—" *This*, which is the only defect remaining, his Majesty, voluntarily and of his mere motion, invites you to cure. Reflect upon the histories of former times—with what difficulties such acts have been obtained, I was going to say extorted, from the Crown by your ancestors—after many struggles—sometimes after more than one negative from the throne. Accept it now with thanks. Every one of your Lordships must feel that gratitude in your own breasts which I have imperfectly attempted to express in the address which I have now the honor to propose for your adoption."[1]

Lord Hardwicke continued steadily to support the government even after the resignation of Mr. Pitt, when, being overruled in the Cabinet respecting a declaration of war against Spain, that haughty minister refused " to be responsible for measures he was no longer allowed to guide." As a reward he had an offer of office, which he thus records in his Diary ;—" 16th November 1761. Lord Bute, by his Majesty's command, offered me the Privy Seal lately resigned by Earl Temple, but I declined it with great duty to the King, and strong professions of zeal for his service, wishing it might be disposed of in such manner as might best promote that service in this difficult and critical conjuncture. This his Majesty was pleased to acknowledge to me the same day in his closet as a very disinterested instance of my zeal for his service, and to enlarge much on his esteem for me, and his protection and favor to me and my family. The Privy Seal was given to the Duke of Bedford."

However, there was a growing coldness between Lord Bute and the Duke of Newcastle, and rumors were afloat

[1] 15 Parl. Hist. 1011, where will be seen the notes still extant in Lord Hardwicke's hand writing, which shows that he continued the practice of writing out his speeches, almost at full length before he delivered them.— With regard to this capital improvement, if he thought it of such importance, he might have explained why he did not himself propose it during the preceding reign.

that the ex-Chancellor was caballing to overthrow the government. Thus he wrote to his son, Lord Royston: "You may possibly have read in the newspapers of my having what is called an '*Opposition Dinner.*' There is no truth in it, for I had only half-a-dozen particular friends. After having been Attorney General ten years, Chief Justice between three and four years, and Chancellor almost twenty, I shall not now contradict all the principles and all the rules of law and order which I have been maintaining all my life."

Nevertheless, Lord Bute, impatient himself to be at the head of the Treasury, that he might have all patronage as well as power in his own hands, having resolved to force out the Duke of Newcastle, the ex-Chancellor suddenly saw things in a very different light, and declared that the policy of the new minister was about to tarnish and render unavailing all the victories won by his predecessor. This changed state of mind was produced by a letter from the Duke, giving an account of an interview with a favorite, in which his Grace had threatened, as he had often before *effectually* done, to resign unless some job were conceded to him, and in which, to his great mortification, he had been taken at his word. Thus piteously complained the ousted place-man to his confidant:—"He answered me dryly that, if I resigned, the peace might be retarded, but he never requested me to continue in office, nor said a civil thing to me afterwards while we remained together."[1] Newcastle felt so wretched out of place, that a few weeks after he opened a negotiation for his return, upon the basis that he should freely renounce the Treasury, and be contented with the Privy Seal—an office without patronage—so that, at the same time, his friend, the Earl of Hardwicke, might be made President of the Council. Such was his Borough interest that Lord Bute listened to the proposal, till, upon consulting with the Secretary to the Treasury, and examining the probable votes in both Houses, it was thought the approaching treaty of peace was sure to be approved of by large majorities. Being finally thrown aside, the Duke went headlong into opposition, took part with Mr. Pitt, caballed in the City, anticipated nothing but disgrace from the pend-

[1] Duke of Newcastle to Lord Hardwicke, May, 1762. Adolph. i. 69. The ostensible dispute was about continuing the subsidy to the King of Prussia.

ing negotiation with France, and resolved to storm the Treasury. Lord Hardwicke would not desert him, and, as far as was consistent with the decorum of his own character, vigorously assisted him in this enterprise.[1]

Parliament meeting on the 25th of November, the preliminary articles of peace, concluded at Fontainebleau on the 3rd of the same month, were laid before both Houses, and on the 9th of December were debated in the House of Lords.[2] After rhetorical orations from the mover and seconder of an address of thanks to his Majesty, Lord Bute spoke with much more than his usual ability, entering at length into the whole course of the negotiations for peace, dwelling upon the terms that had been offered by Mr. Pitt, and contending that those actually concluded were, under all the circumstances, as favorable, and ought to be considered satisfactory by the country. He was answered by Lord Hardwicke in a speech which, considering the difficulties of his situation, displays great talent and dexterity. The criticisms on the several articles have ceased to be interesting, the public, without minute inquiry, having acquiesced in the conclusion that the peace was not a bad one, although, if hostilities had been com-

[1] It is curious that, in writing to the Lord President of the Court of Session on the 12th June, 1763, he represents that he was turned out of the Cabinet, and he tries to mitigate his factiousness:—"As to myself, no great part could be taken from me, because I had none; but that seat which I had been permitted to retain in the King's Council I was excluded from just before the last session of parliament. Your Lordship has undoubtedly heard of me as an opposer. It is true that, in conjunction with several of your Lordship's and my old friends, I have opposed certain particular measures. When I have done so, it has been according to my judgment and conscience, with the greatest duty to the King, and a sincere zeal for his service and that of the public; and I am not ashamed of it."

[2] It may be amusing to present to the reader a specimen of the parliamentary reporting of that day. This debate in the Lords being one of the most important and interesting which ever took place in the House, the following is the fullest account of it published in any journal or periodical work:—"The preliminary articles being read, Lord Wycombe moved an address of thanks to his Majesty. Many objections were made and some severe reflections thrown out against the Earl of Bute, with appearances of heat and animosity. That nobleman defended his own conduct, with temper and decorum, in a well connected speech, delivered with great propriety, to the surprise of many, who did not think him so well qualified in the art of elocution. He gave a detail of the negotiation, and not only avowed himself a warm promoter of the peace, but even expressed a desire that his having contributed to the cessation of hostilities should be engraved on his tomb. He was seconded by the Earl of Halifax, and supported by a great majority."—*15 Parl. Hist. 1252.* Fortunately, we have a sketch of the debate in the handwriting of Lord Hardwicke, which I have made use of.

menced at the proper time against Spain, the House of Bourbon might have been more effectually humbled, and might have been disabled from taking part against us in our impending disputes with our colonies. I shall, therefore, give only a few extracts from his speech which touch on more general topics:—

"I was in hopes that, after so successful a war, and particularly the great advantages gained over the enemy during the present year, a plan of peace would have been produced which would have been satisfactory to all lovers of their country; but rashness and precipitation have marked the negotiation on our part: we have proclaimed that we would have peace at any price or sacrifice; our opponents were made aware that this object was necessary to the party now in power, and the result can only give pleasure to those who regret our victories and envy our greatness. There is one part of the address in which I can most heartily concur—the dutiful professions and assurances given to his Majesty—convinced, from the bottom of my heart, that no prince ever ascended the throne with more virtuous and public-spirited disposition, with greater love for his people and zeal for their happiness, with greater purity of mind and uprightness of heart, untainted even with a wish for any hurtful power, nay, filled with a detestation of it."

He was most successful in his complaint of the preliminary articles being laid before Parliament, that an opinion might be asked upon them; whereas, he contended that, according to precedent and constitutional propriety, the Crown ought to act upon the responsibility of its ministers till a definitive treaty of peace is concluded:—

"Is the Parliament," he said, "to judge of these preliminaries, article by article, and to propose variations and additions? God forbid! 'Tis the prerogative of the Crown to make war and peace. The ministers of the Crown are to act in such matters at their peril. But in this instance the Crown has not yet executed that prerogative. No definitive treaty is made,—consequently no peace is made. We have only the heads, minutes, or notes, of a proposed arrangement between the two nations, by which neither party is bound. In this state of things Parliament ought not to be called upon to interpose. It may be said, that the strong approbation and applause which ministers ask by this address will strengthen their hands in making the definitive treaty. But I assert the direct contrary. I do not say so affectedly, and to maintain the proposition of a day ; but I am really and seriously of opinion, that by this course of proceeding you disable them from doing that right to the King and to the nation for which I make no doubt, they are solicitous. All courts know that an English ministry treats with them under the inspection and animadversion of Parliament. This is a shield of defense to our negotiators against many demands,—a weapon in their hands to enforce others. If they are able to say, ' *We can not do this or that ; the Parliament will not support us*,' a power that wants a peace from you, which is now the case of France, will give submissive attention to that argument. Many material stipulations require to be ascertained, explained, extended, added, or altered, before these preliminaries assume the form of a national compact. But if Parliament sanctions all in the gross, can you expect to succeed in any point which you have to make ? It will be well known on the other side of the Channel, that Parliament can not retract its approbation without stultifying itself, and without upsetting the administration. The noble and skillful person at present his Majesty's ambassador at Paris,[1] when any difference now arises, will talk to the winds. The French minister will laugh in your face, and tell you that ' you are not in earnest, for Parliament has approved of these articles ; you must rest contented with them as they now stand, and with our interpretation of them.' "

Lord Granville, who had chiefly directed the negotiation, and was expected to take the lead in defending the preliminaries, was recently dead, and there was no one to answer these arguments; but whether they influenced any noble Lord's opinion, it was quite certain that they would influence no vote, and Lord Hardwicke found himself so weak in numbers that he did not venture to divide the House, or even[2] to enter upon the Journals a protest against the address. No material inconvenience arose in

[1] The Duke of Bedford.
[2] In the other House, after Mr. Pitt's famous *sitting* speech of three hours and a half, although he was obliged to go away from illness, the opponents of the peace were more adventurous; but they could only muster 65 against 319.

this case from the parliamentary discussion of the preliminaries; the definitive treaty of Paris was satisfactorily concluded on the footing of them,—and, notwithstanding Lord Hardwicke's objections, the same course of proceeding has since been adopted on similar occasions. Indeed, he was guilty of a fallacy in representing a preliminary treaty of peace as a mere *projet* from which either side may draw back, for it terminates hostilities, and, by the law of nations, as far as it goes, it is binding on the parties, although there be certain points between them which remain to be adjusted.

I discover no trace of any debate in the House of Lords on the Definitive Treaty, and the only other speech which we know of Lord Hardwicke having delivered there was on the 28th day of March, 1763, against the very obnoxious bill for levying a duty on cider in the hands of the maker. We have here again a proof of his indefatigable industry on all occasions, which (be it ever remembered) was the great cause of his extraordinary success in life. There are extant, in his own handwriting, notes for a very elaborate *philippic* against this tax. I shall give a few extracts, which I think are more interesting than a finished oration :—

"Shall go upon two great lines of this bill:
 1. I look upon it as an extension and application of the excise laws to improper objects.
 2. I look upon it as an additional land-tax upon the cider counties.
   First Point.
 All former laws; the plan of the Excise—confined to some particular trades or occupations—Do not extend to any subject who may happen to do a particular act in the course of his family affairs.
 Such persons give their names; voluntarily subject themselves to such laws as are or shall be, &c.
 Such dealers have shops, warehouses, outhouses, &c., distinct.
 In this case every person who makes any quantity of cider above, &c. is subjected.
 This arises from laying the tax upon the maker, and not on the first buyer or retailer; and in this the present bill departs from the principle on which excises were admitted, &c." [1]

---

[1] Lord Hardwicke seems to have furnished one of the topics for the celebrated No. XLV. of the "North Briton," published soon after—which, commenting on the King's speech, recommending a "spirit of concord," thus inveighs against the cider tax: "Is the spirit of concord to go hand in hand with the peace and excise through this nation? Is it to be expected between an insolent exciseman and a peer, gentleman, freeholder, or farmer, whose private houses are now made liable to be entered and searched at pleasure? Gloucestershire, Herefordshire, and in general all the cider counties, are not surely the several counties which are alluded to in the speech. The spirit of

He still goes on with his first point at considerably greater length, and then takes up the second of "the land tax on the cider counties," with equal minuteness, bringing forward statistical facts, and trying to show, on principle, that such taxes fall upon the producer—not upon the consumer. We can only judge of the actual speech by the effect it produced, for it was attacked by the *heavy artillery* of Lord Bute. He rose to reply, and his delivery on this occasion was so particularly slow and solemn that Charles Townsend, standing on the steps of the throne, called out in an audible whisper, "*Minute guns!*"[1] These might be considered as announcing the funeral of Lord Bute's ministry. The Cider Bill passed, but it added so much to the unpopularity accumulated upon him and upon his countrymen, by the dismissal of Mr. Pitt, by the inglorious peace, by the royal favoritism on which his administration rested, by Churchill's "Prophecy of Famine," by Wilkes's "Dedication to the New Edition of the Fall of Mortimer," and by the same unscrupulous writer's "North Briton," which had now reached the fortieth number, that the Premier suddenly resigned, and was succeeded by George Grenville. The nation believed that he long continued secretly to direct all the measures of the Court. This suspicion was carried to an extravagant length; but, although he pretended that, having gained all the objects of his ambition, he had betaken himself to "the domestic and literary retirement which he loved," there can be no doubt that, for a considerable time, in ministerial arrangements, he chiefly guided the King; and that he entertained a strong hope of being able ostensibly to resume his position when the prejudices excited against him should have passed away.

Parliament was hurriedly prorogued to prevent discussion; but the closing speech called forth No. XLV. of the "North Briton;" general warrants were issued by Lord Halifax, Secretary of State, to arrest the author, printer, and publisher,—Wilkes was arrested,—Wilkes

concord has not gone forth among them, but the spirit of liberty has, and a noble opposition has been given to the wicked instruments of oppression."

[1] Charles was very impartial between him and the Duke of Newcastle, who were both his near relations, saying, "Silly fellow! silly fellow! I think it as well to be governed by my uncle with the blue ribbon, or my cousin with a green one."

was sent to the Tower,—Wilkes was liberated by the judgment of the Court of Common Pleas; and the cry of "WILKES AND LIBERTY!" resounded throughout the realm. Lord Bute became sensible that some new arrangement was necessary, and opened negotiations with the discarded ministers of George II. By a letter from Lord Hardwicke to his son, we are informed of the attempt made upon him.

"On Friday I was at the levee, a very thin one, to make my bow to the King before going out of town for the autumn. His Majesty was very civil; inquired when I went to Wimple, to which I answered, *on Monday.* I mention this circumstance, because I believe it brought upon me *what follows.* On Sunday noon I had a note from Lord Eg^r. to come to me either *immediately,* or *that night* or on *Monday morning, as early as I pleased.* As I was just stepping into my chariot to dine at Highgate, I named either Sunday night or Monday morning, the last of which took place. His Lordship stayed with me about an hour and a half; began with great civilities and professions of regard, and then told me that he came *by his Majesty's order,* whose good opinion and esteem for me he avowed to represent in the royal words, which were such as it will not become me to repeat. That the King wished to see me again in his council, and he was authorized by his Majesty to offer to place me *at the head of it.* That he (Lord E.) had taken occasion to lay before his Majesty, at different times, what had passed between us in former conversations; and that the King found that, after so long a friendship and connection with the D. of Newcastle, I had some difficulties, upon the point of private honor to break through them. That though his Majesty had reason to be offended with his Grace's late conduct, yet, for the sake of attaining what he so much wished, if the D. of Newc. would accept one of the great offices about the court the King would condescend to it. That his Majesty understood the Duke had declared in the House of Lords, that he would not come again into a ministerial place; and desired *to know my opinion* whether his Grace would return to the King's service upon the foot proposed. I own I did not expect so *direct* a proposition, and made all the dutiful, grateful, but disabling speeches that became me. How little I wished to come into office again, I said, appeared by my having declined the Great Seal in July, 1757, and the Privy Seal in the winter 1761; which I had done with the greatest consideration for his Majesty's service. That, as I had declined to accept an employment, though offered me, whilst all my friends were in court, it was impossible for me to accept one whilst all my friends were out of court. That as to what was said about the D. of Newcastle, my connection with him was avowed and well known; that I might have expressed myself shortly upon former occasions, but I had always described or alluded to others also. That most of, if not all, the great Whig Lords, with whom and their families I had acted for forty years, were now displaced; and I shou only tarnish my own character, at least in ye opinion of ye world, at ye end of my life, and not be of any use to his Majesty, if I separated myself from them. That I rejoiced, for the sake of his Majesty's service, that the proscription was so far taken off from the Duke of Newcastle. That I looked upon it as a good beginning, but there were *others besides his Grace*. As *to the point* on which my opinion was asked, it was too delicate and important for any man to answer, without consulting the person concerned, upon *that very point* directly. Therefore I begged to know how far I might go with the Duke; for I wou^d not exceed his Majesty's permission by one jot. My Lord answered that the King wou^d by no means allow me to acquaint the D. of N. with this, unless I first declared my opinion that *it would do*. To this I said that I was then at a full stand. It was impossible for me to say now that it wou^d do, and how should I know if I could not ask? If I was to hazard a conjecture, it would be that this alone wou^d not do. That things had been suffered to go so far that his Grace himself must have formed connections, &c. However, it was repeated that I must not open one word of this to him. I could not help saying; He will even know of this visit of y^r Lordship's to me; may I own that you have talked to me in the like style as formerly upon my own subject? This was agreed to. . . . .

"He then spoke of the continuance of the cry against Lord B., that he had been hung up in effigie upon a gibbet, at one of the principal gates of Exeter, for this fortnight past, and nobody had dared cut the figure down in all that time. It is immaterial to run into the minutiæ of our conversation; but, in the course of it, my Lord had happened to say that the King could not bring himself to submit to take in a party in gross, as an opposition party. I told him nobody wou^d advise his Majesty to avow the doing of that. But a King of England, at the head of a popular governm^t, especially as of late the popular scale had grown heavier, wou^d sometimes find it necessary to bend and ply a little. That it was not to be understood as being forced: but only submitting to the stronger reason, for the sake of himself and his government. That King William, hero as he was, had found himself obliged to this conduct; so had other princes before him; and so had his Majesty's grandfather, and found his governm^t grew stronger by it. I have now told you the substance of a long conversation. The only material thing besides was that Ld Egremont at last varied a little the form of his restriction, as to the Duke of Newcastle, and put it finally, *that I shou^d not say anything to him of this proposition, till after I had seen or heard from his Lordship again;* and so it was left. When either of those will happen I know not, for his Lordship knew I was fixed to go out of town the next morning, for the autumn, and came to me upon that foundation."

Lord Egremont having died suddenly a few days afterwards, the necessity for a change became more urgent, and a separate negotiation was opened with the Duke of Newcastle. He, too, having refused to desert his friends, the King found it necessary to send for Lord Chatham. We have a very interesting account of what passed between them in the following letter from the ex-Chancellor, which shows that he had greatly improved in the facility and elegance of his English composition since he wrote " PHILIP HOMEBRED " for the " Spectator; " and that, if he had practiced letter-writing, he might have rivaled Horace Walpole:—

"Wimple, Sept. 4, 1763.

" My dear Lord,[1]

" I have heard the whole from the Duke of Newcastle;

[1] His eldest son. This *mylording* of his own son, which would not have been practiced by a Howard or a Spencer, confirms the charge against him that he preposterously piqued himself upon his nobility, and forces us to recollect the poor youth, who, under his mistress's stern orders, brought home cabbages from the greengrocer's, and oysters from the fishmonger's Accord-

and, on Friday morning, *de source*, from Mr. Pitt. But if I was to attempt to relate in writing all that I have heard in two conversations of two hours each, *the dotterells and wheat-ears would stink* before I could finish my letter. Besides it is as strange as it is long, for I believe it is the most extraordinary transaction that ever happened in any Court in Europe, even in times so extraordinary as the present.

"I will begin as the affair has gone on, preposterously, by telling you, that it is all over for the present, and we are to come back *re infectâ*.

"It began as to the substance, by a message from my Lord Bute to Mr. Pitt, at Hayes, through my Lord Mayor, to give him the meeting privately at some third place. This, his Lordship (Lord B.) afterwards altered by a note from himself, saying, that as he did things openly, he would come to Mr. Pitt's house in Jermyn Street in broad daylight. They met accordingly, and Lord Bute, after the first compliments, frankly acknowledged that his ministry could not go on, and that the King was convinced of it; and therefore he (Lord B.) desired Mr. Pitt would open himself frankly, and at large, and tell him his ideas of things and persons with the utmost freedom. After much excuse and hanging back, Mr. Pitt did so with the utmost freedom indeed, though with civility. Here I must leave a long blank to be filled up when I see you. Lord Bute heard with great attention and patience; entered into no defense; but at last said, 'If these are your opinions, why should you not tell them to the King himself, who will not be unwilling to hear you?'—'How can I presume to go to the King, who am not of the council, nor in his service, and have no pretense to ask an audience? The presumption would be too great.'—'But suppose his Majesty should order you to attend him, I presume, sir, you would not refuse it.'—'The King's command would make it my duty, and I should certainly obey it.'

ing to a well-known story, the late Lord Althorp, when a distinguished senator, was thus addressed by his noble father: "Ring the bell, Jack."—*1st Edit.*

In all the copies of the letter heretofore printed, it begins "My dear Lord;" but Mr. Harris, in his Life of Lord Hardwicke, informs us that the original, which he has seen, begins "Dear Royston." "*Dear Phil,*" would have been still better.—(1840.)

"This was on last Thursday sevennight. On the next day (Friday) Mr. Pitt received from the King an open note, unsealed, requiring him to attend his Majesty on Saturday noon, at the Queen's Palace, in the Park. In obedience hereto, Mr. Pitt went on Saturday at noonday, through the Mall, in his gouty chair, the boot of which (as he said himself) makes it as much known as if his name was writ upon it, to the Queen's Palace. He was immediately carried into the closet, received very graciously; and his Majesty began, in like manner as his quondam favorite had done, by ordering him to tell him his opinion of things and persons at large, and with the utmost freedom; and, I think, did in substance make the like confession, that he thought his present Ministers could not go on. The audience lasted three hours, and Mr. Pitt went through the whole upon both heads more fully than he had done to Lord Bute, but with great complaisance and douceur to the King; and his Majesty gave him a very gracious accueil, and heard him with great patience and attention. And Mr. Pitt affirms that, in general, and upon the most material points, he appeared by his manner and by many expressions to be convinced. But here I must again avail myself of my long blank, and make only one general description; that Mr. Pitt went through the infirmities of the peace; the things necessary and hitherto neglected to improve and preserve it; the present state of the nation, both foreign and domestic; the great Whig families and persons which have been driven from his Majesty's council and service which it would be for his interest to restore. In doing this he repeated many names; upon which his Majesty told him there was pen, ink, and paper, and wished he would write them down. Mr. Pitt humbly excused himself, by saying, that would be too much for him to take upon him; and he might, upon his memory, omit some material persons which might be subject to imputation. The King still said he liked to hear him, and bid him go on; but said, now and then, his honor must be consulted; to which Mr. Pitt answered in a very courtly manner. His Majesty ordered him to come again on Monday, which he did, to the same place and in the same public manner."

[Here comes in a parenthesis, that on Sunday Mr. Pitt went to Claremont, and acquainted the Duke of Newcastle with the whole, fully persuaded from the King's manner and behavior that the thing would do; and that on Monday the outlines of the new arrangement would be settled. This produced the messages to the Lords, who were sent for. Mr. Pitt undertook to write to the Duke of Devonshire and the Marquis of Rockingham, and the Duke of Newcastle to Lord Hardwicke himself.]

"But, behold the catastrophe of Monday. The King received him equally graciously; and that audience lasted near two hours. The King began that he had considered of what had been said, and talked still more strongly of his honor. His Majesty then mentioned Lord Halifax for the Treasury, still proceeding upon the supposition of a change.

"To this Mr. Pitt hesitated an objection—that certainly Lord Halifax ought to be considered, but that he should not have thought of him for the Treasury. Suppose his Majesty should think fit to give him the Paymaster's place. The King replied, 'But, Mr. Pitt, I had designed that for poor G. Grenville; he is your near relation, and you once loved him,' To this the only answer made was a low bow. And now here comes the bait. 'Why,' says his Majesty, 'should not my Lord Temple have the Treasury? you would then go on very well.'—'Sir, the person whom you shall think fit to honor with the chief conduct of your affairs can not possibly go on without a Treasury connected with him. But that alone will do nothing. It can not be carried on without the great families who have supported the Revolution government, and other great persons, of whose abilities and integrity the public has had experience, and who have weight and credit in the nation. I should only deceive your Majesty, if I should leave you in an opinion that I could go on, and your Majesty make a solid administration, on any other foot.'—'Well, Mr. Pitt, I see (or I fear) this will not do. My honor is concerned, and I must support it.' '*Et sic finita est fabula.*' 'Vos valete,' but I can not with a safe conscience add, '*plaudite.*' I have made my skeleton larger than I intended at first, and I hope you will understand it. Mr. Pitt professes himself firmly persuaded that My Lord Bute was sincere at first, and that the King was in earnest the first day; but that on the intermediate day,

Sunday, some strong effort was made which produced the alteration.

"Mr. Pitt likewise affirms that, if he was examined upon oath, he could not tell upon what this negotiation broke off, whether upon any particular point, or upon the general complexion of the whole; but that if the King shall assign any particular reason for it, he will never contradict it.

"My story has been so long, though in truth a very short abridgment, that I shall not lengthen it by observations, but leave you to make your own: it will certainly be given out, that the reason was the unreasonable extent of Mr. Pitt's plan—a general rout; and the minority, after having complained so much of proscriptions, have endeavored to proscribe the majority. I asked Mr. Pitt the direct question, and he assured me, that although he thought himself obliged to name a great many persons for his own exculpation, yet he did not name above five or six for particular places. I must tell you that one of these was your humble servant for the President's place. This was entirely without my authority and privity. But the King's answer was, 'Why, Mr. Pitt, it is vacant, and ready for him; and he knows he may have it to-morrow, if he thinks fit.'

"I conjectured that this was said with regard to what had passed with poor Lord Egremont, which made me think it necessary to tell Mr. Pitt in general what had passed with that Lord (not owning that his Lordship had offered it directly in the King's name), and what I had answered, which he, in his way, much commended.

"This obliges me to desire that you will send me by the bearer my letter to you, which you were to communicate to my Lord Lyttleton, that I may see how I have stated it there, for I have no copy.

"I shall now *make you laugh*, though some parts of what goes before make me melancholy, to see the King so committed, and his Majesty submitting to it, &c. But what I mean will make you laugh is, that the Ministers are so stung with this admission, that they can not go on (and what has passed on this occasion will certainly make them less able to go on), and with my Lord Bute's having thus carried them to market in his pocket, that they say Lord Bute has attempted to sacrifice them to his own fears and timidity; that they do not depend upon him, and will have nothing to do with him; and I have been credibly informed that both Lord Halifax and George Grenville have declared that he is to go beyond sea, and reside for a twelvemonth or more. You know a certain cardinal was twice exiled out of France, and governed France as absolutely whilst he was absent as when he was present.

"Yours affectionately,
"HARDWICKE."

While the ex-Chancellor was thus speculating upon changes of administration, and his own return to office, he was struck with a mortal disorder. Hitherto he had enjoyed uninterrupted health, and such attention had he paid to temperance and to exercise when in his power, that, although originally by no means of a robust constitution, he was still active in his body, and the hand of time had been laid so gently on his frame, that he seemed to be only entering into a green old age.

Being made aware that he could not hope to recover, he submitted to the will of Providence with firmness, and even with cheerfulness—gratefully reflecting on the long and singularly prosperous career which he had run.

When parliament again met, he was unable to take part in the stormy discussions which arose out of the prosecution and imprisonment of Wilkes; but his faculties were still unimpaired, and, though confined to his bed, he could occasionally see and converse with his political as well as his private friends.

A resolution being moved and carried in the House of Commons, "that privilege of parliament does not extend to the case of writing and publishing seditious libels," was sent up to the Lords, who were called upon to concur in it. As Mr. Wilkes had attacked Lord Bute so violently and so successfully, he was warmly supported by the opposition—and Pitt in one House, and Earl Temple in the other, boldly resisted the resolution;—but Lord Hardwicke, though a strong party-man to the last, when consulted, expressed a clear opinion "that privilege of parliament does not extend to prevent a member from being prosecuted and imprisoned for any crime; that the words in the common *cantilena*, 'treason, felony, and breach of the peace,' are only put as examples, and that it would be most discredit able to parliament to assert the right of all its members to commit with impunity all misdemeanors which did not amount to an actual breach of the peace." In consequence of this opinion, the Duke of Newcastle, and the peers more immediately connected with him, refused to vote with Lord Temple, or to join in his protest—much to the annoyance of that nobleman.

This was Lord Hardwicke's last interference with politics. Finding that his disease made rapid progress, he deliberately settled his worldly affairs, and then devoted himself to preparation for the awful change which was at hand. Amid the most affectionate attentions of his family, he expired at his house in Grosvenor Square, on the 6th of March, 1764, in the seventy-fourth year of his age. As long as he drew breath his powerful mind remained unclouded, and he was serene and composed. "I saw him in his last moments," wrote his eldest son, "and he looked like an innocent child in his nurse's arms."

According to the directions of his will, he was buried privately at Wimpole, where a monument is erected to his memory, with an inscription, which, after stating the dates of his several promotions, thus eulogizes him:

"The Strength and Quickness of his Parts, joined to an unwearied Application and Industry, recommended him, soon after his entrance into Business, to an extensive course of Practice, and advanced him before the usual Age, to those Inferior Honors of the Robe, from which is open'd the fairest Prospect to the highest. In this Situation as an Advocate and a Servant of the Crown, his Skill in the various Branches of the Law and Constitution, his Eloquence, his Integrity, his Zeal for Justice, and his Candor and Tenderness to the Subject, were universally acknowledged and admired. In each of the Courts where he presided, his Firmness and Dignity, his clear and ready Apprehension, his patient and close Attention, the Compass and Profoundness of his Knowledge, and the Justice of his Decisions, afforded the most valuable Instruction to the Profession, and the Highest Satisfaction to the Parties. His Eloquence in Parliament was natural and manly, his Method exact, his Reasoning powerful and persuasive, his Manner modest yet commanding, his Voice clear and Harmonious; and all these received a luster and a force, almost irresistible, from the acknowledged Integrity of his Character. When he advised in the more Secret Councils of State, his superior Judgment, his long Experience, his Acquaintance with History and Treatise, enabled him to state precisely, to debate fully, and to determine wisely and usefully to the Public those arduous Questions which were the Subject of Deliberation. In his Political Connections, as well as Private Friendships, he was uniform and constant. In his Religious Principles, he was attached to the National Establishment, with that Spirit of Moderation and Charity which becomes a sincere and enlightened Member of a Protestant Communion. In private Life he was distinguished by the Amiableness of his Manners, his engaging Address, and his general Benevolence; ever easy and cheerful in the Conversation of his Family and Friends ; and retaining the Taste of his early Classical Studies, amidst his most laborious and highest Employments. Thus he lived during the Exercise of his Great Offices ; and in his Retirement was honor'd and revered by the whole Nation, and distinguished by the Approbation and peculiar Favor of his Sovereign, till his 74th year ; when a long and painful Disorder, supported by an uncommon patience, and a Strength of Mind unimpaired, put a Period to his Life, March the 6th, 1764."

These are the effusions of filial piety ; but notwithstanding his failings, and the censure to which some parts of his conduct may be liable, he is certainly to be considered a most eminent and meritorious personage in English history. Entering public life very early, he lived to a great age in very interesting times, and he acted an important part in many of the events which distinguished the century in which he flourished. He had heard speeches delivered from the throne by William III. and by George III.; he had seen the reins of government in the hands of Godolphin and in the hands of Pitt ; he had witnessed the rejoicings for the victory of Blenheim and for the capture of Quebec ; his ears had been split with cries of "*Sacheverell and High Church!*" and with cries of "*Wilkes and Liberty!*" he had been acquainted with Bolingbroke and with Burke; he had marked the earliest burst of admiration called forth by the poetry of Pope and by the poetry of Churchill; he himself had been fifty years a member of the Legislature, holding a most distinguished station in either House of Parliament ; he had filled various important offices with singular ability : he had held the highest civil office in the kingdom longer than any of his predecessors (one excepted), since the foundation of the monarchy, and with greater applause than any of his predecessors had ever gained or any successor could hope for ; he had been mainly instrumental in keeping the reigning dynasty on the throne, by the measures which he advised for crushing a dangerous rebellion raised to restore the legitimate line ; he was the great legislator for Scotland, freeing that country from the baronial tyranny by which it had been immemorably oppressed ; in England he was the finisher and almost the author of the immortal Code of Equity to which his name might justly be attached ; though of low degree, in his own lifetime his blood was mingled with that of the Campbells and the Greys, and he established one of the most potent families in the nobility of Britain. Through life, unceasing good luck attended him; but beyond this such results required lofty aspiration, rare intellectual ability, consummate prudence, absolute control of temper, rigid self-denial, and unwearied industry. His chief glory is, that, as a public man, he was ever consistent and upright. Compare him with preceding and with succeeding Chancellors, who started by making themselves formidable as the ultrazealous champions of freedom, and who rose by renouncing and by persecuting the principles which they professed. He was from boy to old man a sound Whig—loving our monarchical form of government, but believing that it exists for the good of the people, and that for the good of the people the prerogatives of the Crown are to be restricted, and are to be preserved.

The heaviest charges I find brought against him by impartial writers, are—love of money, and arrogance of manner in common society:

"He was undoubtedly an excellent Chancellor," says Lord Waldegrave, "and might have been thought a great man had he been less avaricious, less proud, less unlike a gentleman."[1]

"The stately and ceremonious reception of his visitors on a Sunday evening," says Cooksey, "was insipid and disgusting in the highest degree. Stranger as he was to the life and habits of country gentlemen, he treated them with insulting inattention and hauteur. Came they from ever so great a distance, either to visit his Lordship or to see his place, their horses were sent for refreshment to the 'Tiger,' a vile inn near half a mile distant, as I have experienced more than once. He submitted, indeed, like other Lords, sometimes to entertain the *natives*, but with that visible and contemptuous superiority as disgusted rather than obliged them. When in high good-humor, he had two or three stock stories to make his company laugh, which they were prepared and expected to do. One was of his bailiff Woodcock, who, having been ordered by his lady to procure a sow of the breed and size she particularly described to him, came one day into the dining-room, when full of great company, proclaiming, with a burst of joy he could not supress, '*I have been at Royston fair, my Lady, and got a sow exactly of your Ladyship's breed and size.*' He also used to relate an incident that occurred

[1] Mem. p. 20.

to him in a morning ride from Wimple. Observing an elegant gentleman's house, he conceived a wish to see the inside of it. It happened to be that of Mr. Montague, brother to Lord Sandwich, who, being at home, very politely, without knowing his Lordship, conducted him about the apartments, which were perfectly elegant, and expatiated on the pictures, some of which were capital. Among these were two female figures, beautifully painted, in all their native naked charms. '*These ladies,*' says the master of the house, '*you must certainly know, for they are most striking likenesses.*' On the guest's expressing his perfect ignorance. '*Why, where the devil have you led your life, or what company have you kept,*' says the Captain, '*not to know Fanny Murray and Kitty Fisher, with whose persons I thought no fashionable man like you could be unacquainted?*' On my taking leave, and saying, '*I should be glad to return his civilities at Wimple,*' what surprise and confusion did he express on his discovering he had been talking all this *badinage* to Lord Hardwicke!"[1]

Others have given a more favorable view of his manners, representing that "he rose from the fatigues and anxieties of business to the enjoyment of the society of his family and his friends, with the spirit of a person entirely vacant and disengaged, preserving in old age the vivacity as well as appearance of youth, and ever uniting the characters of dignity and amiableness."[2]

The censure of his love of money should be softened by the recollection of the penury from which he had suffered in his youth, and from the consideration that it never exposed him even to the suspicion of corruption. A graver fault, and attended with less palliation, may, I think, be imputed to him in his abandonment of literature and literary men. It might have been expected that, in the breast of one who had been taken to dine at the Kit-Cat, who had acquired credit by writing a paper in the "Spectator," and who had witnessed the glory shed over Lord Somers in his decline by continuing the protector and associate of wits and philosophers, the sacred flame once kindled would have smoldered, ready to burst out when freed from the load of Chancery precedents and official cares. But as he advanced in life he seems to have contracted a contempt for all liberal studies, and to

[1] Cooksey, 101. [2] Life by Chalmers.

have valued men only according to their rank, their riches, and their political influence. I find no trace of his having the smallest intercourse or correspondence, except with lawyers, or the leaders of faction. He obtained a pension for Mallet (a man doing no honor to the country of his birth), under pretense of his literary celebrity, but, in reality, for writing a pamphlet when the nation was exasperated by the ill conduct and disasters of the war, to turn the public resentment and vengeance from the ministry upon Admiral Byng. Dr. Birch, well known as a scholar and historical collector, had been tutor to his sons, and had dedicated the "Thurloe State Papers" to the Lord Chancellor himself. One of his pupils, much attached to him, seeing him neglected and starving, thus ventured to address the great distributor of church patronage:—"From my own acquaintance with him I can only confirm the general character he bears of being a clergyman of great worth, industry, and learning, subsisting at the mercy of booksellers and printers, without any preferment but a small living in the country, which will scarce keep a curate. He is a person of excellent heart as well as head, and, by his diligence and general knowledge in most parts of learning, may be made extremely useful to the public." The reply was an offer of a living in Wales of £30 a year, which Dr. Birch declined accepting. Lord Hardwicke thought it his duty to dispose of ecclesiastical preferments in his gift—with a view to increase his own political influence,—without any scrupulous regard for the interests of religion, and—without the slightest respect for scientific or literary merit.[1] He has had his reward. While Somers, Harcourt, and Murray, are immortalized in the poems of Addison and Pope, Hardwicke was only praised by the dull authors of treatises on the practice of the Court of Chancery, or dull compilers of Chancery reports. With all his titles and all his wealth, how poor is his fame in comparison with that of his contemporary, SAMUEL JOHNSON, whom he would not have received at his Sunday evening parties in Powis House, or invited to hear his stale stories at Wimple! A man desirous of solid fame would rather have written the

[1] When he was actually going out of office, and jobbing in church preferment could be of no avail to him, he gave Dr. Birch a better living in the city of London.

"Rambler," the "Vanity of Human Wishes," "Rasselas,' or the "Lives of the Poets," than have delivered all Lord Hardwicke's speeches in Parliament, and all his judgments in the Court of Chancery; although the Author had been sometimes obliged to pass the night on the ashes of a glasshouse, and at last thought himself passing rich with his £300 pension—while the Peer lived in splendor, and died worth a million.[1]

Beyond his efforts in English prose composition, which I have already mentioned, I am not aware of anything from Lord Hardwicke's pen, except his celebrated letter to Lord Kames. That profound jurist and philosopher, about to publish his treatise on "Equity," sent the "Introduction," explaining his general views on the subject in MS., to the great ex-Chancellor, whose fame was, if possible, higher in Scotland than in his own country. Lord Hardwicke's answer is a very masterly performance,[2] and shows that he might have left some permanent monument of his fame to have placed him in the same category as Sir Thomas More, Lord Bacon, and Lord Clarendon,—great English Judges, who enriched the literature of their country. He not only gives an admirable sketch of the origin of Equity Jurisdiction in England, but enters deeply into the general principles on which the essential distinction between Law and Equity rests, and on which they are respectively to be administered. Unlike mere Chancery practitioners, whom favor or accident has elevated to high judicial office, and who, religiously persuaded that Chancery practice is the perfection of human wisdom,[3] sincerely and strongly think that whatever dif-

---

[1] It is whimsical enough that Johnson himself for a moment wished that, instead of being at the head of English literature, he had been a "law lord." But at other times he showed a consciousness of his own superiority to Chancellors and Peers: "It is wonderful, Sir, with how little real superiority of mind men can make an eminent figure in public life." * Hardwicke is to Johnson as the most interesting Life that could be written of Hardwicke is to Boswell's "Life of Johnson,"—the proportion of a farthing candle to the meridian sun.

[2] June 30, 1759. Lord Woodhouselee's "Life of Lord Kames,' i. 237.

[3] Once, in a conversation I had with a very eminent counsel at the Chancery bar, who wore a silk gown, respecting the effect of "notice to a purchaser of an unregistered deed," I opposed his opinion by citing a decision in point of Chancellor d'Aguesseau. "Ah!" said he gravely, "But had the French Lord Chancellor called in the assistance of the French Master of the Rolls?'

* Bos. iv. 191.

fers from it must be absurd and mischievous,—while he contends, like Lord Bacon,[1] that the administration of law and equity should be committed not to the same court, as in Scotland, but to separate courts, as in England,—he liberally admits that there are partial advantages and inconveniences belonging to both systems, and that there is ground for considerable difference of opinion upon their rival pretensions. He afterwards discusses, in a most luminous manner, the important question, how far in the Prætorian jurisdiction the conscience of the Judge, or *arbitrium boni viri*, is to be controlled,—and beautifully shows the advantage of general rules in restraining caprice as well as corruption, and in letting the world know how civil rights are defined and will be adjudicated.

Lord Hardwicke has been held up by some of his injudicious flatterers as a great classical scholar, and we are referred to a letter which he wrote in the year 1724, "SAMUELI CLERICO," in which he asks the learned Dr. Samuel Clerk to revise an epitaph composed on one of the Bradford family, to whom he was related by marriage, in consequence of a request "a Cocceio uxoris meæ germano, tibi bene noto."[2] But there is nothing in this letter beyond what could be accomplished by a lad who had been at an ordinary grammar school; and Lord Hardwicke must be cited as an instance of success—not in consequence of a finished education, but in spite of a very defective one. By the anxiety with which he gave his own sons the benefit of academical discipline, he showed the consciousness he felt of the unequal fight he had fought from the want of it.

There are extant specimens of his poetical composition, which will perhaps be considered as justifying him in forever renouncing the Muses, and trusting his reputation with posterity to *Atk*. and *Ves. Sr.* Lord Lyttleton had written a copy of verses, addressed to the Countess of Egremont, entitled "VIRTUE and FAME," supposed to be

---

This reminded me of the English tar, who, returning home from a French prison, said to his companion, "Jack, what rum'ns 'em 'ere Frenchmen be . Do you know, Jack, that they call a *horse* a SHOVEL, and a *hat* a CHOPPER?"

[1] "Apud nonnullos receptum est, ut jurisdictio, quæ decernit secundum æquum et bonum, atque illa altera quæ procedit secundum jus strictum, iisdem curiis deputentur; apud alios autem, ut diversis: omnino placet curiarum separatio. Neque enim servabitur distinctio casuum, si fiat commixtio jurisdictionum."—*De Aug. L.* viii. c. 3, aph. 45.   [2] Birch's MSS. Brit. Mus.

a Dialogue between these two ladies, in which VIRTUE, after drawing the character of the best of wives and mothers, concludes by setting FAME right, who thought this must be the wife of a country parson,

> "Who never saw the court nor town,
> Whose face is ugly as her gown.
> 'Tis the most celebrated toast
> That Britain's spacious isle can boast;
> 'Tis princely Petworth's noble dame;
> 'Tis Egremont—go tell it Fame."

Addition extempore, by Lord Chancellor Hardwicke.

> "Fame heard with pleasure—straight replied,
> First on my roll stands Windham's bride;
> My trumpet oft I've rais'd to sound
> Her modest praise the world around;
> But notes were wanting; canst thou find
> A muse to sing her face, her mind?
> Believe, me, I can name but one,
> A friend of your's—'tis Lyttleton.

Again, journeying to London after the death of his wife, he composed the following lines, which he thus entered in his Diary:

"A Wimple iter faciens uxorem nupèr morte abreptam alloquitur, Junii 15° 1762.

> "Conjuge dilectâ privari dùm dolet, heu! me
> Dùm dolet in viduo nocte jacere toro!
> Te rursùm sociam thalami redisse sub astra
> Exopto, notæ te comitemque viæ."

I am sorry that neither from print nor the tradition of Westminster Hall can I collect any personal anecdotes or noted sayings of Lord Hardwicke to enliven my dull narrative of his Life.[1] I suspect that, unlike his immediate successor, studying his dignity very uniformly, and always very observant of decorum, he added little to the "*ana*" of his age. We must not look for the workings of his genius in Joe Miller, but exclusively in the Parliamentary History and the Chancery Reports.

I have now only to state that "he was one of the

[1] There is one story related of him worth mentioning, which shows that he followed the precedent of Lord Chancellor Cowper, in being civil to the House of Cromwell. There being a suit heard before him in which Oliver's grandson was a party, while the opposite counsel was very irrelevantly and improperly inveighing against the memory of the Protector, the Lord Chancellor said, "I observe Mr. Cromwell standing outside the bar there, inconveniently pressed by the crowd; make way for him, that he may sit by me on the bench." It is needless to add, that the representative of the family being so noticed, the orator felt rebuked and changed his tone.

handsomest men of his time, and bestowed great attention to his appearance and dress." There were reports circulated of his gallantries with a Lady B——, and with the celebrated Mrs. Wells ; but for these there was as little foundation as for his conjectured intimacy with Fanny Murray and Kitty Fisher. He was a perfect pattern not only of temperance and sobriety, but also of conjugal fidelity.

Before proceeding to speak of his wife and his descendants, I will further assist the reader to come to a right judgment upon his merits and defects, by presenting characters of him as drawn by three eminent contemporaries who knew him well: the first being his greatest vituperator, the second his most indiscriminate eulogist, and the third speaking of him, I think, in the words of impartiality and truth. Says Horace Walpole :—

" He was a creature of the Duke of Newcastle, and by him introduced to Sir Robert Walpole, who contributed to his grandeur and baseness, in giving him an opportunity of displaying the extent of the latter, by raising him to the height of the former. He had good parts, which he laid out so entirely upon the law in the first part of his life, that they were of little use to him afterwards, when he would have applied them to more general views. On his promotion, he flung himself into politics, but, as he had no knowledge of foreign affairs but what was whispered to him by Newcastle, he made a poor figure. In the House of Lords he was laughed at,—in the cabinet despised."

On the other hand, he is extravagantly praised by another Honorable,—Danes Barrington,—who considers him above all human failing :—

" There is not a report of a single decision of Lord Bacon ; some few, indeed (and those unimportant ones) by Lord Nottingham ; we have hardly a determination of consequence by the great Lord Somers : and though he was succeeded by lawyers of ability and eminence, yet it may be said that we owe the present beneficial and rational system of equity to the peculiar national felicity of the greatest lawyer and statesman of this or, perhaps, any other country, having presided in this Court near twenty years without a single decree having been reversed, either in the whole or any part of it ; an infallibility which in no other instance was ever the lot of humanity."[1]

The Earl of Chesterfield thus mediates between them, and pronounces sentence for posterity:—

" Lord Hardwicke was perhaps the greatest magistrate this country ever had. He presided in the Court of Chancery above twenty years,[2] and in all that time none of his decrees were ever reversed, or the justness of them questioned. Though avarice was his ruling passion, he was never in the least suspected of any kind of corruption—a rare and meritorious instance of virtue and self-denial under the influence of such a craving, insatiable, and increasing passion. He was an agreeable, eloquent speaker in parliament, but not without some little tincture of the pleader. He was a cheerful, instructive companion, humane in his nature, decent in his manners, unstained by any vice (avarice excepted)—a very great magistrate, but by no means a great minister."

His marriage with the young widow turned out most auspiciously. They continued to old age tenderly attached to each other. She contributed not only to his happiness, but to his greatness. " She often humorously laid claim (as she had good right to do) to so much of the merit of Lord Hardwicke's being a good Chancellor, in that his thoughts and attention were never taken from the business of the Court by the private concerns of his family,—the care of which, the management of his money matters, the settling all accounts with stewards and others, and, above all, the education of his children, had been wholly her department and concern, without any interposition of his, further than implicit acquiescence and entire approbation."[3] She was supposed to be very stingy, and foolish stories were circulated to annoy her; but " she would often smile at hearing of *the cold chine being turned and found bare*, of the *potted sawdust to represent lamprey*, and *of the want of Dr. Mead's kitchen*[4] *to be added to Powis House*, and only observe that, uncertain as was the time of Lord Chancellor's dining, and the company that would attend him, yet if it should happen that he brought with him an ambassador or person of the highest

---

[1] Observations on Statutes, 325.   [2] Not quite correct.   [3] Cooksey, 34, 40.
[4] " Oft would he go when summer suns prevail,
To taste the coolness of his kitchen gale."

rank, ne never found a dinner or supper to be ashamed of."

We may judge of the malicious turn given to her domestic arrangements, however deserving of praise, by the charge against her of stealing the purse in which the Great Seal was kept to make a counterpane. The truth is, that this purse, highly decorated with the royal arms and other devices, is, by ancient custom, annually renewed, and is the perquisite of the Lord Chancellor for the time being, if he chooses to claim it. Lady Hardwicke, availing herself of this custom, caused the purse, with its decorations, to be put as embroidery on a large piece of rich crimson velvet, corresponding to the height of one of the state rooms at Wimple. These purses, just twenty in number, complete the hangings of the room, and the curtains of a bed, singularly magnificent. She, therefore, in reality only prepared a characteristic and proud heirloom to be handed down to commemorate the founder of the family.[1]

Lord and Lady Hardwicke had seven children, five sons and two daughters, who all grew up and flourished. Philip, the eldest son, married Jemima Campbell, Marchioness Grey, only daughter of John, Earl of Breadalbane, and granddaughter and heiress of the Duke of Kent, who obtained for her a remainder of his marquisate. This Philip, who became the second Earl of Hardwicke, was a man of letters, and an excellent politician, continuing always a steady adherent of the Rockingham party. Of the accomplished and high-spirited Charles, the second son, it will be my duty to give a separate memoir, as he held the Great Seal of England. Joseph, the third son, being for many years ambassador to the States General, was raised to the peerage by the title of Lord Dover. John, the fourth son, was not inferior in learning or abilities to any of his brothers, but preferred a private station with the enjoyment of several lucrative sinecures conferred upon him by his father. James, the youngest son, was made Bishop of Ely. The eldest daughter having become Lady Anson, and the youngest Lady Heathcote, are said to have been distinguished ornaments of the court of George II. The Chancellor is now worthily represented by his great-great-grandson, the present gallant Earl of Hardwicke."[2]

[1] Cooksey, 39.   [2] Grandeur of the Law, p. 66.

CHAPTER CXXXVIII.

LIFE OF LORD CHANCELLOR NORTHINGTON FROM HIS BIRTH TILL HE RECEIVED THE GREAT SEAL.

MY next Chancellor I can not place in the first rank as a lawyer or a statesman; but he is not despicable in either capacity, and he is a memorable personage in the history of the Great Seal, as he held it nine years, in two reigns,[1] and during the whole of four administrations,—the last of which he overturned.[2]

Robert Henley (afterwards Lord Keeper, Lord Chancellor, Baron Henley, and Earl of Northington) was descended from the ancient family of "Henley of that ilk,' in Somersetshire.[3] In 1660, the elder branch was advanced to the dignity of the baronetage. Before then, a cadet, following the law as a profession, had filled the lucrative situation of "Master of the Court of King's Bench on the Plea Side,"—from the profits of which he left to his family a landed estate of £3,000 a year. He acquired the Grange in Hampshire, which, when afterwards in the possession of his descendant, Horace Walpole speaks of with so much admiration. The house was built for the worthy taxer of costs, when he had become Sir Robert Henley, Knight, by Inigo Jones—presenting a hall and staircase which the world was called upon to admire as "beautiful models of the purest and most classic antiquity."[4]

[1] George II. George III.
[2] Mr. Pitt's, Lord Bute's, Duke of Bedford's, Marquis of Rockingham's.
[3] *i. e.* Taking their surname from the name of a territorial possession belonging to them when surnames first began. Our surnames are chiefly derived from this origin, or from personal peculiarities,—from trades and employments, or from the Christian name of the father or mother. Of these, the first class is the most aristocratic, denoting a descent from an ancient baron, or at least, the lord of a manor.
[4] Lord Henley says, "The critic, however, was, I suspect, misled by the respect due to the name of Jones. The current testimony of all who remember it as it then was, represents it, notwithstanding the merit of individual parts, as, upon the whole, a heavy and gloomy structure, utterly unworthy of the great architect."—*Life of Lord Northington,* p. 5. It is related, that Lord Chancellor Northington, expecting a visit here from George III. and Queen Charlotte, cautioned his daughters against telling their Majesties that the house was built by "INDIGO JONES."
The Grange was sold by the second Earl of Northington to Mr. Drum

His son Robert sat in parliament for the borough of Andover, without acquiring much distinction; but the name of his grandson, Anthony, one of the politest and most accomplished men of his day, frequently occurs in the memoirs and correspondence of the reign of Queen Anne.

Having distinguished himself at Oxford by an early relish for literature, and the great refinement and elegance of his manners, on removing to London he was admitted into the society and friendship of the first wits of the time. He was intimate with the Earls of Dorset and Sunderland, and with Swift, Pope, and Arbuthnot. " It was thought strange," says his biographer, " as every one knew what a secret influence he had on affairs in King William's Court, that he who had a genius for anything great, as well as anything gay, did not rise in the state, where he would have shone as a politician no less than he did at Will's and Tom's as a wit. But the Muses and pleasantry had engaged him. He had something of the character of Tibullus, and, except his extravagance, was possessed of all his other qualities—his indolence, his gallantry, his wit, his humanity, his generosity, his learning, his taste for letters. There was hardly a contemporary author that did not experience his bounty."[1] Garth's " Dispensary" was dedicated to him, and some even ascribed to him the authorship of that poem.[2] He certainly was a contributor to the " Tatler." He first served in the House of Commons for Andover, and afterwards till his death, for Weymouth and Melcombe Regis. He was a strong Whig, and on one occasion came prominently forward as mover of the address to Queen Anne, " that she would confer some dignity in the church upon Hoadly, as a reward for asserting and vindicating the principles of the Revolution." This made him so odious to the Tory administration,

---

mond, and is now the property of Lord Ashburton. But the house has been rebuilt in a most sumptuous style, and not a vestige of the original structure remains. [1] Memoirs of Persons who died in 1711. 8vo. 1712.

[2] There is not much resemblance of character between the father and the son, if there was any truth in the language of this Dedication : " A man of your character can no more prevent a dedication than he would encourage one ; for merit, like a *virgin's blushes*, is still more discovered when it labors most to be concealed. Rather than violate your *modesty*, I must be wanting to your other virtues ; and to gratify one good quality, do wrong to a thousand." The Chancellor, through life, was more remarkable for his *brass* than his *blushes*.

which bore sway for the last four years of Anne's reign, that they made a great effort to deprive him of his seat, first at the election, and then on a petition, but without effect. He married Mary, daughter and coheiress of the Honorable Peregrine Bertie, second son of Montague, Earl of Lindsey, with whom he received a considerable fortune. They had three sons:—Anthony, the eldest, who inherited, and for a time enjoyed, the family estate; Bertie, the youngest, who went into the church; and ROBERT, the subject of this memoir, who was born in the year 1708.[1]

I find no anecdotes of the future Chancellor's childhood, or omens to foretell his coming greatness. Indeed he was pretty well stricken in years before either he himself or others imagined that there would be anything to distinguish him from the ordinary race of mortals who form the chorus in the play of life—without ever fretting and strutting a single hour upon the stage. He was educated at Westminster School. There he formed an acquaintance with the great Lord Mansfield, to whom he was junior about four years; but in consequence of the Chief Justice having spent some time in traveling on the Continent after he had quitted Christ Church, there was only the difference of a few months in their standing at the bar, Murray being the senior by three terms. Another distinguished schoolfellow of theirs was Sir Thomas Clarke, afterwards Master of the Rolls; so that the three highest stations in the law were occupied at the same moment by three Westminster men. Murray and Clarke were both King's scholars; Henley was an oppidan. I have no means of knowing what acquisitions of learning he made, or what disposition he exhibited, till he was transferred to St. John's College, Oxford. There he was entered, and began to reside, on the 19th of November, 1724, in his 17th year.

At this time Alma Mater still lay " dissolved in port," and young Henley, as soon as he was matriculated, piously contracted a great passion for that generous liquor—which adhered to him through life, and made

[1] The most distinguished man of the name before our hero, was Orator Henley, celebrated by Pope. He claimed to be related to the ancient race I have been mentioning; and they would probably have admitted the claim if he had gained his notoriety as a General or a Judge.

him despise claret and all other thin potations. He did not altogether neglect classical learning, but, without being thought at all remarkably deficient in mathematics, he only knew the difference in general appearance between a triangle, a circle, and a square, remaining ignorant of the most common properties of those figures. He chiefly delighted in humor and buffoonery, laying the foundation of that extraordinary collection of droll and not very delicate stories which gave brilliancy to his subsequent career. On the 3rd of November, 1727, he was elected a fellow of All Souls, a distinction for which he was supposed to be chiefly indebted to his powers of amusement. He did not take his degree of Master of Arts till the 5th of July, 1733.

But on the 1st of February, 1728, he was entered of the Inner Temple, and was supposed to begin his juridical studies. We are told that Murray, when he first came to town, "drank champagne with the wits," and that his classic tastes and literary attainments led him to prefer the society of scholars and men of genius to that of his professional brethren. Henley was devoted to the juice of a more powerful vintage, which, in the society he haunted, flowed in very copious streams. Though not devoid of scholarship, and possessing a rich fund of anecdote of a peculiar sort, his conversation was too jovial and boisterous to be endured in the circles where the accomplished Murray shone. Having attended the Courts in the morning, and read a little black letter law on his return, he gave himself to "pleasure in the way he liked it," for the rest of the day, with a few thirsty "All Souls" friends, or some congenial spirits of the Temple. The truth is, that hard drinking was at that time the ruling vice and bane of society, and Henley was not, at his early period of life, fortunate enough to escape the general contagion. He afterwards so far reformed as not to allow his love of wine very seriously to interfere with the pressing business of life, but many a severe fit of the gout was the result of his youthful indulgences. When suffering from the effects of this disease, he was once heard, in the House of Lords, to mutter, after several hobbling and painful walks, with the purse in his hand, between the woolsack and the bar, "If I had only known that these legs were one day to carry a Lord

Chancellor, I'd have taken better care of them when I was a lad."

However, he was a very shrewd fellow; he had an exceedingly good head for law, and, from occasional starts of application, he made much more progress than dull plodders who pore constantly over the "Year Books." Although he never could be called a scientific lawyer, he acquired a competent practical knowledge of his profession, and could get up very reputably all the learning on any particular question with which he had to deal. He was called to the bar, by the Society of the Inner Temple, on the 23rd of June, 1732.[1]

He began with taking a seat in the back row of the Court of King's Bench, where for a long while he had little employment but to take notes, to crack jokes, and to arrange supper parties. From family connections he chose the Western Circuit, of which he afterwards became the leader, but there his progress was very slow.

He had at first a few briefs at Winchester. He showed himself very handy in business, and displayed great skill in cross-examining witnesses, although he was sometimes supposed to take unjustifiable liberties with them. Bishop Newton, who was very intimate with him, as they had been at Westminster together, relates an anecdote of his having cross-examined a broad-brimmed saint, named ZEPHANIAH REEVE, at Bristol, with so much raillery and effect, that the Quaker, forgetting the pacific tenets of his sect, actually sent him a message, insisting on honorable satisfaction, or an apology. Mr. Henley was by no means wanting in courage, but, sensible that he had exceeded the bounds of professional license, and anxious to escape the ridicule of going into the field with such an antagonist, very readily adopted the latter alternative. Many years afterwards, when he was Lord Chancellor, having had a couple pipes of Madeira consigned to him at Bristol, he remembered ZEPHANIAH, and employed him to pay the freight and duty upon them, and forward them to the Grange. "The winter following," says the Bishop, "when the Quaker was in town, he dined at the Chancel-

---

[1] He was afterward admitted of Lincoln's Inn (1745), but this was only to qualify him to hold chambers. The Inner Temple was always his true Inn of Court; and he became a bencher of that Society on being made a King's counsel in 1751.

lor's with a large party of nobility and members of the House of Commons. After dinner the Chancellor related the whole story of his first acquaintance with his friend Reeve, and of every particular that had passed between them, with great good-humor and pleasantry, and to the no little diversion of the company."

In those days the smart junior barristers used to pass their vacations at Bath, a custom not entirely left off when I first knew the profession. Young Counselor Henley was there, the gayest of the gay, and distinguished himself among the ladies in the pump-room in the morning, as well as among the topers in the tavern at night. Here he formed a rather romantic attachment, of which, from his rattling, reckless manner, and his being a professed votary of the god, "ever fair and ever young," he was supposed to be incapable. There was at Bath, for the benefit of the waters, a very young girl of exquisite beauty, who, from illness, had lost the use of her limbs so completely that she was only able to appear in public wheeled about in a chair. She was the daughter and coheiress of Sir John Husband, of Ipsley, in Warwickshire, who, though not "of that ilk," was the last male of a time-honored race, whom Dugdale states to have been Lords of that manor in lineal succession from the Conquest. Henley, struck by the charms of her face, contrived to be introduced to her, when he was still more fascinated by her conversation. His admiration soon ripened into a warm and tender attachment, which he had reason to hope was reciprocal. But it seemed as if he had fallen in love with a *Peri*, and that he must forever be contented with sighing and worshiping at her shrine—when suddenly the waters produced so effectual and complete a cure, that Miss Husband was enabled to comply with the custom of the place by hanging up her votive crutches to the nymph of the spring, and to dance the "minuet de la cour" at the Lower Rooms with her lover. Soon after, with the full consent of her family, she gave her hand to the suitor who had so sedulously attended her. To the end of a long life she continued to enjoy a most perfect state of health, and, their affection remaining unabated, she gave him that first of human blessings, a serene and happy home. The marriage ceremony was performed by his schoolfellow, Bishop Newton,—of which that prelate, in his Memoirs, has the following agreeable recollection: "It happened that he and his lady were married by Mr. Newton, at the chapel in South Audley Street, at which time they were a very handsome couple. Several years afterwards Mr. Newton went one day into Lincoln's Inn Hall while the Court was sitting, to speak with Mr. Murray on some business,—Mr. Henley being next to him, and reading a brief. When he had dispatched his business, and was coming away, 'What,' said Mr. Murray to Henley, 'have you forgotten your old friend Newton, or have you never forgiven the great injury that he did you?' Upon which he started as out of a dream, and was wonderfully gracious to his old schoolfellow, acknowledging that he owed all his happiness in life to him. And, indeed, he had good reason to be happy in his wife and family."[1]

His business not being yet very lucrative, and her father surviving for some years, the newly married couple started with but slender means. Their first residence was a small house in Great James Street, Bedford Row, where they lived for three years very quietly, but very contentedly—in a style congenial to the simplicity of their tastes. After he became Lord Chancellor and Lord Lieutenant for Hampshire, both he and his wife would both look back with pleasing recollection from the Grange and Grosvenor Square to the freedom and frugality of their early establishment near Bedford Row, "where a leg of mutton lasted them three days; the first day hot,—the second day cold,—and the third day hashed."

His further rise was now in great peril by the death of his elder brother Anthony without issue, whereby the family estates in Hampshire and Dorsetshire descended upon him, with the fine house on the south side of Lincoln's Inn Fields, now occupied by the College of Surgeons. Fortunately the property was found much incumbered with debt, or the future Chancellor and Earl would have sunk into a country squire, perhaps distinguished by filling the chair at sessions—petty and quarter. The good management of a few years cleared off, or greatly lightened, the incumbrances, but by this time objects of high ambition had presented themselves to him, and the notion of rural retirement had lost all its attractions.

[1] Newt. Mem.

After his marriage, Henley continued to go frequently to Bath, carrying his wife along with him. He now led comparatively a sober life, but occasionally he would indulge in his old convivial habits, and by his toasts and his stories, and his very agreeable manners, he ingratiated himself so much with the Mayor and Common Council, forming a very small corporation,—with the right of returning members to parliament exclusively vested in them,—that they made him their Recorder, and agreed to elect him at their next vacancy one of their representatives; being swayed, perhaps, not merely by his personal good qualities, but the prospect of his being now able to show his gratitude for their kindness to him. Accordingly, on the dissolution of parliament, which took place in the summer of the year 1747, he was elected a representative for Bath along with Field Marshal Wade, who had gained such notoriety during the recent rebellion.[1]

He became a warm supporter of the party of Frederick, Prince of Wales, designated by the appellation of "*Leicester House*" to which several eminent lawyers were already attached,—particularly Sir Thomas Booth, Chancellor of the Duchy, Dr. (afterwards Sir George) Lee, the eminent civilian, and the Honorable Hume Campbell, afterwards Earl of Marchmont, celebrated as the friend of Pope,—a set who, struggling for a share of the favors of the Crown during the present reign, confidently expected to monopolize the whole in the next.

It is with deep disappointment that, turning to the parliamentary records to ascertain when the new member for Bath made his maiden speech, and by what steps he acquired such a position in the House of Commons as to be appointed Attorney General to the Crown, and afterwards to be intrusted with the Great Seal,—I can not discover, during the ten years he sat in that assembly, his name once mentioned or referred to.[2] It appears, however, from Horace Walpole and contemporary memoir writers, that he was a frequent and active debater. He seems to have been anxious to come forward, as often as he thought he could be of any service to his party, without aiming at oratorical distinction. He was noted as a

[1] 14 Parl. Hist. 77.   [2] See Parl. Hist. xiv. xv.

very steady and consistent politician, so that he did not derive the same benefit from the oblivion of his harangues which might have been enjoyed by some of his successors, who, to further advancement, have spoken with equal ability on both sides of the question discussed.

In 1751, a heavy blow fell upon Leicester House in the sudden death of Frederick. Hume, Campbell, and others, took the opportunity of going over to St. James's, but Henley adhered to the Princess Dowager, and, although he thereby rendered himself obnoxious to George II., he secured his ultimate elevation. Frederick's eldest son (afterwards George III.) being created Prince of Wales, and his establishment being formed, Henley became Solicitor General to his Royal Highness, and at the same time he was appointed a King's counsel. In respect to this last promotion, there being a salary of forty pounds a year annexed to the office, he vacated his seat in the House of Commons; but he was re-elected without opposition.[1]

Henley's silk gown had great success. He not only got into the decided lead on the Western Circuit, but was now in the first business in the Court of King's Bench, both in banc and at nisi prius. He occasionally went into the Court of Chancery in important causes, but, according to the general usage of the eighteenth century, he did not regularly practice there till he became a law officer of the Crown.

So things went on till the year 1756, when Murray insisting on leaving the House of Commons, and being appointed Chief Justice of the King's Bench, the Duke of Newcastle resigned, and a new administration was formed. Leicester House was a party to this arrangement, and Henley succeeded Murray in the office of Attorney General without having previously filled the office of Solicitor General to his Majesty.[2] Now he left the circuit, and transferred himself to the Court of Chancery, where,

[1] 14 Parl. Hist. 77. The inconvenience of vacating a seat in parliament by a silk gown was afterwards obviated by "patents of precedence," or by declaring that the office was to be held "without fee or reward."

[2] Sir Richard Lloyd, the Solicitor under the Duke of Newcastle, was dismissed, but was afterwards made a Baron of the Exchequer. Henley had for his colleague, as Solicitor, the famous Charles Yorke, whose story we shall by and by have to tell.

from the good foundation he had laid in conducting common-law proceedings, from his natural shrewdness and handiness, and from the influence his station was supposed to give him over the Lords Commissioners who held the Great Seal, in the room of Lord Hardwicke, he immediately came into full employment, and was able to cope with the old Chancery counsel, notwithstanding the advantage they enjoyed in being able to make broad assertions as to the settled practice of the Court, and to cite unpublished decisions of the late Lord Chancellor, expressly in point.

He was soon much disturbed by the dismissal of Mr. Pitt and Mr. Legge, and the prospect of himself being turned adrift by the total dissolution of the ministry. By and by he was a little comforted by finding that, with the concurrence of Leicester House, negotiations were opened for a coalition between different parties,—but soon alarmed by the report that Lord Hardwicke, who he thought had a particular spite against him, was to resume the office of Chancellor—and again reassured by the intelligence that Mr. Pitt peremptorily objected to this arrangement. Next followed a confident statement, which was not very disagreeable to him, that Sir Eardley Wilmot, the junior Lord Commissioner, was to be Chancellor; but this was contradicted by that worthy person, who, in a letter to his brother, which was handed about, said, "the acting junior of the commission was a specter I started at, but the sustaining the office alone, I must and will refuse, at all events; I will not give up my peace of mind to any earthly consideration whatever : bread and water are nectar and ambrosia compared with the supremacy of a court of justice."[1] One day, Henley was much excited by hearing that the Great Seal had been offered to Lord Mansfield, and by anticipating that he might accept it, so as to leave the Chief Justiceship of the King's Bench to the Attorney General. Then came certain intelligence that Lord Mansfield having refused the Great Seal, it had been tendered to Sir John Willes, the Chief Justice of the Common Pleas, who was willing enough to accept it, but was standing out for a peerage, which the King objected to, although the last six Chan-

[1] In fact, the offer was not made to Wilmot on this occasion, although it was, and refused (as we shall see), twice over, in the year 1770.

cellors had been Peers, and there had been a general belief that a gagged Keeper or Chancellor would not again be placed on the woolsack.

Henley had not, down to this time, entertained the most distant notion of the Great Seal being offered to himself, as he had only very recently been made Attorney General from practicing in a common-law court, and he felt that he had not sufficient political consequence to aspire to such a dignity. But (as sometimes happens) his mediocrity was the real cause of his elevation. Mr. Pitt knew enough of him from his appearances in the House of Commons to be sure that he could not be formidable in the cabinet,—though considered a fair lawyer, qualified decently to get through the duties of a judicial office;— and under color of paying a compliment to Leicester House, and effectually to bar the return of that old Volpone, Lord Hardwicke, he proposed, with seeming disinterestedness, that the Attorney General, though not politically connected with him, should be the man. Leicester House was rejoiced, and the Duke of Newcastle did not object, being somewhat indifferent about the appointment since he could not procure it for Lord Hardwicke.

The King was obliged to yield any point on which the three parties were agreed; but as Henley, from his connection with Frederick and with the present Prince of Wales, was personally disagreeable to him, he stipulated that the Great Seal must now be taken without a peerage. The offer being made to Henley with this condition, he instantly and joyously accepted it, not even stipulating for a pension, or the reversion of a Tellership to his son, which had been usual on such occasions.[1]

He then thought it would be decent to inform the Chief Justice of the Common Pleas of what had happened. Their interview on this occasion is the subject of one of the stock stories of Westminster Hall. Thus it used to be related with characteristic humor by the late Lord

---

[1] Horace Walpole says, contrary to truth, that he demanded and obtained both: "Willes proposed to be bribed by a peerage, to be at the head of his profession; but could not obtain it. Henley, however, who saw it was the mode of the times to be paid by one favor for receiving another, demanded a Tellership of the Exchequer for his son; which was granted, with a pension of £1,500 a year till it should drop."—*Walp. Mem. Geo. II.* vol. ii. 226. These jobs were afterwards done for him.

Ellenborough:—"Immediately after Willes had refused the Seals, Henley called upon him at his villa, and found him walking in the garden, highly indignant at the affront which he considered that he had received in an offer so inadequate to his pretensions. After entering into some detail of his grievances, he concluded by asking, 'whether, any man of spirit could, under such circumstances, have taken the Seals;' adding, *'Would you, Mr. Attorney, have done so?'* Henley, thus appealed to gravely said, '*Why, my Lord, I am afraid it is rather too late to enter into such a discussion, as I have now the honor of waiting upon your Lordship to inform you that I have actually accepted them.*'"[1]

He was sworn in as Lord Keeper at a Council held on the 30th of June, 1757, and on the first day of Michaelmas Term following, after a grand procession to Westminister Hall, he was duly installed in the Court of Chancery.[2]

[1] Henley's Life of Northington, 34.—Horace Walpole attributed Henley's promotion on this occasion to Mr. Pitt's great desire to make Pratt (afterwards Lord Camden) Attorney General: "One of the most extraordinary parts of the new system is the advancement of Sir Robert Henley. He was made Attorney General by Mr. Fox at the end of last year, and made as bad a figure as might be: Mr. Pitt insisting on an Attorney General of his own, Sir Robert Henley is made Lord Keeper!"—*Horace Walpole to Sir H. Mann*, 3rd July, 1757. This possibly might be an ingredient in Mr. Pitt's determination; but I conceive that his chief motive was to exclude Lord Hardwicke by a man who could not be dangerous.

[2] 30th June, 1757.—"The Lords Commissioners, for the custody of the Great Seal of Great Britain, having delivered the said Great Seal to the King at his Palace at Kensington, on Thursday, the 30th day of June, 1757, his Majesty, about one o'clock the same day, delivered it to Sir Robert Henley, Knight, his Attorney General, with the title of Lord Keeper, who was then sworn into the said office before his Majesty in Council. His Lordship sat at Lincoln's Inn Hall during the Seals, after Trinity Term, and the Seals before Michaelmas Term, 1757. And on Monday, the 7th day of November, being the first day of Michaelmas Term, he went in state from his house in Lincoln's Inn Fields to Westminster Hall, accompanied by the Earl Granville, Lord President of the Council, the Duke of Rutland, Lord Steward of the Household, the Duke of Newcastle, First Lord of the Treasury, the Earl of Hardwicke, the Lord Anson, First Lord of the Admiralty, the Lord Vis. Dupplin, Sir Thomas Robinson, Knight of the Bath, the Master of the Rolls, the Judges, King's Sergeants, King's Counsel, and several other persons. The Lords accompanied him into the Court of Chancery, where (before he entered upon business), in their presence, he took the oaths of allegiance and supremacy, and the oath of Lord Keeper of the Great Seal of Great Britain, the Master of the Rolls holding the book, and the Deputy Clerk of the Crown reading the said oaths; which being done, the Attorney General moved that it might be recorded, and it was ordered accordingly. Then the Lords departed, leaving the Lord Keeper in Court."—*Roll, 1726-1757.*

CHAPTER CXXXIX.

CONTINUATION OF THE LIFE OF LORD NORTHINGTON TILL
THE DEATH OF GEORGE II.

THE new Lord Keeper had nothing to divert him from his judicial duties. His political functions were long in a state of abeyance. He had a pretty strong suspicion in his own mind that he was appointed because he was likely to be quiet in the cabinet, and he did not seek to interfere. Formal meetings of it were occasionally called, which he attended, but he was as little consulted by Pitt about the raising of Highland regiments, or the conduct of the war, as the Six Clerks or the Masters in Chancery. If there had been any debates in parliament, he was precluded from taking part in them; but there were none,—all opposition having vanished for several years, and neither his time nor his attention was in any degree occupied by the sittings of the House of Lords, which generally lasted only while prayers were read, and the question was put "that this House do now adjourn." If a motion was introduced by a speech, it was to vote a monument to a hero who had fallen in battle, or thanks to his surviving comrades; and the Lord Keeper, as Speaker, had only to transmit these thanks, and to read from the woolsack the answers which he received.

Let us follow him then into the Court of Chancery, where his duties were arduous. Here he acquitted himself respectably; but he was contented if he could continue to fill the office, escaping censure,—without aiming at high reputation. He did not follow the example of the fathers of Equity, Lord Nottingham and Lord Hardwicke, who, on coming to the Great Seal, notwithstanding much previous familiarity with the business of the Court in which they were called upon to preside, entered upon a laborious and systematic course of inquiry and of study to qualify themselves for their new situation, that they might discharge its duties in a manner satisfactory to their own minds, and in the hope of being permanently applauded as consummate magistrates. He was satisfied with the stores of professional learning (not inconsiderable) which he had laid in, and with bestowing a reasonable share of pains on the different cases which successively came before him. He always took full notes of the arguments of counsel, and he investigated important questions with much research. Sometimes he wrote out elaborate judgments in his own hand. On the bench he was universally allowed to be impartial and upright. *Laudatus a laudato*, he was pronounced by Lord Eldon to have been "a great lawyer, and very firm in delivering his opinion." He attended Court in the morning with alacrity and cheerfulness, but the evening sittings were a great annoyance to him, from their interference with his convivial pleasures,—and he at last succeeded in abolishing them. With the able assistance of Sir Thomas Clarke, the Master of the Rolls, he contrived pretty well to keep down arrears, although complaints of delay were much louder than in the time of Lord Hardwicke, and the Court was by no means in such good odor with the public. The consequence was that, in all important cases, there was an appeal to the House of Lords. The state of things there was very different from what it had been for twenty years past. The Judge who had pronounced the decree appealed from, had now neither vote nor voice; he could not even ask a question of the counsel at the bar; and a motion being made for a reversal, he could only say, "*the Contents have it.*" Ex-Chancellor Lord Hardwicke always attended, and Lord Mansfield very frequently. It would be wrong to say that they had any inclination to reverse, but they bore no particular good-will to the Lord Keeper, who belonged to a different section in politics from them, and whose authority on questions of Equity they did not consider very high. However, when he acquired a little more experience, and when, being raised to the Peerage, he could freely defend his opinions, he stood higher as a Judge, and appeals from him became more rare. It is said that, after all, "only six of his decrees were reversed or materially altered." [1]

For a long interval after his death, the proceedings of the Court of Chancery in his time had been very insufficiently reported, and when I first entered the profession there were only traditionary recollections of his judgments

Life, 56.

as of his jests;[1] but a few years ago the pious labors of his grandson, my most amiable and accomplished friend, the late Lord Henley, from the Chancellor's own MSS., and from notes taken by several eminent counsel who had practiced under him, produced two volumes of his decisions, which "greatly raised his reputation with those best qualified to estimate it." These show him to have been very bold and very vigorous, and generally very sound; but they are certainly wanting in the depth of thought, in the logical precision, and in the extreme caution, which distinguished the decisions of his predecessor.

I shall give, as a favorable and characteristic specimen of his manner, the judgment delivered by him in the case of *Norton* v. *Relly*,[2] where the bill was filed by a maiden lady residing at Leeds, against a Methodist preacher, and others, trustees named in a deed of gift executed by her to him,—suggesting that it had been obtained by undue means,—and praying that it might be delivered up to be canceled. The "*Tartuffe*" had introduced himself to her notice by a letter, in which he said, that "although unknown to her in the flesh, from the report he had of her he made bold to address her as a fellow member of that consecrated body wherein the fullness of the Godhead dwelt, and that he was coming among them at Leeds, for a little time, to preach the kingdom of God," subscribing himself "her affectionate brother in the flesh." She was prevailed upon to invite him to her house, to accompany him to London, to give him large sums of ready money, and to grant him an annuity charged on her real estates in Yorkshire:—

Lord Chancellor Henley. "This cause, as it has been very truly observed, is the first of the kind that ever came before the Court, and, I may add, before any court of judicature in this kingdom. Matters of religion are happily very rarely the subject of dispute in courts of law or equity." [After expressing his respect for dissenters, he proceeds:] "But very wide is the difference between dissenters and fanatics, whose canting, and whose doctrines, have no other tendency than to plunge their deluded votaries into the very abyss of bigotry, despair, and enthusiasm. And though even against those unhappy and false pastors, I would not wish the

[1] Ambler alone had noticed him. [2] Eden's Rep. ii. 286.

spirit of persecution to go forth, yet are not these men to be discountenanced and discouraged whenever they are properly brought before courts of justice?—men who, in the apostle's language, *go about and creep into people's dwellings, deluding weak women*,—men who go about and diffuse their rant and warm enthusiastic notions, to the destruction not only of the temporal concerns of many of the subjects of this realm, but to the endangering their eternal welfare. And shall it be said that this Court can not relieve against the glaring impositions of these men? That it can not relieve the weak and unwary, especially when the impositions are exercised on those of the weaker sex? This court is the guardian and protector of the weak and helpless of every denomination and the punisher of fraud and imposition in every degree, Here is a man, nobody knows who or what he is; his own counsel have taken much pains modestly to tell me what he is not; and depositions have been read to show that he is not a Methodist. What is that to me? But I could easily have told them what, by the proofs in this cause and his own letters, he appears to be—a subtle sectary, who preys upon his deluded hearers, and robs them under the mask of religion. Shall it be said, in his excuse, that this lady was as great an enthusiast as himself? It is true she was far gone—but not far enough for his purpose. Thus he addressed her, '*Your former pastor has, I hear excommunicated you, but put yourself in my congregation, wherein dwells the fullness of God.*' How scandalous, how blasphemous is this! In coming from London to Leeds he will not come in a stage coach, but must have a post-chaise, and live elegantly on the road at the expense of the plaintiff, who gave him £50 in money, besides presents of liquor—so that his own hot imagination was further heated with the spirit of brandy. He secured a part of her fortune by lighting up in her breast the flame of enthusiasm, and undoubtedly he hoped in due time to secure the whole by kindling another flame of which the female breast is so susceptible; for the invariable style of his letters is '*all is to be completed by love and union.*' Let it not be told in the streets of London that this preaching sectary is only defending his just rights. I repeat, let not such men be persecuted, but many of them deserve to be represented in puppet shows. I have considered this cause not merely as a private matter, but of public concernment and utility. Bigotry and enthusiasm have spread their baneful influence amongst us far and wide, and the unhappy objects of the contagion almost daily increase. Of this, not only Bedlam, but most of the private madhouses, are melancholy and striking proofs. Let it be decreed that the defendant execute a release to the plantiff of this annuity, and deliver up the deed for securing it. I can not conclude without observing that one of his counsel, with some ingenuity, tried to shelter him under the denomination of '*an independent preacher.*' I have tried in this decree to spoil his *independency.*'"

The finest judgment Henley ever delivered is supposed to have been in the case of *Burgess* v. *Wheate*,[1] where the question was, "whether the Crown be entitled by escheat to a trust estate upon the *cestui qui trust* (or person beneficially interested) dying without issue?" He called in the assistance of Lord Mansfield and Sir Thomas Clarke, who differing, he sided with the latter against the escheat, so as to leave the estate to the trustee discharged of every trust,—and his decision has given the rule ever since. But it proceeds on reasonings too technical and abstruse to be introduced here.

He likewise obtained great credit for the rule he laid down respecting *perpetuities*, in the case of *Duke of Marlborough* v. *Earl of Godolphin*. The hero of Blenheim, endeavoring to retain after death a power beyond the limits allowed by law, devised his great estates to trustees for the benefit of several existing persons successively for life, with remainder to their sons in strict settlement; but directed his trustees, on the birth of each son of each tenant for life, to revoke the uses before limited to their respective sons in tail male, and to limit the estates to such sons for their lives :—[2]

Lord Keeper. " It is agreed on all hands that this clause is new, and that, although it has been privately fostered by a particular family, from whom it issued, it never has been adopted by conveyancers. In substance, the testator makes his great-grandson, the present Duke, who was at the date of the will unborn, tenant for life, with a limitation to his sons as purchasers in tail. It is agreed that this could not be done directly by words of limitation,

[1] Eden's Rep. i. 77. [2] Ibid. i. 404.

because, though by the rules of law an estate may be limited, by way of contingent remainder, to a person not *in esse* for life, or as an inheritance, yet a remainder to the issue of such contingent remainder-man, as a purchaser, is a limitation unheard of in law, nor ever attempted, as far as I have been able to discover. Technical reasons, upheld by old repute, and grown reverend by length of years, bear great weight and authority, but a new technical reason appears with as little dignity as an usurper just seated in his chair of state. The common law seemed wisely to consider that real property ought not to be put out of commerce, and should be left free to answer the exigencies of the possessors and their families, and, therefore, would not admit perpetuities by way of entails. The dissipation of young heirs, the splendor of great families, the propriety of annexing sufficient possessions to support the dignities obtained by illustrious persons, afford specious arguments for perpetuating estates by entails; but, in a commercial country, to damp the spirit of industry, and to take away one of its greatest incentives, the power of honorably investing its acquisitions, would produce all the inconveniences against which we have been guarding by fines and recoveries and other devices, now to be considered an essential part of our jurisprudence. The safety of creditors and purchasers requires that the law should be fixed and certain with respect to the limitations of real property in family settlements,—not subject to be questioned upon whimsical inventions, started (though by the ablest men) in order to introduce innovations in fundamentals."

After treating the subject at great length, and with much ability, he decreed that the plaintiff, George, Duke of Marlborough, was entitled to an estate in tail male and not for life only, as John, Duke of Marlborough, had intended; and this decree, on appeal, was affirmed by the House of Lords.[1]

In the case of *Lowther* v. *Cavendish*,[2] respecting the words in a will which will carry leasehold estates along with freeholds, Lord Northington commented rather flippantly on the ruling authority of *Rose* v. *Bartlett* which afterwards drew down upon him this strong censure from Lord Eldon, under the decent disguise that he had been

[1] Life of Lord Northington, Appendix II.   [2] Ambler, 357.

misreported: "I am not disposed to believe that Lord Northington ever made use of the expressions respecting *Rose* v. *Bartlett* which are attributed to him. We all know that he was possessed of great law learning, and a very manly mind; and I can not but think that he would rather have denied the rule altogether than have set it afloat by treating it with a degree of scorn, and by introducing distinctions calculated to disturb the judgments of his predecessors, and remove the landmarks of the law."[1]

But his greatest blunder was in *Drury* v. *Drury*,[2] where he took immense pains to get wrong, holding that "a female marrying under age might renounce the jointure settled upon her, and claim dower and thirds,"—contrary to the practice and understanding of the profession, and contrary to an *obiter* opinion of Lord Hardwicke,—although there was no decision exactly in point. In the course of his rather arrogant judgment, he gave deep offense to the irritable race of conveyancers, by observing, in corroboration of a remark at the bar, that the *conveyancers had not thought about it*,—" which is natural enough, their time being more dedicated to *perusal* than to *thought!*" But they had their revenge when the case was heard upon appeal, in the House of Lords; for Lord Hardwicke moved the reversal in a most crushing speech, in which he said, "The opinion—the course of conveyancers is of great weight. They are to advise, and if their opinion is to be despised, every case must come to law. No! the received opinion ought to govern. The ablest men in the profession have been conveyancers." Lord Mansfield concurred, and the poor Lord Keeper, having put the question, "So many of your Lordships as are of opinion that this decree be reversed, will say, 'CONTENT;' of the contrary opinion, 'NOT CONTENT,'" was obliged to say, "The CONTENTS have it!"

From George II.'s dislike to him, on account of his connection with Leicester House, and from his insignificance in the Cabinet, he probably would have remained a commoner during the rest of this reign, had it not happened that Lord Ferrers thought fit to shoot Mr. Johnson, his steward, and was to be tried before the House of Peers for the murder. A Lord High Steward was to be appointed for the occasion, and he must be a Peer.

[1] *Thompson* v. *Lawly*, 2 Bos. & Pull. 315.   [2] Eden's Rep. ii. 39.

Neither Lord Hardwicke nor Lord Mansfield coveted such a painful pre-eminence, and it had been usual that the holder of the Great Seal, if a layman, should preside at such trials. In consequence, on the 27th of March, 1760, letters patent passed, creating "the right trusty and well-beloved Sir Robert Henley, Knight, a Peer of Great Britain, by the style and title of Baron Henley, of the Grange, in the county of Southampton."

The trial took place in Westminster Hall, on the 16th of April, 1760, and the two following days. "Who," writes Horace Walpole, giving a most amusing narrative of it to his correspondent at Florence, "at the last trials[1] would have believed a prophecy that the three first men at the next should be Henley the lawyer, Bishop Secker,[2] and Dick Grenville?[3] The Judge and criminal were far inferior to those you have seen. For the Lord High Steward, he neither had any dignity, nor affected any. Nay, he held it all so cheap, that he said at his own table t'other day, '*I will not send for Garrick and learn to act a part.*'"[4] There is, no doubt, considerable exaggeration here, from the writer's indiscriminate love of abuse and ridicule; but it must be admitted that his Grace, the Lord High Steward, often carried his dislike of what he called "humbug" to a most unwarrantable length, and, both when sitting publicly on his tribunal, and in private society, did not scruple to violate the rules of decorum and decency.

On this occasion, however, if there were a departure from the heraldic injunctions of "bowing to the cloth of state," or presenting to his Grace his white wand "on the knee," a striking example was given to the world of substantial justice.[5] Were such a case now to come before a jury, there would probably be an acquittal on the ground of *insanity*, although the noble culprit was actuated by deep malice towards the deceased,—although he had con-

---

[1] Alluding to the rebel Lords in 1746.
[2] Now Archbishop of Canterbury.
[3] Now Earl Temple, and as Lord Privy Seal, having precedence of Dukes.
[4] Letter to George Montague, Esq., 19th April, 1760. To another correspondent he says--"Lord Keeper was Lord High Steward; but was not at all too dignified a personage to sit on such a criminal; indeed he gave himself no trouble to figure."
[5] I shall further examine the case in the Life of Charles Yorke, who acted a most important part in it.

trived the opportunity of satiating his vengeance with much premeditation and art,—and although the steps which he afterwards took showed that he was fully sensible of the magnitude and the consequences of his crime.

The Lord High Steward having received the answer from every Peer present, to whom he put the question "*Guilty or not guilty?*"—"GUILTY, UPON MY HONOR," himself standing uncovered at the chair, and laying his hand on his breast, said, "My Lords, I am of opinion that Lawrence, Earl Ferrers, is guilty of the felony and murder whereof he stands indicted, UPON MY HONOR." He then announced to the unfortunate Earl the unanimous verdict of his peers against him.

The address of the Lord High Steward, delivered the following day in passing sentence, has been praised as "one of the best specimens of judicial eloquence in existence—being at once grave, simple, dignified, and affecting."[1]

"Lawrence, Earl Ferrers,

"His Majesty, from his royal and equal regard to justice, and his steady attention to our constitution, which hath endeared him in a wonderful manner to the universal duty and affection of his subjects, hath commanded this inquiry to be made upon the blood of a very ordinary subject, against your Lordship, a Peer of this realm. Your Lordship hath been arraigned; hath pleaded and put yourself on your peers, and they (whose judicature subsists in wisdom, honor, and justice) have unanimously found your Lordship guilty of the felony and murder charged in the indictment. It is usual, my Lord, for courts of justice, before they pronounce the dreadful sentence ordained by the law, to open to the prisoner the nature of the crime of which he is convicted; not in order to aggravate or afflict, but to awaken the mind to a due attention to, and consideration of, the unhappy situation into which he hath brought himself. My Lord, the crime of which your Lordship is found guilty—*murder*—is incapable of aggravation; and it is impossible but that during your Lordship's long confinement you must have reflected upon it, represented to your mind in its deepest

---

[2] Life, by Lord Henley, 44.

shades, and with all its train of dismal and detestable consequences. As your Lordship hath received no benefit, so you can derive no consolation, from that refuge you seemed almost ashamed to take under a pretended insanity; since it hath appeared to us all, from your cross-examination of the King's witnesses, that you recollected the minutest circumstances of facts and conversations to which you and the witnesses only could be privy, with the exactness of a memory more than ordinarily sound; it is therefore as unnecessary as it would be painful to me to dwell longer on a subject so black and dreadful. It is with much satisfaction that I can remind your Lordship that though from the present tribunal, before which you now stand, you can receive nothing but strict and equal justice; yet you are soon to appear before an Almighty Judge, whose unfathomable wisdom is able, by means incomprehensible to our narrow capacities, to reconcile justice with mercy.[1] But your Lordship's education must have informed you, and you are now to remember, that such beneficence is only to be obtained by deep contrition—sound, unfeigned, and substantial repentance. Confined strictly, as your Lordship must be, for the very short remainder of your life, according to the provisions of the late Act, yet from the wisdom of the legislature, which, to prevent as much as possible this heinous and horrid crime of murder, hath added infamy to death, you will be still, if you please, entitled to converse and communicate with the ablest divines of the Protestant church, to whose pious care and consolation in fervent prayer and devotion I most cordially recommend your Lordship. Nothing remains for me but to pronounce the dreadful sentence of the law, and the judgment of the law is, and this High Court doth award, that you, Lawrence, Earl Ferrers, return to the prison of the Tower, from whence you came; from thence you must be led to the place of execution on Monday next, and when you come there you must be hanged by the neck till you are dead, and

---

[1] His Grace thought it unnecessary to disqualify himself as Baron Perrin did upon a similar trial for murder. The prisoner, after the verdict, having still asserted his innocence, the Judge thus modestly began: " Prisoner, you are soon to appear at the bar of a greater, *and, let me add, of an abler Judge;* but, with my limited understanding, I must approve of the verdict, and my duty requires me to pronounce upon you the awful sentence of the law."— *Ex relatione Lord Chief Baron Alexander.*

your body must be dissected and anatomized, and God Almighty be merciful to your soul!"

Henley acted with great propriety between the sentence and execution, doing what he could to gratify the unhappy criminal's last wishes, without saving him from his deserved fate. Horace Walpole writes:—"Two petitions from his mother and all his family were presented to the King, who said, 'As the House of Lords had unanimously found him guilty, he would not interfere.' Last week my Lord Keeper very good-naturedly got out of a gouty bed to present another: The King would not hear him. 'Sir,' said the Keeper, 'I do not come to petition for mercy or respite, but that the £4,000 which Lord Ferrers has in India bonds may be permitted to go, according to his disposition of it, to his mistress, his children, and the family of the murdered man.'—'With all my heart,' said the King, 'I have no objection; but I will have no message carried to him from me.' However, this grace was notified to him, and gave him great satisfaction."[1]

After this trial, although the Lord Keeper was now entitled to speak and vote as a Peer, he was still treated rather contumeliously by his colleagues, and he does not appear to have taken any part in debate or in political intrigue till a new field was opened to him by the accession to the throne of the youthful Sovereign, to whom and to whose father he had been so much devoted.

CHAPTER CXL.

CONTINUATION OF THE LIFE OF LORD NORTHINGTON TILL HE RESIGNED THE GREAT SEAL.

THE death of George II. made a very auspicious change in the position of the Lord Keeper. Hitherto he had been received coldly at Court, and he had been without any political weight. The new King regarded him with great favor as a steady adherent of Leicester House, who might assist Lord Bute in the

[1] Letter to Sir Horace Mann, in which there is an extremely interesting account of the execution.

contemplated change in the administration. On the 16th of January, 1761, on his surrendering the Great Seal into his Majesty's hands, he received it back with the title of "Lord Chancellor," instead of "Lord Keeper,"[1] and he was afterwards created Earl of Northington,[2] and appointed Lord Lieutenant of the county of Southampton.[3]

He took the earliest opportunity to avail himself of the partiality of the reigning monrrch, by asking his permission to discontinue the evening sittings in the Court of Chancery on Wednesdays and Fridays. George III. made a good story, which he used to tell for the rest of his reign, of what passed between him and his Chancellor on this occasion. "I asked him," said his Majesty, "his reason for wishing that these sittings should be abolished. —'Sir,' answered he, 'that I may be allowed comfortably to finish my bottle of port after dinner; and your Majesty, solicitous for the happiness of all your subjects, I hope will consider this to be reason sufficient.'"[4] The permission was graciously accorded—we may suppose an explanation being added that *post-prandian* sittings were becoming generally unpopular, and were unsuited to the changed manners of society.[5]

Lord Bute being at first sworn of the Privy Council—then made Secretary of State—next forcing Mr. Pitt to resign—and, at a short interval, becoming himself Prime Minister, before he had ever spoken in Parliament,[6] and

[1] Geo. 3, 16th Jan. 1761. Memorandum—That the Right Honorable Robert, Lord Henley, Lord Keeper of the Great Seal of Great Britain, delivered the Great Seal to his Majesty in Council, when his Majesty was graciously pleased to redeliver to him the said Great Seal, with the title of Lord Chancellor of Great Britain. Whereupon his Lordship, then in council, took the oaths appointed to be taken instead of the oaths of allegiance, and also the oath of Lord High Chancellor of Great Britain.—*Cr. Off. Min.*, No. 2, p. 1. By another entry, No. 2, p. 4, it appears, that on the first day of the following Hilary Term he took all the oaths over again in the Court of Chancery in Westminster Hall.

[2] 19th May, 1764 —By this title I shall hereafter call him.

[3] 21st August, 1761.

[4] According to other accounts, the Lord Chancellor's answer was still more blunt:—" that I may get drunk, please your Majesty;" or,—"because at that time I am apt to be drunk."

[5] Sir William Grant, when Master of the Rolls, pursued another remedy, by ordering his dinner—with a bottle of Madeira and a bottle of port—to be ready for him at the Piazza Coffee House, at ten at night, when the sittings were over.

[6] It is a curious fact, that when he made his maiden speech he was Prime Minister. His most public previous effort had been in private theatricals.

while only a Scotch Peer,—the Leicester House party, to which Lord Northington had so steadily adhered, was for a brief space triumphant. Although he now had a good deal of influence in the disposal of places, and he took a part in the factious conflicts which divided the Court, still he was not prominent as a politician. He does not seem to have been much consulted about the treaty of peace which it was the great object of Lord Bute's administration to negotiate; and, severely as the preliminaries of Fontainebleau were attacked by Lord Hardwicke, I can not find that he gave any assistance to defend them. He was even silent on the Cider Bill. He spoke, when permitted, in such trenchant fashion, and was so apt to give an advantage to the adversary, that I suspect he was strongly cautioned to remain quiet.

When Lord Bute, having obtained peace abroad, and thrown all England into an uproar, suddenly resigned, and the Duke of Bedford was supposed to be Minister, Lord Northington retained the Great Seal; but while this arrangement continued, he seems strictly to have confined himself to the judicial duties of his office. Having received a personal order from the King that Wilkes should be prosecuted, he left the matter entirely in the hands of the law officers of the Crown.[1] The general warrants were issued by Lord Halifax to arrest the printer and publisher of No. XLV. of the "North Briton," and the successive foolish steps were adopted which brought the Demagogue into such notoriety and importance, without the head of the law being at all consulted.

George Grenville, who was intended to act only a subordinate part in this government, had established a great ascendency, and, acting upon the contracted notions of the constitution of the country which he had imbibed when studying for the bar in a special pleader's office, he threw everything into confusion at home, and he sowed the seeds of that terrible conflict which, after he was in his grave, led to the dismemberment of the British Em-

---

[1] "Lord Chancellor told me had mentioned the 'North Briton' to the King, and that his Majesty had desired him to give directions for the printers being prosecuted. In consequence of which, he had spoken to Lord Shelburne to have a case prepared for the opinion of the Attorney and Solicitor General."—*Journal of the Duke of Grafton.*

pire. It is little to the credit of Lord Northington, that, while he was Chancellor, the ill-omened plan was adopted of taxing America by the British Parliament, and the too famous American Stamp Act was passed. A constitutional lawyer in the cabinet, like Lord Camden, would have reprobated such a measure on principle; and a wary one, like Lord Mansfield, would have disapproved of it as dangerous. But Lord Northington, allowed to enjoy the sweets of his office, gave himself no trouble either about the domestic or colonial policy of the government.

In the midst of the conflicts of faction, the town was amused for a short time by the trial of a Peer on a capital charge. William, Lord Byron, uncle of the illustrious author of "CHILDE HAROLD," having killed a gentleman of the name of Chaworth in a duel fought in a tavern, an indictment for murder was found against him by a grand jury of the county of Middlesex, and was removed, by certiorari, into the House of Lords. Thereupon, the trial was ordered to take place in Westminster Hall, and the Earl of Northington was appointed to preside as Lord High Steward.

On the day appointed, the noble prisoner appearing, attended by the gentlemen jailer and the axe, with the edge turned from him, his Grace addressed to him the following preliminary admonition and comfort:—

"William, Lord Byron, your Lordship is unhappily brought to this bar to answer a heavy and dreadful accusation, for you are charged with the murder of a fellow-subject. The solemnity and awful appearance of this judicature must naturally embarrass and discompose your Lordship's spirits, whatever internal resource you may have in conscience to support you in your defense. It may be, therefore, not improper for me to remind your Lordship that you are to be tried by the fixed and settled laws of a free country, framed only to protect the innocent, to distinguish the degrees of offense, and vindictive only against malice and premeditated mischief. Homicide, or the killing of a fellow-creature, is, by the wisdom of law, distinguished into classes: if it ariseth from necessity or accident, or is without malice, it is not murder; and of these distinctions, warranted by evidence, every person, though accused by a grand jury of the highest offense, is at full liberty to avail himself. As an additional consolation, your Lordship will reflect that you have the happiness to be tried by the supreme jurisdiction of this nation; that you can receive nothing from your peers but justice, distributed with candor,—delivered, too, under the strongest obligation upon noble minds—*honor*. These considerations will, I hope, compose your Lordship's mind, fortify your spirits, and leave you free for your defense."

All the Peers present having agreed in a verdict of "*Manslaughter*," except four, who said *Not Guilty* generally, and privilege of peerage being pleaded in bar of sentence, the Lord High Steward, without, as usual, giving a warning that such a plea could not be available on a second conviction, merely informed the prisoner that he was entitled to be discharged,—broke his white wand in a manner which could not be considered an imitation of Garrick in *Prospero*,—and abruptly adjourned the House.

Now, as at the trial of Lord Ferrers, he was too regardless of forms, but he committed no material mistake of which the accused or the public could complain.[1]

When, at last, the King was so sick of being ruled and lectured by George Grenville, that he preferred Lord Rockingham and the Whigs, without the aid of Mr. Pitt, —a great mistake was committed by them in not insisting on a new Chancellor. They did make Chief Justice Pratt a Peer, by the title of Lord Camden; but if they had given him the Great Seal, they might, from his talents and popularity, have weathered the perils to which they were exposed, and the country, enjoying the benefit of their sound constitutional principles, might have escaped the anarchy and misgovernment which soon followed. But Lord Northington hated them;—while he sat in the cabinet with them, he watched them with jealousy,—and at last he plotted, and he effected, their ruin. As they were to repeal the American Stamp Act, and to censure the proceedings against Wilkes which he had sanctioned, one does not well understand how he should have wished or been permitted to continue in office. But he was a "friend" of the King,—and some were silly enough to think that he might secure to the Government the royal favor and confidence.

The Stamp Act having produced the discontents and

[1] 19 St. Tr. 1177-1236.

disturbances in America which might have been expected from it,—much against the King's wishes, it was to be repealed; but, to mollify him, a preliminary resolution was moved, "that Parliament had full power and right to make laws of sufficient force to bind the colonies." When this came to be debated in the House of Peers, it was objected to by Lord Camden as being not only ill-timed, but as being untrue, on the ground that it might, in its general language, include the power and right to *tax* the colonies, which he strongly denied. "My Lords," he proceeded, "he who disputes the authority of any supreme legislature treads upon very tender ground. It is therefore necessary for me, in setting out, to desire that no inference may be drawn from anything I shall advance. I deny that the consequences of my reasoning will be, that the colonies can claim independence, or that they have a right to oppose acts of the legislature in a rebellious manner, even although the legislature has no right to make such acts. In my opinion, my Lords, the legislature had no right to make this law. The sovereign authority, the omnipotence of the legislature, is a favorite doctrine, but there are some things which you can not do. You can not enact anything against the Divine law. You can not take away any man's private property, without making him a compensation. You have no right to condemn any man by bill of attainder without hearing him. But though the Parliament can not take any man's private property, yet every subject must make contribution: and this he consents to do by his representative. Notwithstanding the King, Lords, and Commons could in ancient times tax other persons, they never could tax the clergy." He then goes on to consider the case of the counties palatine, of Wales, and of Berwick, showing that they never were taxed by Parliament till they sent representatives to the House of Commons; observing that the Irish tax themselves, and that the English Parliament could not tax them. "But," said he, "even supposing that the Americans have no exclusive right to tax themselves, it would be good policy to give it them, instead of offensively asserting a power which you ought never to have exercised. America feels that she can do better without us than we can without her." This was Lord Camden's first speech in the House of Lords.

Lord Northington, leaving the woolsack, commenced in a tone most insulting to the new Peer, and, what was much worse, most insulting to the people of America,—Benjamin Franklin being a listener below the bar:—

"I did not intend," said he, "to trouble your Lordships in this debate, but hearing doctrines laid down so new, so unmaintainable, so unconstitutional, so mischievous, I can not sit silent. Such paradoxes are the result of a heated imagination, accompanied by a facility of utterance and readiness of language. The noble and learned Lord lays it down that the Americans have an exclusive right to impose taxes on themselves. He is to lay down the law for them, and the British Parliament is not to interfere with them. With great submission to the noble and learned Lord, I believe that all except himself will admit that every government can arbitrarily impose laws on all its subjects; there must be a supreme dominion in every state, whether monarchical, aristocratical, democratical, or mixed: to that supreme dominion all must bend. The noble and learned Lord has endeavored to distinguish between the civil power of government and its casuistical power. Every legislature ought to make laws for the safety and the benefit of the whole: but, my Lords, suppose they make a law contrary to this principle, a resistance to such law is at the risk of life and fortune." [After touching upon the power to tax the clergy, and the other illustrations introduced, he proceeded:] "My Lords, I seek for the liberty and constitution of this kingdom no further back than the Revolution: there I make my stand: and in the reign of King William an act passed avowing the power of this legislature over the colonies. As to the expediency of carrying the Stamp Act into execution, does the noble and learned Lord mean that the King has a dispensing or suspending power? The King is sworn by his coronation oath to execute all the laws of this realm. Then the noble and learned Lord would get rid of it by a repeal,—but if you should concur with his Lordship in the expediency of repeal, you will tell twelve millions of your subjects of Great Britain and Ireland that you prefer to them the colonists who have got rich under their protection, and you will soon have these colonies at your door, not merely besieging you as now with petitions, but using the '*argumentum baculinum.*'

What, my Lords, have these favorite Americans done? They have called a meeting of their States, and then have entered into resolutions by which, in my opinion, they have forfeited all their charters. But, my Lords, the nature of the Stamp Act seems to be mistaken. It binds all the colonies to contribute to the expense of the general government incurred in defending them, but it does not control the power each province has to lay internal taxes for local purposes. How could the Americans have acquired the exemption which they claim? If all the great lawyers in Westminster Hall should give an opinion that the King could grant the territory of North America, none could say that the King could put the grantees out of their subjection to the *summum imperium* of Great Britain. My Lords, the colonies are become too big to be governed by the laws they at first set out with. They have, therefore, run into confusion, and it will be the policy of this country to form a plan of laws for them. If they withdraw allegiance, you must withdraw protection; and then the little state of Genoa or of San Marino may soon overrun them."[1]

This coarse invective, the first of the sort delivered in Parliament against "the Rebels," though sure to gratify the King and the "King's friends," was so very indiscreet, and was so evidently calculated to produce resentment and resistance on the other side of the Atlantic, that not only Lord Rockingham and his Whig colleagues were appalled by it, but it gave uneasiness to all moderate Tories who had approved of the Stamp Act, and were still desirous of supporting it.

Lord Mansfield immediately followed, in the hope of repairing or mitigating the mischief: and, notwithstanding his habitual self-command, was unable to conceal his mortification. Thus he gently disclaimed the diatribe of the Chancellor: "I stand up, my Lords, to bring your Lordships to the question before you, which is, whether the proposition enunciated by the noble Duke[2] as to our right to make laws to bind the colonies is, according to what appears from our law and history, true, or not true? It is out of the question whether it was, or was not, expedient to pass the law; whether it be, or be not, expedient to

[1] 16 Parl. Hist. 161–177.
[2] The Duke of Grafton, who moved the resolution.

repeal it. Out of this question, too, are the rules which are to guide the legislature in making a law. This law is made, and the question is, whether you had a right to make it?" Without further reference to the Chancellor, he then goes on, with much calmness, and with arguments to which I have never been able to find an answer, to deny, as far as the *power* is concerned, the distinction between a law to *tax* and a law for any other purpose. The resolution was agreed to, but this debate marred the effect of the repeal of the Stamp Act, and gave a great "*shake*" to the Rockingham administration, by showing that their conciliatory policy was distasteful to the Court.

The Lord Chancellor seems to have remained quiet for the rest of the session, and not even to have spoken when the House of Lords, very properly, rejected the bill passed by the Commons, declaring "General Warrants" to be illegal; leaving this question to be decided (as it was satisfactorily) by the Courts of Common Law.

Soon after the prorogation, it was evident that a political crisis was at hand. The immediate cause of the dismission of the ministry is attributed to an intrigue of the Lord Chancellor Northington, who had long contemplated their feeble state, and meditated their overthrow.[1] He had now personal as well as courtier-like reasons for wishing that there might be a revolution in the cabinet. Those legs, of which he had taken such bad care in his youth, refused to carry the Chancellor any longer between the woolsack and the bar, and he was desirous of making the repose which they demanded as comfortable as possible. His attacks of gout had been of late so frequent and severe, that he found he could no longer hold the Great Seal; yet he was unwilling to retire into private life, and he thought that, in taking an active part in forming a new administration, he should be able to make a good bargain for himself. It may seem strange that he hoped to accomplish his object under the auspices of Mr. Pitt, who had been so odious at Court after his quarrel with Lord Bute, and had expressed a strong opinion against taxing America. But here begins the period of the life of that most illustrious patriot which is the least to

[1] I Adolphus, 225.

his credit. Piqued that there should be a Whig government in which he was not included,—instead of supporting it, he had publicly said, "Lord Rockingham has not my confidence;"[1] and, from his belligerent tendencies, there was an expectation that, if he were once in office, he might be induced to take part against the Americans, and to use the necessary force for subduing them. There is no such bond of political union as a common dislike of the minister. This makes all difference of principle and all past quarrels to be forgotten. George III. and the "Great Commoner" being equally desirious of getting rid of Lord Rockingham, there had been much coquetry between them during some months, and, for the nonce, there was actually considerable good will. Lord Northington was well aware of these reciprocal feelings, and determined to take advantage of them.

The occasion which he seized for effecting his purpose was the preparation of a Code for the government of Canada. A proclamation had issued in 1764, by which all the laws of England were introduced into the French provinces ceded by the peace of Paris; but this rash experiment (as might have been foreseen) caused general discontent and confusion. The papers relating to the disputes had, according to custom, been laid before the Attorney and Solicitor General—most able men—Charles Yorke and De Grey; and they had prepared a very masterly report for the consideration of the cabinet—proposing to leave to the natives their ancient rights of property and civil laws, and to temper the rigor of their criminal procedure by the more equitable and liberal system of English jurisprudence. Soon after the commencement of the recess a cabinet was called to consider this report, and, the Chancellor being confined by a fit of the gout, the meeting took place at his house, in Lincoln's Inn Fields. Contrary to his good humored and courteous, though blunt and careless manner, he was exceedingly cross and peevish on this occasion, and found fault with everybody and everything. He complained that he had been slighted in the affair by Mr. Attorney and Mr. Solicitor; he bitterly criticised and abused their perform-

---

[1] Lord Rockingham's position, at this time, bears a considerable resemblance to that of Mr. Canning, in 1827, when the ultra-Tories and Lord Grey coalesced to eject him.

ance; and he concluded by giving an opinion that no proposition on the subject could be sanctioned by the cabinet until they had procured a complete digest of all the existing laws of Canada,—which would occasion a delay of at least a whole year. His colleagues believed that his waywardness proceeded from the bodily anguish he was suffering, and the meeting broke up without coming to any definite resolution. Next day he refused to attend another cabinet—(as they still supposed) from his great toe being more painful. The rest of the ministers considering the matter very pressing,—that there might not be disturbances at Quebec, as well as at Boston, held two more meetings without him at the Duke of Richmond's house at Whitehall. The Attorney General, who had taken the chief part in framing the Report, being summoned to attend, gave ample information on the principles by which he was guided, and proposed that it should be sent to Quebec for the inspection and consideration of Governor Carlton and the Colonial Crown lawyers, with instructions to return it corrected, according to their judgment, so that it might be in all respects suited to the circumstances and feelings of the province. Every difficulty seemed obviated. In consequence, Lord Egremont, in whose department the business more immediately was, and who had recommended the summoning of the Attorney and Solicitor General, went out of town, declaring his willingness to confide his judgment to their decision. Mr. Attorney, thinking all his cares over till the Morrow of all Souls, and the reassembling of parliament should again make him wish that he could be divided into ten portions to be working in ten places at once,—retired into the country to enjoy the repose of the long vacation.

But the Lord Chancellor, when he heard at night of this last meeting of the Cabinet, loudly exclaimed, "By G—, they shall never meet again!" Next morning, repairing to Richmond, he informed the King "that the Ministers could not go on, and that at all events he himself must resign the Great Seal, and would attend Cabinet Councils with Lord Rockingham no longer." He concluded by advising his Majesty to send for Mr. Pitt,—holding out hopes that there was a change in him, and that he might now be found more pliant and accommodating. The King, without considering too curiously what might follow, being delighted with the prospect of getting rid of the men who had repealed the Stamp Act, and had induced parliament to condemn the proceedings against Wilkes, very willingly adopted this advice, and they manufactured the following letter to "the Great Commoner:"

"Richmond Lodge, July 7, 1766.

"Mr. Pitt,

"Your very dutiful and handsome conduct the last summer makes me desirous of having your thoughts how an able and dignified ministry may be formed. I desire, therefore, you will come for this salutary purpose to town.

"I can not conclude without expressing how entirely my ideas concerning the basis on which a new administration should be erected, are consonant to the opinion you gave on that subject in parliament a few days before you set out for Somersetshire.[1]

"I convey this through the channel of the Earl of Northington; as there is no man in my service on whom I so thoroughly rely, and who I know agrees with me so perfectly in the contents of this letter.

"GEORGE R."

As soon as Lord Northington arrived in town, he forwarded the royal missive, accompanied by the following communication from himself:

"London, July 7, 1766.

"Sir,

"I have the King's command to convey to you his Majesty's note inclosed; and as I am no stranger to the general contents, I can not help adding that I congratulate you very sincerely on so honorable and so gracious a distinction.

"I think myself very happy in being the channel of conveying what I think doth you so much honor, and I am persuaded will tend to the ease and happiness of so amiable and respectable a Sovereign, and to the advantage of this distracted kingdom.

"It is the duty of my office to attend in London (though my health requires air and the country). If, therefore, on your arrival, you want any information,

---

[1] There is no trace of this speech anywhere to be found.

I shall be very ready and willing to afford you all I can.

"I have the honor to be, with great respect,
"Dear Sir,
"Your most obedient,
"Most humble Servant,
"NORTHINGTON."

Mr. Pitt thus answered Lord Northington:

"Tuesday, 10 o'clock, July 8, 1766.

"My Lord,

"I received this morning the honor of your Lordship's very obliging letter inclosing his Majesty's most gracious commands in writing to me. I am indeed unable to express what I feel of unfeigned gratitude, duty, and zeal, upon this most affecting occasion. I will only say, that the remnant of my life, body, heart, and mind, is at the direction of our most gracious and clement Sovereign.

"I will hasten to town as fast as I am able, and will, on my arrival, take the liberty to avail myself of the very kind permission your Lordship is so good as to allow me of troubling you: In the mean time, I beg leave to express, in a word, how truly sensible I am of the great honor your Lordship does me by such favorable sentiments on my subject, and to assure you how proud and happy I am in receiving such flattering marks of friendship and confidence from your Lordship. I am, &c."

And here is his courtly response to the King:

"Sire,

"Penetrated with the deepest sense of your Majesty's boundless goodness to me, and with a heart overflowing with duty and zeal for the honor and happiness of the most gracious and benign Sovereign, I shall hasten to London as fast as I possibly can,—wishing that I could change infirmity into wings of expedition, the sooner to be permitted the high honor to lay at your Majesty's feet the poor, but sincere offering of the little services of

"Your Majesty's
"Most dutiful Subject,
"and devoted Servant,
"WILLIAM PITT."

The particulars of the negotiation are not certainly known, but they may easily be conjectured from the two following letters from Lord Northington to Mr. Pitt:

"London, July 14, 1766.

"Dear Sir,

"I am sorry to find that you are so much out of order, and hope the air will speedily remove that complaint; which I trust wil not be immediately felt, as, by his Majesty's commands, I yesterday wrote to Earl Temple that the King desired to see him in London; and on the other side you will see his answer, received since I began this page. I desire to know when you go to Hampstead; as, if occasion requires, I may be able to communicate accordingly.

"I will apprize the King of your unlucky situation; who was so well satisfied with your dutiful behavior as to feel it accordingly. I am with great respect," &c.

"Sunday, 5 P. M., July 20, 1766.

"Dear Sir,

"Having seen his Majesty after the drawing room to-day, I now sit down to answer your very obliging letter; which, as far as it related to myself, I could not before do.

"The invidious share I have taken in the present business was the result of my sensible feeling for my most gracious Master, and this great commercial and brave country, with which I thought nothing could stand in competition. I therefore determined not to be considerate of myself in any respect, but to stand forth as a public servant, or retire a private man, as either should contribute to the King's service.

"As I suppose you might speak with regard to me in the same style of partial consideration to the King you did to myself, I found his Majesty very desirous that I should take a great office in his administration, to which I assented, and to that you so kindly pointed out. Though no office is so personally inviting as that I am now in, yet is true what I urged that my health can not sustain the Chancery, the woolsack, and state affairs. I need not, after what I said to you, say that the succession of Lord Camden will be most agreeable to myself. Your own thoughts respecting yourself have my full concurrence in, and approbation of, their propriety, and the other persons mentioned have all due respect from me.

"I shall only add that if you lend your advice, as also

your reputation, and the rest of the administration act with cordiality and resolution (from me you shall have the fullest support I can give), I see no difficulties to frighten men.

"I should have made you another visit after I had seen Lord Temple; but I know, in general, how unseasonable visits are to invalids. If you are well enough, I would call at your most convenient hour to-morrow. I have the honor to be, with the greatest respect, dear Sir,
"Your most obedient,
"and most humble Servant,
"NORTHINGTON."

The Chancellor had been the bearer of a communication from the King to Lord Temple, asking him to take office; but his terms could not be acceded to,—and without his co-operation, was formed an administration the most fantastical in its construction, and the most whimsical in its proceedings of any to be found in our annals.[1]

Lord Northington went through the formal ceremony of resigning the Great Seal into his Majesty's hands, at St. James's Palace, on Wednesday, the 30th of July, 1766, and was at the same time declared by his Majesty, PRESI-

---

[1] The following is Horace Walpole's account of Lord Northington's breaking up the Rockingham administration: "On the 7th of July, the Chancellor went into the King, and declared he would resign—a notification he had not deigned to make to the ministers, but which he took care they should know by declaring openly what he had done. When the ministers saw the King, he said, coolly, 'Then I must see what I can do.'"—*Memoirs of King George III.* vol. ii. 334. Sir Denis Le Marchant, the learned editor of this work, says: "Lord Northington's health, and his frequent disagreements with his colleagues, had for some months made him desirous of an honorable and quiet retreat. There is no doubt, both from his own letters and the traditions still extant at the bar, that his habits of hard labor and extreme convivirlty had by this time undermined his constitution much to the deterioration of his temper; and he, perhaps, suspected slights that were never intended. Moreover, the scrupulous sense of public duty, the natural reserve and strict propriety of deportment which characterized Lord Rockingham and Mr. Conway, were by no means to his taste. He must have felt even less easy with such associates than his successor Lord Thurlow did in a later day with Mr. Pitt; and, like him, his usual course in the cabinet was to originate nothing, and to oppose everything. The commercial treaty with Russia, a measure of unquestionable benefit, nearly fell to the ground owing to his unreasonable and obstinate opposition. He would rarely listen to remonstrances from his colleagues; and was on such cold terms with them, as probably justified him in his own mind in breaking up the cabinet so unceremoniously. He was too fearless to stoop to intrigue; and there was no necessity for it on this occasion."

DENT OF THE COUNCIL, with many gracious acknowledgments of his faithful services.

CHAPTER CXLI.

CONCLUSION OF THE LIFE OF LORD NORTHINGTON.

MY Lord President and ex-Chancellor Northington, while laboring for the public good,—in the new arrangements was not forgetful of what was due to himself. As an indemnity for his sacrifice of the Great Seal, it was agreed that, in addition to the salary of his present office, he should receive an immediate pension of £2,000 a year; that on his resignation of this office the pension should be raised to £4,000 a year; and that he should have a reversionary grant of the office of Clerk of the Hanaper in Chancery for two lives, after the death of the Duke of Chandos.

Although Lord Northington held a high appointment at the commencement of this motley administration, his connection with it was fleeting, and this is not the place to tell of the mortification, failure, and eclipsed fame of the "Great Commoner," become Earl of Chatham,—when he found himself, from physical and mental infirmity, unable to control the discordant materials of which he had thought fit to compound his new cabinet.[1]

The only measure of the government in which Lord Northington took any part, was the embargo to prohibit the exportation of corn; and here he exhibited his characteristic rashness and recklessness,—which seemed to be aggravated by age and experience.

On account of the almost unprecedented succession of wet weather in the summer and autumn of 1766, the har-

---

[1] Lord Northington, from the time of his appointment as Lord President, frequently corresponded with the Duke of Grafton, who was at the head of the Treasury. Being at the Grange in September, 1766, he writes to him: "I have not spent my time here without regard to my new employment, having perused the papers which I brought down here, and which have been long in arrear. I am sorry Lord Chatham is laid up; and shall only add, that I think no journey inconvenient which tends to the King's service, or to express the great personal regard with which I am,—My dear Lord," &c.

vest had failed in many parts of England, the price of bread had risen alarmingly, and a famine was apprehended. A foolish proclamation was issued against "forestallers and regraters," which not increasing the quantity of corn, nor lessening the demand for it,—in as far as it had any operation, aggravated the evil by interfering with the operations of commerce. An order was then made by the King in Council, in which Lord Chatham, though absent, concurred, prohibiting the exportation of corn, and laying an embargo on ships loaded with cargoes of corn about to sail for foreign countries, where the scarcity was still more severe. Although it probably would have been wiser to have left the trade in food entirely free, without duty or bounty, the measure was generally approved of, and the government was actuated by the best motive in resorting to it. Still it was contrary to law; for there was no statute to prevent the exportation of any sort of grain, however high the price might be, or to authorize the Crown to interfere on such an occasion. Those concerned in the embargo were therefore liable to actions, and required to be indemnified. This was the rational view of the subject taken by Lord Chatham himself in his maiden speech in the House of Lords, on the first day of the ensuing session. He said, "it was an act of power which, during the recess of Parliament, was justifiable on the ground of necessity;" and he read a passage from Locke on Government, to show that, "although not strictly speaking legal, the measure was right in the opinion of that great friend of liberty, that constitutional philosopher, and that liberal statesman." Upon this footing a bill of indemnity would have passed without difficulty. But Lord Northington, for some unintelligible reason, contended that the measure was strictly legal, and that no indemnity was necessary.¹ He went so far as to main-

[1] The inconsiderate manner in which he had originally agreed to the measure, may be learned from an extract of his letter to the Duke of Grafton, dated 31st August, 1766, " I come now to that part of your Grace's letter which more immediately relates to my office ; the revival of the prohibition of the exportation of corn, by order of council, pursuant to the late act,—which I have not here. And I am of opinion, that it is absolutely fit and necessary, as I stand at present informed." In truth, the order was directly contrary to the late act ; and the President of the Council advises an order, supposed to be framed on an act which he does not see, and with which he is wholly unacquainted ! Surely, we are less slovenly nowadays in our mode of transacting public business.

tain that the Crown had a right to interfere even against a positive act of parliament, and that proof of the necessity amounted to a legal justification. Seemingly unconscious that he was standing up for a power in the Crown to suspend or dispense with all laws, he defied any lawyer to contradict him, and saying "he was no patron of the people," he even went on to throw out a sarcasm against the noble Earl, now at the head of the government, for his past popular courses.

Lord Mansfield, never displeased with an opportunity of chastising Lord Northington, clearly showed that the power he claimed for the Crown was utterly inconsistent with the constitution, and if it ever in any degree existed, was entirely at variance both with the letter and the spirit of the Bill of Rights.[1]

The ex-Chancellor, though, to the amazement of mankind, countenanced by a great constitutional lawyer, who was expected to scout such absurd doctrine, never seems to have rallied from this downset. I can not discover that he again opened his mouth in parliament, although he continued sulkily in office till the close of the following year. Finding that, in the absence of Lord Chatham, there were dreadful distractions in the cabinet, and that he had no weight there, he soon became desirous of retreating to the quiet enjoyment of his pensions and his sinecures.

He communicated his wish to resign to the Duke of Grafton, and they sent a joint representation to Lord Chatham, pointing out "the present state of the King's affairs from the want of his Lordship's support and influence, and from the unfortunate situation of his Lordship's health,—the administration having been rested, *ab initio*, on his Lordship's weight and abilities." They seem to have received a very rough answer from him, as we may conjecture from the following note addressed by Lord Northington to the Duke of Grafton:

"My dear Lord,

"I have the properest sense of your Grace's communication of a letter, most extraordinary, and, as relative to ourselves, most absurd as well as dangerous. My sentiments must remain as they were, in justice to my own honor, my duty to the King and the public, and the peace

[1] 16 Parl. Hist. 245-313.

and quiet of my own mind. I have the honor to be, with the greatest respect," &c.

While Lord Northington's resignation was under consideration, he paid his respects at St. James's, and then sent to the Duke the following account of his reception:

"My dear Lord,

"I was this morning at Court, and had the honor of speaking to ———[1] at the drawing-room, but as he had no commands for me, and several persons of ministry going in, I did not trouble the closet. But I thought it fit to signify to your Grace, that I am convinced from circumstances, that it is wished by *many* to pause till after the session is up. And I could perceive, by the discourse of a noble neighbor of mine, that the thing you are inquiring after is as extensive as I thought it, and too large for your reception. The *many* alluded to above are not of our friends, and it being my permament opinion that we should penetrate through the present cloud, I send this for your better and cooler judgment.

"The S^y was beginning a long account of the state of America, &c., &c. But in the midst of this *hurlothumbo* they were called both in, staid a long time in the closet, and I left them there. . . . My Lord, the affection I bear to your Grace's sentiments, honor, and abilities (and you know I can speak on this occasion only from truth) has induced me to suggest every material circumstance relative to your Grace's conduct in this nice and important crisis, and if my friendship outruns my judgment, I am confident that I shall not only receive your pardon, but thanks for my warmth in endeavoring to express myself, —My dear Lord,

"Your Grace's," &c.

Lord Northington was induced to delay his resignation, and to retreat into the country,—whence he wrote a letter to the Duke, in which, after expressing his satisfaction at having been present when his son was unanimously elected for Hampshire, he says: " though the air and retirement have afforded me some ease, the weather hath as yet debarred me of any relief. I barely walk, and am without strength or appetite. Though I was not surprised that your Grace received no satisfaction in the information you

[1] Word illegible.

inquired after, yet I lament it, as it daily confirms what I have long suspected, that the rancor and intoxication of faction would sap the very foundations of government. The contagion is so widely spread that it is beyond me to know whither to turn to avoid it. I hope, however, your next may afford me more comfort, as I am sensible of your Grace's discernment to discover, and zeal to pursue, every avenue that may open and lead to the stability of your King and country."

A few days after, the Duke wrote to him an enormously lengthy dispatch, giving him an account of negotiations with the Duke of Bedford, Rigby, Conway, Lord Gower, Lord Rockingham, &c., and thus concluding: "one favor I must entreat of your Lordship, who, considering the consequences it is of to the public, must not refuse— which is, though out of office, to assist the cabinet, and particularly myself, with the advice which your ability and great experience in public affairs will make so essential to the King's service." In his answer, Lord Northington says:

"I think myself much obliged to your Grace for communicating to me, in so clear and historical a manner, the progress of political matters since I left London." After tedious comments on recent intrigues, and praising the Duke for continuing in office, he thus concludes: "As to myself, my Lord, I thought it my duty frankly to open my state of health, and its insufficiency to an office so extensive, and of so much attendance: It was but just both to the King and to his ministers, as I was and am morally certain that I shall never re-establish my strength to sustain that burden, but I desire to be laid at the King's feet as one that out of office will be as zealous as in—and as one that will ever to the best of his abilities support his Majesty's government, and, without a compliment, never with so much pleasure as when your Grace is at the head of it."[1]

[1] The Duke, in his Journal, after setting out his own composition *in extenso*, thus proceeds: "It will be proper also to introduce here Lord Northington's answer: We have lived in full and mutual confidence in each other: he had about him the genuine principles of a Whig,* and in all transactions I found him to be a man full of honor, a disinterested gentleman,

* I should be curious to know the definition of a Whig, which would include Lord Northington, who might be a very sound politician, but was as little of a Whig as his successor Thurlow.

Being still pressed by the Duke of Grafton, in the King's name, at least to defer his resignation till the administration might be remodeled, he wrote back, "You are pleased to open the immediate plan of carrying on government in the interim till a better can be formed. . . . . . . I also learn from your Grace's letter that in his Majesty's present situation it is his wish, and your Grace seems to think it will be a convenience, that I should for a time retain the great employment which his Majesty, out of his abundant grace, was pleased to confer on me. I can have but one answer to that, which I must entreat your Grace to lay at the King's feet, 'That I am so sensible of the many and never-to-be-forgotten marks of the King's favor, proceeding from the greatness of his royal mind, which it hath been my good fortune to have received,—that I am disposed to stand whereever I can be of use to his Majesty's affairs till he can model his administration to his best approbation,—and this with all zeal, duty, and cheerfulness.' That, however, I may conceal nothing, I must inform your Grace that I write this from my bed, having yesterday been seized with the gout in my head, which continued till within this hour, with exquisite pain, and is intermitted so as to enable me to write; that yet I think myself better than when I left London, and hope to be able, at no inconvenient distance, to be in London long enough to dispatch any business that may await me at Council. But it will be a fortnight before I can use my own house, and in my present state of health I know not where else to lodge. I have thus answered your Grace with much difficulty, and with a total resignation of myself to the King's commands; and I have only to add, that my wishes for and support of your Grace's honor and glory will always wait upon you."

The Duke of Grafton expressed great satisfaction at the prospect of his retaining office, and sent for his consideration a large bundle of papers respecting the new constitution for Canada. Lord Northington in answer said: "My eyes would not permit me to write to your

and, though much devoted to the King, with great zeal for the constitution. As a lawyer, his knowledge and ability were great; but his manner and speech were ungracious. I shall ever do honor to his memory wherever I hear his name brought forward."

Grace by the last post as I intended, with respect to the affairs of the Canada legislation, and to inform you fully of my ideas on that business. I must first premise that the formation of any plan of that kind can never commence or proceed through the office that I now enjoy, in whatever hands it shall be placed; because the Council can not correspond with any of the King's officers there, to know the true state of that country, which correspondence resides alone in the Secretary of State. When such information is acquired by him, I am of that opinion, that before a plan can be formed, which must necessarily have the sanction of parliament, it is necessary to have the full sense of the King's servants upon that subject, that the measures may have the general support of government, and not be thrown, as they were last year, upon one person not in the least responsible for them. When every information is obtained, I am certain your Grace's penetration anticipates the difficulties to be encountered, from the civil constitution of that province, composed of French, received under a capitulation incorporated with English entitled to a legislation at some time, and who have been encouraged to call for it, by the proclamation, the King's commission, and other excitements. To this as great a difficulty succeeds with regard to a Popish hierarchy, and, of course, a Protestant one; both of which are, in my opinion, delicate subjects: loads too heavy to be sustained by any strength less than that of a concurring administration. I have all along been of this opinion in different administrations, and have been willing to lend my aid to this difficult task. I hope to be able to be in London in about ten days, though I am very indifferent still."[1]

Lord Northington accordingly came to town and remained there a few days; but from a fresh access of his disorder, he was soon again obliged to retire to the Grange, where he experienced a little respite from his sufferings.

At last, on the 23rd of December, 1767, at his earnest entreaty, his resignation was accepted, and Granville, Earl

[1] It has been said, that this letter proves "that a good Chancellor and great lawyer could write in the language, and with the eloquence, as well as propriety, which might better become a common housemaid."—*Law Review*, No. 4. It is marvelous, to be sure, to observe his utter disregard of the common rules of composition.

Gower was appointed President of the Council in his stead.[1]

Being relieved from the anxieties of office, he rallied considerably, although it had been thought that his last hour was at hand. In the course of the following year he was so much better that an effort was made to induce him to re-enter the cabinet. The Duke of Grafton says, in his Journal:—"Hoping that Lord Northington might have considered himself still equal in health to the business of the Privy Seal, his Majesty, in the first instance, made the offer to his Lordship, but which he declined on reasons which were very satisfactory to the King."

The Premier still continued to consult him on public affairs. The following is the last letter of his in my possession, and expresses his sentiments characteristically on the subject of the Middlesex election, which now intensely agitated the public mind:

"Grainge, 10 Dec. 1769.

"My Lord,

"I had the honor of your Grace's by last Sunday's post. I was that day attacked by the gout, and not able to write till now. I am not surprised your Grace expresseth so strong a feeling of the distraction of the times. I have long entertained the same opinion of it, and of its tendency so dangerous to the vitals of this valuable constitution. But, my Lord, the distraction hath so long raged, hath been so much fomented, and in its attack of the supreme power of the nation (the Parliament, I mean) so much neglected (wisely, I must suppose), that it is scarce decent or safe now for an individual to open his sentiments on the subject. Yet it is now come to that pass that it seems totally impossible for the P. to meet and not vindicate its own honor. Doth it want power? Doth it want advice? Thank God the contest is there. Your Grace supposeth I have no idea of the backwardness and lukewarmness of some from whom the K. might expect advice and assistance in his difficulties. I assure your Grace I have long had an adequate one, and very just sentiments of the persons. In this situation your Grace wishes that I would spend the winter in London

---

[1] Lord Henley represents that Lord Northington finally retired in June, 1767 (Life, 54); but I have fixed the date by a reference to the books of the Privy Council.

and give my assistance in the House of Lords. My Lord, I have but one answer, I can not—my health will not enable me to live there this winter, nor if I were there, to attend the House. But, my Lord, were I able, could I? What a figure should I, after the offices I have passed, make, prating on subjects to which I am a total stranger, and on measures in which I do not concur, and about doctrines I know not how adopted! Passive obedience to—a mob! I should, so circumstanced, hurt the service that I have a zeal for,—embarrass your Grace, whom I really honor. Believe me, my Lord, there is nothing to debate upon,—OPORTET AGERE.

"Indeed, my dear Lord, I am advanced in years—my constitution so impaired, that unless I can acquire more strength, must be content to remain the retired, unimportant thing I am.

"In whatever condition, I profess myself to be with equal truth and respect,

"My dear Lord," &c.

During his intervals of ease from his terrible enemy, the gout, he amused himself with making deputy lieutenants, militia officers, and justices of the peace, and getting his old friends round him,—whom he entertained with old port and old stories.

He sunk gradually under his infirmities. When near his end he was reminded of the propriety of his receiving the consolations of religion, and he readily agreed that a divine should be sent for; but when the Right Rev. Dr. ——, with whom he had formerly been intimate, was proposed, he said, "No! that won't do. I can not well confess to him, for the greatest sin I shall have to answer for was making him a Bishop!" The clergyman of the parish was substituted, and the dying ex-Chancellor joined in the ceremonies prescribed by the Church for such a solemn occasion with edifying humility and devotion. Having in *characteristic language*, tenderly taken leave of his weeping daughters, he expired on the 14th of January, 1772, in the 64th year of his age. His remains were interred in the church at Northington, where is to be seen a monument,

"Sacred to the Memory of
ROBERT HENLEY, first Earl of Northington;
JANE, Countess of Northington, his wife;
And of ROBERT, Earl of Northington, their only surviving Son."

The inscription, after warmly praising the virtues of all the three, thus concludes:

"This monument is erected, as a tribute of respect and affection to their parents and their brother, by the R. H. Lady Bridget Tollemache, the R. H. Lady Jane Aston, Mary, Viscountess Wentworth, and the R. H. Lady Elizabeth Eden."

His children may well be excused for piously recording their opinion of the "consummate ability" as well as "inflexible integrity" with which he discharged the duties of all the offices which he filled, but the impartial biographer is obliged to form a more discriminating estimate of his merit.

Endowed with good natural abilities, and possessing very amiable qualities, he was a mere lawyer, seeking only his own advancement, and, though unstained by crimes, —unembellished by genius or by liberal accomplishments —nor very solicitous about the public welfare or even his own fame.

Much praise has been bestowed upon him for consistency as a politician. He certainly was always very faithful to Leicester House, and to the *clique* called the "King's Friends," which sprang out of that connection. But it is difficult to say what the principles were by which he is supposed to have been guided. He seems never to have originated any of the measures of his political associates, but to have been always ready in a very zealous manner to defend such as they favored. He turned out a strong Tory and coercionist, but I apprehend that he would have been as strong a Whig and reconciliationist if the liberal side had been taken by Lord Bute and George III. During the Rockingham administration he could only be considered a spy in the enemy's camp.

He is much more respectable as a Judge. He was not only above all suspicion of corruption or partiality, but, though by no means a profound jurist, his mind was well imbued with the principles of our municipal law; he disposed very satisfactorily of the routine business of his Court, and he could do considerable justice to any important question which arose before him. His judgments are at least remarkably clear, and if they have not the depth they are free from the verbosity and tortuosity of Lord Eldon's, which, dwelling so minutely upon the peculiarities of each case, often leave us in doubt how he has disposed of the points argued before him, and what general rule he means to establish. I do not think that the number of decrees reversed on appeal can be adopted as a criterion of the merits of a Chancellor; and had Lord Northington been raised to the peerage when he received the Great Seal, and had he, like Lord Hardwicke, been the only law Lord, he might possibly have received the same character for infallibility. But, independently of the decisions of the House of Lords against him, the printed reports confirm the tradition, that his boldness in declaring his opinion was not quite equaled by his care and caution in forming it. He may, perhaps, be advantageously contrasted with judges we have read of, who, desperately afraid of committing themselves,—that they may keep out of scrapes, defer giving judgment till both parties are ruined.

I am sorry that I can say nothing for him as a law reformer. But, although he never dreamed of making any attempt to render proceedings in the Court of Chancery cheaper or more expeditious, or to improve any of our institutions, no peculiar blame is to be imputed to him, for he lived at a time when the system of optimism, graced by the inimitable Commentaries of Blackstone, prevailed in Westminster Hall; and half a century elapsed before it was doubted that appearance to a subpœna in Chancery must necessarily be enforced by a commission of rebellion,—that, by the eternal constitution of things, common-law actions must be commenced by *latitat, capias,* or *quo minus,*—or that fraud and trifling violations of property must be checked by the multiplication of capital punishments.

Lord Northington is said to have kept up his acquaintance with the Greek and Latin classics, and to have shown some knowledge of Hebrew. He was singularly unskilled in the composition of English. Indeed, I can discover in him no love of literature, and I should conjecture that when he had got through his official labors he devoted himself to convivial enjoyment or the common gossip of vulgar life. He not only never aimed at authorship, but I do not find that, like Camben, Thurlow, or Wedderburn, he associated with literary men or with artists.

His great delight was to find himself in a circle of lawyers, or common-place politicians, and to indulge in boisterous mirth and coarse jocularity. He himself seems to have possessed a rich fund of humor. Many of his sayings and stories used to be repeated by young students, when

> " 'Twas merry in the hall,
> And beards wagged all."

but would not be found suited to the more refined taste of the present age.¹ He likewise indulged in a bad habit which seems to have been formerly very general, and which I recollect when it was expiring,—of interlarding conversation with oaths and imprecations as intensitives—even without any anger or excitement.

But in spite of these faults, into which he was led by the fashion of the times, he was a strictly moral, and even a religious man. He continued to live on terms of the utmost affection and harmony with his wife, and he composed two beautiful prayers for her use—one soon after their marriage, and the other on the birth of their second child—proofs of his piety and tenderness, which she regarded with enthusiasm till the last hour of her existence. In all the domestic relations he deserves high commendation. He was particularly attached to his daughter,—Lady Bridget, who, with the most perfect feminine delicacy, inherited his powers of humor, and was celebrated for sprightliness of repartee, as well as for her beauty. She was in the habit of reading for her father, and it is said that she could even extract amusement, for the gay society in which she mixed, out of bills, answers and affidavits; but this must have been in ridiculing the proceedings of the Court, and all concerned with them.

Lord Northington in his person, was a remarkably handsome man, of the middle size—rather thin, but, till crippled by the gout, very active and athletic. His portrait, by Hudson, gives him a very agreeable expression of countenance, and represents him, when on the woolsack, with a complexion still fresh and rosy, instead of being, like most of those who have reached this painful elevation, of the color of the parchment they have pored upon—or like Mr. Surrebutter's, in the Pleader's Guide, with

¹ I can not even relate his compliment to the *capacity* of Lady Northington or to the *bright eyes* of his daughter, Lady Bridget.

> "A certain tinge of copper,
> Quite professional and proper."[1]

He enjoyed the lawyer's blessing, a large family—his wife having brought him eight children, three sons and five daughters. Only one son survived him, Robert, the second Earl, who was at an early age elected one of the members for Hampshire, and continued to represent that county till his father's death. He was a fast personal friend and political associate of Charles James Fox, and when the Coalition ministry was formed, in 1783, he was sent as Lord Lieutenant to Ireland, with Mr. Wyndham for Secretary. He is said to have been likely to have succeeded well in this post from the frankness and popularity of his manners, as well as his good sense and firmness; but he was soon removed from it by the ascendency of the younger Pitt.[2] He afterwards died at Paris, on his return from Italy, in July 1786; and, having never been married, the title became extinct.[3]

The daughters all formed high alliances, but they all died without issue, except Lady Elizabeth, married to the eminent diplomatist, Sir Morton Eden, afterwards raised to the Irish peerage by the title of Lord Henley,—whose son, my most valued friend, was the editor of Lord Northington's Judgments, and who, having married a lady adorned with every grace and virtue, the sister of the prime minister Sir Robert Peel, left by her a son, the present representative of his great-grandfather, the Lord Chancellor.

[1] Pleader's Guide, Part I. Lecture vi.
[2] Preface to Eden's "Reports," xxix. Henley's "Life of Northington," 62-64.
[3] The epitaph says, that "he was nominated in MDCCLXXXIV to the arduous and distinguished station of Lord Lieutenant of Ireland: where, in times very difficult, he manifested such talents, assiduity, and firmness as conciliated the love and respect of the nation over which he presided, and gained him the approbation and esteem of his sovereign and his country.'

CHAPTER CXLII.

LIFE OF LORD CHANCELLOR CAMDEN FROM HIS BIRTH TILL THE DEATH OF GEORGE II.

I NOW enter on a most pleasing task. The subject of the following memoir was one of the brightest ornaments of my profession and of my party,—for I glory, like him, in the name of Whig, although, I hope, I have never been reluctant to point out the errors of Whigs, or to praise Tory talent, honor, and consistency. From some of the opinions of Lord Camden I must differ, and I can not always defend his conduct ; but he was a profound jurist, and an enlightened statesman,—his character was stainless in public and in private life—when raised to elevated station, he continued true to the principles which he had early avowed,—when transferred to the House of Peers, he enhanced his fame as an assertor of popular privileges,—when an ex-Chancellor, by a steady co-operation with his former political associates, he conferred greater benefits on his country, and had a still greater share of public admiration and esteem, than while he presided on the woolsack,—when the prejudices of the sovereign and of the people of England produced civil war, his advice would have preserved the integrity of the empire,—when America, by wanton oppression, was for ever lost to us, his efforts mainly contributed to the pacification with the new republic,—and Englishmen, to the latest generations, will honor his name for having secured personal freedom, by putting an end to arbitrary arrests under general warrants, for having established the constitutional rights of juries, and for having placed on an imperishable basis the liberty of the press.

Charles Pratt, afterwards Lord Chancellor and Earl Camden, was descended from a respectable gentleman's family that had been long settled at Careswell Priory, near Collumpton, in Devonshire. The first distinguished member of it was his father, Sir John Pratt, who was an eminent barrister in the reigns of William III. and Queen Anne,—gained considerable reputation by supporting the Whigs in the House of Commons, as representative for

Midhurst,—at the accession of George I. was appointed a puisne Judge of the King's Bench, and in 1718 succeeded Lord Macclesfield as Chief Justice of that Court. The most famous decision in his time was respecting the right of a widow who had married a foreigner to claim parochial relief after his death from the parish in which she was born—thus reported in Sir James Burrow:

> "A woman having a settlement
> Married a man with none,
> The question was, he being dead,
> If what she had was gone?
>
> "Quoth Sir John Pratt, The settlement
> Suspended did remain
> Living the husband, but him dead,
> It doth revive again."
>
> *Chorus of puisne Judges.* ——" but him dead,
> It doth revive again."

He likewise drew upon himself a great share of public attention by the able manner in which he conducted the trial of the famous Christopher Layer for high treason,[1] and by his decided opinion in favor of George I. respecting the Sovereign's control over the education and marriage of his grandchildren.[2]

He was twice married, and had a very numerous family. Charles was the third son by the second wife, daughter of the Reverend Hugh Wilson, a canon of Bangor, and was born in the last year of the reign of Queen Anne. Of his boyhood little is recorded, except that, from his quickness and love of reading, he was considered a lad of promise, and that, from his cheerful and affectionate temper, he was a great favorite among his companions.

When only ten years old, he had the misfortune to lose his father; but this was probably the remote cause of his future eminence. While he was studying the law, and young a the bar, the run of the house of the Chief Justice of England, with the chance of sinecure appointments, would have been very agreeable, but would probably have left him in the obscure herd to which the sons of Chancellors and Chief Justices have usually belonged. His mother intimated to him that the small amount of his patrimony would do little more than, with good man-

[1] Burr. Sett. Cas.; Burn's Just., tit. "Settlement."
[2] 16 St. Tr. 93.   [3] 15 Ibid. 1195.

agement, defray the expense of his education, and that by his own exertions he must make his way in the world.

He was soon after sent to Eton, and, on account of the reduced circumstances of his family, he was placed upon the foundation. But in those days the collegers and oppidans were on the most cordial footing, and here he formed a friendship which lasted through life, and not only led to his advancement, but was of essential benefit to the state—with William Pitt,—then flogged for breaking bounds—afterwards the "Great Commoner" and EARL OF CHATHAM. He likewise had for his playmates Lyttleton and Horace Walpole. At that time, as now, Eton, from its many temptations and gentle discipline, was very ill adapted to a boy idly inclined; yet it was the best school of manly manners, and in the studious the "Genius of the place" fanned the flame of emulation, and inspired a lasting love of classic lore. Fortunately, young Pratt was eminent in the latter category, and here not only was his taste refined, but from his lessons in Livy, and a stealthy perusal of Claudian, he imbibed that abhorrence of arbitrary power which animated him through life.

At the election in July, 1731, he got "King's," and in the following term he went to reside at Cambridge. Being from his earliest years destined by his father to the bar, he had previously been entered of the Society of the Inner Temple.[1] While at the university he did not much meddle with the mathematical pursuits of the place, or even very diligently attend classical lectures, being, from the preposterous privilege of his college, entitled to a degree without examination; but, while most of his Etonian friends sank into indolence, he not only diligently read the best Greek and Latin authors in his own way, but he began that course of juridical and constitutional study which afterwards made his name so illustrious. It is said that while he was an undergraduate several controversies arose in the college respecting the election of officers, and the enjoyment of exclusive privileges, and that he always took the popular side, opposing himself to the encroachments of the master with as much warmth and perseverance as he afterwards displayed on a wider arena.[2]

[1] His admission is dated June 5, 1728. He is designated "Carolus Pratt, generosus filius quintus honorabilissimi Joannis Pratt, Eq.," &c.
[2] This reminds me of a story I have heard of a very distinguished con

In 1735, he proceeded B.A. as a matter of course, and having finished his academical curriculum, took chambers and began to keep his terms in the Inner Temple. I have not been able to learn anything of his habits during this period of his life, but, from what followed, it is quite clear that he had been much more solicitous to qualify himself for business, than to form any connections for obtaining it; and I suspect that, contented with hard reading and a diligent attendance to take notes in Westminster Hall, he did not even condescend to become a pupil in an attorney's office, which had become a common practice since "*moots*" and "*readings*" had fallen into disuse, and "*special pleaders*" had not yet come up. He was called to the bar in Trinity Term, 1738.

But very differently did young Pratt fare from the man whose rapid career had recently been crowned by his elevation to the woolsack. Yorke, the son of an attorney, himself an attorney's clerk, and intimate with many attorneys and attorneys' clerks, overflowed with briefs from the day he put on his robe, was in full business his first circuit, and was made Solicitor General when he had been only four years at the bar. Pratt, the son of the Lord Chief Justice of England, bred at Eton and Cambridge, the associate of scholars and gentlemen, though equally well qualified for his profession, was for many years without a client. He attended daily in the Court of King's Bench, but it was only to make a silent bow when called upon "to move;"—he sat patiently in chambers, but no knock came to the door, except that of a dun, or of a companion as briefless and more volatile. He chose the Western Circuit, which his father used to "*ride*," and where it might have been expected that his name would have been an introduction to him,—but he often declared that his father's memory never brought him a guinea. Spring and summer, year after year, did he journey from Hampshire to Cornwall, without receiving fees to pay the tolls demanded of him at the turnpike gates, which were then beginning to be erected. During the summer circuit, in the year 1741, his nag died, and from bad luck, or from the state of his finances, he was only able to replace him by a very sorry jade. With difficulty did he get back to

temporary, who is said, when he was entitled to *fags* at Eton, to have summoned them before him, and formally to have *emancipated* them.

London—whence he thus wrote to a friend :—' Alas! my horse is lamer than ever,—no sooner cured of one shoulder than the other began to halt. My losses in horseflesh ruin me, and keep me so poor that I have scarce money enough to bear me in a summer's ramble; yet ramble I must if I starve to pay for it."

In the beginning of the following year he had a glimpse of good fortune, being retained in the famous Chippenham election case as counsel for the sitting members. But facts, law, and arguments were wholly disregarded. This was the death-struggle of Sir Robert Walpole. All looked with impatience to the division, for which there had been on both sides most strenuous efforts. There were brought down the halt, the lame, the blind, the moribund. It was discovered that, not by the eloquence of Pratt, but by the good management of the Opposition "whipper-in," the Government was to be beaten. As the tellers began their office, Sir Robert beckoned to Mr. Rolt, the member whose return was questioned by a ministerial petition, to sit near him, and entered freely into conversation with him, animadverting on the ingratitude of several persons who were now voting with the Opposition, although he had greatly obliged them, and declaring that he should never again sit in that House.

In a few days after, Pratt wrote the following letter to a brother barrister in the country, with whom he was on very intimate terms:—

' Feb. 6, 1741 (2).

" Dear Davies,

"I am afraid you think me dead, for you can't think I have forgot you if I am alive. I thought it better to execute your orders than write idle letters without doing your business: so that if you have received your wine, and it proves good, you'll excuse the want of a foolish epistle to forerun it. I have of late been much taken up with a petition in the House of Commons, wch has taken up a great deal of time. It was the Chippenham Election: and y^r humble serv^t was employed ag^t the Court for ye sitting members. The last division in this famous petition put an end to Sr Rob^{ts} reign and glory, for he then left the House of Commons, gave up the cause, and next day resigned all his places. So that I am complimented by many persons as having assisted in giving the last blow to this great man,—a compliment wch I don't desire the credit of, but am content with the honor of having served my clients faithfully. I dare say you imagine that we in town know all that is to happen upon this great change, and expect to hear from me a compleat list of the new ministers, and the future plan of their measures. The town is full of this discourse, and every man has already settled the government as he wishes it may be settled. But I assure you that as yet we remain in as profound an ignorance of what is to be as you do in the country, therefore I shan't amuse with any of ye idle reports that are current, wch are as various as the inclinations and wishes of those men are upon whose hopes or dispositions these reports are grounded. This is fact, that Sr Robt Walpole is created Earl of Orford, and his natural daughter by his last wife before the marriage made a lady to give her the rank of an earl's daughter, wch otherwise her bastardy w^d prevent her from taking. This is a ridiculous circumstance in ye patent, and makes some people smile and others angry. It is said, too, that he has a pension of £4,000 for life settled. Thus far his retreat has been honorable: how far it will be safe for the future, I can't tell; but most people think there will be some angry notions at the meeting of ye Parl^t—perhaps impeachments, but probably they will end in nothing. Mr. Pulteney has refused everything: he will continue, he says, a lover of his country, and do his utmost to support the family and any good administration. This is a great character if he can persist in it. Most people think the Tories will get nothing by the change, but will be left in the lurch. No talk yet of a reconciliation between the King and Prince.

"Y^{rs} most affectionately,
"C. PRATT."[1]

However, if our aspirant thought that business was now to pour in upon him, he was greviously disappointed, for several years passed away without his receiving another brief.

To cheer him up, his school and college friend, Sneyd Davies, addressed to him a poetical epistle, in which the poet dwells upon the worthlessness of the objects of hu-

[1] Letter kindly furnished to me by Major Evans, of Eyton Hall.

man ambition, and points out to him the course of the bright luminaries then irradiating Westminister Hall:

> "Who knows how far a rattle may outweigh
> The mace or scepter? But as boys resign
> The play-thing, bauble of their infancy,
> So fares it with maturer years; they sage,
> Imagination's airy regions quit,
> And under Reason's banner take the field,
> With resolution face the cloud or storm,
> While all their former rainbows die away.
> Some to the palace, with regardful step
> And courtly blandishment, resort, and there,
> Advance obsequious ;—in the senate some
> Harangue the full-bench'd auditory, and wield
> Their list'ning passion (such the power, the sway
> Of Reason's eloquence!)—or at the bar,
> Where Cowper, Talbot, Somers, Yorke before
> Pleaded their way to glory's chair supreme,
> And worthy fill'd it. Let not these great names
> Damp, but incite; nor Murray's praise obscure
> Thy younger merit. Know, these lights, ere yet
> To noonday luster kindled, had their dawn.
> Proceed familiar to the gate of Fame,
> Nor think the task severe, the prize too high,
> Of toil and honor, for thy father's son."[1]

He persevered for eight or nine years; but, not inviting attorneys to dine with him, and never dancing with their daughters, his practice did not improve, and his "*impecuniosity*" was aggravated. At last he was so much dispirited that he resolved to quit the bar,—to return to the seclusion of his college,—to qualify himself for orders,—and to live upon his fellowship as he might, till, in the course of time, he should be entitled to a college living, where he might end his days in peace and obscurity. This plan he certainly would have carried into execution, if he had not thought that it was fit he should announce it to the leader of his circuit, who had always been kind to him. This was Henley, afterwards Lord Northington, who, first in his usual jesting manner, and afterwards with seriousness and feeling, tried to drive away the despair which had overwhelmed his friend, and prevailed so far as to obtain a promise that Pratt would try one circuit more.[2]

[1] Dodsley's Collection, vol. vi.
[2] I find in the *European Magazine* for July, 1794, a supposed account of the dialogue between them, which I consider entirely fictitious. Here is a specimen of it: "Henley heard him throughout with a seeming and anxious composure, when, bursting out into a horse-laugh, he exclaimed, in his strong

At the first assize town on the next circuit, it so happened that Pratt was Henley's junior (by contrivance it was suspected) in a very important cause, and that, just as it was about to be called on, the leader was suddenly seized with an attack of gout, which (as he said) rendered it necessary for him to leave the court and retire to his lodgings. The lead was thus suddenly cast upon Pratt, who opened the plaintiff's case with great clearness and precision, made a most animated and eloquent reply obtained the verdict, was complimented by the judge, was applauded by the audience, and received several retainers befere he left the hall. His fame traveled before him to the next assize town, where he had several briefs, —and from that time he became a favorite all round the circuit.[1] Although Henley continued senior of the "Western" for several years longer, till he was made Attorney General, Pratt's success was facilitated by an opening from the removal of two inferior men, who had long engrossed a great share of the business. Employment in Westminster Hall soon followed; for in new trials and other business connected with the circuit he displayed such great ability, and such a thorough knowledge of his profession, that in cases of weight he was soon eagerly sought after to hold "second briefs," although he never seems to have had a great share of routine business,—which, with less éclat, is attended with more profit.[2]

The first case in which he attracted the general notice of the public was in the memorable prosecution of a printer by Sir Dudley Ryder as Attorney General, under the orders of the House of Commons, in consequence of some remarks

manner, 'What! turn parson at last! No, by G—, Charles, you shan't be a P—— neither! You shall do better for yourself, and that quickly, too. Let me hear no more of this canting business of turning parson; you have abilities that run before us all, but you must endeavor to scour off a little of that d——d modesty and diffidence you have about you to give them fair play.'" The writer knew so little of Pratt's real history as to represent tha he was afterwards introduced for the first time by Henley to Pitt.

[1] My friend Mr. Dampier, Vice-Warden of the Stannaries, writes to me,— "Sir James Mansfield, who was of K. C., and ab^t 19 years jun^r to Ld C., used to tell me that he remembered Ld C. on the West. Circuit, and that his rise was very sudden and rapid, after a long time of no practice; but once having led a cause in the west, he became known, and was immediately in full business, on the circuit."

[2] His name does not occur in the Reports nearly so frequently as those of some others who are long since forgotten.

on their commitment of the Honorable Alexander Murray for refusing to kneel at their bar. Lord Chief Justice Lee, the presiding Judge, intimated his opinion that the jury were only to consider whether the defendant published the alleged libel (which was clearly proved to have been sold by him in his shop at the Homer's Head in Fleet Street), and whether " the S—r " meant " the Right Honorable Arthur Onslow, the Speaker of the House of Commons," and the " H—h B—ff" meant " Peter Leigh, gentleman, then High Bailiff of the city of Westminster?" Pratt was junior counsel for the defendant, and following Ford, a distinguished lawyer in his day, whom he greatly eclipsed, he showed that *ex animo* he entertained the opinion respecting the right of juries which he subsequently so strongly maintained against Lord Mansfield, and for which, after a lapse of forty years, he triumphantly struggled against Lord Thurlow in the last speech he ever delivered in parliament. He told the jury that they were bound to look to the nature and tendency of the supposed libel, and to acquit the defendant, unless they believed that he intended by it to sow sedition, and to subvert the constitution in the manner charged by the prosecutors :

" Are you impanneled," said he " merely to determine whether the defendant had sold a piece of paper value two-pence? If there be an indictment preferred against a man for an assault with an intent to ravish, the intent must be proved; so if there be an indictment for an assault with intent to murder, the jury must consider whether the assault was in self-defense, or on sudden provocation, or of malice aforethought. The secret intention may be inferred from the tendency; but the tendency of the alleged libel is only to be got at by considering its contents and its character; and, because, ' S—r ' means ' *Speaker*,' and ' h—h-b—ff ' means ' *high-bailiff*,' are you to find the defendant guilty, if you believe in your consciences that what he has published vindicates the law, and conduces to the preservation of order?" He then ably commented upon the absurdity of this prosecution by the House of Commons, who, arbitrarily and oppressively abusing the absolute power which they claimed, would not even tolerate a groan from their victims. Said he, " There is a common proverb,—and a very wise Chancellor affirmed that *proverbs are the wisdom of a people*,—LOSERS MUST HAVE LEAVE TO SPEAK. In the Scripture, Job is allowed to complain even of the dispensations of Providence, the causes and consequences of which he could not comprehend. As complaints are natural to sufferers, they may merit some excuse where the infliction is by the act of man, and to common understandings seems wanton and tyrannical. A gentleman of high birth and unblemished honor is committed to a felon's cell in Newgate, because, being convicted of no offense, he refuses to throw himself before those for whom he did not feel the profoundest respect, into that attitude of humility which he reserved for the occasion of acknowledging his sins, and praying for pardon, before the throne of the Supreme Ruler of the Universe. Must all be sent to partake his dungeon who pity his fate? The Attorney General tells a free people that, happen what will, they shall never complain. But, gentlemen, you will not surrender your rights, and abandon your duty. The fatal blow to English liberty will not be inflicted by an English jury."

The Attorney General having replied, and Lord Chief Justice Lee having reiterated his doctrine, by which everything was to be reserved to the Court, except *publication* and *innuendoes*, the jury retired, and, being out two hours, returned a general verdict of NOT GUILTY. When the Attorney General could be heard, after the shout of exultation which arose, he prevailed upon the Chief Justice to call back the jury, who were dispersing, and to put this question to them:—" Gentlemen of the jury, do you think the evidence laid before you, of the defendant's publishing the book by selling it, is not sufficient to convince you that the said defendant did sell this book?" The foreman was at first "a good deal flustered;" but the question being repeated to him, he said, in a firm voice, all his brethren nodding assent, " Not Guilty, my Lord; not guilty! That is our verdict, my Lord, and we abide by it!" Upon which there was a shout much louder than before; and the Court broke up.[1] The controversy respecting the rights of juries was not settled till the passing of Mr. Fox's Libel Bill in 1792; but, after this expression of public feeling, the practice of requiring

---
[1] 18 St. Tr. 1203–1230.

persons summoned to the bar for breach of privilege to fall down on their knees was discontinued by both Houses of Parliament.[1]

For several years Pratt went on steadily in the ordinary progress of a rising lawyer. Without a silk gown, he was now one of the leaders of the Western Circuit, and, being considered peculiarly well read in parliamentary law, he was the favorite in all cases of a political aspect. He had a great share of election business before the House of Commons, which for the present he preferred to a seat in that assembly.

From some cause not explained (some uncharitably said from the apprehension that he might rival the Honorable C. Yorke, now making a distinguished figure at the bar) he was not a favorite with the Chancellor, but he was at last made a King's Counsel, upon a report which he never authorized, that he intended permanently to practice in the Court of King's Bench. When with his silk gown he went over to the Court of Chancery, as eminent counsel then sometimes did, and he was actually beginning to interfere with Charles Yorke, he was treated with much civility, but with marked disregard, by Lord Hardwicke, who plainly, though not tangibly, showed that he never listened to anything which Pratt said.[2]

I do not find that he attached himself to any particular section in politics, but he was on a footing of familiar intimacy with the great Whig chiefs, particularly with his old schoolfellow Pitt, who was in the habit of consulting him respecting questions of a legal or constitutional nature which from time to time arose.

He was likewise in the constant habit of associating with artists and men of letters. Although he did not yet enjoy the sweets of domestic life, this must have been an agreeable portion of his existence, for, free from the anxieties of office, he had achieved an enviable station in society, the pleasures of which were enhanced by recollecting the despair into which he had formerly been plunged; he was courted by friends, and respected by

[1] On the trial of a peer for felony it is still put down in the programme,— that is, " to kneel when arraigned:" but this ceremony is not insisted on in practice.

[2] On the authority of Sir James Mansfield, from the relation of Lord Camden himself. He added, that " Lord Mansfield so enlarged the practice of K. B. that counsel did not leave his Court."

opponents; highly satisfied with the present, he had brilliant prospects before him. The disgrace brought upon the country by the imbecility of the Government might disquiet him; but his solicitude was mitigated by the consideration that this Government was becoming daily more unpopular, and that it might be replaced by one patriotic and powerful, in which he himself might be called to take a part.

At last Mr. Pitt was at the head of affairs with dictatorial authority. Resolved, both on public and private grounds, that his old Etonian friend should now be provided for, he thought it might be too strong a measure at once to give the Great Seal to a man at the bar, who had never been a law officer of the Crown, nor had sat in parliament; but he declared that Pratt should be Attorney General in the place of Sir Robert Henley, who was to be made Lord Keeper. Against this arrangement Charles Yorke, who had been appointed Solicitor General the November preceding, and whose father was mainly instrumental in constructing the new ministry, strongly protested, as derogatory to his rights and his dignity; but Pitt was firm, maintaining that, from standing at the bar and merit, Pratt ought long ago to have been raised to the honors of the profession. Yorke, although in a manner very ungracious, and although still retaining a grudge against Pratt for this supposed slight, agreed to serve under him as Solicitor.—Mr. Attorney received the honor of knighthood.

In those days the law officers of the Crown had no anxiety about a seat in parliament; they were not driven to canvass popular constituencies, with the danger of being thrown out, and the certainty of a large hole being made in their official earnings. Sir Charles Pratt was put in for the close borough of Downton, which he continued to represent without trouble or expense, till he was made Chief Justice of the Court of Common Pleas.

He now flourished in the Court of Chancery, and he was an overmatch for the heavy Equity pleaders who for twenty years had been sleeping over "Exceptions" and "Bills of Revival."[1]

[1] During the four years that he afterwards practiced in this Court, there is hardly a reported case in which his name is not mentioned as counsel.—See Eden's R. p., temp. Northington.

To share his prosperity and to solace his private hours, being too much occupied to go into gay company, he, though "on the shady side of forty," resolved to take a wife. The courtships of some of my Chancellors have been amusing; but, having to *relate* not to *invent*, I can only say of this union (which I believe to have been highly prudent and respectable, but quite unromantic), that the lady of his choice was Elizabeth, daughter and coheir of Nicholas Jefferys, Esq., of Brecknock Priory, who brought considerable wealth into the family, and in compliment to whom one of its titles was afterwards selected. They are said to have lived together in harmony and happiness; but throughout the whole of Lord Camden's career we have to regret that very few personal or private anecdotes of him have been handed down to us. We must be contented with viewing him on the stage of public life.

It is a curious fact that, although he was afterwards such a distinguished orator in the House of Lords, during the whole time that he sat in the House of Commons his name is not once mentioned in the printed parliamentary debates. This arises partly from the very imperfect record we have of the proceedings of the legislature during this period of our history, there being only one octavo volume for the twelve years from 1753 to 1765,—partly from the cessation of factious strife during Mr. Pitt's brilliant administration, and partly from Pratt's style of speaking being rather too calm and ratiocinative for the taste of the Lower House,—so that while he remained there he was merely considered "*par negotiis, neque supra,*"—equal to carrying through the law business of the Government, and fit for nothing more,—no one dreaming that hereafter he was to rival Chatham, and that Mansfield was to quail under him.

The only occasion when he seems to have attracted much notice as a representative of the people was in bringing forward the excellent bill—which unfortunately proved abortive—for amending the "Habeas Corpus Act," in consequence of a decision that it did not apply, unless where there was a charge of *crime*—so that in many instances persons illegally deprived of their liberty by an agent of the Crown could not have the benefit of it. Horace Walpole tells us, that "the Attorney General declared himself for the utmost latitude of the habeas corpus," and adds, that " it reflected no small honor on him, that the first advocate of the Crown should appear as the first champion against prerogative." The bill having easily passed the Commons, where it was warmly supported by Pitt, was (as I have had occasion to mention elsewhere)[1] rejected by the Lords, in deference to the opinion of the "law Lords," who then opposed all improvement, and likewise to gratify the strong prejudices of the King, who had openly declared against it, and who, throughout the whole course of his reign, most conscientiously and zealously opposed every measure, domestic or colonial, that had in it the slightest tincture of liberality.[2]

Pratt, while Attorney General, conducted two government prosecutions, still professing and acting upon the great principles of justice for which he had so boldly struggled when defending those who had been prosecuted by his predecessors. The first was against Dr. Hensey for high treason, in corresponding with the King's enemies and inviting them to invade the kingdom. The trial took place at the bar of the Court of King's Bench, before Lord Mansfield and the other Judges of that Court. Mr. Attorney, in opening the case to the jury, having read several letters which had been written by the

[1] Ante, p. 206.
[2] It is a curious fact, that, with regard to law reform, the two Houses have recently changed characters. I will not presume to praise the assembly to which I have now the honor to belong, as far as politics may be concerned; but, in jurisprudential legislation, I say boldly, they are greatly in advance of the other House—which has become the great obstacle to improvement. I will give a few instances. The late Libel Bill (generally called in Westminster Hall "Lord Campbell's Libel Bill"), which originated in the House of Lords, was deprived in the House of Commons of some of its most important clauses for the protection of private character and the liberty of the press. In the session of 1845 the House of Commons threw out bills, which, being approved of by the Lord Chancellor and all the law Lords, had passed the House of Lords unanimously—1. To abolish "Deodands," that disgraceful remnant of superstition and barbarism; 2. To allow a compensation to be obtained by action where a pecuniary loss is sustained from death caused by the negligence of another, so that a railway company might be compelled to make some provision for orphans whose father has been killed by their default; and 3. To permit actions to be commenced against persons who, having contracted debts in England or Ireland, have gone abroad to defraud their creditors, and there spend the funds remitted to them from home,—which at present the law can not touch.—(1846.) In the Session of 1847 I was able to carry Bills 1 and 2; but Bill 3, chiefly meant for the benefit of Ireland, is considered by Irish Members derogatory to the dignity of that country.—(1849.)

prisoner to the French Government during the war, and which he contended were treasonable, said—

"These letters, and translations of them, being laid before you, you, gentlemen, will be proper judges of their destructive tendency; indeed (under the sufferance of the Court) you are the only judges of this fact. Proof being given that they are in the handwriting of the prisoner, and were sent off by him,—if you are of opinion, from a fair construction of their contents, that his object was to solicit and to encourage the landing of a French army on our shore, then he is guilty of the crime laid to his charge by this indictment;—but otherwise it will be your duty to acquit him, whatever opinion you may form of his character, and whatever suspicions you may entertain of his conduct."

The jury having found a verdict of "*guilty*," the Attorney General consented that the day for the execution should be appointed at the distance of one month. The prisoner, after being several times respited, was finally pardoned—a striking instance of the clemency of the Government, and a strong contrast with the execution of Byng under the late administration.[1]

The only *ex officio* information which he filed was against Dr. Shebbeare for a most seditious and dangerous publication, entitled "A Letter to the People of England," containing direct incentives to insurrection. Horne Tooke, no enemy to the liberty of the press, approves of the prosecution, saying, that "if ever there was an infamous libel against the Government, surely it was that."[2] The trial came on in Westminster Hall, before Lord Mansfield. In opening the case to the jury, the Attorney, although using rather quieter language, adhered to the doctrine for which he had struggled with such brilliant success in his first great speech in the *King* v. *Owen*, and expressly told the jury that he desired them, besides the evidence of publication, and the *innuendoes*, to consider the language of the libel, and not to find a verdict for the Crown unless they were convinced that it had a direct tendency to a subversion of the public tranquillity—from which they might fairly infer that the defendant published it "maliciously and seditiously," as charged in the information; but he added, that "he did not wish for a conviction if

[1] 19 St. Tr. 1342-1389. [2] 20 Ibid. 708.

any man in the world could entertain a doubt of the defendant's guilt." At the distance of many years, he stated with pride, in his speech in the House of Lords, on Fox's Libel Bill, the marked manner in which he had intimated his opinion to all the world "that the criminality of the alleged libel was a question of fact with which the Court had no concern."[1]

Pratt conducted with the same propriety the prosecution of Lord Ferrers for murder, before the House of Lords. Thus he opened, with touching simplicity and candor: —" My Lords, as I never thought it my duty in any case to attempt at eloquence where a prisoner stood upon trial for his life, much less shall I think of doing it before your Lordships: give me leave, therefore, to proceed to a narrative of the facts." These he proceeds to state with great perspicuity and moderation, as they were afterwards fully proved by the witnesses. The laboring oar on this occasion, however, fell to the Solicitor General Yorke, who so ably repelled the defense of insanity.[2]

The labors of the law officers of the Crown were very light at the close of the reign of George II., for all opposition in parliament was annihilated: from the universal popularity of a triumphant government, seditious libels were unknown,—and there were no Government prosecutions, except in the Court of Exchequer against unlucky smugglers.

CHAPTER CLXIII.

CONTINUATION OF THE LIFE OF LORD CAMDEN TILL HE RECEIVED THE GREAT SEAL.

ON the demise of the Crown, all things for some time went on very smoothly. Pratt prepared the proclamation of George III. His patent as Attorney General was renewed by the young Sovereign, and no great alarm was excited by the circumstance of Lord Bute, who had been groom of the stole to the Prince, being sworn a Privy Councillor. But when this nobleman was made Secretary of State, and began with the air of a

[1] Annual Register, 1758.   [2] 19 St. Tr. 885.

royal favorite to interfere actively with the patronage and with the measures of the Government, it was discovered that Whig rule was coming to an end. The Stuarts having fallen into utter contempt, so that the return of their persons was no longer to be dreaded, there was to be a restoration of their maxims of government. Being of "good Revolution principles," which had been openly stated as a recommendation to office during the last two reigns, now made a man be looked upon at Court very coldly, and "the divine indefeasible right of kings" became the favorite theme,—in total forgetfulness of its incompatibility with the parliamentary title of the reigning monarch. A breaking up of the combination of the few great families who called themselves "*the Whig party*,"—who had for many years monopolized the patronage of the Crown,—and who had on various occasions exhibited the vices with which they had formerly been in the habit of reproaching the Tories,—would have been a most laudable exploit; but unfortunately the Sovereign was determined to transfer power from one faction, kept in check by professing liberal principles, to another imbued with a love of absolutism,—although the leaders of it while in opposition had occasionally spoken the language of freedom,—which they were now eager to disclaim.

Pratt being resolved to maintain his own principles, happen what would,—as the proposal to make the Judges irremovable at the commencement of a new reign was laudable by carrying into effect the intention of the Act of Settlement, and as he was not called upon to do any thing in parliament or in Westminster Hall inconsistent with his notions of duty,—he continued in his office of Attorney General even when his chief—strongly condemning the foreign policy now adopted—had resigned. If he had continued Attorney General till No. XLV. of "The North Briton" was published, he must then have thrown up his office, for he would sooner have thrust his hand into the fire than advised or defended general warrants to seize the printer and publisher, or countenanced any of the violent proceedings against Wilkes, which shortly rendered the Government so odious and contemptible, and introduced factious struggles almost unparalleled in our annals.

But in the lull before the storm died Lord Chief Justice

Willes, and the Attorney General laid his head upon "the cushion of the Common Pleas." It was rather agreeable to the Sovereign and the ministers that he should be placed in a Court in which it was thought that no political cases could come, and he could do no mischief with his "wild notions of liberty." Accordingly, his patent as Chief Justice was immediately made out; and having qualified himself by submitting to the degree of the coif,[1] on the 23rd of January, the first day of Hilary Term, 1762, he took his seat in the Court of Common Pleas. Here, it so turned out, there were soon more political cases than during many years after came before the Court of King's Bench,—where he would by no means have been trusted. He himself anticipated nothing but repose in his new office; and he really thought that his political life was at an end. Thus he writes to his old friend Davies: "I remember you prophesied formerly that I should be a Chief Justice, or perhaps something higher. Half is come to pass: I am Thane of Cawdor, but the greater is behind; and if that fails me, you are still a false prophet. Joking aside—I am retired out of this bustling world to a place of sufficient profit, ease, and dignity; and I believe that I am a much happier man than the highest post in the law could have made me." He then little expected that before long the prophet might have exclaimed to him "Thou hast it now, King, Cawdor, Glamis—all!"

Lest he should never have a better opportunity, in the Court of Common Pleas, of proclaiming his adherence to constitutional principles, a question of practice arising during his first term, viz., "whether the Judges could refuse a plea *puis darrein continuance*," the Chief Justice said, "Such discretion is contrary to the genius of the common law of England, and would be more fit for an Eastern monarchy than for this land of liberty. *Nulli negabimus justitiam.*"[2]

But, ere long, he had to adjudicate upon a case that excited more interest in the public mind than any that had occurred in a court of law since the trial of the Seven Bishops.

On the morning of Saturday, 30th of April, 1763, John

---

[1] He was called along with Sergeant Burland. *Emblema annuli—Tu satis ambobus.*—2 Wilson, 136. [2] Ibid. 137. *Paris v. Salkeld.*

Wilkes, the member for the Borough of Buckingham, was arrested under Lord Halifax's general warrant to "seize the authors, printers, and publishers of the North Briton, No. XLV., together with their papers." As soon as a copy of the warrant could be obtained, while he was still in his house in Great George Street, in custody of the messengers, Sergeant Glyn, in the Court of Common Pleas, moved for, and obtained for him, a writ of *habeas corpus*, returnable immediately,—the Chief Justice observing, "that this was a most extraordinary warrant." The Solicitor to the Treasury, who was present, having reported what had passed to the Secretary of State, Mr. Wilkes, before the writ could be served on the messengers, was committed a close prisoner to the Tower, and the officers of the Secretary of State returned that "he was not in their custody." On the Monday a *habeas corpus* was obtained, directed to the Lieutenant of the Tower.

The metropolis was now in a state of almost unparalleled excitement. At the sitting of the Court, on the Tuesday morning, Mr. Wilkes was brought into Court by the Lieutenant of the Tower, who, without noticing in his *Return* the "general warrant" under which the arrest took place, merely set out the commitment to the Tower of Mr. Wilkes, as "the author and publisher of a most infamous and seditious libel, entitled the North Briton, No. XLV., tending to inflame the minds and to alienate the affections of the people from his Majesty, and to excite them to traitorous insurrections against the government." Thus the question of the legality of general warrants was for the present evaded: but Sergeant Glyn moved, that Mr. Wilkes should be set at liberty, "*first*, on the ground that it did not appear that there had been any information on oath against him before his commitment; *secondly*, that no part of the libel was set forth to enable the Court to see whether any offense had been committed; and, *thirdly*, that he was privileged from arrest as a member of parliament." After a learned argument by counsel, and a vaporing speech from Mr. Wilkes himself, the Court took time to consider; and, on the Friday following, the Lord Chief Justice Pratt delivered their unanimous opinion, overruling the first two objections, and thus dealing with the last:—

"The third matter insisted upon for Mr. Wilkes is, that he is a member of parliament (which is admitted by the King's Sergeants), and so entitled to privilege to be free from arrests in all cases *except treason, felony. and actual breach of the peace;* and we are all of opinion that he is entitled to that privilege, and that he must be set at liberty. The Seven Bishops were most unjustly ousted of their privilege, three of the Judges deciding that a seditious libel was an actual breach of the peace. 4 *Inst.* 25 says, 'the privilege of parliament holds, unless it be in three cases, viz., treason, felony, and the peace. Privilege of parliament holds in information for the King, unless in the cases before excepted.' The case of an information against Lord Tankerville for bribery (4 *Anne*) was within the privilege of parliament. We are all of opinion that a libel is not a breach of the peace: it tends to a breach of the peace, and that is the utmost. But that which only tends to a breach of the peace can not be an actual breach of it. In the case of the Seven Bishops, Judge Powell, the only honest man of the four Judges, dissented, and I am bound to be of his opinion, and to say that case is not law—but it shows the miserable condition to which the state was then reduced. Let Mr. Wilkes be discharged from his imprisonment."

A great part of the population of London being in Westminister Hall, Palace Yard, and the adjoining streets, a shout arose which was heard with dismay at St. James's.[1]

As the authorities then stood, I think a court of law was bound to decide in favor of privilege in such a case; but although I must condemn the servile desire to please the King and his ministers, by which both Houses were actuated on the reassembling of parliament, I can not but approve the resolution to which they jointly came, and which, I presume, would now be considered conclusive evidence of the law, "that privilege of parliament does not extend to the case of writing or publishing seditious libels."[2] I do not think that privilege of parliament should in any respect interfere with the execution

[1] 2 Wilson, 151-160; 19 St. Tr. 982-1002.
[2] 15 Parl. Hist. 1365.—I am not aware whether the privilege was claimed in cases of libel after conviction, so as to prevent sentence of imprisonment. The Earl of Abingdon, and other members of parliament, have since been sentenced to imprisonment for libel without question.

of the criminal law of the country. Little inconvenience arises from the immunity of members of parliament from arrest for debt, and this is necessary to protect them in the discharge of their public functions.

The immense popularity which Lord Chief Justice Pratt now acquired, I am afraid, led him into some intemperance of language, although his decisions might be sound. Many actions were brought in his Court, and tried before him, for arrests under general warrants; and, the juries giving enormous damages, applications were made to set aside the verdicts, and to grant new trials. It might be right to refuse to interfere, but not in terms such as these:—

"The personal injury done to the plaintiff was very small, so that if the jury had been confined by their oath to consider the mere personal injury only, perhaps twenty pounds would have been thought damages sufficient: but the jury saw before them a magistrate exercising arbitrary power over all the King's subjects—violating Magna Charta, and attempting to destroy the liberty of the kingdom by insisting on the legality of this general warrant; they heard the King's counsel, and saw the Solicitor to the Treasury endeavoring to support and maintain the legality of the warrant in a tyrannical and severe manner. These are the ideas which struck the jury on the trial, and I think they have done right in giving exemplary damages. To enter a man's house under color of a nameless warrant in order to procure evidence, is worse than the Spanish inquisition—a law under which no Englishman would wish to live an hour;—it was a most daring attack on the liberty of the subject. ' Nullus liber homo capiatur vel imprisonetur, nec super eum ibimus—nisi per legale judicium parium suorum vel per legem terræ.' An attempt has been made to destroy this protection against arbitrary power. I can not say what damages I should have given if I had been upon the jury."[1]

Mr. Wilkes's own action being afterwards tried before Lord Chief Justice Pratt, he said,—

"The defendants claim a right, under a general warrant and bad precedents, to force persons' houses, break open escritoires, seize papers where no inventory is made of the things taken, and no persons' names specified in

[1] 2 Wils. 206, 207. *Huckle* v. *Money.*

the warrant, so that messengers are to be vested with a discretionary power to search wherever their suspicions or their malice may lead them. As to the damages, I continue of opinion that the jury are not limited by the injury received. Damages are designed not only as a satisfaction to the injured person, but likewise *as a punishment to the guilty, and as a proof of the detestation in which the wrongful act is held by the jury.*"[1]

The jury having given £1,000, a bill of exceptions was tendered to the direction—but the Chief Justice refused to receive it, as it came too late after verdict.

In *Leach* v. *Money*,[2] however, the question as to the legality of general warrants was regularly raised. There, Lord Chief Justice Pratt having given a similiar direction, a bill of exceptions was duly tendered and carried by writ of error into the King's Bench. It was in arguing this case that Dunning laid the foundation of his splendid fame. Lord Mansfield having, in the course of the argument, thrown out an opinion against the legality of the warrant, the Attorney General Yorke contrived to be beaten on a by-point; but, without a formal judgment, general warrants have ever since been considered illegal, although they were sanctioned by a uniform usage of ancient standing in the office of the Secretary of State.[3]

Another very important case was brought before the Court of Common Pleas while Pratt presided there, in which the question was distinctly raised, "whether, on a charge of libel, the Secretary of State may grant a warrant to *search for, seize, and carry away papers;*" and in support of this practice, too, a long course of precedents was proved. But, after protracted arguments, the Chief Justice said,—

"The warrant was an execution in the first instance without any previous summons, examination, hearing the plaintiff, or proof that he was the author of the supposed libels,—a power claimed by no other magistrate whatever (SCROGGS, Ch. J., always excepted); it was left to the discretion of the defendants to execute the warrant in the absence or presence of the plaintiff when he might have no witness present to see what they did, for they were to seize all papers, bank bills, or any other valuable papers

[1] 1 Wils. 244; *Beardmore* v. *Carrington.*   [2] Burr. 1692.
[3] 19 St. Tr. ,982-1002.

they might take away if they were so disposed. If this be lawful, both Houses of Parliament are involved in it; for they have both ruled that, in such matters, they are on a footing with all the rest of the King's subjects. In the case of Wilkes, a member of the House of Commons, all his books and papers were seized and taken away: we were told by one of these witnesses, that 'he was obliged by his oath to sweep away all papers whatsoever.' If this be law, it would be found in our books, but no such law ever existed in this country; our law holds property so sacred, that no man can set his foot on his neighbor's close without his leave. The defendants have no right to avail themselves of the usage of these warrants since the Revolution,—that usage being contrary to law. The Secretary of State can not make that law which is not to be found in our books. It must have been the guilt or poverty of those on whom such warrants have been executed that deterred or hindered them from contending against the power of a Secretary of State and the Solicitor to the Treasury, as such warrants could never have passed for lawful. It is said to be better for the Government and the public to seize the libel before it is published. If the legislature be of that opinion, they will make it lawful. As yet our law is wise and merciful, and supposes every man accused to be innocent till he is tried by his peers and found guilty. Upon the whole, we are of opinion that this warrant is wholly illegal and void."[1]

Pratt, while a common-law Judge, certainly was of signal service to his country. He not only arrested some flagrant abuses in his own time, but he laid down principles upon which other flagrant abuses still continuing, such as the opening of private letters at the Post-office by order of the Secretary of State, may still be reached and remedied.

It would appear from the Reports that there were few cases of importance, not of a political nature, debated in the Common Pleas while Pratt was Chief Justice. The most important, perhaps, was *Doe* v. *Kersey*,[2] in which he maintained, in opposition to the other Judges of his own Court, and also to a unanimous decision of the King's

[1] *Entick* v. *Carrington;* 19 St. Tr. 1002–1030.
[2] See *Doe d. Hendson* v. *Kersey*, 4 Burn. Eccl. Law, 97; *Wyndham* v *Chatwynd*, 1 Burr. 414.

Bench, that witnesses to a will must be disinterested when they attest it, and that it is not enough that their interest is removed before they come to prove it. Although he was overruled, the legislature adopted his opinion, by enacting that the moment of attestation is the period to regard in considering their credibility. In no other case was there a final difference between him and his brethren on the bench, and all his contemporaries unite in bearing testimony to the combination of dignity, impartiality, and courtesy with which he presided over the proceedings of his Court.[1]

After the liberation of Wilkes, and the condemnation of "general warrants" and "search warrants for papers," Pratt became the idol of the nation. Grim representations of him laid down the law from sign-posts. Many busts and prints of him were sold, not only in the streets of the metropolis, but in provincial towns and remote villages. A fine portrait of him, by Sir Joshua Reynolds, with a flattering inscription, "in honor of the zealous assertor of English liberty by law," was placed in the Guildhall of the city of London. Addresses of thanks to him poured in from all quarters, and most of the great municipalities of the empire presented him with the freedom of their corporations. English journals and English travelers carried his fame over Europe; and one of the sights of London which foreigners went to see, was THE GREAT LORD CHIEF JUSTICE PRATT.

On the formation of the Rockingham administration, although the leaders unfortunately consented to have Northington for their Chancellor, they wished to court popularity, and to give a pledge that they meant to follow a different course of policy at home and abroad from their predecessors, who prosecuted Wilkes and taxed the colonies. Accordingly, their first act was to raise the popular Judge to the peerage, by the style of "Baron Camden, of Camden Place, in the county of Kent."[2] The property from which he took his title had belonged to the celebrated antiquary of that name, and had passed, through several

[1] 2 Wilson, 275–292; *Entick* v. *Carrington;* 19 St. Tr. 1073.
[2] The Duke of Grafton, in his "Journal," says, "One of the first acts of our administration was to obtain from his Majesty the honors of a peerage for the true patriot, Lord Chief Justice Pratt, which the King had the condescension to grant to our earnest entreaties; the news of which was received by the nation with much applause."—Part II. p. 47.

changes of ownership, into the possession of the Pratts.

The new Peer took his seat in the House of Lords on the first day of the following session, being looked at with a jealous eye both by Lord Northington, who had opposed his elevation, and by Lord Mansfield, who instinctively dreaded a contest for the supremacy which he had enjoyed there since the death of Lord Hardwicke.

I have already mentioned Lord Camden's maiden effort upon the right to tax America, where he was so rudely assailed by the Lord Chancellor.[1] The declaratory bill being brought in, he on a subsequent day opposed it in a set speech, upon which he had taken immense pains, —which has been rapturously praised, and some passages of which are still in the mouths of schoolboys,—but which I must acknowledge seems to me to exhibit false reasoning and false taste. Having begun by alluding to the charge against him, as "the broacher of new-fangled doctrines, contrary to the laws of this kingdom and subversive of the rights of Parliament," he thus proceeded:

"My Lords, this is a heavy charge, but more so when made against one stationed as I am, in both capacities as a Peer and a Judge, the defender of the law and the constitution. When I spoke last, I was indeed replied to but not answered. As the affair is of the utmost importance, and in its consequences may involve the fate of kingdoms, I have taken the strictest review of my arguments, I have re-examined all my authorities—fully determined, if I found myself mistaken, publicly to own my mistake and give up my opinion; but my searches have more and more convinced me that the British Parliament has no right to tax the Americans. I shall not criticise the strange language in which your proposed declaration is framed; for to what purpose, but loss of time, to consider the particulars of a bill, the very existence of which is illegal,—absolutely illegal,—contrary to the fundamental laws of nature, contrary to the fundamental laws of this constitution—a constitution grounded on the eternal and immutable laws of nature,—a constitution whose center is liberty, which sends liberty to every individual who may happen to be within any part of its ample circumference? Nor, my Lords, is the doctrine new; it is as old as the constitution; it grew up with it; indeed, it is

[1] Ante, p. 264.

its support; taxation and representation are inseparably united. God hath joined them, no British Parliament can put them asunder; to endeavor to do so, is to stab our very vitals. My position is this—I repeat it—I will maintain it to my last hour—taxation and representation are inseparable; this position is founded on the laws of nature; it is itself a law of nature; for whatever is a man's own, is absolutely his own; no man has a right to take it from him without his consent, either expressed by himself or representative; whosoever attempts to do it, attempts an injury; whosoever does it commits a robbery;[1] he throws down and destroys the distinction between liberty and slavery. Taxation and representation are coeval with, and essential to, the constitution. I wish the maxim of Machiavel were followed—that of examining a constitution, at certain periods, according to its first principles; this would correct abuses and supply defects. To endeavor to fix the æra when the House of Commons began in this kingdom, is a most pernicious and destructive attempt; to fix it in Edward's or Henry's reign, is owing to the idle dreams of some whimsical, ill-judging antiquarians. When did the House of Commons first begin? When, my Lords?—it began with the constitution. There is not a blade of grass growing in the most obscure corner of this kingdom which is not—which was not ever—represented since the constitution began; there is not a blade of grass which, when taxed, was not taxed by the consent of the proprietor." [He then examines, at great length, the arguments drawn by analogy from Ireland, Wales, Berwick, and the Counties Palatine; and, having treated with merited scorn the miserable crotchet that America was virtually represented in the House of Commons, he thus concluded:] "The forefathers of the Americans did not leave their native country and subject themselves to every danger and distress, to be reduced to a state of slavery; they did not give up their rights; they expected protection, not chains, from their mother country; by her they believed they should be defended

---

[1] These words offended George Grenville, the author of the Stamp Act, so much, that he complained of them in the House of Commons, pronouncing them, with great emphasis, to be "a libel upon parliament;" and threatening to bring the printer of the speech to the bar for punishment. But no further notice was taken of it.—*Almon's Biographical Anecdotes*, i. 377.

in the possession of their property and not despoiled of it. But if you wantonly press this declaration, although you now repeal the Stamp Act, you may pass it again in a month; and future taxation must be in view, or you would hardly assert your right to enjoy the pleasure of offering an insult. Thus our fellow-subjects in America will have nothing which they can call their own, or, to use the words of the immortal Locke, *What property have they in that which another may by right take, when he pleases, to himself.*"[1]

Although the Stamp Act was most properly repealed, and nothing could exceed the folly of accompanying the repeal of it with the statutable declaration of the abstract right to tax, I confess I do not understand the reasoning by which, admitting that the British Parliament had supreme power to legislate for the colonies, a law passed to lay a tax upon them, though it may be unjust and impolitic, is a nullity. I agree that it may be put upon the footing of an act of attainder without hearing the party attainted in his defense, or an act to take away a man's private property without compensation; but could Lord Camden, sitting as a Judge, have held such acts to be nullities—hanging for murder the sheriff who assisted at the execution in the one case, or in an action of trespass recognizing the property of the original owner in the other? Would not a statute oppressively encroaching on the personal liberty of the colonists, or wantonly interfering with the exercise of their industry, be in all respects as objectionable as a statute enacting that " their deeds, and contracts shall be void, unless written on paper or parchment which has paid a duty to the state?" Nor do I see how our constitutional rights would be at all endangered by acknowledging the undoubted fact, that representation was unknown in this country till the end of the reign of Henry III., and that the Commons did not till long after sit in a separate chamber as an independent branch of the legislature. The assertion that all property and that all classes were represented in England, rather favors George Harding's doctrine, "that the Americans were actually represented by the knights of the shire for Kent, because the land in America was all granted by the Crown, to be held in socage of the manor

[1] 16 Parl. Hist. 177.

of East Greenwich in that county." However, our patriot displayed a noble enthusiasm on this occasion, and perhaps one ought to be ashamed of critically weighing the expressions which he used.[1]

With the exception of opposing the Declaratory Act, Lord Camden gave the Rockingham administration his cordial support; and he was free from the imputation to which Mr. Pitt was subject, of assisting the Court in getting rid of men who were sincerely anxious to conciliate America.

When Lord Northington at last abruptly brought on a crisis, and Mr. Pitt was sent for to form a new administration, Lord Camden was on the Midland Circuit. A communication was immediately opened between them; and Lord Camden expressed his willingness to co-operate in any way for the public good. The state of his mind, and the progress of the negotiation, will best be disclosed by the following letters written by him to Mr. T. Walpole, a common friend :—

"July 13, 1766. Nottingham.

" Dear Sir,

" I thank you for your intelligence, which turns out to be true, as the same post brought me a letter from the Chancellor to the same effect, though more authentic and circumstantial. Mr. P. then is come. May it be prosperous! But I foresee many difficulties before an administration can be completly settled. You are near the scene of action, and as likely to be intrusted by the great man as anybody; or, if not, must of course be so conversant with those who know, as to hear the best intelligence. My old friend, the C^r, has taken so much laudable pains to leave his office, that he must, in my opinion, remain. The D. of N., and your friend the Marquess,

---

[1] Junius, in his first letter, which appeared on the 21st of January, 1769, six years before hostilities commenced, severely reflected on the speeches of Mr. Pitt and Lord Camden in this debate, and accused them of thereby separating the colonies from the mother country: " Mr. Pitt and Lord Camden were to be the patrons of America, because they were in opposition. Their declaration gave spirit and argument to the colonies; and while, perhaps, they meant no more than the ruin of a minister, they, in effect, divided one-half of the empire from the other." I can not agree with this unscrupulous writer in imputing improper motives to them, but I do agree with him in condemning their assertion, " that the authority of the British legislature is not supreme over the colonies in the same sense in which it is supreme over Great Britain."—See Junius's Letter, 5th October, 1771.

must give way: but I do not believe Mr. P. will wish to remove the rest in office, unless, perhaps, they, in a pique, should scorn to hold on under his appointment, which I do not expect. It is an untoward season of the year, everybody out of town—and expresses must be sent for concurrence and concert to poor gentlemen who are at their country houses, without friends or advisers near; so they must, in some measure, follow the dictates of their own judgment, which may be more likely to mislead than direct. I am unable to conjecture; but if I am not much mistaken, the E. T. will accede.

"I can send you nothing in return for your intelligence, unless I could suppose you could be interested with stories of highwaymen and housebreakers. Perhaps you will not be displeased to hear that I am well and in good spirits—have had much traveling and little business—that one-third of my circuit is over, and that I am, let matters be settled or unsettled, most sincerely yours,

"CAMDEN."

"July 19, 1766. Leicester.

"Dear Sir,

'I am arrived late at this place, and find letters from you and Nuthall, pressing me to leave the circuit. I am willing enough to quit this disagreeable employment, but I think I ought not, upon a private intimation, to depart from my post. If you will by letter, or by express if you please, only tell me that Mr. Pitt would wish to see me, I will come to town at a moment's warning. Ld T. is gone. If Mr. Pitt is not distressed by this refusal, or if he is provoked enough not to feel his distress, I am rather pleased than mortified. Let him fling off the Grenvilles, and save the nation without them.

"Yours ever, &c.
"CAMDEN."

"July 20, 1766. Leicester

"Dear Sir,

"I have slept since I wrote to you; and having taken the advice of my pillow upon the subject of my coming to town, I remain of the same opinion, that I ought not at this time to quit my station, uncalled and uninvited. If Mr. P. really wants me, I would relieve his delicacy by coming at his request, conveyed to me either by you or Mr. Nuthall; but I suspect the true reason why he has not desired me to come, is because, as things are just now, he does not think it fitting. Sure Mr. P. will not be discouraged a second time by Lord T.'s refusal. He ought not for his own sake, for it does become him now to satisfy the world that his greatness does not hang on so slight a twig as T. This nation is in a blessed condition if Mr. P. is to take his directions from Stowe. A few days will decide this great affair, and a few days will bring me back of course. In the meantime, if my sooner return should be thought of any consequence, I am within the reach of an express. I was catched at Chatsworth by the D. of Devon and his 2 uncles, and very civilly compelled to lye there; but not one word of politics.

"I am, &c.
"CAMDEN."
"Warwick, July 24, 1766.

"Dear Sir,
"I am much concerned to find that Mr. Pitt's illness hangs upon him so long, and the wishes of the public by that means disturbed. He must set his hand to the plow, for the nation can not be dallied with any longer. L T.'s wild conduct, though Mr. P. is grievously wounded by it, may, for aught I know, turn out to be a favorable circumstance to reconcile him more to the present ministry, and of which corps he must form, as he always intended, this our administration. Indeed this inclination is one of the principal grounds of difference between the two brothers. Ld T. having closely connected himself with that set of men whom he opposed so inveterately, I have heard very authentically from the Stowe quarter, that one of the chief points upon which they broke was upon the promotion of Ld G., and recommended by Ld T. to be Secretary of State, under the color of enlarging the bottom, and reconciling all parties. That since he asked nothing for his brother G., he had a right to insist upon this promotion. The other, on the contrary, put a flat negative upon all that connection. Ld T. was very willing to go hand-in-hand with Mr. P. *pari passu*, as he called it, but would acknowledge no superiority or control. This was continually and repeatedly inculcated, not to say injudiciously, if he really intended to unite, because such declarations beforehand must create an incurable jealousy, and sow disunion in the very moment of reconciliation.

He taxes Mr. P. with private ingratitude, and is offended that two or three days elapsed before he was sent for. This is public talk at his Lordship's table, and therefore requires no secresy. Tnere are now, or will be in a few days at Stowe, the two Dukes of B. and M., with their ladies, Sir J. Amherst, and the royal guests. Therefore Ld T. is declared not the head of that party, for that is an honor he must never expect, but a proselyte received among them. Let not Mr. P. be alarmed at this formidable gathering of great men. The King and the whole nation are on the other side. I hope to be in town next Wednesday. In the meantime, believe me, &c.,

"CAMDEN."

When he arrived in town, on the conclusion of the circuit, he found the whimsical arrangement nearly completed,—according to which Mr. Pitt, becoming a Peer, was to be Lord Privy Seal and Prime Minister, the Duke of Grafton was to be First Lord of the Treasury, Lord Northington was to be President of the Council, Sir Charles Saunders was to be First Lord of the Admiralty, and Lord Shelburne and General Conway were to be Secretaries of State. The Great Seal was offered to Lord Camden, and, without hesitation, he accepted it,—stipulating only (as he reasonably might), that on giving up a lucrative situation, which he held during good behavior, he should have a retired allowance of £1,500 a year, and the reversion of a tellership for his son.[1] Although there were strange and discordant elements in the new Cabinet into which he was to enter, he reasonably supposed that he must be secure under the auspices of that great man who had formed it, and who had himself, through life, been the devoted friend of liberty.

Believing that the Lord Privy Seal would reduce into insignificance the Heads of the Treasury and of the Admiralty, and the Secretaries of State, he anticipated, with certainty, the speedy conciliation of America, the

---

[1] In a letter to the Duke of Grafton, dated 1st August, 1766, he says—
"The favors I am to request from your Grace's dispatch are as follows :—
 "1. My patent for the salary.
 "2. Patent for £1,500 a year upon the Irish establishment, in case my office should determine before the tellership drops.
 "3. Patent for tellership for my son.
 "4. The equipage money ; Lord Northington tells me it is £2,000. This I believe, is ordered by a warrant from the Treasury to the Exchequer."

increased humiliation of the House of Bourbon, and the return of tranquillity at home, by the abandonment of the unconstitutional policy which had marked the measures of Government since the commencement of the present reign. He thought that Pitt's second administration was to be as prosperous as the first,—if, from its pacific tendency, it should be less brilliant. For himself, he calculated that, with such a chief, the political functions of his office would require little time, and cause little anxiety,—so that, concurring in the measures of a powerful as well as liberal Government, he might chiefly devote himself to the discharge of his judicial duties, and to the improvement of our jurisprudence.

At a council held at St. James's on the 30th of July, 1766, Lord Camden received the Great Seal from his Majesty, with the title of Lord Chancellor.

CHAPTER CXLIV.

CONTINUATION OF THE LIFE OF LORD CAMDEN TILL HE BECAME AN EX-CHANCELLOR.

LORD CAMDEN'S appointment to the woolsack gave almost universal satisfaction;[1] and he had more doubts than any one else as to his own sufficiency. He deemed it lucky that he had the long vacation to refresh his recollection of Equity, and to get up the cases which had recently been decided in the Court of Chancery, while he had been a common-law Judge.

He held sittings before Michaelmas Term in Lincoln's Inn Hall, and on the 6th of November, the first day of the term, after a grand procession from his house in Lincoln's Inn Fields to Westminster Hall, he was there installed in his office with all the usual solemnities.[2]

[1] Lord Shelburne, in a letter to Mr. Pitt, dated 10th July, 1766, says, in a "P.S. You must permit me to add how happy I am in the choice of a Chancellor—and murmurs only come from the ultra-Tories."

[2] "30th July, 1766. Robert, Earl of Northington, Lord High Chancellor of Great Britain, having delivered the Great Seal to the King, at his Palace of St. James's, on Wednesday, the 30th day of July, 1766, his Majesty the same day, delivered it to Charles, Lord Camden, Chief Justice of the Common Pleas, with the title of Lord High Chancellor of Great Britain; who was

As an Equity Judge, Lord Camden fully sustained the reputation he had acquired while presiding in the Court of Common Pleas. When he pronounced a decree upon the construction of a will, or the liability of a trustee, he was not received with shouts of applause from hundreds of thousands of persons assembled round the Court, as when he ordered the liberation of WILKES, or adjudged the illegality of "general warrants;" but he now conciliated the calm respect and good opinion of all parties by his extensive legal information, by his quickness of perception and soundness of understanding, by the perspicuity with which his opinions were propounded, by the patience and impartiality which he uniformly displayed, and by his dignified politeness, which appeared more graceful by contrast with the unrefined manners of his predecessor. Although without the qualification, now considered indispensable and all-sufficient for the Equity bench, of having passed many years in the drudgery of drawing bills and answers, his mind was deeply imbued with the general principles of jurisprudence ; he had studied systematically the Roman civil law,—he was acquainted with the common law of England in all its branches, the most familiar and the most abstruse,—his time in his earlier years after entering the profession not having been engrossed by "*præproprera praxis*,"—instead of a hurried attention to a great variety of points, he had acquired the habit of deliberately investigating great questions,—as a Nisi Prius leader he possessed the faculty

then sworn into the said office before his Majesty in Council. His Lordship sat in Lincoln's Inn Hall during the Seals before Michaelmas Term ; and on Monday, the 6th day of November, being the first day of Michaelmas Term, went in state from his house in Lincoln's Inn Fields to Westminster Hall, accompanied by the Earl of Northington, Lord President of the Council, the Duke of Grafton, First Lord of the Treasury, the Earl of Bristol, Lord Lieutenant of Ireland, the Earl of Shelburne, and the Right Honorable Henry Seymour Conway, two of his Majesty's principal Secretaries of State, the Lord Viscount Barrington, Secretary of War, Lord Edgecombe, Treasurer of the Household, Sir Charles Saunders, Knight of the Bath, First Lord of the Admiralty, the Master of the Rolls, the Judges, King's Sergeants, King's Counsel, and other persons of quality. The Lords accompanied him to the Court of Chancery, where (before he entered upon business), in their presence, he took the oaths of allegiance and supremacy, and the oath of Chancellor of Great Britain, the Master of the Rolls holding the book, and the Deputy Clerk of the Crown reading the said oaths : which being done, the Attorney General moved that it might be recorded, and it was ordered accordingly. Then the Lords departed, leaving the Lord Chancellor in Court."—*Cr. Off. Min.*, No. 2, p. 14.

of sifting evidence and dealing rapidly and skillfully with facts,—he had taken infinite pains to make himself master of Equity doctrines and practice,—and for some years he had been first in business, as well as in rank, at the Chancery bar. In those days the notion had not sprung up that a common lawyer was unfit to be an Equity Judge, and Lord Camden was allowed to discharge his duty most admirably, even by hoary fixtures of the Court, such as AMBLER, who had "practiced as a barrister for upwards of forty years, of which thirty were employed in the Court of Chancery, under five Lord Chancellors, three sets of Commissioners, and five Masters of the Rolls."[1]

But we must appreciate his merits chiefly by the general testimonies in his favor from his contemporaries; for, when Chancellor, he was most unfortunate in the want of a "vates sacer." Not unfrequently his chief reporter, after a brief statement of the arguments of the defendant's counsel, thus deals with a judgment on which the Judge had bestowed infinite labor, and which was admired for its learning, precision, and lucid arrangement: "And Lord Camden being of the same opinion, which he delivered at large, the bill was dismissed."[2] But though these chroniclers only give us his dry conclusions of law in the fewest and most ordinary words, we may form a notion of his style and manner from a "Reminiscence" of BUTLER. "I distinctly remember," said he, Lord Camden's presiding in the Court of Chancery. His Lordship's judicial eloquence was of the colloquial kind—extremely simple,—diffuse but not desultory. He introduced legal idioms frequently, and always with a pleasing and great effect. Sometimes, however, he rose to the sublime strains of eloquence; but the sublimity was altogether in the sentiment; the diction retained its simplicity; this increased the effect."[3] About his dress and manner he seems to have been very little solicitous. "He wore a tie wig in Court," says a contemporary, "and has been frequently observed to garter up his stockings while counsel were the most strenuous in their eloquence."[4]

I do not think that during the time he held the Great

[1] Preface to Ambler, vi.
[2] Ambler, 660. Dickens is generally more provokingly deficient.
[3] Butler's Reminiscences [4] Political Anecdotes, 385.

Seal (only three years and a half) he added much to our Equity code. I do not find questions of greater importance settled by him, than that a bequest to "the most necessitous of my relations" shall go among the *next of kin*, according to the Statute of Distributions, without any inquiry into their circumstances;[1] and that by a bequest "of all the testator's pictures," (he having at the making of his will a good collection), after-purchased pictures shall pass.[2]

Only one of his decrees was reversed, and the general opinion has been that the reversal was wrong. A testator having devised freehold estates to certain uses, and bequeathed a leasehold messuage to trustees to convey to the uses of the freehold, "so that they should not separate," suffered a recovery of the freehold estates, whereby, as to them, the will was revoked, Lord Camden held, that the bequest of the leasehold was revoked also.[3] This decree was reversed on appeal; but Lord Eldon said, in *Southey* v. *Somerville*,[4] that "he should be disposed to agree with the opinion of Lord Camden rather than the judgment of the House of Lords;" and, on principle, I conceive it must be assumed (however contrary to the fact), that the testator knew and intended all the consequences of the recovery which he suffered.[5]

Lord Camden's plans for legal reform were defeated by the unhappy turn which politics and parties took (so contrary to his seemingly well-founded expectations) almost from the moment of his elevation to his present office. He had intended, under the auspices of Lord Chatham, again to bring forward his Habeas Corpus Bill, with some other measures to improve the administration both of criminal and civil justice; but the great luminary to whose light and influence he had trusted was eclipsed, and for a time seemed blotted out of the system, so that darkness was spread over the political world, and chaos seemed to have come again.

Lord Chatham had scarcely called into existence his motley administration,—pleasantly depicted by Burke as "a cabinet so curiously inlaid—such a piece of diversified

---

[1] *Wedmore* v. *Woodroffe*, Ambler, 636. [2] Ibid. 640.
[3] *Darley* v. *Darley*, Ibid. 653. [4] 13 Ves. Jr. 492.
[5] 3 Br. P. C. 365; and see *Carrington* v. *Payne*, 5 Ves Jr. 404; *Lowndes* v. *Stone*, Id. 649; *Ware* v. *Polhill*, 11 Ves. Jr. 280.

mosaic—such a tesselated pavement without cement—
here a bit of black stone, and there a bit of white, which
had a chance of coherence only from the controlling
genius of its framer,"—when, by fresh and aggravated
attacks of his old malady, the gout, he was almost disabled from attending to public business; and soon after,
on account of a nervous disorder which is supposed even
to have affected his mind, he was long seen only by his
wife and his medical attendants. The consequence was,
that Lord Camden's situation soon most became embarrassing and distressing. After a period of utter confusion, the members of the Government from whom
he most differed got the ascendency; and, from the protracted hope of the restoration of his friend, who nominally continued in office, he was cut off from the resource
of resigning and going into opposition.

The first difficulty which arose after the formation of
the new government was from the scarcity and apprehension of famine, produced by the failure of the harvest.
The price of provisions was rapidly advancing, and the
greatest alarm prevailed in the public mind. The prime
minister was confined to his bed at Bath. A proposal
being made that the exportation of corn should be prevented, the Chancellor recommended that this object
should be effected by an order of the King in council.
Lord Chatham, who was still able to communicate with
his colleagues by letter, concurred in this advice, and the
measure was carried into effect. It was popular in itself,
but rendered odious by the manner in which it was defended. I have already mentioned the scrape into which
the Government was on this occasion precipitated by the
indiscretion and intemperance of Lord Northington, now
President of the Council.[1] He ought to have been
thrown overboard, and the foundering vessel would have
righted. Lord Camden thought that he must be supported, and was so far misled by his zeal to serve a colleague as to persuade himself (in trying to persuade
others) that the act of interfering with lawful commerce,
although against an express statute, was not only justifiable from expedience, so as to entitle the parties concerned in it to be protected by an indemnity, but was in
itself strictly legal, and without any indemnity, might be

[1] Ante, 274.

defended in a court of justice. According to the evidence of credible witnesses present, he at last worked himself up to say:—

"The necessity of a measure renders it not only excusable, but legal; and consequently a judge, when the necessity is proved, may, without hesitation, declare that act legal which would be clearly illegal, where such necessity did not exist. The Crown is the sole executive power, and is therefore intrusted by the constitution to take upon itself whatever the safety of the state may require during the recess of parliament, *which is at most but a forty days' tyranny*. The power exercised on this occasion was so moderate, that Junius Brutus would not have hesitated to intrust it even to the discretion of a Nero."[1]

He now received from Lord Temple the severest chastisement ever inflicted upon him:—

"Forty days' tyranny!" exclaimed his opponent. "My Lords, tyranny is a harsh sound. I detest the very word, because I hate the thing. But is this language to come from a noble and learned Lord, whose glory it might and ought to be to have risen by steps which Liberty threw in his way, and to have been honored as his country has honored him, not for trampling her under foot, but for holding up her head? I have used my best endeavors to answer the argument of the 'forty days' by argument founded on principles; I will now give the noble and learned Lord one answer more, and it shall be *argumentum ad hominem*. That noble and learned Lord has said, I believe, on other occasions, and he has said well, *the price of one hour's English liberty none but an English jury could estimate*—and juries under his guidance have put a very high value upon it, in the case of the meanest of our fellow subjects when oppressed by the servants of the state. But 'forty days' tyranny' over the nation by the Crown! Who can endure the thought? My Lords, less than 'forty days' tyranny,' such as this country has felt in some times, would, I believe, bring your Lordships together without a summons, from your sick beds, faster than our great patriots themselves, to get a place or a pension, or both,[2] and, for aught I know, make the subject of

[1] Lord Charlemont's Correspondence, p. 22.
[2] Lord Camden was often taunted with his retired allowance under the name of "pension."

your consultation that appeal to Heaven which has been spoken of. Once establish a dispensing power, and you can not be sure of either liberty or law for *forty minutes*."[1]

Lord Mansfield, more calmly but not less forcibly, pointed out the fallacy and the dangerous consequences of the Chancellor's reasoning, and on this occasion gained a signal triumph over his rival. There can be no doubt that Lord Camden was confounding acts which the law says may be lawfully done in a case of necessity—with acts done in violation of the law for the public good ; and that his doctrines led inevitably to a power in the Crown to suspend or repeal all laws, without the previous or subsequent sanction of parliament. The doctrine has never since been contended for; and whenever ministers, for the safety of the state, have acted contrary to law, they have thrown themselves upon parliament, and asked for a bill of indemnity.[2]

---

[1] Adolph Hist. i. 290.

[2] "The opposition acknowledged the rectitude of the measure; but we were not to be justified on the ground on which the Cabinet thought fit at first to take up the business, by supporting it as maintainable under the Salus Populi Suprema Lex, and we had the mortification, after two days' debate, to stoop to a Bill of Indemnity, which ought to have been proposed in the beginning.....In the struggle for and against the necessity of passing the Indemnity Bill, it was curious to see Lord Mansfield bestriding the high horse of Liberty, while Lord Chatham and Lord Camden were arguing for the extension of prerogative beyond its true limits ; and it was in these debates that the upright Chancellor, in the warmth of speaking, inadvertently made use of the expression, 'that if it was tyranny, it was only a tyranny of forty days.'"—*Duke of Grafton's Journal.*

"With regard to Lord Camden, the truth is, that he inadvertently overshot himself, as appears plainly by that unguarded mention of *a tyranny of forty days*, which I myself heard. Instead of asserting that the proclamation was legal, he should have said ' My Lords, I know that the proclamation is *illegal*, but I advised it because it was indispensably necessary to save the kingdom from famine ; and I submit myself to the justice and mercy of my country.' Such language as this would have been merely rational and consistent ;—not unfit for a lawyer, and very worthy of a great man."—PHILO JUNIUS, 15th Oct. 1771.

We are amazed at Lord Camden's "FORTY DAYS' TYRANNY," but it is remarkable that there is hardly any public man who has not, at some time or other, indiscreetly used some expression which has passed into a by-word against him. I might mention Lord Melbourne's "heavy blow and great discouragement to the Church," Lord John Russell's "finality of the Reform Bill," and Lord Lyndhurst's "aliens in blood, language, and religion." I myself had the honor of having 50,000 copies of a speech, which I made in the House of Commons when Attorney General, printed and industriously distributed in every borough in England among freemen possessing the right of voting for members of parliament, because I very indiscreely said (what was

The government, rendered unpopular by this exhibition, was soon entirely deprived of all assistance from Lord Chatham, who was unable to attend either the debates in the House of Lords or the meetings of the Cabinet, and, shut up in his house at Hayes, refused to correspond on business with his colleagues or with the King. In a fit of national fatuity, which we can only explain by supposing that it was inflicted as a special visitation from Heaven for the sins of the people,—within a few months after the repeal of the American Stamp Act, there was passed, without opposition, and almost without public observation, the fatal act imposing a duty on tea and other commodities when imported into the colonies,—which led to the non-consumption combination,—to the riots at Boston—to civil war—to the dismemberment of the empire. How Lord Camden should have suffered it to pass through the House of Lords in silence, I profess myself utterly at a loss to conjecture: it was not only impolitic, but, according to his doctrine, it was *ultra vires parliamenti*, and to be treated as a nullity; for to justify this by calling it "a commercial regulation," would only be rendering more contemptible his flimsy and fallacious distinction between a power to regulate commerce, and a power to impose a tax.[1]

After Parliament was prorogued, Lord Camden had very nearly been deprived of the Great Seal when he had held it little more than a year,—and, for his fame as a minister, there is great reason to regret his continuance in office. Lord Chatham's health was deemed irrecoverably gone, and Charles Townshend, with the concurrence of the King, had arranged a new administration, in which he himself was to have been First Lord of the Treasury, and Charles Yorke was to have been his Lord Chancellor,—when the plan was rendered abortive by his sudden and lamented death, in the flower of his age.

very true) that the "right of freemen to vote was the *plague-spot* on our representative system."

[1] Ten years afterwards, when the sowing of the wind was producing the whirlwind, Lord Camden being taunted with his sanctioning of the tax, he said: "I confess as mere matter of supposition, the conjecture is plausibly supported, but the fact was entirely otherwise. I never did, or ever will give my consent to raising any tax in any form on the people of America for the purpose of raising a revenue to be under the disposal of the British parliament."—18 Parl. Hist. 1222. His confidential correspondence with the Duke of Grafton had not then commenced.

Then followed the arrangement called the "Duke of Grafton's administration," in which he was recognized as Prime Minister. Lord Chatham still retained the Privy Seal, and was supposed to be a member of the Cabinet; but he remained entirely sequestered from public business, under circumstances which will never be fully explained.

Lord Camden did not concur in all the opinions of the First Lord of the Treasury, but greatly preferred him to the Duke of Bedford, Lord Shelburne, or any other Whig leader, and the closest friendship was established between them. To this we are indebted for the letters I am about to introduce, which will be found to throw a new light upon the state of parties, and the history of the country from this time, till the reins of government were placed in the hands of Lord North.

An important question soon arose, whether the Great Seal of Ireland should be held by an Irish or an English lawyer? Lord Townshend was then Lord Lieutenant, and, for the sake of popularity, being naturally desirous of having an Irishman, had brought over the Duke of Grafton to the same opinion. However, Lord Camden, being consulted by him, wrote back the following answer:—

"Bath, Sept. 27, 1767.

" My dear Lord Duke,

" I have since the receipt of your Grace's letter turned my thoughts upon the subject of it with the most serious attention, and am displeased with myself for not agreeing altogether with your Grace in conferring the Irish Seal upon an Irishman. I will readily confess I am not a competent judge of this question, for want of knowing the true state of that country, the manner in which it has been governed of late years, the power and influence of the several connections, and, above all, the importance of the Irish bar in the House of Commons there: and there fore it is very likely that your Grace may be much bettei enabled than myself to form a true judgment upon the utility and policy of complimenting the Irish with the high office. Your Grace, however, has a right to my poor opinion, such as it is; and indeed, my Lord, I am very loth to give up to the unreasonable demands of two of those barristers (however eminent) the last, as well as most important law office in that kingdom, which England hitherto has thought fit to reserve to herself. All the chiefs upon each bench were formerly named from hence; the Irish have acquired the King's Bench, and the late Lord Lieutenant, for the first time, made them a present of the Chief Baron; and there has not for many years been an instance of a puisne judge sent from this country: I believe Baron Mounteney was the last.

"Thus, by degrees, has this country surrendered up all the great offices of the law, except only the Common Pleas and the Great Seal; and I much doubt whether this country acquires any advantage by all these concessions.

"In the last session, Mr. Flood moved a general censure upon the characters and capacity of the Judges sent from England, with a view, no doubt, of inflaming the people against all these nominations, in hopes of extending their encroachments to a total exclusion of the English from the Irish bench; and now, such is the danger of precedent, they threaten general opposition (for so I understood from Lord Clare) if this favor is refused, and your Grace seems to think it will be an affront upon the next Council there.

"Jocelyn and Bowes, though both Englishmen, are honored with the appellation of Irish for the present purpose, and are cited as precedents in their favor. I am very apprehensive, that if your Grace should indulge now the Irish in this *demand* (for I can call it by no other name), the precedent will bind England forever; for national favors once conferred can never be resumed. Ireland has reason enough to be discontented with the mother country: the popular party are sure to distress the Castle to some degree every session, and the method has been hitherto to win over the leaders in the House of Commons by places, pensions, and honors, which has enabled the Lord Lieutenant for the time being to close his particular session with ease to himself; at the same time that it has ruined the King's affairs, and enraged the people. The next successor is involved in the same difficulties, and his convenience has been complimented by the like measures; till, at last, by this profusion of rewards the Government has nothing to give, and is left beggared, and consequently unsupported. In such a state of things would your Grace wish to pursue such a plan, and grant now, before the opening of the session, the highest post in the law to one member only of the House of Commons (for only one can have it), whose removal afterwards to make room for an Englishman (let his behavior be ever so obnoxious) would be a most odious and unpopular measure in that country? An Englishman in the office is expected to remain an Englishman, and is permitted; an Irishman anglicised would never be endured. Indeed, my Lord, the very yielding, in my humble opinion, would be a weakening of Government, and be more pernicious than the most troublesome session.

"I am truly sensible of Lord Townshend's embarrassments, and foresee that, if he should not obtain this boon, he must expect to meet with some very disagreeable struggles. But, I dare say, his zeal, courage, and ability are equal to the whole, and I am sure he will cheerfully undertake what he has accepted, though your Grace should adhere to our first opinion, of keeping the Seal, for the present, in commission.

"Your Grace will be pleased to consider that the Chancellor, Chief Baron, and Chief Justices, are called to the Council in Ireland in the quality of statesmen, and that the Council in that country is an assembly of equal importance of either of the branches of the legislature. If the Lord Lieutenant is surrounded with Irish only filling these offices at the board, he is subject to be overruled in every quarter by the great chiefs of the law, in which case I doubt he must submit.

"But if your Grace should at last be determined to name an Irishman, you will please to consider whether Sir A. Malone is not clearly the properest person. He has not indeed applied for it, but I understand he would be happy with the offer; and such is the deference to his superior character, that every one of those gentlemen who has applied have put themselves only in the second place after him. So that, if your Grace is resolved upon an Irishman, 'Detur dignissimo!' Let it carry with it a march of public spirit, at the same time that it is a management of parties. I know your Grace will forgive my frankness: this is my present opinion, though I will most willingly submit to a contrary determination, and when your Grace has done it, I shall say in public that it is well done; indeed, I shall go near to think so, because I am sure the decision will be taken by those who understand Ireland better than I do.

"I presume your Grace has asked Lord N———'s [1] opinion upon this subject; that will have great weight with me, as well as your Grace. He used to think as I do, as did Lord Chatham; but different circumstances may well bring about a change of opinion.

"I know your Grace will be anxious to hear some news of Lord Chatham; if I had been able to have given you any authentic intelligence of his amendment to any considerable degree, I should have wrote before. The whole country in his neighborhood report him much better; but his knocker is tied up, and he is inaccessible. I read a letter from Lady Chatham yesterday, who is so fearful of owning my Lord to be better, that she retracts it, even while she is admitting it in the same sentence, and conveys hopes of his recovery while she forbids them. I verily believe he is considerably mended.

"I propose to be in town on Monday morning, the 7th of next month, to prorogue the Parliament, at eleven o'clock in the morning, if your Grace will be so good as to order the proper preparations,—to go to Court,—to swear in Lord North, and set out immediately for my return. I hope this will be permitted.

"I have the honor to be, with the most perfect respect and esteem, your Grace's

"Most obedient faithful Servant,
"CAMDEN."

Lord Townshend still pressed very hard for the appointment of an Irish lawyer, and, in a letter to Lord Camden, said,—" This measure is the very criterion of an odious or a popular administration; if the concession is not granted, it will be a proof of my own insignificance, and the safest course will be for me to confess it to all mankind." Lord Camden, therefore, wrote to the Duke of Grafton:—
" When such language is used, there are but two things to be done—to quarrel or to submit. The first being, at this time, to the last degree improvident and dangerous, which his Lordship well knows, makes the latter necessary. However, the Cabinet resolved on resistance, as

[1] Lord Northington's.

appears by the following letter from Lord Camden to the Duke of Grafton :—

"I find by your Grace's letter, and one I received from Lord Shelburne, that I am called upon to name a person for the Irish Seal. He must be eminent, and one who at this ticklish juncture would be every way fit for the office. I doubt it will be too much for me, in such a dearth of men willing to accept, to recommend one who will answer that description, nor dare I undertake it without the sanction of a cabinet. The whole business is, indeed, a state question, and does not properly fall within my department."

Mr. Sergeant Hewitt, afterwards Lord Lifford, was fixed upon. The Duke of Grafton says, in his Journal,—

"Lord Northington's opinion concurred so fully with Lord Camden's on the disposal of the Great Seal of Ireland, that the Cabinet was persuaded not to give way to Lord Townshend's reasoning in favor of an Irish lawyer's holding it; and I am persuaded that our firmness gave more real consideration to his Lordship's situation, and dignity and weight to his government, than any yielding of his own would have effected. Before Parliament met, Mr. Sergeant Hewitt accepted the Seal, with every good disposition to discharge properly the great trust put into his hands, and his learning as a lawyer sanctioned our expectations from the appointment. He was a true Whig, and bore a character to which all parties gave their assent of respect; and though his speeches in parliament were long, and without eloquence, they were replete with excellent matter and knowledge of the law. His conduct in Ireland, under the peerage of Lifford, soon gained the esteem of the public."

Lord Camden's views on this subject were tinged by the prejudices which then subsisted in England, respecting the subjection of Ireland. The two countries must now be considered on a footing of perfect equality, and the only consideration is, what is most conducive to their mutual interest? That great statesman, Lord Wellesley, proposed (I think wisely) as a solution of this question,— that there should be one bar for England and Ireland; and that while lawyers practicing in England should be occasionally appointed to preside in the courts of justice in Ireland, lawyers practicing in Ireland should be reciprocally appointed to preside in the courts of justice in England.

Public affairs remained in a state of considerable tranquillity, till the sudden reappearance in England of the notorious John Wilkes, which threw the whole nation into a ferment. After the popularity he had acquired by establishing the illegality of " general warrants " and of " the seizure of papers by the authority of the Secretary of State," he had been convicted of publishing seditious and obscene libels; he had been outlawed, and he had lived in exile. Having failed in negotiations to obtain a pardon, he now boldly presented himself at the hustings as a candidate to represent the city of London in parliament. Defeated there, he started for Middlesex, and he was returned for this county by a great majority, being supported by a mob who compelled all who appeared in the streets and highways to join in the cry of " Wilkes and liberty!" The Government was most seriously alarmed, and Lord Camden, with the other ministers being summoned to attend a meeting of the Cabinet, wrote the following letter to the Duke of Grafton ;—

"Bath, April 3, 1768.

" My dear Lord Duke,

" Whatever vexation and inconvenience I may feel at this unexpected summons, which calls me from hence above a week before the time, yet, I shall, without fail, give my attendance at the time appointed. The event is disagreeable and unforeseen, for I am persuaded that no person living, after Wilkes had been defeated in London, would have thought it possible for him to have carried his election for the county of Middlesex. Sure, I am, that if the Government had arrested him while he was a candidate, this step would have secured his election, and would have been considered as the cause of his success. I can not pretend, at this distance, without further information, to advise what proceedings are now necessary, as the only subject for consideration seems to be, what measures are to be taken by the House of Commons at the meeting of Parliament. If the precedents and the constitution will warrant an expulsion, that perhaps may be right. A criminal flying his country to escape justice—a convict and an outlaw! That such a person should in open daylight, thrust himself upon the country as a candidate, his crime unexpiated—is audacious beyond description. This is the light in which I consider the affair; the riot only inflaming the business, and not showing the weakness of the Government more than any other election riot in the kingdom. But it would be well to consider what may be the consequences if W. should be re-elected. That is very serious. I take it for granted that he will surrender, and receive judgment in the K. Bench, the first day of the Term,—when, I suppose, the outlawry will be reversed, and he will be imprisoned. We expect him at this place to-night, where, I suppose, he intends to remain till the Term ; and this town is not a little alarmed lest the same spirit of violence should follow him hither. But, I trust, we are not mad enough here to follow the example of the metropolis. Whatever may be the heat of the present moment, I am persuaded it will soon subside, and this gentleman will lose his popularity in a very short time after men have recovered their senses.

" I am," &c.

At the Cabinet all present appear to have acquiesced in the determination that Wilkes should immediately be expelled the House of Commons; but when it appeared that the demagogue, instead of submitting to his sentence, meant to insist that the outlawry was erroneous,—that all the proceedings against him were void,—and that he was entitled to be treated as an innocent man,—the Chancellor quailed, and thus addressed the Premier:

" 20th April, 1768.

" My dear Lord,

" I dare say you have been informed of what passed to-day in the Court of King's Bench, and that Mr. W. is still at large. His counsel, however, promised that he should be forthcoming in custody, and then move to be bailed ; sue out a writ of error and reverse the outlawry. They gave notice, likewise, that they intended, after they had got rid of the outlawry, to move in arrest of judgment. Your Grace will be pleased to perceive that Mr. W. stands at present convicted only by verdict; and if there shall appear to be any material defect in the record, that the judgment must be stayed ; in which case he must be discharged, and he becomes a freeman upon this prosecution as much as if he had never been convicted. I dare say your Grace will see, upon this short representation, that till judgment is finally pronounced against Mr. W. by the Court, no man has a right to pronounce him guilty. This appears to me a real difficulty attending the measure, which yesterday we thought so clear. For how can the House expel a member, either as an outlaw or a convict, while the suit is pending, whereas he may turn out at last to be neither the one nor the other? I am afraid, considering the necessary delay in courts of law, it will be impossible for the King's Bench to give judgment before the Parliament meets, and therefore it deserves the most serious consideration whether the proposed measure should be pursued while the obstacle stands in the way.

"I have the honor," &c.

The motion for the expulsion was accordingly deferred till, the outlawry being reversed, sentence of imprisonment for a year and ten months was pronounced on Wilkes, and he insulted Parliament by a virulent libel, which, at the bar of the Lower House, he avowed and boasted of. His expulsion was then carried, and a new writ was ordered to elect another representative for Middlesex. This proceeding, though impolitic, can not be considered unlawful or unconstitutional; for there might be a presumption that his constituents would not have elected a person guilty of such misconduct, and it might be fair to give them an opportunity of determining whether they would still have him for their representative.

I am glad to think that the subsequent proceedings respecting the Middlesex election were not sanctioned by Lord Camden; for I believe that all mankind are now agreed that the House of Commons acted illegally and unconstitutionally in again expelling Mr. Wilkes for a supposed offense committed before his re-election,—in declaring him disqualified to serve in parliament,—and in seating Mr. Luttrell as representative for Middlesex, although he had only a small minority of the electors in his favor. The Chancellor is by no means exempted from blame for consenting to belong to an administration which overruled his opinion upon such questions. Although we may account for his continuing in office while he could be considered as having Lord Chatham for a colleague, it does astonish us exceedingly that he still condescended to hold the Great Seal after his great Chief had resigned, and was at open enmity with the Government. But he was placed in a most painful situation; Lord Chatham was still unable to appear in parliament, and there was no statesman with whom he thought he could better co-operate for the public good than the present head of the Treasury.

The three following letters to the Duke of Grafton explain the removal of Lord Shelburne from the Government, the consequent resignation of Mr. Pitt, and Lord Camden's perplexity:—

"29th Sept. 1768.

"I understand your Grace's plan is fixt, and I saw plainly the last time I was in town that Lord S——'s removal was determined. What can I say to it, my dear Lord? It is unlucky.

"The administration, since Lord Chatham's illness, is almost entirely altered, without being changed, and I find myself surrounded with persons to whom I am scarce known, and with whom I have no connection. Lord Chatham is at Hayes, brooding over his own suspicions and discontents. His return to business almost desperate, inaccessible to everybody, but under a persuasion (as I have some reason to conjecture) that he is given up and abandoned. This measure, for aught I know, may fix his opinion, and bring him to a resolution of resigning. If that should happen, I should be under the greatest difficulty.

"I am truly, my dear Lord, distressed. I have seen so much of courts that I am heartily tired of my employment, and should be happy to retire upon a scanty income if an honorable opportunity offered to justify my retreat to the King and your Grace; but that step I will never take without your consent, till I find I have not the King's favor and your confidence, unless I should be forced by something more compelling than the Earl of S——'s removal.

"After all, though your Grace is so good as to relieve me from any opinion on the subject, yet the case being stated as it is, that either your Grace or the Earl must quit, my opinion is clear, in a moment, that your Grace must remain. I am," &c.

"14th Oct. 1768.

"My concern upon the intelligence contained in your Grace's letter is inexpressible, and though I was apprehensive that Lord Shelburne's dismission would make a deep impression upon Lord Chatham's mind, yet I did not expect this sudden resignation. I will still live in hope that his Majesty's letter may produce an alteration, because there is a possibility, though at the same time I do not flatter myself with any sanguine expectations. Your Grace and I feel for each other. To me I fear the blow is fatal, yet I shall come to no determination. If I can find out what is fit for me to do in this most distressed situation, that I must do; but the difficulty lies in forming a true judgment. Whatever my decision may be, I will never resign my active endeavors to support the King's service, or my unchangeable attachment to your Grace. This most unfortunate event will throw the King's affairs into a state of utter distraction. Perhaps order may spring up out of this confusion. I do assure your Grace that my mind is at present in too great an agitation to be soon settled, and therefore I do not give myself leave to form any opinion concerning my own conduct: I shall wait with impatience to hear the conclusion, and am, with the truest zeal and attachment," &c.

"Bath, 16th Oct. 1768.

"Your Grace's intelligence does not surprise me: I expected it, and predetermined my own journey to London before I had the honor of your Grace's letter. Unfortunately one of my children is so ill that I must wait a day or two before I set out, in order to see what turn her distemper will take. I propose, however, to be in town on Wednesday next, or Thursday at the latest.

"Nothing could give me so much satisfaction as to join with your Grace in one line of conduct, and yet I see plainly that our situations are different, and the same honor due to the King and regard to the public operating upon two minds equally aiming at the same end, may possibly draw us different ways; but I dare say your Grace will believe me, in all events and circumstances, what I really am, with all respect and unfeigned attachment," &c.

On his return to London he heard such an account of Lord Chatham as to convince him that the country was for ever deprived of the services of this illustrious patriot—and, agreeing to support the present Government, he prevailed on Mr. Dunning to follow his example.[1]

The dispute with the colonies was now assuming a very alarming aspect, the act so heedlessly passed to impose a duty on goods imported into America having produced the discontent and the resistance which might have been expected from it. Lord Camden's views upon the subject were most liberal and enlightened, and, if he had been listened to, he would have saved the empire from civil war and dismemberment. In the prospect of the meeting of parliament, having been consulted by the Prime Minister respecting the King's speech, he thus replied:—

"As to North America, before a speech can be sketched upon the subject, it is necessary to know what measures the King's ministers intend to pursue, for the speech and the address must mark the outlines of these measures.

"I was a long time in hopes that Massachusetts Bay would have been the only disobedient colony. It would have been no difficult matter to have dealt with them if the others had sat still and remained passive; but I am deceived in that expectation, for it is now manifest that the whole continent will unite and make it common cause. We are drifted by I know not what fatality upon Mr. Grenville's ground. We are pressed on the one hand by the declaratory law, and on the other, by the colonies' resolute denial of parliamentary authority. The issue is now joined upon the *right*, which, in my apprehension, is the most untoward that could have been started—fatal to Great Britain if she miscarries—unprofitable if she succeeds. For if it is (as I believe your Grace thinks with me it is) inexpedient to tax the colonies, as we all maintained when the Stamp Act was repealed—after both sides are half ruined in the contest, we shall at last establish a right which ought never to be exerted.

"If the Americans are able to practice so much self-denial as to subsist only for one twelvemonth without British commodities, I do very much fear that they will carry their point without striking a blow. Patience and perseverance in this one measure will ruin us; and I am the more apt to dread this event, because it seems to me

[1] Note to the Duke of Grafton, dated 4th Nov. "I sat late in Court, and have just dined. Mr. Dunning stays in his office at my request."

that the colonies are more sober, and consequently more determined, in the present opposition than they were upon the Stamp Act. For, except only the riots at Boston, I see nothing like active rebellion in the other provinces. If this should happen, the merchants and manufacturers here at home will be clamorous, and half our own people will be added to the American party.

"Your Grace will ask, upon this representation of things, *what is to be done?* Indeed, my dear Lord, I do not know what is best to advise. The parliament, I presume can not repeal the Act in question, because that would admit the American principle to be right and their own doctrine erroneous. Therefore I conclude the parliament will not repeal, consequently must execute the law, and this of course must be the language of the Speech.

"The method how to execute it is the next consideration, and here I am as much at a loss. There is no pretense for violence anywhere but at Boston. That is the ringleading province, and if any country is to be chastised, the punishment ought to be leveled there. I have been sometimes thinking, that if the Act was repealed in favor of the other provinces, excepting Massachusetts Bay, and there executed with proper rigor, such a measure might be successful. But I am aware that no man, perhaps, but myself, could be brought to relish such a concession, as almost everybody else holds the declaratory law to be a second fundamental one, never to be departed from.

"I submit to the declaratory law, and have thought it my duty, upon that ground, as a minister, to exert my constitutional power to carry the Duty Act into execution. But as a member of the legislature, I can not bring myself to advise violent measures to support a plan so inexpedient and impolitic, and I am very much afraid (I speak this confidentially to your Grace) that if a motion should be made to repeal the bill I should be under the necessity to vote for it. But there are so few in my way of thinking, that such a motion is not to be expected.

"I am very sensible that a difference of opinion upon a subject so serious and important may be prejudicial to the administration, and I lament the occasion, being persuaded that a most perfect union among us is essential, and I will labor to effect it with my best endeavors. But I do fear, most exceedingly, that upon the American question the Bedfords and myself will be too far asunder to meet. I must maintain my own ground. The public knows my opinion and knows theirs. Neither of us can be inconsistent with ourselves.

"This letter is to your Grace only. You are my Pole Star, Lord Chatham being eclipsed. I had rather see your Grace at the head of government than any other man in the kingdom, and therefore I have disclosed to you my whole heart upon this ill-fated business. I am sensible that my sentiments do not altogether coincide with your Grace's opinion.

"There is nothing I dread so much as a war with America. I shall be very happy to know the result of your councils in town upon this subject.—Corsica is rather a delicate than a difficult business."[1]

Lord Camden's advice was entirely disregarded. He had, in like manner, quarreled with his colleagues respecting the Middlesex election. Still he made an effort to save Dunning, who, continuing in office at his request, had given great offense to Lord North, now leader of the House of Commons, by insisting on one occasion that Wilkes should be heard before he was condemned. Thus he appealed to the Premier:—

"10th Dec. 1768.

"I had an opportunity, after I saw your Grace yesterday, of hearing an account of what passed in the House of Commons, and I find the debate turned upon this: 'Whether they should vote the paper a libel before Wilkes was heard in his defense?' and that this was no question on the merits, but only discourse upon the mode of proceeding: that the Solicitor General thought, if Mr. Wilkes was to be heard, he ought regularly to be at liberty to speak to the nature and quality of the paper, as well as to the fact of writing and publishing. And indeed, my dear Lord, I am of the same opinion; and I do verily believe that no lawyer can hold a different lan-

[1] We owe the foregoing letters to the circumstance of the Chancellor having passed the autumn at Bath, while the Prime Minister was at Euston: "Lord Camden and myself unfortunately saw less of each other than in other summers—both of us profiting by a retreat into the country of the leisure which a recess from Chancery and Treasury business offered."—*Duke of Grafton's Journal, 1768.*

guage. The Solicitor said that, difficult as the task would be for Mr. W. to maintain an argument that the paper was no libel, yet he ought not to be precluded from that argument,—which he would be if the House determined it to be a libel. I do not see how they can, consistent with the terms of justice, pronounce the paper to be a libel till they have heard him. Now, my dear Lord, give me leave to say that Lord North should not be quite so much offended with Mr. Dunning, because the matter before the House was rather a discourse upon the method of proceeding than a measure of administration. I do not believe Mr. D. will be so base as to remain in office, and not to be hearty in the support of administration. I have the honor," &c.

This application was successful, and Dunning continued in office till after Lord Camden's own removal.

The Ministers found they were getting into such tremendous difficulties respecting the Middlesex election by contemning the Chancellor's advice, that the Prime Minister wrote to him, specially inviting him to attend a Cabinet to be held upon the subject. The following was his answer:—

"9th January, 1769.

" My dear Lord,

" I have the honor of your Grace's letter, and will certainly attend the meeting of the King's servants on Wednesday morning next. I do wish, most heartily, that the present time could be eased of the difficulties that Mr. W.'s business has brought upon the Government: a fatality has attended it from the beginning, and it grows more serious every day. Your Grace and I have unfortunately differed. I wish it had been otherwise. It is a hydra, multiplying by resistance, and gathering strength by every attempt to subdue it. As the times are, I had rather pardon W. than punish him. This is a political opinion, independent of the merits of the cause.

"I am very glad to hear the holidays have given your Grace so happy a respite. They have been to me a perfect paradise, as I have employed my whole time in studying the Douglas cause, and my mind has been totally vacant from political vexations.

" I have the honor," &c.

He attended the meeting, but with no good effect. The

Duke of Grafton treated him with perfect civility, and was inclined to be governed by his opinion; but what he laid down respecting the law and the constitution was scornfully received by all the others.—From thenceforth he constantly absented himself from the Cabinet when the two great subjects of internal and colonial policy were to be discussed—Wilkes and American coercion.

The public were not then in possession of these secrets. For two years it was remarked that he preserved an impenetrable silence in parliament, unless when, as Speaker, he put the question, and declared the majority; but no one suspected that he had, in reality, ceased to be a member of the Government.[1]

At last, when Parliament reassembled in the beginning of January, 1770, the Lord Chancellor spoke out. Lord Chatham, after his resignation,—to the astonishment of all mankind, not only experienced a considerable relaxation of his bodily infirmities, but recovered the full energy of his gigantic intellect. On the first day of the session he was in his place, though supported on crutches and swathed in flannel, and having delivered a most violent speech against the measures of the Government, affirming that the liberty of the subject had been invaded, not only in the colonies, but at home, he moved as an amendment to the address, that "the House would with all convenient speed take into consideration the causes of the present discontents, and particularly the proceedings of the House of Commons touching the incapacity of John Wilkes, Esq., depriving the electors of Middlesex of their free choice of a representative."[2]

Lord Mansfield having taken up the defense of the Government, and insinuated that all their measures must be considered as having the full approbation of the noble and learned Lord who held the Great Seal—"ever consid-

---

[1] The reports of the debates respecting the Middlesex election and America at this time generally conclude with the words, "The Lord Chancellor was silent."—16 Parl. Hist. 477.

[2] It was in this debate that he so strikingly contrasted modern peers with their ancestors who had won Magna Charta: "Those iron barons (for so I will call them when compared with the silken barons of modern days) were the guardians of the people; yet their virtues were never engaged in a question of such importance as the present. A breach has been made in the constitution—the battlements are dismantled—the citadel is open to the first invader—the walls totter—the constitution is not tenable. What remains, then, but for us to stand foremost in the breach to repair or perish in it?"

ered the champion of popular rights,"—the Lord Chancellor left the woolsack, and, in a burst of indignation, tried to defend his conduct and his consistency:—

"I accepted the Great Seal," said he, "without conditions: I meant not, therefore, to be trammeled by his Majesty——I beg pardon—by his Ministers; but I have suffered myself to be so too long. For some time I have beheld, with silent indignation, the arbitrary measures of the Minister; I have often drooped and hung down my head in Council, and disapproved by my looks those steps which I knew my avowed opposition could not prevent. I will do so no longer; but openly and boldly speak my sentiments. I now proclaim to the world, that I entirely coincide in the opinion expressed by my noble friend, whose presence again reanimates us, respecting this unconstitutional and illegal vote of the House of Commons. If, in giving my opinion as a Judge, I were to pay any respect to that vote, I should look upon myself as a traitor to my trust, and an enemy to my country. By their violent and tyrannical conduct, Ministers have alienated the minds of the people from his Majesty's government—I had almost said, from his Majesty's person. In consequence, a spirit of discontent has spread itself into every corner of the kingdom, and is every day increasing; insomuch, that if some methods are not devised to appease the clamors so universally prevalent, I know not, my Lords, whether the people in despair may not become their own avengers, and take the redress of grievances into their own hands." [1]

The amendment being negatived, Lord Rockingham moved that the Lords be summoned for the following day, when he should make a proposal of great national importance; but it being evident that, after this scene, the Government could not go on, Lord Weymouth, the Secretary of State, moved an adjournment for a week. Lord Temple said:—

"The House well knows for what purpose the Lords opposite want an adjournment; it is to settle the disordered state of the administration, which is now shattered in a most miserable manner, and, in all likelihood, will soon fall to pieces. Their particular object is to dismiss the virtuous and independent Lord who sits on the

[1] 1 Adolphus, 390; 16 Parl. Hist. 644; Gent. Mag. Jan. 1770.

woolsack, and to supply his place with some obsequious lawyer who will do as he is commanded." Lord Shelburne added : " After the dismission of the present worthy Chancellor, the Seals will go a begging : but I hope there will not be found in the kingdom a wretch so base and mean-spirited as to accept of them on the conditions on which they must be offered."

The ministerial crisis which followed was one of the most exciting and memorable in our party annals. Lord Chatham, Lord Temple, and Lord Rockingham were now reconciled, and, taking the same view of the questions which then divided the nation, might have formed a strong government, with Lord Camden for their Chancellor,—on the basis of American conciliation, and of the reversal of the unconstitutional judgment at home, that a commoner was rendered disqualified to represent the people by a vote of the House of Commons. But the Court was determined to make a vigorous effort to concoct an administration that would push on its favorite policy at home and abroad. The main difficulty was to prevail upon a lawyer of any reputation to take the Great Seal, as successor to Lord Camden,—particularly after the late denunciations in the House of Lords against all who should think of degrading themselves by basely doing so. Lord Camden, under the advice of his friends, determined that he would not voluntarily resign.

Through persuasions, and with a result which I shall have to detail in the life of Charles Yorke, he was induced in an evil hour to accept the offer pressed upon him, although he condemned his own act at the instant, and soon fatally repented of it.

On Tuesday, the 16th of January, 1770, about seven in the evening, Lord Camden, in pursuance of a summons he had received for that purpose, attended at the Queen's Palace, and there surrendered the Great Seal into the King's own hands. He slept sounder that night than he had done for many months.

The very extraordinary circumstances in which he had been placed must apologize for his political conduct while in office. I am afraid it can not be strictly justified.

To the last hour of his holding the Great Seal, the exercise of his judicial functions met with universal approbation. I ought not to pass over without notice the admirable manner in which he disposed of appeals and writs of error in the House of Lords. Lord Mansfield, on those occasions, generally sat along with him. To the honor of my profession, and for the credit of the decisions of the tribunal judging in the last resort in this country, it should be known that, however strongly law Lords may differ on questions of party politics, they have always zealously co-operated in the endeavor satisfactorily to dispose of the juridical business of the House; and, with a few exceptions,—when the lay Peers have exercised their strict right, and tried to prevail by numbers,—justice has been administered there with entire purity, and on the most enlightened principles. Lord Camden and Lord Mansfield sometimes attacked each other in debate so sharply as almost to render a resolution necessary, that "they should be required to give an assurance that *the matter should not go further*, or that they be taken into the custody of the Black Rod"—yet they never had the slightest difference of opinion in any case argued by counsel before them.

Soon after Lord Camden had taken his seat on the woolsack, came on the famous writ of error in *Harrison v. Evans*, in which the question was, "whether a Dissenter was liable to a fine for not serving a corporate office which he was disqualified for serving by the Corporation Act, he not having taken the sacrament of the Lord's Supper according to the rites of the Church of England?" This arose out of an ingenious scheme to raise a tax upon the Dissenters in the City of London for the purpose of building the MANSION HOUSE, which by law they could never enter. In the City courts judgment was given that the defendant was liable to the penalty of £600. Lord Mansfield moved the reversal of the judgment, in one of the finest specimens of forensic eloquence to be found in our books. Having shown that, as the person whom the citizens pretended to choose for sheriff could not serve the office (as they well knew), this was merely an attempt to punish him for being a Dissenter, he said,—"Conscience, my Lords, is not controllable by human laws, nor amenable to human tribunals. Persecution, or attempts to force conscience, will never produce conviction, and can only be calculated to make hypocrites or martyrs." Lord Camden, rejoicing to hear such noble sentiments from the

Lord Chief Justice of the King's Bench, heartily concurred in them, and by the unanimous judgment of the House a great triumph was given to religious liberty.[1]

So when Wilkes's case came to the bar of the House of Lords, Lord Camden and Lord Mansfield agreed on the two points which were raised on the record:—1. "That the Solicitor General, when the office of Attorney General is vacant, has authority by law to file a criminal information;"[2] and, 2. "That a defendant being convicted of two misdemeanors, may at the same time be sentenced to two periods of imprisonment, the second to commence after the expiration of the first."[3]

But Lord Camden attracted chief notice while Chancellor by his judgment in the great Douglas cause, which, in Scotland, had almost led to a civil war between the supporters of the opposite sides, and in England even had excited more interest than any question of mere private right had ever done before. Archibald Douglas, the apellant, had been brought up as the son of Lady Jane Douglas, and her husband, Sir John Stewart,—being supposed, along with his twin-brother, Sholto, who died an infant, to have been born in Paris, when their mother, after having long been married and remained childless, was in her forty-ninth year;—and, if such was his birth, he had a right to the immense estates of his maternal uncle, the late Duke of Douglas, and was the heir general of the Douglas family, one of the most illustrious in Europe. The Duke of Hamilton, the heir male of the Douglases, and in default of issue of the Lady Jane, entitled to all their domains, as well as those of the Hamiltons, which he inherited through a female, insisted that these two children were spurious, and had been purchased from a glass manufacturer and a rope-dancer, at Paris,—brought an action in the Court of Session in Scot-

[1] 16 Parl. Hist. 313; 3 Brown's Parl. Cas. 465; Life of Sir Eardley Wilmot, 73.

[2] After the resignation of Charles Yorke as Attorney General, before a successor had been appointed, Sir Fletcher Norton, as Solicitor General, had filed the information against Wilkes for composing and publishing the *North Briton*, No. XLV.

[3] Being convicted on this information, and on another for composing and publishing the " Essay on Woman," besides being fined, he was sentenced on the first to be imprisoned ten calendar months, and on the second to be imprisoned twelve calendar months, to be computed from the determination of the first imprisonment.

land to establish his right,—and there had a majority of the judges in his favor.¹ The appeal was heard in the session of 1769, and drew vast crowds to the bar of the House of Lords to listen to the weighty and eloquent argumentation of Thurlow, Wedderburn, and the other most eminent advocates of the age. It was conjectured that the law Lords were for the appellant, but the great body of the Peers had attended the hearing of the appeal, and were to take part in the decision; there had been much canvassing for the "Douglases" and the "Hamiltons," and a great degree of suspense existed down to the very morning of the judgment.

It astonishes us very much to be told, that when the order of the day had been read by the clerk for the further consideration of the cause of the *Duke of Hamilton* v. *Douglas*, the Duke of Newcastle " opened the debate," and that " he was answered by Lord Sandwich, who spoke for three hours with much humor, and scandalized the Bishops, having, with his usual industry, studied even the midwifery of the case, which he retailed with very little decency."²

Lord Camden then thus began,—there being such silence while he spoke, that a handkerchief would have been heard to drop, notwithstanding the crowds in attendance :³—

"My Lords, the cause before us is, perhaps, the most solemn and important ever heard at this bar. For my own share, I am unconnected with the parties; and having, with all possible attention, considered the matter, both in public and private, I shall give my opinion with that strictness of impartiality to which your Lordships have so just and equitable claim. We have one short question before us,—Is the appellant the son of the late Lady Jane Douglas, or not? I am of the mind that he is; and own that a more ample and positive proof of the child's being the son of a mother, never appeared in a court of justice, or before any assize whatever." After

¹ The fifteen Judges of the Court of Session divided 8 to 7—the Lord President Dundas being in the majority.
² Horace Walpole's " Memoirs of George III.," vol. iii. 303.
³ " Lord Mansfield, it had long been discovered, favored the Douglases; but the Chancellor Camden, with dignity and decency, had concealed his opinion to the very day of the decision."—*Horace Walpole's Memoirs of George III.*, vol. iii. 303.

very ably stating the *prima facie* case from the marriage of the parents, and their acknowledging the appellant as their son, he minutely analyzed the evidence to contradict and to corroborate it, and thus (*rondeau fashion*) concluded:—" The question before us is short, 'Is the appellant the son of Lady Jane Douglas, or not?' If there be any Lords within these walls who do not believe in a future state, these may go to the death with the declaration that they believe he is not. For my part, I am for sustaining the positive proof which I find weakened by nothing brought against it: and, in this mind, I lay my hand upon my breast, and declare that, in my soul and conscience, I believe the appellant to be her son."

Lord Mansfield followed—*haud passibus æquis*—making the worst speech he ever delivered—so bad a speech as to bring suspicion upon the judgment—for he did little more than dwell upon the illustrious descent of the Lady Jane, and the impossibility of any one with such a pedigree being guilty of such a fraud as palming a supposititious child upon the world.' The House agreed to the reversal without a division, but five lay Peers signed a protest recording their opinion that "the appellant was proved not to be the son of Lady Jane Douglas." [2]

[1] It is hardly possible that the account we have of Lord Mansfield's speech on this occasion can be full and correct, particularly as it does not contain the charges against Andrew Stewart, which were made the subject of the famous " Letters."

[2] Horace Walpole thus states the result:—" The Chancellor then rose, and with leading authority and infinite applause told the Lords he must now declare that he thought the whole plea of the Hamiltons a tissue of perjury, woven by Mr. Andrew Stewart, and that, were he sitting as judge in any other Court, he would order the jury to find for Mr. Douglas; and that, what that jury ought to do on their oaths, their Lordships ought to do on their honors. This speech, in which it was allowed he outshone Lord Mansfield, had the most decisive effect. The latter, with still more personal severity to Stewart, spoke till he fainted with the heat and fatigue. At ten at night the decree was reversed without a division."—*Memoirs of George III.*, vol. iii. 304.

I believe the general opinion of English lawyers was in favor of the decision of the Court of Session in Scotland; but this was produced a good deal by Lord Mansfield's wretched argument, and the very able letters of Andrew Stewart, the Duke of Hamilton's agent, whose conduct had been severely reflected upon. I once studied the case very attentively, and I must own that I came to the conclusion that the House of Lords did well in *reversing*. There was undoubtedly false evidence in support of the appellant; but it would have been too much in such a case to act upon the maxim, "false in one thing, false in all things," so as to deprive him of his birthright from misconduct to which he was not privy. There seems to be no doubt that the

Before finally quitting Lord Camden's Chancellorship, I must advert to the manner in which he disposed of his judicial patronage—always an important consideration in scanning the merits or demerits of Chancellors; and I am happy to say, that, instead of corrupting or enfeebling the bench by political job or personal favor, he acted steadily for the public good, on the maxim, *Detur digniori*. When about to leave the Common Pleas, he succeeded in having the learned and virtuous Sir Eardley Wilmot appointed to succeed him—whom he thus addressed:

"5th August, 1766.

"I have the King's orders to acquaint you with his intention of removing you to the Chief Justiceship of the Common Pleas, if it be agreeable to you. As Mr. Morton is not yet determined to yield up to you the Chief Justiceship of Chester, I would advise you to *repose yourself in the Common Pleas* till that desired event happens. *I assure you it is a place of perfect tranquillity.* I do most sincerely congratulate you on this nomination, and beg leave to inform you that you owe as much to Lord Northington and to Lord Chatham as to myself. I have been under a treaty with George Cooke ever since I came to town, the particulars of which you shall know when you come. I have withstood his bribe, being determined never to defraud my successor upon my death-bed: his necessities are extreme as well as my punctilio: However, it is now in your hands rather than in mine;[1] for I do not consider myself any longer in conscience, though I am in law, Chief Justice of the Common Pleas.

"I am with great truth, &c.

"CAMDEN."

The times were too distracted to allow of any systematic amendment of the law; but it should be recorded that, under the auspices of Lord Chancellor Camden, passed the "Nullum Tempus Act," by which an adverse

Lady Jane, notwithstanding her advanced age, was pregnant and had a miscarriage subsequent to the birth of the appellant; and insuperable difficulties attended the theory of his being the son of Madame Mignon. Being in possession of his *status*, I think the evidence was insufficient to deprive him of it—and the strong family likeness satisfactorily established seems to prove that the conclusion of law concurred with the fact of his physical origin.

[1] This relates to an office in the Court which then, and long after, the Chief Justice might lawfully sell.

enjoyment of property for sixty years gave a good title against the Crown, whereas the maxim had before prevailed, "*nullum tempus occurrit Regi,*"—according to which obsolete claims might be set up, and vexatious proceedings instituted by the government against political opponents.[1]

About the same time likewise passed the famous "Grenville Act," by which the decision of contested elections was transferred from the House of Commons as a body, to select committees sworn to do justice between the parties.[2] The chief merit of the measure belongs to its author, whose name it bears, but from his colleague at the head of the law he had encouragement and assistance in preparing it.

Thus Lord Camden, while in office, must be allowed to have deserved well of his country. He rendered her still more important services when reduced to a private station.

CHAPTER CXLV.

CONTINUATION OF THE LIFE OF LORD CAMDEN TILL HE WAS FIRST APPOINTED PRESIDENT OF THE COUNCIL.

PASSING over for the present the intrigues for the disposal of the Great Seal, which accompanied and followed Lord Camden's resignation of it, we must now regard him as an opposition leader, banded with Lord Chatham, Lord Rockingham, and other Whig Peers, strenuously to resist the measures of the new Government with Lord North at the head of it. At the commencement of their operations he was placed rather in an awkward predicament in a debate which arose on Lord Marchmont's famous midnight motion,[3] "that any interference of the Lords respecting the Middlesex election would be unconstitutional." Lord Chatham having bitterly reflected on the measures of the Government respecting Wilkes, Lord Sandwich took occasion to charge

---

[1] Stat. 9 Geo. 3, c. 16.   [2] 10 Geo. 3, c. 16.
[3] It was on this occasion that Lord Chatham exclaimed, "If the constitution must be wounded, let it not receive its mortal stab at this dark and midnight hour."

the late Chancellor with duplicity of conduct, because he had permitted those proceedings which had given so much disgust, and which he and his friends now so loudly condemned. Lord Camden answered him, by declaring upon his honor, "that long before Mr. Wilkes's expulsion, and also before the vote of incapacity, on being asked his opinion by the Duke of Grafton, he had pronounced it both illegal and imprudent,"—adding that "he had always thought so, and had often delivered his opinion to that effect."[1] The Duke of Grafton, however, declared that although the Chancellor had once before the expulsion said it would be impolitic or ill-timed, he never had expressed his sentiments on the vote of incapacity, but whenever that subject was agitated he had withdrawn from the council board, thereby declining to give any opinion upon it; and Lord Weymouth, another member of the Cabinet, asserted that the Chancellor had withheld his advice and assistance from his colleagues on every mention of expulsion and incapacity:—

Lord Camden. "Before the silence to which the noble Lords allude, I had repeatedly given my opinion upon the impropriety of the measures we have been discussing. But when I found that my opinion and my advice were rejected and despised, and that these measures were to be pursued in spite of every remonstrance I could make, I did withdraw myself—under the conviction that my presence would only distract, without preventing them. I was never further consulted upon them directly or indirectly because my opinion was well known—but I was ever ready to express my opinion boldly and openly on every question debated in council, and humbly, but firmly, to give my best advice to my Sovereign for the public good."[2]

When Lord Chatham introduced his bill for reversing the decision of the House of Commons which disqualified Mr. Wilkes, and seated Mr. Luttrell as member for Middlesex, Lord Camden warmly supported it against the vigorous attacks of Lord Mansfield. After stating the course pursued, he thus proceeded:—

"What, then, hindered the House from receiving Mr. Wilkes as their member? I am ashamed to guess at it,—

[1] As far as the original expulsion goes, Lord Camden had forgotten his first opinion. Ante, p. 331.   [2] 16 Parl. Hist. 824.

merely because they would act in an arbitrary, dictatorial manner, in spite of law or precedent, against reason and justice. A secret influence had said the word—'*Mr. Wilkes shall not sit,*' and the *fiat* was to be obeyed, though it tore out the heart-strings of this excellent constitution. The judgment passed upon the Middlesex election is a more tyrannical act than any which disgraced the twelve years' suspension of parliaments in the reign of Charles I.; and, though this bill may be rejected (as we are all sensible how a majority can supersede reason and argument), I trust in the good sense and spirit of the people of this country—that they will renew the claim of their inherent and inalienable right to a true and free representation in parliament." [1]

Soon after, arose the personal controversy between Lord Camden and Lord Mansfield respecting the law of libel. A motion having been made in the House of Commons, respecting the direction given to the jury on the trial of Woodfall, for publishing JUNIUS'S " Letter to the King," Lord Mansfield desired that the House of Lords might be summoned, as "he had something to communicate to their Lordships." On the day appointed, he contented himself with saying that he had left a paper with the Clerk of the House; that the paper contained the opinion of the Court of King's Bench in the case of *Rex* v. *Woodfall;* and that their Lordships might read it, and take copies of it, if they pleased. Lord Camden asked him if he meant to have the paper entered on the Journals. He said, "No, no! only to leave it with the clerk."—*Lord Camden.* " My Lords, I consider the paper delivered in by the noble Lord on the woolsack[2] as a challenge directed personally to me and I accept it; he has thrown down the glove, and I take it up. In direct

---

[1] 16 Parl. Hist. 963, 1306. No other discussion respecting Lord Camden's conduct while Chancellor, or his dismission, appears in the printed parliamentary debates. But the Duke of Grafton, in his Journal says; " At this time Lord Chatham's virulence seemed to be directed against myself: he persisted for some days in the intention of charging me in parliament with having advised the removal of Lord Camden, on account of his vote in the House; nor was he dissuaded from this till Lord Camden had assured him that he knew so perfectly that the advice did not come from me, that he should, if his Lordship made the motion, think it incumbent on him to rise in his place and declare that he well knew it was not from my advice."

[2] The Seals were now in commission, and Lord Mansfield presided as Speaker in the House of Lords.

contradiction to him, I maintain that his doctrine is not the law of England. I am ready to enter into the debate whenever the noble Lord will fix a day for it. I desire and insist that it may be an early one. Meanwhile, I propose the following questions to the noble and learned Lord upon his paper, to each of which I expect an answer." He then read six questions, respecting the Chief Justice's notions as to the jury being at liberty to consider whether the paper charged to be libelous, be of a criminal or innocent character. Lord Mansfield replied that "this mode of proceeding was taking him by surprise; that it was unfair; and that he would not answer interrogatories." Lord Camden then pressed for a day to be appointed for the noble and learned Lord to give in his answers, and said he was ready to meet him at any time. Lord Mansfield pledged himself that the matter should be discussed. The Duke of Richmond having congratulated the House on the prospect before them, begged that the day might be fixed.—*Lord Mansfield.* "I have only said I will hereafter give my opinion; and as to fixing a day, I will not fix a day." The matter here dropped and never was resumed. Lord Mansfield's want of moral courage holding him back from a renewal of the contest, and Lord Camden thinking he had gained a sufficient triumph.[1]

The morning after this encounter, he received the following kind and flattering inquiry from Lord Chatham:—

"Pall Mall, Wednesday.

" My dear Lord,

" I am anxious to know how you do after the noble exertion of yesterday. What your Lordship did was transcendent; and as you were not quite well, I am solicitous to hear of you;—though, after recollection, I think I ought to inquire how my Lord Mansfield does."[2]

The ex-Chancellor continued most zealously to discharge his public duty, and was indefatigable in his attendance in the House of Lords, and in hearing causes in the Privy Council when summoned to attend there; but, till the rupture with the American colonies was approaching, he seems from this time seldom to have taken a prominent part in the debates.

When the Royal Marriage Act was brought forward in

[1] 16 St. Tr. 1317, 1321.   [2] MSS. of Marquis Camden.

1772, he strongly opposed it. He admitted that some regulations were necessary to prevent the misalliance of those near to the throne; but he disapproved of the proposed enactments, and he strongly pointed out the inconvenience and injustice which might arise from the proposal to extend them to all the descendants of George II., who, according to the common process of descent, might be expected in a few generations to extend to many thousands. He mentioned that he knew an undoubted legitimate descendant of a King of England who was then keeping an ale-house. His manliness deserves great credit, considering that the reigning Sovereign was resolved to carry the bill as originally framed, against the advice of several of his Ministers,—and had expressed himself personally offended with all who questioned its wisdom.

In 1774, came on judicially in the House of Lords the great question of literary property,—" whether, at common law, authors have a perpetual copyright in their works?" Lord Camden denied the claim; and, on his opinion, the judgment was pronounced, by which only a limited monopoly is enjoyed, as conferred by the legislature. I give a specimen of his speech, which has been loudly praised, but which I must own appears to me, though founded on right principle, to be rather declamatory :—

" If there be anything in the world common to all mankind, science and literature are in their nature *publici juris*, and they ought to be free and general as air or water. They forget their Creator as well as their fellow-creatures who wish to monopolize his noblest gifts and greatest benefits. Why did we enter into society at all, but to enlighten one another's minds, and improve our faculties for the common welfare of the species? Those great men, those favored mortals, those sublime spirits, who share that ray of divinity which we call *genius*, are intrusted by Providence with the delegated power of imparting to their fellow-creatures that instruction which Heaven meant for universal benefit: they must not be niggards to the world, or hoard up for themselves the common stock. We know what was the punishment of him who hid his talent; and Providence has taken care that there shall not be wanting the noblest motives and incentives for men of genius to communicate to the world the truths and discoveries, which are nothing if uncommunicated. Knowledge has no value or use for the solitary owner; to be enjoyed it must be communicated: *scire tuum nihil est, nisi te scire hoc sciat alter.* Glory is the reward of science; and those who deserve it scorn all meaner views. I speak not of the scribblers for bread, who tease the world with their wretched productions; fourteen years is too long a period for their perishable trash. It was not for gain that Bacon, Newton, Milton, Locke, instructed and delighted the world. When the bookseller offered Milton five pounds for his PARADISE LOST, he did not reject the offer and commit his piece to the flames, nor did he accept the miserable pittance as the reward of his labors; he knew that the real price of his work was *immortality*, and that posterity would pay it. Some authors are as careless of profit as others are rapacious of it, and in what a situation would the public be with regard to literature if there were no means of compelling a second impression of a useful work! All our learning would be locked up in the hands of the Tonsons and Lintots of the age, who could set what price upon it their avarice demands, till the whole public would become as much their slaves as their own wretched hackney compilers." [1]

He afterwards opposed the bill introduced to extend the period of copyright,[2] and it was thrown out. But I think he was romantically unjust to literary men, and the controversy is at last well settled by the exertions of my friend, Sergeant Talfourd[3]—so that literature may now be pursued as a liberal profession, offering to those who succeed in it the means of honorable support, and of making an adequate provision for their families.

After the time when Lord Camden was removed from the office of Chancellor, till the Duke of Grafton quitted office and joined the Opposition in 1776, they were political enemies, but they continued private friends. I will here introduce a few extracts from the letters of the former, showing the familiar intimacy which subsisted between them.

The ex-Premier having accepted the office of Lord

[1] 17 Parl. Hist. 992. *Donaldson* v. *Becket.* [2] Ibid. 1,402.
[3] Stat. 5 & 6 Vic. c. 45.

Privy Seal under Lord North, the ex-Chancellor sent him a letter of congratulation, in which he says:—

"If I was not more afraid of public calumny than of any private or particular displeasure, I should certainly, as I intended, pay my respects to your Grace next week, which your Grace must now excuse me from doing, because that would look more like courting your fortune than seeking your friendship. Notwithstanding which, I shall still hold myself engaged, if you please, to spend a day with your Grace at Wakefield Lodge some time in the summer. And when everybody sees, as they will in a month or two, that I am neither partaking your good fortune, nor paying homage to it in the moment of your preferment, I shall set at nought every other suspicion that jealousy and malversation may raise against my conduct."

To an invitation from the Duke to visit him, Lord Camden returned the following answer:—

"Deal, June 23, 1775.

"Your Grace is too great a man to feel the comfort of so private a retreat as I am enjoying, and of not being under the daily temptation of a plentiful table, when the digestion always suffers in proportion as the appetite is provoked. I am advancing apace towards the state of a steady and invincible abstinence, and begin to think I may be able to withstand all the allurements both of meat and drink. But I am sure to be in danger the moment I set my foot in Wakefield Lodge. If I should find myself sufficiently fortified to meet and resist this temptation by the month of August, I shall endeavor to take advantage of your Grace's invitation, for I should be extremely happy to keep alive that friendship which had commenced in politics, and has never been violated, though unluckily interrupted, by the same cause."

The next letter in the series is without date, but must have been written soon after:—

"Mine and your Grace's old friend, the Earl of Chatham, still continues extremely ill. I am satisfied, from the account I hear from time to time (for he sees nobody), he can never recover his health so far as to be fit for any active business—so miserably is he reduced by age and sickness. I am, thank God, remarkably well, but your Grace must not seduce me into my former intemperance. A plain dish, and a draught of porter (which last is indispensable), are the very extent of my luxury. I have suffered a good deal, and have studied stomach disorders to such purpose, that I think I am able to teach your Grace (who are yet young) how to arrive at a strong and healthy old age,—which, I hope, will be your lot for the sake of the public as well as of your friends."

When the Duke of Grafton, seeing the injustice of the American war, and alarmed by the unskillful manner in which it was carried on, joined Lord Chatham, Lord Rockingham and Lord Shelburne, in trying to put an end to it, Lord Camden again wrote to him, with the most unbounded confidence on all subjects. The following is the desponding view taken by the ex-Chancellor of public affairs in the beginning of the year 1776:—

"I am so satisfied of the efficacy of Bath for my constitution, that I am determined to make it another visit next spring; nor shall any consideration of politics restrain me; for, indeed, my dear Lord, the chance of doing good is at an end. So many circumstances have combined, like so many fatalities, to overturn this mighty empire, that all attempts to support it are weak and ineffectual. Who could have imagined that the Ministry could have become popular by forcing this country into a destructive war, and advancing the power of the Crown to a state of despotism? And yet this is the fact, and we, the minority, suffer under the odium due only to the Ministers, without the consolation either of pay or power. America is lost, and the war afoot. There is an end of advising preventive measures, and peace will be more difficult to make than war was. For your Grace justly observes that the claims of the Americans, if they are successful, will grow too big for concession, and no man here will venture to be responsible for such a treaty. For I am persuaded it will be the fate of England to stoop, though I do not know the minister to apply so humiliating a remedy. Shall we ever condescend to make that country a satisfaction for damages? and yet she will never treat without it. What, then, must be our conduct in parliament? I am at a loss to advise. I thought from the beginning of the year secession was the only measure left. I still think the same: but I will enter the lists of a more active opposition if that shall be thought best. I wish it were possible for the whole body to unite; but union is only understood and practiced on the other side of the Atlantic. That would be respectable, and perhaps formidable; but I do not expect to see it. Absence would look more like union to the public, and might, perhaps, join us at last into a confederacy.[1] If motions are to be made, they should be in concert, and we ought to protect and defend each other from attacks, like real friends: else, like other broken forces, we shall be put to the rout."

A few days later, Lord Camden added:—

"I shall persist to the last in giving my testimony against this pernicious war, though I neither expect success nor popular applause; but it will be no inconsiderable consolation to hear my name joined to your Grace's, let the event turn out as it may."

In the autumn of this year Lord Camden visited Ireland, where he had a daughter married to Mr. Stewart, the ancestor of the present Marquess of Londonderry. Thence he thus addressed the Duke of Grafton:

"The colonies have now declared their independence. THEY ARE ENEMIES IN WAR, AND FRIENDS IN PEACE; and the two countries are fairly rent asunder. What then are we?—mere friends or enemies to America. Friends to their rights and privileges as fellow-subjects, but not friends to their independence. This event does not surprise me: I foresaw it. The Ministers drove it on with a view of converting a tyrannical and oppressive invasion into a national and necessary war; and they have succeeded too well: and now I expect the Opposition will be called upon to join with them in one cause, and we shall be summoned as Englishmen to unanimity. But if your Grace should see a French war to grow out of this civil dispute, which I expect and believe to be unavoidable, our provinces will then be leagued with our enemies in an offensive war against Great Britain. In such a situation a private man may retire, and lament the calamities which he endeavored faithfully to prevent. But how can

---

[1] It is surprising to find this great constitutional lawyer recommending secession from parliament—a measure wrong in principle, and which has invariably been injurious to the party resorting to it.

he give an active opposition to measures that self-preservation will then stamp with necessity? I have but one line to pursue if I am to bear my part, and that is a reunion with America, almost at any rate. '*Si possis, recte: Si non, quocunque modo.*' But I do not expect the ministry, the parliament, or the nation, will adopt any such system. So that what with the general fear in some of incurring the popular odium, and in others of seizing this opportunity '*to make their fortunes by shifting their position*,' according to Lord Suffolk's phrase,—the minority next winter will dwindle to nothing."

In the beginning of 1777 he writes—

"From politics, my dear Lord, I am almost entirely weaned. I can not prevail upon myself to go with the tide, and I have no power to struggle against it. War must now decide the question between the two countries, both sides having too much offended to be ever forgiven. But, hopeless as I am, I shall be always at your Grace's command, and ready to contribute my poor endeavors for the public. And yet I suspect I shall spend more time this year at the playhouse and opera than the House of Lords."

Notwithstanding Lord Camden's despair, arising from the violent policy adopted by the Government, and the passion for coercing the colonists which still prevailed in the nation, he nobly seconded Lord Chatham in all the efforts of that illustrious patriot to bring about a reconciliation between the mother country and the colonies. He spoke at great length in every debate upon America, and many of his speeches during this interval are preserved. But although they were most exciting when delivered, the interest of them has nearly died away, and I can only venture to give a few extracts from them to show their extraordinary merit.

In opposing the bill for cutting off commerce with the New England States, which so soon led to hostilities, he said:—

"Some of your Lordships inform us that it is a bill of mercy and clemency,—kind and indulgent to the Americans,—calculated to soothe their feelings, and to favor their interests. But, my Lords, the true character of the bill is violent and hostile. My Lords, it is a bill of irritation and insult. It draws the sword, and in its necessary consequences plunges the empire into civil and unnatural war."[1]

On the Duke of Grafton's motion respecting the British forces in America, he said:—

"I was against this unnatural war from the beginning. I was against every measure that has reduced us to our present state of difficulty and distress. When it is insisted that we aim only to defend and enforce our own rights, I positively deny it. I contend that America has been driven by cruel necessity to defend her rights from the united attacks of violence, oppression, and injustice. I affirm that America has been aggrieved. Perhaps as a domineering Englishman wishing to enjoy the ideal benefit of such a claim, I might urge it with earnestness, and endeavor to carry my point; but if, on the other hand, I resided in America—that I were to feel the effect of such manifest wrong, I should resist the attempt with that degree of ardor so daring a violation of what should be held dearer than life itself ought to enkindle in the breast of every freeman."[2]

Speaking a second time in this same debate, after he had been loudly reproached for the violence of his language, he said:—

"Till I am fairly precluded from exercising my right as a Peer of this House, of declaring my sentiments openly, of discussing every subject submitted to my consideration with freedom, I shall never be prevented from performing my duty by any threats, however warmly and eagerly supported or *secretly suggested*. I do assure your Lordships I am heartily tired of the ineffectual struggle I am engaged in. I would thank any of your Lordships that would procure a vote of your Lordships for silencing me; it would be a favor more grateful than any other it is in the power of your Lordships to bestow; but until that vote has received your Lordships' sanction I must still think, and as often as occasion may require continue to assert, that Great Britain was the aggressor, that our acts with respect to America were oppressive, and that if I were an American I should resist to the last such manifest exertions of tyranny, violence, and injustice."[3]

---

[1] 18 Parl. Hist. 436.   [2] 18 St. Tr. 947.
[3] 18 St. Tr. 954. See also 18 Parl. Hist. 36, 164, 209, 271, 292, 422, 436

Lord Camden, in his correspondence with the Duke of Grafton, afterwards gives an account of a serious illness of Lord Chatham, which was kept secret from the world, and seems to have been a prelude to the closing scene of his glorious career. In a P.S. to a letter, dated July 27, 1777, he says:—

"Since I wrote this I have received a melancholy account of a stroke received to-day by Lord Chatham, as he was riding. He fell from his horse, and lay senseless for ten minutes. The message to-night is, that he is very much recovered. Whether this was apoplectic, paralytic, or gout in the stomach, I can not learn. I wish it may not prove fatal. The public has lost him, and I fear he and England will perish together."

In a few weeks after, he gives this statement of Lord Chatham's recovery and of his plans:

"I thought it better to wait till I could give you some satisfactory account of my neighbor Lord Chatham's health, and his intentions at the opening of parliament. If your Grace thinks, as I do, that the Earl's recovery may, upon some possible event, give a new turn to public affairs, you will not be sorry to hear that he is now (though it seems almost miraculous) in bodily health and in mental vigor, as equal to a strenuous exertion of his faculties as I have known him these seven years. His intention is to oppose the address, and declare his opinion very directly against the war, and to advise the recalling the troops, and then propose terms of accommodation wherein he would be very liberal and indulgent, with only one reserve and exception, viz., that of subjection to the mother country: for he never could bring himself to subscribe to the independence of America. This, in general, will be his line, and this he will pursue if he is alone. I should imagine your Grace would have no objection to concur with this plan, though it is certain beforehand that all the breath will be wasted, and the advice overruled by numbers. Yet it would be right to stand firm upon the same ground, and not depart an inch from our steady purpose of opposing this war forever. Thus much I thought it my duty to impart to your Grace. For my own part I still continue in the same

454, 656, 675, 811, 901, 953, 1222, 1278, 1284; vol. xix. 337, 394, 625, 640, 652, 664, 738, 860.

state of despondency, hoping nothing and fearing everything."

On the memorable 7th of April, 1778, when Lord Chatham fell senseless on the floor of the House of Lords in a dying effort to save his country, Lord Camden, who was prepared to follow him in the debate, eagerly ran to his relief, and joined in the vote of adjournment to which the House immediately came. A few days after, in a letter to the Duke of Grafton, he wrote the following account—the most graphic and the most authentic extant—of that solemn scene:

"April, 1778, N. B. Street.

"My dear Lord,

"I can not help considering the little illness which prevented your Grace from attending the House of Lords last Tuesday to have been a piece of good fortune, as it kept you back from a scene that would have overwhelmed you with grief and melancholy, as it did me and many others that were present: I mean Lord Chatham's fit, that seized him as he was attempting to rise and reply to the Duke of Richmond; he fell back upon his seat, and was to all appearance in the agonies of death. This threw the whole House into confusion; every person was upon his legs in a moment, hurrying from one place to another, some sending for assistance, others producing salts, and others reviving spirits. Many crowding about the Earl to observe his countenance—all affected—most part really concerned; and even those who might have felt a secret pleasure at the accident, yet put on the appearance of distress, except only the Earl of M., who sat still, almost as much unmoved as the senseless body itself.[1] Dr. Brocklesby was the first physician that came; but Dr. Addington, in about an hour, was brought to him. He was carried into the Prince's chamber, and laid upon the table, supported by pillows. The first motion of life that appeared was an endeavor to vomit, and after he had discharged the load from his stomach that probably brought on the seizure, he revived fast. Mr. Strutt prepared an apartment for him at his house, where he was carried as

---

[1] It appears by the Journal that there were only two Earls bearing titles beginning with an M. present that day—the Earl of Marchmont and the Earl of Mansfield. I am much afraid that the latter is alluded to; he only is represented as sitting, in Copley's famous picture of this scene.

soon as he could with safety be removed. He slept remarkably well, and was quite recovered yesterday, though he continued in bed. I have not heard how he is to-day, but will keep my letter open till the evening, that your Grace may be informed how he goes on. I saw him in the Prince's chamber before he went into the House, and conversed a little with him, but such was the feeble state of his body, and, indeed, the distempered agitation of his mind, that I did forebode that his strength would certainly fail him before he had finished his speech. In truth, he was not in a condition to go abroad, and he was earnestly requested not to make the attempt; but your Grace knows how obstinate he is when he is resolved. He had a similar fit to this in the summer; like it in all respects, in the seizure, the retching, and the recovery; and after that fit, as if it had been the crisis of the disorder, he recovered fast, and grew to be in better health than I had known him for many years. Pray Heaven that this may be attended with no worse consequences. The Earl spoke, but was not like himself; his speech faltered, his sentences broken, and his mind not master of itself. He made shift, with difficulty, to declare his opinion, but was not able to enforce it by argument. His words were shreds of unconnected eloquence, and flashes of the same fire which he, Prometheus like, had stolen from heaven, and were then returning to the place from whence they were taken. Your Grace sees even I, who am a mere prose man, am tempted to be poetical while I am discoursing of this extraordinary man's genius. The Duke of Richmond answered him, and I can not help giving his Grace the commendation he deserves for his candor, courtesy, and liberal treatment of his illustrious adversary. The debate was adjourned till yesterday, and then the former subject was taken up by Lord Shelburne, in a speech of one hour and three-quarters. The Duke of Richmond answered; Shelburne replied; and the Duke, who enjoys the privilege of the last word in that House, closed the business, no other Lord, except our friend Lord Ravensworth, speaking one word; the two other noble Lords consumed between three and four hours. And now, my dear Lord, you must with me lament this fatal accident; I fear it is *fatal*, and this great man is now lost forever to his country; for, after such a public and notorious exposure of his decline, no man will look up to him, even if he should recover. France will no longer fear him, nor the King of England court him; and the present set of ministers will finish the ruin of the state, because, he being in effect superannuated, the public will call for no other men. This is a very melancholy reflection. The opposition, however, is not broken, and this difference of opinion will wear off; so far, at least, the prospect is favorable. I think I shall not sign the protest, though, in other respects, I shall be very friendly. I have troubled your Grace with a deal of stuff, but the importance of the subject will excuse me.

"Your Grace's, &c.

"CAMDEN.

"P. S. I understand the Earl has slept well last night, and is to be removed to-day to Downing Street. He would have gone into the country, but Addington thinks he is too weak."

On the day when the debate was resumed, Lord Camden was silent; and it was remarked, that thenceforth during the rest of the struggle with America, being deprived of his great associate,—from grief, or despair of doing good, he hardly ever addressed the House.

However, when the bill to mark the gratitude of the nation for the immortal services of Lord Chatham was opposed by the Lord Chancellor Apsley, although the King professed to approve of it, Lord Camden's indignation burst forth, and he exclaimed:—

"The noble and learned Lord on the woolsack has praised very deservedly—I hope with no insidious intention—the memory of the Duke of Marlborough, but seems entirely to have forgotten the victories of the deceased Earl. I will remind the noble and learned Lord that while he, who it is now wished to treat with neglect, *as if by some accident alone he had been elevated to an office he was incompetent to fill*, ruled the destinies of this mighty empire, from the extremest east to the setting sun; in every quarter of the globe—to earth's remotest bounds—were the arms of England borne triumphant;—our operations on the sea and on the land were invariably accompanied by extension of territory and extension of commerce, and we had at once all the glories of war and all the enjoyments of peace. But, my Lords, what I consider a more substantial claim to your admiration and your gratitude, he was ever the assertor of liberty, and the defender of the rights of Englishmen at home and abroad. Had his advice been followed, the country would now have been free, tranquil, and happy; and it is only by returning to his principles that we can be rescued from the state of degradation and suffering to which, by despising them, we have been reduced."[1]

It is not very creditable to the House that, at the division, the attendance of Peers was so small—perhaps the dinner hour had arrived—but the bill was carried by a majority of 42 to 11.

Lord Camden warmly supported Lord Rockingham's motion for a censure on the manifesto of our Commissioners in America which put the country under martial law—when he took occasion to reprobate the cruel manner in which hostilities were conducted, and, still more, the arrogant tone in which this cruelty was defended:— " Were not tomahawks and scalping-knives considered the proper instruments of war? Was not letting loose savages to scalp and murder the aged and the impotent, called *using the instruments of war which God and nature have put into our hands?*" Then, in the spirit of his departed friend, he counseled that, instead of trying to lay waste America, we should immediately strike a blow against France, evidently preparing to take part against us. " Distress France," said he ; ." render her incapable of assisting America. Attack France immediately; attack her powerfully by sea. England is still mistress of the ocean. To wound America is to wound ourselves. To aim a blow at France is to prevent a blow from being aimed at us by an inveterate enemy." The motion being negatived by 71 to 37, he drew up a spirited protest, which was signed by almost all the Whig Peers.[2]

When the indecisive engagement off Ushant took place in the summer of 1778, Lord Camden, in a letter to the Duke of Grafton, showed much sagacity in penetrating the intentions of France and Spain to assist the Americans:—

" Keppel's engagement with the French fleet is only the beginning of this cursed war. I don't apprehend the French avoided the action through fear, but policy, and

[1] 19 Parl. Hist. 1239. [2] 20 Parl. Hist. 43.

that they came out of Brest only to provoke Keppel to make the first assault, so as to be justified in America, by maintaining England to be the aggressor, and so to bring the war within the case of their treaty of alliance, by which America is bound to assist, and, indeed, to be a principal in the French war, and Keppel's chasing will be called the *first assault*. These are my politics, for I am, as I always have been, persuaded that France was determined at all events to make the war, and I am equally certain that Spain will join, notwithstanding the Spanish ambassador's journey hither, which is no better than an imposture, and that too shallow to impose on any but children and our ministers."

In the session of 1779, Lord Camden entered into a laborious exposure of the abuses of Greenwich Hospital, which were rendered famous as the subject of Lord Erskine's first speech at the bar—and he was of essential service in rendering this noble establishment more beneficial for our brave seamen.

He then made an effort to obtain liberal measures for Ireland, which being withheld, up sprang the volunteers, who petitioned with arms in their hands:—" I hope and believe," said he, " notwithstanding the ill-treatment the Irish have received from this country, which has brought upon them an accumulation of distresses and calamities, they will still retain their affection and attachment for England. Let us meet them with generous kindness. Nothing should be done by halves—nothing niggardly—accompanied with apparent reluctance." [1]

Soon after, in a debate on pensions and sinecures, being taunted about his own *pension*, or, as we should call it, "retired allowance," he said "he received it for long services, and in lieu of a valuable office (Chief Justice of the Common Pleas), and it would be a hardship to his family to lose it, and the reversion which was to supersede it; but if they must be included in a measure for clearing away abuses, he should rejoice in it, however the loss might distress him, when he reflected on the great and permanent advantages which would thereby accrue to his country." [2]

In the autumn of this year Lord Camden proposed to

[1] 20 Parl. Hist. 670.   [2] Ibid. 1363.

the Duke of Grafton a new plan of operations to be pursued by the Opposition:—

"A conversation with your Grace upon the state of the kingdom at present, will give me as much satisfaction as I am capable of receiving upon so hopeless a subject. If your Grace can suggest any plan of proceeding for the Opposition, likely to change the Court system or animate the public, I shall be happy to adopt as well as to promote it. For my own part, I confess fairly my own opinion that the opposition to the Court is contracted to a handful of men within the walls of parliament, and that the people without doors are either indifferent or hostile to any opposition at all. Whether this singular and unexampled state of the country is owing to a consciousness among the people that they are as much to blame as the ministers, and are ashamed to confess their own error, or whether, in truth, they hold the Opposition so cheap as to think the kingdom would suffer instead of mending by the exchange, or, from a combination of all these motives, choose to suffer patiently rather than encounter the troubles that are apt to follow upon a general disturbance: whatever is the cause of that slavish resignation which is predominant at present, the fact is, they do not desire a change. What then is to be done in order to obtain some degree of popularity? I shall make a simple answer by saying, '*Nothing!*' and yet perhaps that nothing, if well conducted, might have a stronger operation than the vain repetition of those feeble efforts that have hitherto been made in parliament by perpetual wrangles, personal animosity, abuse, and bad language, for this attack has been returned twofold upon us, and has set the parties against each other like a couple of prize-fighters combating for the entertainment of the gazing public, who are greatly diverted by a blow soundly given or dexterously parried, without a wish for the victory of either of the combatants. This has been the conduct of Opposition hitherto. If, on the other hand, a firm and temperate Opposition in short speeches, a few debates without rancor, could be established, such a course might probably restore us to the good opinion of the public, and then the distress of the times might work them into an opinion that the Opposition mean really the good of the whole. This or any idea may serve to talk of, but, to say the truth, I have no hopes left for the public; the whole people have betrayed themselves, and are not worth fighting for."

In the session of 1780 Lord Camden delivered a very long and animated speech in answer to Lord Thurlow, now Chancellor, who was resolved to throw out a bill which the Commons had passed almost unanimously, to disqualify Government contractors from sitting in their House. He began by observing that "his noble and learned friend on the woolsack had maintained his opposition to the bill in contradiction to the clearest principles of the constitution, indeed, to every rule of common sense and common experience, and to the whole system of parliamentary jurisprudence. His noble and learned friend had expressed himself in very strong language against innovation, and had rallied their Lordships to the post of danger, as if the constitution were to be overturned; but might not the same opposition have been given in the same words to bills now universally acknowledged to be necessary to preserve the purity and efficiency of our representative system,—the Place Bill, the Pension Bill, and the Bill for disqualifying officers of the Excise or Customs from sitting in the other House, because they may be preferred or dismissed at the pleasure of the Crown? Would his noble and learned friend have called these measures '*idle and fanciful suggestions, the frenzy of virtue and the madness of ideal perfection?*'" The bill was rejected by a majority of 61 to 41,—a decision which rendered the Lords very odious, the Commons a few days before having passed the famous resolution moved by Dunning—"That the power of the Crown has increased, is increasing, and ought to be diminished."[1]

A debate took place, in the beginning of 1781, on the King's message relative to the rupture with Holland, which made the situation of public affairs still more difficult and alarming. There being, as yet, no symptom of any change of policy on the part of the government, Lord Camden, rising with great solemnity, and speaking in a tone of the deepest grief, said:—

"He rose from a call of duty, for the last time, and whatever might be the event of this final effort to save his country, at least to mitigate her distresses and misfor-

[1] 21 Parl. Hist. 340, 414-459.

tunes, he should retire from his fruitless attendance in that House with this consolation, that he had discharged his duty to the best of his poor abilities so long as it promised to be productive of the smallest or remotest good, and that he declined giving their Lordships any further trouble where hope was at an end, and when zeal even had no object which could call it into activity. He regretted that he had not formed the resolution earlier, as he should thus have been saved from much chagrin and a series of the most mortifying disappointments, for he had been able in no degree to prevent or retard the ruin which now seemed impending." [1]

He interfered no further with any political question during this protracted session; but in the recess which followed, there was such a loud expression of public opinion against the war, and such strong rumors were circulated of Lord North's wish to retire, that when parliament re-assembled, he attended to make another effort for peace. His speech, on supporting the amendment moved by Lord Shelburne, was, I think, decidedly the best he ever delivered in Parliament, and it is fully and correctly reported; but, to its credit, there is no passage in it which I can select for quotation. Instead of aiming at fine sentences (the sin which most easily beset him), he confined himself to a simple and rapid narrative of facts,—from which he deduced the incapacity of ministers, and attempted to show that the only chance of saving the empire from final ruin, as well as dismemberment, was by an immediate change of men and of measures.

The extraordinary merit of this speech is said to be demonstrated by the eulogy which it extorted from the unwilling Thurlow, who followed in the debate:[2] but, with more doubtful claims to praise, it might possibly have been very favorably criticised by this dissembler, who, under the guise of bluntness, had ever a keen eye to his own advantage, and who, seeing a change approaching, was rather willing to soothe opponents, and to show that his enmities were placable. Whatever might be his motives, he thus began:—

"I must acknowledge, my Lords, the great abilities of the noble and learned Lord who has just sat down. I

[1] 21 Parl. Hist. 1060.
[2] See Lord Brougham's "Statesmen of George III.," 3rd series, 177.

affirm that, to the best of my judgment, I never heard a more able discourse within these walls: the premises were openly and clearly stated, and the deductions followed without constraint or false coloring. I trust that the noble and learned Lord will receive these as my real sentiments, for I am not at any time much in the habit of traveling out of the business before the House, to keep up the trivial forms of debate—much less to pay particular personal compliments to any man."

He then proceeded to combat the amendment,—which was negatived by 75 to 31,—but which he well knew embodied the sentiments of a majority of both Houses.[1]

The crisis soon arrived;—Lord North declaring in the House of Commons, on the day fixed for Lord Surrey's motion on "the state of the nation," that "his Majesty's ministers were no more."[2] Now was formed the second Rockingham administration, and the Whigs, till they quarreled among themselves, were completely in the ascendant. There was considerable difficulty in disposing of the Great Seal. Lord Camden might, no doubt, have resumed it with the full concurrence of all sections of the party, but for twelve long years he had been unaccustomed to daily judicial drudgery; he was now verging upon seventy, and his attacks of the gout were becoming more frequent and more severe. He, therefore, preferred the office of President of the Council.

It has always been unaccountable to me, that, on his declining the Great Seal, it was not given to Dunning, a most consummate lawyer, as well as a great debater, and a zealous Whig. If *he* unaccountably preferred the Duchy of Lancaster, the subordinate office conferred upon him, why was not the Great Seal given to Sir Fletcher Norton, who had become a favorite with the Rockingham Whigs, and was most eager for judicial elevation? The King, no doubt, was desirous that Thurlow should still be the "Keeper of his conscience," so that he might have a "*friend*" in the Cabinet; but his wishes at that moment might easily have been controlled. I suspect that the Shelburne and Rockingham sections continued distinct even at the formation of the government, Dunning belonging to the former, and Norton to the latter, and that neither would agree to the appoint-

[1] 22 Parl. Hist. 637-679.   [2] Ib. 1214.

ment of the other's lawyer to the woolsack. This jealousy was openly manifested in a few days, for, although it be the province of the prime minister to "take the King's pleasure" with regard to the creation of peers, Dunning was made Baron Ashburton on the advice of Lord Shelburne, without the knowledge of Lord Rockingham; whereupon Lord Rockingham immediately insisted that Norton should be made Baron Grantley. Thus the Great Seal remained in the clutch of Thurlow, who hated all Whigs of all degrees with a most perfect hatred, and could not possibly be expected cordially to act in a Government founded on principles which he had uniformly and vehemently opposed.

CHAPTER CXLVI.

CONTINUATION OF THE LIFE OF LORD CAMDEN TILL THE KING'S ILLNESS IN 1785.

THE inconvenience of having Thurlow for Chancellor was soon experienced by the new Government. Lord Rockingham and Lord Shelburne both agreed upon the propriety of carrying the "Contractors' Bill," which had been lately rejected,—and by way of redeeming their pledges, and maintaining their popularity, the reintroduction of it was one of their first measures. In the House of Lords it was fiercely attacked by the "Keeper of the King's conscience," who was thus answered by his colleague, Lord Camden, the new Lord President of the Council:—

"My Lords, I must express my astonishment at the laborious industry exerted by the noble and learned Lord on the woolsack; I can only suppose that he wishes to eke out a long debate, which (confining ourselves to solid and rational discussion) might in my humble apprehension, have terminated in half an hour. The bill presents to my mind but one idea; it is simple and obvious The noble and learned Lord said its principles should be examined, and in that single observation of all he addressed to you, I agree with him. I believe there is no noble Lord present who doubts of the existence of 'undue influence' in one shape or another, however denominated, or whatever aspect it may lately have assumed. A very distinguished member of the other House,¹ now transferred into this on account of his great talents and inflexible political integrity, moved a resolution which was carried against the minister by a considerable majority,—'That the influence of the Crown has increased, is increasing, and ought to be diminished.' This is a full recognition on record of the existence of that evil which the principle of the bill was calculated to remove. I will not say that an improper or corrupt influence has ever in any instance operated on any of your Lordships. My regard for the purity and dignity of this assembly forbids me to entertain such a suspicion. Nevertheless, I most heartily concur in the resolution of my noble and learned friend, which we must not allow to remain a dead letter, but make the foundation of practical improvement. I can hardly believe that the noble and learned Lord was serious in denying the existence of all public corruption. Thank God! as far as my means and poor capacity could be exerted, I have uniformly set my face against it. I can assure your Lordships that the hope of assisting to remove this cause of our national misfortunes constituted one of the prime inducements for my taking a part in the administration. My colleagues in office, who entered into the King's councils along with me, I am sure are animated by a firm and unanimous resolution to reform all abuses, to promote public economy, and to give their Sovereign and the nation such proofs of their sincerity as must put it out of the power of any set of men to deprive them of their only means of solid support. The noble and learned Lord has tried to compel your Lordships to reject this bill because you rejected a similar bill two years before. He seeks to deprive you of the exercise of your understanding, and to deprive the public of all advantage from the removal of prejudice and the advancement of knowledge. The bill is different in some of its provisions, and your Lordships are considering it under altered circumstances. This bill is part of a general plan of reform. To effectuate so great a work, my friends have been invited by the public voice to take office. If

¹ Dunning, Lord Ashburton. See 21 Parl. Hist. 340, 6th April, 1780; majority 233 to 215.

this bill be thrown out, there is an end of the present administration; they would be no more. Having failed in our expectations, *we* being unable to carry the measures which while in opposition we recommended to those in power, the nation would regard us with indignation if we continued to draw our salaries while we are under the dictation of those whom we despise. Corrupt and incapable as the last ministers were, I am free to confess, my Lords, that in that case it would be much better that they should be restored to power. They may possibly amend; but by remaining in office without the confidence of parliament and under the necessity of abandoning our objects, we should become daily more degraded and more contemptible, and we should not only ruin our own characters, but extinguish all confidence in public men, essentially injure the country, and take away all hope of better times."

Thurlow continued a most vexatious opposition to the bill in the committee,—denouncing it as "a jumble of contradictions;" but Lord Camden left the further defense of it to the two new law Lords, Lord Ashburton and Lord Grantley, and they fleshed their maiden swords in various rencounters with the "blatant beast" who tried to tread them down. In some of the divisions the ministerial majority was not more than *two*. The bill was carried, but the Administration was much shaken by this sample of the manner in which it was to be thwarted by the "King's friends." [1]

Lord Camden's next speech in the House of Lords was in support of the bill to declare the legislative independence of Ireland, which had become necessary from the determined efforts of the Irish "Volunteers," in consequence of moderate and reasonable concessions being long denied to the sister kingdom. This measure was prudent under existing circumstances, with a civil war raging, and foreign enemies multiplying around us; but any prudent statesman might have foreseen that it could not permanently be the basis of the connection between the two islands. The parliament of Ireland and the parliament of Great Britain being equally supreme and independent, they must ere long differ on questions of vital importance, without an arbiter to reconcile them; and if, from any

[1] 22 Parl. Hist. 1356–1382.

calamity, the power of the Crown should be in abeyance, every tie which bound them together would be severed. Lord Loughborough urged, "that when there was no check upon the Irish parliament but the mere VETO upon bills, and the government of each country was to move in perfect equality, his Majesty would not be King in Ireland in any different manner from that in which he might be sovereign of any other separate territory. The contiguity of position might preserve a more constant intercourse between the subjects of both, and the communion of rights unite them more closely to each other; but it was a possible case, that their interests might be supposed to be conflicting, and what then was to prevent their separation?"

Lord Camden not being able to solve these difficulties, and not venturing to hint at the remedy of a legislative union, regretted "that any debate had arisen on the subject; saying, that unanimity would have given the best chance of efficiency to a measure that must pass." He spoke much of the virtues of the Irish, and the hardships they had suffered. "The right of binding Ireland by a British statute could not be exercised. Why then should the right be claimed? His noble and learned friend had not suggested any other practical course than to agree to this bill. There was no difficulty in renouncing our right of judicature; so far it was a matter entirely for the consideration of the Irish: and as they now had a House of Lords consisting of men of great wisdom, knowledge, and integrity, assisted by their Judges, supposed to be well qualified to advise in matter of law, they were quite right in wishing to decide their own lawsuits at home. With regard to legislation there was more difficulty; but the present demand from the parliament of Ireland only echoed the voice of a brave, a generous, and an *armed* people; and he dreaded what might ensue if its justice or expediency were questioned."[1] The bill was very properly passed, with little more discussion; but, within seven years, upon the mental malady of George III.—according to the doctrine which prevailed, that it lay with the two Houses of Parliament to supply the deficiency—there might have been a choice of two different regents for the

[1] 23 Parl. Hist. 44. See Lord Camden's letter on this subject, 13th Aug. 1784, post.

two islands; and in point of fact, the two islands were about to appoint the same regent by very different means, and with very different powers.

Soon afterwards came the disruption of the Whig goverment, by the death of the Marquis of Rockingham, and the appointment of Lord Shelburne to succeed him. Lord Camden was of opinion (and, I must say, with due deference to such names as Fox, Burke, and Lord John Cavendish, was rightly of opinion) that there was no sufficient ground for ministers to throw up their employments in a crisis of such danger to the state. The new Premier was not generally popular; but he was of liberal principles, he was of good abilities, he was a magnificent patron of learning and genius; and the Rockinghams, though personally disliking him, had been sitting with him in the same cabinet. A denial of the right of the King, under these circumstances, to prefer him, was something very much like an entire extinction of the royal authority by a political junto. Lord Camden, therefore, retained his office of President of the Council till he was ejected by the formation of the "Coalition Ministry." He was much grieved to be separated from political friends to whom he was sincerely attached,—and chagrined to be brought into closer contact with Lord Thurlow, whose consequence in the Cabinet was much enhanced; but he earnestly superintended the negotiations for peace, and labored to bring them to a favorable issue.[1]

Soon after the formation of Lord Shelburne's Government, it was in great danger from internal dissensions. The Duke of Grafton had been induced by Lord Camden to join it, and to accept the Privy Seal. Probably forming an exaggerated notion of his own importance, from his superior rank, and the political station he had once filled, he thought himself slighted, and thus disclosed his griefs to his old friend :—

[1] While the negotiations for peace were going on, it would appear that the President of the Council was confidentially consulted respecting the different articles. There was now, as there had been at antecedent periods, a disposition to restore Gibraltar to Spain; but this he strenuously resisted. "With Lord Camden," says the Duke of Grafton, "I had much conversation; he appeared to me to lean now considerably to the opinion that Gibraltar is of more consequence to this kingdom, and that the views of its ministers ought in future to look to the possession of it as an object of more value than at first imagined; as likewise that the cession of it, even on good terms, would be grating to the feelings of the nation."—*Journal, 1782.*

"I begin to feel now what I have thought often before —that a Lord Privy Seal, who is not known and understood to be *confidentially trusted* and *consulted* by the principal minister, cuts but a silly figure at a cabinet. If he is wholly silent, and tacitly comes in to all that is brought there, he becomes insignificant—as he is deemed officious and troublesome if his opinions urge him to take a more active part than his office appears to call from him. I have too much warmth and zeal in my disposition not to be drawn into the latter; and my spirit revolting at the former, I find that I must make my retreat if my suspicions should be realized, and that the Earl of Shelburne circumscribed his confidence towards me within the bounds of great *civility* and *appearance of communication.*" [After at great length stating the means by which he had connected himself with Lord Shelburne, and his supposed ill usage, he says,] "I had once resolved, from a dislike to suspense, to have told you all I thought and felt on the subject; but it is knowing too little of mankind to think that opinions or real confidence can be forced. You may as well force love, and I was and think I shall remain silent. However, it has eased my mind in some degree to have opened my design to your Lordship. We have moved so much on the same principle, that I can not help wishing to hear what you say about me. My case is particular: recollect the situation I have been in, and that, thank God! I have nothing I want, and nothing I fear from any minister; and, above all, that my domestic peace and happiness ought to be most the object of my wishes and pursuits; and then say, my dear Lord, if I am not right."

Thus Lord Camden replied:—

"I have seen and observed with infinite concern that Lord S. has by no means treated your Grace with that confidence I expected, after you had so earnestly labored to support his new administration, not only by taking so important a post in it yourself, but by keeping others steady who were wavering at that critical moment. I am myself an instance and a proof of your Grace's endeavors, for your persuasion had more force with me than any other motive to remain in my present office. I was therefore disappointed, seeing the Earl of S. so negligent in his attention to your Grace; as if, when his administration was settled, he had no further occasion for those to whom he was indebted for the credit of his situation. Your Grace's real importance demanded the openest communication, and your friendship the most confidential return, and therefore I can not be wholly without suspicion that his Lordship means to take a line, and pursue a system, not likely to meet with your Grace's approbation; and if he does, I am not surprised at his reserve: for where there is a fundamental difference of opinion there can be no confidence. However, I will not suffer my suspicions to operate with me till I have demonstration by facts. Lord S. continues to make professions of adhering to those principles we all avowed upon the first change, and he has pledged himself publicly to support them—in which respect it is but reasonable to wait some time for the performance of his promises. At the same time I do readily admit your Grace's dignity, rank, and former situation require something more, and you ought not, as Duke of Grafton, to submit to so under a part with the Earl of Shelburne as to be Privy Seal without confidence. But considering the perilous condition of the public at this conjuncture, I should be much concerned if your Grace was to take a hasty resolution of retiring just now, because your retreat would certainly be followed by other resignations, and would totally *unwhig* the administration, if I may use the expression;[1] and this second breach, following so quick upon the first, would throw the nation into a ferment. It will not be possible when the parliament meets, for Lord S. to conceal or disguise his real sentiments; and if it should then appear that the government in his hands is to be rebuilt upon the old bottom of influence, your Grace will soon have an opportunity of making your retreat on better grounds than private disgust.

"I am not more fortunate than your Grace in sharing his Lordship's confidence. Yet though 'I am bound only for three months,' and have the fair excuse of age to plead, I would not willingly risk the chance of any disturbance at this time by an abrupt resignation, but

---

[1] The only other occasion I recollect of this word being used was when Mr. Fox, on the King's illness, having contended that the heir apparent was entitled as of right to be Regent, Mr. Pitt, smacking his thigh, exclaimed, "For this doctrine I will '*unwhig*' him for the rest of his days."

would rather wish, if such a measure should hereafter become necessary, to take it in conjunction with others upon public grounds.

"I am, besides, but too apprehensive that more than one of us will be ripe for it, perhaps before the session. Lord K., I know from certainty will quit after the campaign. The D. of R.'s discontent is marked in his countenance; and if the Whigs should desert, neither G. C., nor Mr. Pitt, nor even Mr. T., would have the courage to remain behind. I do not, my dear Lord, conceive it possible that a cabinet composed as ours is, can be of long duration; especially if Lord S. confines his confidence to one or two of those possibly obnoxious to the others. I have had a long friendship for the Earl, and can not easily be brought over to act a hostile part against him, and for that, as well as other reasons, can not help expressing my own wishes that your Grace may wait awhile; at least till you have received most evident conviction of his indifference to your opinions and assistance."

The Duke of Grafton says: "Lord Camden's advice prevailed, and I readily acquiesced in his opinion on this occasion, as I was always inclined to do on most others."[1] Thus harmony was restored, and Lord Shelburne's Government went on with some vigor till the preliminaries of peace were signed.

Mr. Fox and Lord North, by their ill-starred union, having then obtained in the House of Commons a large majority, and passed a vote of censure on the terms agreed to, parties were thrown into a state of unexampled confusion. Lord Shelburne was still unwilling to retire, and hoping to create a difference between the chiefs associated for his overthrow, meditated to form a coalition himself, either with the one or the other of them. Meanwhile his colleagues strongly pressed him to resign. The Duke of Grafton demanded an audience of the King, and, acting singly, though with the approbation of Lord Camden, surrendered the Privy Seal into the King's hands, on account of his disagreement with the head of the Cabinet. His Grace, after relating his conversation with George III., gives a very lively sketch of the state of the ministry at this time:—

[1] Journal, Aug. 1782.

"Previously to my going to St. James's, Lord Camden called on me, and imparted all that he found himself at liberty to say of a very serious conversation he had that morning with the Earl of Shelburne, who had sent for Lord Camden, as he now and then did when he found himself in difficulties, and on this occasion to consult Lord Camden on the part it became the Earl to take. The substance of Lord Camden's advice was decisive, and nearly this: that Lord Shelburne should retire, as unfortunately it plainly appeared that the personal dislike was too strong for him to attempt to stem, with any hope of credit to himself, advantage to the King, or benefit to the country; that he had it in his power to retire now with credit and the approbation of the world, for whatever the acts and powers of united parties had expressed by votes in parliament, &c., still the nation felt themselves obliged to him for having put an end to such a war by a peace which exceeded the expectations of all moderate, fair-judging men. Lord Camden further said to his Lordship, that he might add luster to his retreat by prevailing on the King to call on the body of the Whigs to form an administration as comprehensive as could be. Lord Camden went further, by saying, that if Lord Shelburne could not be prevailed on to take either of the steps which would give him most credit with the world, and that he was still from engagement or inclination instigated to stand as minister, he had nothing better to advise than that his Lordship should, with manly courage, avow a close junction with Lord North's party, if he could so manage it. This, indeed, might enable his Lordship to carry an administration which a middle way and a partial junction never would effect. Lord Camden added, that he thought the last scheme to be that which ought, if possible, to be avoided. I observed to Lord Camden that I was clear, notwithstanding the advice, that Lord Shelburne preferred it to all the others, and that such would be his decision. The object of sending for Lord Camden, I believe, was with the hopes to draw him into his opinion if he was able, and by no means to take his advice unless it could be made to coincide with the part he was decided to take, though he did not perceive that it was now too late for his plan to succeed. Lord Camden freely acquainted Lord Shelburne that he could not remain at any rate, that the whole was new modeled, and that he must claim his right of retiring at three months, and which had been stipulated at Lord Rockingham's death. Lord Camden urged to him strongly that the propriety of his coming to his decision before two days were expired: the other inclined to see the event of as many months.—On the 21st, Lord Camden called on me in the morning, and, after much lamentation on the alarming state of public matters, he told me that he was fully determined to quit his office, but that he should take every precaution to make it particularly clear that his resignation should not be interwoven with Lord Shelburne's retreat: he was anxious that his Lordship's conduct on the present occasion should neither guide his in reality nor in appearance. Lord Camden's decision pleased me much, as I told him, for his character entitled him to take his own part whenever he thought the ground good and honorable, without being actuated by the decision of any person whatever."

Lord Camden accordingly resigned in a few days after, and Mr. Fox and Lord North remaining steady to their engagements, notwithstanding all the attempts which were made to disunite them, Lord Shelburne was obliged to retire,—the Cabinet was stormed,—and, for a brief space, the "Coalition Ministry" was triumphant.

Lord Camden now went into violent opposition, and listed himself under the banner of the younger Pitt, delighted to recognize in him the brilliant talents and the lofty aspirations of the friend of his youth, his political patron, and the associate of his old age—with whom he had long fought the battles of the Constitution.[1]

When Mr. Fox's India Bill, after its most stormy passage through the Commons at last reached the House of Lords, it was violently assailed by the Ex-Chancellor, who denounced its principles as being an arbitrary infringement of the property and the rights of the greatest Company in the world. "This bill," he said, "was tantamount to a commission of bankruptcy or a commission of lunacy against them: it pronounced them to be unable to proceed in their trade, either from want of property,

[1] It might truly have been said of Lord Chatham and Lord Camden that "in many a glorious and well-foughten field they kept together in their chivalry."

or from want of mental capacity. The only argument for this violent measure was that of *necessity*—which had been used by the worst kings and the worst ministers for the most atrocious acts recorded in history. The only necessity for the bill was that ministers might preserve their power and increase their patronage. The author of the bill was himself to appoint to every office in India. The influence of the Crown had been, to a certain degree, curtailed by late reforms, but now it would be infinitely greater than when one section of the present Government had beaten the other on the resolution that 'the influence of the Crown had increased, was increasing, and ought to be diminished.' He lamented the death of the Marquis of Rockingham, who, had he survived, would have adhered steadily to the doctrines of Whiggism, and he lamented still more deeply that some of those who called themselves his friends should now favor a measure so inconsistent with the principles which it had been the labor of that great man's life to establish."[1]

The bill being rejected in the House of Lords by a majority of 95 to 76, the "Coalition Ministry" being dismissed, and William Pitt, at the age of twenty-four, being made Prime Minister, it was expected that Lord Camden would immediately have resumed his office of President of the Council,—and this would have happened had he not waived his claim, that he might facilitate the new arrangements. Earl Gower, afterwards Marquis of Stafford, although he had never had the slightest intercourse with Mr. Pitt, entertained a great admiration of his talents and his character, and sent him a message by a confidential friend that, "desiring to enjoy retirement for the rest of his life, he had no wish for any office, but that in the present situation of the King, and distressed state of the country, he would cheerfully take any office in which it might be thought he could be useful." His name and experience were likely to be of great benefit to Mr. Pitt at this moment,—particularly as Lord Temple, after holding the Seal of Secretary of State for a few days, had thrown it up. The Presidency of the Council, with high rank and little work, was thought the post which would be most suitable and agreeable to Lord Gower. He was accordingly appointed to it, and held it during the stormy

[1] 24 Parl. Hist. 190.

session which ensued, when the young minister, supported by the King and the nation, fought his gallant fight against the combined bands of Tories and Whigs, who had vowed his destruction.

Although the rejection of the India Bill by the Lords had put an end to the "Coalition Ministry," there was perfect tranquillity in their House for the rest of the session, while the storm was raging in the House of Commons—insomuch that Lord Camden, although prepared to support the new Administration, had no occasion to come forward once in their defense. When the session was closed by a prorogation, and, parliament being dissolved, the people pronounced decidely against the Coalition, Mr. Pitt's difficulties were over, and he was in the proudest situation ever occupied by a minister under an English sovereign.

Lord Gower's assistance might now have been dispensed with, but his taste of office had pleased him, and he felt no inclination to withdraw again into private life. Lord Camden would not put the the Government to any inconvenience by an impatient desire to resume his office, and during the recess he paid a long visit to Ireland, with the double object of seeing his favorite daughter, and of acquiring information to enable him to assist in carrying the important measures which the minister was about to bring forward for the establishment of a free trade between the two countries.

While there he wrote the Duke of Grafton the following letter on Parliamentary Reform, giving a most interesting view of the state of public feeling among the Irish, after they had obtained "independence:"—

"There is one question which seems to have taken possession of the whole kingdom, and that is the reform of parliament—about which they seem very much in earnest. Those who wish so much for that reformation at home, can not with much consistence refuse it to Ireland, and yet their corrupt parliament must be considered the only means we have left to preserve the union between the two countries. But that argument will not bear the light, and no means ought, in my opinion, to be adopted too scandalous to be avowed. I foresaw when we were compelled to grant independence to Ireland, the mischief of the concession, and that sooner or later a civil war would be the consequence—a consequence ruinous to England, but fatal to Ireland, for she must at all events be enslaved either to England or France. This people are intoxicated with their good fortune, and wish to quarrel with England to prove their independence. Big with their own importance, and proud of their 'Volunteers,' they are a match, as they imagine, for the whole world. But as Galba describes the Romans—'Nec totam servitutem pati possunt, nec totam libertatem.' This misfortune would never have happened if our government had not been tyrannical and oppressive."

On Lord Camden's return to England, a negotiation was opened for his restoration to the Cabinet. He consented on the condition that an effort should be made to induce his old chief, the Duke of Grafton, to join the Administration. Mr. Pitt was pleased with the proposal, for he still professed himself to be a stout Whig, and he wished to have some counterbalance in his government to the Sidneys, the Gowers, and the Thurlows. The plan was to transfer Lord Gower to the Privy Seal, and to make Lord Carmarthen resign his office of Secretary of State. Lord Camden thus writes to the Duke of Grafton, giving him an account of the negotiation:—

"Mr. P. told me he had mentioned to Lord G. his wish that he would consent to exchange his office for the Privy Seal, and believed he should find no difficulty in obtaining that compliance; that he had not yet found an opportunity of sounding Ld C., as it was not easy for him to make such a proposal as might tempt him to retire from his present situation, but that it was upon his mind, and that your Grace as well as myself might be assured the very moment any vacancy in the Cabinet could be procured that your Grace would condescend to accept, it should be done. I must do Mr. Pitt the justice to say he expressed as earnest a desire as myself to a close and intimate political conjunction with your Grace, and saw clearly the great utility of the Cabinet having so clear a Whig complexion as our accession would give it."

In a subsequent letter, Lord Camden, after speaking of the negotiation for the resignation of Lord Carmarthen, says:—

"If that difficulty is removed, I should hardly allow your Grace's plea of disability, or fear, to undertake so arduous an employment to have the weight of an insurmountable objection. If that was sufficient in your Grace, who are now in the very vigor of your age and the ripeness of your understanding, to warrant a refusal, what can be said to me, who am in the last stage of life, when both mind and body are in a state of decline, and are every day tending towards total incapacity? In reality, such is my backwardness to embark in business, that nothing but the comfort of your Grace's support and co-operation could have prevailed upon me to alter my determined purpose (for so it was till I was overruled) for final retirement. And I am afraid, if I know my own feelings, I should perhaps be pleased at my heart, and almost thank your Grace, if you should, by withdrawing yourself, give me an honest excuse for breaking off.—I have read the Dean of St. Asaph's trial, and confess I have seen nothing libelous in the paper, and am, besides, more displeased with Judge Buller's behavior than I was formerly with Lord Mansfield's. Something ought to be done to settle this dispute; otherwise the control of the press will be taken out of the hands of the juries in England, and surrendered up to the Judges."

It was found impossible to prevail on Lord Carmarthen to retire. This disappointment Lord Camden communicated in a letter to the Duke of Grafton, in which, after stating that no vacancy could then be made for him in the Cabinet, he thus proceeds:—

"And now, my dear Lord, what part does it become me to take? I don't ask your advice, because I have taken my part already, and have agreed to come in; but I will state my own difficulties, and the true reason that prevailed upon me, at last, to accept. I am more averse than ever to plunge again into business in the last stage of my life. I do not like the Cabinet, as composed: the times are full of difficulty, and the C. not much inclined to persons of our description. Add to this, my own aversion to business, now almost constitutional from a habit of indolence; and, above all, the want of your Grace's support, the only circumstance that made me enter into this engagement after I had, over and over again, given a positive denial. These, you must allow, were weighty considerations; and yet, though I was fairly released by Mr. Pitt's failing to make that opening he had engaged to make, and your Grace's postponing your acceptance till the end of the session, yet, when I consider that Mr. Pitt would be cruelly disappointed and perhaps, in some sort, disgraced upon my refusal, after he had engaged Lord Gower to exchange his office, and that I was pressed in the strongest manner by all my friends, and more particularly by your Grace, who was pleased to think my coming forward would be useful to the public, and help to establish the Administration, I took the resolution to vanquish my reluctance, and to sacrifice my own ease to the wishes of other men."

It was still some weeks before the arrangement was completed, and then Lord Camden, after informing the Duke of Grafton that Lord Gower had at last actually exchanged the Presidency of the Council for the Privy Seal, adds:

"I am now called upon to fill up the vacancy. I go to it with a heavy heart, being separated from your Grace, with whom I had intended to have closed my political life—*iterum mersus civilibus undis*, at a time of life when I ought to have retired to a monastery; but as the die is cast, I will go to the drudgery without any more complaining, and do my best: as I have lost all ambition, and am happily not infected with avarice, and as my children are all reasonably provided for according to their rank and station, I can have no temptation to do wrong; and therefore though, in my present situation when I do not ask the employment but am solicited to accept it, I might, after the fashion of the world, put some price upon myself, I am determined neither to ask nor to accept any favor or emolument whatever for the sacrifice of my own ease.

"I have employed myself of late in examining with some attention the proceedings of the Court of King's Bench in the libel cause of the Dean of St. Asaph, thinking it probable it might have been brought by writ of error into our House; but they have taken care to prevent that review by arresting the judgment, and so the great question between the Judge and the jury in this important business is to go no further, though it is strengthened by a solemn decision of the Court, which never happened before. This determination, in my poor opinion, strikes directly at the liberty of the press and yet is likely to pass *sub silentio*. The newspapers are modest upon the subject, because Mr. Erskine is not to be commended by one party, or Lord Mansfield run down by the other. Thus your Grace see that public spirit is smothered by party politics."

Lord Camden, notwithstanding some affectation of reluctance, very cheerfully resumed his office of President of the Council, and continued to fill it during a period of nine years, always co-operating most harmoniously and zealously with the "Heaven-born Minister," who, although he began to be nicknamed "Billy Pitt the Tory," and although his zeal for reform did cool considerably, cannot be accused of bringing forward any measures which a Whig might not have supported, till the aged Lord President had disappeared from the scene.

The session of 1785 was chiefly occupied with the measures to establish free trade with Ireland, which were so creditable to their author—the first English minister who was a pupil of Adam Smith. However, they were furiously opposed by the English manufacturers, with Mr. Peel, the father of the great Sir Robert, at their head,—foretelling entire ruin to England if the laws against the importation of Irish manufacture were removed,—as, from the low price of labor and the lightness of taxation in Ireland, cotton might be spun, muslin woven, and every sort of fabric finished there at an infinitely cheaper rate than in England;—so that, if the proposed abolition were agreed to, English industry would be paralyzed, grass would grow in the streets of Manchester, and we should become a nation of paupers. Mr. Peel threatened that he would remove, with his capital and his family, to the sister isle, which was thus to be so highly favored at the expense of the mother country. In the House of Lords, these views were zealously supported by Lord Stormant and other Peers. But the resolutions were defended, in a masterly speech, by Lord Camden. He said:

"That, to his knowledge, nothing but the strongest necessity could have induced the Minister to undertake a measure so weighty, which, however conducted, was sure to be productive of murmurs and discontent among many who, upon all other subjects, were disposed to be his warmest supporters."

He then drew an affecting picture of the present

wretchedness of Ireland—he described her great natural advantages—he explained her wrongs—he sought to create alarm by her loud demands of redress:

"The tranquillity of the empire," said he, "is at stake The Irish will next lay their greviances at the foot of the throne; and importune the Sovereign of both countries to take part with the one against the interest, or rather the prejudices, of the other. Here is the foundation of a civil war. Does it not become the providence of the Government to guard against such an emergency? The discontents of the Irish are in proportion to their sufferings."

Having detailed the proposed regulations for establishing free trade between the two islands, he considered the objection to them:

"With respect to the argument of cheapness of labor, which has given such terrors to the manufacturers," he observed, "I confess I see it without alarm. This cheapness of labor must only continue during the rudeness of art; and, in the meanwhile, the rich and manufacturing country must enjoy the benefits of superior skill. There the finished article will be cheaper. As to Mr. Peel, and the other intelligent witnesses examined at your bar, who threaten to emigrate to Connaught, I feel no uneasiness. If they really should form spinning establishments in that wild region, they may do much to civilize and improve it; and in Lancashire their place may be supplied by others equally enterprising and respectable. They are not more reasonable than our manufacturers of silk and iron, who call upon us to lay such duties upon these articles, when exported from Irelaud, that the Irish may be excluded from competition in supplying them to the American market. These requests may all be traced to their true source—the itch of monopoly. Let us not have protecting duties on one side of the water, with retaliating prohibitions on the other, which will foster growing enmity between us, to the delight and aggrandisement of our common enemies."

Still there were thirty votes in the negative; and a protest was signed, I am sorry to say, by Lord Derby, Lord Fitzwilliam, and other Whig Peers.

When Mr. Pitt again brought forward his motion for a reform in Parliament, Lord Camden gave him all the assistance and encouragement in his power; and the following letter, urging the Duke of Grafton to compel one of his members, who was rather doubtful, to vote for the measure, affords, I think, strong evidence of the Premier's sincerity:—

"My dear Lord,

"I find myself under a necessity of troubling your Grace, at Mr. Pitt's request, upon a question which I have always thought of the highest importance to the Constitution, I mean the Reform of Parliament. And, if your Grace thinks upon the subject as I do, you will lend your aid by imparting your wishes to such of your friends as are likely to pay attention to your opinion. Mr. Pitt is not assured how Mr. Hopkins stands inclined to this measure, but is very anxious to obtain his concurrence, unless he is really and conscientiously averse to it. At least he wishes, and would think that he may not unreasonably hope, that he would give his vote for bringing in the Bill. When I have said this, I have said all that becomes me to say on this occasion, adding only that Mr. Pitt's character, as well as his administration, is in some danger of being shaken, if his motion is defeated by a considerable majority. I do confess myself to be warmly interested in the event, upon every consideration, and that, perhaps, is the best apology I can make your Grace for giving you this trouble, leaving it entirely to your own wisdom to judge how far it would be fitting or agreeable to your Grace to communicate your wishes to Mr. Hopkins.

"I am," &c.

I will here introduce two letters written at this time, showing, in an amusing manner, how an application used to be made, and evaded, to promote a Bishop. The individual to be translated was Hinchcliffe, who, since the year 1769, had held the poor see of Peterborough, where he had been placed by the Duke of Grafton, when Premier. The first letter is to his Grace from Lord Camden:—

"I was forced to wait some days before I could meet with an opportunity of conferring with Mr. Pitt, and when he had, after a full conversation, explained himself, though I think I perfectly understood the substance, I would not venture to put my own sense upon his words.

I begged that he would at his first leisure put it down in writing—which I have this day received. But I should not care to send it by the common post, unless I should have your Grace's commands for that purpose. To say the truth, I do wonder a little upon reflection, that we have hazarded our correspondence as we have done by the post. I will only add, that the answer, as far as I can judge, will give your Grace satisfaction. Courtly expressions and complimental civility are of course, and go for nothing; but I am much mistaken indeed if Mr. P. is not as sincere in his intentions as he is cordial in his expressions."

The following is the Prime Minister's courteous and cautious reply:—

"Downing Street, Feb. 4, 1786.

"My dear Lord,

"In answer to the communication your Lordship was so good to make to me from the Duke of Grafton, I should be greatly obliged to you if you will assure him that, from the desire I entertain of showing every possible attention to his Grace's wishes, he may rely on my being happy to find an opportunity of recommending the Bishop of Peterborough to his Majesty for advancement on the Bench. His Grace not having particularly mentioned any specific object, and it being difficult to foresee the arrangements which may be taken till a vacancy happens in some of the most considerable sees, I can do no more than express my general inclination to meet his Grace's wishes as far as circumstances will allow. Indeed I think there is every reason to suppose that in the course of no very long time, openings must occur which may admit of some desirable promotion being proposed to the Bishop, and it will give me great pleasure whenever it can be done to his Grace's satisfaction.

"I am ever,
"My dear Lord,
"With great attachment and regard,
"Most sincerely yours,
"W. Pitt."

"The Rt Honble Lord Camden."

As might have been foreseen, Hinchcliffe lived and died Bishop of Peterborough.[1]

[1] However, he was solaced with the Deanery of Durham.

On the 13th of May, 1786, Lord Camden's services to the Minister were recognized by his being raised in the peerage; he was created Viscount Bayham, of Bayham Abbey, in the County of Sussex, and Earl Camden.

His chief antagonist in the House of Lords, in his later years, was Lord Loughborough, who was in hot opposition from the dissolution of the "Coalition Ministry," till he went over with the "Alarmists" at the commencement of the French Revolution. Against him he ably defended the East India Judicature Bill,[1] the Excise Bill,[2] and other measures of Government; but Mr. Pitt's ascendency was now so triumphant, that the Lords had little to do but to amuse themselves with Mr. Hasting's trial, and they had no other debate of permanent interest till the nation was thrown into consternation and confusion, in the year 1788, by the King's illness.

CHAPTER CXLVII.

CONTINUATION OF THE LIFE OF LORD CAMDEN TILL THE BREAKING OUT OF THE FRENCH REVOLUTION.

WHEN the Sovereign, supposed to be upon the throne, with the scepter in his hand, ruling his people, was actually in a straight waistcoat, under the control of keepers,—the royal authority being in complete abeyance, some measures were indispensably necessary for the purpose of reviving it. Mr. Pitt, aware of Lord Thurlow's intrigue with Carlton House to retain

---

[1] 26 Parl. Hist. 131.

[2] Being then in his 72nd year, he took occasion to declare that his youthful sentiments in favor of the liberty of the subject remained unaltered. "I allow that the extension of the excise laws is dangerous, and fraught with multifarious mischiefs. It unhinges the constitutional rights of juries, and violates the popular maxim that 'every man's house is his castle.' I have long imbibed these principles; I have been early tutored in the school of our constitution, as handed down by our ancestors, and I shall not easily get rid of early predilections. They still hang hovering about my heart. These are the new sprouts of an old stalk. Trial by jury is indeed the foundation of our free constitution; take that away, and the whole fabric will soon moulder into dust. These are the sentiments of my youth,—inculcated by precept, improved by experience, and warranted by example. Yet, strange as it may appear to your Lordships, the necessity of the change obliges me to give my assent to the present bill," &c.—*26 Parl. Hist. 177.*

the Great Seal in case of a Regency, placed all his confidence in Lord Camden for carrying through his plan,—whereby the two Houses were to assert their right to provide as they should think fit for the exercise of the prerogatives of the Crown, and a bill was to be passed, according to the usual forms of the Constitution, appointing the Prince of Wales Regent, under severe restrictions,—to disable him, as much as posible, from conferring favors on the political party, to which his Royal Highness was attached.

On the 20th of November, the day on which Parliament met after the prorogation, the Chancellor having announced the royal indisposition, Lord Camden moved an adjournment for a fortnight,—and that a letter of summons should be written to every Peer, requiring his attendance. In the meanwhile he presided at a meeting of Privy Council, attended by all Privy Councillors of whatever party,—at which the King's physicians, being examined, all agreed that he was wholly incapable of meeting Parliament, or attending to public business, but differed as to the probability of his recovery. On the appointed day, Lord Camden laid the examination before the House, When they had been read, he observed,—

"The melancholy state of his Majesty's health is sufficiently evinced; and as the physicians can not give your Lordships any assurance as to the time when he may recover, it is incumbent on the two Houses of Parliament to proceed to make some provision to supply the deficiency in the legislature, and to restore energy to the executive government. Yet, previously to such a necessary and important step, I shall take the liberty of moving for a committee to search for precedents in similar cases. According to rumor, it had been laid down in another place 'that the course of proceeding under such circumstances was prescribed by the common law and the spirit of the constitution, viz. that the heir apparent, being of age, was entitled to assume the legal authority as a matter of right, and to exercise it as long as his Majesty's disability shall continue, as upon a demise of the Crown.' —If this be the common law, it is an entire secret to me. I never read or heard of such a doctrine. Those that broached it should have been ready to cite their authorities. They may raise expectations not easily laid, and may involve the country in confusion. The assertion of this doctrine, however, is a strong argument in favor of my motion, for we shall thus have an ample opportunity of considering the precedents on which it rests."

Lord Loughborough mentioned the extraordinary assertion hazarded elsewhere, " that the Prince of Wales, the heir apparent to the throne, has no more right to take upon himself the government during the continuance of the unhappy malady which incapacitates his Majesty, than any other individual subject,"—contending that an elective regency was inconsistent with an hereditary monarchy. Thurlow at this moment thought it convenient to deny the Prince's right,—and, after a short reply from Lord Camden, his motion was carried.[1]

On the 23rd of December, after the report of the committee, Lord Camden moved the Resolution, " That it is the right and duty of the Lords spiritual and temporal, and Commons of Great Britain, now assembled, and lawfully, fully, and freely representing all the estates of the people of this nation, to provide the means of supplying the defect of the personal exercise of the royal authority, arising from his Majesty's indisposition in such manner as the exigency of the case may appear to them to require." After a long debate, it was carried by a majority of 99 to 66, and was followed by another resolution, moved by Lord Camden, " That it is necessary for the two Houses to determine in what manner the royal assent shall be given to a bill for settling the regency."[2]

On a subsequent day he moved, " That for the purpose of providing for the exercise of the King's royal authority during the continuance of his Majesty's illness, in such manner and to such extent as the circumstances of the nation may appear to require, it is expedient that his Royal Highness the Prince of Wales, being resident within the realm, be empowered to exercise and administer the royal authority in the name and on the behalf of his Majesty, subject to such limitations and exceptions as shall be provided." He thus began:—" It is with deep concern that I find a task of such unprecedented weight has devolved upon me. I stand up most reluctantly to address your Lordships on this occasion, feeling every day stronger and stronger reasons to wish to retire from the

[1] 27 Parl. Hist. 654–675.   [2] Ibid. 853.

hurry of business to repose and contemplation. I trust, my Lords, that this is the last act of my political life. I must not shrink from my duty, for the safety of the monarchy and the public tranquillity are at stake." Having recapitulated the proceedings that had been taken since his Majesty's illness began, and the resolutions of the two Houses respecting their right to appoint a Regent with such powers as they might confer upon him, he detailed the plan of regency which the ministers proposed, explaining and defending the regulations for the custody of the King's person, for preserving the household appointments as they then stood, and for preventing the Regent from creating Peers. He allowed that the Heir Apparent was the fittest person for the two Houses, in their discretion, to select for Regent; but insisted on the propriety of putting him under restrictions while there was any probability of his Majesty being restored to the throne. The objection, that inconvenience might arise from so materially curtailing the power and patronage of the Crown, he answered by observing that "if the Regent's administration was conducted on good principles, it would meet with general support; and if its measures were unconstitutional, there should be no facility given to carrying them through." Notwithstanding powerful arguments to show that our constitution might suffer serious detriment from the election of a Regent by the two Houses, with such powers as they were pleased to bestow upon him, and from tampering with the prerogatives of the Crown, which were not supposed to be greater than were necessary to carry on the government for the public good, Lord Camden carried his motion by a majority of 94 to 68; but a strong protest was signed by the Duke of York and almost all the Peers who voted in the minority.[1]

Lord Camden's next speech was respecting the *mode* in which the Regent should be "elected or appointed." He declared that "amidst a choice of evils, the proposal of his Majesty's ministers, which he was to explain, appeared to him to be the least objectionable, and most fit

[1] 27 Parl. Hist. 1075-1094. In the course of this debate Lord Camden got into a scrape, in obviating the objection to the suspension of the power of making Peers, by saying, that "on any urgent call for a peerage it might be conferred by Act of Parliament,"—a proceeding which appeared to their Lordships so unconstitutional and republican, that he was obliged to explain and retract.

to be adopted, because the most reconcileable to the principles [*quære*, forms?] of the constitution. He was open to conviction, and was ready to adopt any other which their Lordships might deem preferable; but something must immediately be done to resuscitate the legislature, and to rescue the people from the condition—of which they were beginning loudly to complain—of being without a government. He was aware that the plan he was to recommend had already been made the subject of much ridicule. 'A phantom!' 'a fiction!' 'a forgery!' and various other contemptuous appellations had been bestowed upon it. Let those who objected to it in this House show how, otherwise, the constitution could again be put into a state of vigor and activity. The delay that had already taken place had revolted the public mind, and the nation loudly called on Parliament to interpose its authority. But, circumstanced as it at present was, Parliament could not take a single step;—without the King, it was a mere headless, inanimate trunk;—the royal assent was essential to legislation. The King upon his throne in that House, or by Commissioners appointed under the Great Seal, must sanction their proceedings,—which otherwise had no legal operation. The first step to be taken was to open the parliament by the King's authority. The law declared that, in person or by representative, the King must be there, to enable them to proceed as a legislative body. That his Majesty, from illness could not attend personally, was a fact too well known to be disputed. When the King could not attend personally, the legal and constitutional process was to issue letters patent under the Great Seal. In the present dilemma, therefore, he recommended that the two Houses should direct letters patent to be issued, under the Great Seal, authorizing Commissioners to open parliament in the name of his Majesty. He must use the liberty to say, that those who treated this proposal with ridicule were ignorant of the laws of their country. A '*fiction*' it might be termed, but it was a fiction admirably calculated to preserve the constitution, and, by adopting its forms, to secure its substance. Such a commission being indispensable, by whom was it to be ordered? The King's sign-manual, the usual warrant for it, could not be obtained. Would it be said that the Prince of Wales could command the Lord Chancellor to put the Great Seal to the commission? Both Houses had recently resolved that the Heir Apparent has no such right. Would the Lord Chancellor himself venture to do it of his own accord? Undoubtedly he would not. The commission must be ordered by some authority, for, being once issued with the Great Seal annexed to it, it commanded implicit obedience, and the law would admit no subsequent inquiry respecting its validity. He was opinion that it was in the power of the two Houses to direct the Great Seal to be put to the commission, and in their power only. The Great Seal was the high instrument by which the King's *fiat* was irrevocably given; it was the *clavis Regni*, the mouth of royal authority, the organ by which the Sovereign spoke his will. Such was its efficacy, that even if the Lord Chancellor, by caprice, put the Great Seal to any commission, it could not afterwards be questioned. In so doing he would be guilty of a misdemeanor, but the Judges must give effect to it.[1] If an act of parliament receive the royal assent by a commission under the Great Seal, '*Le Roy le voet*' being so pronounced, it is added to the statute-book, and becomes the law of the land, which no one may question. Thus the '*phantom*' would prove a substantial benefit, and the '*fiction*' would end in the reality which all good men desired." His Lordship then went on to explain, and to rely upon, the precedent at the commencement of the reign of Henry VI., when, the Sovereign, being an infant of nine months old, the Great Seal was placed in his hand, or his hand was placed on the Great Seal, and it was supposed to be given by him to the Master of the Rolls; whereupon many commissions were sealed by it, and the government was carried on under its authority. He concluded by moving, "That it is expedient and necessary that letters patent for opening the Parliament should pass under the Great Seal."[2]

At the request of the Duke of York, Lord Camden agreed that the names of the Prince of Wales and of the other princes of the blood should be omitted from the commission, as they all condemned this mode of proceeding, and the motion was carried without a division. Accordingly, on the following day, a commission under

[1] Till repealed by *scire facias*.   [2] 27 Parl. Hist. 1123-1133.

the Great Seal, was produced in the name of his most gracious Majesty, George III., by which his Majesty was made to declare, that, "*it not being convenient for him to be personally present*, he authorized certain Commissioners to open the Parliament in his name, and to declare the causes of Parliament being summoned by him." The Commons attending at the Bar of the House of Lords to hear the commission read, the Commissioners declared the causes of the summons to be, " to provide for the care of his Majesty's royal person, and for the administration of the royal authority." The two Houses did not go through the form of agreeing upon an humble address to his Majesty, in answer to his gracious speech by his Commissioners; but the Regency Bill was immediately brought in. " The Phantom" did not the second time appear to make the bill a law; for, after it had passed the Commons, and while it was in committee in the Lords, it was stopped by the King's convalescence; and George III. remained above twenty years on the throne before there was such a recurrence of his malady as to render it necessary to resort to similar proceedings.[1]

From the course then adopted, and carried through, I presume, it is now to be considered part of our constitution, that if ever, during the natural life of the Sovereign, he is unable, by mental disease, personally to exercise the royal functions, the deficiency is to be supplied by the two Houses of Parliament, who, in their *discretion*, will probably elect the heir apparent Regent, under such restrictions as they may please to propose,—but who may prefer the head of the ruling faction, and at once vest in him all the prerogatives of the Crown. On the two occasions referred to in the reign of George III., the next heir being at enmity with the King and his ministers, this was considered the loyal and courtly doctrine, and, from its apparent advancement of the rights of Parliament, there was no difficulty in casting odium upon those who opposed it: but I must avow that my deliberate opinion coincides with that of Burke, Fox, and Erskine, who pronounced it to be unsupported by any precedent, and to be in accordance with the principles of the Polish, not the English, monarchy. The two Houses of Parliament

[1] 27 Parl. Hist. 1297. See Parl. Deb. xviii. 1102; ante, vol. i. p. 23.

would be the proper tribunal to pronounce that the Sovereign is unable to act; but then, as if he were naturally, as well as civilly, dead, the next heir ought, as of right, to assume the government as Regent, ever ready to lay it down on the Sovereign's restoration to reason,—in the same way as our Lady Victoria would have returned to a private station if, after her accession, there had appeared posthumous issue of William IV. by his Queen. It is easy to point out possible abuses by the next heir as Regent, to the prejudice of the living Sovereign,—but there may be greater abuses of the power of election imputed to the two Houses, whereby a change of dynasty might be effected. I conceive, therefore, that the Irish Parliament, in 1789, acted more constitutionally in acknowledging the *right* of the next heir,—in scouting the fiction of a commission, or royal assent, from the insane Sovereign, —and in addressing the Prince of Wales to take upon himself the government as Regent.

After the King's recovery, Lord Camden adhered (with one memorable exception) to the resolution he had announced, that, on account of his advanced age, he would no longer take part in the debates of the House of Lords· but he remained in his office, and steadily supported the Administration by his counsels. It has been suggested that, in his extended connection with Mr. Pitt, he abandoned the liberal principles for which he had so long struggled. But this charge is, I think, entirely without foundation. He had been called away to a better state of existence before the commencement of the trials for high treason which disgraced the country in the end of the year 1794,—and I am not aware of any measure adopted with his sanction which might not have been brought forward under Lord Chatham or Lord Rockingham. Bishop Watson accuses him of an entire subserviency at this time to the supposed illiberal policy of the Government. "I asked him," says the Bishop, "if he foresaw any danger likely to result to the Church establishment from the repeal of the Test and Corporation Acts; he answered at once, '*None whatever;* Pitt was wrong in refusing the application of the Dissenters, but he must now be supported.'"—I never attach much importance to what is supposed to have fallen from any man in the laxity of private talk; but supposing this reminiscence to be quite correct, and that no qualification or circumstance to vary the effect is forgotten, might not the President of the Council, without sacrificing the Dissenters or his own consistency, hesitate about breaking up the Government on their account, and wait for a more favorable opportunity to do them justice? The Bishop might have been softened by another anecdote which he relates of Lord Camden about the same time:—" I remember his saying to me one night when Lord Chancellor Thurlow was speaking, contrary, as I thought, to his conviction, *' There now, I could not do that; he is supporting what he does not believe a word of.'* " [1]

Lord Camden, like many very sincere and steady friends of liberty, was much appalled by the excesses of the French Revolution, and was alarmed lest our free institutions, the growth of ages, and the result of reason and experience, might be endangered by reckless Jacobin innovation. Any expressions which he might use while laboring under such impressions are not to be nicely weighed for the purpose of making out a charge of inconsistency against him. Burke having sent him a copy of his "Appeal from the New to the Old Whigs," received from him the following answer:—

"Brighton, August 5, 1791.

"Sir,

"I have received with great pleasure your last publication, which, as it professed to be sent by the author, I determined to read through with the utmost attention, that I might afterwards proportion my thanks to the value of the present.[2] I have done so, and am ready to declare my perfect concurrence in every part of the argument, from the beginning to the end, and return you my warmest thanks for presenting me with so valuable a performance, though perhaps my acknowledgment of its merit may lose some part of its grace by my being an interested party, as I am, in the success of the doctrine. The commendation of one convert (and I have no doubt there will be many) would be a stronger testimony of its value than the applause of hundreds that needed no conviction. I, for instance, like many others, have always thought

[1] Bishop Watson's Memoirs, p. 162.
[2] I must confess that, for conscience sake, I follow just the opposite rule—always returning thanks when I have read the title-page.

myself an old Whig, and hold the same principles with yourself; but I suppose none, or very few of us, ever thought upon the subject with so much correctness, and hardly any would be able to express their thoughts with such clearness, justness, and force of argument. I am, therefore, as well as them, better instructed how to instruct others than I was before.

"There is only one passage in your book that gives me the least concern, and that is where you talk of retiring from public business. For though, as a member of the Administration, I might be well enough pleased at the Opposition's losing one of its ablest assistants, yet I shall be sorry to see the Parliament deprived of so strenuous an advocate for the constitution.

"As an old Whig, therefore, and not as a minister, give me leave to subscribe myself,
"Your most obliged and obedient servant,
"CAMDEN."

CHAPTER CXLVIII.

CONCLUSION OF THE LIFE OF LORD CAMDEN.

LORD CAMDEN showed his sincere and unabated attachment to his early political principles by his zealous support of Mr. Fox's Libel Bill, which otherwise never would have passed the House of Lords. Near the close of the session of 1791, Thurlow threw it out, under pretense that there was not time to consider it, but not before Lord Camden had made an admirable speech in its favor, showing that the jury were the proper judges of the seditious tendency of any writing called a seditious libel. He said,—"I have long endeavored to define what is a seditious libel, but have not been able to find any definition which either meets the approbation of my own mind, or ought to be satisfactory to others. Some judges have laid down that any censure of the government is a libel. Others say, that it is only groundless calumnies on government that are to be considered libels; but is the judge to decide as a matter of law whether the accusation be well or ill founded? You must place the press under the power of judges or juries, and I think your Lordships will have no doubt which to prefer." [1]

In the following year the bill again came up from the Commons, and Thurlow did his best to defeat it. He summoned the judges, and obtained from them an unanimous opinion that the question of "libel or no libel?" was one of pure law, for the Court alone,—and two law Lords, Lord Bathurst, an ex-Chancellor, and Lord Kenyon, the Chief Justice of the King's Bench, combined with him to extinguish the rights of juries. But the veteran champion of those rights was undaunted. "Nothing can be more refreshing to the lovers of liberty, or more gratifying to those who venerate the judicial character, than to contemplate the glorious struggle for his long-cherished principles with which Lord Camden's illustrious life closed. The fire of his youth seemed to kindle in the bosom of one touching on fourscore, as he was impelled to destroy the servile and inconsistent doctrines of others—slaves to mere technical lore, but void of the sound and discriminating judgment which mainly constitutes a legal, and above all a judicial mind." [2]

In the memorable debate which decided the fate of the bill,—rising in his place slowly and with difficulty,—still leaning on his staff, he thus began:—"I thought never to have troubled your Lordships more. The hand of age is upon me, and I have for some time felt myself unable to take an active part in your deliberations. On the present occasion, however, I consider myself as particularly, or rather as personally, bound to address you—and probably for the last time. My opinion on this subject has been long known; it is upon record; it lies on your Lordships' table: I shall retain it, and I trust I have yet strength to demonstrate that it is consonant to law and the constitution." His voice, which had been at first low and tremulous, grew firm and loud, and all his physical as well as mental powers seemed animated and revived. He then stated, with his wonted precision, what the true question was, and he argued it with greater spirit than ever. Alluding to his favorite illustration, from a trial for murder, he said, "A man may kill another in his own defense, or under various circumstances, which render the killing no murder. How are these things to be explained?—by the

[1] 29 Parl. Hist. 731. [2] Lord Brougham's Lives of Statesmen, iii. 178.

circumstances of the case. What is the ruling principle? —The intention of the party. Who decides on the intention of the party? The judge? No! the jury. So the jury are allowed to judge of the intention upon an indictment for murder, and not upon an indictment for a libel!!! The jury might as well be deprived of the power of judging of the fact of of *publication*, for that, likewise, depends upon the *intention*. What is the oath of the jury? Well and truly to try the *issue joined*—which is the plea of *not guilty* to the whole charge." In going over the cases, when he came to *Rex* v. *Owen*, in which he gained such distinction as counsel for the defendant, he explained how he had been allowed to address the jury, to show the innocence of the alleged libel. "Then," said he, "came *Rex* v. *Shebbeare*, where as Attorney General, I conducted the prosecution. I went into court predetermined to insist on the jury taking the whole case into their consideration; and so little did I attend to the authority of the judges, that, in arguing the character of the libel, I turned my back upon them, directing all I had to say to the jury-box. In the days of the Charleses and Jameses, the doctrine now contended for would have been most precious; it would have served as an admirable footstool for tyranny. So clear is it that the jury are to decide the question of '*libel or no libel?*' that if all the bench, and all the bar, and the unanimous voice of Parliament, were to declare it to be otherwise, I could not change my opinion. I ask your Lordships to say, who shall have the care of the liberty of the press? The judges, or the people of England? The jury are the people of England. The judges are independent men! Be it so. But are they totally beyond the possibility of corruption from the Crown? Is it impossible to show them favor in any way whatever? The truth is, they possibly may be corrupted—juries never can! What would be the effect of giving judges the whole control of the press? Nothing would appear that could be disagreeable to the Government. As well might an act of parliament pass, that nothing shall be printed or published but panegyrics on ministers. Such doctrines being acted upon, we would soon lose every thought of freedom. If it is not law, it should be made law—that in prosecutions for libel, the jury shall decide upon the whole case. In the full catalogue of crimes, there is not one so fit to be determined by a jury as libel." Before he concluded, he took an opportunity to pay a just tribute of respect to his old rival, Lord Mansfield, now almost in the tomb, into which he himself was so soon to follow him. "Though so often opposed to him," said he, "I ever honored his learning and his genius; and, if he could be present, he would bear witness that personal rancor or animosity never mixed with our controversies. When, after this last effort, I shall disappear, I hope that I, too, may have credit for good intentions with those who differ from my opinions, and that, perhaps, it may be said, *through a long life he was consistent in the desire to serve his country.*'" This speech was warmly complimented by all who followed, on both sides, in a two-nights' debate, and gained a majority of 57 to 32 for the second reading of the bill.

The general expectation was, that it would be allowed to pass silently through its subsequent stages; but Thurlow trying to damage it in committee by a nullifying amendment, Lord Camden was again called up, saying, that "he would contend for the truth of his position, as to the right of juries in cases of libel, to the last hour of his existence, *manibus pedibusque.* When he had reiterated his argument, the amendment was rejected.

Lord Chancellor.—" I trust the noble and learned Lord will agree to a clause being added to the bill, which he will see is indispensably necessary to do equal justice between the public and those prosecuted for libels. This clause will authorize the granting of a new trial, if the Court should be dissatisfied with a verdict given for the defendant."

Earl Camden.—" What! after a verdict of acquittal?"
Lord Chancellor.—" Yes!"
Earl Camden.—" NO, I THANK YOU!!!"'

These were the last words he ever uttered in public. The bill, in its declaratory form, was then suffered to pass through the committee, and to be read a third time; Lords Thurlow, Bathurst, and Kenyon, signing a strong protest against it. This is to be honored as a great example of a law Lord boldly declaring and acting upon his own deliberate and conscientious conviction upon a question of law, contrary to the unanimous opinion of the

[1] 29 Parl. Hist. 1404-1534.

judges when asked their advice for the assistance of the House.—Now that the mist of prejudice has cleared away, I believe that English lawyers almost unanimously think that Lord Camden's view of the question was correct on strict legal principles; and that the act was properly made to *declare* the right of the jury to determine upon the character of the alleged libel, instead of *enacting* it as an innovation.

No law ever operated more beneficially than that which had been so long and so violently opposed by legal dignitaries. It put an end to the indecent struggle, in trials for libel, between the judge and the jury, which had agitated courts of justice near a century; it placed the liberty of the press on a secure basis· all the predictions that it would encourage seditious publications and attacks on private character have been falsified; and we have now the best definition of a libel—"a publication which, in the opinion of twelve honest, independent, and intelligent men, is mischievous and ought to be punished." The bill bears the name of Mr. Fox, because he introduced it into the House of Commons, while the merit of it is claimed by the admirers of Erskine, on account of his glorious fight for the rights of juries in the case of the Dean of St. Asaph; but Pratt had struggled successfully for its principle long before these names were ever heard of, and to him we must ascribe its final triumph.[1] His perseverance is the more meritorious, as he might have had a plausible pretext for taking a contrary course, from the multiplication of seditious writings, and the democratic movement then supposed to threaten the public tranquillity; but he wisely thought that the vessel of the state is best prepared to encounter a storm by making a *jettison* of abuses.

Lord Camden survived two years. Although his mental faculties remained unimpaired, he did not again appear before the public. He would have been glad to resign his office, but it was not convenient that a vacancy should be made in the Cabinet, and "the King claimed a continuation of his services while he was so well able to perform them." Every possible indulgence was shown him. Cab-

[1] It is said that Lord Camden had prepared the draught of Mr. Fox's Libel Bill many years before, but kept it back till he saw there was a chance of carrying it.—*Europ. Mag.* Aug. 1794. p. 93.

inets were often held at his house; and draughts of deliberation were sent to him into the country, where he now for the most part resided.

His private friendships continued to be cherished with unabated ardor. Thus, a few weeks before his death, he addressed the Duke of Grafton:—

"I am more restored than I ever expected to be, and, if I can combat this winter, perhaps may recover so much strength as to pass the remainder of my days with cheerfulness: but I do not believe it possible ever for me to return to business, and I think your Grace will never see me again at the head of the Council Board. It is high time for me to become a private man and retire. But, whatever may be my future condition, whether in or out of office, I shall remain with the same respect and attention,

"Your Grace's most faithful friend," &c.

He then made a short excursion to Bath, to try the benefit of the waters; but the *stamina* of life were gone, and his spirits were broken by bodily debility. While there, he met his old political antagonist, Welbore Ellis, now Lord Mendip, who, although his senior, had a constitution still unbroken. Meeting in the pump-room, the courtier said to the patriot, "I hope you are well, and in the enjoyment of a happy old age." "Happy!" said Lord Camden, in a fit of temporary despondency, "how can a man be happy who has survived all his passions and all his enjoyments?" "Oh, my dear Lord," was the reply, "do not talk so: while God is pleased to enable me to read my Homer in my ordinary hours, and my Bible at my better times, I can not but be thankful and happy."

He saw that he must now only look for happiness in a better world, and to meet his end in the midst of his family and his friends, he soon after removed to his town residence in Hill Street, Berkeley Square. Here he gradually sunk, more through the gentle pressure of time than any particular disorder. He quietly breathed his last on the 13th of April, 1794, in the eighty-first year of his age, —exactly thirteen months after the decease of his great rival, Lord Mansfield, who had attained the more venerable age of eighty-nine.

His remains were deposited in the family vault, in the

parish church of Seal, in Kent. A monument has there been erected to his memory, with an epitaph, which, after stating his age, and the various offices he held, thus concludes in language which, though dictated by the piety of an affectionate son, posterity will repeat:—

"Endowed with abilities of the highest order, with learning deep and extensive, with taste discriminating and correct, with talents in society most instructive and agreeable, and with integrity universally acknowledged, he lived beloved by his family and friends, respected and venerated by his country, and died universally regretted by all good men."

Among all the Chancellors whose lives I have written, or who are yet in prospect before me, there is no one whose virtues have been more highly estimated than Lord Camden's. We may conceive how he was regarded in his own age, from the character of him by Horace Walpole, ever anxious, by sarcasms and sneers, to lower even those whom he professed to exalt:—"Mansfield had a bitter antagonist in Pratt, who was steady, warm, sullen, stained with no reproach, and a uniform Whig. Nor should we deem less highly of him because private motives stirred him on to the contest. Alas! how cold would public virtue be if it never glowed but with public heat! So seldom, too, it is that any consideration can bias a man to run counter to the color of his office, and the interests of his profession, that the world should not be too scrupulous about accepting the service as a merit, but should honor it at least for the sake of the precedent."

A contemporary writer says:—"He was blessed by nature with a clear, persuasive, and satisfactory manner of conveying his ideas. In the midst of politeness and facility, he kept up the true dignity of his important office: in the midst of exemplary patience, (foreign to his natural temper, and therefore the more commendable,) his understanding was always vigilant. His memory was prodigious in readiness and comprehension: but, above all, there appeared a kind of benevolent solicitude for the discovery of truth, that won the suitors to a thorough and implicit confidence in him."[1]

I find nothing hinted against him as a judge, except "that he was a little too prolix in the reason of his decrees, by taking notice even of inferior circumstances, and

[1] Almon's Anecdotes, vol. i. p. 384.

viewing the question in every conceivable light." The same objector adds: "This, however, was an error on the right side, and arose from his wish to satisfy the bar, and his own mind, which was, perhaps to a weakness, dissatisfied with its first impressions, however strong." Both as an Equity and Common-Law Judge his authority continues to be held in reverence by the profession.

As a politician, he is to be held up as a bright example of consistency and true patriotism to all future generations of English lawyers, and the high honors which he reached should counteract the demoralizing effect of the success which has too often attended tergiversation and profligacy,—when these calculations are aided by the recollection that such success, however brilliant, will neither secure permanent admiration or real happiness.

Lord Camden's eloquence is not free from tinsel—but still it is characterized by sterling vigor of thought, richness of imagery, and felicity of diction. Like most great English lawyers, and unlike most great French and Scotch lawyers, he never aimed at literary distinction. His only known printed production was "An Inquiry into the Process of Latitat in Wales." But he had a great taste for reading, which did not confine itself to legal and antiquarian lore. It is said that throughout life he was a devourer of romances, including the interminable tomes of Scuderi—and that the "Grand Cyrus" and "Philidaspes" furnished him many an evening's repast, for which his appetite was sharpened by the juridical labors which had occupied the morning. Late in life he learned Spanish, to read the romances in that language; having exhausted those written in English, French and Italian.[1] Although he never pretended to be a poet, he would sometimes good-naturedly pen *vers de société*. Giving a party on Twelfth Night to a number of young persons, he required that all the company in turn must produce four lines on the character they should respectively draw. He himself drew a young barrister, in wig and gown, and thus addressed him:—

> "Lawyer, attend to me, and I'll unfold
> How brass and silver shall make sterling gold;
> My nostrum shall all alchemy surpass.
> If your tongue's silver, and your forehead **brass**."

---
[1] Pursuit of Literature, p. 61.

In his youth, he followed the example of Lord Chancellor North in devoting himself, as a relaxation from study, to music, in which he seems to have made great proficiency; for, his friend Davies planning an opera to be set to music by Handel, we find him offering to assist with his advice respecting the genius of musical verse, the length of the performance, the numbers and talent of the singers, and the position of the choruses—in the language of an accomplished adept in the science of harmony.

He was not a member (I should have been glad to record that he was) of "*the Literary Club*," and he never seems to have been intimate with Johnson or Goldsmith, or any of the distinguished authors of his day. "Goldsmith, in his diverting simplicity, complained one day, in a mixed company, of Lord Camden. '*I met him,*' said he, '*at Lord Clare's house in the country, and he took no more notice of me than if I had been an ordinary man.*' The company having laughed heartily, Johnson stood forth in defense of his friend. '*Nay, gentlemen,*' said he, '*Dr. Goldsmith is in the right. A nobleman ought to have made up to such a man as Goldsmith, and I think it is much against Lord Camden that he neglected him.*'"[1] However, we learn likewise from the inimitable Boswell, that Lord Camden was on a footing of great familiarity with him "whose death eclipsed the gaiety of nations." "I told him," says this prince of biographers, "that one morning when I went to breakfast with Garrick, who was very vain of his intimacy with Lord Camden, he accosted me thus: '*Pray now did you—did you meet a little lawyer turning the corner, eh?*' '*No, sir,*' said I; '*pray what do you mean by the question?*' '*Why,*' replied Garrick, with an affected indifference, yet as standing on tip-toe, '*Lord Camden has this moment left me. We have had a long walk together.*' JOHNSON: '*Well, sir, Garrick talked very properly. Lord Camden was a* LITTLE LAWYER *to be associating so familiarly with a player.*'"[2] But in another mood, Johnson would have highly and deservedly praised the LITTLE LAWYER for relishing the society of a man who was a most agreeable companion, and of high intellectual accomplishments, as well as the greatest actor who ever trod the English stage.

Lord Camden is said to have been somewhat of an epi-

---

[1] Boswell's Life of Johnson, iii. 336.   [2] Ibid.

curean—indisposed towards exertion, bodily or mental, unless when roused to it by the necessity of business, or the excitement of strong feeling—and to have taken considerable pains in supplying his larder and his cellar with all that could best furnish forth an exquisite banquet. It is certain that he was himself always extremely temperate, forming a contrast in this and other particulars with his immediate predecessor on the woolsack—for his conversation was ever polished and decorous. He seems to have been most amiable in private life, and to have had in a distinguished degree

> ———" that which should accompany old age—
> Honor, love, obedience, *troops of friends*."

With many political opponents, he was without a personal enemy.

Lord Camden was in stature below the middle size, but well proportioned and active. We have several exquisite portraits of him. That painted for the City of London, by Reynolds, is one of the finest specimens of the English school. Judging from these, his physiognomy, without marked features or deep lines, was more expressive of gentleness of disposition and frank good-humor than of profound thoughtfulness or stern resolution.

With the exception of an occasional slight fit of the gout, he enjoyed uninterrupted health. He had never had the smallpox, and it is related of him, as a weakness, that he was always much afraid of taking that disorder—his terrors being greatly aggravated when his friend, Lord Waldegrave, died of it at the age of fifty.[1]

He left a son, John Jeffreys, who, in 1812, was created Marquess Camden and Earl of Brecknock, and who was not only distinguished for his public services, but for the disinterested renunciation of the legal profits of his tellership, beyond a very limited amount, to the great benefit of the public revenue.

Lord Chancellor Camden is now represented by his grandson, the present Marquess, who, out of respect for his own virtues, and for the memory of his ancestors, has been decorated with the garter which his father wore.[2]

[1] Nich. Lit. An. viii. 533.   [2] Grandeur of the Law, 27.

CHAPTER CXLIX.

LIFE OF LORD CHANCELLOR CHARLES YORKE FROM HIS BIRTH TILL HE WAS RETURNED AS A MEMBER OF THE HOUSE OF COMMONS.

WERE it not for the melancholy spectacle which presents itself at the end of the vista, I should start on this new excursion into the field of biography with alacrity and delight. The subject of the present memoir was possessed of the finest talents,—of the most varied accomplishments,—of every virtue in public and in private life;—but when he seemed to have reached the summit of his lofty ambition he committed a fatal error, and the grave closed upon him under circumstances the most afflicting. His end was "doubtful," and it has cast a shade over the whole of his career, which ought to have appeared so brilliant. The attainment of the Great Seal proved his destruction. "As if there were contagion in the touch, instant disappointment, anguish and death—such was the strange and melancholy fate of Charles Yorke. The allegory of the Eastern monarch devoting one day to supreme felicity, yet finding every hour perversely darkened with chagrin and sorrow,—the fable of the Persian fruit—sweet to the eye, and ashes to the taste,—were only the image and symbol of this great lawyer's miserable destiny."[1]

There are some examples in England of a great lawyer having a great lawyer for his son; but in most of these,—as in the case of Sir Nicholas Bacon,—the father had died while the son was very young, leaving him to struggle for a subsistence. Charles Yorke, the second son of the great Lord Hardwicke, was born on the 10th of January, 1723, in a splended mansion in Great Ormond Street. His father, then Attorney General, and making a larger income than had ever fallen to the lot of an English barrister, continued near forty years afterwards to fill the highest offices of the law, accumulating immense wealth, and able to make a splendid provision for all the members of his

[1] Law Magazine, LXI., where will be found an able vindication of his memory from the charge preferred by Junius.

family. Yet Charles,—even under the enervating influence of a sinecure place which was conferred upon him—from a noble love of honorable distinction, exerted himself as strenuously and perseveringly as if, being the son of a poor Scotch clergyman, who could give him nothing beyond a good education, he had depended entirely on his own exertions for his bread and for his position in the world.

Like Lord Bacon, he was most fortunate in his mother, who, while his father was absorbed in professional and official duties, watched over his education with great discretion as well as tenderness. She brought up all her children in thrifty habits, and taught them the most valuable of all virtues—the virtue of self-denial. The boys, instead of going to Eton, where they were in danger of learning idleness, extravagance, and contempt of parental rule, were sent to a most excellent private school at Hackney, kept by the Rev. Dr. Newcome, a sound classical scholar, and a strict disciplinarian. Here Charles remained from childhood till he was seventeen; and here he must have acquired the taste for literature, and the steady habit of application, for which he was afterwards remarkable. He was then removed to Ben'et (now Corpus Christi) College, Cambridge, where his elder brother had been an undergraduate two years; and he was placed, like him, under the tuition of the pains-taking Dr. Birch. Little aided by academical rules, he now devoted himself to study with enthusiasm, and he soon gave extraordinary proofs of his progress.

I doubt not that, upon the whole, Cambridge, as a place of education, has derived benefit from the mathematical and the classical tripos since established, and the other distinctions at present held out to rouse emulation and to encourage industry; but a spontaneous, genuine, ardent love of knowledge, which sometimes springs up in those happily born, and is fostered by the mutual converse of kindred minds, perhaps formerly led to a higher degree of mental cultivation and really valuable attainment. While Charles Yorke was an undergraduate, there was probably a good deal of general idleness among Cantabrigians, and few could have gone through what now would be considered a creditable examination in the Greek measures or the higher mathematics; but I question whether all the present resident members of the University could compose the "Athenian Letters."

This work, consisting of two quarto volumes, I have lately perused, and I strongly recommend it to all who would, in a most agreeable manner, extend or refresh their acquaintance with the institutions, the literature, the manners, and the distinguished men of Greece at the most interesting period of her history. To it Charles Yorke was the principal contributor before he had completed his twentieth year, and, considering the knowledge of books and men which his contributions exhibit, I own they seem to me a more wonderful instance of precocity than the early Latin verses of Cowley and Milton, which clever schoolboys can so closely imitate.

The undertaking was commenced under the auspices of Dr. Birch, as an exercise to his pupils, for the purpose of imprinting their reading on their memories, and initiating them in English composition, so miserably neglected at our universities. Cleander, an agent of the King of Persia, is supposed to be resident in Athens during the Peloponnesian war, and to carry on a correspondence, not only with his court, but with his brother living at home, and with private friends in Egypt and other provinces of the Persian empire. These letters are stated, in a lively preface written by Charles Yorke, to be translations from a MS. in the library at Fez, in the King of Morocco's dominions, the supposed deposit of vast treasures of Oriental learning.

They were first printed at Cambridge, in the years 1739 and 1740, but were communicated only to a limited number of friends, under the strictest injunctions of secresy, "from an ingenuous diffidence which forbade the authors, most of them extremely young, to obtrude on the notice of the world what they considered only a preparatory trial of their strength." In 1781 a new edition was published, still only for private circulation—the editor paying a merited compliment to him "of whose talents, virtues, and services, the world was unfortunately deprived when they were most wanted, both by his own profession and by the public." The real authorship of the different letters was now disclosed. "The work was supposed to be genuine, and a translation from an old Arabic version; but when a due interval of time has elapsed the truth may be owned; the illusion vanishes; it is a masquerade which is closed; the fancy dresses and the dominoes are returned to the respective wardrobes; the company walk about again in their proper habits, and return to their proper occupations in life." [1]

A copy of this edition having been transmitted by the younger brother of Charles Yorke, created Lord Dover, to the author of the celebrated "Travels of Anacharsis," BARTHELEMI returned an answer, which (after making all due allowance for French politeness) must be considered a high testimony to the merits of our young countryman:—"Si je l'avois connu plutot, ou je n'aurois commençé le mien, ou j'aurois taché d'approcher de ce beau modèle. Pourquoi ne l'a-t-on pas communiqué au public? Pourquoi n'est-il pas traduit dans toutes les langues? Je sacrifierois volontiers mes derniers jours au plaisir d'en enrichir notre littérature, si je connoissois mieux les finesses de la langue Anglaise." [2]

I will give, as a specimen, a "private and confidential" letter from "CLEANDER to HYDASPES, first Chamberlain of the King of Persia," upon the contrast between the manners to which he had been accustomed and those he saw in his travels:—

"The first question you would, probably, have me resolve is, what peculiar difference I find in the manners of Greece and Persia; since custom has placed as many marks of distinction in the civil manners of every nation as Providence has displayed in the natural bodies of each individual. I will tell you, then. A Persian would find nothing more surprising than the unbounded freedom of action and conversation which reigns here. The councils of the Great King are impenetrable, we discover nothing of them till they take effect; whilst here everything is known long before it is put in execution, and canvassed with as much liberty in common conversation as in the assemblies of the people. We approach our mighty monarch with positions of adoration, and address him in

---

[1] Pref. xv. ed. 1798. There having been some surreptitious editions, this last edition, most splendid and correct, was given to the world by the late Earl of Hardwicke.

[2] Lord Mansfield's acknowledgment for his copy is touching:—" Give me leave to return you my warmest thanks for the ATHENIAN LETTERS.
———" ' Veteres revocamus amores.
Atque olim amissas flemus amicitias.'"

language which is used to the Deity. At Athens, the magistrates are distinguished more by being virulently abused than by any mark of authority. Pericles himself is sure to be the object aimed at by every one who writes either scandalous libels to be dispersed about the city, or performances designed for public representation. The actors themselves sometimes appear upon the stage in masks, which are made exactly to resemble the face of the person ridiculed. The Persian magnificence appears most at their entertainments; the Athenian at their solemn festivals. The Asiatic feasts are remarkable for the vast quantities of provisions, the costliness of the preparations, and the sumptuous furniture; the chief recommendation of the Greek one is the elegance and variety of the conversation, which induced an Athenian to make this observation: 'Our entertainments not only please when we give them, but the day after.'[1] The Asiatic taste and grandeur appear in the palaces of their princes and satraps; the Grecian in the temples of their gods and the public buildings. Not a nobleman in Persia but shows his rank by the richness of his dress and the number of his attendants; whereas here you can not distinguish a citizen from a slave by his habit; and the wealthiest Athenian, the most considerable person in the city, is not ashamed to go to market himself. In Persia the eyes of all are turned towards the Sovereign, and they regulate their conduct by his: in the free republics of Greece, the people are king, and resemble other monarchs in their bad qualities more than in their good ones; for they are fickle and imperious, severe and obstinate."

In these letters Charles Yorke gives a lively representation of the different views that may be taken of Spartan manners. Thus he praises:—

"The Spartans banished Ctesiphon for saying he could talk a whole day upon any question. A rhetorician told one of their kings that eloquence was the most excellent gift to mankind: he answered,—'You do well to say so, because when you are commanded silence, you are useless.' . . . . I observed when I conducted the ambassador of Lacedæmon to the royal chamber, agreeably to the usual ceremony, he dropped a ring which he wore

[1] This reminds me of a moral sentiment I have heard given as a toast in Scotland: "May Evening's *diversions* bear Morning's *reflections*."

upon his finger, and in stooping to recover it, made an awkward reverence to our monarch. Podarchus stood as a candidate a few months since to supply a vacancy in the chosen troop of the 300, and, upon finding he was not chosen, he went out from the presence of the Ephori with much seeming gaiety, and in a fit of laughter. They called him back, and inquired the reason of it. He answered,—' he could not help congratulating the state in silence on being possessed of 300 braver and better citizens than himself.' At the last Olympian games, another Spartan, being asked whether his victory there would be of any service to him, he replied,—' Yes, for it would recommend him to a station before the King in battle.' The statues of the gods are all in armor, to intimate that the people place their confidence in military force. Their sacrifices are made with uncommon frugality, because they imagine the Deity is more moved by the sincerity than the incense of the worshiper. The only prayer they offer up at the altar is, that they may receive good things for their good actions. All mourning ceases in eleven days. No one is allowed an inscription on his monument except he dies in the field. They set so much a higher value on a victory gained by stratagem than by force, that in the former case they sacrifice an ox to Mars, and in the latter no more than a dunghill cock."

But thus their great lawgiver is censured, in describing the results of his institutions:—

"The Spartans are a proud and severe people. Let them thank Lycurgus, who has made them so. Unlike the rest of the admired sages who have given salutary laws to the world, instead of enlarging the minds of an ignorant race, he has more effectually contracted them. Instead of teaching them a little condescension to others, they have learned only to set a value upon themselves. Instead of polishing them into an ease and benevolence of temper, he has reformed them out of it, and for the sake of avoiding the refinement of luxury, he has introduced a neglect of that humanity in the lesser offices of life, which adds such a relish to the enjoyment of it."

In the letters there are frequent allusions to contemporaneous English politics. Thus Charles Yorke, in another letter from Cleander to Hippias, on "Ostracism," evidently points at the resolution then generally entertained to drive Sir Robert Walpole from the helm :—

"No mischiefs are to be wondered at in that state where a man's merit, instead of gaining him the love of his citizens, recommends him to nothing but disgrace. Good Heavens! can there be a surer sign of universal frenzy in a commonwealth than the punishing of great virtues with a severity only due to the basest vices, and rewarding high services and the noblest achievements with such black unthankfulness?"

But we must follow the youthful author in his academical career. Avoiding Jacobite roysterers and the fellows of Trinity—"such a parcel of stupid drunken sots that the like was not in the whole kingdom,"[1]—not very regular at lecture, and sometimes missing chapel,—but rising in summer with the sun, and in winter lighting his own fire long before day; following with intense ardor the course of study which he preferred; taking no relaxation but a walk with a brother Athenian, in which they planned a dispatch to or from Babylon,—he spent his time most pleasantly and most profitably on the banks of the Granta. In 1742, he took his degree of M.A. as a nobleman, and left the University without his merits being fully known, for he was only talked of as having agreeable manners, although "one of a set who were great *saps* and rather *exclusive*."

He now seriously began the study of the law. His father, on account of the sprightliness he had displayed even in his nurse's arms, having from his infancy destined him for the bar, had entered him of the Middle Temple, while yet in his 14th year.[2] Thence he had been transferred to the "Honorable Society of Lincoln's Inn," of which he became a distinguished ornament.[3] He

---

[1] Language of Dr. Bentley, the Master of that College.

[2] "The Honble Charles Yorke, Esqre., 2nd son of the Right Honble Philip, Lord Hardwicke, Baron of Hardwicke, in the county of Gloucester, Lord High Chancellor of Great Britain, was specially admitted into the Society of the Middle Temple, the 1st day of December, 1735."

[3] "Lincoln's Inn.—The Honourable Charles Yorke, Esquire, second son of the Right Honble Philip, Lord Hardwicke, Baron of Hardwicke, in the county of Gloucester, Lord High Chancellor of Great Britain, is admitted into the Society of this Inn, the 23rd day of October, in the sixteenth year of the reign of our Sovereign Lord, George the Second, by the Grace of God of Great Britain, France, and Ireland, King, Defender of the Faith, &c., and in the year of our Lord 1742."

had contrived to keep some terms there while he was still an undergraduate. To free him from the temptations and distractions of Powis House,' where the Chancellor now lived in great splendor, our student had a set of chambers assigned to him in Stone Buildings, Lincoln's Inn, from which he was not to migrate to the paternal mansion except on "high days and holidays," by special invitation.² He had not the advantage of sitting at a desk in an attorney's office; but he had often breathed a legal atmosphere, from which he had unconsciously imbibed many legal notions;—and the Chancellor, observing his acuteness and aptitude for instruction on all subjects, took pleasure in expounding to him the elements of jurisprudence, and making him comprehend the bearings of any constitutional question which agitated the public mind.

Thus instructed, he made a rapid progress; and, by attending the Courts in the morning, and devoting himself to Littleton and Plowden in the evening, he laid the

---

¹ On the south side of Grosvernor Square.
² Occasionally he wrote to his father, but in language so cold, stiff, and formal, that we should be shocked by it, if we did not bear in mind the conventional modes by which respect was still usually testified by children to parents. I give one specimen:

"Lincoln's Inn, Jan. 25, 1742-3.
"My Lord,
"On taking possession of my chambers last night, several thoughts came into my mind, some of which have so near a relation to your lordship, that I would flatter myself that it may not misbecome me to open them. And the first which naturally arose in it, were my most grateful acknowledgments for the time your goodness allowed me to continue in the University, before you called me to the study of the Law; in which, tho' I have not made the improvements I could wish, yet I hope that little attention I have given to letters may be of lasting use to me, by inspiring me with a principle of rational ambition, and furnishing me with means to attain the proper objects of it.

"Your great example in that scene of life which I am preparing to enter, suggests many things to me, which it is fitter for me to weigh than to explain; only thus much I am free to declare, that no advice or destination, not even your Lordship's, could have induced me to think of the Bar, if I had not previously determined to exert my utmost diligence in the *studious*, and all the courage and abilities I am master of in the *active* part of the profession. This is what I have sometimes been desirous of saying, but as the subject is to me very interesting, I have rather chosen to entrust it to paper, which will be more unmoved than myself in the delivery of it. I need not desire your Lordship, who is so used to distinguish the expression of men from their intentions, to lay no weight on mine, till a few years shall prove them to be the genuine dictates of my heart. I am with the truest respect and affection,
"Your Lordship's most obliged and dutiful Son, "CHAS. YORKE."

foundation of his professional eminence. Although he never was considered a deep black-letter lawyer, he acquired the faculty of knowing where all the learning on any point that might arise was to be found, and he could prepare himself successfully to enter the lists against men who ignorantly rejoiced to think that science had never taught them to stray beyond the precincts of Westminister Hall. Even now he did not abandon his literary tastes; and, by avoiding frivolous amusements, and attending strictly to the improvement of small sections of time wasted by most others, he could, without detriment to his professional progress, keep an assignation with an eminent tragic actor or painter, and carry on a clandestine correspondence with a critic or a poet. These were his dissipations.

He had formed a great intimacy with the author of the "Divine Legation of Moses," and this tyrant of the literary world was to him condescending, bland, and courteous. There is happily preserved to us C. Yorke's very interesting answer to a letter of Warburton, accompanying a presentation copy of the first volume of a new edition of his great work:—

"July 1, 1742.

"Dear Sir,

"I was pleased, on returning home the other day after an excursion of a few weeks, to find your first volume waiting for me, with a most agreeable letter from yourself, full of kindness and vivacity. To speak the truth, I had been meditating before I received yours to say something to you on the very piece you allude to; but you have prevented me in it;—I thought only of congratulating you, but you seem to require condolence.—And surely without reason. What signifies it that your adversaries are not worth contending with? It is a proof that men of sense are all on your side.—Like the specters whom Æneas encountered, you can not hurt them by any weapons; but it should be remembered, on the other hand, they do not injure but tease, and will follow you the less the more you endure and despise them. You should forgive them, too, for you began hostilities. The only provision in the constitution of things for the *dull* is the *indolence* of the ingenious. Therefore, when a man unites great application to great parts, throws down the fences of prejudice, and strikes out new paths in knowledge, they confederate against him as a destroyer of their merit, and a dangerous invader of their property.

"After all, it is a serious and melancholy truth, that when speculative errors are to be reformed, and received opinions either rationally opposed or defended, the matter can not be attempted without much censure. The discreet upbraid you with imprudence, the prejudiced with absurdity, and the dull with affectation. It is a censure, however, which generally arises from interest; for the works of such as you contribute to bury many useless volumes in oblivion.

"I rejoice that you approve of the further remarks I sent you on a few passages in Tunstall's *Epistle;* not only on account of your candor in doing it, but because your sagacity has confirmed what I had thrown out, by two or three very eloquent turns of argument. Whenever you treat a subject, you leave nothing to be said after you, and for that reason can always improve upon others. But this is a trifle. The new edition of your book shows that you can even improve upon yourself. Tully, I think, says of his behavior in the office of friendship—'*cæteris satisfacio quam maximè, mihi ipsi nunquam satisfacio.*' And in writing, it is one mark of superior understanding not to be contented with its own produce.

"Your correspondence is exceedingly acceptable to me. When I am conversing with you on subjects of literature or ingenuity, I forget that I have any remote interest in what is going forward in the world, nor desire in any time of life to be an actor in parties, or as it is called somewhere '*subire tempestates reipublicæ.*' But when I find everybody inquiring to-day concerning the report of the secret committee yesterday,[1] this passion for still life vanishes; *agilis fio et mersor civilibus undis.*

"I am, dear Sir, with the greatest affection and esteem,
"Your most obliged
"and faithful Servant,
"CHARLES YORKE."[2]

This seems to me to be a very wonderful production, considering that the writer was only nineteen years of age.

[1] This refers to the Report of the Secret Committee on the conduct of Sir Robert Walpole,—in which it was thought Lord Chancellor Hardwicke might be implicated.—*12 Parl. Hist.* 788.   [2] Warburton's Letters, 495.

He appears thoroughly to have understood the foibles as well as the merits of his correspondent; and the advice he gives him is remarkable, not only for its boldness, but the felicity of expression in which it is conveyed. We must likewise admire the eagerness with which, notwithstanding his literary enthusiasm, he was ready to plunge into the waves of party strife.

Yet he had occasional struggles between his love of a life of contemplation and a life of action. In a subsequent letter to Warburton, he says,—

"The din of politics is so strong everywhere, that I fancy it must have penetrated into your retirement. It tempts me sometimes, in an indolent fit, to apply Lord Bacon's words to myself,—'that I discover in me more of that disposition which qualifies to hold a book than to play a part.' Yet, if you come to London this spring, you will find me engaged in what properly concerns me; but your company, whether enjoyed by letter or personally, will always draw me back to my old studies—*frustra leges et omnia jura tuentem*."

His letters in this correspondence contain not only examples of bold criticism, but of daring speculation on theological subjects, consistent always with a belief in the great truths of revealed religion, but using considerable freedoms in proposing an allegorical interpretation of Scripture.[1] From his marvelous proficiency,—from the ripeness of his judgment, as well as the extent of his reading, and the variety of his attainments,—we must greatly doubt whether there has been any improvement in the system of education for the bar and for public life since his time. Had his training been a century later, he would still have been plodding for his degree without having begun the study of the law,—and he would have known nothing beyond what is to be learned in the narrow bounds of the modern University curriculum; whereas, we behold him in reality, not only a sound scholar, but a fine writer, and qualified to enter into competition for fortune and fame with the most distinguished lawyers and statesmen.

His rising merit was described by a veteran politician, and exquisite judge of character, now living in retirement,—who thus addressed him:—

[1] See "Selections from Warburton's Literary Remains."

"Houghton, 24th June, 1743.[1]

"Dear Charles,

"This place affords no news, no subject of amusement and entertainment to fine men. Persons of wit and pleasure about town understand not the language, nor taste the charms, of the inanimate world. My flatterers here are all mutes. The oaks, the beeches, and chestnuts seem to contend which shall best please the lord of the manor. They can not deceive, they can not lie. I, in return, with sincerity admire them, and have as many beauties about me as take up my hours of dangling, and no disgrace attends me because I am sixty-seven years of age. Within doors we come a little nearer to real life, and admire, on the almost speaking canvas, all the airs and graces which the proudest of the ladies can boast. With these I am satisfied, as they gratify me with all I wish, and all I want, and expect nothing in return which I can not give. If these, dear Charles, are any temptations, I heartily wish you to come and partake of them. Shifting the scene has sometimes its recommendations, and from country fare you may possibly return with a better appetite to the more delicate entertainment of a court life.

"Dear Charles, yours most affectionately
"ORFORD."

Charles Yorke was called to the bar by the Honorable Society of Lincoln's Inn, in Hilary Term, 1743.[2] Though

---

[1] Hardwicke MSS.

[2] "At a Council held the 1st day of February, 1745,—Ordered, That the Honble Charles Yorke, Esqre., one of the Fellows of this Society, being of full standing, having performed all his exercises, and observed the rules of this Society, be called to the Bar this Term, first paying all his arrears and duties to this Society."

The following entries respecting him are likewise found in the books of the Society:—

"At a Council held the 8th day of May 1754,—Ordered, That the Honble Chas^s Yorke, Esqre., one of his Majesties Council learned in the law, be invited to the Bench of this Society; and Mr. White and Mr. Hanmet, two of the Masters of the Bench, are desired to attend with this order, and report his answer to the next Council; and if the said Mr. Yorke do accept of this invitation, he is, according to the rules of this Society, to pay all his arrears and duties to the Treasurer of this Society, before he be called to the Bench."

"At a Council held the 28th day of November, 1755,—Ordered, that the Honble Charles Yorke, Esqre., be Treasurer for the year ensuing."

"At a Council there held the 29th day of November, 1756,—Ordered, That the Honble Charles Yorke, Esqre., Soll^r Genl, be Master of the Library for the year ensuing."

still in his minority,[1]—he almost immediately got into considerable practice. It was a great advantage to him, no doubt, to be the son of the Lord Chancellor; but, as has been proved by frequent instances, this would have availed him nothing without the power of self-denial, the talents, and the energy which he displayed.

According to the usage then universally followed, he must have gone some circuit; but I can not discover which he selected, or how he fared in the provinces. During term time, in London, he was so overwhelmed with briefs, that he was obliged to abandon the society and the correspondence of his friends. Hilary Term, 1744, approaching, thus he writes to Warburton: "As business is coming in apace, I know not when I shall have an opportunity of conversing with you at large upon paper, unless I busy the present in a mannei to me the most entertaining in the world."

As might be expected, it was chiefly in the Court of Chancery that the solicitors were disposed to employ him—not always from the purest motives. However, he never assumed any airs from his near relationship to the Judge, nor was there ever, as far as I can trace, any well-grounded complaint of his receiving undue favor there. His father was proud of him, and had been particularly delighted with his Athenian Letters; perhaps thinking truly how much better "Cleander" wrote than "Philip Homebred;" but allowed him fairly to fight his own way at the bar, neither taking any indirect means to push him forward, nor, when he heard him argue at the bar, treating him in any respect differently from other counsel.[2]

As yet, the fame of our aspirant was confined to the precincts of Westminister Hall and Lincoln's Inn; for then, unless there were a state trial, no notice was taken of any judicial proceedings in any journal or periodical publication: but, while in his twenty-second year, he suddenly burst upon the public as a bright legal luminary. At this early age, he published the best juridical treatise that had appeared in the English language.

[1] The same evening he wrote to his brother Joseph,—" I was this day called to the Bar—very unequal to the task, and against my own opinion. However, I determined to submit, and there is an end."
[2] Yet it appears that Lord Camden suspected that Lord Hardwicke withheld silk gowns for the advantage of his son Charles, and slighted the young gentleman's competitors.—Ante, p. 297.

The spirit of Jacobitism had become very strong; there were general discontents in the public mind, and an invasion from France, to assist the Pretender, was daily expected. Lord Hardwicke, the Chancellor, thought it was necessary to render the laws against treason more stringent, by making it treason to correspond with the sons of the Pretender, and by continuing forfeiture and corruption of blood in cases of treason; so that all the honors and all the property of any one convicted of treason should for ever be lost to his children and his family. Against this last enactment there was a strong feeling, which the Chancellor's precocious son undertook to combat;—not from an ungenerous nature, but from a desire to stand by his father, whose opinions he was bound to reverence. Accordingly, during the fervor of men's minds upon the subject, he brought out anonymously, but allowing himself to be soon discovered as the author, "Some Considerations on the Laws of Forfeiture for High Treason."

Of all the departments of literature, jurisprudence is the one in which the English had least excelled. Their treatises of highest authority were a mere jumble—without regard to arrangement or diction. Now, for the first time, appeared among us a writer who rivaled the best productions of the French and German jurists. He was not only an admirer, but a correspondent, of Montesquieu; and he had caught a great share of the President's precision, and of his animation. In this treatise, he logically lays down his positions, and enforces them in a train of close reasoning,—without pedantic divisions, observing lucid order,—and drawing from the history and legislation of other countries the most apposite illustrations of his arguments. The following may be considered a fair specimen of the work; although, without a perusal of the whole of it, an adequate idea can not be entertained of the excellence of the plan on which he proceeds, or of the felicity with which that plan is executed:—

"It is not the purpose of this essay to attempt a justification of any instance in which the law of forfeiture may, in some countries, have been carried to an extremity, as little to be reconciled with principles of policy as of clemency or justice. Among the Persians and Macedonians, not only the criminals convicted of treason were put to death,

but all their relations and friends. The descendants of
Antiphon, the orator, were disqualified from advancing
themselves, by their own merit, to estates and offices in
Athens. The posterity of Marius's faction were excluded
by a law of Sylla from the same privileges When these
are laid out of the case, what is the force of the answer?
It clearly resolves into this,—that those rights, and the
power of transmitting property, which are derived from
the favor of society, may not be bestowed upon such
terms as shall bind the possessor to his duty, and for the
breach be subjected to forfeiture. As to the corruption
of blood, it may suffice to say thus much of it here: that
if a man is not capable of transmitting property acquired
by himself to an heir, it seems a necessary consequence in
reason, which is the ground of law, that he shall not be
capable of receiving from an ancestor either to enjoy or
to transmit; for, however society may effectuate any
man's compassionate intention who would make a gift to
the traitor's posterity, yet the law, which is consistent
upon every occasion, and only to be moved by considerations that affect the whole, will not make an effort of itself to supply that connecting link in the chain of descent
which has been struck out of it for the traitor's infamy
and the public benefit. Thus society, by making the loss
of those rights it confers upon every man a penalty for
the greatest crime which can be committed against his
country, interests every relation and dependant in keeping him firm to the general tranquillity and welfare; at
the same time, it gives him an occasion of reflecting that
when he sets about it he must break through every private as well as public tie, which enhances his crime, while
it is an aggravation of his punishment. Nay, more, he
may hope to escape from the justice of his country with
his own life if that alone were to be forfeited; but the
distress of his family will pursue him in his securest
thoughts, and abate the ardor of revolution. Many instances there are of men not ashamed to commit base and
selfish enormities, who have retained a tenderness for
their posterity by the strong and generous instinct of
nature. The story of Licinius Macer, who was father to
the great orator, is very remarkable, as related by a
Roman annalist. Having gone through the office of
Prætor, and governed a province, he was accused, upon

returning home, of extortion and abuses of his power. The very morning of his trial he strangled himself, after having sent word to Cicero, who was preparing to plead against him, that being determined to put an end to his life before sentence, the prosecution should not go on, and his property would be saved to the benefit of his son. Upon the whole, then, where is the wrong? It is agreeable to justice to bestow rights upon condition. It is the wisdom of governments to lay hold on human partialities."—He tries to soften the law's harshness, with which, notwithstanding his assumed boldness, he is evidently a little shocked, by observing how rarely it would be brought into practice; that it would be "like Goliath's sword in the Temple, not to be taken down but on occasions of high necessity—at other times, *in tabulis tanquam in vaginâ reconditum.*"

At the present day, while all must be charmed with his learning, his ingenuity, and his eloquence, I do not think that his reasoning will carry general conviction. He greatly exaggerates the moral guilt of the treason against which the law was to be directed—that of trying, from mistaken principle, to restore the exiled royal family,—which he confounds with the treason inveighed against by the Roman writers—that of conspiring to subvert public liberty for individual aggrandizement;—he utterly fails in his attempt to prove that the children are not punished for their father's crime, by being made infamous and cast destitute on the world;—and though a regard for the public tranquillity may require that a man shall try to bring about a revolution, whatever may be the established government, at the risk of his own life, no reasoning can persuade us that it is just or politic to involve his posterity in his ruin.

However, Charles Yorke's performance was rapturously applauded; his father, in defending the bill in the House of Lords, made an excellent speech, all the topics of which were known to be taken from it[2]—and the solicitors

---

[1] See 17 Geo. 2, c. 39.
[2] At first it was attributed to Warburton, Sherlock, and other eminent writers. The author thus cautioned Warburton: "I continue absolutely convinced of the importance of secrecy, and if any inquiry should be made, that even a false scent should be encouraged." But when it was much applauded, the Chancellor wrote to a friend: "The secret of Charley's book is

had no longer any scruple in giving briefs to the Chancellor's son, who had shown such acquaintance with his profession, as well as such general ability. He was now in full practice at the bar, and considered likely to outstrip his father in rapid promotion; but in such matters there is much of chance and accident, and Sir Dudley Ryder remaining Attorney-General, and Murray Solicitor, years rolled on without a vacancy.

Meanwhile, he was nearly snatched away by a violent illness, from which his recovery was almost miraculous. Giving an account of his health to his brother, the Colonel, who was then serving abroad, he says,—" It pleased the providence of God to turn the crisis of my disorder in such a manner as to preserve my life; yet if I am not mistaken, should it ever be my lot to die of a fever, I have nothing more to feel than what I did, except it be the stroke of instant death itself." [1]

CHAPTER CL.

CONTINUAION OF THE LIFE OF LORD CHANCELLOR CHARLES YORKE TILL HE WAS APPOINTED SOLICITOR GENERAL.

CHARLES YORKE commenced his senatorial career in the autumn of 1747, and continued a member of the House of Commons till within a few hours of his death. He first represented the snug borough of Reigate, which had passed under the grant by King William to his grand-uncle, Lord Chancellor Somers, and now belonged to his cousins, the Cockses. He succeeded his elder brother, who was elected for the county of Cambridge.

On this occasion there was addressed to him, by Mr. Edwards, the following

SONNET.

"Charles, whom thy country's voice applauding calls
  To Philip's honorable vacant seat,
  With modest pride the glorious summons wait,

---

out, and everybody talks of it as his—much to his commendation—as indeed it deserves."—*Aug. 1745.* [1] July, 1747.

> And rise to fame within St. Stephen's walls.
> Now wear the honors which thy youth befalls
>   Thus early claim'd from thy lov'd learned retreat;
>   To guard those sacred rights which elevate
> Britain's free sons above her neighbor thralls.
> Let Britain, let admiring Europe see
>   In those bright parts which erst too long confin'd
>   Shone in the circle of thy friends alone,
> How sharp the spur of worthy ancestry
>   When kindred virtues fan the generous mind
> Of Somers' nephew and of Hardwicke's son." [1]

From the scanty accounts handed down to us of parliamentary proceedings in the middle of the eighteenth century, it is very difficult to discover what was his success in debate. Although he sat in parliament twenty-three years—in the "Parliamentary History" his name is only mentioned five times.[2] We know, from contemporary writers, that he was a smart orator, and had a considerable position in the House; but it is pretty clear that he did not support the reputation he had acquired at the bar and by his pen; and that he remained at a vast distance behind the "silver-tongued Murray," whom he strove to emulate.

His maiden speech was upon a law bill; and all that we know of it is from a letter of Dr. Birch to the Hon. Philip Yorke, containing this statement as part of the news of the day: "Your brother, Charles, opened his mouth on Monday, in the House of Commons, with some success, upon the Bill for the Relief of Protestant Purchasers' Trustees, &c., of Papists' Effects; against which he urged such a weight of objections, that the patrons of it, Lord Gage and Mr. Fazakerley, abandoned it without any reply; and the committing of it was postponed."[3]

At the meeting of parliament, in November, 1748, he was selected to second the address moved by Lord Barrington,—the following short sentence being the whole record of his performance: "The Honorable Charles Yorke, second son of Lord Chancellor Hardwicke, rose and seconded, in a very able speech, the motion of the noble Lord."[4] However, in a letter from Mr. Etough to Dr. Birch, preserved in the British Museum, we have this testimony in its favor: "The figure Charles Yorke made

---

[1] Cooksey, 163.
[2] 14 Parl. Hist. 267, 325, 1008, 1275; 15 Parl. Hist. 270.
[3] Hardwicke Papers; 14 Parl. Hist. 266. [4] 14 Parl. Hist. 325.

the first day of the session is an agreeable piece of news. Nothing can be more pleasing than such accounts of young men, who have the additional character of probity and virtue."[1]

In 1751, he took a leading part in defending the Regency Bill, introduced on the death of Frederick, Prince of Wales, whereby the Princess Dowager was to be appointed Regent during the minority of her son, afterwards George III.; but (to gratify the King's dislike of her, and his partiality for his younger son) she was to be under the control of a council of Regency, with the Duke of Cumberland at the head of it. In answer to a speech of Mr. Prowse, violently attacking the measure as unconstitutional, thus spoke Charles Yorke :—

"Sir, as the bill now under consideration is designed to be, and certainly will be, a precedent for all future ages, I hope that honorable members, who speak for it, or against it, will leave the person thereby to be appointed Regent entirely out of the question. If the present conjuncture were only to be considered, I believe that, looking to the character and disposition of the amiable Princess named, no gentleman would think of laying her under any restraints or regulations; no one would hesitate a moment in agreeing to invest her, not only with sovereign, but with absolute sway; because it would only be extending the power to do good. But when we are framing institutions for the government of society, we must not consider persons, but things. For this reason our ancestors have chosen, and have handed down to us, a limited[1] rather than an absolute monarchy. They knew, as well as we, that a wise, active, and just king might be trusted with absolute power; that the more absolute he was, the better it would be for society; but they considered how difficult, if not impossible, it was to refuse to a bad king the authority that had been given to a good one. For the same reason a regency during the minority or incapacity of a king has always, by our constitution, been laid under still greater restraints and limitations. I care not for the theory of the constitution, so much dwelt upon by the honorable gentleman who spoke last. From histories, records, and precedents alone can we know what the constitution really is in practice,

[1] MSS. 4326 B.

and I defy any one to show that a regent or protector has ever been intrusted with a full and absolute sovereign power—I mean, as full and absolute a power as our kings have usually been intrusted with. The Duke of Gloucester, indeed, on the death of Edward IV., usurped a sole regency with absolute power; but no man will contend that his power was legal or constitutional; and the use he made of it can never, I am sure, be any encouragement for the Parliament to follow that precedent. Even the good Earl of Pembroke, in the miniority of Henry III., when appointed Regent, was restrained from making grant under the Great Seal; and his successful governments was owing to his own wisdom, not the unlimited power conferred upon him. The honorable gentleman admits, that when the King's person or his right to the Crown may be in danger, the power of the Regent ought to be restrained by a council of regency, But is it not obvious, that this argument can be least used where it is most wanted? When the Duke of Lancaster was appointed Regent, in the minority of Richard II., was it urged that his ambition might prompt him to murder the infant King, and to usurp the Crown? No, Sir; the argument made use of on that occasion was, that the constitution forbade the appointment of a regent with sovereign power, though, in charity, supposed to be a good regent,—for the same reason that we limit the authority of a supposed good king. So a council of regency was created in the infancy of Henry VI., when the Duke of Bedford was appointed Regent, and in his absence the Duke of Gloucester. If the Lords who appointed another Duke of Gloucester Protector, with sovereign power, in the minority of Edward V., had not been guided more by resentment against the Queen-mother and her relations than the rules of our constitution, the Plantagenet line might still have been upon the throne. There is here no slight intended to the Princess. In the three minorities to which I have referred, the mother of the infant sovereign was entirely passed over in the appointment of a regent;—and a striking proof is given of his Majesty's sense of the known virtues of the Princess by proposing her as Regent. If she is to be laid under restraints, this does not proceed from any jealousies we can entertain of her character. These restraints are only such as every wise king would choose to lay upon himself. Would any wise king choose to make peace or war, to prorogue or dissolve parliaments, or to remove any great officer of state, or appoint bishops or judges, without consulting men who have worthily served their country, and who are the most capable of giving good advice to the Crown? As to the council of regency, their power is merely restrictive; they have no active power; they can not so much as meet except when called by the Regent, and when they do meet they can take nothing under consideration but what her Royal Highness may recommend to them; they can act in nothing; their resolutions will signify nothing without her concurrence; and if they should refuse to consent to any act necessary for the good of the kingdom, they are removable on the joint address of the two Houses of Parliament. This formidable council of regency will, therefore, rather be a security to the Regent than an obstruction to any of her measures; for, though by our state maxim 'the King can do no wrong,' I doubt whether that maxim can be applied to one who is appointed to govern, as Regent, in the King's name; and therefore it may much import the Princess, when Regent, that she should be able to make it appear, by an authentic document, that what she does has been thought by responsible advisers to be the most proper and necessary measure for the public good. I would willingly invest her Royal Highness with the full exercise of all the prerogatives of the Crown, if this course were not absolutely inconsistent with our constitution, and if there were not an apprehension that the precedent, on some future occasion, might be attended with the most fatal consequences. This alone makes me do violence to my own inclination, and compels me to banish from my thoughts the personal qualities of the illustrious lady now to be appointed Regent. If others would consider the Regent as a constitutional abstraction, I am fully persuaded that there would be a general unanimity as to the appointment and powers of the council, and no one would propose a course which would be quite novel in our history, and the remote consequences of which might bring upon the authors of it the curses of posterity."[1]

[1] 14 Parl. Hist. 1008.

Horace Walpole, in an account of this debate sent to his correspondent at Florence, says, " Lord Strange and Sir Roger Newdigate both spoke against the bill; and Charles Yorke, a young lawyer of good parts, *but precise and affected*, for it."[1] I must own that there is a good deal of flippancy as well as sophistry in this smart harangue, and that the orator is rather gently handled by the critic. Murray followed in a more statesmanlike strain,—and, upon a division, the "council clause" was carried by a considerable majority.

Soon after, Charles Yorke received his first professional advancement in being appointed counsel to the East India Company, when he must have felt infinitely more delight than on afterwards receiving the Great Seal.[2]

The next occasion on which we can trace him in the House of Commons was the first day of the session of 1753, when he moved the address. We, accustomed to see some tender scion of nobility brought forward for such a task, are surprised to find it assigned to a practicing lawyer who had been several years in parliament. He seems to have been a good deal laughed at for proposing "to acknowledge his Majesty's *wisdom*, as well as goodness, in pursuing measures calculated to preserve the general tranquillity of Europe." The Earl of Egremont moved that the words "wisdom as well as" be left out, and other members violently censured the measures which were supposed to show such " wisdom as well as " goodness; but the amendment was negatived, and the address carried, without a division.[3]

In the same session, Charles Yorke restored and extended his reputation by a spirited defense of his father, when attacked for bringing forward the famous " Marriage Act." Henry Fox, its great opponent, having dilated very offensively on " the chicanery and jargon of the lawyers, and the pride of their Mufti," went on to apply to the Chancellor the story of a gentlewoman at Salisbury, who, having a sore leg, sent for a country surgeon, who pronounced that it must be cut off; " the gentlewoman, unwilling to submit to the operation, sent for another

[1] Letter to Sir H. Mann, May, 1751; Hor. Walp. Mem. Geo. II. p. 108.
[2] 28th July, 1751. His brother John, in a letter of this date says, "Charles has been this morning to visit the Directors—foes and friends. As a specimen of what is to follow, he is invited to meet them at Pontac's to-morrow to dine upon a turtle." [3] 14 Parl. Hist. 1275.

more merciful, who said he could save her leg, and that no operation was necessary; the surgeons conferred; the ignorant one said, 'I know it might be saved, but I have given my opinion, my character depends upon it, and we must carry it through;'—so the leg was cut off." Charles Yorke, rising in great anger, thus began: "It is new in parliament—it is new in politics—it is new in ambition." —He then proceeded to draw a lofty character of his father, and, describing in glowing terms the height to which he had raised himself by his merit, concluded by telling Fox how imprudent it was to attack a man so capable of vindicating himself and retaliating upon his accuser. Mr. Fox, in reply, tried to raise a laugh against him, by repeating and playing upon his words, "Is it new in parliament to be conscientious? I hope not. Is it new in politics? I am afraid it is. Is it new in ambition? It certainly is to attack such authority."[1] However, the House sympathized with the pious son, and these gibes were considered in bad taste. When the amended bill came back to be discussed in the Lords, the Chancellor introduced his famous attack upon Fox by a very touching allusion to the manner in which he had been defended elsewhere by one near and dear to him, and in which "the incendiary had been punished."[2]

This quarrel made so deep an impression on the mind of Fox, that though generally a good-natured man,— when he heard at Nice, many years after, of Charles Yorke's death, and the melancholy circumstances which attended it, he thus wrote to a correspondent with an affectation of querulousness, but with real malignity:— "I never envied Mr. Yorke while he lived, but I must take leave to envy him and everybody else when they are dead: I comfort by persuading myself it is happier to wish for death than to dread it, and I believe every one of my age does one or the other. But I do not find myself near a natural death, nor will you see me hanged, though

---

[1] Fox was luckier in an encounter with another lawyer in the same debate. He held in his hand a copy of the bill, in which were written in red ink the amendments moved by some members who pretended to be its friends. The Solicitor General, standing near him while speaking, said, "How bloody it looks!" Fox answered, "Yes; but thou canst not say I did it:
'See what a rent the learned Casca made,
Through this the well-beloved Brutus stabb'd.'"
[2] 15 Parl. Hist. 84; Hor. Walp. Geo. II. 299.

I verily think they will never leave off abusing me." And writing soon after to George Selwyn, who delighted in looking at old friends when laid out for burial, he says, with savage jocularity, "Yorke was very ugly while he lived—how did he look when he was dead?"[1]

The last important speech of Charles Yorke was delivered in the year 1754, upon the subject of extending the "Mutiny Act" to the East Indies, when all the old arguments being brought forward about standing armies and martial law, he ably showed the necessity of keeping up a military force in those remote regions, and the impossibility of doing so unless soldiers might be tried by a military tribunal for an infraction of the Articles of War.[2] Although no other fragments of his eloquence are to be found in the regular records of the proceedings of Parliament, we know from contemporary memoirs that he continued to speak, and to be respectfully listened to, in the House of Commons, on every constitutional question which arose till near the close of his career.

Meanwhile, amidst all the distractions of business, and the anxieties of ambition, he preserved his better tastes, and he was glad to escape from the wrangling of lawyers, and the slang of the House of Commons, to criticism and philosophy. He still kept up a close intercourse, by visits and letters, with Warburton. On one occasion, having been disappointed in the hope of finding him at Prior Park, he thus shows the impression made upon him by this picturesque place, where the "humble Allen" had entertained POPE:—"The natural beauties of wood, water, prospect, hill and vale, wildness and cultivation, make it one of the most delightful spots I ever saw, without adding anything from art. The elegance and judgment with which art has been employed, and the affectation of false grandeur carefully avoided, make one wonder how it could be so busy there without spoiling anything received from nature." After controverting an emendation by Warburton of the text of *"Measure for Measure,"*[3] he pro-

---

[1] Hor. Walp. Lett. iv.   [2] 15 Parl. Hist.
[3] The Duke in the character of a friar, says to Claudio, in order to prepare him for death, and dissuade him from a reliance on his sister's intercession with Angelo,—
 "Do not *satisfy* your resolution with hopes that are fallible."
The divine proposes to read "falsify;" but the lawyer shows that "satisfy," in the sense of *discharge*, is the true reading.

ceeds to give him some excellent and much-needed advice,—to be less acrimonious in his controversies with brother authors.

"It is to be expected, where any writer has the marks of an original, and thinks for himself, producing *de suo penu* things wholly new to most understandings, that some will have their difficulties to propose; others their tenets to maintain; and few will give a ready assent to truths which contradict prevailing notions, till time and posterity have wrought a gradual change in the general state of learning and opinions. What wonder, then, that many should write against you? How natural that you should defend! It was expected from you. The zeal for knowledge is commendable: the deference to mankind becomes you. But here lies the mischief. You and your adversaries stand upon unequal ground. They engage with that best friend and second on their side—vulgar prejudice. Let their insinuations be ever so malignant, provided they write *dully* they gain the character of writing *coolly!* How natural that you should expostulate! If your expostulations have been sometimes too warm, they were not the bitter overflowings of an ill-natured mind, but the unguarded sallies of a generous one. Yet even such sallies are not forgiven you: not because those you answer have deserved better, but because sensible and candid men are disposed to think too well and too highly of you to forgive that in you which they would overlook in others. And therefore could nobody permit you to reverence yourself as much as I do, you would wait with patience that period when '*Answers*' will be forgotten; unless, (according to the epigram of Martial) you choose to give flies a value and an immortality by entombing them in amber. It is to flatter me exceedingly to intimate that I have contributed to lead you into those sentiments in which the very tædium of controversy, and the pursuit of noble designs, must necessarily confirm you."[1]

Subsequently, when he had acquired high reputation in public life and the most brilliant prospects were before him, thus he addresses the great scholar and divine:—"I endeavored to convince myself it is dangerous to converse with you, for you show me so much more happiness in the quiet pursuits of knowledge and enjoyments of

[1] Warburton's Correspondence, 498

friendship than is to be found in lucre or ambition, that I go back into the world with regret, where few things are to be attained without more agitation, both of reason and the passions, than either moderate parts or a benevolent mind can support." [1]

He proved the sincerity of his friendship for Warburton, by obtaining for him the "preachership" of Lincoln's Inn, which was in this instance, and so often has been, the stepping-stone to a bishopric; and by prevailing upon his father, who had ceased to have much respect for literature, to give him a prebendal stall. Thus writes the prebendary-elect to his crony Hurd:—"Last Sunday the Chancellor sent me a message with the offer of a prebend of Gloucester, as a mark of his regard, and wishes it had been better. I desired Mr. Charles Yorke to tell him that no favors from such a hand could be unacceptable. Yorke of his own mere notion told me he intended to write to the Master of the Rolls to recommend you in case of a vacancy. He does not know the force of his interest, but he shall push it in the warmest manner." Hurd was disappointed at the Rolls, but by the interest of Charles Yorke, who adopted him into his friendship, and prized him more highly than posterity has done, he succeeded Warburton in the preachership of Lincoln's Inn, which in his case likewise led to a mitre. Upon this occasion he wrote to Warburton, saying,—"It will be an election unanimous; but as little attentions please, I shall endeavor to prevail upon him, when I have the pleasure of seeing him, to *mount timber* on Sunday as a compliment to the benchers." [2] Warburton thereupon warily suggested to Hurd,—"Mr. Yorke may be right in your not being too punctilious about sermons at first. But take care not to accustom them to works of supererogation, for, as puritanical as they are, they have a great hankering after that Popish doctrine."

Charles Yorke likewise kept up a constant correspondence with the President Montesquieu. Having expressed to him a wish to renounce public life for literary leisure, he received the following answer:—

" Une noble ambition convient aux jeunes gens, le repos

---

[1] Warburton's Correspondence, 505.
[2] This was in vacation time, and it is the duty of the preacher of Lincoln's Inn to officiate only during the terms.

à un âge plus avancé ; c'est la consolation de la perte des agrémens et des plaisirs. Ne négligez pas des talents qui vous sont venus avant l'âge, et qui ne doivent point etre contraires à votre santé, quoiqu'ils sont votre nature meme. Vous vous souvenez des belles choses que dit Cicéron, dans son Livre des Offices, contre les philosophes, et combien il les met au dessous de la vie active des citoyens et de ceux qui gouvernent la république ; et on ne peut pas le soupçonner d'avoir eu de l'envie contre ceux qui s'attachoient à la philosophie ; puis qu'il étoit lui-meme un si grand philosophie ; le meme, dans un autre endroit, appelle Archiméde un petit homme ; et Platon n'alla en Sicile que pour faire voir à l'univers qu'il étoit non seulement capable de donner des loix à une république, mais de la gouverner. Continuez donc une profession que vous faites avec tant de gloire ; continuez une profession qui fait qu'en vous regardant on se souvient toujours de votre illustre père ; continuez une profession qui fait voir que dans un âge trés-tendre vous avez pu porter le poids de la réputation sans vous courber."

The President afterwards sent him a copy of his works, with this polite epistle :—

"Monsieur, man très-cher et très-illustre Ami,

"J'ai un paquet de mes ouvrages, bons ou mauvais, à vous envoyer ; j'en serai peut-etre le porteur ; il pourra arriver que j'aurai le plaisir de vous embrasser tout à mon aise. Je remets à ce tems à vous dire tout ce que je vous écrivois. Mes sentimens pour vous sont gravés dans mon cœur, et dans mon esprit, d'une manière à ne s'effacer jamais. Quand vous verrez Monsieur le Docteur Warburton, je vous prie de lui dire l'idée agréable que je me fais de faire plus ample connoissance avec lui ; d'aller trouver la source du sçavoir, et de voir la lumière de l'esprit. Son ouvrage sur Julien m'a enchanté, quoique je n'ai que de très-mauvais lecteurs Anglois, et que j'ai presque oublié tout ce que j'en sçavois. Je vous embrasse, Monsieur. Conservez-moy votre amitié ; la mienne est éternelle.

"MONTESQUIEU.

"à Paris, ce 6 Juin, 1753."[1]

[1] In sending a copy of this letter to Warburton, Yorke observes,—" His heart is as good as his understanding in all he says or writes ; though he mixes now and then a little of the French *clinquant* with all his brightness and solidity of genius, as well as originality of expression."—*Corresp.* p. 507.

In the autumn of the same year, Charles Yorke left England with the intention of visiting the President at his château in Gascony, and accompanying him to Bordeaux, that he might see how justice was administered in the parliament there; but he was recalled home before this object could be accomplished. The President thus expressed his disappointment:" J'aurois été bien heureux de passer quelque tems avec vous à Labrede; vous m'aurez appris à raissonner, et moy je vous aurois appris à faire du vin et à planter des chenes, sous lesquels quelque druide se mettra quelque jour; mais quand je serois aussi jeune que vous, je ne verrois point cela." He then goes on to talk of their common friend "Monsieur le Docteu *Walburthon*"—to whom he promises a copy of the *Esprit de Lois*, and a cask of wine, in return for his new edition of Pope.

I ought not to pass over a misfortune which had befallen him, the severity of which I can the better appreciate from having been visited by a similar one myself.[1] In the night of the 5th of July, 1752, a fire sudenly burst out from his staircase in Stone Buildings, Lincoln's Inn. He narrowly escaped with his life, but he suffered an irreparable loss, in which the whole nation participated—the invaluable State Papers, in thirty volumes folio, collected by his grand-uncle, Lord Somers, and made over to him, having been all reduced to ashes. Warburton says: "They were full of very material things for the history of those times, which I speak upon my own knowledge."[2] Perhaps posterity had a heavier loss in the destruction of Charles Yorke's own MSS.; for although he was too modest to talk much of them, it was gener-

---

[1] When I was Attorney General, my chambers in Paper Buildings, Temple, were burnt to the ground by fire in the night time, and all my law books and MSS., with some valuable official papers, were consumed. Above all, I had to lament a collection of letters written to me by my dear father, in a continued series, from the time of my going to College till his death in 1824. All lamented this calamity except the claimant of a peerage, some of whose documents (suspected to be forged) he hoped were destroyed; but, fortunately, they had been removed into safe custody a few days before, and the claim was dropped.

[2] Lord Hardwicke, in a letter written next day, says, "My son Charles was forced to run down stairs in danger of suffocation, with nothing on but his shirt and breeches, and in that condition took shelter in his friend Mr. Clarke's chambers on the other side of the square. He lost every thing, and came home to me almost as naked as he came into the world. But what affects him most is the loss of his library and all his MSS. and papers."

ally believed that he had prepared for the press several law treatises, which would have rivaled the fame of the "Considerations on Forfeiture for Treason;" and Cowper's verses, on a like misfortune which befell Lord Mansfield, might have been addressed to him:

> "And Murray sighs o'er Pope and Swift,
> And many a treasure more,
> The well-judged purchase and the gift
> That grac'd the letter'd store.
>
> "Their pages mangled, burnt, and torn,
> The loss was his alone;
> But AGES YET TO COME SHALL MOURN
> THE BURNING OF HIS OWN."

He soon got a new set of chambers, and furnished his shelves with new copies of such books as could be obtained from the booksellers; but—even in consulting reports and law treatises—for years there was almost daily something annoyingly reminding him of those he had lost,—which were made valuable to him by notes and scratches, and with every page of which he had formed an endearing familiarity.

For this, or some better reason, he became tired of a bachelor's life, and, being now in his thirty-third year, he resolved to enter the holy state of wedlock. The object of his choice was Catherine, only child and heiress of William Freeman, Esq., of Aspeden, Herts, a granddaughter of Sir Thomas Pope, Bart., of Tittenhanger. To her he was united on the 19th of May, 1755,[1] and with her he lived most happily till, after bringing him three children, she was snatched away to an early grave.

Though still what we in our time should consider quite a youth at the bar, who ought to be pleased with the prospect of gradually getting into a little business, he compared his father's progress with his own, and he was exceedingly dissatisfied to think that he was not yet made a judge, or a law officer of the Crown. So far back

---

[1] On this occasion, his brother, Colonel Yorke, wrote to their sister, Lady Anson,—" I rejoice that Charles is going to be married at last. If I had governed him for some years since, he should have been married sooner and been less in love. I hope his contingencies will not fall in soon, for I shall be sadly disappointed if he does not rise to where I intend he shall be: and I am afraid, if he is too much at his ease, that his ambition will cease to operate." He received a letter of felicitation from Mr. Pitt, with this wish,— "May you find matrimony just what I have found it, the source of every comfort and of every joy."

as 1747, he had had a feather put into his cap by being made Solicitor General to the Prince of Wales. But his only other Government preferment hitherto had been the grant of Clerk of the Crown to him jointly with his brother John Yorke, the grasping Chancellor being desirous to keep this good thing in the family as long as possible. Disappointed at not sooner obtaining the real honors of the profession, Charles now talked of leaving it altogether, and taking entirely to the political line, in which he flattered himself he might rise to be Prime Minister. It appears that he had infused his discontented notions into his friends. Warburton writes to Hurd, "Yorke, who has spent the holidays with me, has just now left me to return to the bar, whose nature, virtue, and superior science in any age but this would have conducted their favorite pupil to the bench."[1]

At last an opening appeared to have arisen. On the 25th of May, 1756, died Sir Dudley Ryder, Chief Justice of the King's Bench, the day before he was to have kissed hands on being raised to the peerage, and it was expected that this would make an immediate move in the law. But the assistance of Murray, the Attorney General, was so essentially necessary to the Duke of Newcastle's government in the House of Commons, that, although he demanded the Chief Justiceship as of right, the office was kept vacant six months, in the hopes of bribing him to forego his claim. In the mean while the Chancellor being supposed to have all the law appointments at his disposal, his son earnestly pressed that now some arrangement might be made whereby he might be promoted. On the 2nd of June, 1756, thus wrote Mr. Potter, the son of the Archbishop, to Mr. Pitt :—

"Charles Yorke, who has long had a wish to quit the profession, has taken advantage of this opportunity, and has sternly insisted with his father, that, unless he makes him Solicitor General now, he will immediately pull off his gown. The Chancellor yields, and has promised either to make him Solicitor, or to consent that he shall quit the profession and be a Lord of the Admiralty. I think I know which side of the alternative the Chancellor will take. On Murray's leaving the bar, and Charles Yorke becoming Solicitor General, he would get at least £4,000

[1] Warb. Corresp.

per annum. The Chancellor will compute now much that exceeds the salary of a Lord of the Admiralty, and the vices of the family will probably operate, so as to keep poor Charles in the only train in which he can be of any consequence."¹

Murray having at length obtained the Chief Justiceship by the threat of withdrawing from public life, the administration was subverted, and Lord Hardwicke resigned the Great Seal. But he contrived that the desired promotion should be bestowed upon his son, who, on the 6th of November, 1756, was sworn in Solicitor General.²

CHAPTER CLI.

CONCLUSION OF THE LIFE OF LORD CHANCELLOR CHARLES YORKE.

THE first public duty cast upon Charles Yorke, after his promotion, was to make a complimentary speech on the elevation of a rival. Murray, the Chief Justice elect, was to take leave of the Society of Lincoln's Inn previous to going through the preliminary form of being made a Sergeant at Law, that he might thereby be qualified to become a Judge. Mr. Solicitor, being then the Treasurer or head of the Inn, according to ancient usage presented the departing member with a purse of gold as a retaining fee, and addressed him in a flowing oration, extolling his eloquence, his learning, and his qualifications for the high judicial office which he was about to fill. The very words of the answer are preserved, from which we may judge of the talent and the courtesy exhibited on both sides:—

¹ Chatham Correspondence, i. 160.
² The retiring Chancellor represented it as the spontaneous act of the King. Writing to a friend, he says, "Your congratulations on my son's promotion to the office of Solicitor General are extremely obliging, not only to me but to him. The King, my gracious master, who accepted my resignation with those demonstrations of goodness which related by me might have the appearance of vanity, was pleased to do it as a mark of his approbation of my long and faithful, though unmeriting service. I had made it my firm resolution neither to ask nor accept any pecuniary or lucrative advantage—but of this favor I own I am proud."

"I am too sensible, Sir, of my being undeserving of the praises which you have so elegantly bestowed upon me, to suffer commendations so delicate as yours to insinuate themselves into my mind; but I have pleasure in that kind partiality which is the occasion of them. To deserve such praises is a worthy object of ambition; and from such a tongue, flattery itself is pleasing. If I have had in any measure success in my profession, it is owing to the great man who has presided in our highest Court of judicature the whole time I attended the bar. It was impossible daily to come into his presence without catching some beams from his light. The disciples of Socrates, whom I will take the liberty to call the great lawyer of antiquity, since the first principles of law are derived from his philosophy, owe their reputation to their having been the reporters of the sayings of their master. If we can arrogate nothing to ourselves, we may boast the school we were brought up in; the scholar may glory in his master, and we may challenge past ages to show us his equal. My Lord Bacon had the same extent of thought, and the same strength of language and expression, but his life had a stain. My Lord Clarendon had the same abilities, and the same zeal for the constitution of his country; but the civil war prevented his laying deep the foundations of law, and the avocations of politics interrupted the business of the Chancellor. My Lord Somers came the nearest to his character; but his time was short, and envy and faction sullied the luster of his glory. It is the peculiar felicity of the great man I am speaking of, to have presided near twenty years and to have shone with a splendor that has risen superior to faction, and that has subdued envy. I did not intend to have said so much upon this occasion; but with all that hear me, what I say must carry the weight of testimony rather than appear the voice of panegyric. For you, Sir, you have given great pledges to your country, and large are the expectations of the public concerning you. I dare to say you will answer them."

For us Lincoln's-Inn men, this was, indeed, a proud day. The greatest of Common-Law Judges, on his own inauguration, spoke so eloquently of the greatest of Equity Judges now in retirement, after a judicial career of unequaled length and brilliancy,—and held out seemingly well-founded anticipations that the son who was addressed would rival his father's glory. All three were members of Lincoln's Inn, and the scene was acted in Lincoln's Inn Hall, amidst a crowd of barristers and students, many of whom, if fortune had been propitious to a display of their talents, would have been hardly less distinguished.

In the following year, the Solicitor General expected further promotion, but was doomed to a severe disappointment. After some months of anarchy which followed the resignation of the Duke of Newcastle and Lord Hardwicke, during which the Great Seal was in commission, and there was a perpetual shifting of the principal offices of state, the Court was obliged to surrender at discretion to Mr. Pitt, who then formed his famous Administration. He bore no good-will to the House of Yorke, and, although he would not dismiss Charles from the office held by him, he insisted on making his old schoolfellow, Pratt, Attorney General. This was most highly distasteful to Mr. Solicitor; but after consulting his father and his friends, he consented to swallow the bitter pill presented to him. Pratt was his senior at the bar, and had now risen into high reputation, so that it was no degradation to serve under him. They acted with apparent cordiality, though it was said that Yorke never forgot the affront, and was actuated by the recollection of it in his intrigue against Lord Camden, when he was himself to have become Chancellor under Charles Townshend, and in the negotiation which closed his own career, when, in an evil hour he actually received the Great Seal, that Lord Camden might be cashiered.

Opposition being now annihilated, the Attorney and Solicitor General had very light work in the House of Commons, and their official duty chiefly consisted in advising the Government (which they did most admirably) upon numerous questions of international law, arising during the prosecution of the war.

The first great occasion when they appeared together in public was on the trial of Dr. Hensey, at the King's Bench bar, for high treason, in carrying on a correspondence with the French, and inviting them to invade the realm. It was the part of the Solicitor General to sum up the evidence for the Crown, but he declined to do so, reserving himself for the general reply on the whole case, —a course which Lord Mansfield and the whole Court held he was entitled to pursue. His reply was distinguished by extreme moderation and mildness of tone, as well as perspicuity and force of reasoning. The prisoner was convicted,—but, on account of extenuating circumstances, he was afterwards pardoned.[1]

The only other state prosecution in which Pratt and Charles Yorke were jointly engaged was that of Lord Ferrers, before the House of Peers, for the murder of his steward, of which I have given an account in the Life of Lord Northington, who then presided as Lord High Steward.[2] The Solicitor General's reply on this occasion is one of the finest forensic displays in our language, containing, along with touching eloquence, fine philosophical reasoning on mental disease and moral responsibility.

"In some sense," said he, "every violation of duty proceeds from insanity. All cruelty, all brutality, all revenge, all injustice, is insanity. There were philosophers in ancient times who held this opinion as a strict maxim of their sect; and, my Lords, the opinion is right in philosophy, but dangerous in judicature. It may have a useful and a noble influence to regulate the conduct of men;— to control their impotent passions;—to teach them that virtue is the perfection of reason, as reason itself is the perfection of human nature;—but not to extenuate crimes, nor to excuse those punishments which the law adjudges to be their due."

Every Peer present said, "Guilty, upon my honor;" and when the unhappy culprit had expiated his offense at Tyburn, homage was done throughout the world to the pure and enlightened administration of criminal justice in England.

About this time Charles Yorke sustained a blow which long rendered tasteless all the applause with which his efforts were crowned. He lost the chosen partner of his fate, whose participation of his good fortune gave it all its value. When a little recovered, he described his anguish, and the sacred source of his consolation, in a letter to his friend Warburton, which has unfortunately

[1] 19 St. Tr. 1342–1382.   [2] Ib. 945; ante, p. 256.

perished. We may judge of its tone from the language of Warburton in transmitting it to Hurd:—

"This morning I received the inclosed. It will give you a true idea of Yorke's inestimable loss, and his excellent frame of mind. He has read, you will see, your Dialogues. And was he accustomed to speak what he does not think (which he is not), at this juncture he would tell his mind, when laboring with grief.

> 'Nam veræ voces tum demum pectore ab imo
> Ejiciuntur, et eripitur *Persona*, manet res.'" [1]

Upon the accession of George III., Charles Yorke was continued in his office of Solicitor General, and, from feeling rather a dislike to Mr. Pitt, he seems early to have attached himself to Lord Bute. He saw without regret the resignation of the "Great Commoner;"[2] and when Pratt was "shelved," as was supposed, in the Court of Common Pleas, the Attorney Generalship was joyfully conferred upon the Solicitor, who was expected unscrupulously to go all lengths against Wilkes.

He derived little satisfaction from this elevation. It was soon seen that Lord Bute's Administration could not stand, and he was involved in disagreeable intrigues for the recall of the Duke of Newcastle or Mr. Pitt to office. On one occasion, Lord Lyttleton came to him as the emissary of the Court to tempt him, by an offer of the Great Seal, to influence his father and his family to support the "favorite." In an account which he sent of this interview to his father, he says:—

"I added with respect to the *thing* itself, that if I could suppose the King would ever do me the honor hinted, I should not be afraid to accept it, though I should think it

---

[1] Warb. Corr. 292.

[2] Warburton, in a letter to Mr. Pitt, written soon after, tries to remove from his mind the impression made by some of Yorke's manifestations of satisfaction on this occasion:—

"Prior Park, October 17, 1761.

...."The Solicitor General has just now left this place after a visit to me of a few days. I should be unjust to him on this occasion to omit saying that to me he ever appeared to hold you in the highest honor, and your measures (as soon as ever the effects appeared) in the highest esteem. I ought in justice to add further, that he deceived me greatly if, at that very time when your just resentments were about breaking out against the Duke of Newcastle, he did not use his best endeavors, both with the Duke and his father to repair their treatment and to procure you satisfaction. But he had not then that influence with them which he has had since."—*Chat. Corresp.* ii. 161.

too early and in many respects not eligible at this time. I inquired how Lord Mansfield stood, and whether he might not be thought of? He answered that Lord M. would feel nothing personally as to me, because he would see that it was impossible for him to have the Great Seal *rebus sic stantibus.* Lord Lyttleton said that if such an offer came, I could not with honor refuse it; he thought Lord B.'s prudence, with absolute favor, might weather the conjuncture, and that the D. of N. ought to reflect he never could be a minister in *power* as he had been in the late reign; and that it would be, above all, absurd for him to make himself the instrument of Mr. Pitt's power, which would be the consequence of opposition." After enlarging on the difficulties of his situation, and his reluctance to be associated with the Duke of Newcastle, he thus concludes: "If it is a measure to resign, and I am to go *ad latus* of Mr. Pitt, I shall incline strongly to attend the bar no more, which I may *now* quit without loss of honor in the world, and might perhaps attend hereafter with some profit, but more vexation." Lord Hardwicke wrote in answer,—" There is no great ground at present for any public parliamentary opposition; the unpopularity of the *Scotchman* can not in form be taken up in parliament till it breaks out and is exemplified in material instances of conduct. From hence you may conclude it is scarce probable that you will be put under the difficulty you apprehend about *resignation*, and this brings me to the only point in which I differ from you. I mean your idea of quitting the bar in case you should think fit to quit your office, which last I do by no means foresee. But if it should so happen, my opinion upon consideration is, that it would be unadvisable in the highest degree for you to leave the bar. It will be giving up the most independent and I think the most advantageous profession in England without any occasion; for you would not find your prospects much lessened by the loss of your office; but you would find your own consideration and importance much diminished by the loss of your profession. My Lord Granville used to say, that the first man at the bar in opposition was equal to the first man upon the bench. I don't carry it so far; but I really think that the first man at the bar in *opposition* is, *cæteris paribus*, equal to the first man in the bar in *place.*"

Meanwhile, Mr. Pitt tried to gain him over by lures which are described in a letter of Lord Hardwicke:—

"As to Mr. Attorney General, he said he had the greatest esteem and friendship for him, which had increased as their acquaintance had proceeded, which was of long standing: that he had never done anything to forfeit his reciprocal friendship, however he had been misunderstood. He owned that he had a great regard for Lord C. J. Pratt, but never in prejudice to him, and wished Charles to live upon good terms and in confidence with his Lordship: that the only competition which could arise between them was in case of a change of the Great Seal, either by the disability of the present possessor or any other contingency: that he should give or avow his opinion to the King, and the public would be well served by either, but his original acquaintance was with Mr. Attorney, and it would be unbecoming in him, and he should be ashamed to attempt anything to his prejudice."[1]

But all the attempts which were made on the death of Lord Egremont to bring back the Whig ministers of George II. having failed, Charles Yorke thought that it was full time for him to resign.

He has been too severely blamed for his proceedings while first law officer of the Crown. He did file the criminal informations for "No. 45 of the North Briton," and for the "Essay on Woman;" but few will deny that the one publication was seditious, or that the other was obscene. He was not consulted by Lord Halifax about issuing "general warrants," and he might have been pardoned for saying that they were *primâ facie* legal, as they had been issued by all Secretaries of State since the Revolution, however inconsistent they might be with the principles of the constitution. Although he ought to have opposed the folly of burning libels by the common hangman, which led to such serious riots and mischief, it should be recollected that this was a practice then approved by grave statesmen. He was fully justified in proceeding to outlawry when the demagogue had fled from justice,—and no further step had been taken in the affair when he threw up his office of Attorney General.

[1] June, 1763

On his retirement, there seems to have been a general eagerness to do him honor. The Duke of Newcastle next day wrote to him, saying—" I must congratulate you upon the most honorable and most unusual mark of attention and respect which you received yesterday, both from the bar and from my Lord Chancellor." [1] He made way for Sir Fletcher Norton, who was appointed Attorney General on the formation of the Administration which was called the "Duke of Bedford's," but in which George Grenville, fatally for our colonial interests, soon gained the ascendency.

Freed from the trammels of office (as has often happened), Charles Yorke raised his reputation as a debater. Although his name is not afterwards once mentioned in the "Parliamentary History," we know from contemporary letters and incidental notices that he condemned the issuing of "general warrants," but that he strenuously contended that privilege of parliament does not extend to the case of seditious libel. On this last subject he gained the victory over Pratt, and rivaled Pitt himself, who was in the habit of exalting or disparaging the power of the House of Commons, as it suited his purpose. We have a lively sketch of the "Privilege Debate" from Horace Walpole:—

"Mr. Pitt, who had the gout, came on crutches, and wrapped in flannels, but was obliged to retire at ten at night, after making a speech of one hour and fifty minutes; the worst, I think, I ever heard him make in my life. For our parts, we sat till within ten minutes of two in the morning; yet we had but few speeches, all were so long. Charles Yorke shone exceedingly. He had spoken and voted with us the night before; but now maintained his opinion against Pratt. It was a most able and learned performance; and the latter part, which was oratoric, uncommonly beautiful and eloquent. You find I do not let a partiality to the Whig cause blind my judgment. That speech was certainly the masterpiece of the day. Norton would not have made a figure if Charles Yorke had not

---

[1] His fee-book shows that he had made the last year of his Attorney Generalship, £7,322 8s. 6d., but that his early receipts had not been by any means so great as might have been expected: 1st year, £121; 2nd, £201; 3rd and 4th, between £300 and £400 in each; 5th, £700; 6th, £800; 7th, £1,000; 9th, £1,600; 10th £2,500; in 1757, when Solicitor General, £3,400; 1758, £5,000.

appeared; but, giving way to his natural brutality, he got into an ugly scrape." [1]

In the course of these discussions, Dunning, who had a great spite against the Yorkes, made a violent attack both on the father and the son. "If I were," said he, "to characterize a late great Chancellor, I should say that I can not think he merited the appellation of a patriot, having ever regarded him as a decent, circumspect, prerogative lawyer; that he leaned, in his notions, too much towards aristocracy; that he seemed, in his politics, to approach much nearer to the principles of the Earl of Clarendon than of Lord Somers; and that, at last, upon what public principles I could never learn, he joined the Opposition, after having been in all things with the Court for forty years before. I could never determine whether he had, or had not, a good conception of our foreign interests, although I always imagined he had a thorough one of all the domestic connections among us. I might ask whether his Lordship did not uniformly, throughout his life, pursue his own private interest, and raise the greatest fortune, and provide the most amply for his family, of any lawyer who ever lived; and whether, during his administration, the judicial promotions were not disposed of upon ministerial motives, or agreeably to professional desert? I might, nevertheless, and ought to add, that the same illustrious personage was blessed with a good temper and great worldly prudence, which are the two handmaids-in-ordinary to prosperity; that his whole deportment was amiable; that he possessed, in general, the soundest understanding in matters of law and equity, and the best talents for judicature I had ever seen; and that he might be cited as an example, in this country, of the perfect picture of a good judge, which my Lord Bacon hath so admirably drawn. He was free from the levities, vices, and excesses which frequently disfigure men of a lively and fruitful fancy. His station did not require, nor his

[1] Horace, afterwards writing to Lord Hertford, says: "Mr. Yorke's speech in our House, and Lord Mansfield's in your's, carried away many of the opposition." Mr. Onslow, in a letter to Lord Hardwicke, wrote: "Mr. Yorke has this moment closed the noblest performance that was ever heard—in answer to the most beastly and brutal speech of Norton, who said he would treat the opinion of parliament in this matter as the opinion of a drunken porter. Nothing ever met with such applause as C. Yorke. Pitt is in love with him, and so we are all."

genius furnish him with imaginative wit or eloquence, and, perhaps, had he possessed a true taste for the fine arts and the polite parts of literature, he would never have been so extensive a lawyer, to which, however, the plainness of his education might have somewhat contributed. In short, we may say that Lord Somers and he seem to have been, in every respect, the reverse of each other." Afterwards he went on with the son:—" I do not mean to forget that a certain candid lawyer united his best endeavors to strangle the *Habeas Corpus Bill;* but then he did it in so delicate and qualified a manner, that surely he can not expect to have his pass for a first-rate part upon the occasion. Ticklish times, or political struggles, always bring to light the real abilities of men, and let one see whether a man owes his reputation and rank to family interest, and an attention to please, or to real great parts, a sound judgment, and true noble spirit. People of the latter class become for ever more considerable by opposition; whereas the former, by degrees, sink to common men when deprived of artificial support, and should therefore never quit, for one moment, a Court; or if, by connection or chance, they are compelled so to do, should return to it again as fast as possible."[1] To these tremendous sarcasms, rendered more cutting from being edged with seeming candor. Yorke is said to have made a spirited reply, but, unfortunately, it is lost to us. We are only told that, passing over with slight notice the disparaging strictures on himself, he vindicated his father from all the charges brought against him. With respect to the abuse of judicial patronage, he cited the names of Ryder, Lee, Strange, Foster, Pratt, Denison, and Wilmot, promoted by him—" a series of almost sacred names requiring no epithets." Of the ex-Chancellor's private virtues he took rather a lofty estimate; but his judicial merits, which it was impossible to appreciate too highly, he justly held up to the admiration of mankind.[2]

The Attorney General, on his resignation, appeared at

---

[1] This is one of the best specimens of Dunning's eloquence preserved to us. Although he was for years such a brilliant debater in the House of Commons, we can judge of his powers almost exclusively by the impression which they produced. It is a curious fact, that when he went into the House of Lords he utterly failed. Lord Mansfield and Lord Brougham are nearly the only lawyers who have succeeded equally in both assemblies.

[2] See Law Mag. No. lxi. p. 87.

first outside the bar in a stuff gown, for he had not had a silk gown before his promotion to be a law officer of the Crown, and the practice had not yet been introduced of making the person so promoted likewise a King's counsel, so that he may not be reduced to the ranks when he loses office.[1]

But the administration now in power, wishing to soften the ex-Attorney General's hostility to them, offered him a "patent of precedence,"—to move next after the Attorney General for the time being—which he accepted as a fair mark of respect for his professional eminence. Yet this was proclaimed at White's to be a proof of tergiversation. "Opposition," writes a correspondent of George Selwyn, "seems to be on its death-bed; the Yorkes have left it; Charles Yorke has been squeamish, and would not return to his old post again, but kisses hands to-morrow for his patent of precedency. He as acted as most lawyers do out of their business,—with as much absurdity, and as little knowledge of the world, as the fellow of a college." "When Charles Yorke left us," says Horace Walpole to Lord Hertford, "I hoped for the desertion of Charles Townshend, and my wish slid into this couplet —

"To the Administration.
"One Charles, who ne'er was ours, you've got, 'tis true;
To make the grace complete, take t'other too."

In the same strain, Single-Speech Hamilton writes to Calcraft:—"Mr. Yorke's patent of precedency, by himself and his friends, is stated as a piece of very disinterested conduct, but is considered by all the rest of the world in a very different light His having a promise of being Chancellor is asserted and denied, exactly as people are differently affected to him; but the opinion of his being to succeed his brother as Teller of the Exchequer gains credit. . . . . Mr. Yorke seemed to be so much ashamed of his patent, that he did not come to kiss hands for it on Friday, which you know was a crowded day at court."[2]

While Mr. Grenville was in vain trying to tax America, and to extinguish Wilkes, Charles Yorke, without sup-

---
[1] To correct this in Dunning's case, when he ceased to be Solicitor General, Lord Mansfield, with the general concurrence of the outer bar, called to him to move immediately after the Recorder of London.
[2] Dec. 1, 1764; Chat. Corr. 299, n.

porting him, did not very actively oppose his measures, and chiefly confined himself to his practice at the bar, which continued undiminished, although he was now without the *prestige* of office. Having won the great Downing College cause, a letter of thanks, in Latin, was forwarded to him by the public orator of the University of Cambridge, under a vote of Convocation, to acknowledge his services, formerly in establishing their privilege of printing books, and more recently in obtaining a decree by which a great estate was secured to them for building and endowing a new college. This testimony was peculiarly grateful to him, as strengthening the ties which for generations connected his family with the University which they had so much adorned. Soon after, he was elected one of its representatives in Parliament.

Although out of office, he was still exposed to flattery; and thus he was addressed by the famous Dr. Dodd, who was then a candidate for the preachership of Lincoln's Inn, expecting soon to be a bishop instead of dying as a malefactor:—" I am satisfied that all my endeavors will be fruitless without your interest, which is (and indeed, from your superior merit, ought to be) most powerful. I humbly and earnestly entreat your support and concurrence. This granted, I shall not doubt of success: this denied me, I shall give up the pursuit. I have, indeed, little to urge to engage your favor; a desire to deserve well of my fellow creatures is my best plea." But Hurd was preferred.

On the formation of the first Rockingham Administration, consisting of most virtuous men, with the most patriotic intentions, Charles Yorke joined them,—resuming his office of Attorney;—and, oh! if he had never deserted them! In that case his career might have been prosperous to its termination, and he might have left an unclouded name to posterity. He did long steadily adhere to them, although he was fatally seduced from them at last. He zealously co-operated in the repeal of the Stamp Act, and the other popular measures of this short-lived government.

While he was Attorney General the second time, the writ of error came to be argued before the Court of King's Bench in the famous case of *Money* v. *Leach*, to determine the validity of "general warrants."[1] He was rather in a delicate predicament; for his own opinion, which he had expressed in parliament, was against them, and Lord Mansfield, without absolutely committing himself, had intimated pretty strongly during the discussion an agreement on this question with Lord Camden. Yet, as counsel for the Crown, he was bound to contend that the King's messenger was not liable to the action for false imprisonment brought by the plaintiff for having been arrested under a general warrant, as one of the publishers of the "North Briton, No. 45." From this dilemma, Mr. Attorney dexterously extricated himself by magnifying another objection raised to his justification, and allowing the judgment of the Court to pass against him on that, while he left the main question without any formal adjudication.[2]

In the spring of 1766, an intrigue was going on for bringing in Charles Yorke as Chancellor to a new Cabinet. Thus writes Lord Shelburne to Mr. Pitt, giving an account of a conversation he had had with Lord Rockingham :—

"In regard to the Duke of Newcastle and Mr. Yorke, though he had reason to believe they might be brought into everything that was desired, yet it was to be wished that it should be proposed with a certain degree of reserve. I observed, or at least thought, he avoided saying whether the Seals were to be Mr. Yorke's object, but seemed carefully to adhere to such general terms as I have mentioned."[3]

In July, 1766, when the Rockingham Administration was unfortunately routed, Yorke, still at variance with Pitt, who constructed the motley Cabinet which succeeded, again resigned his office of Attorney General, which he never resumed,[4] and he remained in opposition till the ever deplorable moment when he consented to accept the Great Seal.[5]

[1] Burrow, 1692.   [2] 19 St. Tr. 1027.   [3] 24th Feb. 1766.
[4] He was succeeded by De Grey, afterwards Lord Walsingham. It would appear that an effort was then made to induce him to continue in office. Lord Chatham in a P. S. to a letter to the Duke of Grafton, on the formation of this Ministry, says,—

"I saw Mr. Yorke yesterday; his behavior and language very handsome: his final intentions he will himself explain to the King in his audience tomorrow."—*MSS. of Duke of Grafton.*

[5] He and his family were much chagrined because he had not long before

At the time of his last resignation, he narrowly missed the office of Chief Justice of the Common Pleas. On Pratt's elevation to the woolsack, this was given to Sir Eardley Wilmot. The ex-Attorney General, without his "pillow," preserved his good-humor, and thus addressed his more fortunate friend:—

"Tittenhanger, August 11, 1766.

"Dear Sir,

"I know not whether you are yet Chief Justice of the Common Pleas in form, but give me leave to congratulate you and the public on your advancement. The kind and uniform friendship which you have shown me, makes me feel a real pleasure on the occasion. *Dieu vous conserve dans sa sainte garde, et moi dans votre amitié!*"

A copy of an elegant edition of Cicero accompanied this letter as a present, which is preserved, with the following inscription upon it in Sir Eardley's handwriting:—

"THE GIFT OF THE HONORABLE CHARLES YORKE.
"Quem tu Dea tempore in omni,
Omnibus ornatum voluisti excellere rebus."

Still Yorke retained his literary tastes and friendships, and he was more delighted with a new book than with a well indorsed brief. Thus he writes to Warburton, now in lawn sleeves:—

"Feb. 2, 1767.

"My dear Lord,

"I can not resist the impulse of thanking you in three words for the perusal of your new discourses, as well as your last letter. All the fruits of your friendship are pleasing to me. The book was most eagerly devoured. How do you manage always to say something new upon old subjects, and always in an original manner? The

---

replaced Lord Northington on the woolsack. In the Diary of the second Earl of Hardwicke is to be found this passage: "It can not be sufficiently repeated, that he resumed the office of Attorney General on an express promise from the King's own mouth, that he should be Lord Chancellor by the end of next session; and when my brother begged of his Majesty (as decency and duty required) that he would not engage himself so far, the King replied, 'I will pledge myself to you.' The King likewise, previous to this conference, wrote a letter to Lord Egmont, to be shown my brother, in which he entered into the same kind of engagement; but the letter itself I never saw, nor had Mr. Y. a copy of it. Certain it is, that his friends had it in their power at that juncture to have made him Chancellor, as Lord Northington was generally disliked; but they wanted his assistance in the House of Commons, where they had no able speaker in the law line."

bookseller favored me with it just on the eve of the 30th of January, and within three days of Candlemas; one of them the greatest *Civil Fast* in England, and the other the greatest Religious Festival of Antichrist. Your Lordship has furnished me with such meditations for both, that I must add it to the account of my obligations,
"And remain always,
"Your Lordship's most faithful
"And affectionate humble Servant,
"C. YORKE."[1]

He had for a client the celebrated David Garrick, from whom he refused a fee till it was forced upon him, and whom he often invited to his house. At one of these visits there was a discussion on a passage of Shakespeare, which next day drew forth the following epistle:—

"Xmas Day.
"Sir,
"As it is my greatest pride to be thought of favorably by Mr. Yorke, I would not chuse to appear ignorant at his table; and therefore I have taken the liberty to explain something which I said in the warmth of conversation yesterday. My good friend Mr. Wray rides always so swift a nag, that whoever strives to follow him will be apt to stumble. This was my case, when we talked about Hamlet and the 'mobled Queen.' He asked me, what was 'mobled?' I answered, *Clouted*. But something running in my head, and the demon of criticism (slipping down with ye Burgundy) possessing me at ye instant, I said, Is it not *mob-led?* When I returned home, and was looking into a memorandum book, where I had collected every scrap about Shakespeare, I found that I had met with this interpretation of 'mobled' in some pamphlet or other, and that I had written under it, Absurd and ridiculous; and most certainly it is so. Dr. Warburton says—Mobled, or mabled, signifies veiled; Johnson—Huddled, or grossly covered. Capel has it, Ennobled queen, wch I don't understand. Shakespeare certainly means, wretchedly clad :

——————' A clout upon that head,
Where late the diadem stood,' &c.

"I have taken the liberty to say thus much, lest I

[1] Warb. Corr. 509.

shou^d be thought too ignorant by those I had the honor to converse with yesterday.

"I am, most gratefully, Sir,
"Your most obedient and very humble servant,
"D. GARRICK.

"If you wou^d likewise turn ye edge of Mr. Wray's wit from me upon this occasion, my mind will be at peace."

At this time he carried on a correspondence with Stanislaus Augustus, the unfortunate King of Poland, to whom he seems to have complained of his loss of office and his dreary prospects. He received the following consolation and advice, in a letter addressed "à M. Yorke, ci-devant Avocat Général :"—

"Mon cher Charles Yorke,

"Vous serez toujours Charles Yorke, tel titre que vous preniez, ou que vous résigniez; et c'est le nom que j'aimerois toujours le plus à vous donner parce qu'il convient le mieux à la sincère et intime amitié dans laquelle nous avons vécu, et dont le sentiment durera autant que moi-meme. Comme j'écris plus amplement à votre frère l'Ambassadeur, et que je compte dire aux deux frères ce que je dis à l'un (en vertu de cette union digne des temps Patriarchals que j'ai tant admirée dans votre famille), je ne répète pas ici sur Harris que j'ai été charmé de connaitre et d'accueillir avec distinction, ni sur ma situation présente qui redevient très critique. Tout ce que je vous dirai c'est, que si jamais on vous offrait la Couronne de la Pologne, je ne vous conseille pas de l'accepter, pour peu que vous aimiez votre repos. Puissiez-vous, mon cher et digne ami, jouir bien à votre aise de cet *otium cum dignitate* pour lequel vous etes a tous égards si bien qualifié—et dont les douceurs apparemment ne deviendront jamais mon partage! Puissais-je pour soulagement dans ma pénible carrière avoir au moins encore une fois le plaisir de vous embrasser! J'ajoute cette prière a celle que je fais tous les jours: 'Seigneur, donnez de la sagesse, du courage, et de la patience, à mesure que vous me donnez de la peine.' Adieu, mon ami, pour cette fois.

"S. A. R.

"Varsovie, 20 Mars, 1768."

So happy had he been with his first wife, that he had again entered the married state, being united to Agneta, daughter of Henry Johnson, Esq., of Berkhampstead, a lady of great accomplishments, with whom he lived happily, and who brought him a son, the late Sir Joseph Yorke, of the royal navy, said to have been the delight of the quarter-deck, and whom I remember the delight of the House of Commons.

The ex-Attorney General now had a charming villa near Highgate, where his family resided, and to which he eagerly retired as often as the Court of Chancery and Parliament would permit. There Warburton paid him a visit in June, 1769. The following letter, notwithstanding its lively tone, can not be read without melancholy, when we recollect that the meeting which it describes was the last that ever took place between the two friends, —and that a terrible catastrophe was at hand:

"Last Thursday we dined with Mr. and Mrs. Yorke, at Highgate. It was not a good day; but we walked on his terrace and round his domain. He has improved it much. But, in contempt of your *latebræ dulces*, you enter the terrace by the most extraordinary gate that ever was. His carpenter, I suppose, wanting materials for it, got together all the old garden-tools, from the scythe to the hammer, and has disposed them in a most picturesque manner to form this gate, which, painted white, and viewed at a distance, represents the most elegant Chinese railing, though I suspect the patriotic carpenter had it in his purpose to ridicule that fantastic taste. Indeed, his new-invented gate is full of recondite learning, and might well pass for Egyptian interpreted by Abbé Pluche. If it should chance to service the present members of the Antiquarian Society (as it well may), I should not despair of its finding a distinguished place among their future '*Transactions*' in a *beautiful copperplate*. I was buried in these contemplations when Mr. Yorke, as if ashamed of, rather than glorying in, his artificer's sublime ideas, drew me upon the terrace. Here we grew serious; and the fine scenes of nature and solitude around us drew us from the Bar of the House and the Bishop's Bench to the memory of our early and ancient friendship, and to look into ourselves. After many mutual compliments on this head, I said,—'that if at any time I had been wanting in this sacred relation, I had made him ample amends by giving him the friendship of the present preacher of Lincoln's Inn.' His sincerity made him acknowledge the greatness of the benefit; but his politeness made him insist upon it 'that it was not a debt which he had received at my hands, but a free gift.' Let it be what it will, I only wish he may show the world he knows the value of it. This I know, that his father, amidst all his acquaintance, chose the most *barren* and *sapless*—on which *dry plants* to shower down his more *refreshing rain*, as Chapman very sensibly calls it."[1]

These two worthy divines certainly valued their legal friend on account of his personal good qualities, but likewise on account of the rich church patronage which they believed would belong to him, for they confidently expected that he would one day hold the Great Seal, like his father, and, by heaping preferment upon them, make a better use of it.

Charles Yorke's last great appearance before the public as an advocate was at the bar of the House of Lords, in the famous Douglas cause; when, along with Wedderburn, he strenuously, though unsuccessfully, strove to support the judgment of the Court of Session, which had been pronounced against the legitimacy of the claimant.

Horace Walpole, ever eager to disparage all who bore the name of Yorke, giving an account of this trial in his "Memoirs of George III." says,—" Mr. Charles Yorke was the least admired. The Duchess of Douglas thought she had retained him; but, hearing he was gone over to the other side, sent for him, and questioned him home. He could not deny that he had engaged himself to the House of Hamilton. 'Then, Sir,' said she, 'in the next world whose will you be, for we have all had you?'"[2] But there can be no doubt that, in pleading for the respondent, he acted according to the rules of professional etiquette and of honor; and that he displayed ability and eloquence not surpassed by any who joined in the noble strife.

After the judgment of reversal, he very handsomely came forward to vindicate Andrew Stewart, the Duke of Hamilton's agent in conducting the cause, from the aspersions cast upon him by Lord Mansfield and Lord Camden. Thus he wrote to him, intending that the letter should be made public:—

[1] Warb. Corr. 432.   [2] Vol. iii. 302.

"Let me beg of you one thing as a friend—not to be too anxious, nor feel too much because things impertinent or injurious are said of yourself. Can any man exert his talents and industry in public or private business without staking his good name upon it? or at least exposing himself to the jealousy of contending parties, and even to their malice and detraction?"—"All who study the cause must be convinced of the purity of your intentions, and the integrity and honor of your conduct."—"The sincere opinion of a friend, declared on such occasions so trying and important, is the genuine consolation of an honest mind. In such causes an advocate is unworthy of his profession who does not plead with the veracity of a witness and a judge."

Whether in or out of office—while Charles Yorke maintained the independence of the bar, he behaved with great courtesy to the Judges before whom he practiced:— "It was impossible," says George Hardinge, "to conceive any deportment more graceful in good manners for the bench than Mr. Yorke's towards Lord Camden, as long as the latter held the Seals,—and these attentions were mutual. Indeed, the Court and the Bar were upon terms of the most amiable intercourse imaginable"[1]

Although Charles Yorke had been professedly in opposition since the last resignation of his office of Attorney General, in July, 1766, he was supposed at times to have coquetted with the Ministry, but latterly he had allied himself more closely with the Rockingham Whigs. His elder brother, the second Earl of Hardwicke, was a most zealous member of that party. After Lord Chatham's resuscitation, which followed his resignation, the two sections of the Whig party were reconciled, and formed a formidable opposition to the Court, now bent on taxing America, and trampling on the liberties of the people by persisting in the perpetual disqualification of Mr. Wilkes to sit in parliament. If all the Whigs remained true and steady to their engagements, the greatest hopes were entertained that the illiberal members of the Cabinet might be compelled to resign, that America might be conciliated, and that tranquillity and the constitution might be restored at home.

With this prospect opened the session of 1770; when,

[1] MS. Life of Lord Camden.

Lord Chatham, having again thundered against ministerial corruption and imbecility, Lord Camden made his startling disclosure, that for years he had absented himself from the Council while the most important subjects of colonial and domestic policy were debated there, because he utterly condemned the course which his colleagues were obstinately pursuing.[1] The total surrender of the Government depended upon whether any lawyer, of decent character and abilities, could be found to succeed him. Lord Shelburne, knowing this, had declared in the House of Lords, "that the Seals would go a-begging; but he hoped there would not be found in the kingdom a wretch so base and mean-spirited as to accept them on the conditions on which they must be offered."[2] This was on the night of Tuesday, the 9th of January.

A meeting of the Opposition leaders was held next morning, when they resolved that Lord Camden should be requested to hold the Great Seal till he should be dismissed; and that all their influence should be used to prevent any lawyer of character from agreeing to accept it. Simultaneously, the King and his "friends" determined that if Lord Camden did not voluntarily resign, he should be dismissed, and that a successor to him must be found at any price. Lord Mansfield would have been the first object of their choice, but in less ticklish times he had expressed a firm purpose never to exchange his permanent office of Chief Justice of the King's Bench for the fleeting *éclat* of the Chancellorship.[3] The great effort to be made was to gain over Charles Yorke, whose secession would add much credit to their cause, and materially

---

[1] Horace Walpole says,—"The Duke of Grafton accused him of having made no objection to Luttrell's admission; his friends affirmed he had; and Lord Sandwich allowed that he had reserved to himself a liberty of acting as he pleased on every question relating to Wilkes. The Chancellor's mind certainly fluctuated between his obligations to Lord Chatham and the wish to retain his post. The Duke of Grafton's neglect determined the scale."—*Walp. Mem. Geo. III.*, iv. 42.

[2] Horace Walpole represents that General Conway tried to prevail upon the Duke of Grafton to continue Lord Camden in office, and that the Duke "told him he was to see a person of consequence at night on that subject." "That person," said Horace to Conway, "is Charles Yorke, who is afraid of being seen going into the Duke's House by daylight."—*Memoirs of George III.*, iv. 44.

[3] Horace Walpole says,—"It had been thought necessary to make Lord Mansfield the compliment of offering him the Seals;" but if this offer was then repeated it must have been an empty form.

damage the Whigs. A letter was immediately written to him, making an overture in very general terms, and in the evening of the following day, a long interview took place between him and the Duke of Grafton. The Great Seal was now distinctly offered to him ; and when he talked of his past political connections, a hope was held out to him of the admission of some of his friends into the Cabinet, and of the adoption of a more liberal policy. He required time for consideration, but seemed in a humor so complying, that the Duke of Grafton made a very favorable report to the King of the state of the negotiation. Charles Yorke, however, having stated what had passed to a meeting of Whigs at Lord Rockingham's, they pronounced the whole proceeding treacherous and deceitful ; they foretold that, as soon as he had been inveigled to leave his party, the Court would treat him with contumely, and they prevailed upon him to give them a pledge that he would be true to them. He returned to the Premier. and declared that he positively declined the Great Seal, Being then asked if he had any objection to see the King, who had condescendingly expressed a wish to confer with him, he said " he felt bound as a faithful subject to obey what he considered a command from his Sovereign," and he showed such alacrity in yielding to the wish as to create a belief in the Duke's mind that he had voluntarily solicited the interview. It took place at St. James's, on Saturday, the 13th of January. The particulars of the conversation are not known, but as yet Charles Yorke remained firm, and the King, with deep concern, wrote to the Duke of Grafton that he had been able to make no impression on the obstinate lawyer.

This refusal caused great joy among the Whigs, and news of it being sent to Hayes, where Lord Chatham then was, he thus wrote:—

"Wednesday, Jan. 17, 1770

" Mr. Yorke's refusal is of moment ; and I can readily believe it, from my opinion of his prudence and discernment. No man with a grain of either would embark in a rotten vessel in the middle of a tempest, to go he knows not whither. I wish our noble and amiable Chancellor had not been so candid as to drag the Great Seal for one hour at the heels of a desperate Minister, after he had hawked it about with every circumstance of indignity to the holder of it."

Before this wish was expressed, the prudence and the virtue of Charles Yorke had been overpowered. The Ministers had abandoned all hope of gaining him, and were thinking of pressing the Great Seal on Sir Eardley Wilmot, or De Grey, the Attorney General;[1] but the King himself, without consulting them, with great dexterity and energy made an attempt, which at first seemed crowned with brilliant success, though it terminated so fatally.

On Tuesday, the 16th of January, there was a levee at St. James's, and Charles Yorke thought it his duty to attend for the purpose of testifying his loyalty and personal respect for the Sovereign. To his great surprise he met with a very gracious reception, and the lord in waiting informed him that his Majesty desired to see him in his closet when the levee was over. He hardly thought it possible that the offers to him should be repeated, but he resolutely determined at all events to be faithful to the engagements into which he had entered. Again led into temptation, he was undone. Long after he entered the King's closet he firmly, though respectfully, resisted the solicitations by which he was assailed —urging, by way of excuse, his principles, the opinions he had expressed in parliament, his party connections, and the pledge he had given to his brother. But he could not stoutly defend his reasons against a royal opponent, who naturally thought himself entitled to the services of all born under allegiance to the English crown, and who could not well appreciate objections to the performance of the duties of a subject. The King made some impression by declaring, that, with such a Chancellor as he

[1] Horace Walpole thus notices the lawyers who might have been thought of for Chancellor at this time :—" Norton had all the requisites of knowledge and capacity, but wanted even the semblance of integrity, though for that reason was probably the secret wish of the Court. He was enraged at the preference given to Yorke; yet nobody dared to propose him even when Yorke had refused. Sir Eardley Wilmot had character and abilities, but wanted health. The Attorney General De Grey, wanted health and weight, and yet asked too extravagant terms. Dunning, the Solicitor General, had taken the same part as his friends Lord Camden and Lord Shelburne. Of Lord Mansfield there could be no question; when the post was dangerous, his cowardice was too well known to give hopes that he could be pressed to defend it."—*Mem. Geo. III.*, iv. 49.

wished, an administration might soon be formed which the nation would entirely approve. He added,—" My sleep has been disturbed by your declining. Do you mean to declare yourself unfit for it? If you will not comply, it must make an eternal breach between us. Rescue me from the degrading thraldom to which I am reduced." The yielding disputant had no answer to make to this appeal; his virtue cooled as his loyalty was inflamed: unable longer to resist,—without making any stipulations for himself, with respect to pension or tellership,—he sank down on his knees in token of submission,—and the King, giving him his hand to kiss, hailed him as " Lord Chancellor of Great Britain."

Charles Yorke, by his Majesty's command, then proceeded to the house of the Duke of Grafton, to inform him of what had happened. The minister, all astonishment, could not believe his own ears, and hurried down to St. James's—where the King fully confirmed the news of the victory which had been won. According to the representation of the second Earl of Hardwicke, Charles Yorke had not yet the courage to disclose his lapse to his old political associates, and, the whole of this day, declared to them that he had refused all the King's offers; but he seems to have been in such an excited and disturbed state of mind as hardly to have been conscious of what he said or did.

The same evening the Great Seal was taken from Lord Camden, and the next day a council was held, at the Queen's House, for delivering it to the new Chancellor, and administering to him the oaths of office.

As he was never installed in Westminister Hall, nor ever sat in the Court of Chancery, there is no entry respecting him as Chancellor to be found in the Close Roll, or in the records of the Crown Office; but the following minute appears in the books of the Privy Council:—

"At the Court at the Queen's House, the 17th of January, 1770.

" Present, the King's Most Excellent Majesty in Council:

" His Majesty in Council was this day graciously pleased to deliver the Great Seal to the Right Honorable Charles Yorke, Esquire, who was thereupon, by his Majesty's command sworn of his Majesty's Most Honorable Privy Council, and likewise Lord High Chancellor of Great Britain, and accordingly took his place at the board."

At the same time a warrant was signed by the King for a patent raising him to the peerage, by the title of Baron Morden, of Morden, in the county of Cambridge.

In the course of this day Lord Chancellor Charles Yorke drove to his brother's to communicate to him what he had done. It so happened that Lord Rockingham, Lord Hardwicke, and the other leaders of opposition, were then holding a meeting to concert measures against the Government. He was introduced to them, and unfolded his tale. We are told that it was received with a burst of indignation, and that all present upbraided him for a breach of honor. According to Lord Hardwicke's Diary, he again called in the evening of the same day, when the brothers conversed more calmly. But it is certain that when he went home his mind was sorely harassed with the severity of the reproaches which had been cast upon him.

That very night it was announced that he was dangerously ill; and at five o'clock in the evening of Saturday the 30th of January, three days after he had been sworn in Chancellor, he was no more. His patent of nobility had been made out and was found in the room in which he died, but the Great Seal had not been affixed to it, so that the title did not descend to his heirs. He expired in the forty-eighth year of his age.

A suspicion of suicide immediately arose, and a controversy has ever since been maintained on the question whether that suspicion was well founded. Fortunately, it is no part of my duty to give an opinion upon a subject so delicate and so painful. Would to God that I could entirely avoid it! I shall content myself with stating the authorities on both sides, leaving the reader to draw his own conclusion. In our time, on a death so sudden occurring, a coroner's inquest would be held as a matter of course; but no coroner's inquest was held, although it would appear that the body was exhibited by order of the family to check the circulation of the rumors which were afloat.

About three weeks after the event, there came out, in the "Public Advertiser," a letter to the Duke of Grafton from JUNIUS,[1] in which that unscrupulous writer, alluding to the dismissal of Lord Camden and the death of Charles Yorke, says,—

"One would think, my Lord, you might have taken this spirited resolution[2] before you had dissolved the last of those early connections which once, even in your opinion, did honor to your youth—before you would oblige Lord Granby to quit a service he was attached to—before you had discarded one Chancellor and killed another. To what an abject condition have you labored to reduce the best of Princes, when the unhappy man who yields at last to such personal instance and solicitation as never can be fairly employed against a subject, feels himself degraded by his compliance, and is unable to survive the disgraceful honors which his gracious Sovereign had compelled him to accept! He was a man of spirit, for he had a quick sense of shame, and death has redeemed his character. I know your grace too well to appeal to your feelings upon this event; but there is another heart, not yet, I hope, quite callous to the touch of humanity, to which it ought to be a dreadful lesson for ever."

In the following year Junius reiterated the charge :—

"Enough has been said of that detestable transaction, which ended in the death of Mr. Yorke. I can not speak of it without horror and compassion. To excuse yourself, you publicly impeach your accomplice, and to *his* mind, perhaps, the accusation may be flattery. But in murder you are both principals. It was once a question of emulation; and if the event had not disappointed the immediate schemes of the closet, it might still have been a hopeful subject of jest and merriment between you."[3]

Sir Nathaniel Wraxall, commenting on this passage, says: "The transaction to which Junius refers is one of the most tragical which has taken place in our time. Mr. Yorke closed his existence in a manner strongly resembling the last scene of the lamented ——," mentioning the name of an illustrious man, who, in a fit of mental aberration, arising from deep grief, had shortened his days.

Jeremiah Markland, on the 5th of February, 1770, thus wrote to Mr. Bowyer :—

[1] Feb. 1770.   [2] The Duke's own resignation.
[3] Letter to the Duke of Grafton, 22nd June, 1771.

"Your letter of February 1 gave me a new and melancholy light concerning the last Chancellor who died . . . ! But the spirit which appears in many of our nobility, and the cession of one great wicked man, whose parts I was afraid (and there was more reason for the fear than, I presume, was generally apprehended), had got an entire superiority over the weakness of another, have made me very easy as to political matters. I had expressed my apprehensions in many political squibs and crackers, which I had occasionally let off; but shall now suppress them as unnecessary. The last was this :—

> '*To the D of G.*
> ' How strangely Providence its ways conceals!
> From Pratt it takes, Yorke it takes from, the Seals
> Restore them not to Pratt, lest men should say
> Thou'st done one useful thing in this thy day.' " [1]

Horace Walpole, in his "Memoirs of the Reign of George III.," says :—

"After struggling with all the convulsions of ambition, interest, fear, horror, dread of abuse, and, above all, with the difficulty of refusing the object of his whole life's wishes, and with the despair of recovering the instant, if once suffered to escape—Charles Yorke, having taken three days to consider, refused to accept the Seals of Chancellor." [2] . . . "Mr. Conway acquainted me, in the greatest secresy, that the Duke of Grafton, dismayed at Yorke's refusal of the Great Seal, would give up the administration. Not a lawyer could be found able enough —or if able, bold enough—or if bold, decent enough—to fill the employment." . . . "What was my astonishment when Mr. Onslow came and told me that Yorke had accepted the Seals! He had been with the King overnight (without the knowledge of the Duke of Grafton), and had again declined; but being pressed to reconsider, and returning in the morning, the King had so overwhelmed him with flatteries, entreaties, prayers, and at

---

[1] Nichols's Literary Anecdotes, vol. iv. 298. See likewise "The Whisperer," Feb. 17, 1770.

[2] Horace Walpole is very inaccurate as to dates in this part of his Memoirs. For example, he represents the speeches respecting the dismissal of the Chancellor and the acceptance of the Seals by another lawyer, made in the House of Lords on the 9th of January, the first day of the session, as made on the 15th of January, when Lord Camden was substantially dismissed, and Charles Yorke had twice refused to succeed him.—*Mem. Geo. III.*, iv. 48.

last with commands, and threats of never giving him the post if not accepted now, that the poor man sank under the importunity, though he had given a solemn promise to his brother, Lord Hardwicke, and Lord Rockingham, that he would not yield. He betrayed, however, none of the rapaciousness of the times, nor exacted but one condition, the grant of which fixed his irresolution. The Chancellor must, of necessity, be a Peer, or can not sit in the House of Lords.[1] The coronet was announced to Yorke, but he slighted it as of no consequence to his eldest son, who would probably succeed his uncle, Lord Hardwicke, the latter having been long married, and having only two daughters. But Mr. Yorke himself had a second wife, a very beautiful woman, and by her had another son. She, it is supposed, urged him to accept the Chancery as the King offered, or consented that the new peerage should descend to her son, and not to the eldest. The rest of his story was indeed melancholy, and his fate so rapid as to intercept the completion of his elevation. He kissed the King's hand on the Thursday;[2] and from Court drove to his brother, Lord Hardwicke's; the precise steps of the tragedy have never been ascertained. Lord Rockingham was with the Earl. By some it was affirmed that both the Marquis and the Earl received the unhappy renegade with bitter reproaches. Others, whom I rather believe, maintained that the Marquis left the house directly, and that Lord Hardwicke refused to hear his brother's excuses, and, retiring from the room, shut himself into another chamber, obdurately denying Mr. Yorke an audience. At night it was whispered that the agitation of his mind, working on a most sanguine habit of body, inflamed of late by excessive indulgence both in meats and wine, had occasioned the bursting of a blood-vessel, and the attendance of surgeons was accounted for by the necessity of bleeding him four times on Friday. Certain it is, that he expired on the Saturday, between four and six in the evening. His servants, in the first confusion, had dropped too much to leave it in the family's power to stifle the truth; and though they

---

[1] Horace is here inaccurate in his law as well as his facts.
[2] This, again, is a mistake, for the Great Seal had actually been delivered to him on Wednesday, the 17th of January; and it was on the evening of this same day that he drove to Lord Rockingham's.

endeavored to color over the catastrophe by declaring the accident natural, the want of evidence, and of the testimony of surgeons, to color the tale given out, and which they never took any public means of authenticating, convinced everybody that he had fallen by his own hand—whether on his sword, or by a razor, was uncertain."[1]

Cooksey, a relation of the Hardwicke family, on the mother's side, in his "Life of Lord Hardwicke," gives an account of Lord and Lady Hardwicke's children; and, after introducing Philip, the eldest son, thus proceeds:—

"Being a capital supporter of the principles and party which was headed by the amiable Marquis of Rockingham, there was no post or office in administration to which he might not have been appointed, as there were none to which his abilities would not have done honor. That body of respected and real patriots generally held their private meetings and consultations at his Lordship's house in St. James's Square; and it was at one of those that his brother appeared with the Seals which his Majesty had prevailed on him to accept, on the resignation of Lord Camden. The expressive silence with which he was received and dismissed by that illustrious assemblage of his friends, made him but too sensible of their disapprobation of his conduct. His self-condemnation of it, also, and horror of consequential shame and diminution of his high character, proved fatal to his life. His last moments gave Lord Hardwicke an occasion of expressing his nice sense of honor and refined delicacy, The Seals, and the patent creating him Baron Morden, were on a table in the apartment of the dying Chancellor. 'What hinders,' said one of his friends, 'the Great Seal being put to this patent, while his Lordship yet lives?' 'I forbid it,' said his noble brother. 'Never shall it be said of one of our family, that he obtained a peerage under the least suspicion of a dishonorable practice.' The biographer then introduces the second son: 'Charles, who, after displaying the most shining abilities in the several law offices of Solicitor and Attorney General, was unhappily appointed Lord Chancellor of England on January 17, 1770; which appointment, not being attended with the approbation of his friends or his own, had such effect on his feelings as to render life insupportable. He quitted it

[1] Mem. of Geo. III., iv. 48–53.

on the 20th of the same month, to the inexpressible grief of all good men who knew him. Happily he leaves a son, heir to his virtues and the honors and great estates of his family.' " [1]

Belsham, in his History of the Reign of George III., thus describes the last hours of Charles Yorke:—

"Lord Camden having in the course of the debate condemned, in decisive terms, the proceedings of the House of Commons, and actually divided on this occasion with Lord Chatham, was immediately compelled to relinquish the Great Seal; but such was the political consternation prevailing at this crisis, that no person competent to the office could be persuaded to accept it. Mr. Yorke, Attorney General, son of the late Lord Chancellor Hardwicke, a man of the highest professional ability, had given, as was reported and believed, a positive assurance to the Earl, his brother, that he would not, upon any terms, listen to the offers of the Court; but, upon being sent for by the King and earnestly solicited, he at length, in a fatal moment, *consented*, and a patent was immediately ordered to be prepared for his elevation to the peerage, by the title of Lord Morden. On repairing to the residence of his brother, in order to explain to him the motives of his acceptance, he was *refused admission;* and, in the agitation of his mind, unable to endure the torture of his own reflections, he in a few hours put an end to his existence." [2]

Other compilers of Memoirs and Magazines, which have been subsequently given to the world, have repeated the story, without any corroboration of it. But much weight must be given to the following very interesting extract from the MS. journal of the Duke of Grafton:

"Parliament was to meet on the 9th of January, 1770. The necessity of having a Chancellor to vindicate the law authority of the Cabinet was dinned into my ear in most companies I frequented; and it was particularly remarked that Mr. Charles Yorke had taken no part in the whole business of the Middlesex election that need preclude him from joining in opinion with the decisions of the Commons. Such insinuations were very irksome to me, and about the Court I was still more harassed with them.

[1] Cooksey, 43.   Belsham i. 303.

At last, when I was passing a few Christmas holidays at Euston, Lords Gower and Weymouth came down on a visit. They informed me that the King, on hearing their intention of going to Euston, had expressly directed them to say, that the continuation of the Lord Chancellor in his office could not be justified, and that the Government would be too much lowered by the Great Seal appearing in opposition, and his Majesty hoped that I should assent to his removal, and approve of an offer being made to Mr. Yorke. My answer, as well as I recollect, was, that 'though it did not become me to argue against his Majesty's remarks on the present peculiar state of the Great Seal, I must humbly request that I might be in no way instrumental to dismissing Lord Camden.'

"In a few days after my arrival in London the session opened, when the Lord Chancellor spoke warmly in support of Lord Chatham's opposition to the address; and while we were in the House, Lord Camden told me that he was sensible the Seal must be taken from him, though he had no intention to resign it. At St. James's it was at once decided that the Seal should be demanded; but, at my request, Lord Camden held it for some days, merely for the convenience of Government, during the negotiation for a respectable successor. No person will deny that Mr. Charles Yorke, Sir Eardley Wilmot, and Mr. De Grey, would, any of them, have filled the high office of Lord Chancellor with the full approbation of Westminster Hall. They were all three thought of for it, though Sir Eardley's infirm state of health, accompanied by an humble diffidence of himself, which had been a distinguishing mark in his character through life, forbade the hopes of his acceptance.

"While I continued in office it was my duty as well as desire to exert myself in endeavoring to render the King's administration as respectable as I was able, though I lamented and felt grievously the loss of Lord Camden's support, from which I derived so much comfort and assistance; yet I was satisfied that the lawyers I have mentioned were men equal to discharge the duties of a Chancellor. I therefore received the King's commands to write to Mr. Yorke directly. I saw him the next day. He received the offer of the Great Seal with much gratitude to his Majesty, but hoped that he should be allowed to return his answer when he should have given it a day's consideration. Mr. Charles Yorke remained with me between two and three hours, dwelling much on the whole of his own political thoughts and conduct, together with a comment on the principal public occurrences of the present reign. When he came to make remarks on the actual state of things, after speaking with much regard of many in administration, he said that it was essential to him to be informed from me whether I was open to a negotiation for extending the administration, so as to comprehend those with whom I had formerly and he constantly wished to agree. My answer was, that he could not desire more earnestly than myself to see an administration as comprehensive as possible, and that this object could only be brought about by the union of the Whigs—adding that I should be happy to have his assistance to effect it. Mr. Yorke appeared to be pleased with this answer, and after many civilities on both sides we parted. On his return to me the next day, I found him a quite altered man, for his mind was then made up to decline the offer from his Majesty, and that so decidedly that I did not attempt to say any thing further on the subject. He expressed, however, a wish to be allowed an audience of his Majesty. This was granted, and at the conclusion of it the King, with the utmost concern, wrote to acquaint me that Mr. Yorke had declined the Seal. On his appearing soon after at the levee, his Majesty called him into his closet immediately after it was over. What passed there I know not, but nothing could exceed my astonishment when Lord Hillsborough came into my dressing-room in order to tell me that Mr. Yorke was in my parlor, and that he was Lord Chancellor through the persuasion of the King himself in his closet. Mr. Yorke corroborated to me what I had heard from Lord Hillsborough, and I received the same account from his Majesty as soon as I could get down to St. James's.

"Mr. Yorke stayed but a little time with me, but his language gave me new hopes that an administration might shortly be produced which the nation would approve. How soon did this plausible hope vanish into a visionary expectation, only from the death of Mr. Yorke before he became Lord Morden, or we could have any preliminary discourses on the measures he earnestly desired to forward! I had long been acquainted with Mr. Yorke, and held him in high esteem. He certainly appeared less easy and communicative with me from the time of his acceptance to his death than I might expect, but it was natural to imagine that he would be more agitated than usual when arduous and intricate business was rushing at once upon him. I had not the least conception of any degree of agitation that could bring him to his sad and tragical end. Nor will I presume to conjecture what motives in his own breast, or anger in that of others, had driven him to repent of the step he had just taken. By his own appointment I went to his house about nine o'olock in the evening, two days, as I believe, after Mr. Yorke had been sworn in at a council board summoned for that purpose at the Queen's House. Being shown into his library below, I waited a longer time than I supposed Mr. Yorke would have kept me without some extraordinary cause. After above half-an-hour waiting, Dr. Watson, his physician, came into the room; he appeared somewhat confused—sat himself down for a few moments, letting me know that Mr. Yorke was much indisposed with an attack of colic. Dr. Watson soon retired, and I was ruminating on the untowardness of the circumstances—never suspecting the fatal event which had occurred, nor the still more lamentable cause ascribed for it by the world, and, as I fear, upon too just ground.

"I rung the bell, and acquainted one of the servants that Mr. Yorke was probably too ill to see me, and that I should postpone the business on which I came to a more favorable moment. Mr. Yorke, I believe, was a religious man: It is rare to hear of such a person being guilty of an action so highly criminal. It must, therefore, have been in him a degree of passionate frenzy bearing down every atom of his reason. You will not wonder that I can not think on the subject without horror still."

On the other hand, it is said that besides an exposure of the body to prove that the death was natural, a detailed statement was published by the relations of the deceased, satisfactorily explaining all the circumstances which led to the suspicion; but, after diligent inquiry, I have not been able to procure a copy of it.

Among the papers of the second Earl of Hardwicke

was found the following document, entitled "Private Memorial," and bearing the date Dec. 30, 1770:—

"I shall set down on this paper the extraordinary and melancholy circumstances wch attended the offer of the Gr. Seal to my brother in Jany last. On the 12th of that month he received, on his return from Tittenhanger, a note from the D. of Grafton, desiring to see him. He sent it immediately to me, and I went to Bloomsbury Square, where I met my brother John, and we had a long conversation with Mr. Yorke. He saw the D. of Grafton (by appointment) in the evening, and his Grace made him (in form and with^t personal cordiality) an offer of the Gr. S., complaining heavily of Ld Camden's conduct, particularly his hostile speech in the H. of Lords the 1st day of the session. My brother desired a little time to consider of so momentuous an affair, and stated to the Duke the difficulties it laid him under. His Grace gave him till Sunday in the forenoon. He (Mr. Y.) called on me that morning (the 14th), and seemed in great perplexity and agitation. I asked him if he saw his way thro' the clamorous and difficult points upon wch it would be immediately expected he should give his opinion, viz., the Middlesex election, America, and the state of Ireland, where the Parliament had just been prorogued, on a popular point. 'He seriously declared he did not, and that he might be called upon to devise measures of a higher and more dangerous nature than he sho^d chuse to be responsible for. He was clearly of opinion that he was not sent for at the present juncture from predilection, but necessity ; and how much soever the Gr. S. had justly been the object of his ambition, he was now afraid of accepting it.' Seeing him in so low and fluttered a state of spirits, and knowing how much the times called for a *higher*, I did not venture to push him on, and gave into the idea he himself started, of advising to put the Gr. Seal in commission, by wch time wo^d be gained. He went from me to the D. of Grafton, repeated his declining answer, and proposed a commission for the present, for wch precedents of various times were not wanting. The D. of Grafton expressed a more earnest desire that my brother sho^d accept than he did at the first interview, and pressed his seeing the King before he took a final resolution. I saw him again, in Montague House

Garden, on Monday, the 15th, and he then seemed determined to decline, said a particular friend of his in the law (Mr. W.) had rather discouraged him, and that nothing affected him with concern but the uneasiness which it might give to Mrs. Y.

"On Tuesday forenoon (the 16th) he called upon me in great agitation, and talked of *accepting*. He changed his mind again by the evening, when he saw the King at the Queen's Palace, and finally declined. He told me, just after the audience, that the K. had not pressed him so strongly as he expected; that he had not held forth much prospect of stability in administration; and, that he had not talked so *well* to him as he did when he accepted the office of Attorney General, in 1765. His Majesty, however, ended the conversation very humanely and prettily, that "after what he had said to excuse himself, it would be cruelty to press his acceptance."' I must here solemnly declare that my brother was all along in such an agitation of mind, that he never told me all the particulars wch passed in the different conversations, and many material things may have been said to him w$_{ch}$ I am ignorant of. He left me soon after, to call on Mr. Anson and L$_d$ Rockingham, authorizing me to acquaint everybody that he had declined, adding discontentedly, that 'It was the confusion of the times wch occasioned his having taken the resolution.' He appeared to me very much ruffled and disturbed, but I made myself easy on being informed that he would be quiet next day, and take physick. He wanted both *that* and bleeding, for his spirits were in a fever.

"On Wednesday morning (the 17th) I accidentally met with several friends, and told them what I then thought my brother's resolution. Some approved, all acquiesced, nobody much wondered at it. The state of things appeared very fluctuating and uncertain; several resignations had happened, more were talked of, and I had been favored with no private communications from any quarter (but Ld Rockingham's) to direct my judgment. That very morning, instead of taking his physick, he left it on the table, after a broken night's rest, and went to the levee, was called into the closet, and in a manner *compelled* by the K. to accept the Gr. S., with expressions like these: 'My sleep has been disturbed by y^r declining; do you mean to declare yrself unfit for it?' and still stronger afterwards: 'If you will not comply, it must make an eternal breach betwixt us.' At his return from Court, about 3 o'clock, he broke in unexpectedly on me, who was talking with Ld R., and gave us this account. We were both *astounded* (to use an obsolete, but strong word) at so sudden an event, and I was particularly shocked at his being so overborne in a manner I had never heard of, nor co^d imagine possible between prince and subject. I was hurt *personally* at the figure I had been making for a day before, telling everybody, by his authority, that he was determined to decline; and I was vexed at his taking no notice of me, or the rest of the family, when he accepted. All these considerations working on my mind at this distracting moment, induced me (Ld Rock. joining in it) to press him to return forthwith to the King, and to intreat his M^ty either to allow him time till next morning to recollect himself, or to put the Gr. S. in commission, as had been before resolved upon. We co^d not prevail. 'He said he co^d not in honor do it. He had given his word, had been wished joy,' &c. Mr. John Yorke came in during this conversation, and did not take much part in it, but seemed quite confounded. After a long altercative conversation, Mr. Yorke (unhappily then Ld Chancellor) departed, and I went to dinner. In the evening ab^t 8 o'clock, he called on me again, and acquainted me with his having been sworn in at the Queen's House, and that he had then the Gr. S. in the coach. He talked to me of the title he intended to take, that of *Morden*, wch is part of the Wimple estate; asked my forgiveness if he had acted improperly. We kissed and parted friends; a warm word did not escape either of us. When he took leave, he seemed more composed, but unhappy. Had I been quite cool, when he entered my room so abruptly at 3 o'clock, I sho^d have said little, wished him joy, and reserved expostulation till a calmer moment. I was heartily grieved, and expressed it too *sharply*, that he had not represented plainly to the K. the bad situation of his affairs, owing entirely to the imprudent and *hollow* conduct of the court. I thought, having been so ill-used before, he had no reason to conceal wholesome truths now, when he was called upon not from choice, but necessity, and to replace a man whom the K. had greatly flattered to retain in his service not long before. This I was authentically informed of not long after. It came from Bob Pratt.

"On Thursday, the 18th, I went to Richmond to compose my thoughts, and to consider what part I sho^d take, for I was afraid that, in the manner my brother had come in, the public w^d consider him as carrying the family to Court in his pocket. Mr. John Yorke and the Dean of Lincoln spent part of the day in Bloomsbury Square, and he proposed to the former the taking a place in the Ad^{ty}, wch the other civilly and gently declined, upon wch Mr. Yorke said, 'Then it w^d be the ruin of him.' He said little to them, and appeared quite oppressed and melancholy. In the meanwhile, I had conversed with Dr. Jefferys, and he gave a very friendly and right opinion, 'that I sho^d do my best to support the part wch my brother had taken.' I came to town with that *resolution*, Friday, in the forenoon, and am persuaded that had I found Mr. Y. as I left him, matters w^d have ended quite otherwise than they *did*. He was taken very ill that morning, and when I saw him in the evening of the 19th, he was in bed, and too much disordered to be talked with. There was a glimmering of hope on the 20th, in the morning; but he died that day, ab^t 5 in the evening.

"The patent of peerage had passed all the forms, except the Gr. Seal, and when my poor brother was asked if the Seal sh^d be put to it, he waved it, and said, 'he hoped it was no longer in his custody.'

"I can solemnly declare, that except what passed at my house on the Wednesday forenoon, I had not the least difference with him thro' the whole transaction; not a sharp or even a warm expression passed, but we reasoned over the subject like friends and brothers, reciprocally communicating our respective ideas and intelligence. Seeing the state of mind he was in, I was rather of opinion that he sh^d let the Gr. Seal be put in commission, and give his opinion freely as a private man in the H. of C. on the point of disqualification, in wch I knew he differed entirely with Ld Rockingham and his party. In short, the usage he met with in 1766, when faith was broke with him, had greatly impaired his judgment, dejected his spirits, and made him act below his superior knowledge and abilitys. He w^d seldom explain himself, or let his opinion be known in time, to those who were ready to have acted with him in the utmost confidence. After the menacing language used in the closet, to compel Mr. Yorke's acceptance, and the loss wch the King sustained by his death at that critical juncture, the most unprejudiced and dispassionate were surprised at the *little* or rather *no* notice that was taken of his family; the not making an offer to complete the peerage was neither palliated nor justified in their opinion. It was due to the *manes* of the departed, from every motive of humanity and decorum. Ld Hillsborough told a friend of mine indeed, that the K. had, soon after his death, spoken of him with *tears in his eyes*, and inquired after his family; but it w^d surely not have misbecome his M^ty, conscious of the *whole* of his behavior to an able, faithful, and despairing subject, to have expressed that concern in a more particular manner, and to those who were so deeply affected by the melancholy event. A worthier and better man there never was, nor more learned and accomplished in his own profession, as well as out of it. What he wanted was the calm, firm judgment of his father; and he had the misfortune to live in times wch required a double portion of it. Every precaution was taken by me to prepare him for the offer, and to persuade him to form some previous plan of conduct, but all in vain. He w^d never explain himself clearly, and left everything to chance, till we were *all* overborn, perplexed, and confounded in that fatal interval wch opened and closed the negotiation with my brother. With him the Somers line of the law seems to be at an end; I mean of that set in the profession who, mixing principles of liberty with those proper for monarchy, have conducted and guided that great body of men ever since the Revolution

> ' Manibus date lilia plenis,
> Purpureos spargam flores, et fungar inani
> Munere vir.'

"1781. I have reason to think, from what L^d H—gh hinted to me this winter, that some means were used wch I was ignorant of, to bring my brother to court when the Gr. S. was forc'd upon him." [1]

[1] Considering the statement which had been made by Junius, and often repeated before this entry was written, we must be surprised that the circumstances of the death of Charles Yorke are not here more specifically stated. The writer's great object seems to have been to justify himself from the charge of having acted harshly to his unhappy brother. From lapse of mem

Adolphus, in his History of the Reign of George III., gives the following account of Charles Yorke's appointment and his death, without hinting at the current rumor:—

"The Seal was taken from Lord Camden and offered to Mr. Yorke, who had twice filled the office of Attorney General with the greatest reputation for talents and integrity. The unsettled state of parties, and the gloomy complexion of affairs, naturally occasioned him to feel considerable reluctance at undertaking the office at that particular time. Nothing, probably, would have overcome his repugnance but the earnest manner in which his acceptance of the Great Seal was pressed upon him by the King himself, as most essential to his service. Thus urged, Mr. Yorke determined to obey the commands of his Sovereign without reversionary conditions or stipulations. He was immediately raised to the peerage by the title of Baron Morden, of Morden, in Cambridgeshire; an honor he did not live to possess, as the patent was not completed before his death, which occurred three days after he received the Great Seal." [1]

But an express, and seemingly authentic, contradiction is given to the imputation of suicide, by Craddock, a writer of credit, who, in his Memoirs, twice touches upon the subject; "Mr. Sheldon," says he, "and his brother, were very rich men. Mr. S. married a relative of Mr. Charles Yorke, for a short time Lord Chancellor. Mr. Sheldon's eldest son, through the Reverend Mr. Sparrow, of Walthamstow, became intimate with me, and was frequently at my house in summer. After the dreadful death of Mr. Yorke, the newpapers more than hinted that he committed suicide, and this was mentioned at my table, not knowing Mr. Sheldon was his nephew. Mr.

oiy, at the distance of nearly a whole year, he makes a mistake as to the day on which the King's levee was held; and, unless he had been misled by the incoherent narration delivered to him on Tuesday, the 16th, he must have confounded materially his recollection of what happened on that and the following day. He represents his brother as either willfully concealing facts, or being in a state of great distraction. I, therefore, can not consider the Diary as of much weight in this painful controversy.

[1] Vol. i. 397. I must observe, however, that the silence of this historian, notwithstanding his good information and general accuracy, is less to be relied upon in the present instance, as he confesses he suppressed what would be hurtful to the feelings of George III.—such as his Majesty's first attack of insanity in 1765, which rendered the Regency Bill necessary. (Vol. i. 175.)

Sheldon replied to the gentleman, 'I pledge you my honor, my relative did not cut his throat.' When Mr. Sheldon was out of the room, the gentleman regretted that he had mentioned the circumstance, but said he was utterly astonished at Mr. Sheldon's denial. A gentleman then said, 'I believe I know the truth from Mr. Sheldon. After Mr. Charles Yorke left his Majesty, and had accepted the Seals, it was said Lord Rockingham and others expressed much resentment. Lord Rockingham, for himself, expressly denied that he said anything. However, Mr. Charles Yorke went privately to his sideboard, and took out a bottle of some very strong liquor. He was subject to a severe stomach complaint. This liquor brought on violent sickness, and in the paroxysm he broke a blood-vessel. After his death he was laid out, and the neck exposed to several persons, purposely permitted to view the corpse.' This, I rather think, was the whole truth."[1]

In a subsequent volume of his work, Craddock incidentally mentions "Mr. Yorke, who was afterwards, for a short time, Lord Chancellor;" and then he adds, "Having just alluded to the short life of the much-regretted Mr. Yorke after he was Lord Chancellor, I think it incumbent upon me to contradict the reported manner of his death, on the authority of one of his own family. He certainly was much agitated, after some hasty reproaches that he received on his return from having accepted the Seals, and he hastily took some strong liquor which was accidentally placed near the sideboard, and, by its occasioning great sickness he broke a blood-vessel. The friend from whom I received the account assured me that he was present when the corpse was left openly in the chamber, that the attendants might gratify their curiosity, and see that his death could not be truly attributed to the direct means which had been so publicly and so confidently asserted."[2]

I must likewise observe, that in an able article on the "Life of the Honorable Charles Yorke," published in the "Law Magazine," so recently as the year 1843, the imputation is strenuously negatived, and this account is given of the event:—"Stung with the coldness and reproaches of his party after his acceptance of the Great

[1] Crad. Mem. iv. 252.   [2] Ib. v. 92.

Seal, Mr. Yorke returned home in a state of extreme agitation, and drank freely of some spirits, which, in conjunction with the nervous excitement, occasioned a violent paroxysm of sickness. In the throes of his illness, he ruptured a blood-vessel."

The charitable conclusion may possibly be drawn that the unfortunate Charles Yorke died from the accidental bursting of a blood-vessel, and that he is only to be blamed for a want of due firmness in not adhering to his engagements.

Even those who think that the testimony that he died by his own hand preponderates, must pity while they condemn him, and must still regard his memory with respect. Heaven forbid that such an act should be justified or palliated; but there is not in the annals of human error an instance of a violation of religious duty so mixed up with virtuous feelings, and so demonstrating the excess of noble qualities. His acceptance of the Great Seal was wrong, but did not proceed from sordid motives. He made no condition for pecuniary grants to himself, which, if he had asked them, would have been showered down upon him. Nor does he at all seem to have been seduced by the love of power or splendor. He quitted a strong and united party to join one that was crumbling to pieces; and if he had survived he could hardly have expected long to enjoy his elevation. He was overpowered by royal blandishments, and a momentary mistake as to the duty of a good subject. But he was soon struck with deep remorse, and his love for honest fame was demonstrated by his being unable to survive the loss of it. Many holders of the Great Seal, to obtain it, have disregarded engagements as binding, and violated principles as sacred; yet, having clutched it, have suppressed the stings of conscience, and reveled in the fruits of inconsistency and treachery. Such men, who live without honor, and die a natural death without repentance, may have more to answer for in the sight of a just and merciful God, than he who, in the anguish of self-reproach, sought by a voluntary death to make atonement for the offense which he had committed.

All must join in the admiring, without qualification, nearly every portion of his prior career. The brilliant promise which he gave of proficiency in early youth, he fully realized in manhood. He is not of the same caliber as Lord Bacon, Sir Thomas More, and Lord Somers; but for the combination of professional knowledge and liberal accomplishments, he is at the very top of the second class of English lawyers. As an advocate, as a law officer of the Crown, and as a member of the House of Commons, he was almost equal to his father; and if he had enjoyed the good fortune to preside for twenty years on the bench as his father did, I make no doubt that he would have rivaled his father's fame as a magistrate. In literature, he was infinitely beyond him. I have already shown that he was a very considerable master of English prose composition,—having a style easy, elegant, and forcible, and with much more of genuine Anglicism than we generally find at a time when the public taste was corrupted by the inversions and the measured sententiousness of Johnson.

Dabbling in poetry, his efforts, perhaps, deserve only to be denominated "Vers de Société;"—but I do not know any succeeding (as there were few preceding) Chancellors who could have equaled the following specimens of them:—

"*Lines* (in imitation of Pope) *supposed to be addressed by a Lady deceased to the Author of a Poem in honor of her Memory.*

"Stript to the naked soul, escap'd from clay,
From doubts unfetter'd and dissolv'd in day,
Unwarm'd by vanity, unreach'd by strife,
And all my hopes and fears thrown off with life,
Why am I charmed with friendship's fond essays,
And, though, unbodied, conscious of thy praise?
Has pride a portion in the parted soul?
Does passion still the formless mind control?
Can gratitude outpant the silent breath,
Or a friend's sorrows pierce the gloom of death?
No! 'tis a spirit's nobler taste of bliss
That feels the worth it left, in proofs like this.
Thou liv'st to crown departed friends with fame,
And, dying late, shalt all thou gav'st reclaim."

"*To a Lady, with a present of Pope's Works.*

"The lover oft, to please some faithless dame,
With vulgar presents feeds the dying flame;
Then adds a verse of slighted vows complains,
While she the giver and the gift disdains.
These strains no idle suit to thee commend,
On whom gay loves with chaste desires attend;
Sure had he living view'd thy tender youth,
The blush of honor and the grace of truth,

Ne'er with Belinda's charms his song had glowed,
   But from thy form the lov'd idea flowed:
His wanton satire ne'er the sex had scorn'd,
   For thee, by virtue and the muse adorn'd."

"Stanzas, in the manner of Waller, occasioned by a Receipt to make Ink, given to the author by a Lady.

" In earliest times, ere man had learn'd
      His sense in writing to impart,
With inward anguish oft he burn'd,
      His friend unconscious of the smart.

" Alone he pin'd in thickest shade,
      Near murmuring waters sooth'd his grief,
Of senseless rocks companions made,
      And from their echoes sought relief.

" Cadmus, 'tis said, did first reveal
      How letters should the mind express,
And taught to grave with pointed steel
      On waxen tables its distress.

" Soon was the feeble waxen trace
      Supplied by ink's unfading spot
Which to remotest climes conveys
      In clearest marks the secret thought.

" Blest be his chemic hand that gave
      The world to know so great a good;
Hard that his name it should not save
      Who first pour'd forth the sable flood.

" 'Tis this consigns to endless praise
      The hero's valor, statesman's art,
Historic truth and fabling lays,
      The maiden's eyes, the lover's heart.

" This kindly spares the modest tongue
      To speak aloud the pleasing pain;
Aided by this, in tuneful song,
      Fond vows the virgin paper stain."[1]

Charles Yorke was a member of the Royal Society, but though distinguished in literature, I do not believe that he ever showed any taste for science. He always continued to delight in the society of men of letters, and was desirous of serving them. Hurd was indebted to him for promotion as well as Warburton. He did not waste his time in field sports and frivolous amusements. All the leisure he could spare from professional and political occupations he allotted to intellectual pursuits and enjoyments.

I find only one jest of his recorded, and it does not make us regret that he did not oftener aim at humor. After being returned member of the University, he went

[1] See also " Ode to the Honorable Miss Yorke, on her copying a portrait of Dante;" Cooksey's Life of Lord Hardwicke, 35 Annual Register, 1770.

round to pay his respects to the members of the senate. Among them was an old "Fellow" proverbial for having the largest and most hideous face that was ever seen. Mr. Yorke thus addressed him:—" Sir, I have great reason to be thankful to my friends in general, but confess myself under particular obligation to you for the very *remarkable countenance* you have shown me on this occasion."

Although Henry Fox spitefully says, " Yorke was very ugly while he lived,"—according to his portraits, the likeness of him on his tomb, and a figure of him in wax, still preserved, his countenance was intellectual and pleasing. Though his features were plain, his smile is said to have been soft and captivating; and his eye and mouth, in particular, indicated to a physiognomist his high mental qualities. He must have had much goodness of heart, for a numerous body of friends were very warmly attached to him. His untimely end caused a tremendous sensation in the metropolis, and political opponents joined in deeply deploring it. George Hardinge says,—" I saw Lord Camden just after Mr. Yorke's death, and I never in my life observed him so melancholy as that event made him. All their competitions and jealousies were at an end, and he lamented him in tears, and spoke of him with undissembled esteem."[1]

I should have mentioned that his remains were interred in the parish church of Wimpole, where there is erected a splendid monument to him by Scheemaker, bearing an inscription, which, after stating his birth and earlier promotions, thus proceeds :—

" The Great Seal was delivered to him, January 17th, 1770, at a juncture very unfavorable for his accepting it. He died, after a short illness, on the 20th of that month. He possessed uncommon Endowments, natural and acquired ; was a complete Master of his own Profession, as practiced in both parts of the United Kingdom ; had an extensive knowledge of Polite Literature, and understood with accuracy the Modern as well as Ancient Langauges. His Style in Composition and Speaking was nervous, elegant, and clear, and his Invention and Learning often furnished him with arguments which had escaped the Ingenuity of others. He was heard with attention and conviction, both in the Senate and at the Bar. His Mind was of a humane and liberal turn ; and both in his public and private Station, he always acted upon Principles of Virtue and Honor. With these Talents and Qualities, we justly lament that the Public was deprived of his Abilities at a juncture when they might have been of the greatest use, and the Crown of his Service in a

[1] MS. Life of Lord Camden.

Station to which he had been long destined, and which he would have eminently adorned.

"This Monument is erected to his Memory by his most affectionate and afflicted Brother, PHILIP, Earl of HARDWICKE."

Considering that these are the sentiments of one who had so loved him from infancy, and so deeply lamented the close of his career, they are most solemn and affecting.

Charles Yorke, from his life and from his death, will always be interesting in English history. " His moral and intellectual worth, literary merits, legal renown, and, more than all these, his gentle goodness and attaching qualities of heart, shed a calm and placid light, even at this interval of time, over his memory, like the pure ray of some distant star, which the mists, raised by earth, have for a time obscured from our view."[1]

The Great Seal not having been put to the patent for creating him Baron Morden before he expired, this peerage only reminds his descendants of the additional honors they might have acquired. His eldest son, soon after coming of age, represented the county of Cambridge in parliament, till the death of his uncle, the second Earl of Hardwicke, in 1790, when he succeeded to all the honors and estates of the family. On his death, without male issue in 1834, they devolved on the present Earl of Hardwicke, whose father, the late gallant and good-humored Vice-Admiral, Sir Joseph Yorke, M.P., was the youngest son by the second marriage of Lord Chancellor Charles Yorke.[2]

[1] Law Mag. No. lxi. 95.
[2] Ante, p. 236 ; Grandeur of the Law, 66.

There is a labored panegyric on the subject of this memoir, which, coming from a very eminent lawyer who had frequently heard him plead at the bar, possesses sufficient interest to justify me in copying it in a note, although it be written in a turgid and almost bombastic style :—" That modern constellation of English jurisprudence, that elegant and accomplished ornament of Westminister Hall in the present century (1792), the Honorable Charles Yorke, Esq.; whose ordinary speeches as an advocate were profound lectures ; whose digressions, from the exuberance of the best juridical knowledge, were illuminations; whose energies were oracles; whose constancy of mind was won into the pinnacle of our English forum at an inauspicious moment; whose exquisiteness of sensibility at almost the next moment from the impression of imputed error stormed the fort even of his cultivated reason, and so made elevation and extinction contemporaneous ! and whose prematureness of fate, notwithstanding the great contributions from the manly energies of a Northington and the vast splendors of a Camden, and notwithstanding also the accessions from the two rival luminaries which have more latterly adorned our equitable hemisphere [Thurlow and Wedderburn], causes an almost insuppliable interstice in the science of English equity. To have been selected

CHAPTER CLII.

LIFE OF LORD CHANCELLOR BATHURST FROM HIS BIRTH TILL HE WAS MADE A PUISNE JUDGE.

COMPENSATION is sometimes made for a scanty share of natural abilities by great success in the world. Thus, justice is done to the individual, while the pride of rewarded genius is tempered, and a balm is applied to the wounded self-complacency of those who have been unfortunate. For such wise purposes, Henry Bathurst—little qualified for any intellectual pursuit—became a Member of the House of Commons, one of the twelve Judges, a Commissioner of the Great Seal, Lord Chancellor, Lord President of the Council, and an Earl,—and when he had been raised to the first magistracy in the kingdom, he retained that situation for a much longer period than More, Bacon, Clarendon, or Somers. To his credit be it remembered, that he reached such a height without a dishonorable action. The portion of plain common sense bestowed upon him was unmixed with any vicious propensity; and his career, if it was without brilliancy, was without reproach. The proximate causes of his success may be considered harmless manners,

---

as the friend of such a man was nearly *instar omnium* to an English lawyer. Even to be old enough to have received the impression of Mr. Charles Yorke's character as a lawyer from the frequency of hearing his chaste, delicate, and erudite expressions in the discharge of professional duty, is some source of mental gratification."—HARGRAVE'S *Preface to Hale*, p. clxxxi.

This effort of an industrious black-letter conveyancer at fine writing was thus justly satirized in " The Pursuits of Literature :"—

" With HARGRAVE to the Peers approach with awe,
And sense and grammar seek in Yorke and law."

There is a disparaging character of Charles Yorke by Horace Walpole, to which, from the author's prejudices against all the Yorkes little weight can be given :—" Yorke's speeches in parliament had for some time, though not as soon as they ought, fallen into disesteem. At the bar his practice had declined, from a habit of gluttony and intemperance, as I have mentioned. Yet as a lawyer his opinion had been in so high repute, that he was reported to have received 100,000 guineas in fees. In truth his chief practice had flourished while his father was not only Lord Chancellor, but a very powerful minister. Yorke's parts were by no means shining. His manner was precise, yet diffuse; and his matter more sententious than instructive. His conduct was timid, irresolute, often influenced by his profession, oftener by interest. He sacrificed his character to his ambition of the Great Seal, and his life to his repentance of having attained it."—*Mem. Geo. III.*, iv. 53.

sober habits, family interest, and the mediocrity of his parts, which, preventing envy and jealousy, made him to be regarded with favor by men in power, and to be preferred to others who might have given trouble by entertaining an independent opinion, and who might from dependents have risen into rivals. It should likewise be borne in mind that, as far as the public could observe, he performed almost decently the duties of the offices in which, to the surprise of mankind, he was placed,—affording a memorable example of what may be accomplished by dull discretion.[1]

The subject of this memoir was the second son of Allen, Lord Bathurst, who acted a distinguished part in public life during four reigns, and is celebrated in prosaic verses by Pope, and in poetical prose by Burke. The family are said to have come from Germany, and to have resided at "Batters," near Luneburg, from which originally they took their name. On coming to England they had a grant of a tract of forest land in Sussex, which was at first called "Batters Hurst," and then "Bathurst." Their castle here was demolished, and they lost almost the whole of their property during the wars of the Roses, so that for some generations they fell into obscurity. But they were revived by commerce; and Sir Benjamin Bathurst, their chief in the reign of William III., rose to be Governor of the East India Company, and treasurer of the household to Princess Anne, of Denmark.

Allen, the long-lived,—his son,—having studied at Trinity College, Cambridge, under the then Master, Dean Bathurst, his uncle, was returned to parliament, when hardly of age, for the borough of Cirencester, and became a partisan of the Tories. As a reward for his services, he was raised to the peerage,—being one of the batch of twelve, made in 1711, to support the Peace of Utrecht,— who, when they were introduced into the House of Lords, were asked, in legal phraseology addressed to a jury, "if

---

[1] "Have you not observed," writes Swift to Bolingbroke, "that there is a lower kind of discretion and regularity, which seldom fails of raising men to the highest stations in the court, the church, and the law? Did you never observe one of your clerks cutting his paper with a *blunt ivory knife?* Did you ever know the knife to fail going the true way? Whereas if he had used a *razor* or a *penknife*, he had odds against himself of spoiling a whole sheet. I have twenty times compared the notion of that *ivory implement* to those talents that thrive best at court."

they would speak by their foreman?" He continued an active debater in that House above half a century,—almost invariably in opposition to the successive Whig administrations formed under the first two princes of the House of Brunswick. But he lived to see better times, when Tory ascendency was to be restored. In 1757 he was appointed treasurer to George III., then Prince of Wales; and when that Sovereign came to the throne, although the venerable Tory Peer declined office on account of his infirmities, he had a pension granted to him of £2,000 a year, and he was in due time advanced to an Earldom. He was spared to behold his son, well-stricken in years, sitting on the woolsack as Lord High Chancellor; being the only individual, except the father of Sir Thomas More, on whom such a felicity was ever conferred. But he was less distinguished as a statesman than as the intimate associate of Swift, Prior, Rowe, Congreve, Arbuthnot, Gay, Addison, and Pope,—still keeping up an intimate acquaintance with the most distinguished of the succeeding generation of men of letters.

We have an interesting relation of the manner in which he became acquainted with the author of Tristram Shandy:—" He came up to me one day," says that lively writer, "as I was at the Prince of Wales's court:—'I want to know you, Mr. Sterne, but it is fit that you should know also who it is that wishes that pleasure. You have heard of an old Lord Bathurst, of whom your Popes and Swifts have sung and spoken so much. I have lived my life with geniuses of that cast, but have survived them; and, despairing ever to find their equals, it is some years since I have cleared my accounts and shut up my books, with thought of never opening them again. But you have kindled a desire in me of opening them once more before I die, which now I do; so go home and dine with me.' This nobleman, I say, is a prodigy; for at eighty-five he has all the wit and promptitude of a man of thirty; a disposition to be pleased, and a power to please others, beyond whatever I knew,—added to which a man of learning, courtesy, and feeling."

The aged Peer had indeed the most elegant tastes, and the most jovial manners,—offering a striking contrast to Henry, who was rather abstemious and sullen—insomuch that when, after supper, the son had retired, the father would rub his hands, and say to the company, "Now that *the old gentleman* is gone to bed, let us be merry, and enjoy ourselves."

To him was inscribed Pope's epistle "On the Use of Riches," in which he is thus addressed:—

> " The sense to value riches, with the art
> To enjoy them and the virtue to impart
> Not meanly, not ambitiously pursued,
> Not sunk by sloth, nor rais'd by servitude;
> To balance fortune by a just expense,
> Join with economy magnificence;
> With splendor charity, with plenty health;
> O, teach us, BATHURST, yet unspoiled by wealth!
> That secret rare between the extremes to move
> Of mad good-nature and of mean self-love."

But a more striking tribute to his memory is to be found in the famous speech delivered, a few months before his death, by Burke, on Reconciliation with America.[1] The orator, with the imagination of a true poet, having drawn the attention of the House to the rapid growth of the colonies, and the respect with which, on account of their wealth and population, they ought to be treated, thus proceeded:—

"Mr. Speaker, I can not prevail upon myself to hurry over this great consideration. It is good for us to be here. We stand where we have a vast view of what is and what is past. Clouds, indeed, and darkness rest upon the future. Let us, however, before we descend from this noble eminence, reflect that this growth of our national prosperity has happened within the short period of the life of man. It has happened within sixty-eight years. There are those alive whose memory might touch the two extremities. For instance, my Lord Bathust might remember all the stages of the progress. He was in 1704 of an age at least to be made to comprehend such things. He was then old enough *acta parentum jam legere, et quæ sit poterit cognoscere virtus.* Suppose, Sir, that the angel of this auspicious youth, foreseeing the many virtues which made him one of the most amiable, as he is one of the most fortunate men of his age, had opened to him in vision that when in the fourth generation, the third prince of the House of Brunswick

[1] This speech was delivered on the 22nd of March, 1775, and he died on the 15th of September following.

had sat twelve years on the throne of that nation which (by the happy issue of moderate and leading councils) was to be made Great Britain, he should see his son, Lord Chancellor of England, turn back the current of hereditary dignity to its fountain, and raise him to a higher rank of peerage, while he enriched the family with a new one—if, amidst these bright and happy scenes of domestic honor and prosperity, that angel should have drawn up the curtain and unfolded the rising glories of his country, and, while he was gazing with admiration on the then commercial grandeur of England, the genius should point out to him a little speck, scarce visible in the mass of the national interest, a small seminal principle, rather than a formed body, and should tell him—'Young man, there is America—which at this day serves for little more than to amuse you with stories of savage men and uncouth manners; yet shall, before you taste of death, show itself equal to the whole of that commerce which now attracts the envy of the world. Whatever England has been growing to by a progressive increase of improvement, brought in by varieties of people, by succession of civilizing conquests and civilizing settlements, in a series of seventeen hundred years, you shall see as much added to her by America in the course of a single life!' If this state of his country had been foretold to him, would it not require all the sanguine credulity of youth, and all the fervid glow of enthusiasm, to make him believe it? Fortunate man, he has lived to see it! Fortunate, indeed, if he lives to see nothing that shall vary the prospect, and cloud the setting of his day!"

But, however reluctantly, in obedience to my duty I must now attend to a much less interesting character, and explain in what manner the most improbable part of the vision was realized. "The auspicious youth" was married to Catherine, daughter and heiress of Sir Peter Apsley, by whom he had four sons and five daughters."[1]

[1] He was, or pretended to be, rather alarmed by the fecundity of his wife. In a letter to Swift, alluding to the Dean's scheme for relieving the miseries of the Irish by fattening their children for the table, he says,—" I did immediately propose it to Lady Bathurst as your advice,--particularly for her last boy, which was born the plumpest and finest thing that could be seen; but she fell into a passion, and bid me send you word that she would not follow up your direction, but that she would breed him to be a parson, and he should live upon the fat of the land; or a lawyer, and then instead of being eat himself he should devour others. You know women in a passion never mind

For Henry, the second son, I must bespeak, during a short space, the patience of the reader, although, as he had no striking qualities, good or bad, and as he met with no remarkable vicissitudes of fortune, I can not expect to excite in his favor the sympathy of any class of readers.

He was born on the second of May, in the year 1714. I know not, and I must own I have not taken much pains to ascertain, at what school he was educated. He probably passed through it with little flogging and little distinction. At the usual age he went to Christ Church, Oxford,—where nothing more is known of him than that he took his degree of B. A. in 1733.

Being at this time a younger brother, he was destined to the bar, and he was entered of Lincoln's Inn. The discipline there had become what it has since continued; moots and readings have fallen into disuetude, and no other means of instruction substituted for them, the only qualification for being licensed as an advocate was—eating a certain number of dinners in the Hall.

This *curriculum* being completed by Mr. Bathurst, he was called to the bar in the year 1736. He rode the Oxford circuit, and sat in the Court of King's Bench but, although he was very regular in his habits, he seems to have had little business beyond a few briefs given him by favor.

While still in his twenty-second year he was returned to serve for the family borough of Cirencester. It is said that a lawyer ought not to enter parliament till he has fair pretensions to be made Solicitor General; but I do not believe that young Bathurst's professional progress was at all impeded by his political pursuits, and without being in parliament he probably would never even have had a silk gown. He sat in the House of Commons for Cirencester, and for the county of Gloucester, from 1736 to 1751, a period of fifteen years—during the whole of which he is hardly ever mentioned as having taken part in debate.

In 1741, he is said to have opposed the Bill for forcibly

what they say; but as she is a very reasonable woman, I have almost brought her over to your opinion, and have convinced her that, as matters stood, we could not possibly maintain all the nine; she does begin to think it reasonable that the youngest should raise fortunes for the eldest."

manning the Navy. His short speech is reported, and I suspect invigorated, by Dr. Johnson, for it has the true Johnsonian flow:—

"Sir, that this law will easily admit, in the execution of it, such abuses as will overbalance the benefits, may readily be proved; and it will not be consistent with that regard to the public, expected from us by those whom we represent, to enact a law which may probably become an instrument of oppression. The servant by whom I am now attended may be termed, according to the language of this bill, a seafaring man, having been once in the West Indies; and he may, therefore, be forced from my service and dragged into a ship, by the authority of a justice of the peace, perhaps of some abandoned jobber, dignified with the commission only to influence elections, and awe those whom excises and riot acts can not subdue. I think it, Sir, not improper to declare that I would by force oppose the execution of a law like this; that I would bar my doors and defend them; that I would call my neighbors to my assistance; and treat those who should attempt to enter, without my consent, as thieves, ruffians, and murderers."[1]

Though Mr. Bathurst spoke rarely, he was a constant attender in the House, and his vote might always be reckoned upon by the opponents of Sir Robert Walpole. He joined the Leicester House party, and in 1745 was made Solicitor General to the Prince of Wales, on which occasion the rank of King's counsel was conferred upon him, and he put on a silk gown.

In 1749, he opposed the grant of an indemnity to the citizens of Glasgow for the loss they had sustained in the late rebellion, contending that they ought to have made a stouter resistance to the rebels, and that such indemnities would lessen the disposition to oppose foreign or domestic enemies—and pointing out the burning of Penzance by the Spaniards, in the reign of Elizabeth, and of Teignmouth, with all the ships in its harbor, by the French, in the reign of William III., when no compensatiou from parliament was made to the sufferers, or asked by them.[2] The same session, he spoke upon his favorite subject, the manning of the navy, condemning the plan

[1] 12 Parl. Hist 93. He is represented as having said a few words on two other occasions respecting this bill. (Ibid. 105, 120.) [2] 14 Parl. Hist. 527.

brought forward by Ministers for that purpose.¹ In 1750, he delivered a long oration about the demolition of the port of Dunkirk, a favorite topic for the assailants of successive governments for half a century.²

Meanwhile, he continued steadily to attend the courts in Westminster Hall, and to go the Oxford circuit, though with little encouragement.

While at the bar, he was engaged in one *cause célèbre*,— the trial, at Oxford, of Miss Blandy for the murder of her father,—which he had to conduct for the Crown as the leader of the circuit. This is the most horrid parricide to be found in our criminal annals, and I hope it will remain for many generations without a parallel. Mr. Bathurst's address to the jury has been much praised for its eloquence —and, as it certainly contains proof of good feeling, if not of high talent and refined taste, I have pleasure in copying the best passages of it. After making some observations upon the prosecution being carried on by order of the King, and upon the immense concourse of people assembled, he thus proceeded :—

"Miss Blandy, the prisoner at the bar, a gentlewoman by birth and education, stands indicted for no less a crime than that of murder; and not only for murder, but for the murder of her own father, and for the murder of a father passionately fond of her, undertaken with the utmost deliberation; carried on with an unvaried steadiness of purpose, and at last accomplished by a frequent repetition of the baneful dose administered with her own hand. A crime so shocking in its own nature, and so aggravated in all its circumstances, as will (if she be proved to be guilty of it) justly render her infamous to the latest posterity, and make our children's children, when they read the horrid tale of this day, blush to think that such a creature ever existed in a human form. I need not, gentlemen, point out to you the heinousness of the crime of murder. You have but to consult your own breasts, and you will know it. Has a murder been committed? Who has ever beheld the ghastly corpse of the murdered innocent, weltering in its blood, and did not feel his own blood run slow and cold through all his veins? Has the murderer escaped? With what eagerness do we pursue! With what zeal do we apprehend! With what joy do we

---

¹ 14 Parl. Hist. 553–557. ² Ibid. 698.

bring to justice! And when the dreadful sentence of death is pronounced upon him, everybody hears it with satisfaction, and acknowledges the justice of the Divine denunciation that '*Who sheddeth man's blood, by man shall his blood be shed.*' If this, then, is the case of any common murderer, what will be thought of one who has murdered her own father? who has designedly done the greatest of all human injuries to him from whom she received the first and greatest of all human benefits? who has wickedly taken away his life to whom she stands indebted for life? who has deliberately destroyed, in his old age, him by whose care and tenderness she was protected in her helpless infancy? who has impiously shut her ears against the loud voice of nature and of God, which bid her 'honor her father,' and instead of honoring him has murdered him?—in shortly opening the case, that you may the better understand the evidence, although I shall rather extenuate than aggravate, I have a story to tell which I trust will shock the ears of all who hear me. Mr. Francis Blandy, the unfortunate deceased, was an attorney-at-law, who lived at Henley, in this county. A man of character and reputation, he had one only child,—a daughter,—the darling of his soul, the comfort of his age. He took the utmost care of her education, and had the satisfaction to see his care was not ill bestowed, for she was genteel, agreeable, sprightly, sensible. His whole thoughts were bent to settle her advantageously in the world. In order to do that, he made use of a pious fraud (if I may be allowed the expression), pretending he could give her £10,000 for her fortune. This he did in hopes that some of the neighboring gentlemen would pay their addresses to her; for out of regard to him she was, from her earliest youth, received into the best company; and her own behavior made her afterwards acceptable to them. But how short-sighted is human prudence! What was intended for her promotion, proved his death and her destruction." He then went on to state the following facts:—"Captain Cranstoun, an officer of the army, of a noble family in Scotland, but of a most profligate character, being stationed with a recruiting party at Henley,—for the sake of Miss Blandy's expected fortune, pretended to fall in love with her, and paid his addresses to her. She being soon deeply attached to him, accepted his offer, but the father positively refused his consent. The lovers then resolved to poison him—and Captain Cranstoun sent Miss Blandy some Scotch pebbles with a powder to clean them, which was white arsenic. To prepare the world for what was to happen, according to the superstition of the times, they had pretended to have heard supernatural music in the house, and to have seen an apparition which foreboded his death. She first administered the poison to her father in his tea, and when it caused him exquisite anguish, and seemed to be consuming his entrails, she gave him a fresh dose of the poison in the shape of gruel, which she said would comfort and relieve him. As he was dying, the cause of his death was discovered and communicated to him. He exclaimed, 'Poor love-sick girl! what will not a woman do for the man she loves?' She said, 'Dear Sir, banish me where you will, do with me what you please, so that you do but forgive me.' He answered, 'I do forgive you, but you should, my dear, have considered that I was your own father; but, oh, that that villain, who hath eat of the best and drank of the best my house could afford, should take away my life and ruin my daughter!' She then ran for the paper containing the powder, and threw it into the fire, thinking it was destroyed; but it remained unconsumed, and produced her conviction. How evidently the hand of Providence has interposed to bring her to this day's trial, that she may suffer the consequence! For what but the hand of Providence could have preserved the paper thrown by her into the fire, and could have snatched it unburnt from the devouring flame? Good God! how wonderful are all thy ways! and how miraculously hast thou preserved this paper, to be this day produced in evidence against the prisoner, in order that she may undergo the punishment due to her crime, and be a dreadful example to all others who may be tempted in like manner to offend thy Divine Majesty!"

Some witnesses being called for the defense, Mr. Bathurst replied, and thus concluded:—

"Gentlemen, you are sworn to give a true verdict according to the evidence laid before you. If upon that evidence she appears to be innocent, in God's name let her be acquitted. But if upon that evidence she appears to be guilty, I am sure you will do justice to the public and acquit your own consciences."

There was a verdict of *guilty* on the clearest proof of premeditation and design: but (to show the worthlessness of the dying declarations of criminals, and the absurdity of the practice of trying to induce them to confess) she went out of the world with a solemn declaration, which she signed and repeated at the gallows, that she had no intention of injuring her father, and that she thought the powder would make him love her and give his consent to her union with Captain Cranstoun.[1]

Mr. Bathurst continued leagued in politics with those who placed all their hopes of preferment on the accession of a new Sovereign. At the commencement of the session of 1751 he opposed the address, and, to recommend himself to the Prince, leveled several sarcasms at the King—sneering at the courtly language which the House was called upon to adopt:—

"We must not," said he, "express our acknowledgments to his Majesty without calling them our *warmest* acknowledgments; we must not talk of his Majesty's endeavors, without calling them his *unwearied* endeavors. Thus I could go on, Sir, with my remarks through the whole of this address; and all this without knowing anything of the facts we thus so highly extol. How a minister might receive such high-flown compliments without knowledge, or how this House may think proper to express itself upon the occasion, I do not know; but I should be ashamed to express myself in such a manner to my Sovereign; nay, I should be afraid lest he should order me out of his presence for attempting to put upon him such gross flattery."[2]

Frederick soon after dying suddenly, Mr. Bathurst went over, with a number of his party, to the Court, and in consequence he was, in 1754, made by Lord Hardwicke a puisne Judge of the Court of Common Pleas.

[1] 18 St. Tr. 1118-1194. [2] 14 Parl. Hist. 805.

CHAPTER CLIII.

CONTINUATION OF THE LIFE OF LORD BATHURST TILL HE RESIGNED THE GREAT SEAL AND WAS MADE PRESIDENT OF THE COUNCIL.

BY reading, attendance in Court, and going the circuits, Mr. Justice Bathurst had picked up a little law without much practice: he had industriously made a sort of Digest of the rules of evidence and the points generally arising at the trial of actions;[1] he was quiet and bland in his manners, and he possessed a great share of discretion, which enabled him on the bench to surmount difficulties, and to keep out of scrapes. With these qualifications he made a very tolerable puisne.[2] When sitting alone, he ruled points of law as rarely as possible, leaving them mixed up with facts to the jury: and sitting in banc, he agreed with the Chief Justice and his brethren, or (if the Court was divided) with the Judge who was supposed to be the soundest lawyer.[3] Notwithstanding his Tory education and his attachment to the Government, he concurred in the judgment of Lord Camden for the liberation of Wilkes, and against general warrants. In a case in which it was held that a bond in consideration of past cohabitation is good in law, he pleased the sanctimonious by enriching his judgment with quotations from the books of Exodus and Deuteronomy, to prove that "wherever it appears that the man was the seducer, a provision for the woman shall be upheld."[4]— The murmurs against his appointment as a political job died away, and there was a still weaker Judge made after him to keep him in countenance.[5]

But although people ceased to wonder that he had been

[1] This was afterwards enlarged by Mr. Justice Buller, and published under the name of "Buller's Nisi Prius."
[2] Walter Scott used to tell a story in point. The heir apparent of a considerable family in Scotland having been, though almost fatuous, called to the bar, and there being some talk in the servants' hall about the profession of an advocate, an old butler exclaimed,—"It canna' be a very kittle tred, for our young laird is ane."
[3] See Wilson's Common Pleas Reports.
[4] Turner v. Vaughan, 2 Wils. 339.
[5] When Graham was made a Judge, Law, then at the Bar, said,—"He puts Rook on a pinnacle." Rook till then had been considered very incompetent.

put upon the bench as a pnisne Judge, no one ever dreamed of his going higher.—A puisne Judge he did remain for fifteen long years, when, according to our modern system, he would have been entitled to retire on a pension. But nothing can be more fantastical than the distribution of prizes in the lottery of legal promotion.

The triumph at Court on the acceptance of the office of Chancellor by Charles Yorke, was turned into deep dismay by his sudden death. The Great Seal was earnestly pressed upon Sir Eardley Wilmot, Chief Justice of the Common Pleas, but he resolutely refused to accept it, partly from a dislike of politics, partly from disapprobation of the measures of the Government, and partly from considering how precarious must have been the tenure of his new office. A strong appeal was again made to Lord Mansfield, and he was implored, by consenting to be Chancellor, to rescue the King from his difficulties, and to restore vigor to the Government, so much weakened by the secession of the Marquis of Granby, the Duke of Manchester, Dunning, and all the liberals who had gone out with Lord Camden; but the wary Scot would not leave his seat in the King's Bench, which he so much adorned, and which he held for life. He advised that the Great Seal should be put into commission, and he consented to preside on the woolsack as Speaker of the House of Lords. This course was adopted.[1]

A strange selection was made of Commissioners, which could not have been by his advice,—unless, indeed, (as was suggested), he wished them to be entirely under his own control,—three puisne Judges, of fair character, but very moderate abilities and learning, and almost en-

[1] The difficulty of disposing of the Great Seal at this juncture led to the resignation of the Duke of Grafton. After relating his fruitless negotiations, thus he addresses his son, Lord Euston:—" You will feel for me in this distressing dilemma: you will perceive that I left nothing untried to bring the vessel to tolerable trim: and when you consider that, quitted by Lord Camden, and at the same time by Lord Granby, I had no reliance in the Cabinet but on General Conway only, I know you will think that, under such circumstances I could not proceed and be of service to the King and to the country; and recollect that the hopes of co-operation with Mr. Yorke to bring about an essential addition of right, principle, credit, and support, vanished of course with himself. I laid before his Majesty directly my difficulties, and observed that they were such as compelled me to retire from my office, though it would be my full desire to give all assistance to his Majesty's Government."—*Journal.*

tirely unacquainted with the practice of Courts of Equity: Sir Sidney Stafford Smythe, from the Exchequer; Sir Richard Aston, from the King's Bench; and, last and least, the Honorable Henry Bathurst, from the Common Pleas.[1] The profession stood aghast at this arrangement, and the anticipation of failure was exceeded by the reality.

The Court of Chancery had not been in such a state since Cromwell's time, when the bench there was occupied by MAJOR LISLE and COLONEL FIENNES. No one of the three Commissioners had any confidence in himself or in his colleagues. In the regular hearing of causes, they got on tolerably well by a mutual agreement to hold their tongues, and to consult Lord Mansfield as to the framing of their decrees; but, on "Seal Days," when they were peppered by motions to be disposed of at the moment, they could not conceal their consternation. A single incompetent Judge sitting by himself may take advantage of the tone of the counsel addressing him, of the countenance of the bystanders, and of hints from the officers; but the difficulties of the three Lords Commissioners were multiplied by their numbers, and the conflicting devices which they adopted to conceal their ignorance.

In one easy case, which attracted much public notice, and in which they had the good luck to be unanimous, they gained a little *éclat*. The bill was filed by the celebrated Macklin against some booksellers, who employed Mr. Gurney, the short-hand writer, for the fee of one guinea, to go to the playhouse and take down from the mouths of the actors, the words of his farce, entitled "*Love à la Mode*," lately brought out upon the stage, but never printed. The copy thus obtained they were about

---

[1] "January 23, 1770.
"Sir Sidney Stafford Smythe, K^{nt}., ⎫ a Baron of the Exchequer.
Sir Richard Aston, K^{nt}., ⎬ a Judge of the King's Bench.
The H^{on}. Henry Bathurst, ⎭ a Judge of the Common Pleas,
being by letters Patent, dated the 21st Jan^y, 1770, appointed Commissioners for the custody of the Great Seal of Great Britain, upon the 23rd of the same month came into the Court of Chancery at West^r Hall, and in open Court took the oaths of allegiance and supremacy, and also the oath of office, the same being administered by the Deputy Clerk of the Crown,—Mr. Holford, the Senior Master in Chancery present, holding the book. Which being done, Mr. Attorney General prayed that it might be recorded, which the Court ordered accordingly."—*Cr. Off. Min. B.*, No. 2, fol. 16.

to publish in the "Court Miscellany, or Gentleman and Lady's Magazine," and a motion was made for an injunction to prevent them from doing so. The defendants' counsel contended, that in such a case a Court of Equity ought not to interfere, but leave the plaintiff to his remedy at law, as he had lost all property in the piece by acting it, and he had not sustained, and he could not sustain, any damage, the representation on the stage being benefited rather than injured by additional publicity. But the Lords Commissioners, without hearing a reply from the counsel for the plaintiff, held that the acting was no publication to deprive him of his remedy, and Lord Commissioner Bathurst said—"The printing it before the author has printed it, is doing him a great injury. Besides the advantage from the performance, he has another means of profit—and irremediable mischief is about to be done to his property. This is a strong case for an injunction." *Perpetual injunction ordered.*[1]

But the solemn judgments of the Lords Commissioners, although supposed to be sanctioned by the authority of Lord Mansfield, were not always approved of, and they and he were particularly censured for a reversal of the decree of the Master of the Rolls in the great case of TOTHILL *v.* PITT.[2] This suit arose out of the will made by Sir William Pynsent, in favor of Mr. Pitt, as a mark of the testator's sense of the patriotic services of " the Great Commoner," and involved the right to a considerable amount of personal property bequeathed to him, along with the estate of Burton Pynsent. The case coming on at the Rolls, before Sir Thomas Sewell, a very eminent Equity Judge, he decided in favor of Mr. Pitt— on the clear and well-established rule of law, that " where the words of a will give an express estate tail in a freehold, the same words applied to personalty will give the whole interest—to avoid a perpetuity, which the law abhors." After this decree had been acquiesced in for six years, an appeal was brought against it before the present Lords Commissioners of the Great Seal. I am wholly at a loss to account for the reversal which they pronounced ; for I utterly, and most seriously and unfeignedly, discard the notion which prevailed at the time, that they or their

[1] Ambler, 694 ; see Murray *v.* Elliston, 5 B. & A. 737 ; Morris *v.* Kelly, 1 J. & W. 656. [2] Dickens, 431.

assessor must have been influenced by political enmity to the respondent. The reversal caused a burst of surprise, and he immediately appealed against it to the House of Lords. The Judges, being summoned, gave an unanimous opinion in favor of the now appellant, and, with the concurrence of Lord Mansfield himself, the reversal was reversed, and the original decree was affirmed.[1]

After the learned Trio had gone on for a twelvemonth, floundering and blundering, the public dissatisfaction was so loud that some change was considered necessary. What was the astonishment of Westminster Hall, and of the public, when it was announced that his Majesty had been pleased to deliver the Great Seal to the Honorable HENRY BATHURST, a Judge of the Common Pleas, as Lord Chancellor, and to raise him to the peerage, by the title of Baron Apsley, of Apsley, in the county of Sussex!

It was thought vain again to solicit the acceptance of the Great Seal by any legal dignitary who had already acquired judicial reputation, and there were then objections to introducing into the House of Lords "the majestic sense of Thurlow, or the skillful eloquence of Wedderburn." Bathurst, from his birth and family connections, was very acceptable to the party in power; he was a man of inoffensive manners, and of undoubted honor and fidelity; and his insignificance was not disagreeable—being regarded as a guaranty that he would give no trouble in the Cabinet.

He was sworn in at a council at St. James's, the first day of Hilary Term. Two days after, he led a grand procession from his house in Dean Street to Westminster Hall, attended by the great officers of state and many of the nobility, and he was duly installed in the Court of Chancery.[2]

[1] Brown's Parliamentary Cases, vii. 455.
[2] "23rd January, 1771.

"The Lords Commissioners for the custody of the Great Seal of Great Britain, having delivered the said Great Seal to the King at his palace of St. James's, on Wednesday, the 23rd of January, 1771, his Majesty, about one o'clock the same day, delivered it to Henry Bathurst, Esqr., with the title of Lord Chancellor of Great Britain, who was thereupon, by his Majesty's command, sworn of the Privy Council, and likewise Lord High Chancellor of Great Britain, and took his place at the board accordingly. And on Friday, the 25th of Jan^y, he went in state from his house in Dean Street to West^r. Hall, accompanied by Earl Gower, President of the Council, Earl of Suffolk,

His proper title in the peerage at this time was Lord Apsley, and so continued till the death of his father, in 1775, when, his elder brother having previously died without issue, the earldom of Bathurst descended upon him; but I shall use the freedom to denominate him Lord Bathurst from the commencement of his Chancellorship.

Many thought that he must now entirely break down; but, on the contrary, he got on tolerably well. The Chancery galley was less unsteady than when *three* unskillful pilots were employed at the helm. There was entire confidence placed in the new Chancellor's integrity and earnest desire to do what was right; the Attorney and Solicitor General who practiced before him were desirous of supporting him, and he himself, placing just reliance on the liberality and honor of the Chancery bar, acted on the belief that there would be no gross attempt made to mislead him. In weighty cases he was in the habit of calling in the assistance of common-law judges, and being governed by their advice.

He likewise leaned constantly on Sir Thomas Sewell, the Master of the Rolls—never showing any arrogance or false pretension. In one important cause, having required the inferior Judge to sit as assessor, and heard his opinion, he said, with disarming candor—"I ought to apologize for keeping the matter so long before the Court; at first I differed in opinion with his Honor, but he hath now convinced me, and I entirely concede to his Honor's opinion, and am first to thank him for the great trouble he hath taken on the occasion."

Still the appointment was justly complained of as resting on political convenience, without regard to the interests of the suitors. As long as Lord Bathurst held the Great Seal, deep grumblings were uttered, and bitter sarcasms were leveled against him.

In all companies was repeated the saying of Sir Fletcher

---

rd Privy Seal, Earl of Hillsborough, one of the principal Secretaries of State, Marquess of Carnarvon, the Earls of Litchfield, Marchmont, Poulett, Strafford, the Lords Bruce and Boston, and Sir John Eardley Wilmot, K^{nt}.; where, in their presence, he took the oaths of allegiance and supremacy, and the oath of Lord High Chancellor of Great Britain, the Master of the Rolls holding the book, and the Deputy Clerk of the Crown reading the said oaths. Which being done, the Solicitor General moved that it might be recorded, and it was ordered accordingly."—*Minute Book*, No. 2, fol. 18.

Norton, who, when he heard of Lord Commissioner Bathurst being declared Lord High Chancellor, exclaimed, "What the three could not do, is given to the most incompetent of the three!"

Sir Charles Hanbury Williams inserted the new Chancellor in the band of Tories who

> " Were curs'd and stigmatiz'd by power,
> And rais'd to be expos'd."

Stories were invented and circulated respecting the Chancellor, which showed the low estimation in which he was held. It was said that his Lordship, on Wilkes being elected Lord Mayor of London, had threatened, in the exercise of the royal prerogative, when the profligate patriot was presented for confirmation, to disallow the choice of the citizens,—till told that this would be Wilkes's reply: " I am fitter for my office than you are for yours, and I must call upon the King to choose another Lord Chancellor."—Again, when he got into a controversy with a soldier's widow, about a spot of ground at Hyde Park Corner, and she having filed a bill against him, he gave her a sum of money to relinquish her claim, a witty barrister was represented to have observed, " Here is a suit by one old woman against another, and the Chancellor has been beaten in his own Court!"

There is a passage in Boswell's Life of Johnson, which shows still more strikingly the opinion of well-educated men upon this subject. The biographer having mentioned the introduction of Sir Alexander Macdonald to the Lexicographer, in the year 1772, thus proceeds:— " Sir Alexander observed, that the Chancellors in England are chosen from views much inferior to the office, being chosen from temporary political views. JOHNSON : ' Why, Sir, in such a government as ours, no man is appointed to an office because he is the fittest for it, nor hardly in any other government; because there are so many connections and dependencies to be studied. A despotic prince may choose a man to an office merely because he is the fittest for it.' " Such a conversation would not have occurred during the Chancellorship of Lord Hardwicke or Lord Somers.[1]

I give one other testimony from a popular work pub-

---

[1] Boswell, ii. 160.

lished shortly before the close of Lord Bathurst's career as Chancellor:—

"He traveled all the stages of the law with a rapidity that great power and interest can alone in the same degree accelerate. His professional character in his several official situations was never prominently conspicuous, till that wonderful day when he *leaped* at once into the foremost seat of the law. Every individual member of the profession stood amazed; but time, the great reconciler of strange events, conciliated matters *even here*. It was seen that the noble Earl was called upon from high authority to fill an important office, which no other could be conveniently found to occupy. Lord CAMDEN had retired without any abatement of *rooted* disgust, far beyond the reach of persuasion to remove. The great CHARLES YORKE, the unhappy victim of an unworthy sensibility, had just resigned the Seals and an inestimable life together; where could the eye of administration be directed? The rage of party ran in torrents of fire. The then Attorney and Solicitor General were at the moment thought ineligible. Perhaps, too, the noble Lord then at the head of affairs, and who was yet untried, had a policy in not forwarding transcendent abilities to obscure his own. Every such apprehension vanished upon the present appointment. This man could raise no sensation of envy as a rival, or fear as an enemy." [1]

Strange to say, he continued in the office of Lord Chancellor between seven and eight years. We have a very imperfect record of his judicial performances during this period. His reporters are *Ambler* and *Dickens*, and both together hardly give more space to the whole of his Chancellorship than is occupied by a single term of Lord Eldon or Lord Cottenham. He does not seem to have settled any point of much importance, and I can only find one case of general interest which came before him. —The widow of Philip Stanhope having sold to Dodsley, the bookseller, for £1,500 "Lord Chesterfield's Letters to his Son," which were advertised for publication, the executors of Lord Chesterfield, who was lately deceased, filed an injunction. The defendant first insisted that a person to whom a letter is written, or his representatives,

[1] Strictures on Eminent Lawyers, p. 76; Ambler, from p. 696 to p. 772; a Dickens, from p. 432 to p. 544.

may publish it without, or against the consent of, the writer or his representatives; and then tried to make out that at any rate in this case the late Lord Chesterfield, having recovered back some papers which he wished to burn, had expressly given permission to Mrs. Stanhope to make what use she pleased of those letters written by him to her late husband, after she had observed to him that "they would make a fine system of education if published," and that the only objection he offered was, "that there was too much Latin in them." But "the LORD CHANCELLOR was very clear that an injunction ought to be granted: That the widow had no right to print the letters without the consent of Lord Chesterfield or his executors: That she had obtained neither the one nor the other: That Lord Chesterfield, when he declined taking the letters, and said she might keep them, did not mean to give her leave to print and publish them. He cited the case of Mr. Pope's letters to be published by Curl, and Lord Clarendon's Life advertised by Dr. Shebbeare." *Injunction ordered till hearing, but recommendation given to the executors to permit the publication in case they saw no objection to the work on having a copy of it delivered to them.*[1]

The letters were published accordingly, and, upon the whole, there would have been ground for lamentation if they had been suppressed. Upon them chiefly depends the literary reputation of Lord Chesterfield; and, notwithstanding the noted saying of Dr. Johnson concerning the "morals" and "manners" which they teach, and although they are disfigured by passages highly exceptionable, they contain many useful observations on life, and they may be turned to good advantage in the education of youth. Our indignation against the writer is much softened by considering the characteristic faults of his son, to whom they were addressed.[2]

[1] Ambler, 737; Thompson and others, executors of the Earl of Chesterfield, v. Stanhope and Dodsley.
[2] Lest I should be supposed to give any countenance to the fashionable immorality to be found in these Letters, I copy, for the benefit of my young readers, the epigram describing their result:—

"Vile Stanhope—Demons blush to tell—
In twice two hundred places
Has shown his son the road to hell,
Escorted by the Graces.

Without able assistance, Lord Bathurst would have made sad work of the appeal business in the House of Lords. He had never been engaged in a Scotch case, and was utterly ignorant of Scotch law, so as not to know the difference of a holding *a me* from a holding *de me;* and the solemn decisions of the fifteen Judges of the Court of Session were to be reviewed by him. But Lord Mansfield, taking compassion upon his destitute condition, or influenced by a regard for the credit of the Government or the interests of justice, attended the hearing of these cases, and they were very satisfactorily disposed of.

The only very important English case which he had to deal with in the House of Lords was one in which he could not conveniently lean on Lord Mansfield; as it was a writ of error from a judgment of the Court of King's Bench on the grand question of literary property. But the twelve Judges were called in, and, adopting the opinion of a majority of them, "that authors have now no property in their works except what the legislature confers," the Chancellor had an easy task to perform in moving a reversal. "Having declared that he was wholly unbiassed, he entered into a very minute discussion of the several citations and precedents relied upon at the bar; and, one by one, described their complexion, their origin, and their tendency; showing that they were foreign to any constructions which would support the respondents in their argument. He then gave a history of the bill passed in Anne's reign for the protection of literary property, which, he said, was drawn up by the advice of Swift and Addison; and concluded with de-

> "But little did th' ungenerous lad
> Concern himself about them;
> For base, degenerate, meanly bad,
> He sneak'd to hell without them."

And I will give as an antidote the touching exhortation of my countryman, BURNS:—

> "The sacred lowe o' weel-plac'd love
> Luxuriantly indulge it;
> But never tempt th' illicit rove,
> Tho' naething should divulge it
> I waive the quantum o' the sin,
> The hazard of concealing:
> *But, och! it hardens a' within,*
> *And petrifies the feeling!*"

claring, that he was clearly of opinion with the appellants."[1] The reversal was carried, after a long debate, however, several lay peers and bishops taking part in it on opposite sides.

The only other important judicial proceeding in which Lord Bathurst was concerned is the trial of the Duchess of Kingston, before the House of Lords, for bigamy. The offense being in point of law *felony*, he was, on this occasion, created Lord High Steward, and Westminister Hall was fitted up with as much grandeur as when Charles I. was tried there before LORD PRESIDENT BRADSHAW and the "High Court of Justice,"—although, in this instance, it was known that a conviction could only lead to an admonition "that the lady should not do the like again."

When she first appeared at the bar, and courtesied to the Peers, his Grace the Lord High Steward thus addressed her:—

"Madam, you stand indicted for having married a second husband, your first husband being living; a crime so destructive of the peace and happiness of private families, and so injurious in its consequences to the welfare and good order of society, that by the statute law of this kingdom it was for many years (in your sex) punishable with death; the lenity, however, of later times has substituted a milder punishment in its stead.[2] This consideration must necessarily tend to lessen the perturbation of your spirits upon such an awful occasion. But that, Madam, which, next to the inward feelings of your own conscience, will afford you most comfort, is, reflecting upon the honor, the wisdom, and the candor of this high Court of criminal jurisdiction. It is, Madam, by your particular desire that you now stand at that bar. In your petition to the Lords, praying for a speedy trial, you assumed the title of Duchess Dowager of Kingston, and you likewise averred that Augustus John Harvey whose wife the indictment charges you with being, is at this time Earl of Bristol. On examining the records, the Lords are satisfied of the truth of that averment, and have accordingly allowed you the privilege you petitioned

---

[1] 17 Parl. Hist. 1001, 1400.
[2] Formerly women were hanged for all *clergiable* felonies however trifling because they could not plead that they were *clerks*.

for, of being tried by your peers in full Parliament; and from them you will be sure to meet with nothing but justice, tempered with humanity." [1]

The great question was, whether a sentence of the Ecclesiastical Court, which had been obtained, adjudging that there had been no prior marriage, was binding upon the House of Lords in the present proceeding? This having been most learnedly and ably argued by Thurlow and Wedderburn on the one side, and Wallace and Dunning on the other, the Lord High Steward, by the authority of the House, submitted it to the Judges. They gave an opinion in the negative, and the trial was ordered to proceed.

It was then proved by the clearest evidence that the Duchess, when Miss Chudleigh, and a maid of honor, had been secretly married to the Honorable Mr. Hervey, at that time a lieutenant in the navy, now Earl of Bristol, and that they lived together some days and nights, although afterwards, repenting of what they had done, they collusively tried to have the marriage declared null in the Ecclesiastical Court; and that she had afterwards been married to Evelyn Pierrepont, Duke of Kingston. The Lords unanimously found her guilty—one Lord adding, " erroneously, not intentionally." *Lord High Steward:* "Madam, the Lords have considered the charge and evidence brought against you, and have likewise considered of everything which you have alleged in your defense; and upon the whole matter their Lordships have found you guilty of the felony whereof you stand indicted. What have you to allege against judgment being pronounced upon you?" She having prayed the privilege of the peerage, to be exempt from punishment, and, after argument, a resolution being passed that she was entitled to it, the Lord High Steward said to her: " Madam, the Lords have considered of the prayer you have made, and the Lords allow it. But, Madam, let me add, that although very little punishment, or none, can now be inflicted, the feelings of your own conscience will supply that defect. And let me give you this informa-

---

[1] The difficulty would be to try for bigamy a lady married to a peer, whose first alleged husband was and continues a commoner. Quacumque viâ datâ she must be acquitted; for if there was no prior marriage, she is innocent; and if there was, the second marriage is void, so that she is no peeress, and the Lords have no jurisdiction.

tion, likewise—that you can never have the like benefit a second time, but another offense of the same kind will be capital. Madam, you are discharged, paying your fees."

His Grace then broke his white wand, and dissolved the Commission. In this solemn farce, which amused the town for three days, he was allowed to have played the easy part of Lord High Steward very creditably.[1]

Lord Chancellor Bathurst made no attempt to amend the law, or to reform the abuses of the Court of Chancery; but all notion of legal reform had disappeared during the last half of the eighteenth century; and it is a curious fact, that no general order was made by any Chancellor from Lord Hardwicke down to Lord Loughborough.[2]

Lord Bathurst was a member of the Cabinet which originated and carried on the most important and the most disastrous war in which this country was ever engaged—the war with our American colonies, by which the empire was dismembered; but I do not believe that he was answerable for any of the imprudent measures of Lord North's administration, except by assenting to them. He probably took no active part in the discussions in council respecting *conciliation* or *coercion*—and, when blood began to flow, he offered no opinion respecting the manner in which the war should be conducted. Even in parliament he very rarely spoke, except on some subject connected with the law; and, unlike Lord Camden and some other lawyers, who have greatly extended their oratorical fame when placed among the Peers, he seems never to have been well listened to in either House.

His maiden speech as a Lord was in defense of the Royal Marriage Act, which was framed, exactly as we now see it, under the directions of King George III., and which, although several of his ministers disapproved of it, his Majesty was resolutely determined to carry through without any alteration, so that his family might not again be degraded by misalliances—as he thought that it had lately been. Lord Bathurst, although when Attorney General to Frederick, Prince of Wales, his master being at variance with George II., he had seen great reason to doubt the asserted authority of the King respecting the marriage of his descendants, now, as Chancellor to George

[1] 20 St. Tr. 355–651.   [2] See Beame's Orders.

III., had all his doubts cleared up, and thus, in answer to the Marquis of Rockingham, he addressed their Lordships:—

"I confess, my Lords, that I had a share in drawing this bill, and I should be unworthy of the situation which I have the honor to fill if I were not prepared to justify every clause, every word, and every letter in it; and I am free to confess that I will not give my consent to any amendment whatever that may be proposed to it. Better than alter it, throw it out. But your Lordships will see its importance to the state. The King's right to the care of the royal family, and the approbation of their marriage, rests on the public good, and can not be doubted. As to who are the royal family, all the descendants of George II. are;—and so is the Prince of Wales. They are paid out of the civil list, and therefore they are of the royal family. If any inconvenience arise, parliament will take care to remedy it a hundred years hence. The power may be abused; but so may all power. It is not against religion to annul marriages—as we know by the general Marriage Act, from which the marriages of the royal family are excluded. The public necessity now requires that they should be regulated, and no mode would be effectual, other than that which this bill prescribes." [1]

At the commencement of the new parliament, in November, 1774, a scene was enacted which must have afforded some amusement to those who recollected Sir Fletcher Norton's biting sarcasm upon the appointment of Bathurst as Chancellor. The same Sir Fletcher Norton being elected Speaker of the House of Commons, had to appear before the same Chancellor at the bar of the House of Lords, to "disqualify himself," and to pray that the Commons might be directed to make a worthier choice. However, this was not the occasion to retaliate; and the Chancellor, in expressing his Majesty's approbation of the choice of the Commons, declared that "no person in Mr. Speaker's situation ever stood less in need of apology." [2]

In the course of the same session the Chancellor supported the bill for cutting off the commerce of the rebellious provinces in America, with the rest of the world; and the measure of sending Hanoverian troops to Gibral-

[1] 17 Parl. Hist. 389.   [2] Ib. 32.   [3] Ib. 456.

tar and Minorca, the legality of which turned on the just construction of the "Act of Settlement."[1]

The Americans having now declared their "*Independence,*" and there being open hostilities with them, a great difficulty arose as to the treatment of prisoners taken by us in battle. We still said they were the *King's subjects* who were guilty of "levying war against him in his realm." But if so, they ought immediately to have been brought to trial for high treason, and they could not legally be detained in custody. To have treated them as *prisoners of war* would have been to acknowledge the authority of Congress as the legislature of a separate state. To have executed them as *traitors* would not only have been contrary to the rules laid down by jurists respecting the mode of conducting a contest which assumes the aspect of civil war, but would inevitably have led to retaliation, there being many "loyalists" in the power of the "rebels." To extricate the Government from this dilemma, the Chancellor brought in "A Bill to suspend the Habeas Corpus Act with respect to his Majesty's subjects taken fighting against him in America;"—whereby power was given to detain them in custody without bringing them to trial. He said, "If ever there was a bill that deserved the appellation of humanity, it was this. It was certainly necessary that some punishment should be inflicted on persons taken in the act of enmity against us; but what ought it to be? Since it was plainly not expedient that they should be discharged, and not politic, from the apprehensions of retaliation, to put them to immediate death, what was the alternative? In his opinion, the only just medium had been adopted—that of preserving them till the conclusion of the war—so that their offense might still be visited upon them without endangering the lives of our fellow-subjects now in a similar situation in America."[2] The bill passed, though strongly opposed by the Duke of Richmond and other Peers.

Lord Bathurst was always desirous of getting up Lord Mansfield to defend the Government, and of avoiding a personal conflict with Lord Camden; but in the session of 1778 he was driven to give his opinion in favor of the legality of a plan which Ministers had adopted, of allowing regiments to be raised and maintained by individuals

[1] 17 Parl. Hist. 815.   [2] 19 Ib. 52, 561.

without the authority of parliament,—contending that, although the "Bill of Rights" declared that "to keep up a standing army in time of peace was contrary to law, this not being a time of peace, the provision did not apply to it." Lord Camden was now very severe upon him, insisting "that the arguments in support of the measure from the woolsack would lead to the utter subversion of the constitution, and that to raise troops without the consent and during the sitting of parliament was not only illegal and unconstitutional, but a violation of the fundamental privileges of parliament." The subject was resumed on a subsequent day, when Lord Camden reiterated his doctrine, but the Lord Chancellor did not venture again to take the field against him.[1]

After the calamitous surrender of General Burgoyne and his army at Saratoga, the Earl of Thanet having produced in the House of Lords a letter to him from the victorious American General GATES, recommending peace between the two countries, and having moved that it should be laid upon the table, "the Lord Chancellor asked their Lordships if it could possibly be deemed right to accept a letter which held out such terms as were not only exceedingly unequal, but grossly insulting? What! acknowledge the independency of America! and withdraw our Army and our fleet! Confess the superiority of America, and wait her mercy! He desired the House to consult their own feelings for an answer."[2] The motion, though supported by the Duke of Manchester and the Duke of Grafton, was negatived without a division.

Soon after, the Chancellor showed that he could be excited by great provocation, and that with a larger stock of moral courage to support him, he might have made a better figure in life. The Earl of Effingham, making a motion for papers respecting the public ex-

---

[1] 19 Parl. Hist. 625.
[2] Ibid. 734, 742. Notwithstanding this public declaration which the Chancellor considered it his duty to make in parliament, it appears from letters which I have seen, but which I am not at liberty to make public, that on the 9th of December, 1777, he had strongly expressed his private opinion to Lord North, on the necessity of opening a negotiation with the Americans for the acknowledgment of their independence, and that he had subsequently tendered his resignation because his advice was rejected. This correspondence is very creditable to Lord Bathurst, and shows that he was much respected by his colleagues.

penditure, and anticipating the rejection of it, declared, "that if the proofs of the extravagant and wasteful conduct of administration were denied him there, he would take care to produce them elsewhere. The public had a right to know in what manner their money was spent, and he would furnish them with information. It was in vain, he saw plainly; to attempt in that House to move for anything which the Ministers were not willing to give. In the present instance, the First Lord of the Admiralty knew his strength in a division. He would go below the bar, and take with him his—he had liked to have said—servile majority; he should not, therefore, rest satisfied, but would use proper means to come at the truth, which he would certainly communicate to the public."—The Lord Chancellor, leaving the woolsack *in great warmth*, thus spoke:—

"My Lords, I feel myself called on to support the honor of the House. If such language is allowed to pass unnoticed, your Lordships will no longer be moderators between the King and the people. The noble Earl has talked of a *servile majority;* are your Lordships to be so grossly insulted without even administering a rebuke? I have sat in this House seven years, and never before heard so indecent a charge—a servile majority! The insinuation is not warrantable. I, for one, have been in the habit of voting for the measures of Government; but will any noble Lord venture to say that I am under undue influence? The Ministers of the Crown know that the place I hold is no tie upon me; they know that I always act freely according to my conscience. I was born heir to a seat in this assembly;[1] I enjoy a peerage by hereditary right. I could not, therefore, sit silent, and hear the noble Earl talk of a *servile majority*. I am amazed that the members of the Government should so long have suffered themselves patiently to be traduced. In future, I hope

[1] This is not strictly correct, although the peerage had been conferred upon his family three years before his birth, as he was a younger brother till he had reached manhood. I have know a few, and a very few, peers who have gained distinction, though born to a peerage; the late Lord Holland, the present Earl of Derby, and others, might be held out as examples—but almost all the peers who have displayed much energy and talent in my time, have either themselves been created peers or were born before their fathers were created peers, or had begun their career as younger brothers. The *res augusta domi* is not so hard to struggle with as the enervating influence of wealth and high position without the necessity for exertion.

they will know how to check such a strain of invective. The Ministry, my Lords, will always have a majority,—they being independent and the majority independent,—for the moment that the Opposition have a majority, the Ministry will be no more."[1]

So great was the superiority of numbers which the Government still commanded, that Lord Effingham, to conceal the weakness of his party, suffered the motion to be negatived without a division.

I mention with great pain Lord Bathurst's next public exhibition, for hitherto he has appeared, if not a bright, a worthy and amiable man. After the glorious death of Chatham, which caused such public enthusiasm, and extinguished all enmity against him in almost every bosom,—insomuch that King George III. himself professed to be friendly to the making of some provision for his family,—when the bill for this purpose, which passed with much applause through the Commons, came up to the Lords, the Lord Chancellor (I am afraid from an illaudable desire to please the Court) did his best to throw it out, and opposed it in a most unfair manner, by pretending that, although purely a money bill, it might be properly amended by their Lordships. "The deceased Earl's services," said he, "when actually minister, I will not depreciate; but they were sufficiently rewarded. A few years after, he accepted the high post of Privy Seal, with great emoluments, at a time when it was well known his bad state of health rendered it impossible for him to assist his Majesty's councils. Having drawn an invidious comparison between Lord Chatham and the Duke of Marlborough, although himself one of the ministers who had wasted so many millions in the fruitless contest with America, he meanly resorted to the cant that "this was not a proper time to be lavish of the people's money." "But," he added, "what operates powerfully with me against the bill is, that the provision is for the family of him who is supposed to have done the services. Why was not the reward given to him in his lifetime? Because the answer would have been, 'he has had reward enough already from what his Sovereign has done for him.' I never can agree, that by either rejecting or amending a money bill we invade the privileges of the other House,

[1] 19 Parl. Hist. 995.

for we are as much trustees for the people as the Commons. The King has assented to the bill; but, addressed as he was by the other House, he was in a great measure obliged to assent—and we can not suppose that his Majesty will be offended by our exercising our right to reject or amend it. The grant did not spontaneously come from the Crown, as it ought to have done, and would have done if there had been any ground for it. Before I conclude, I must use the freedom to declare that I see no cause to despond because the Earl of Chatham is no more. There still remain as firm well-wishers to their country, and men as capable of doing it real service."[1] I have shown, in the Life of Lord Camden, the merited chastisement inflicted upon the author of this most ungracious and foolish effusion.[2]

Lord Bathurst's last speech in the House of Lords, as Chancellor, was in opposition to a motion of the Duke of Bolton, for an address to his Majesty, "to implore him that he would be graciously pleased to defer the prorogation of Parliament until the present very dangerous crisis may be happily terminated." This was warmly supported by Lord Camden, who drew a most melancholy picture of the state to which the country had been reduced by the misconduct of Ministers, and forcibly pointed out the necessity of a change both of measures and of men to preserve our national independence.

---

[1] The Earl of Chatham is dead, but Earl Bathurst survives!!! At any rate, our Chancellor thought it was fitter to imitate the King of England than the King of Scotland:

> "This news was brought to Edinburgh,
> Where Scotland's King did reign,
> That brave Earl Douglas suddenly
> Was by an arrow slain.
>
> "O heavy news! King James did say;
> Scotland can witness be,
> I have not any captain more
> Of such account as he.
>
> "Like tidings to King Henry came
> Within as short a space,
> That Percy, of Northumberland,
> Was slain in Chevy Chase.
>
> "Now, God be with him, said our King,
> Sith 'twill no better be;
> I trust I have within my realm
> FIVE HUNDRED AS GOOD AS HE."

[2] Ante, p. 362.

The Chancellor followed, and attempted to answer him, but seems to have entirely failed, if he did not actually break down. He confined himself to some technical remarks on the mode in which parliament may be summoned at common law and by the statute, and on the inconvenience which would be felt if the two Honses were merely to adjourn, instead of being prorogued. The motion was negatived by a majority of 42 to 20, but the Opposition Peers being triumphant in the debate, it was thought indispensable that the Government should be strengthened in the House of Lords.

The following day the prorogation took place, and as soon as the ceremony was over, a Council was held at St. James's, when the Great Seal was surrendered by Lord Bathurst, and was delivered to Thurlow, the Attorney General, as Lord Chancellor, the ex-Chancellor being declared President of the Council.

This proceeding seems to have been very precipitate: it was not accompanied with any other changes, and I am unacquainted with its secret history. One would have expected that, having tided over the session, Lord Bathurst, notwithstanding his inefficiency, would have been allowed to retain his office till after the long vacation, and till parliament and the Court of Chancery were to meet again in November. He had not had any difference with Lord North, or any of the other ministers, and they were conscious that he had done his best to serve them. I suspect that, from the approaching war against France and Spain, and the questions which were anticipated with neutral powers, some advice was required in the Cabinet upon international law, which might be given in a bolder tone, and acted upon with more confidence. It is very much to be deplored that, when the disputes with the colonies were ripening into civil war, and when sound constitutional councils might have saved the state, there sat in the cabinet one of the weakest, though one of the worthiest of our Chancellors.

His most meritorious act while he held the Great Seal (which I have much pleasure in commemorating) was his giving spontaneously a commissionership of bankrupts to Sir William Jones,—still, notwithstanding brilliant talents and stupendous acquirements, struggling with pecuniary difficulties. Soon after Lord Bathurst's resignation, came out the "Translation of the Orations of Isæus," dedicated to the ex-Chancellor. The dedicator, a little at a loss for topics of public commendation, dexterously takes shelter under the supposed modesty of his patron, and preserving at once a character for gratitude and for sincerity, contents himself with saying:—

"I check myself, therefore, my Lord, with reluctance, and abstain from those topics to which the overflowing of my zeal would naturally impel me; but I can not let slip the opportunity of informing the public, who have hitherto indulgently approved and encouraged my labors, that although I have received many signal marks of friendship from a number of illustrious persons, to whose favors I can never proportion my thanks, yet your Lordship has been my greatest, my only benefactor; that, without any solicitation or even request on my part, you gave me a substantial and permanent token of regard, which you rendered still more valuable by your obliging manner of giving it, and which has been literally the sole fruit that I have gathered from an incessant course of very painful toil."

While Lord Bathurst held the Great Seal, an attempt was in vain made to corrupt him by a secret offer to Lady Bathurst of three thousand guineas for the living of St. George's, Hanover Square. The offer was traced to the famous Dr. Dodd, then a King's chaplain, and he was immediately dismissed from that situation. This Chancellor is allowed to have disposed of his church patronage very creditably, although on one occasion he incurred considerable obloquy by conferring a chaplaincy on Martin Madan (the translator of Juvenal), whose heterodox opinions and indifferent morals were then generally notorious, and who afterwards gave such serious offense to the Church by the publication of his "Thelyphthora" in favor of the doctrine of polygamy.[1]

[1] Lives of Eminent English Judges, p. 36.

CHAPTER CLII.

CONCLUSION OF THE LIFE OF LORD BATHURST.

LORD BATHURST continued President of the Council nearly four years, till the formation of Lord Rockingham's Administration—when he resigned with Lord North. During this disastrous interval, although he was still a member of the Cabinet, he did not take a leading part in public affairs, and he seldom opened his mouth in the House of Lords,—Thurlow, his successor, treating him with very little consideration or courtesy. In 1779, he made a speech in defense of the management of Greenwich Hospital, when he was very roughly handled by Lord Camden, but rescued by Lord Mansfield.[1] Soon after, he came forward to resist the Duke of Richmond's motion about the Civil List Expenditure, contending that, "if a system of economy was to be adopted, it should not begin with the Crown, the splendor of which should be maintained by an ample revenue for the honor and dignity of the empire."[2]

In the following session, Government being hard pressed upon the occasion of Lord Shelburne's motion for an address to his Majesty praying to be informed " by whose advice the Marquis of Carmarthen and the Earl of Pembroke had been dismissed from the office of Lord Lieutenant by reason of their conduct in parliament,"— Lord President Bathurst said :—

" He could declare with truth, that, after upwards of thirty years' public service, he did not know that he had ever made an enemy, or given just cause of offense in any public character he had filled. He disapproved of removing persons from their appointments under the Crown, except for misconduct or incapacity, but he thought the present motion highly objectionable, as it went to intrench on the King's prerogative of choosing his own servants: this, like other prerogatives, might be abused, but it was necessary for the public good; and there was no pretense for saying that it had been abused in the present instance, as there was nothing to distin-

[1] 20 Parl. Hist. 569.   [2] Ibid. 1259.

guish the removals, which formed the subject of the present debate, from a continued stream of precedents since the Revolution down to the present day."[1]

The Lord President was the organ of the Government in the House of Lords respecting the proceedings to be taken in consequence of Lord George Gordon's riots. On the 2nd of June, 1780, their Lordships, in approaching Westminster Hall, were in serious danger from the violence of the mob, and it was with the utmost difficulty, and after much ill-usage, that they could force their way through Palace Yard. On their assembling in their own chamber, we are told by an eye-witness that "it is hardly possible to conceive a more grotesque appearance than the House exhibited. Some of their Lordships with their hair about their shoulders; others smothered with dirt; most of them as pale as the ghost in Hamlet, and all of them standing up in their several places, and speaking at the same instant; one Lord proposing to send for the guards; another for the justices or civil magistrates; many crying out, *Adjourn! adjourn!* while the skies resounded with huzzas, shoutings, hootings, and hissings in Palace Yard. This scene of unprecedented alarm continued above half an hour." News was then brought that Lord Boston had been dragged from his coach, and was undergoing the most cruel ill-usage from the rabble, who detained him a prisoner.

Lord Bathurst showed great courage, and rose from the ministerial benches to implore order, and to make a regular motion,—but he could not procure a hearing. Lord Townshend offered to be one that would go in a body to the rescue of their brother peer. The Duke of Richmond, however, as a piece of pleasantry—somewhat ill-timed—suggested that if they went as a House, the mace ought to be carried before the noble and learned Lord on the woolsack, who (the Bishops being excused) should go at their head, followed by the Lord President of the Council, the next in rank who could fight. Lord Mansfield, then acting as Speaker in the absence of the Lord Chancellor, declared his readiness to do his duty. Just at that moment Lord Boston entered, with hair all disheveled, and his clothes almost covered with hair-powder and mud,

[1] 21 Parl. Hist. 22⁵.

occasioned by the ill-treatment he had experienced. After some further tumultuous discussion, Lord Bathurst moved an adjournment, which was carried. The House gradually thinned, most of the Lords having either retired to the coffee-houses, or gone off in hackney-carriages, while others walked home under favor of the dusk of the evening—leaving Lord Mansfield, in the seventy-sixth year of his age, alone and unprotected, save by the officers of the House and his own servants.

Next day, "Earl Bathurst called the attention of the House to the great fall from dignity which their Lordships had suffered the preceding day, in consequence of the gross insults and violence offered to many of their Lordships' persons by the rioters and unruly mob which had assembled in the streets, and not only interrupted the members of that House in their way to it, and prevented many from coming to do their duty in parliament, but had obliged others, after a compulsory adjournment, to steal away, like guilty things, to save themselves from being sacrificed to lawless fury. Their Lordships had witnessed the insults and violence offered to the persons of several of their Lordships; but others had been still greater sufferers; in particular, a right reverend Prelate (the Bishop of Lincoln) had been stopped in the street,—had been forced out of his coach, the wheels of which were taken off,—and, having sought refuge in a private house, had been followed by the mob, and had been obliged to make his escape in disguise. Before their Lordships proceeded to any other business, it behoved them to do something for the recovery of their dignity, by bringing the offenders to justice." He concluded by moving an address to his Majesty, praying "that he would give immediate directions for prosecuting in the most effectual manner the authors, abettors, and instruments of the outrage committed yesterday in Palace Yard and places adjacent." After a debate, in which the Government was severely blamed for negligence in not taking proper measures to secure the peace of the metropolis, the motion was agreed to. He afterwards moved that the Judges should prepare a bill "to indemnify sheriffs and jailers for the escape of prisoners during the late tumults," as these officers of the law were now liable for very heavy fines and punishments, without having been guilty of any negligence. The bill was brought in and passed without opposition.[1]

Lord Bathurst's last considerable effort on the stage of public life appears to have been one of his best. In the debate respecting the rupture with Holland, in answer to a violent attack on Ministers by the Duke of Richmond, he said—

"That measures in support of the dignity of the Crown, the rights of Parliament, and the national safety, were arraigned in the most indecent terms, and when all other means of defeating them failed, then noble Lords predicted national ruin, which they said was brought about by ministerial corruption. This he would never allow to pass by in silence, it being evidently the language of disappointed ambition. All their Lordships who supported the Government were involved in the general accusation. Was it possible to sit in the House, day after day, without feeling the strongest emotions of well-founded indignation? The noble Lords to whom his Majesty had intrusted the direction of his affairs, were basely and unjustly vilified—their characters scandalously and indecently traduced—charged with being wicked at one time, and incapable at another, according as it corresponded with the views, or answered the purposes, of their accusers—as having entered into a conspiracy against the liberties of their country, and leagued for its destruction. He had for a long series of years served his Sovereign in various capacities, and he could lay his hand upon his heart, and with truth affirm that he had ever acted for the good of his country according to the best of his abilities; and that there was nothing the Crown had to bestow which could induce him to give a vote contrary to his conscience. He had enough to put him above the poor temptations of patronage and emolument; and he believed there was not a single noble Lord, who had supported the measures asserted to be carried by the mere force of corruption, who did not act from motives equally honorable and conscientious as himself. But it was plain whence all this arose—a wicked ambition—a lust of power—a thirst after the emoluments of office—from corruption and the worst species of corruption, for it was incurable—a corruption of the heart. Measures were opposed be-

[1] 21 Parl. Hist. 672-698.

cause they were said to be the King's measures; Ministers were traduced merely because they were Ministers; the object of the Opposition was to storm the Government, reckless of consequences—but, what grieved him more than private persecution or public accusation, the dearest interests of the country were sacrificed in the conflict. He trusted, however, that the good sense of the nation would see that such conduct flowed from party rage—the result of political despair and factious disappointment."

The Duke of Richmond retaliated, alluding to the time when Lord Bathurst was in opposition:—

"The noble and learned Lord speaks from long experience. His early struggle was tedious and mortifying—full of disappointment, and clouded with despair. No man is a better judge of the various operations of the human mind under such circumstances. So he concludes that a wicked, corroding ambition, whetted and inflamed by unavailing attempts, and ending in a state of political despair, is accompanied with malice and personal enmity, and 'that worst species of corruption—a corrupt heart.' But the noble and learned Earl is a Tory; he was then in opposition to the Whigs. Whoever opposes *his* friends, whether in or out of place, must act from factious motives and a *corrupt heart*."[1]

Lord Bathurst did not reply, nor afterwards venture to stand forward as the champion of the Court.

We next find him, while carrying through a Government bill for imposing a stamp on almanacs, engaged in an altercation with Thurlow, the Chancellor, who seems always to have thought that he had a privilege to oppose the measures of every Government with which he was connected, and to assail any of his colleagues. The Chancellor complained bitterly of the manner in which the bill was worded, saying that "several clauses were contradictory and unintelligible."

The Lord President tried to explain and defend them:

Lord Chancellor: "I am very sorry to say that the explanation of my noble and learned friend affords no satisfactory answer to my objections. Indeed, I am so dull of apprehension as to be unable to understand him. I do

[1] 21 Parl. Hist. 1013.

suspect, my Lords, that the framer of the first clause accidentally omitted the word 'not,' and that he really meant to forbid the doing of the very thing which is here commanded.¹ It appears to me a gross mistake, and I must beg your Lordships '*not*' to give your sanction to nonsense."—*Lord President:* "The proposed amendment of the noble and learned Lord on the woolsack would defeat the whole object of the bill, which is sufficiently plain to those who are willing to discover it."

The Lord Chancellor attacked other clauses, but met with no support, and Lord Bathurst succeeded in carrying his bill without any amendment.²

Such conflicts shook an Administration now tottering to its fall. Lord North, personally, had been for some time eager to withdraw, but was prevailed upon to retain office from the King's insuperable dislike to the Opposition leaders, and his threat to abandon England and the English crown rather than consent to the independence of America. At last the Government was in a minority in one House, and, on a motion of which notice had been given by Lord Shelburne, was threatened with the same fate in the other. To avert the coming storm, Lord North announced that "his Majesty's Ministers were no more."

Lord Bathurst, always downright and sincere, did not, like Thurlow, intrigue to continue in office with those to whom he had been opposed on all the most important principles on which the state was to be governed, and instantly resigned with his chief, intending now to enjoy the repose of private life. There was yet no parliamentary allowance for ex-Chancellors, and he declined the grant of a pension. But he had been able to procure a tellership of the Exchequer and other valuable sinecures for his son.

During a few years following, he occasionally attended in his place in the House of Lords, but he did not mix in the party contests which ensued, and he was never excited to offer his opinion on either side, by the animated discussions on the Peace of Paris, on the Coalition between Mr. Fox and Lord North, on Mr. Fox's India

---

¹ This reminds one of the proposal—for the purpose of making precept and faith square with practice—to take "not" from the COMMANDMENTS, and to put it into the CREED.   ² 22 Parl. Hist. 538-548.

Bill, on the Regency Question, on the French Revolution, or on the commencement of the war with the French Republic, which he lived to see.

He seems only to have spoken once after his retirement from office—in opposing a bill for the relief of insolvent debtors; which, according to his narrow views; he considered unjust to creditors and ruinous to trade.[1] But it should be recollected that such notions were then very generally entertained, and that Mr. Burke, by condemning imprisonment for debt, was so far in advance of his age, that he was considered a dangerous innovator, and on this ground chiefly lost his election for the city of Bristol.[2]

Lord Bathurst spent his last years entirely in the country, and, after a gradual decay, expired at Oakley Grove, near Cirencester, on the 6th day of August, 1794, in the eighty-sixth year of his age. His remains were interred in the family vault there, and a monument to his memory was erected in the parish church, with this simple and touching inscription, which he himself had composed:—

"In Memory of HENRY, EARL BATHURST, Son and Heir of Allen, Earl Bathurst, and Dame Catherine, his wife.
"His ambition was to render himself not unworthy of such Parents."

Although of very moderate capacity, he always acted a consistent and honorable part; and, never having deserted his principles or his party, or engaged in any unworthy intrigue to aggrandize himself, the blame can not rest upon him that he was placed in situations for which he was incompetent.

I hope I shall not be expected to enter into any analysis of his character as a judge, as a statesman, or an orator, for in his mental qualities and accomplishments he is really not to be distinguished from the great mass of worthy men who, when alive, are only known to their families and a small circle of friends, and who are forgotten as soon as the grave has closed over them. He is praised for his temperate and regular habits, and for the dignity and politeness of his manners. In public

[1] 23 Parl. Hist. 1100.
[2] Even when I was Attorney General, and brought in a bill to abolish imprisonment for debt, I was only able to carry it as to *mesne process*, leaving cases *after judgment* for subsequent legislation.

life (as he often boasted) he made no enemies, and in private life he was universally beloved.

He remained a bachelor till forty, when he married a widow lady, who, in four years, died without bringing him any children. In 1759 he took for his second wife, Tryphena, daughter of Thomas Seawen, Esq., of Maidwell, in the county of Northampton, and by her (besides other issue) had a son, Henry, the third Earl, a distinguished statesman, who ably filled high offices under George III. and under George IV. both as Regent and King. The Lord Chancellor Bathurst is now represented by his grandson, Henry George, the present and fourth Earl.[1]

[1] Grandeur of the Law, 70. I may be accused of having omitted to mention what is perhaps the most memorable act in the life of Lord Chancellor Bathurst,—that he built Apsley House at Hyde Park Corner, the town residence of the illustrious Duke of Wellington,—where stood the "Hercules Pillars," the inn frequented by Squire Western.

www.ingramcontent.com/pod-product-compliance
Lightning Source LLC
Chambersburg PA
CBHW032027150426
43194CB00006B/179